Katerina CLARK

MAYAKOVSKY

A Biography

MAYAKOVSKY

A Biography

Bengt Jangfeldt

TRANSLATED BY HARRY D. WATSON

THE UNIVERSITY OF CHICAGO PRESS
CHICAGO AND LONDON

BENGT JANGFELDT is a Swedish author and researcher. He is the author of several books, including *The Hero of Budapest: The Triumph and Tragedy of Raoul Wallenberg*.

HARRY D. WATSON is an author and translator who lives in Scotland.

Frontispiece: photograph of Mayakovsky by Avraam Sterenberg (ca. 1919–20) (detail of fig. on p. 249, below).

The University of Chicago Press, Chicago 60637
The University of Chicago Press, Ltd., London
English translation © 2014 by Harry D. Watson
All rights reserved. Published 2014.
Printed in the United States of America

23 22 21 20 19 18 17 16 15 14   1 2 3 4 5

ISBN-13: 978-0-226-05697-5 (cloth)
ISBN-13: 978-0-226-18868-3 (e-book)
DOI: 10.7208/chicago/9780226188683.001.0001

Originally published as *Med livet som insats: berättelsen om Vladimir Majakovskij och hans krets* by Wahlström and Widstrand, Stockholm, Sweden. © Bengt Jangfeldt, 2007. Published in the English language by arrangement with Bonnier Rights, Stockholm, Sweden.

LIBRARY OF CONGRESS CATALOGING-IN-PUBLICATION DATA
 Jangfeldt, Bengt, 1948– author.
 [Med livet som insats. English]
 Mayakovsky : a biography / Bengt Jangfeldt ; translated by Harry D. Watson.
  pages cm
 In English, translated from Swedish.
 "Originally published as Med livet som insats : berättelsen om Vladimir Majakovskij och hans krets by Wahlström and Widstrand, Stockholm, Sweden. © Bengt Jangfeldt, 2007"—Title page verso.
 Includes bibliographical references and index.
 ISBN 978-0-226-05697-5 (cloth : alkaline paper)—ISBN 978-0-226-18868-3 (e-book)
 1. Mayakovsky, Vladimir, 1893–1930. 2. Poets, Russian—20th century—Biography. 3. Futurism (Literary movement)—Soviet Union. I. Watson, Harry D., translator. II. Title.
 PG3476.M312J3413 2014
 891.71'42—dc23
 [B]

                                                                            2014015931

♾ This paper meets the requirements of ANSI/NISO Z39.48–1992 (Permanence of Paper).

I have had the privilege of knowing personally many of Mayakovsky's closest friends, some of them quite well—Lili Brik and Vasily Katanyan, Roman Jakobson, Lev Grinkrug, Luella Krasnoshchokova, Galina Katanyan, Rita Rayt, Tatyana Yakovleva, and Veronika Polonskaya.

This book is dedicated to the memory of these people, who have given me so much.

CONTENTS

YOUR THOUGHT,

DAYDREAMING IN A BRAIN GONE SOFT,

LIKE SOME FATTENED-UP LACKEY ON A GREASE-STAINED

COUCH,

I'LL TEASE AGAINST THE BLOODIED SHREDS OF MY HEART;

I'LL JEER ALL I WANT, INSOLENT AND CAUSTIC.

THERE ISN'T A SINGLE GRAY HAIR IN MY SOUL,

NOR ANY GENERIC TENDERNESS!

THUNDERING THE WORLD WITH THE MIGHT OF MY VOICE,

I GO FORTH, GORGEOUS,

TWENTY-TWO YEARS OLD.

TENDER PEOPLE!

YOU PLAY YOUR LOVE ON VIOLINS.

THE BRUTE BANGS HIS OUT ON KETTLEDRUMS.

BUT YOU CAN'T TURN YOURSELVES INSIDE OUT, LIKE I CAN,

TO BE PURE LIPS AND NOTHING ELSE!

Vladimir Mayakovsky, from the prologue to "A Cloud in Trou-
sers" (trans. James H. McGavran III)

The door between the two rooms had been taken off its hinges to make more space. Mayakovsky stood leaning against the doorframe. He took a small notebook from the inside pocket of his jacket, glanced in it and stuck it back in his pocket again. For a while he said nothing. Then, his eyes sweeping over the room as if it were an enormous auditorium, he read out the prologue, and asked—not in verse, but in prose, in a low, unforgettable voice:

You think malaria makes me delirious?
It happened.
In Odessa, it happened.

(TRANS. GEORGE REAVEY)

We raised our heads and did not take our eyes off this miracle until it was all over.

Vladimir Mayakovsky had been writing poetry for several years, but this reading of "A Cloud in Trousers" at the apartment of Lili and Osip Brik in July 1915 marked the beginning of a new stage in both his literary and his private life. "The Briks were entranced by his verses and fell in love with them once and for all," remembered Lili's younger sister, Elsa, who was present at the reading. For Mayakovsky, the encounter with Lili and Osip Brik was a turning point in his life that he was later to describe as "a most joyous date."

By the summer of 1915, the World War had been raging for a year, and it was obvious to most people that it would be followed by sweeping political and social changes. In the aesthetic sphere—in literature, painting, and music—the revolution was already a fact, and Russia was in the vanguard of this process. The composer Igor Stravinsky was enjoying great success in Paris, as was the Ballets Russes under Sergey Diaghilev; and in the field of art the Russians were in the front line, with names like Vasily Kandinsky, Mikhail Larionov, Vladimir Tatlin, and Kazimir Malevich, all of whom in their own way contributed to the groundbreaking development of Russian art in these years.

One of the starting shots for the "modern breakthrough" was fired in 1909, when the Italian Filippo Tommaso Marinetti proclaimed Futurism, a movement heralding a general revolt against the cultural heritage in literature as well as art and music. Futurism had an enormous impact in Russia, where its most interesting development was in the field of literature.

One of the participants in this movement was Vladimir Mayakovsky, who at the time of his meeting with Lili and Osip Brik was only twenty-two years old but, despite his youth, one of Futurism's leading figures. In Boris Pasternak's poignant definition, "since childhood he was the spoilt creature of a future that yielded to him quite early on and seemingly with no great effort." When this future arrived two years later, it was spelled Revolution—next to the two world wars the Russian Revolution was the most emblematic political event of the twentieth century. With all his talent and passion, Mayakovsky plunged into this enormous social and political experiment, which had the classless Communist society as its final goal. No other writer is as indissolubly linked with the Russian Revolution as Mayakovsky.

In this struggle for a new and more just society, he was joined by a generation of like-minded people who had grown up with the Revolution as an all-absorbing idea. To this generation belonged Lili and Osip Brik, who were as inseparably united with Mayakovsky as he himself was with the Revolution. It is impossible to talk about Mayakovsky without talking about them, and vice versa. During the 1920s, the constellation Mayakovsky-Brik became the very embodiment of the aesthetic and political avant-garde—and of a new, avant-garde morality. Mayakovsky was the main poet of the Revolution, Osip, one of the leading cultural critics, and Lili, with her liberal attitude toward love and sex, the symbol of modern woman, freed from the moral fetters of bourgeois society.

From that overwhelming evening in July 1915 onward, Mayakovsky, Lili, and Osip Brik were inseparable. For fifteen years, they lived together in one of the most remarkable and legendary relationships in the history of Russian literature—for fifteen years, until the sunny day in April 1930 when a pistol bullet tore their lives to pieces. And not only theirs: the bullet that penetrated Vladimir Mayakovsky's heart also shot to pieces the dream of Communism and signaled the beginning of the Communist nightmare of the 1930s.

It is this vortex of political, literary, and private storms that this story of Vladimir Mayakovsky and his circle is about.

VOLODYA

1893–1915

**Through us time's horn rings out in wordplay.
The past is stifling. The Academy and
Pushkin are more baffling than hieroglyphics.
Chuck Pushkin, Dostoyevsky, Tolstoy, etc.,
overboard from the ship of the Present.
We alone are *the face* of *our* time.**
A Slap in the Face of Public Taste

Vladimir Mayakovsky was Russian but spent his childhood in the Caucasian province of Georgia, which had been under Russian sovereignty since the end of the eighteenth century. The population consisted mainly of Georgians but also of peoples from neighboring provinces and countries: Armenians, Turks, Russians. In the east Georgia borders on Azerbaijan, and the Black Sea forms the border to the west.

He was born on 19 July 1893 in the village of Bagdady in western Georgia, not far from the provincial capital of Kutaisi.* His father, Vladimir Konstantinovich, was a

---

* Dates in the book are given consistently in terms of the Gregorian calendar which was in use in the western world. In the nineteenth century the difference between the Gregorian calendar and

Mayakovsky in 1913 at the age of twenty (detail of photo on page 11).

master forester and, according to family legend, was descended from the legendary Zaporozhian Cossacks. According to the same source, the name Mayakovsky stemmed from the fact that most members of the family on his father's side were tall and powerfully built—*mayak* means "lighthouse" in Russian. His mother, Alexandra Alexeyevna, came from Ukraine. Vladimir—or Volodya, as he was called—had two sisters, Lyudmila, who was nine years older than himself, and Olga, who was three years older. (A brother, Konstantin, had died of scarlet fever at the age of three.) The family came from the minor aristocracy but were wholly dependent for their living on the father's salary, which provided a reasonable living without any luxuries.

Vladimir Konstantinovich—a big man with broad shoulders, like his forebears—was a cheerful, friendly, sociable, and hospitable person with black hair and a black beard. He was full of energy and found it easy to talk to people. He spoke with a deep bass voice; according to his daughter, his speech was "full of proverbs, wordplay, and witticisms," and he knew "innumerable events and anecdotes that he would relate in Russian, Georgian, Armenian, and Tatar, in all of which he was fluent." At the same time he was extremely sensitive and impressionable, with a fiery temperament and a tendency to mood swings that were "frequent and violent."

Mayakovsky's mother was the opposite of her husband in every way: reserved, thin, fragile, but strong willed. "With her character and her inborn tact Mother neutralized Father's impetuosity, hot temper, and mood swings," according to Lyudmila: "Never once in our life did we hear her as much as raise her voice." She had chestnut-colored hair and a high forehead, and a rather thrusting jaw. Volodya resembled his mother in looks, but in build and disposition he was like Vladimir Konstantinovich, who passed on to his son his temperamental nature and his sensitivity. From his father Volodya also inherited his dark bass voice.

---

the Julian, which was used in Russia until 1918, was twelve days, and in the twentieth century, thirteen days. According to the so-called old style, Mayakovsky was born on 7 July.

Volodya Mayakovsky with his parents and sisters Lyudmila (*standing*) and Olga in the revolutionary year 1905.

The little mountain village where Volodya spent his first years consisted of around two hundred small farms and had fewer than a thousand inhabitants. It lay in a deep, longish valley surrounded by high, steep mountains covered in forests which were full of bears, roe deer, wild boar, foxes, hares, squirrels, and all sorts of birds. Volodya learned to love animals at an early age. The houses were surrounded by large vineyards and a wealth of fruit trees: apple, pear, apricot, pomegranate, and fig. In direct contrast to the abundance of the natural world were the deficiencies in the administrative resources of the village, which had a post office but neither a school nor a doctor. It was twenty-seven kilometers to the nearest town, Kutaisi, and the only public transport was by coach. When Olga and Konstantin fell ill with scarlet fever, it took so long for the doctor to reach Bagdady that the boy was dead by the time he got there.

The family house stood a little out of the way on the edge of the village, on the right bank of the Khanis-Tschalis River. According to Volodya's siblings, it resembled "a gold miner's house somewhere in California or the Klondyke." There were three rooms, one of which was the master forester's office. Directly underneath was the surging water of a pebbly mountain stream. The children spent a lot of time outside, and Volodya soon taught himself to swim and ride. He was particularly fond of dangerous games and pastimes, the more dangerous the better. Along with his sister Olga he loved to climb trees and cliff faces and rush around on the narrow mountain paths that coiled around the sheer drops.

The imagination and inventiveness that Volodya showed in his games prefigured the rich creativity that he would later demonstrate. The same applies to another trait that manifested itself very early, when he was only five years old: his ability to recite poetry. His father lacked a higher education but loved literature and often read aloud to his family such classics as Pushkin, Lermontov, and Nekrasov. Although Bagdady was a long way from the public highways, relatives often came to visit, especially in the summer, and on these occasions Vladimir Konstantinovich used to ask Volodya to read aloud for their guests. The boy was not yet able to either read or write but his phenomenal memory made it easy for him to learn things by heart. He recited both well and expressively. To exercise his voice he used to creep inside the large wine amphora which lay on its side on the ground and recite poems to Olga, who stood outside playing the part of the public.

In his learning of poems, just as in his games, there was a strong element of competition. Volodya wanted to be the best at any price and liked to participate in the games of the grown-ups. One game was a sort of "ship comes laden with lines of poetry": the first player begins to read a poem, stops in the middle and throws a handkerchief to the next person, who has to try to finish the poem. Or they had to find as many words as possible beginning with a particular letter. Volodya's competitiveness was matched by an unbridled energy which made him never want to stop playing. "Volodya was often obstinate and had the ability to persuade the adults to yield to his wish to continue the game," his mother recalled. "At such times he would also usually take it upon himself to organize the whole game and carry with him those who were already tired and who didn't want to play any more." He brought the same passion and impatience to all kinds of games: cards, dominoes, croquet, and more besides. In October 1904 Olga reported to her sister Lyudmila that Volodya had "become terribly obsessed with playing dominoes" and that he had already managed to win a whole album full of foreign stamps. Here we see the contours of a dominant trait of Mayakovsky's character, his love of gambling, which we will have reason to return to more than once.

As Bagdady lacked educational facilities, Mayakovsky's eldest sister, Lyudmila, had been sent at an early age to a boarding school in Georgia's capital, Tbilisi, and in 1900 her mother and Volodya moved to Kutaisi so that he could start his schooling there. He was seven years old by then. After two years' preparatory study he was accepted into what the Russian school system called a "gymnasium." His studies went well, and he distinguished himself particularly in drawing. Lyudmila took lessons from a Kutaisi artist who found Volodya so promising that he taught him for nothing. "Before long Volodya was almost competing with me at drawing," Lyudmila remembered, and "we began to get used to the idea that he would be an artist."

Just as striking as Volodya's talent for drawing and reciting poetry was his total lack of musicality. He could not hold a note and was utterly uninterested in music, he was never seen to go near the piano and never wanted to dance. "When the young people gathered at our house and the dancing started, Volodya was asked to join in too," his mother recalled: "He always said no thanks and instead went to his friends in the yard next door to play *gorodki*," a kind of skittles.

TO MOSCOW!

In the winter of 1906, when Volodya was twelve, his father died of blood poisoning at the age of forty-nine. He had pricked himself with a needle while sewing documents together. Volodya was the youngest of his children, but he was very mature for his age and took an active part in the preparations for the funeral. "He took care of everything and never lost his composure," Lyudmila recalled.

The death of their father was devastating for the family, not least for the son, who from this time onward, according to Lyudmila, "became more serious" and "regarded himself as grown-up." The way in which his father had died left a deep impression on the sensitive boy's psyche. He was afflicted with an intense fear of infection which in later life developed into a phobia about cleanliness. He always had his own soap and his own rubber drinking cup with him, and on his travels he always carried a folding rubber bathtub. He avoided public transport, disliked shaking hands with people, and never grasped a door handle with his bare hand, preferring to use his jacket pocket or a handkerchief. He always lifted a tankard of beer with his left hand so as to be able to drink from the side that no one else's lips had touched—a trick made easier by the fact that he was ambidextrous.

Their father's death also had an immediate effect on the family's financial situation. For the past two years Lyudmila had been studying at the Stroganov school of applied arts in Moscow, and in order to provide for her Alexandra Alexeyevna and the children who were still living at home also moved there. In Moscow, Alexandra got by on her widow's pension and by letting out rooms to students. Volodya and Olga earned their keep by painting boxes, Easter eggs, and other objects. Volodya also drew advertising placards for a firm of chemists.

Mayakovsky's registration card at the Moscow police, 1908.

Mayakovsky had already read a fair amount of radical literature while studying at the gymnasium in Kutaisi, but it was thanks to the family's lodgers that he first came into contact with convinced socialists. When he was in his fourth year at the gymnasium he joined a social-democratic study circle, and a year or so later he became a member of the party's Bolshevik wing. At the same time he was expelled from the gymnasium because of unpaid termly fees.

During the following two years, 1908–9, Mayakovsky devoted more or less the whole of his time to political activity. He read and disseminated illegal literature among bakers, shoemakers, and typographers. The police carried out surveillance on him, and although he was only fifteen or sixteen, he was arrested several times. During one raid he ate a bound notebook containing addresses to prevent it from falling into the hands of the police. His first two periods of detention were short lived, one month in each case, but on the third occasion he spent six months in jail, five of them in solitary confinement.

His time in Butyrki prison brought about a change in Mayakovsky's life. If he had previously read mostly political literature, his reading now took a different turn. "An incredibly important time for me," he wrote later: "After three years of theory and practice I now immersed myself in literature." He read the classics—Byron, Shakespeare, Tolstoy—but without great enthusiasm. As for the Symbolist poets Andrey Bely and Konstantin Balmont, he appreciated their modern form of writing but was put off by their themes and metaphorical language. The reality he sensed should be depicted in another way! He tried, but it didn't work. When he was freed in January 1910 the guards confiscated a notebook full of poems, something he later declared that he was grateful for.

Between arrests Mayakovsky had studied at Stroganov's school of applied arts, just like his sister. But he had been banned from the school because of his political activities. Nor had he graduated from the gymnasium. He now felt that he wanted to get an education, something that he saw as incompatible with continued work for the party. "I was faced with the prospect of devoting my whole life to writing leaflets propounding ideas taken from books that were politically correct but which were not the result of my own thinking. If you were to shake out of me all I had read, what would be left? The Marxist dialectic. But had not this weapon ended up in hands that were too immature for it? It is a weapon that is easy to use if one only has like-minded people to deal with. But if one encounters opponents?" The quotation is from 1922, but the problem Mayakovsky hints at is no rationalization. The conflict between art and politics troubled him right from the start; it was to color all his actions and hasten his death.

Mayakovsky gave up his political activity, but as he had doubts about his literary talent, his liberation from politics was followed by a resumption of his painting. After four months at Zhukovsky's art college, which he felt was too traditional, he began studying in the studio of another artist, Pyotr Kelin, where he prepared for his application to the College of Painting, Sculpture, and Architecture— the only college which did not demand any political "certificate of reliability." After his second attempt, he was accepted in August 1911 for the college's model class.

THE MARVELOUS BURLYUK

Mayakovsky was eighteen when he started at the college and he soon became known for his self-confidence and cheek. He was vociferous, quick-witted, and capable of devastating rejoinders, and as nervy and impatient in his speech as in his movements. He could never sit still on a chair but rushed around the whole time with a cigarette in the corner of his mouth. The dominant impression he made was strengthened by his height—he was about six foot three. His pushiness meant that many people found him quite unbearable—he was liked only by those who suspected or understood "his enormous personality, which exceeded all bounds." The challenging image he presented was underlined by a consistently Bohemian style of dress: long, unkempt hair, a broad-brimmed black hat pulled down over his eyebrows, a black shirt and black cravat—a Byronic hero in search of his artistic identity.

But his cheek and provocativeness reflected only one side of Mayakovsky's character. Basically, as a friend from the painting school explained, he was an extremely sensitive person—something he tried hard to hide under a mask of arrogance and an uncouth exterior. Anyone who knew Mayakovsky closely could testify that his aggressiveness was a defense mechanism. Boris Pasternak, for example, gave a telling definition of Mayakovsky's "brashness" as the result of a "farouche timidity" and his "pretence of will-power" as the consequence of a "lack of will, phenomenally suspicious and prone to a quite gratuitous gloom."

But Mayakovsky never gave any outward sign of this side of his personality, so when he came across David Burlyuk at the painting school—a fellow artist who was slightly older than Mayakovsky but equally sure of himself—the potential for conflict was there. Burlyuk, a Cubist, was also hit by Mayakovsky's poisoned arrows. "An unkempt, unwashed giant with the definite air of a hooligan about him constantly persecuted me, as a 'Cubist,' with his jokes and witticisms," Burlyuk recalled. "It went so far that I came close to resort-

Mayakovsky as a student at the College of Painting, Sculpture, and Architecture in the fall of 1911.

ing to fisticuffs, especially as I was interested in sport at that time and in Müller's [gymnastic] system and so I could look after myself in any confrontation with this enormous, long-legged youth with his dusty velvet blouse and his glowing, mocking dark eyes." How-

In this picture from 1913, we see, in the upper row, Nikolay Burlyuk, his brother David, "the Father of Russian Futurism," and Mayakovsky. *Sitting:* Velimir Khlebnikov and the Futurists' two "maecenases," the aviator Georgy Kuzmin and the musician Sergey Dolinsky, who published the almanac *A Slap in face of Public Taste* and Mayakovsky's first book of poetry, *I!*

ever, it all ended happily, and Burlyuk and Mayakovsky became the best of friends in the "life-and-death battle between the old and the new in art and life which was then raging around us," as Burlyuk put it.

It was Burlyuk who discovered Mayakovsky's talent for poetry. When Mayakovsky recited a poem to Burlyuk in the course of a walk in the autumn of 1912, he was so uncertain of his ability that he claimed it was written by an acquaintance. But Burlyuk saw through the deception and declared that Mayakovsky was a poet of genius. The discovery was equally bewildering for both of them. Even if Mayakovsky had written a little poetry during his time in prison, he had no actual apprenticeship behind him, but, according to Burlyuk, appeared "like Pallas Athena as an accomplished poet." For Mayakovsky, this nocturnal promenade along the boulevard by the Passion Monastery in Moscow was to determine the direction of his future creativity. "I abandoned myself to poetry," he remembered. "That evening, quite unexpectedly, I became a poet."

A COMPULSIVE GAMBLER

Burlyuk became the authority that Mayakovsky's as-yet-unfocused talent needed to help him find his way. He read French and German poetry to Mayakovsky and supplied him with books—and money. Mayakovsky was so poor that he could not afford to go to the dentist and the contrast between his youth and his rotten teeth was striking: "When he spoke or laughed all you saw was some brown, corroded and crooked, spiky stumps," noted Burlyuk's wife Marusya. Burlyuk, by contrast, came from a well-to-do family—his father was the steward of a Ukrainian estate—and he gave Mayakovsky fifty kopecks a day to save him from starving.

When the money still did not go far enough, he went hungry and slept on park benches. To get enough food for the day he played cards—and billiards, a game at which he was almost unbeatable. The white heat of competition, the readiness to hazard everything, was in Mayakovsky's blood: he was a passionate gambler who spent every free moment at the card or billiard table. He was like this throughout his life, even when it was no longer necessary for his survival. Wherever he found himself, the first thing he did was to seek out the billiard halls and sniff out other card fiends. He was a compulsive gambler, one who simply couldn't stop himself.

"Playing cards with Mayakovsky was awful," recalled Nikolay

A merry Mayakovsky in Kiev in 1913. It has not been possible to establish with certainty the identity of the young lady who provoked his toothless smile.

Aseyev, a young poet who got to know Mayakovsky in the spring of 1913 and who was just as much in thrall to the gambling bug as Mayakovsky himself. "For he could not grasp that losing was just as natural and as possible a part of gambling as winning. He saw losing as a personal insult, something that could not be put right":

It was a sort of boxing without fists, in which the individual ex-changes of blows were only a preparation for the knock-out punch. He was incapable of fighting physically. "I can't fight," was his an-swer when I asked if he had ever been in a fight. When I asked why not, he replied: "If I start, I'll end up killing someone." That was how he summed up his temperament and his massive strength. So he could only fight in exceptional cases. When he played cards, on the other hand, his temperament and his strength were balanced by his opponent's temperament and patience. But of course he sensed how much stronger he actually was. So every time he lost he felt it as an insult, an accident, a stroke of blind fate.

Mayakovsky took his opponent's breath away, he staked every-thing, bluffed, and did not rise from the table until he had won or been forced to acknowledge that he had lost. He played with his nerves at full stretch, and when the tension was released—another close friend recalled—he would "pace up and down the room weeping."

Mayakovsky gambled the whole time, and on anything. If there was no gaming table in the vicinity he would devise a wager. How many paces to the next block? What will be the number of the next tram to come round the corner? Once, Aseyev recalled, they got off the train a station early to see who could reach the next set of signals first without starting to run. When they arrived there simultane-ously they tossed a coin to decide who had won. But the important thing for Mayakovsky was not the gold ruble they wagered for; it was that he did not lose.

As far as obsessive-compulsive disorders were concerned, May-akovsky's gambling addiction was matched only by his phobia about cleanliness. The burgeoning poet was, in other words, a deeply neurotic young man, and this impression was strengthened by his enormous consumption of cigarettes, as many as a hundred a day. But even his smoking was a form of neurosis, and not dictated by dependence on nicotine. Although he always had the stump of a cigarette dangling from the corner of his mouth—he did not use matches, lighting each cigarette from the stub of the last one—he never inhaled.

DANGEROUS FUTURISTS

When David Burlyuk first met Mayakovsky, who was eleven years his junior, he already had a career as an artist behind him. He had shown his work at several exhibitions of modern art, both in Russia and abroad (for example, at Der Blaue Reiter in Munich). He was a central figure in the Russian artistic avant-garde and one of the men behind the artists' society Jack of Diamonds, which in the years 1912 to 1916 organized a series of notable exhibitions in Moscow and Petersburg. The Jack of Diamonds group, whose most prominent members were painters like Ilya Mashkov, Pyotr Konchalovsky, and Aristarkh Lentulov, regarded Cézanne as their master and were sometimes known as post-Cézannists.

Burlyuk promptly introduced Mayakovsky into these circles. They started making joint appearances and in November 1912 Mayakovsky had his first public outing as a poet, artist, and propagandist for the new currents in painting and poetry. One month later Mayakovsky made his debut in the Futurists' first almanac, *A Slap in the Face of Public Taste*, with the very same two poems that he had recited for Burlyuk: "Night" and "Morning," experimental poems strongly influenced by the formal language of modern painting. It was in that almanac that four of the leading representatives of the Russian literary avant-garde appeared for the first time within the same covers—Vladimir Mayakovsky, David Burlyuk, Velimir Khlebnikov and Alexey Kruchonykh. If readers found these experiments in poetic form incomprehensible, they could learn from the manifesto, "A Slap in the Face of Public Taste," that this was because the Futurists had "thrown Pushkin, Dostoevsky, Tolstoy, etc., overboard from the ship of the Present" and announced: "*We* alone are *the face* of *our* time." The old art was dead, and its place had been taken by "Cubo-Futurism": Cubism in pictorial art, Futurism in verbal art. As several of the Russian Futurists were both painters and poets, the formula was particularly apt.

The Futurists' criticism of the prevailing norms was first and foremost aesthetically motivated, but it was also a social protest. Unlike previous generations of artists and writers, who were largely recruited from the upper class of the big cities, the Russian avant-

During the tour of the Russian provinces during the winter of 1913–14, Mayakovsky and his friends often dressed in tails and top hat, in stark contrast to their revolutionary aesthetic program. In order to further challenge "public taste," they sometimes appeared in war paint, like Vasily Kamensky in the photograph at left.

garde came from the middle class or underclass and, moreover, from the provinces. The aesthetic rebellion thus had a social dimension which gave it extra strength and legitimacy.

It was quite natural, therefore, that Mayakovsky and Burlyuk should decide to set off on a recitation and lecture tour of Russian provincial towns. The tour was a response to the threat of expulsion

When the tragedy *Vladimir Mayakovsky* was published in 1914, it was in a typically Futurist layout, where typefaces and upper- and lowercase letters interacted freely, in full accordance with the manifesto "The letter as such" from 1913: "Ask any wordwright and he will tell you that a word written in individual longhand or composed with a particular typeface bears no resemblance at all to the same word in a different inscription. After all, you would not dress all your young beauties in government overcoats!" The drawing, by David Burlyuk's brother Vladimir, pictures Mayakovsky in his striped black-and-yellow blouse.

from the art college which was hanging over them. But there was also another, more important motive: Futurism was a big-city phenomenon, and the tour was a way of getting the new aesthetic known out in the country districts, where the movement was mostly seen as a joke and ridiculed as totally incomprehensible and meaningless—if it was known at all. Since the Futurist poets had difficulty finding publishers and were forced to bring out their books themselves, often in small editions of three to five hundred, there were few people outside of Petersburg and Moscow who had read them.

The tour lasted for three and a half months, from mid-December 1913 to the end of March 1914. With them were the poet Vasily Kamensky, and, for a shorter time, the "Ego-Futurist" Igor Severyanin. They read poems, lectured about the latest directions in art, and showed lantern slides of their own work and that of others, such as Picasso. The Futurist message was strengthened by the challenging dress of the performers: they wore radishes in their buttonholes and had planes, dogs, and cabbalistic signs painted on their faces. Mayak-ovsky for the most part was clad in a yellow blouse, sewn from "three ells of sunset" (as he described it in the poem "The Snob's Blouse"). "Degenerate types," one journalist thought, "with brands on their faces like outright criminals."

Interest in the touring company was enormous, and the scandals were many. The public responded to the provocations of the Futurists with whistles and boos, but also with applause and laughter. On one occasion the performance was stopped after the local police chief was informed about Mayakovsky's catalog of crimes. On another occasion, in Kiev, it was allowed to go ahead but in the presence of the governor-general, the chief of police, eight police commissars, sixteen assistant commissars, twenty-five police supervisors, sixty police constables inside the theater and fifty mounted police out-side. "Mayakovsky was in raptures," Kamensky recalled: "What poets apart from ourselves have been honored with such a state of war? . . . Ten policemen for every poem read. That's what I call poetry!"

In other words, the tour achieved its aim: the movement became known, and the battle for the new art was raised to a higher level. Interest was increased by the fact that the founder of Futurism, the Italian Filippo Tommaso Marinetti, visited St. Petersburg and Mos-cow while they were halfway through their tour. Despite the fact that the Russian Futurists, keen to stress the independence of the Russian movement, did everything they could to disrupt and sabotage Mari-netti's appearances, they had no objection to the extra publicity that the scandals brought in their wake.

But the tour also had another consequence. The attacks that May-akovsky and Burlyuk had made on the established authorities made their position at the art college untenable, and in the end the college authorities saw no alternative but to expel them—a decision which in Maykovsky's case had the advantage that he could now devote himself full-time to the art form for which he had the greatest talent: poetry.

IT HAPPENED IN ODESSA

Despite his talent for poetry, Mayakovsky was still best known for causing scandals and for being a generally shameless character. The poet Benedikt Livshits, who was close to the Futurists during these years, has given a vivid description of what could happen when Mayakovsky kicked over the traces, like for example during a lunch at the home of Mrs. Dobychina, a prominent art collector: "During the lunch he directed a torrent of sarcastic remarks at the hostess, made a fool of her husband, a reserved man who meekly endured his insults, teasingly broke off pieces of sponge cake with fingers that were red with the cold, and when "D" lost patience and said something about his dirty nails, he answered her so rudely that I thought we would be asked to leave there and then."

Despite or perhaps because of his arrogance, Mayakovsky exerted a powerful attraction on the opposite sex and had many affairs, some of them serious, some less so. Right from the time of their earliest encounters, Burlyuk was struck by the way Mayakovsky boasted about his many conquests. He was "not very choosy about the objects of [. . .] his passion," which, according to Burlyuk, he slaked either with middle-class women who deceived their husbands "in the countryside, in hammocks and swings" or with the "newly kindled and untamed fire of young female students."

Mayakovsky's split personality also manifested itself in his relationships with women. His provocative and shameless manner concealed a lack of confidence, shyness, and a feeling of not being appreciated or understood. His sexual voracity seems to have been just as much the result of his need for acknowledgement as of his obviously well-developed libido. The young women who had relationships with Mayakovsky during these years are unanimous in their testimony. He loved to challenge and provoke, but sometimes he dropped the mask of insolence and cynicism. "He was attentive to all [the girls]," one of them recalled, "but always in a careless way, as if he regarded them as lesser beings. He talked to them about trivia, asked them out for a ride in a horse-drawn carriage and then forgot all about them." He was cynical in his view of women and was capable of describing a woman unceremoniously as "a piece of mutton." Although in private he was gentle and tender, smiling his "toothless smile," it only took an outsider to show up for his hackles to rise.

The attraction that Mayakovsky exerted on female university and art college students was matched only by the disgust he inspired in

In the winter and spring of 1913, Mayakovsky spent a lot of time with the young painter genius Vasily Chekrygin and the siblings Lev and Vera Shekhtel. The photograph shows Mayakovsky with Vera and the fifteen-year-old Chekrygin.

their parents. His artist friends included the brother and sister Lev and Vera Shekhtel, whose father, Fyodor Shekhtel, was one of Russia's leading Art Nouveau architects. In 1913, with help from the siblings, Mayakovsky brought out his first collection of poems, the lithographed *I!*, with drawings by Lev (under the pseudonym of Zhegin) and the fifteen-year-old prodigy Vasily Chekrygin.

"My parents were shocked by his provocative manner," remembered Vera, who had an intense romantic relationship with Mayakovsky in the spring and summer of 1913. Vera's father did what he could to stop Mayakovsky from going out with her, but it made no difference, and during one of his unwelcome visits his relationship with Vera was consummated; she became pregnant and was sent abroad for an abortion.

As far as we know, this was the first time Mayakovsky had made a woman pregnant, but it was not the last. In the winter of 1913–14 he had two love affairs, one of which left its mark in the form of yet

In Mayakovsky's first book, the lithographed *I!*, the poems were transcribed and illustrated by Lev Shekhtel and Vasily Chekrygin, who made this drawing. The print run was three hundred copies.

another unwanted pregnancy. The eighteen-year-old student Sonya Shamardina, who got to know Mayakovsky in the autumn of 1913, penned a detailed portrait of her two-years-older boyfriend:

> Tall, strong, self-confident, stylish. Still rather youthfully angular and broad across the shoulders. He had a characteristic way of moving, a little crookedly, by suddenly lifting one shoulder, and then he really looked broad-shouldered.
>
> A large, masculine mouth with its eternal cigarette, which he shifted from one corner of his mouth to the other. His laugh was abrupt and peculiar.
>
> I wasn't bothered by his rotten teeth. On the contrary, they seemed to underline his inner being, his own special beauty.
>
> Especially when—unabashed, with lofty contempt for the middle-class, scandal-seeking public—he read out his poems: "And yet," "But would you be able to?," "Love," "I will sew myself black trousers from the velvet of my voice"...
>
> He was handsome. Sometimes he asked: "Am I not handsome?"...
>
> A blouse in a warm yellow color. Another with black and yellow stripes. Frayed trousers with a shiny backside.

Sonya Shamardina.

Sonya became pregnant and had a late abortion in the winter of 1914, but she concealed both this and her pregnancy from Mayakovsky. When they saw each other again in the summer of that same year, Mayakovsky was working on a poem which had been conceived during the Futurist tour that same winter. Sonya remembered how he paced up and down the room mumbling lines of verse. This was how he "wrote," by beating out the rhythm with his footsteps.

Even if the object of the poet's love in the poem is called Mariya, it is likely that some of her features were borrowed from Sonya. But the principal model was a sixteen-year-old girl with that very name—Mariya Denisova—whom Mayakovsky fell head over heels in love with during an appearance in Odessa in January 1914. According to Vasily Kamensky, Mariya made him lose his head altogether. "Mariya had made such a huge impression on us that, when we got back to the hotel, it was ages before we managed to calm down," he remembered. "Burlyuk maintained a profound silence and kept his gaze fixed on Volodya, who was agitatedly pacing to and fro in the room, not knowing what to do with himself, what to do with this wave of love which had suddenly burst over him. . . he rushed from one corner to another repeating in

Mariya Denisova, whose beauty Mayakovsky in "A Cloud in Trousers" compared to that of Mona Lisa: "You said, / 'Love, / money, / passion, / Jack London'— / but all I saw was: / you're a Gioconda / that has to be stolen!"

an undertone: 'What am I to do? How should I act? But isn't it just stupid? . . . Shall I tell her what's what, straight off? Then she'll be frightened.'"

Mariya also came to the Futurists' next two performances, and her presence made Mayakovsky "lose his head completely"—"he couldn't sleep at night and didn't let us sleep either," Kamensky recalled. But when Mayakovsky at last declared his love, on the same day on which the Futurists left town to continue their tour, the result was bitter disappointment: Mariya had already promised herself to another (and indeed got married later that same year).

One evening all three Futurists, Mayakovsky, Burlyuk, and Kamensky drew portraits of Mariya. Reproduced here are Mayakovsky's (*previous page*) and Burlyuk's. On the back of Burlyuk's drawing, there is a cryptogram that has been deciphered thus: "I love you . . . dear sweet adored kiss me do you love me?"—a trace of Mayakovsky's declaration of love.

However short the acquaintanceship with Mariya was, it gave Mayakovsky the fuel for his first longer poem (*poema* in Russian) and one of the foremost lyric achievements of his whole career. The lines "You think malaria makes me delirious? / It happened. / In Odessa, it happened" were inspired by her.

LILI

2

1891–1915

**After even the briefest meeting with Osya
I realized that I loved no one but him.**
Lili Brik

Just as happened with Mayakovsky, Lili and Osip Brik were swept along by the revolutionary tide of 1905. They were children of the same time and the same country—but not of the same social class, which made their confrontation with raw Russian reality rather less dramatic. Whereas Mayakovsky served three prison sentences, Osip was punished with a short-lived expulsion from school, and while Mayakovsky was spending five months in solitary confinement, Osip's knowledge of such things was confined to the facts he assembled in order to be able to write an essay on the subject for his law exams. On the other hand, the Briks were exposed to the capriciousness of the authorities for reasons which had nothing to do with their political views, but with the fact that they were not ethnic Russians, but Jews.

Lili Yuryevna Kagan was born in Moscow on 11 November 1891. Her given name—unusual in Russia—

Lili photographed on her twenty-third birthday, 11 November 1914.

was inspired by a biography of Goethe that her father was reading when she was born. One of the German author's lovers was called Lili Schönemann. But mostly the Russian form of the name, *Lilya*, was used.

Her father, Yury Alexandrovich Kagan (1861–1915) had been born to a Jewish family in Libau in Kurland (now Latvia), which was a part of the Russian Empire. His Jewish name was Uri. The family were poor and unable to finance his studies. In order to acquire a higher education, therefore, he made his way—on foot!—to Moscow, where he took a law degree. However, as career opportunities for Jews in tsarist Russia were extremely limited, Yury Alexandrovich was not allowed to practice as an advocate but was represented in court by his non-Jewish colleagues. Indignant at these injustices, he came to specialize in "Jewish matters," including accommodation issues. In the Russian Empire, Jews were confined to particular areas and not allowed to live in the major cities unless they underwent baptism or were promoted to the status of "merchant of the first guild." He also worked as a consultant to the Society for Dissemination of Correct Information about Jews. As a result of her father's—and the family's—exposed position, Lili's attitude to Jewishness was, in her own words, "strained from the very beginning." However, Yury Alexandrovich did not concern himself exclusively with Jewish issues; among other things, he also worked as a legal adviser to the Austrian embassy.

Her mother, Yelena Yulyevna (née Berman, 1872–1942), was also from Kurland (Riga), and grew up in a Jewish family which spoke German and Russian. She was extremely musical and studied piano at the Moscow Conservatory. The fact that she failed to achieve the professional career she was destined for was not due to her origins, however. She married while still a student and consequently was never awarded a final diploma. "My childhood memories are set to music," Lili recalled. "There was not a single evening when I did not fall asleep to the sound of music. Mother was an excellent musician and spent every free minute playing [the piano]. There were two grand pianos in the salon, and for long periods they were played eight handed, and almost every evening a quartet was arranged." Yelena Yulyevna was a Wagner enthusiast and went to the festival in

Bayreuth as often as she could. Her other favorite composers included Schumann, Tchaikovsky, and Debussy.

Her musicality was inherited by her daughter: "Before I was a year old I was regarded as a musical prodigy," Lili remembered. From the age of six she was given lessons by her mother, which led to a growing distaste for music. This effect is not unusual when children are taught by their parents, but in Lili's case her reaction was also a manifestation of a strongly developed feeling of independence unusual for her age. She

Lili with her younger sister Elsa, ca. 1900.

could not bear any external pressure. Not even a professional piano teacher could prevail upon her. When she finally realized that it was the instrument, not the teacher, that was the problem, she asked if she could begin playing the violin instead. She practiced like one possessed and made great strides, thanks to her teacher, Grigory Kreyn, and despite her father's opposition ("Today the violin, tomorrow the drum!"). But when, as a gesture of reconciliation, Yury Alexandrovich gave Lili a violin case as a birthday present, the fire went out and she immediately became "bored stiff with the violin." We see here evidence of another of her character traits: however quickly she became enthused by something, she could just as suddenly lose interest, become "bored stiff." She always needed new sources of stimulation.

When Lili was five she acquired a sister, Elsa, who was born in October 1896. Every year the girls and their parents traveled to cities and spas in Western Europe: Paris and Venice, Spa and Thuringia, Nådendal and Hangö. Little is known about Lili's early childhood years, but a letter she wrote at the age of ten to her maternal aunt Ida and uncle Akiba Danzig gives an indication of her defiant mindset:

"Forgive me for not writing for such a long time but if you knew how boring it is you wouldn't demand so much of me."

OSIP

"The year of 1905 began with my accomplishing a revolution in the fourth year of gymnasium," she remembered. "We were forced to wear our hair in plaits on the tops of our heads, my plaits were heavy, and I had a headache every day. One day I persuaded the girls to come to school with their hair down, and we went in to morning prayers with that hairstyle." This stratagem met with opposition not only from the school authorities but also from her father, who shouted that if she left the house with her hair down it would be over his dead body—not because he did not understand her but because he was afraid she would get into trouble. She sneaked out via the kitchen stairs.

The protest was childish, but revolution was in the air. In the winter of 1905 the "first Russian revolution" had broken out and the protests against the power of the tsar infected schoolchildren too. Lili and her friends organized meetings at home and in the gymnasium, demanded freedom for Poland and set up a course in political economy. The course was conducted by the brother of one of Lili's school friends, Osip Brik, who was in the eighth year of the Third Gymnasium and had just been expelled for revolutionary propaganda. All the girls attending the course were in love with him and they would carve his pet name Osya on the school bench. But Lili was only thirteen and had other things on her mind than boys.

The course did not last long. A state of emergency was soon declared in Moscow, and people covered their windows with blankets and tried to stay indoors. Yury Alexandrovich slept with a revolver on his bedside table. As Jews, the Kagan family were particularly exposed and on one occasion, when there was a rumor of a coming pogrom, for safety's sake they spent two nights in a hotel.

Osip Maximovich Brik was born in Moscow on 16 January 1888. His father, Maxim Pavlovich, was a merchant of the first guild and therefore, as a Jew, entitled to live in Moscow. His firm, Pavel Brik Widow & Son dealt in jewelry and—first and foremost—in coral. Osip's

Osip's father Maxim Brik photographed during one of his business trips to Irkutsk in Siberia.

mother, Polina Yuryevna, was an educated woman, fluent in languages and liberal like her father; according to Lili she knew the works of the nineteenth-century radical Alexander Herzen by heart.

What was sold as "corals" was in actual fact a special kind of sand which was transformed into coral-like small stones, and which was found in the Bay of Naples. The discovery made the Brik family into millionaires. "Coral" was sold not so much in Moscow as in Siberia and Central Asia, to which Maxim Pavlovich traveled several times a year.

That Osip was a gifted young man is shown by the fact that he attended Moscow's Third Gymnasium, which, in accordance with the prevailing quota system, took in only two Jewish boys each year. And his expulsion was obviously short lived, as he left the gymnasium in the summer of 1906 with an "excellent" for conduct on his certificate.

The other Jewish boy who was admitted to the school in 1898 under the quota system was called Oleg Fröhlich. With three other classmates they formed a closed circle of friends who stayed together during the whole of their time at gymnasium. Their emblem was a five-pointed star, and they did everything together: went on binges, courted young girls, made fun of their teachers. "The friends were inseparable, they weren't a group or a society but a gang," Lili recalled. "They had a language all of their own. They spoke with one voice and sometimes scared the living daylights out of those around them."

But the "gang of five" did not simply indulge in teenage pranks; they were radical and idealistic, and on one occasion they clubbed

The high-school student Osip Brik, the girls' dream prince.

together to buy a sewing machine for a prostitute. They were also interested in literature. Their ideal was Russian Symbolism, which was at its height at the turn of the century, and Osip wrote Symbolist-inspired poems himself. He also wrote a novel with two of his friends. It bore the title *The Wrestling King* and was distributed by the town's newspaper vendors. However much solidarity with his cronies meant to Osip, the young Miss Kagan made a big impression on him. "I began to receive phone calls from Osip," Lili said. "I spent Christmas Eve with the Briks. Osya took me home and suddenly asked me, in

Lili on vacation with the family in 1906, when she received the letter from Osip that she tore into pieces. Her father is the man on the left; next to him, in black, is her mother, and, to the right of her, leaning against the basketwork chair, Lili herself. The little girl sitting in the sand is Elsa.

the carriage: 'Don't you think, Lili, that there's something more than friendship between us?' I didn't think there was, I had quite simply not given it a moment's thought, but I liked the way he put it and, taken by surprise, replied: 'Yes, I do.'" They began to see each other, but some time later Osip explained that he had been mistaken and did not love her as much as he had thought. She was thirteen, he was seventeen, he found it more interesting to discuss politics with Lili's father than to go out with her, and she was jealous. But after a while the relationship revived and they began to see each other again. "I wanted to be with him every minute of the day," Lili wrote, and she did "everything that a seventeen-year-old boy must have found vulgar and sentimental": "When Osya sat in the window I immediately sat in an armchair at his feet. On the sofa I sat by his side and held his hand. He would stand up abruptly, pace up and down the room, and in all this time, about half a year, he only kissed me once, on the throat, awkwardly, almost as a joke."

Lili spent the summer of 1906 with her mother and little sister, Elsa, in the spa of Friedrichroda in Thuringia. Osip promised to write to her every day, but despite Lili's repeated and despairing reminders, there was no word from him. When at last she received a letter, its contents were such that she tore it into pieces and stopped writing herself. This was exactly what Osip had been hoping for, but for Lili his tepid wording came as a shock. She began to lose her hair and developed nervous facial tics which she would never be rid of. A few days after her return from Moscow they met in the street. Osip had acquired pince-nez, and she thought he had become older and uglier. They stood and chatted, and although Lili was trying hard to appear uninterested, she suddenly heard herself say: "But I love you, Osya." Despite everything he had subjected her to, it was clear to her that it was only Osip she loved, that she could love. In the years that followed she had many love affairs, and sometimes she even came close to marrying, but she only needed to see Osip to break with her suitor. "After even the shortest encounter with Osya I realized that I didn't love anyone but him."

ABORTION IN ARMAVIR

Mathematics came easy to Lili and she left high school in 1908 with the highest mark in the subject: 5+. "After high school I wanted to go on to Professor Guerrier's higher courses for women, in the mathematics faculty. In the final examinations I had done so brilliantly in mathematics that the rector asked papa to call round for a chat and urged him not to let me waste my mathematical talent."

As Jewish girls were not accepted by Guerrier without a school-leaving certificate, Lili began studying at the Lazarev Institute for Boys, where, among a hundred boys, there were only two girls, one of whom, according to Lili, was "unspeakably ugly." "When I was translating Julius Caesar, the headmaster helped me by translating from Latin to French in a whisper, whereupon I blurted the Russian

Lili during the vacation in Germany in the summer of 1906.

translation out loud. In natural history I was asked what color my blood was, where my heart was located, and if there were occasions when it beat faster. . . . When the history teacher caught sight of me he would start to his feet and offer me a chair. I didn't need to answer a single question but still got a top mark. The boys were intensely jealous of me."

In 1909 Lili started at the mathematics faculty, but her interest in the subject gradually waned, and the following term she began studying at the Moscow Institute of Architecture, where a sculpture class had just been set up. Here, she studied painting and plastic art.

Lili's father knew the headmaster of the Lazarev Institute, but that was not why she enjoyed such success with the male teachers. Although she was not conventionally pretty—her head, for example, was disproportionately big for her body—from her earliest years she was extremely alluring to men of all ages, not least because of her blinding smile and her large dark eyes. Perhaps no one has depicted her appearance and temperament better than her own sister. Lili's hair had "a dark red color, and her round eyes were nut-brown," writes Elsa, continuing:

> She had a large mouth with perfect teeth and a glowing complexion, as if she was illuminated from within. She had a neat bust, round hips, long legs and very small hands and feet. She had nothing to hide; she could have gone around completely naked; every little part of her body was admirable. Moreover, she liked going around with nothing on at all; she was completely lacking in shame. Later, when she was going to a ball, mama and I liked to watch her getting dressed, putting on her underclothes, fastening her silk stockings and pulling on her little silver shoes and the lilac dress with the square décolletage. I was dumb with admiration when I looked at her.

It was in the summer of 1906, Lili recalled, that the attentions began in earnest. While she was on a visit to Belgium a young student asked for her hand. "I said no without giving him the ghost of a chance, but I received a postcard in Moscow with a picture of ivy and the caption: 'Je meurs où je m'attache [I die where I get stuck].'" If the flirtation was serious on the student's part it was anything but on Lili's; she was only fourteen years old. But her exceptional powers of attraction were a constant source of anxiety to her parents, and Lili was forced to write one letter of rejection after another to lovesick admirers, often at her mother's dictation.

Two years later, just as Lili was preparing for her school-leaving examinations, her music teacher Grigory Kreyn turned up again, and they started seeing each other. They played the violin together and discussed music. Lili was impressed by his outspoken views on the classics: Beethoven was repulsive, Tchaikovsky vulgar, and Schubert would have been better off if he had spent his life in an pub. One day Kreyn robbed her of her innocence while his girlfriend was busy washing up in the next room. "I didn't want to," she recalled, but "I was seventeen and afraid of appearing bourgeois."

Lili became pregnant. The first person she confided in was Osip, whose immediate reaction was to offer to marry her. But when she realized, after a sleepless night, that the offer was probably dictated by pity, she declined. Instead she asked her mother to go away with her, but without telling her that she was pregnant. As Yelena Yulyevna disliked Kreyn, she was glad of the opportunity to take Lili out of his sight and suggested that they travel to Nice or Italy. But instead Lili asked if they could go to Armavir in southern Russia, where she hoped that Aunt Ida, with her sober temperament, would have a calming influence on her mother.

In fact, the opposite occurred. When Lili told them she was pregnant and moreover wanted to keep the baby, her mother and aunt were distraught and demanded that she have an abortion. The mood was scarcely improved by the telegram which arrived from her father in Moscow: "KNOW EVERYTHING. WRETCH HAS SENT ME THE LETTERS." Convinced that Lili had been taken away against her will, Kreyn had sent her father the letters she had written to him, in order to show how much they loved each other.

Abortions were forbidden in Russia, but the number of illegal interventions was considerable, and it increased dramatically during the first years of the century. The abortion was carried out by a doctor whom Lili's paternal uncle knew in a railway hospital outside Armavir, which, according to Lili, was "an absolute hotbed of lice."

Afterward, when the doctor offered to restore Lili's maidenhead, she protested violently. But her mother prayed and begged and assured Lili that one day she would fall in love and want to conceal her shame from her future husband. Despite her daughter's protests—"But I am not going to deceive the man I fall in love with"—the procedure was carried out. Lili reacted with her usual defiance. When, several days later, the doctor removed the stitches, she rushed straight into the toilet and robbed herself of her innocence again, this time with her finger.

After the abortion Lili did not want to return to Moscow. Instead, she went to another maternal aunt in Tbilisi. On the train she made the acquaintance of an officer, whom she flirted with all night long, sitting on a packing case full of cackling geese. When the officer learned that Lili was Jewish, he tried to reassure her by saying that it didn't really matter, as she was a woman—with a bit of luck she could make a Christian marriage. "He was very aggressive with his attentions," Lili recalled. "He even took out a revolver and threatened to shoot me if I didn't agree to kiss him, but I didn't do it and still survived." The flirtations continued in Tbilisi: a rich Jew asked for Lili's hand and promised her 2000 rubles a month for clothes alone, and a Tatar prince who had been educated in Paris tried to talk her into accompanying him on a trip to the Caucasus mountains. Lili was not entirely unwilling but her aunt put her foot down.

After Georgia, Lili and her mother and Elsa converged on Katowice in Prussia (present-day Poland), where Yelena Yulyevna's brother lived. Not even Uncle Leo could resist Lili's precocious charms but threw himself at her and demanded that she marry him. Lili complained bitterly to her mother that she could hardly say two words to a man without his asking for her hand. "You always say that it's my fault and now it's your own brother, what have I done?" Yelena Yulyevna was justifiably outraged by her brother's behavior but did not know whether to laugh or cry. Perhaps she realized that her daughter was right when she insisted that she was not always to blame herself for all the uncontrolled outpourings of emotion that followed in her wake.

The convalescent trip continued to a sanatorium outside Dresden. The patients consisted of "young people suffering from nicotine poisoning, old maids, a scraggy Rumanian lady with pimples and a name ending in 'esco,' and then me," recalled Lili, who immediately attracted lustful glances from the male convalescents. A Herr Becker, who was married, tried unsuccessfully to get her drunk, and a young lieutenant who claimed to hate Jews declared he was ready to marry in a synagogue for her sake. When the old maids began whispering that Lili had visited the toilet with two men she was interrogated on the subject by the sanatorium's *Frau* but categorically denied having done so.

Back in Moscow, Lili resumed her studies with Professor Guerrier; but she could not forget what had happened at Armavir—the assault on her physical and emotional integrity which had taken place with her mother's consent had wounded her deeply. For a long time she had been hoarding a glass jar of potassium cyanide in the drawer of her writing desk. One morning she swallowed the whole contents, waited for a minute or so, and then began crying hysterically. After a whole day in bed she went to school again the following morning.

Lili could not understand why she had not died. Later she found out that her mother, in the course of searching for letters from Kreyn, had opened the drawer of her writing desk, found the poison, washed out the glass jar, and filled it with soda powder. Then she had followed Lili at a distance for several days, afraid that she would throw herself under a tram.

The person who had given Lili the bottle with a death's head and two crossed bones on the label was called Osip Volk. He was the son of a rich saddler and so in love with her that he wanted her to die so that he could kill himself afterward.

WOMAN IN A CORSET

The turbulence of the last few years made Lili long to leave Moscow. She also wanted to continue her sculpture studies. One of the "jeunesse dorée" she went around with was Genrikh Blumenfeld, a young artist who had studied painting in Paris. Harry, as he was called—having been born in the United States—was two years younger than Lili, barely eighteen years old, but his was a personality that glowed in

Lili's beau, Harry Blumenfeld

any company or context. When the young painter with the agitated features spoke about older masters, or drawing, or form, or Cézanne, or the paths that the new art was taking, everyone listened as if spellbound. According to Lili, "everything, including his outward appearance, was unusual": "A very dark complexion, hair black and brilliantined; eyebrows like wings; light-gray eyes, a gentle and intelligent gaze; a protruding lower jaw and an enormous, lascivious mouth with downward-pointing corners which almost seemed as if they didn't belong to him."

Once it had been decided that Lili would study sculpture abroad, she contacted Harry, who advised her to go to Munich, since, according to him, she was too young for Paris. He had her completely in his power: she was impressed by his drawings, and his conversation was so inspiring that it brought a blush to her cheeks. Once when she picked up his powder compact to apply some powder, he screeched: "What are you doing, I have syphilis!" With that exclamation he won her heart, and during the last two weeks before she left for Munich they began an intimate relationship, without a thought for his illness. When she visited the Briks to say her farewells, for the first time it was not Osip who was the focus of her thoughts. Lili was thinking of herself, full of new feelings and new dreams. Osip begged her not to go, but in the late spring of 1911 she traveled to Munich in company with her mother and Elsa. A few months later, Harry followed her.

In Munich Lili rented a small furnished room and began studying at the Studio Schwägerle, one of the city's most respected artists' studios. She sculpted every day from half past eight until six, and once a week she had drawing. Working beside her in the studio was a young girl from Odessa, Katia, who was barely a year older than Lili but very advanced for her age. When on occasions she spent the night at Lili's there would be fondling and caresses, and Lili gradually became more adept in the secrets and techniques of love.

It was Katia who introduced Lili to Alexey Granovsky, a theater student of her own age who was in Munich to study theater directing with Max Reinhardt. They started seeing each other, went to cafés, and ate colossal amounts of *Mocca-Eis*, they visited museums and secondhand bookshops, and Granovsky showed her his theater sketches and notes on direction. They spent the nights together in his little apartment, and each morning Lili took a taxi home. This routine was broken when Harry, whose arrival she was expecting, and Osip Volk, who was totally unexpected, appeared simultaneously in Munich. "I was run off my feet," Lili recalled. "They all had to be kept unaware of each other's existence. Osip was staying in a hotel, but I rushed around looking for a studio for Harry, and Granovsky was just Granovsky."

After a while Lili managed to dispatch Volk to Moscow. Faced with a choice between Granovsky and Blumenfeld, she preferred the latter. She was not in love with him, but he fascinated her and she felt sorry for him. Eventually Granovsky also took his leave and Lili was left alone with Harry.

Harry had come to Munich to paint Lili, in the guise of *Venus* and *Woman in a Corset*. She posed naked for the Venus painting, lying on a chalk-white starched sheet spread over a divan. *Woman in a Corset* was based on Rubens's paintings of the Madonna and Child but differed from its models in that Lili was clad in a red corset with sheer black silk stockings. However, the paintings appear never to have been completed, and the sittings came to an end of their own accord because of Harry's severe headaches, a side-effect of syphilis. The pain only eased toward evening, when they made love. According to Lili, Harry was "monstrous in his erotomania" and forced her into acts she had never before taken part in or even heard of. The doctor warned Lili that Harry was very infectious and she must be extremely careful. Yet they often had intercourse. "I was so dreadfully sorry for him," she explained.

MADLY IN LOVE

By the middle of December 1911 Lili was back in Moscow again. On the very day of her arrival she bumped into Osip Brik at the Artists' Theater, and they agreed to meet at a Jewish charity ball the following day. After a few minutes' conversation with Osip she told him yet again that she loved him. The next day they took a walk through the town. "I told him about Munich, Harry, and my work," she recalled. "We went into a restaurant, sat down in a private room, ordered a pot of coffee, and then Osip asked me straight out to be his wife. I said yes."

Lili's parents, exhausted from the frights their eldest daughter had given them over the years, were very pleased with her decision. Osip's father and mother were abroad and had to be informed by letter. Osip wrote to them on 19 December:

> I can no longer conceal from you what fills my heart; I cannot help sharing with you my infinite happiness, although I know that this news will make you anxious; that is why I have not written before. [. . .] But I cannot hide it from you any longer. I have become engaged. My fiancée, as you can no doubt guess, is Lili Kagan. I am madly in love with her, and always have been. And she loves me as no woman in the world has ever loved. You cannot imagine, dear papa and mama, in what a happy state I find myself at present. I beg you to act in this matter as I have dreamed that you will. I know you love me and wish me the greatest good luck. You should therefore know that this good luck has now materialized. [. . .] As soon as you receive this letter, telegraph me your blessing immediately; only then can I feel completely happy.

What Maxim Pavlovich and Polina Yuryevna telegraphed, however, was not a blessing but the diametrical opposite. Lili's rackety biography was no secret as far as they were concerned, and Osip's father asked him to think twice before taking such an important step. Lili had an artistic nature, he felt, and what Osip needed was a calm and peaceful home. His mother, who knew even more about Lili's past, was in a state of shock.

To calm his parents down, Osip wrote them another letter. After the opening sentence, "As I expected, you have been very surprised and worried by the news of my engagement to Lili," he went on:

Lili, my fiancée, young, pretty, educated, from a good family, a Jewess, is frightfully in love with me, is that not enough? Her past? But the past, what is that? Childish games resulting from a passionate temperament. What modern woman has not done as much? And for my own part? I have certainly not had such a good time as she has, but I have no problem forgetting every trace of past and future affairs, since I love Lili. It is even easier for her, as she has only loved me. [. . .] In conclusion, I wish to express my conviction that if, as I believe, you entertain some preconceived ideas about Lili, then these will vanish as soon as you come to know her better and see how she loves me, and, most important of all, how I love her and how happy we are together.

Osip was serious about his plans to marry, and his parents were reluctantly forced to accept the fact. "I won their hearts by asking for a Steinway as a wedding present instead of a diamond ring," Lili recalled. "From this they drew the conclusion that I was cultivated and unselfish."

In the weeks following their engagement Lili and Osip met every day and philosophized the nights away. The decisive confirmation that they were made for each other came in their conversations about the supernatural: "Osip listened to me then, in a state of high excitement, went over to the desk, took out a notebook full of writing and started reading out, in almost exactly the same words, what I had just said." In January Osip went off to Siberia on business for the family firm while Lili busied herself fitting out the apartment which her parents had rented for them in central Moscow.

The wedding took place on 11 March 1912. Lili and Osip were Jewish but they were not religious and did not wish to marry in the synagogue. Instead they were married in the Kagan household by Moscow's rabbi, who, however, had to promise not to make a speech—otherwise Lili would terminate the ceremony! But her father had warned his friend the rabbi about Lili's "whims," and the wedding proceeded without incident. Osip rattled off a prayer he had learned specially for the occasion and the rabbi rounded off the solemn ceremony with the sour comment: "I hope I have not detained the happy couple too long."

Everything points to the fact that Lili and Osip were deeply in love. In letters to their friends Osip wrote that he could not be without her "for a minute" and was "unspeakably happy" that she had agreed to be his wife. Yet Osip knew more than most about Lili's colorful biography and had even offered to marry her when another man had made her pregnant. Lili's pleasure in sexual experimentation, which would have caused most men to have second thoughts, seems not to have frightened Osip off.

One of the reasons that Osip was not disturbed by Lili's promiscuity seems to have been that he did not associate love with sex. If Lili had "a heightened curiosity about sex," as a female friend expressed it, the opposite seems to have been true of Osip, who seems not to have been particularly bothered by the fact that this curiosity was not satisfied even after their marriage. "We never slept in the same bed; he couldn't, didn't like it, said that he didn't get any rest that way," Lili explained. Moreover, Osip had a character trait that would become accentuated with the years: his moral relativism. "I can't get my head round his moral physiognomy," wrote Pyotr Mzhedlov, one of the "gang of five," to another member of the group, Oleg Fröhlich, in the same year in which Osip and Lili got married.

CARAVANSARIES AND BROTHELS

Osip studied law at Moscow University for four years and took his final diploma in the spring of 1911. His assignment was a paper on solitary confinement. Its conclusion was radical for its time: "Society is powerless in the face of crimes which have already been committed, and no influence exerted on the perpetrator will lead to the desired result; only social reforms which basically make criminal behavior impossible can give mankind victory over this evil."

Osip's thesis was intended to deal with the sociological and legal status of prostitutes—widespread prostitution was the subject of innumerable discussions and writings during these years. He walked

Lili and Osip as newlyweds, with Elsa (left).

round the boulevards of Moscow collecting material, got to know many prostitutes, and supported them in their dealings with the police and clients. But he demanded no "recompense" for his services, which made a big impression on the girls, who flattered him with the pet name "sugar daddy." The thesis was never written, however.

After a few months' military service in the summer of 1911 Osip seems to have worked for a time as a lawyer, but after his marriage he gave up the law and instead began to work for the family firm. The head office was in Moscow, but the trade in coral was mostly carried on in other places, which entailed many long journeys to remote parts of the Russian Empire.

On a few occasions Osip took Lili with him on these trips. The first summer after their wedding they visited the market at Nizhny Novgorod, where Pavel Brik Widow & Son had booth number 15 in the caravansary. The living quarters were above the shop. Every morning when Osip went downstairs to work, he locked the door from the outside. The rules were strictly Islamic: women were not allowed out alone and even on visits to the toilet Lili was accompanied by a guard. But in the evenings they went out to an entertainment venue together: "The merchants disported themselves like kings, and the number of diamonds adorning the young and strikingly beautiful Jewess in Spanish costume [who performed] increased with every night," Lili recalled. That same winter they traveled to Chita and Verkhneudinsk in Siberia (near the border with China and Mongolia), where the firm of Brik was also represented at the market. The customers were Buryats, who apart from coral also bought clocks without works, which they used as cases.

For two autumns in a row, in 1912 and 1913, Osip and Lili traveled around in Turkestan. On one occasion they invited the young poet Konstantin Lipskerov to accompany them—"Even then we had a touch of the Maecenas about us," Lili commented later. Osip had been there before, but for Lili it was a strange new world. They were inundated with presents in the Oriental manner; they drank green tea and ate flatbread and pilaf till they choked on it. Just as in the caravansary in Nizhny Novgorod, men and women lived strictly separate lives. Once, when Lili and Osip were visiting a rich merchant, before they sat down to table the merchant went over to the women's part of the house to tell them that another woman was visiting. "When he returned," Lili recalled, "he was in very high spirits and was carrying a newborn baby in his arms. He had been to Moscow and had come back but had had so much to do that he had not had time to look in on the women. He didn't even know that one of

Lili and Osip in Turkestan with the poet Konstantin Lipskerov and a Turkmen boy.

them was pregnant, but the little boy turned out to be two months already."

Life in Turkestan was exotic, and Lili was inquisitive and adventurous. One day an acquaintance offered to take her to his sister so she could see how a Turkmen woman lived. Lili accepted, and they went to the old part of Samarkand. While they were sitting drinking tea, eating sweetmeats, and having a quiet chat, they heard a frantic knocking, and a man whom Lili knew burst in panting and with a terrified expression: someone had seen her with a strange man and concluded that she had been abducted in order to be sold.

On another occasion, this time in company with Osip, Lili visited a brothel in Samarkand. Whether it was Lili's sexual or Osip's sociological curiosity that lay behind the initiative is a moot point, but their interest in such things was not entirely new kindled—during their trip to Paris in the winter of 1912–13 they had visited a *maison de rendez-vous* where they had studied a sex show with a lesbian couple.

In Samarkand brothels were a relative novelty; hitherto men had satisfied their needs with the help of long-haired young boys, so-called *bachi*, who danced and entertained in the teahouses. The

A typical teahouse (*chai-khana*) at the river in Kokand in Turkestan.

brothels were in a street outside the city—the only place where one could see women without veils. Lili's description of a brothel in Samarkand in 1912 is worth quoting:

> The street is illuminated with colored lights; on the verandas sit women, mostly Tatars, playing instruments resembling mandolins or guitars. It's quiet and still and there are no drunks. We called on the richest and best-known of them. She lives with her old mother. There are cords suspended from the low ceiling of the bedroom, and all her dresses are hanging from the cords. Everything is Oriental, but in the middle of the room stands a nickel-plated double bed.
>
> We were received in the traditional Central Asian manner. The low table is groaning with fruit and Oriental sweetmeats on a bewildering array of dishes. The tea is green. The musicians come in, sit on their hunkers, and our hostess begins to dance. Her gray dress reaches the floor, the sleeves are so long that you can't see her hands, and the collar hides her throat, but when she begins to

move, it becomes apparent that it is only the collar that is buttoned up, the dress is slit down to her knees and without a single clasp. She has nothing on underneath, and the least movement reveals her naked body.

DESERTER

Lili and Osip were genuinely interested in literature, paintings, music, the theater, and ballet, and they often read aloud to each other: Russian, German, and French classics, Nietzsche's *Thus Spake Zarathustra* and Kierkegaard's *In Vino Veritas*. They also liked Italian literature and studied Italian for a while. Osip's ex libris showed Paolo embracing Francesca, with the relevant quotation from Dante's *Divine Comedy*: "And that day we read no more." In other words, the Briks belonged to what is usually called the educated middle classes. But they were far from devoting themselves exclusively to cultural activities. They lived a carefree life which also included less demanding activities such as variety shows and car trips—a fashionable pursuit at the beginning of the century—and an interest in horse racing led them to wear out the seats in the grandstands as much as those in the theaters. There was no lack of money. Osip came from a prosperous home, and Lili had received a dowry of 30,000 rubles, corresponding to almost £230,000 in today's money. A third of it went into

Osip's ironic ex libris, with the text from Dante's *Divine Comedy*: "And that day we read no more."

furnishing their apartment, and they had no trouble dissipating the rest.

The people they socialized with came from the same well-heeled and often decadent milieu, and several of them were decidedly eccentric. These included the Albrecht family, which had one of the first motorcars in Moscow, an enormous English bulldog, a snake, and a female ape named after Don Juan's first wife, which was given manicures like any other lady. Their daughter was a lesbian, but unfaithful to her "husband" Sonya with men as well as women. Obsessed with Casanova, she dreamed of landing up in hell so she could meet him there.

Another original acquaintance was Zinaida Stilman, who despite being small and rotund with birthmarks on one cheek had been married five times and was courted by Grand Duke Dmitry Pavlovich. Once when Lili asked her if it was true that she lived with men for money, she asked with unfeigned astonishment: "Why, Lili Yuryevna, would it be better to do it for nothing?"

On their trips to Turkestan Osip and Lili became so fascinated by the culture and people of Central Asia that they thought seriously about settling there for a few years. But their plans were frustrated by the First World War, which broke out in the summer of 1914. One day before the declaration of war Lili and Osip boarded a Volga steamboat and did not return to Moscow until Osip's father had telegraphed to say that the first companies had gone off to the front and they could come home again. Lili would later attribute their flight to their "defeatism" and lack of "patriotic fervor."

While they waited for Osip's fate to be decided, the first transports with wounded men began to arrive in Moscow. Like so many others, Lili and Osip's sister Vera went on accelerated courses to train as nurses. The hospitals were full of soldiers who had had their legs amputated, and Lili later recalled with horror how she had been obliged to cut bandages from suppurating wounds.

Through his acquaintance with the famous tenor Leonid Sobinov, Osip managed to arrange to serve with a motorized company in Petrograd (as St. Petersburg had been renamed after the outbreak of war). In the autumn of 1914, accordingly, he and Lili left Moscow and moved to the capital, where initially they lived in a two-room apartment with full board on Zagorodny Prospekt. Later, in January 1915, they moved to an equally large apartment on Zhukovsky Street. Both addresses were right in the center of the city.

Despite his service with the motorized company, the threat of service at the front had not been wholly averted. On the advice of their friend Misha Grinkrug, Osip contacted the company clerk, a corrupt individual who was highly regarded for both the moderateness of his demands and for keeping his word. Company clerk Ignatyev hinted to Osip

Osip in the uniform he would soon hang up.

that he had the power to decide whether he was to remain in Petrograd or not. "Oh well, a man can live at the front too," said Osip in a defiant bid to stop Ignatyev bumping up the price. "Of course, but not for so long," replied Ignatyev. Osip appreciated this rejoinder and immediately gave him twenty-five rubles.

In order to keep in with Ignatyev, Lili and Osip sometimes invited him home for lunch. This proved to be a good investment, as it was not long before the army command decided that all Jews should be dispatched to the village of Medved in the Novgorod administrative district—"so as not to ruin the motorized company's pretty scenery," in Lili's words. Medved had a military colony founded by the reactionary minister of war Arakcheyev a hundred years earlier. The barracks culture typical of Nicholas I's reign permeated the whole atmosphere. It was no coincidence that a concentration camp for Japanese prisoners was set up in Medved during the Russo-Japanese War of 1904–5.

The Twenty-Second Division was stationed there as well as one of the Russian Empire's five disciplinary battalions. It was to one of these that Osip was to be sent, for forward posting to the front.

The disciplinary battalion in Medved was notorious all over Russia, and Lili declared that if Osip let himself be led off under escort like a thief or patricide then she was neither his wife nor his friend and she would never forgive him. The prospect was less than enticing, and Osip immediately sought out Ignatyev, who received another twenty-five rubles and saw to it that he was admitted to hospital. When the danger was over it emerged that Osip's name had disappeared from the rolls, and after a while the army forgot he existed. As he made no effort to remind them, he was to all intents and purposes a deserter and forced to go into hiding. He never went to the theater, never visited his parents in Moscow, and spent as little time out of the house as possible—he was "lower than the grass, quieter than the water," as the Russian expression has it. He passed the time constructing houses and other objects with playing cards: a theater, a tram, and a car, among other things—a hobby which Osip, with his versatile talents, brought to perfection.

During their early days in Petrograd, according to Lili, they socialized mostly with "distant relatives of Osip's relatives," some of whom were as uneducated as they were rich. One day one of them took Lili out to the tsar's summer palace at Tsarkoye Selo. Opposite Lili in the train compartment was a strange man who glanced at her from time to time. His beard was dirty and his nails black, but he was dressed in a long caftan with a gaudy silk lining, high boots and a handsome beaver cap, and he had a cane with a costly handle. "I studied him for a long time, quite shamelessly, while he glanced furtively at me. His eyes were bright blue, his gaze cheerful. Suddenly he snorted into his beard."

The man was Grigory Rasputin, the mystical monk with a hypnotic influence over the imperial family, especially the tsarina. On the return journey they ended up in the same compartment, and Rasputin invited Lili to come and call on him in his apartment in Petrograd, where hordes of admiring, credulous women gathered to be cured by the illiterate miracle worker. She was welcome to bring her husband with her, he added. Lili was, as usual, up for a bit of adventure, but Osip was as indifferent as she was enthusiastic and said he could not even understand her curiosity—"Surely everyone knows what a bunch of robbers that lot are."

As long as Osip was serving with the motorized company, Lili was alone during the day. She usually strolled along the quays to the Hermitage, where she would walk around for hours. In the end, she was as familiar to the attendants as the objects in the museum were to her. She often continued on to the Guards' Society department store, where she drank coffee and ate sandwiches. Sometimes she went to the cinema, irrespective of what was showing. "You cannot imagine how lonely I am here!" Lili wrote to Oleg Fröhlich in January 1915: "I have no one to talk to all day." Eventually her enforced idleness and depression made her desperate. One day, while out walking, she bumped into two young men from Moscow's beau monde and accompanied them to an operetta. Afterward they went to a restaurant, where they drank huge quantities of wine; Lili got drunk and described her experiences with Osip in the brothel in Paris. Her two suitors offered to show her a similar establishment in Petrograd and when she awoke next morning it was in a room with an enormous bed, a mirror in the ceiling, carpets and drawn curtains. She had spent the night in a notorious *maison de rendez-vous* in Apothecary Lane. She rushed straight home and confessed everything to Osip, who in a calm voice advised her to have a bath and forget the whole thing.

WHAT IS TO BE DONE?

Where other men's wives would have made every effort to hide their shame, Lili immediately told Osip what she had been up to, just as she had done when she discovered that she was pregnant. Osip, for his part, reacted coolly and rationally where other men would have been beside themselves with jealousy. And when Lili discovered that one of the young men was boasting about his conquest all over town, she bawled him out in public so that everyone could hear. She made no secret of her affairs and was never ashamed of them, and Osip reacted to them with an almost incomprehensible calmness, apparently not at all wounded in his masculine self-esteem. When Lili described these first years with Osip as the "happiest" of her life, she must surely have been referring not just to the love between them but also to the fact that Osip allowed her a degree of freedom she could not conceive living without, and which most other men would never have accepted.

Lili's emancipation reflected the independent turn of mind of a woman who refused to let herself be governed by prejudice and outside authority. But her relaxed attitude to sex was not only a question of personal inclination; it must be seen in a larger social context. The years following the revolution of 1905 were characterized by a strong interest in issues regarding sexuality, marriage, free love, contraception, and prostitution. The same problems were being discussed elsewhere in Europe. But the Russian debate needed no inspiration from outside; the reality at home provided enough fuel to keep it going.

Russian radicalism had its roots in two of the most influential novels of ideas to come out of the 1860s: Ivan Turgenev's *Fathers and Sons*, whose hero, the nihilist Bazarov, distanced himself from all of society's values; and Nikolay Chernyshevsky's *What Is to Be Done?*, perhaps the most important contribution to the debate about women's emancipation in Russia. Chernyshevsky's novel is about women's liberation from all kinds of oppression—by their parents, men, the institutions of society—and their right to study, work, and love. Marriage should be egalitarian, which among other things means that a woman should be able to live with men other than her husband, and have a bedroom of her own. "Who can own another person? A coat or a pair of slippers, yes. But this is nonsense!" Jealousy, Chernyshevsky avers, is "a perverted emotion, a false emotion, a wretched emotion." The secret behind every lasting relationship is both partners' awareness that the other one has the right to leave when they are no longer in love. The truly radical nature of Chernyshevsky's thinking is demonstrated by the fact that not only his heroine, Vera Pavlovna, but also her male counterpart respects these rules.

What Is to Be Done? was a source of inspiration for generations of Russian women and men. During the last decade of the nineteenth century the tensions in society became greater, and although the social order in Russia was difficult to upset, in 1905 the first Russian revolution broke out. However, the revolt was quelled, and despite certain political reforms the ensuing decade was to be marked by

stern political repression. Many radicals, like the proletarian writer
Maxim Gorky, were forced into exile, while other political activists
went underground and operated illegally. After years of engagement
with social and political issues young people in particular were as-
sailed by despair and resignation, and instead devoted their energies
to private problems. This mood was exacerbated by a social trend
which swept over Europe and which found more fertile soil in Russia
than anywhere else: decadence. In the cultural and intellectual realm
it found expression in the cult of "pure art" and in different forms
of occultism; in "life," it took the form of a libertine attitude to love
and sexuality which bordered on the amoral.

Free love and untrammeled love relationships were praised in
novel after novel. The best known of these was Mikhail Artsybashev's
Sanin of 1907, which applauded hedonism and total sexual expres-
sion. In the words of Richard Stites, a specialist in the history of the
Russian women's movement, "young people vented their blocked
energies in sexual adventures and carnal excesses, covering their
compulsive behavior with the vulgar Saninist notion of pleasure for
its own sake." The attitude toward sex during the first years of the
twentieth century was so nonchalant that, according to one Russian
writer, there were educated women for whom a love affair was no
more memorable than "a chance dinner companion and the menu
in the restaurant where they happened to dine."

It was in this social climate that Lili and Osip formed their view of
sexuality, marriage and domestic life; it is against this background
that their values and actions must be seen.

ELSA

Mayakovsky moved in circles associated with the artists' group Jack
of Diamonds, and so did Lili's sister, Elsa. For a short period she even
took lessons from Ilya Mashkov, who on one occasion is said to have
commented favorably on her drawings. Here she fell in love with Lili's
old suitor Harry Blumenfeld, who had begun as a pupil in Mashkov's
studio after returning from Munich and who is described in Elsa's
diary as "lecherous" but with "wonderful eyes." But her love was not
returned, Harry loved another—and besides Elsa was well aware that

The teenage-chubby Elsa, who complained to her diary that she was not beautiful enough: "God has given me the desire for love, He has created my soul for love, but He has not given me a body made for love."

her mother would never allow Harry to court her. Knowing that he had syphilis also made it easier to suppress her feelings for him.

Elsa's diary from 1912–13 bears witness to a large degree of self-absorption and a highly developed little-sister complex. She is sixteen or seventeen and compares herself in every way to Lili, whom she admires and wants to be like: "I ought to have been born really pretty. I think I wouldn't have needed much money then, I mean, not that I wouldn't have needed it, but like Lili I wouldn't have given it a thought." But their relationship was a complex one. At the same time as she complains that her big sister "as usual" pays no attention to her and does not care what she says, she delivers the following devastating characterization of herself: "I am shameless, insufferable, and never satisfied. The very image of Lili."

While Lili and Osip were traveling in Turkestan, she lived at their place and was affected by "strange thoughts" that "floated in the air" in their apartment. She had "sensual dreams," she wrote in her diary. She was "not exactly perverse" but rather "had a yen for indecent things, as long as they are not positively repulsive." She often fell in love, but her feelings were not seriously reciprocated and she suffered from what she perceived as an unattractive outward appearance: "God has given me the desire for love, He has created my soul for love, but He has not given me a body made for love."

It was in this—rather chubby—teenage body that Elsa first encountered Vladimir Mayakovsky at the home of the pianist Ida Khvas, who was a student at the Moscow Conservatory and a close friend of some of the Jack of Diamonds group. As the Kagan and Khvas families were friendly, Elsa and Lili had known Ida and her sister Alya since they were children.

According to Elsa, the meeting took place in the autumn of 1913, but the date is uncertain. In any event it was in the summer of 1914 that they began to see each other on a more regular basis. Now, after the Futurist tour that had attracted so much attention, Mayakovsky was no longer clad in frayed trousers with a shiny seat, but in a top hat and black overcoat, and on his promenades along the Moscow boulevards he swung an elegant walking stick. But he was just as incorrigible as ever, and Yury Alexandrovich and Yelena Yulyevna, in common with all the other parents, were deeply shocked by his coarse manner. This is how Elsa describes a lunch in the parental home:

> Volodya is quiet and polite and from to time he addresses mama with phrases like "Forgive me, Yelena Yulyevna, I seem to have scoffed all the beef patties . . ." and he categorically refuses to start up a conversation with papa. Toward the end of the evening, when my parents were about to go to bed, Volodya and I went into papa's study. . . . But mama didn't go to sleep, she waited for Volodya to finally take his leave and several times she came in in her dressing gown to chase him out the door: "It's time to go, Vladimir Vladimirovich . . ." Volodya wasn't offended, but he was stubborn and didn't go.

One might think that Yelena Yulyevna had been chastened by Lili's stormy youth, but not so: she was dismayed by Elsa's relationship with Mayakovsky and wept.

In the summer of 1914 Elsa accompanied her mother and father to Germany, where Yury Alexandrovich underwent an operation for cancer. When the war broke out they found themselves in a sanatorium outside Berlin and were obliged to return somewhat hastily to Russia. Back in Moscow, and recovered from his operation, Lili and Elsa's father resumed his legal career. But his health deteriorated again and a year later, in June 1915, he died.

During their father's convalescence Elsa had introduced Lili to Mayakovsky, who took the liberty one day of calling on them in their little apartment in Zhukovsky Street. He had come from the seaside resort of Kuokkala in Finland—then a Russian grand duchy—where he was spending the summer. He immediately began to boast that no one wrote better poems than he did but that no one understood them or recited them as they ought to be recited. When Lili asked to be allowed to try, he gave her "Mama and an evening murdered by the Germans." She read the poem as Mayakovsky wanted it to be read but when he asked if she liked it, she replied: "Not particularly." "I knew that one is supposed to praise writers," Lili recalled, "but Volodya's impudence annoyed me." Osip, who had bronchitis and was lying on the sofa reading a newspaper, turned his face to the wall and drew a blanket over himself to show that he thought Mayakovsky ought to go.

As opposed to Lili's and Osip's ostentatious indifference, Elsa's enthusiasm knew no bounds. She was obsessed by Mayakovsky's poems, which she knew by heart, and she defended him furiously against anyone who questioned his talent. After her father's funeral she lived for a time with Lili and Osip, who, however, would have greatly preferred Elsa to stop seeing him. As Mayakovsky occasionally called on her at Zhukovsky Street, the conflict eventually came to a head: "the Mayakovsky problem" had to be solved one way or another. The only way Elsa could rescue her relationship with Mayakovsky was to convince her sister and brother-in-law of his greatness as a poet, and the best way to achieve that would be if he were given an opportunity to read his poems to them. However, Lili and Osip stood firm and begged Elsa not to ask him to give a reading. But she paid no attention, "and so, for the first time," Lili recalled, "we got to hear 'A Cloud in Trousers.'"

The conflict was resolved, but not in the way that Elsa had imagined.

3

A CLOUD IN TROUSERS

1915–1916

Thief of my heart,
Who have stripped it of everything,
Who have tortured my soul in delirium,
Accept, my dearest, this gift—
Never, perhaps, shall I think of anything else.
Vladimir Mayakovsky, "The Backbone-Flute"
(trans. George Reavey)

"Mayakovsky did not change his pose once," Lili remembered. "He did not look at anyone. He complained, raged, mocked, demanded, became hysterical, pausing between the sections.

"Afterward he sits at the table and asks me for tea, with studied casualness. I hurry to pour him some from the samovar, I am silent, while Elsa says triumphantly: 'What did I tell you?'"

The first to pull himself together was Osip, who declared that Mayakovsky was a great poet even if he never wrote another line. He took from Mayakovsky his notebook with "A Cloud in Trousers" in it and did not let go of it the whole evening. When Mayakovsky

The artist Boris Grigoryev's painting with the neutral title *The Stranger* in all probability depicts Mayakovsky. It was painted in 1916, when it was shown at an exhibition arranged by the group The World of Art.

finally asked for it back, it was in order to dedicate the poem "To Lili Yuryevna Brik." This was the first time that a poem by Mayakovsky was crowned with her name, but it would not be the last. Before it was all over, he would dedicate each volume of his collected works to Lili.

Lili and Osip were probably the first to hear the final version of "A Cloud." Mayakovsky had previously read versions of the poem to, among others, Maxim Gorky, the literary critic Korney Chukovsky, and the painter Ilya Repin, and always with the same shattering effect. Gorky, for example, started to weep and was "both frightened and moved" by the author's way of "bursting into sobs like a woman." When he told Mayakovsky that he faced "a great but difficult future," the poet replied grimly that he wanted "to have the future today," adding, "I want no future without joy, and I feel no joy." He spoke, Gorky recalled, "as if with two voices, now like a pure lyric poet, now sharply satirical": "It was as if he did not know himself and was afraid of something. . . . But it was obvious that he was a person with a very special emotional life, very talented and—unhappy."

THE THIRTEENTH APOSTLE

What was it that reduced Gorky to tears and made Lili hail "A Cloud in Trousers" as something new and long awaited in literature? To anyone who was familiar with Mayakovsky's earlier poems, "A Cloud" was unexpectedly "un-Futurist." To be sure, it contains bold imagery and a series of neologisms, but it is not a formally complex experimental poem of the kind he was notorious for. What was new about it was its message and tone, which were more Expressionist than Futurist.

Gorky's comment about Mayakovsky's "two voices" hit the nail on the head. A few weeks after the reading at Lili and Osip's, Mayakovsky had an article published under the title "About the Two Mayakovskys." It opens with Mayakovsky introducing himself in the way he believes he is perceived by the public: a shameless cynic, provocateur, and self-publicist "whose greatest pleasure is to pounce, in his yellow blouse, on people who are nobly preserving their modesty and decency behind correct greatcoats, tails, and lounge suits." But behind the shameless cynic, provocateur, and self-publicist of twenty-two there lurks another person, he explains, "the totally unknown poet Vladimir Mayakovsky" who wrote "A Cloud in Trousers"—whereupon he cites a series of quotations from the poem which bear witness to a wholly different side of his personality.

Three years later, after the Revolution, Mayakovsky would describe the message of the poem's four sections in the following slogans: "Down with your love," "down with your art," "down with your system," "down with your religion." There is no such systematic method or symmetry in the poem, but if one substitutes the ideologically motivated pronoun "your" with the first person singular, the description may be said to be correct. "A Cloud in Trousers" deals with these things, but not about "your"—that is, capitalist society's—but about *my*, Mayakovsky's, pain-filled, unrequited love, *my* aesthetic ascent of Golgotha, *my* revolt against injustices, *my* struggle against a cruel and absent God.

"A Cloud" is one long monologue in which the poet in the first person turns toward—and mostly against—the world outside, everything that is "not-I." It begins with Mayakovsky, in Whitmanesque style, cheekily praising himself:

No gray hairs streak my soul,
No grandfatherly fondness there!
I shake the world with the might of my voice,
and walk—handsome,
twenty-two-year-old.

Already, here in the prologue, the reader is being prepared for the abrupt changes from one emotional state to another which permeate the poem:

If you wish,
I shall rage on raw meat
—or, as the sky changes its hue—
if you wish,
I shall grow irreproachably tender:
not a man, but a cloud in trousers!

The poem's first section is about his love for a young woman,

"Mariya," for whom Mariya Denisova was one of the models. Waiting for her to arrive for a rendezvous in a hotel, Mayakovsky hears a nerve jump out, "like a sick man from his bed," and begin to dash about "with a couple more /. . . in a desperate dance," so violent that the plaster falls from the ceiling in the room below:

> Nerves—
> big nerves,
> tiny nerves,
> many nerves!—
> galloped madly
> till soon
> their legs gave way.

When Mariya finally appears and explains that she is going to marry someone else, Mayakovsky is calm, "like the pulse / of a corpse." But his calmness is hard won; inside, there is another person who wants to break out of his "I." He is "gloriously ill"—that is, in love—and his heart is in flames. When the firemen come rushing in, Mayakovsky urges them to "climb lovingly when a heart's on fire" and tries to put out the fire himself by pumping "barrels of tears from my eyes." When he can't get it to stop, he braces himself "against my ribs," the rib cage breaks, but "you can't leap out from a heart"—one cannot be free from the eternal longing for love: "Moan / into the centuries, / if you can, a last scream: I'm on fire!"

In the next section, his mood is quite different: the despairing poet whose heart was on fire now appears in the role of a futuristic rebel and stamps *nihil* "upon every achievement":

> I never want
> to read anything.
> Books?
> What are books?

The time is past for authors who boil "a broth / of love and nightingales" while "the tongueless street merely writhes / for lack of something to shout or say." Modern life, the modern city, can only be celebrated by poets of the new era, "creators within a burning hymn— / the hum of mills and laboratories." However, Mayakovsky's way is strewn with thorns. The Futurists' tour of 1913–14 is presented as a road to Golgotha, where

> not a man
> but
> shouted:
> "Crucify,
> crucify him!"

Mayakovsky's poetic talent is dismissed, his contemporaries "mock" him "like a prolonged / dirty joke." But the future is his, and in a messianic prophecy he sees "whom no one sees, / crossing the mountains of time." He sees "a year" approaching, "in the thorny crown of revolutions":*

> And when,
> with rebellion
> his advent announcing,
> you step to meet the savior—
> then I
> shall root up my soul;
> I'll trample it hard
> till it spreads
> in blood—and offer you this as a banner.

The third section develops the theme of the earlier parts, but the subject matter of rebellion is clearer. The clouds resemble "workers in white" who "went their way / after declaring a bitter strike against the sky," and Mayakovsky urges all "famished ones, / sweating ones, / servile ones, / mildewed in flea-ridden dirt" to rebel. But his feelings are contradictory. Although he has seen "whom no one sees," "noth-

---

* These lines were deleted by the censor. In the uncensored edition of 1918 Mayakovsky replaced the vague "a [certain] year" with "the year nineteen hundred and sixteen." He was keen to show that he had forecast the Revolution but at the same time did not wish to appear suspiciously exact in his prophecy.

ing," he says, "will happen": the sky is "playing Judas again / with a handful of treachery-spattered stars."

He squeezes himself into a corner of taverns "with vodka drenching my soul and the cloth." From an icon on the wall another Mariya, the mother of God, spreads light from her halo over the revelers. History repeats itself; once again Barabbas is preferred over her son, that is, Mayakovsky:

> Deliberately, perhaps,
> I show no newer face
> amid this human mash.
> I,
> perhaps,
> am the handsomest
> of your sons.
> . . .
>
> I, who praised the machine and England,
> I am perhaps quite simply
> the thirteenth apostle
> in an ordinary gospel.

Even if Mayakovsky's protest does not lack social dimensions, it is at heart about a rebellion of a more fundamental kind, an existential rebellion directed against time and a world order which make human beings' lives a tragedy. This is even more clearly the case in the final section of the poem, where Mayakovsky's plea for love is again dismissed in lines whose prophetic contents the author was fortunately unaware of: "I and my heart have never lived till May, / in that life we have lived / there are only a hundred Aprils."

The one who bears responsibility for Mayakovsky's unhappy, impossible love is none other than God the Father, who has provided human beings with hands and a head but "didn't see to it / that one could without torture / kiss, kiss and kiss":

> I thought you a great big god almighty,
> but you're a dunce, a minute little godlet.

Watch me stoop
and reach for a shoemaker's knife
in my boot.

Swindlers with wings,
huddle in heaven!
Ruffle your feathers in shuddering flight!
I'll rip you, reeking of incense,
Wide open from here to Alaska!

Love drives people to the edge of madness and suicide, but space is dumb and no answer is forthcoming. The way of the world cannot be disturbed; rebellion is in vain and is met with silence: "The universe sleeps, / its huge paw curled / upon a star-infested ear."

"A Cloud in Trousers" is a youthful, insubordinate monologue which reminded Pasternak of Dostoevsky's young, rebellious fictional heroes and made Gorky exclaim that "he had only read such a conversation with God in the Book of Job." Despite certain weaknesses in composition and structure, the poem is an impressive achievement, given that Mayakovsky was only twenty to twenty-one years old when it was written. With its emotional charge and groundbreaking figurative language it occupies a central place in his writings and is moreover an excellent compendium of all the important themes in his oeuvre, both before and after. Several of these themes—madness, suicide, the struggle with God, man's existential exposure—were already pithily formulated in the play *Vladimir Mayakovsky*, written two years earlier: an expressionistic, Nietzschean drama published under the subtitle *A Tragedy*. Significantly enough, *Vladimir Mayakovsky* was not the name of the author but the title of the play. "Art was called tragedy," Pasternak commented: "The right name for it. And the tragedy was called 'Vladimir Mayakovsky.' The title concealed a simple discovery of genius—that the poet is not the author but the subject of a lyricism addressing itself to the world in the first person." When Mayakovsky was asked why the play bore his name, he answered: "It is the name of the poet in the play who is doomed to suffer for all." The poet is a scapegoat and redeemer—alone, rejected by the multitude, he takes this burden on himself precisely because he is a poet.

When an extract from "A Cloud" was printed in the Futurist almanac *The Archer* in February 1915, its genre was described as "tragedy," and in the article "About Different Kinds of Mayakovsky," the writer referred to the poem as his "second tragedy." He thereby established a direct connection between the poem and the play, a connection which is made all the clearer by the fact that "A Cloud" originally had the title "The Thirteenth Apostle," who was none other than Mayakovsky himself. When the author was forced by the censorship to change the title, he chose "A Cloud in Trousers," another of his incarnations. In all three cases—"Vladimir Mayakovsky," "The Thirteenth Apostle," and "A Cloud in Trousers"—the titles were thus synonymous with the authorial persona, a concept quite natural for a poet whose whole oeuvre was deeply autobiographical.

A DREADFUL HOOLIGAN

Although authorities like Maxim Gorki and Korney Chukovsky expressed their admiration for "A Cloud," Mayakovsky had had difficulty finding a publisher for the poem. When Brik heard this, he offered to pay for it to be printed and asked Mayakovsky to find out what it would cost. The Futurist poets were poor and constantly in search of sponsors, and to begin with Mayakovsky saw Osip too as a potential Maecenas. He therefore mentioned a higher price for printing than had actually been asked, and pocketed the difference. Many years later, when he found out that Lili and Osip knew he had cheated them, he was deeply ashamed.

Mayakovsky soon came to realize that Osip was not the usual moneybags but someone whose interest in Mayakovsky and in Futurism was genuine. However it was a very recent interest. Apart from their one previous face-to-face meeting with Mayakovsky, Lili and Osip had only seen him once in public. In May 1913, when the Symbolist poet Konstantin Balmont returned to Russia after several years in exile, a soiree was organized in his honor. Among those who performed was Mayakovsky, who welcomed Balmont "on his enemies' behalf." He was booed by the audience, and among those booing were Lili and Osip.

Now, in 1915, Mayakovsky already had a reputation as a promising poet, but he was still not widely known. The few poems he had written had only been published in newspapers or obscure Futurist calenders, and when *Vladimir Mayakovsky* was performed in St. Petersburg in the autumn of 1913, Lili and Osip were living in Moscow. In actual fact there were few people who knew of Mayakovsky other than as a Futurist scandalmonger.

His recitation of "A Cloud" blew away Osip and Lili's skepticism in one fell swoop. *A Cloud in Trousers* came out as a book in September 1915, with the final dedication "To You, Lilya" on the title page, the publisher's name OMB—Osip's initials—on the cover, and a new description of its genre: not "tragedy" but "tetraptych"—a composition in four parts, recalling a tripartite icon, a *triptych*. The edition ran to 1,050 copies. Several pages, which the censor perceived as blasphemous or politically sensitive, had been replaced by dots. "We knew 'A Cloud' by heart," Lili remembered, "anticipated the proofs like a lover's meeting, and filled in the censored parts by hand. I loved the flame-colored cover, the typography, and the dedication and had my copy bound by the best bookbinder in the most expensive leather binding available with gold lettering and dazzling white endpapers of moiré. Mayakovsky had never been involved in anything like this before and was pleased beyond measure." But sales were sluggish—according to Mayakovsky, because "most consumers of poetry were unmarried women and ladies, who couldn't buy the book because of its title"—the erotic subtext of which was strengthened by the semantic ambiguity of the Russian word for "trousers," *shtany*, with its nuance of "underpants."

"Too bad that you didn't like Mayakovsky's book," Osip wrote to Oleg Fröhlich, "but I think you simply haven't read it properly. Or perhaps you're put off by the coarse style and the lapidary form.— Personally speaking, for four months I have done nothing but read that book. I know it by heart and feel it to be one of the greatest works of genius in world literature. . . . Mayakovsky is at our place day and night and has shown himself to be a colossal personality, even if of course he isn't fully formed yet. He is only 22 and a dreadful hooligan."

"The Briks were mad about the poems and fell in love with them once and for all" and Mayakovsky "fell in love once and for all with

Lili," were, as we have seen, Elsa's summing-up of Mayakovsky's reading of "A Cloud." As Lili's little sister, she had always stood in her shadow, and sometimes, as in Harry Blumenfeld's case, even inherited her passions. But this time it was the other way round: from now on, Mayakovsky had eyes only for Lili.

THE METAMORPHOSIS

Before the reading at Osip and Lili's home, Mayakovsky had spent the summer in Finland, on the Karelian Isthmus, where many Petersburgers had their dachas. Gorky had his house at Mustamäki, and Ilya Repin and Korney Chukovsky lived not far away at Kuokkala. Directly after meeting Lili, Mayakovsky declared to Chukovsky that he was going to start a new life, as he had met a woman he would love until his dying day, "the only one." "He said it so solemnly that I immediately believed him," Chukovsky recalled, "although he was 22 years old and although at a superficial glance he appeared so fickle and dissipated."

After his visit to Petrograd Mayakovsky intended to return to Kuokkala. But instead he rented a furnished room at the Palais Royal on Pushkin Street by Nevsky Prospect, a hotel he usually stayed in during his visits to Petersburg and which was close to Lili's and Osip's apartment. He lived there until the beginning of November, when he moved to Nadezhdin Street, which was even closer, only five minutes' walk away.

Mayakovsky and Lili started meeting, in his apartment or in some *maison de rendez-vous*. He liked the unusual setting, the red plush, the gilded mirrors. They were inseparable, sailing out to the islands in the Petersburg delta, walking along Nevsky Prospect, Mayakovsky in a top hat, Lili in a big, black hat with feathers. They spent the nights strolling along the quays. Lili was a woman who made all the other women he met seem uninteresting, and his love for her changed his life in a trice.

After years of a hard and impoverished Bohemian existence, Mayakovsky found in Lili and Osip Brik the companionship which he had been looking for since his father's death nine years earlier: a world of adults who accepted him and gave him a feeling of security. Yet they were so unlike, had such different backgrounds. They were rich; he was poor. They had grown up in the center of Moscow, he had grown up in the provinces (moreover, in a remote part of the empire). They had undergone higher education, were well mannered and well read; he had almost no education, his reading had been rudimentary and unsystematic, and his spelling left a lot to be desired. They had traveled around Europe since they were little and spoke several foreign languages; he had never been abroad and apart from Russian spoke only Georgian.

Lili and Osip immediately grasped Mayakovsky's greatness as a poet but had a problem with his uncouth manners, which contrasted so strikingly with their own admittedly unconventional but at heart solidly bourgeois lifestyle. The same was true of Osip's mother, who found Mayakovsky just as difficult as Lili's mother did. On one visit to Lili and Osip, Polina Yuryevna had brought with her a large hamper from Yeliseyev, Petrograd's finest delicatessen, with caviar, confectionery, fruit, and a large melon. "We were just opening it," Lili recollected, "when Volodya came in, caught sight of the melon, and with a triumphant cry of 'Wow, that's what I call a melon!' he downed it in one go. Polina Yuryevna never took her eyes off Volodya . . . and they were glowing with indignation."

Mayakovsky was as artless as a child and immoderate in everything he undertook. In fact, he was "not Lili's type in the least" and she exerted herself to "remodel" him, as a friend, Roman Jakobson, put it. She saw to it that he had his long hair cut and got rid of his yellow blouse, and a dentist was given the task of making new teeth for him. The metamorphosis is obvious in the first photograph of Mayakovsky and Lili together, where he is wearing a cravat and an English belted overcoat. If the makeover appealed to Lili, there were others who saw it as an assault on his identity. "I well remember that when I saw his even row of teeth, jacket, and tie, I thought that it had all been done for Lili's sake," commented Sonya Shamardina: "For whatever reason, I was disturbed by this. I couldn't stop thinking about his mouth with the bad teeth—so strongly was that mouth connected, to my mind, with his whole poetic persona."

Lili did what she could to restyle Mayakovsky, but there was also an adjustment in the other direction. Mayakovsky introduced Lili

There is a big contrast between the "hooligan" Mayakovsky in Grigoryev's painting and his appearance just a few months after he met Lili.

and Osip to his friends. Vasily Kamensky, David Burlyuk, Velimir Khlebnikov, Boris Pasternak, Nikolay Aseyev, and other young poets began to frequent the apartment on Zhukovsky Street—as did artists like Pavel Filonov and Nikolay Kulbin. Boris Pasternak, who during those years was under an almost hypnotic influence from Mayakovsky and who would soon leave the Futurists' circle, felt himself in comparison with Mayakovsky to lack "both meaning and value."

The Futurists were not the only ones who came calling in the little two-room apartment, which soon developed into a literary salon, if in miniature format. Another welcome guest was the poet and songwriter Mikhail Kuzmin, who would perform his songs on the Briks' grand piano. Another of Lili's and Osip's friends was one of the leading dancers of the time, Yekaterina Geltser—ballet was an old passion of both Osip and Lili. Osip had long been interested in it from a theoretical perspective, and at the end of 1915 Lili began

Lili loved the ballet and started taking lessons with Alexandra Dorinskaya, who before the war had performed with Diaghilev's Ballets Russes in Paris.

to take lessons with Alexandra Dorinskaya, who before the war had danced with Nijinsky in Diaghilev's Ballets Russes in Paris.

The apartment was small and felt even smaller because of the grand piano, which was crowned by Osip's card constructions. On one wall there hung a large roll of paper where guests left their visiting cards in the form of amusing verses or drawings. With her charm and peculiar beauty Lili was the natural focus of the salon. She was a "lady"—well brought up, well read, stylish—but at the same time totally unprejudiced and unpredictable in her reactions and replies. She left no one unmoved. Nikolay Aseyev describes his initial impressions of her as follows:

> I was led [by Mayakovsky] into an apartment like no other, shimmering with hand-painted fabrics, ringing with poetry, newly written or just declaimed, and a hostess with brightly glistening,

intense eyes and the ability to persuade and surprise with unheard-
of opinions, her own, not dredged up from elsewhere or borrowed
from recognized authorities. We—myself, Shklovsky, and, if I
remember correctly, Kamensky—were bewitched by those eyes,
those comments, which moreover were never forced on one but
were always uttered as if in passing, but which always hit the mark,
right in the bull's eye.

BREAD!

At the beginning of September 1915, shortly before *A Cloud* came off
the presses, there was another big change in Mayakovsky's life: he
was called up for military service. Like most other authors, including
the Futurists, Mayakovsky had been dragged along in the national
hysteria which erupted in August 1914. According to the future Nobel
Prize winner Ivan Bunin, on the day that war was declared Mayak-
ovsky climbed onto the monument to the Russian general Skobe-
lev and recited patriotic verses, and according to the poet Vladislav
Khodasevich he was even supposed to have incited a hate-filled mob
to go and attack German shops in Moscow. But when he volunteered
his services, he was turned down on the grounds of his "political
unreliability." His patriotic needs were satisfied instead by writing
poems and propaganda verses which he illustrated with drawings
and which were printed as bills and postcards—a sort of illustrated
broadsheet, which in Russian is called *lubok*. Elsa remembers how
he used to pace to and fro in the room mumbling verses while she
practiced the piano, and Ida Khvas has described how they trailed
around Moscow collecting money for wounded soldiers.

For Mayakovsky, the war was not only a struggle on the military
field of battle but also an aesthetic challenge—and opportunity.
Alongside his war poems, during a few weeks in the autumn of 1914
Mayakovsky wrote about ten articles in which he hailed the war as
a purifying bath out of which a new human being would be born.
"The war is not a meaningless murdering but a poem about a lib-
erated and uplifted soul," he wrote: "Russia's human foundation
has changed. The strong men of the future have been born." Now "a
whole new cycle of ideas is entering the world" and what has been

regarded as poetry up till now "should be forbidden in wartime just like cabarets and the sale of intoxicating drinks." The war has shown that "the strong men of the future," that is, the Futurists, were right: the old language is no longer capable of describing a new reality. To think that it's sufficient to rhyme words like "machine-gun" or "cannon" in order to go down in history as a contemporary poet is an illusion. "The important thing for a poet is not what but how," Mayakovsky declared in a characteristic phrase—"the word is a goal in itself."

Whether or not it was Mayakovsky's glowing patriotism that persuaded the authorities to change their minds about his "political unreliability" is unknown, but in any case he was called up in the autumn of 1915. Thanks to his new friends he was offered the opportunity to keep Osip company in the motorized division. According to certain sources he was helped by Gorky, but it is not unreasonable to suppose that the scribe Ignatyev also had a finger in the pie. As Mayakovsky was a trained artist, he was given work as a draftsman. But he was still short of money and was forced to ask his mother for winter clothes and help in buying his uniform.

Even if his military service involved certain restrictions, Mayakovsky was able to stay on at the Palais Royal, and his socializing with Lili, Osip, and other friends continued with almost undiminished intensity. During the autumn he and Osip collected material for a Futurist almanac, *Vzyal*, which appeared in December. The title is the Russian verb "take" in the past tense, "took" or "taken," and it refers to a phrase in the almanac: "Futurism has taken Russia in an iron grip." "Volodya had long been wishing to give that name to someone: a son or a dog," Lili remembered. "Now it became a magazine instead."

Apart from Mayakovsky, the contributors included Pasternak, Khlebnikov, and Viktor Shklovsky, a young student at the university in Petrograd with new revolutionary ideas about literature. *Vzyal* also saw Osip's debut as a critic, with the article "Bread!," in which he describes contemporary Russian poetry—which he himself not so long ago had revered!—as sickly pastry ("Blok's snowballs," "Balmont's good eclairs," and so on), which moreover are baked in foreign ovens. Things are otherwise now!—

Rejoice, shout louder: we have bread again! Don't rely on your servants, go yourself and queue up for Mayakovsky's book *A Cloud in Trousers*. Slit the pages carefully, so that—like a starving man who does not want to miss a single crumb—you will not miss a single letter in this bread-book. But if you are so poisoned that sound food cannot cure you, then you might as well die—die of your own diabetes.

FLUTE

"A Cloud" had a printed dedication to Lili, but it was not she who had inspired the poem. From now on she was the sole heroine in Mayakovsky's poems. During the autumn of 1915 Mayakovsky worked on a new poem, "The Backbone-Flute." "'Flute' was written slowly, each section being followed by a solemn recitation," Lili remembered: "First it was read to me, then for Osya and me together, then for everyone else. That's how it was the whole time with everything Volodya wrote." One of Lili's greatest talents was that very ability to listen—she had an exquisite ear for poetry and was prodigally generous to anyone with creative talent. The book appeared in February 1916 under the name of the publishing firm OMB and with the printed dedication "To Lili Yuryevna Brik."

That Mayakovsky worshipped Lili goes without saying; that much is apparent in his love poems from these years: "The Backbone-Flute," "Lilichka!," and a poem with the unpoetic title "To the Whole Book." What these poems have in common is the violent alternation between euphoria and deepest despair, between the joy that love confers and the feeling that it is not reciprocated. Without Lili, he writes in "Lilichka!," there is neither sea nor sun, and the only sound that gladdens him is the sound of her "beloved name." In "The Backbone-Flute" he sings a "a redhead / with rouged lips"; he places his cheek "burning like the Sahara" under her feet and presents her with a crown in which his words "spell a rainbow of shudders":

> I am fated to be a tsar—
> on the sunlit gold of my coins
> I shall command my subjects

to mint
your precious face!
But where
the earth fades into tundra,
where the river bargains with the north wind,
there I'll scratch Lili's name on my fetters,
and in the darkness of hard labor kiss them again and again.

But the poet has blasphemed, he has shouted that God does not exist,
and the beloved woman in fact reveals herself as God's punishment,
for she is married and does not love him:

This day, on visiting you,
I sensed
something wrong in the house.
You had concealed something in your silks,
and the smell of incense expanded in the air.
Glad to see me?
That "very"
was very cool.
Confusion broke the barrier of reason.
Burning and feverish, I heaped on despair.
Listen,
there is no way
you can hide a corpse.
Pour out that terrible word like lava on my head!
Every muscle
in your body
trumpets
like a megaphone:
it's dead, it's dead, it's dead.
It can't be,
Answer me.
Don't lie!

The conclusion is loftily pathetic:

Thief of my heart,
Who have stripped it of everything,
Who have tortured my soul in delirium,
Accept, my dearest, this gift—
Never, perhaps, shall I think of anything else.

Even if one cannot simply equate the reality of the poem with that of life, there can be no doubt that these lines are strongly autobiographical: it was in this way that Mayakovsky experienced his relationship with Lili. "Love, jealousy, friendship were for Mayakovsky feelings of hyperbolical strength," Lili wrote. "He was reluctant to speak of them" but "wrote, all the time, unceasingly, poems in which all his pain was depicted whole."

But what of Lili? How did she feel about Mayakovsky's emotional assault? When "The Backbone-Flute" was finished, Mayakovsky invited her to his little one-room apartment in Nadezhdin Street. With his winnings from gambling and the fee for a magazine article he had bought roast beef at Yeliseyev's, almond pastries from De Gourmet, three pounds of cherries in liqueur and chocolate from Kraft, and flowers from Eilers. He had polished his shoes and put on a nice tie. After the reading, when Lili explained how much she liked him, he burst out: "Like? No more than that? Why don't you love me?" Lili explained that of course she loved him—but secretly she was thinking: "It's Osya I love."

This account is taken from a fragment of memoir in which Lili depicts herself in the third person. It has characteristics of fiction but builds on her diaries and comes very close to the psychological truth. She continues by describing how Mayakovsky follows her home, so tense and low spirited that Osip wonders what has happened:

Mayakovsky sobbed, cried out, and threw himself full length against the sofa. His enormous body lay on the floor; he buried his face in the cushions and pressed his hands to his head. He howled his heart out. Lilya bent over him in consternation. "Stop, Volodya, don't cry. You're at the end of your tether after writing poetry like that from morning till night." Osya rushed out to the kitchen for water. He sat on the sofa and tried to lift Volodya's head up. Volo-

dya lifted his face, wet with tears, and pressed himself against Os-
ya's knees. Through his sobs he yelled: "Lilya doesn't love me!" He
tore himself away, stood up, and ran out into the kitchen. There he
groaned and cried so loudly that Lilya and Osya took refuge in the
furthest corner of the bedroom.

The first years of Mayakovsky's and Lili's life together were thus
difficult for both of them. Mayakovsky "crowned" Lili in his poems,
but she became worn out and irritated by his highly strung emotions.
His attentions were so intrusive that she felt them to be "an actual as-
sault": "In two and a half years I literally didn't have a quiet moment."
When Mayakovsky wrote yet another long poem about tortured love,
"Don Juan," Lili had had enough: "I didn't know it was being written.
Volodya recited it to me unexpectedly as we were walking along the
street—the whole thing by heart. I got angry because it was about
love again—as if I wasn't fed up with it! Volodya tore the manuscript
from his pocket, shredded it into tiny pieces and let the wind blow it
away along Zhukovsky Street."
Even if the manuscript was ripped apart it is likely that fragments
of the text came to be used in other poems, like for example this one:

You didn't soil your hands in grubby murder.
You
only let slip:
"In a soft bed
he,
fruit,
wine in the palm of the night table."
Love!
You were only in my
fevered
brain!

The quotation is from the poem "To the Whole Book," the lyrical fore-
word to Mayakovsky's first collection of poems, *Simple as a Mooing*,
whose title in turn is a quotation from the tragedy *Vladimir Mayak-
ovsky*. As an introduction to a poetry anthology, "To the Whole Book"

In his poem "The Backbone Flute," Mayakovsky wrote: "I am fated to be a tsar— / on the sunlit gold of my coins / I shall command my subjects / to mint / your precious face!" This is how he himself "minted" Lili, in a drawing from 1916, the same year that the photo on the next page was taken.

is a remarkable choice, especially as the poem—and, through the title of the poem, the whole book—is dedicated to Lili. The lines inside the quotation marks have a concrete biographical background and refer to Lili's and Osip's wedding night as Lili described it to Mayakovsky. The volume came out in October 1916. However platonic the relationship between Lili and Osip was at this time, Mayakovsky still saw Osip as a rival in the competition for Lili's favors and as an obstacle to the establishing of a steady relationship with her. Lili, on her part, no doubt used the marriage argument for her own ends, to keep him at a distance.

"I saw right away that Volodya was a poet of genius, but I didn't like him," Lili wrote in a text which became known only after her death. "I didn't like loud-mouthed people—outwardly loud-mouthed. I didn't like the fact that he was so big that people turned to look at him in the street, I didn't like the fact that he listened to his own voice, I didn't even like his name—Mayakovsky—so noisy and so like a pseudonym, a vulgar one at that."

There was one conversation in particular that she found repellent. A rape had taken place and Lili thought the man ought to be shot, but Mayakovsky said that "he understood him, that he could rape a woman himself, that he understood there might be occasions when one couldn't restrain oneself, that if he was with a woman on a desert island, etc." Lili reacted with disgust: "Of course I don't remember the exact words that were spoken, but I see, I see the expression on his face, his eyes, his mouth. I remember the feeling of repugnance. If Volodya hadn't been such a poet, our acquaintanceship would have ended there."

Whatever the strength of Lili's feelings for Mayakovsky, it was not to be expected that she would change her view of love and sexuality the minute that he came into her life. Just like before, she had several suitors and made no secret either of them or of her unquenchable love for Osip. One of those who paid court to her for many years was Lev ("Lyova") Grinkrug, whom she knew from Moscow and who came to visit her in Petrograd just about every weekend. Grinkrug belonged to one of the few noble Jewish families in Russia—his father was a doctor and had been granted a hereditary title for his contributions during the Russo-Turkish war of 1877–78. Lev Alexandrovich himself had trained as a lawyer and worked in a bank. Although his courtship was discreet and he was no Don Juan, Mayakovsky's extreme jealousy meant that he was dreadfully tortured by Lev's closeness to Lili.

It was quite different for Osip. He had never demonstrated jealousy, and physical relations between himself and Lili had ceased even before she met Mayakovsky. "It happened by itself," Lili confided, adding that she and Osip "loved each other too deeply to attach any importance to it." This explanation is no doubt a rationalization. In all likelihood there were other, deeper motives behind the repression of the physical side of their relationship. Perhaps it was simply that Osip and Lili did not match each other on the sexual plane. But she loved him deeply, at least as deeply as Mayakovsky loved her, and she could not envisage living without him—perhaps for the very reason that he maintained this emotional distance from her.

NERVES GALLOPED MADLY TILL SOON THEIR LEGS GAVE WAY

Mayakovsky and Elsa had been seeing each other for about a year before he fell in love with Lili. But however ardent and intimate Elsa tried to portray their relationship in her memoirs, it was of a quite different kind from that between Mayakovsky and her big sister. A female friend of the Kagan sisters was of the opinion that Elsa "magnified" the relationship. When, shortly after falling in love with Lili, Mayakovsky was asked if he had also been in love with Elsa, he replied "No, no." According to one of those who knew Elsa best, Roman Jakobson, the relationship was characterized by "brotherly tenderness."

Elsa's successful attempt to persuade Lili and Osip of her friend's poetic greatness had the immediate and paradoxical consequence that she and Mayakovsky hardly saw each other again. "It is hard to believe, but once and for all Lili and I have no friends in common," Elsa wrote to him in September 1915, continuing: "If you only knew how sad it feels! I who became so attached to you, and now suddenly you are a stranger."

Mayakovsky's answer was to send her *A Cloud in Trousers* with the dedication "To sweet, delightful Elitchka from her devoted V[ladimir]

V[ladimirovich]." Elsa thanked him for the book but said she was convinced it was Lili's idea to send it. "You would never have hit on the idea by yourself," she added, clearly offended.

The sisters competed over most things, not only Mayakovsky, and seldom saw each other. Lili was married in Petrograd; Elsa lived with her mother in Moscow, where she was studying architecture, and besides, the war was on, which made it harder to meet. But meet they did on 31 December 1915 at a "Futurist New Year celebration" in Lili and Osip's apartment. The Christmas tree was decorated with *A Cloud in Trousers* and Mayakovsky's yellow blouse made out of paper. As the apartment was so small the tree was suspended upside down from the ceiling. The guests sat cheek by jowl along the walls and the food was served over their heads, straight from the open door. Everyone was dressed up: Lili in a kilt with red stockings, bare knees and a marchioness's wig; Mayakovsky was a "hooligan" with a red muffler and a shillelagh in his hand; Viktor Shklovsky was a sailor, Vasily Kamensky had painted half a mustache on his upper lip and a little bird on his cheek and had sewn multicolored shreds of material onto his jacket. Elsa had a hairpiece in the form of a tower, crowned with a feather which reached right up to the ceiling. The evening, or night, ended with Kamensky proposing to Elsa, who was pleasantly surprised but declined.

According to Lili it was the first time anyone had proposed to Elsa, who lacked Lili's power of attraction and was often unlucky in love. "Whoever I like doesn't like me, and vice versa," she wrote to Mayakovsky in October 1916. During the summer she came close to taking poison, she reported, but now life was just repellent in general. The letter was Elsa's reply to *Simple as a Mooing*, which Mayakovsky had sent her. "Apart from the fact that it has a humorous feel to it, it reminds me of so much," she wrote. "On almost every page I meet a dear old acquaintance. I remember everything: where and when I heard it from you." She wanted very much to meet with Mayakovsky and wondered if he was thinking of coming to Moscow. "I am unwilling to write this as I am afraid of what the answer will be. Is it altogether out of the question for you? I would be so glad!"

To her surprise, Mayakovsky replied: "Very sorry that I can't come to Moscow in the near future, forced therefore unfortunately to postpone my implacable intention to hang you for your gloomy mood. The only thing that can save you is to come here as soon as possible and beg my forgiveness in person. Elik, seriously, come here immediately. I'M SMOKING. This is the limit of my social and personal activity." (Obviously, Mayakovsky had tried to give up smoking—probably at Lili's insistence.)

Lev ("Lyova") Grinkrug, for a short time Lili's lover, remained a true friend throughout her whole life. He died in Moscow in 1987 at the age of ninety-eight.

During the next two and a half months Mayakovsky and Elsa exchanged no fewer than eleven letters without Mayakovsky's once revealing anything about his feelings. Elsa was grateful to hear from him at all but wondered on one occasion why he wrote nothing about himself. "Are you not able to?" she asked, thereby touching on an important character trait of this outwardly so "loudmouthed" individual: his "unique reserve," as Lili put it. "Mayakovsky never liked talking about himself," David Burlyuk commented in a form of words which was repeated by Ida Khvas, with the additional comment: "he seldom even talked about his mother and sisters." So the fact that Mayakovsky never touched on his feelings or romantic problems in letters or conversation ought therefore not to surprise us.

Although Elsa lived in Moscow, she was naturally aware that relations between Mayakovsky and her sister did not always run smoothly. She knew Lili, she knew Mayakovsky, she read his poems and knew how tortured he was. And she saw her chance to entice him back. Although she was well aware how touchy Mayakovsky was about any mention of other men in Lili's vicinity, she stoked his jealousy. Lev Grinkrug—she told him—was "in a gloomy mood," and she wondered if this could possibly be because Lili was "nasty to him."

Elsa's letters are long and personal, Mayakovsky's short and terse. But on 19 December 1916 she received a letter which frightened her:

> Dear little Elik!
> Come at once!
>   Forgive me for not writing. It doesn't mean anything. Just at the moment you are in fact the only human being I think of with love and tenderness
>   I kiss you hard hard
>   Volodya
>   "Nerves galloped madly till soon their legs gave way"
>   Answer *at once*
> I beg you

The last sentence is printed in large letters right across the first page of the letter. "Your letter made me so anxious that I decided to leave immediately," Elsa replied on 21 December by return of post. "I absolutely want to meet you! I can sense something in the air that ought not to be there and when I think about you, it's always with a feeling of unease." The unease was caused by the lines "Nerves galloped madly till soon their legs gave way" from "A Cloud in Trousers." "I was nineteen years old," Elsa recalled, "and up till that time I had never traveled anywhere without mother's permission, but this time I simply told her, without explaining the reason, that I was going to Petrograd." The very next day she was sitting on the train.

They met in Mayakovsky's room in Nadezhdin Street. Elsa remembered: a sofa, a chair, on the table a bottle of wine. Mayakovsky sits at the table, stalks round the room without saying a word. She sits on the sofa in the corner waiting for him to say something, but he is silent, rams something into his mouth, wanders about, hour after hour. Elsa doesn't know why she came in the first place and wants to leave. A male acquaintance is waiting down at the front door.

> "Where are you off to?"
>   "I'm leaving."
>   "Just don't dare."
>   "Don't you dare say 'don't dare' to me!"

We began to quarrel. Volodya was furious and held me there by force. I tore myself away; I wasn't going to stay there for anything! I dashed to the door, pulled on my fur coat, and rushed out. I was on my way down the stairs when Volodya roared past. "Pardon, madame . . ." and doffed his hat.

When I came out onto the street Volodya was already sitting in the sled, beside Vladimir Ivanovich, who had been sitting waiting for me. Mayakovsky explained, impudently and unashamedly, that he intended to spend the evening with us, and immediately began to joke with me and to tease Vladimir Ivanovich, who of course couldn't give tit for tat. Who could compete in this sport with Mayakovsky? And we really did spend the evening together, all three of us, having supper and going to some variety show . . . both laughter and tears! But what a difficult and gloomy person Mayakovsky was.

There is one thing that Elsa does not mention: that her weeklong stay in Petrograd led to the resumption of her relationship with Mayakovsky. Immediately after returning home she wrote a letter to him in which she told him that she had cried on the train home and been utterly inconsolable and "mama didn't know what to do with me"— "And it's all your fault, you devil!" Mayakovsky had promised to come to Moscow, and she was waiting impatiently for him: "I love you a lot, do you still love me?" When she had received no answer by 4 January 1917, she wrote yet another despairing letter: "You're not coming, I know it! . . . At least write that you love me as much as before." But Volodya came. On the same day that Elsa sent the letter from Moscow he obtained three weeks' leave from the motorized company and traveled to Moscow. There he met his mother and his sisters—and, naturally, Elsa. It is not hard to imagine the feeling of triumph she must have enjoyed—after all, she had succeeded in enticing Mayakovsky away from Lili, if only for a while.

What Elsa was frightened of when she read the lines about the legs of his nerves giving way was that Mayakovsky would take his own life. That particular time around the New Year of 1917 was a "dramatic phase" in Mayakovsky's life, and he was "very gloomy," as Roman Jakobson recalled. Several suicide attempts or threats to commit suicide belong to this period. "How often I heard the word 'suicide' from Mayakovsky," Lili recalled. "It was pure terror." Early one morning she was awakened by a telephone call: "I'm going to shoot myself. Good-bye, Lilik."

She dashed over to his room in Nadezhdin Street. Mayakovsky opened the door. On the table lay a revolver. "I fired," said Mayakovsky, "but the revolver clicked. The second time I couldn't make up my mind and waited for you instead." Her nerves frayed, Lili took Mayakovsky home with her to Zhukovsky Street. Once there, he forced her to play preference. They played furiously, and he wore her out by constantly declaiming Anna Akhmatova's lines "What has your beloved done with you, / What has your beloved done." Lili lost the first trick, then, to his great delight, all the remaining ones.*

"When he became as hysterical as that, I either tried to calm him down or else I became angry with him and begged him not to frighten and torment me." Lili was not exaggerating: the idea of suicide runs, as we shall see, like a red thread through Mayakovsky's life and writings.

THE WORD IS RESURRECTED AND A NEW BEAUTY IS BORN

If relations with Mayakovsky were complicated, Elsa could draw comfort from the courtship of an old childhood friend—the same Roman Jakobson who bore witness to Mayakovsky's "gloominess" at this time. The Kagan and Jakobson families lived only a few blocks from each other in Myasnitskaya Street in Moscow and were intimate acquaintances. Like the Kagan family, Jakobson belonged to the Jewish elite of Moscow. His father was a prominent wholesaler nicknamed "the rice king." Elsa and Roman were exactly the same age, and when their mothers were pregnant with them, they used to joke that if they had a boy and a girl, they ought to marry each other. Roman had never had any close contact with Lili—the difference in their ages was too great—but he and Elsa had spent a lot of time

---

* According to Lili's memoirs, this episode occurred in 1916, but there is good evidence that it happened in the following year, when we can read in Mayakovsky's notebook: "18 July 8:45. All of a sudden nothing to live for. 11 October 4:30. End." In a letter from 1930 Lili also talks about Mayakovsky's suicide attempt "thirteen years ago."

During their pregnancy, Elsa's and Roman's mothers used to joke that if they gave birth to a boy and a girl the children would marry. They did not, although Roman very much wanted to. In this picture from 1903, we see the seven-year-old Roman (*to the left*) and Elsa (*with curly hair*) in the company of Lili and Roman's cousins.

together, not least because they had the same French teacher, Mademoiselle Dache. But they had not seen each other for many years when, at the end of 1916, they were united in what Jakobson later described as a "deep, intense friendship."

One day in January 1917 Roman and Elsa were about to go to the theater. While Roman waited for Elsa to get changed, he sat browsing through a couple of books that she had handed him. One of them was *The Backbone-Flute*, the other, a volume of essays about the language of poetry, both of them published by Osip Brik. Roman Jakobson was studying philology, dialectology, and folklore at Moscow University. He was only twenty years old but already had the reputation of being a genius. As early as 1913 he had written his first precocious literary manifesto under the influence of the most radical Futurists, Kruchonykh and Khlebnikov, and the following year he was visited by the seventeen-year-older painter Kazimir Malevich, who had heard about his theories (although they had not been published) and wanted to discuss them with him. Two years later, at the age of eighteen, Jakobson was one of the founders of the Moscow Linguistic Circle and became its first chairman.

When Jakobson now read the articles in the volume published by Osip, he was struck by the similarities to his own thoughts about poetic language. "Shortly after getting my hands on these two books, in the middle of January 1917, I went to Petrograd. Elsa gave me a letter for Lili. Zhukovsky Street, where they lived, wasn't far from the station, and I went straight to their house and stayed, if I remember correctly, for five days. They refused to let me go," he recollected: "Everything was extremely bohemian. The table was spread all day long with sausage, bread, cheese, and—the whole time—tea. The samovar was carried in at regular intervals." When he returned to Moscow Elsa, overcome, noted in her diary" "Roman has returned from Petrograd. He too, unfortunately, already belongs to the Brik camp."

In mid-February Jakobson once again traveled to Petrograd. It was *maslenitsa*, Shrove Tuesday, and Lili had invited him for *bliny* with butter. Among the other guests were the literary scholars Boris Eikhenbaum, Yevgeny Polivanov, Lev Yakubinsky, and Viktor Shklovsky. During the nibbles and the toasts, OPOYAZ, the Society for the Study of Poetic Language, was founded. It was a pancake day with undreamed-of consequences for the development of Russian literary studies.

The driving force was Viktor Shklovsky, who often called on the Briks. He was the same age as Mayakovsky and a student at Moscow University, and was generally looked on as a prodigy. He had attracted attention as early as 1914 with his pamphlet *The Resurrection of the Word*. In this piece Shklovsky attacked old-fashioned literary theorists who maintained that literature was a reflection of either life (realism) or of a higher reality (symbolism). He claimed that the object of literary research ought instead to be "literature in itself," that which makes literature literature: rhymes and speech

From the summer of 1914 on, Korney Chukovsky kept a guestbook where his visitors, among them Mayakovsky, left their greetings in the form of poems, drawings, and the like. The book was called "Chukokkala," a combination of his last name and the village in Finland where he lived, Kuokkala. The one who invented the word was the artist Ilya Repin, who had his studio in Kuokkala and left many traces in "Chukokkala," among them a portrait of the twenty-one-year-old Viktor Shklovsky, who visited Chukovsky in June 1914.

sounds in poetry, composition in prose, and so on. "Art is always free from life, and its color has never reflected the color of the flag over the city's fortress," as he would later pointedly formulate his credo.

In his theoretical reasoning, Shklovsky was influenced by the Futurist poets' ideas about "the self-sufficient word," "the word in itself." The old forms are worn-out, "automatized"; they have lost their effectiveness and no longer make any impression. What is needed is new forms, "arbitrary" and "derived" words. The Futurists are creating new words from old roots (like Khlebnikov), "making them red-hot with rhymes" (Mayakovsky), or altering their intonation with the help of verse rhythm (Kruchonykh). "New, living words are being born," writes Shklovsky in *The Resurrection of the Word*, and "ancient word-gems are recovering their former lustre. This new language is incomprehensible, difficult, it can't be read in the way one reads 'The Stock-Exchange News.' It does not even resemble Russian, but we are all too prone to demand of poetic language that it should be comprehensible." Now that new aesthetic directions are beginning to emerge, it is not the theoreticians but the artists who will show the way.

One such artist was Mayakovsky, and when *A Cloud in Trousers* was published, Shklovsky was one of the first reviewers. In Mayakovsky, he wrote in the almanac *Vzyal*, "the street, which previously lacked artistic expression, has found its words, its form." The new human being that Mayakovsky represented "does not crouch" but "shouts." "A new beauty is on its way to being born, and a new drama will be born which will be played in the town squares."

The second review of "A Cloud" was written, as we have seen, by Osip, who after meeting Mayakovsky was gripped by a fervent interest in Futurist poetry. "We approved only of poetry," Lili recalled. "We were as if drunk. I knew all Volodya's poems by heart, and Osya completely devoured them." Through his acquaintance with Shklovsky Osip was drawn into the circle of young philologists and literary scholars who were aiming to achieve the same revolution in their fields as the Futurists were doing in poetry, and in August 1916 he published the volume which so shook Roman Jakobson as he sat waiting for Elsa to change for the theater.

Osip was not trained in literature or languages but familiarized himself with the relevant issues with impressive speed. Already in the second volume, which contained essays on poetic language and came out in December 1916 (also under the publisher's imprint of OMB), he was presenting an epoch-making theory about consonantal "sound repetitions" in poetry. "He had an exceptional talent," Roman Jakobson recalled. "Everything was like a crossword" for him. Although he knew only a few words of classical Greek, he quickly reached conclusions about Greek verse which, according to one specialist, were "astonishing."

Just as striking as his genius was another characteristic of Osip's: his "lack of ambition," in Roman Jakobson's words, or "insufficient willpower to finish anything"—as Shklovsky put it. He hatched ideas on a conveyor belt but was never particularly interested in seeing them through to fruition. Instead he gladly shared his ideas with friends and colleagues. But was it really only a question of "lack of ambition"? "He liked me," Jakobson recalled, "but when I came and told him that I was threatened with being classed as a deserter he replied: 'You are neither the first nor the last.' And did nothing. Was his want of ambition deep down an expression of something else? An exaggerated caution? The inherited instinct of the Russian Jew not to stick his neck out unnecessarily? Indifference? According to Viktor Shklovsky, Brik was a "retiring and remote person." One example of this was his method of avoiding military service. And he was utterly rational: "If Brik had his leg cut off, he would attempt to prove that it was more comfortable that way."

WAR AND THE WORLD

At the same time as the Briks' two-room apartment was seething with discussion of modern poetry, the streets were seething with social unrest. In the summer of 1916 the front had as good as collapsed and the fortunes of war had turned, and the following summer the Russian army was even able to go on the offensive—but the home front showed more and more signs of dissatisfaction and disenchantment. There was a severe shortage of food and other goods, and inflation was three times higher than wage rises. The inflation was partly due to poverty in the countryside (income per capita was only a seventh of that in England), partly to decreasing tax revenues, partly because the production of vodka had been forbidden after the outbreak of war (the tax on alcohol had accounted for a quarter of the state's revenue from taxation!). At the same time rubles were being printed at an ever-increasing rate without being covered by the gold reserves.

The effects of inflation and want were felt almost exclusively by the population of the towns, and especially the cities of Petrograd and Moscow, which were a long way from the agricultural areas. The landowning peasants on the other hand were major beneficiaries of the rising prices of grain, cattle and horses, which were requisitioned by the state, and in economic terms they were the winners of the war. In the autumn of 1916 the Ministry of Police warned that the situation was beginning to be reminiscent of 1905 and that a new revolt could be under way. The causes were partly the inability of the regime to deal with the economic problems, partly the tension between town and country. At the same time dissatisfaction also began to spread within the army, which until now had been loyal to the regime. Desertion began to take place on a massive scale, and by the beginning of 1917 more than a million soldiers had thrown away their uniforms and made their way home.

The demonstrations in Petrograd, which initially were economically motivated, changed character by the end of 1916 and became more outspokenly political. Demands for political reform were also made in the Russian parliament, the *duma*, but Tsar Nicholas II turned a deaf ear to them. The German-born Tsarina Alexandra Fyodorovna was generally regarded as being a bad influence on her husband, and the monk Grigory Rasputin was active in the corridors of power. As it was not possible to get rid of the tsarina, a group of right-wingers decided to remove Rasputin in a conspiracy that included a member of the royal family. In the night of 16/17 December he was murdered in Prince Yusupov's palace in Petrograd.

Two days later Mayakovsky wrote his "nerves letter" to Elsa. Neither here nor in letters to other people at this time are there any references to the world outside his own, private world. It is as if he lived in a world populated only by himself and his feelings. Even if some letters have probably been destroyed or disappeared, so many are preserved from other periods that it is possible to discern a distinct pattern: the political, social reality is almost never commented on.

However, events in society did not pass him by without leaving a trace. The torments of war are reflected—as are those of love—in his poetry. In 1916 and 1917, alongside all the satirical verses and propaganda poems, Mayakovsky wrote a new long poem, "War and the World." In this poem, the title of which is a paraphrase of Tolstoy's *War and Peace*—"world" and "peace" are the same word in Russian—Mayakovsky's former rather primitive view of the war is replaced by an existential meditation on its folly and terrors. The guilt is a collective one and the poet, Vladimir Mayakovsky, not only the scapegoat but also sharing the responsibility. He therefore makes a personal plea to mankind for forgiveness—perhaps as penance for the propagandistic exaggerations he was guilty of in the initial phase of the war: "Mankind! / My dear ones! / For Christ's sake, / For Christ's debt, / Forgive me!"

At the same time he sees a new time dawning. The notion that the old world was doomed to destruction was widespread in Russia around the turn of the century, not least among writers. Just as in "A Cloud in Trousers," Mayakovsky's understanding of man's existential vulnerability is balanced by a messianic conviction that a new and more harmonious world order is approaching:

> And he,
> the free human being
> I keep speechifying about—
> is coming,
> believe me, believe me!

Закованная фильмой.
Лили Брик
Маяковскій.
Акц. „Нептун" Общ.
Нептун
Нептун

4

THE FIRST REVOLUTION
AND THE THIRD

1917–1918

**Long live the political life of Russia
and long live an art free of the state!**
Vladimir Mayakovsky in March 1917

"I returned to Moscow utterly convinced that we were in for a revolution," Roman Jakobson remembered. "That was quite clear from the atmosphere in the university." But it was not just the students who had had enough. On 8 March 1917 a peaceful demonstration was held in Petrograd in connection with International Women's Day. The female demonstrators demanded bread and peace. In the next few days further demonstrations were held, only to be violently put down. On 12 March the garrison in the Paul barracks voted to refuse to obey orders to shoot at civilians, and before the day was out large parts of Petrograd were in the soldiers' hands. On 13 March the revolt spread to Moscow. Two days later, on 15 March, Nicholas II abdicated.

The monarchy was abolished, and a provisional government was set up. The February revolution, as it is

The poster for *Fettered by Film* that plays such an important role in the film itself. The drawing was made by Mayakovsky.

known, since it began in February according to the Julian calendar, was a fait accompli. On 8 March Elsa wrote a letter to Mayakovsky in which, for once, she commented on life outside her own chamber: "Dear uncle Volodya, what exactly is going on; it's simply fantastic!" She told him that Roman, who had had such a clear premonition of what was going to happen, had joined the militia, and, armed with a gun, had arrested six police constables. As a student at Moscow University he had been called upon to help maintain order on the streets.

The revolution was greeted with great enthusiasm in broad swaths of society, and hopes of far-reaching changes were high. There was a general feeling of freedom in the air, of a political spring. The atmosphere is well captured in a letter that the philosopher Lev Shestov wrote to his family in Switzerland a week after the upheaval:

> All that people can talk about here is the marvelous events that are unfolding in Russia. No one who didn't see it with their own eyes can imagine how it happened. Especially in Moscow. As if by an order from above, everybody decided as one man that it was necessary to change the old order. Then everything happened in one week. If there were some clashes in Petrograd, in Moscow it was one long festival. . . . With a calm that signifies great and solemn events, and in less than a week, this whole enormous country over threw the old and embraced the new.

The new government was faced with concrete demands: the food-supply situation had to be improved and the war either won or brought to an honorable conclusion. But exactly what form the politics of the future should take in posttsarist Russia, no one knew. The dominant sensation in the spring of 1917 was one of liberation, of euphoria.

For Mayakovsky and other writers and artists, the revolution aroused hopes that they would be allowed to do their work without interference from official censors and academies. March 1917 saw the founding of the Union of Cultural Workers, in which every political and aesthetic strand was represented, from conservatives to anarchists, from backward-looking aesthetes to the most radical Futurist groupings. Mayakovsky was elected to the ruling council as the writers' representative, which caused quite a stir. Why a controversial Futurist and not a world-renowned author like Maxim Gorky? The explanation was that Gorky had agreed to join a government commission and was therefore accused of having sold out the interests of those working in the cultural field. The new union fought for the independence of art and artists from the state, and those who cooperated with the government were regarded as collaborators. "The motto of myself and all the rest of us is—long live Russia's political life and long live an art free from the state!" Mayakovsky declaimed two weeks after the February revolution: "I do not say no to politics, but there is no room for politics in art."

In regard to their view of art's independence from the state, there was no difference between the left and right wings of the Cultural Union. The same was true of attitudes to the war, where the union's "left-wing block"—to which Mayakovsky belonged—was just as much in favor of national defense as most of the others. Mayakovsky, who in January had been awarded the medal For Zeal, declared proudly that Russia had not only "the world's best art but also the world's best army." Accordingly, there was no problem about uniting patriotism with aesthetic avant-gardism and political radicalism. There were high hopes that the new government would also lead to a change in the fortunes of war.

In the poem "Revolution," published in May 1917 in Maxim Gorky's recently founded newspaper *New Life*, the organ for "social-democratic internationalists," Mayakovsky welcomed the revolution as a triumph for "the socialists' great heresy." But he belonged to no political party—the brand of socialism he supported was libertarian, with a strongly anarchistic bent. At this time, his political views were not more distinct than that. On one occasion when he had collected money for the families of victims of the revolution, he handed it over to the editorial staff of a newspaper published by the liberal "cadet" party (as the Constitutional Democrats were called, from the abbreviation of their name, KD).

Many people, delirious with joy at the fall of tsardom, entertained unrealistic expectations about the future. Mayakovsky's somewhat airy-fairy view of the potential of the February revolution is clear from an episode which stuck in his friend Nikolay Aseyev's mind. For the first time in Russian history, anyone could put himself forward for election, and Moscow was covered in placards and lists of candidates. Alongside posters for the main parties adorning the facades were proclamations from less established political associations such as various anarchist groups and other more or less obscure organizations like the Cooks' Trade Union. One day when Aseyev and Mayakovsky were out looking at the posters, Mayakovsky suddenly suggested drawing up a candidates' list of his own, which would consist of Futurists. He himself would head the list of candidates, Kamensky would be in second place, and so on. "When I, in my ignorance, protested that no one would vote for us, Vladimir Vladimirovich replied thoughtfully: 'The devil only knows, the way things are just now. Just think if I was elected president . . .'"

If Mayakovsky's view of the world was romantic and unconnected to reality, Osip had a well-developed feel for the political game. There is reason to believe that already at this early date he had a more positive attitude to Bolshevism than Mayakovsky. When Lenin returned to Russia in April 1917 after more than ten years in exile, he was met at the Finland station in Petrograd by jubilant crowds. Among them was Osip, who had made his way there out of curiosity. "Seems crazy—but dreadfully convincing," was his verdict, preserved for posterity by Roman Jakobson, who for his part spent this fateful night for Russia drinking cognac and playing billiards with Mayakovsky and other friends.

BOLSHEVIK VANDALISM

The poem "Revolution" was dedicated to Lili, and Mayakovsky's adoration of his beloved also shines forth in other poems. But by and large we know very little about their relationship during these revolutionary years. On 8 August Mayakovsky was granted leave of absence from the motorized company because of problems with his teeth, and at the end of September he traveled to Moscow. From here he wrote a letter to Lili and Osip. It was addressed to both of them and gives no hint of any special intimacy between him and Lili.

The letter was sent to 7 Zhukovsky Street, apartment 42. The next letter was sent to the same address but with another apartment number. This letter is from December 1917. Between them lay not only a calendar distance of four months, but a historic abyss: the Bolshevik seizure of power in October.

In the summer and autumn of 1917 it had become increasingly obvious that the provisional government which had been set up after the February revolution—and which had changed its form and shape several times during the spring and summer—was incapable of dealing with the momentous issues facing the country. The war was going so badly that plans were drawn up for the evacuation of Petrograd, and the Bolshevik party's demands for land reform won more and more support from the people. The Bolsheviks' coup on the night of 7 November (25 October) meant that the eight-month-long democratic experiment was over.

The new revolutionary situation meant that the old society's laws were abolished more or less overnight. Chaos broke out, and many of the better-off fled the country headlong. It is these two factors in combination that explain why, in the autumn of 1917, Lili and Osip could leave their two-room apartment and move into one with six rooms in the same building. As the army was in a state of disintegration, Osip no longer needed to stay in hiding on account of his desertion, and the larger apartment became vacant because the earlier tenant had gone (fled? been shot?). Mayakovsky was also released from military service immediately after the October coup.

A few weeks after seizing power, the Bolshevik party called a meeting to try to set up a collaboration with the country's cultural workers. Among the few writers and artists who heeded the call were, apart from Mayakovsky, the poet Alexander Blok and the theater director Vsevolod Meyerhold. However, the plans of People's Commissar of Enlightenment Anatoly Lunacharsky for a state-run cultural council met with the same resistance as the provisional government's thoughts on the same lines. A week later, when the Union of Cultural Workers discussed the question, Mayakovsky expressed his attitude in a phrase which does not reflect any enthusiasm: "One is obliged to welcome the new rulers and enter into contact with them."

Brik and Mayakovsky belonged to the political left, even if they were not members of any party. They were close to Maxim Gorky's Mensheviks (social democrats) and contributed to his newspaper

New Life, and in May Osip was appointed editor in chief of a socialist satirical magazine, *The Wheelbarrow*, although in the event it never appeared. But the dividing lines between the various socialist parties had not yet been drawn up, and people belonging to different parties and factions socialized freely. Changing one's party allegiance was also common. People were united more by their detestation of everything that could be described as bourgeois than by common ideas about how the new society was to be built. And as regards aesthetic questions, it was still total freedom from the state that counted. Writers and artists were solid in their resistance to attempts by the Bolshevik party to acquire control over cultural life. For many of them, moreover, it was only a question of time before the Bolsheviks were toppled from power—so why negotiate with them?

If Mayakovsky's attitude was one of wait-and-see, Osip's role in the game of cultural politics was more complicated. It was he who was entrusted with the task of presenting Lunacharsky's proposal to the Union of Cultural Workers. Although Osip had only known the people's commissar of enlightenment since May, he was now acting as the middleman between the Bolshevik government and the cultural workers.

As it was far from obvious that the Bolsheviks had come to stay, Osip's decision to accept the role of middleman involved a significant degree of political risk. But it can also be seen as the expression of a well-developed political intuition. That the Bolsheviks perceived Osip as one of them emerges from the fact that, on 26 November, he was elected to the Petrograd city council on the Bolshevik list, which was headed by Lunacharsky. However, there is no information about his participation in the work of the council.

Was Osip a Bolshevik? The question cannot be answered with a simple yes or no. In an article called "My Position" published in *New Life* on 5 December, he stated that he was not a member of the Bolshevik party and his election had come as a complete surprise, as no one had asked his permission. He was a "cultural worker" and claimed not to know whether or not the policies being implemented by the Bolsheviks were good or bad. "The arrests of dissidents, attacks on the written word and the press, and comparable examples of physical violence are not characteristic only of the Bolsheviks," he writes, with the assaults by the tsarist regime on its political opponents fresh in his mind. It is not this that upsets him; what he is complaining about is the Bolsheviks' cultural program, which he sees as "impossible."

The background was that the Bolshevik party had lent its support to the workers' organization Proletkult, which espoused a view of culture directly opposed to that of the Futurists. The ideologues of Proletkult maintained that the workers did not understand "modern" art and literature and had to have the revolutionary message presented in more comprehensible—read "classical"—forms. "The sole correct way to proceed," Osip explained, is therefore to "tirelessly follow one's own cultural line, be present wherever culture is under threat and steadfastly defend it against all forms of vandalism, including the Bolshevik version." Although he is not a member of the party and has no intention of subordinating himself to any party discipline or participating in any political meetings, he should therefore not refuse his "unexpected election."

The letter testifies to the duplicity of Brik's attitude to the new ruling powers. He is not a member of the Bolshevik party but is willing to act as a Bolshevik on the city council if this can help undermine the Bolsheviks' cultural policies. So he accepts his election, not out of political conviction, but for tactical reasons. Do we not sense here yet another expression of Osip's "moral relativism"?

Even if there were differences of opinion between Brik and Lunacharsky, they still seem to have spoken roughly the same language. Not so with Mayakovsky, who, in Osip's words, "could not agree with the people's commissar of enlightenment." The conflict with Lunacharsky was in actual fact so serious that, around the end of November and the beginning of December, Mayakovsky left Petrograd and moved to Moscow.

The cause of the conflict emerges from Mayakovsky's reaction to Osip's article. "I read Oska's letter in *Novaya Zhizn*, breathing with nobility," he wrote to Osip and Lili in the first letter of his that survives from Moscow: "I should like to receive one like it." Mayakovsky's enthusiasm for Osip's "noble" letter was in actual fact the first expression—after October 1917—of a conviction which was fundamental for his aesthetics and for that of the avant-garde in general: there can be no revolutionary content without a revolutionary form.

When it became clear to him that Lunacharsky was refusing to give the Futurists priority of interpretation in the discussion of aesthetic matters, he chose to leave the field.

TO RUSSIA

It is clear from the poem "Revolution" that Mayakovsky regarded the February revolution as his own: "We have won! Long live us! / Lo-o-ong li-i-ive us!" The October Revolution was hailed with no such dithyrambs. In fact, he wrote only a dozen or so poems during the next two years, until the autumn of 1919. His reservations about the Bolsheviks' view of culture thus had a direct parallel in his partial poetic paralysis.

The two revolutionary poems that Mayakovsky wrote in the autumn of 1917, "Our March" and "Ode to the Revolution," reflect the general revolutionary frenzy and do not express support for any concrete political line. But he also wrote a poem with a quite different message, "To Russia."

The I of the poem, a transoceanic ostrich "with feathers of meter and rhyme," is stupid enough to bury his head in his "resounding plumage," that is, to devote himself to writing poetry. He does not belong in his snowy "monsterland" (*urodina* is a neologism combining *urod* [monster] and *rodina* [homeland]), but buries himself deeper into his plumage until he sees an imaginary South Sea island. But even in the ostrich's homeland his fantasy is trampled underfoot and he is seen as a foreign bird—people's attitude toward him oscillates between bewilderment and adoration. Utopia is exposed as a fiction, and at the end of the poem he is back in the wintry urban landscape of the opening lines. Nothing has changed and he gives up: "So take me then in your ice-cold grip! / Let the wind's razor blade shave off my feathers. / I might as well disappear, / a stranger from the other side of the ocean, / into the madness of all Decembers."

On the surface, "To Russia" is about the poet's role in society and society's attitude to the poet.* Read in this way, it can be seen as a

---

* In Soviet times, the poem was purposely dated to 1915 or 1916, since Mayakovsky was not supposed to have written a poem critical of the new socialist society.

poetic commentary on Osip's criticism of the Bolsheviks' utilitarian view of culture and as a defense, albeit a resigned one, of form and fantasy. (That Mayakovsky could simultaneously write such different poems as "Our March" and "Ode to the Revolution," on the one hand, and "To Russia," on the other, should not be seen as surprising—it is an expression of the ambivalence which characterized his attitude to the Revolution.) On a deeper level, "To Russia" is a variant of a central theme in Mayakovsky's writing: the poet with his imagination and his "resounding plumage" is always "transoceanic," always a stranger, wherever he finds himself.

THE POETS' CAFÉ

Mayakovsky got an opportunity to show off his "feathers of meter and rhyme" after moving to Moscow. In the autumn of 1917, with financial backing from the millionaire restaurateur Nikolay Filippov, Vasily Kamensky had set up a platform for poets called The Poets' Café in an old laundry off Tver Street, in the heart of Moscow. The interior consisted of a stage and some crudely carved furniture. The walls were decorated by Mayakovsky, Burlyuk, and other artists and covered in more or less comprehensible quotations from the Futurists' works. The Poets' Café deliberately harked back to the traditions of prewar times from the artists' café The Stray Dog in St. Petersburg, and the public was provoked by the same scandalous methods as during the heyday of Futurism. One symbol of continuity was that Mayakovsky went back to wearing his yellow blouse, which had been packed away since he had met Lili.

The public arrived late, after the theater. The platform was open to all. Apart from the elite corps of Futurists there were also guest appearances by singers, poets, dancers, actors. Vladimir Holtzschmidt, "Life's Futurist," entertained the public by breaking boards over his head. In mid-December Mayakovsky reported to Lili and Osip: "The café up to now has been a very pleasant and jolly institution. [. . .] Chock-full of people! Sawdust on the floor. On the platform, ourselves. [. . .] We beg the public to go to hell. Share out the money at midnight. [. . .] Futurism is very popular."

"Café Futurism" coincided with the most militant and at the same

Burlyuk and Mayakovsky (*standing, at left*) in the Poets' Café (from the film *Not Born for Money*).

time most pluralistic phase of the revolution, in which different anarchist groups played a central role. The anarchists, who were occupying several houses in the neighborhood, were often spotted in the Poets' Café—as were the security police, the Cheka. Lev Grinkrug, who visited the café almost every evening, remembers scenes with anarchists where shots were fired.

It was no coincidence that the anarchists frequented the Poets' Café. The Futurists' "ideology" was an antiauthoritarian, anarchistic socialism, and the anarchists often used the café as a meeting place. In *The Futurists' Newspaper*, which was published on 15 March 1918, Mayakovsky, Burlyuk, and Kamensky declared that Futurism was the aesthetic equivalent of "anarchist socialism," that art must get out onto the streets, that the Academy of Art must be shut down and art separated from the state. Only a "revolution of the spirit" can free mankind from the fetters of the old art!

The spiritual revolution was the *third revolution* that was to follow after the economic and political upheavals—a spiritual transformation without which the revolution was incomplete. The first two revolutions had been successful, but in the realm of culture "old art" still ruled, and the Futurists exhorted "the proletarians of the soil and the factories" to carry out a "third bloodless but brutal revolution, the Revolution of the Spirit." The idea of a spiritual revolution was in the air. The leading Symbolist Andrey Bely wrote in 1917 that "the revolution in the means of production is a reflection of the revolution but not the revolution itself," an idea which was developed in the revolutionary socialist newspaper the *Banner of Labor*.

The anarchism of "Café Futurism" did not only consist of slogans, but also found practical expression. In March 1918, at a time when the anarchists were occupying private houses in Moscow on an almost daily basis, Mayakovsky, Kamensky, and Burlyuk took over a restaurant which they wanted to convert into a club for "individual-anarchist creativity." However, they were thrown out only a week later, and the project ran into the sand.

"Café Futurism" ended abruptly on 12 April 1918, when the Poets' Café was shut down. The end of anarchist Futurism coincided almost to the day with the Cheka's liquidation of political anarchism, which occurred on 12 April. The two events, which in all probability were connected, marked the end of the Russian Revolution's anarchistic period in both politics and culture.

MAN

In the midst of the most hectic café period, in February 1918, Mayakovsky brought out his new poem, "Man," under the imprint ASIS (Association for Socialist Art) and with money from a few friends, among them Lev Grinkrug. The other, uncensored edition of "A Cloud in Trousers" came out at the same time and under the same imprint.

When at the end of January Mayakovsky recited "Man" at a private poetry evening on the theme "Two Generations of Poets Meet," it caused a sensation. Those present included large sections of the Russian poetic Parnassus: Symbolists such as Andrey Bely, Konstantin Balmont, Vyacheslav Ivanov, and Jurgis Baltrušaitis; the Futurists David Burlyuk and Vasily Kamensky, and some other poets who defied any such categorization, like Marina Tsvetayeva, Boris Pasternak, and Vladislav Khodasevich. "Poets read in order of seniority and without much apparent success," Pasternak recalled: "When it came to Mayakovsky's turn, he got up, curved one arm around the edge of the empty shelf at the back of the divan, and began reciting 'Man.' Like a bas-relief [. . .] he towered above the people that were seated or standing there. And now with one arm propping his handsome head, now bracing his knee against the bolster, he recited a work of uncommon profundity and exalted inspiration."

Opposite Mayakovsky sat Andrey Bely, who listened as if trans-fixed. When the reading was over, he rose, shaken and pale, and declared that he could not imagine how poetry of such power could be written at such a time. The reading at the Polytechnic Museum a few days later was equally successful. "I had never heard Mayakovsky read like that," recalled Roman Jakobson, who was there with Elsa: "He was very nervous, wanted to get everything out and read quite exceptionally. . ." Bely was also present at this reading, and he repeated his words of praise: after the Symbolists, Mayakovsky was the outstanding Russian poet. It was a recognition he had long been waiting for.

"Man" was written during the course of 1917. Work on the poem began during the spring and finished sometime toward the end of the year, after the October Revolution. The almost one-thousand-word poem thus occupies a central place in Mayakovsky's oeuvre from a chronological point of view: on the threshold between the old times and the new. But it has an almost equally central status thematically. Nowhere does Mayakovsky's existential alienation find more desperate expression than here.

The structure of the poem is modeled on the life of Jesus, and it is divided into sections like "Mayakovsky's Nativity," "Mayakovsky's Life," "Mayakovsky's Passion," "Mayakovsky's Ascension," "Mayakovsky in Heaven," "Mayakovsky's Return," "Mayakovsky to Eternity." The religious connection is emphasized by the typography of the cover, where the author's surname and the title are intertwined like a cross.

Mayakovsky's birthday—"the day of my descension"—was the most mundane of days. No one thought to notify a distant star that there was something to celebrate. And yet it is an event of the same caliber as Christ's birth. Every movement Mayakovsky makes is a

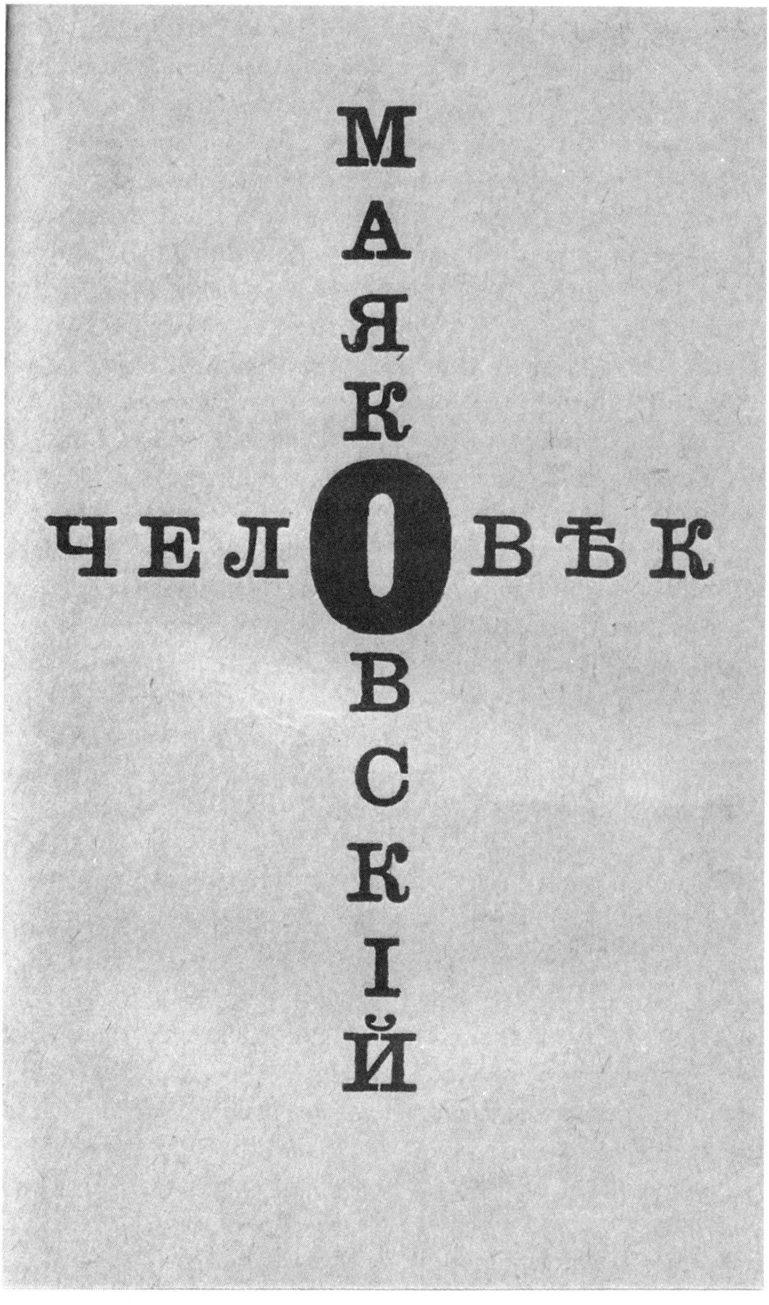

МАЯКОВСКІЙ

ЧЕЛОВѢКЪ

On the cover of *Man*, the name of the author and the title are shaped as a cross, a fitting symbol for this Christ parable, which ends with Mayakovsky standing "embraced by fire, / on the pyre of an impossible love / that never burns down."

miracle; his hands can enfold any throat, his tongue form any sound it wants; he possesses an intellect that sparkles like precious stones; he can change winter into summer and water into wine. Within his magic sphere everything becomes poetry—stout washerwomen are transformed into "daughters of the sky and the dawn"; the baker's buns are bent into the necks of violins; the bootlegs that the shoemaker is working on become harps. Everything is the result of Mayakovsky's birth: "It is I / who hoisted my heart like a flag. / A matchless wonder of the twentieth century!" Faced with this miracle, pilgrims come streaming from Our Lord's grave, and Mecca empties of the faithful.

However, far from everybody is equally impressed by the poet's transforming power. The real world, represented by "bankers, tycoons, and doges," feels under threat and goes on the attack: If everything is "heart," what have they accumulated heaps of money for? And who gave him permission to sing? Who asked the days to bloom in July? No, lock up the sky behind bars, twist the earth into streets, poison the tongue with gossip! Chased into the "earthly pen" the man/poet drags along his "daily yoke," his brain oppressed by "The Law" and with "Religion" like a chain over his heart. He is locked inside a "senseless story"; all fantasy is proscribed; everything is ruled by money. Everything, large and small, drowns in the golden maelstrom of money: geniuses, hens, horses, violins, elephants. On an island in the middle of this whirlpool lives the "Ruler of All," the poet's "rival" and "invincible enemy," in thin stockings with small, fine polka dots, elegant trousers, and a natty tie that "glided down from his enormous neck / over the globe of his belly."

Although Mayakovsky's enemy bears the clichéd characteristics of the bourgeois, it would be too simplistic to reduce the "Ruler of All" to a social or economic phenomenon. In Mayakovsky's poetic world the concept "bourgeois" is first and foremost a symbol—for stagnation, conservatism, repletion. "To be bourgeois / is not to own capital, / scatter gold coins around. / It is the dead man's heel / on the young ones' throat, / it is the mouth stuffed full with fat," as he defined the phenomenon a couple of years later, in the poem "150,000,000." The "Ruler of All" is "the universal bourgeois," whose cheap and vulgar taste dominates and corrupts the world. The conclusion that Mayakovsky formulates in "Man" can stand as a motto for the whole of his work:

> Revolutions shake the bodies of kingdoms,
> the human herd changes drovers,
> but you,
> uncrowned lord of the hearts,
> not a single rebellion can disturb!

The Ruler's power of attraction is so strong that even the poet's beloved is seduced by it. He tries to stop her, but it is too late, she is already with Him. His skull shines; He is completely hairless; only on his final finger joint do three small hairs peek out from under a jewel. She bends over his hand, and her lips whisper the names of the hairs—one is called "Little Flute," the other "Little Cloud"; the third is called after some other work by the poet. In this way, not only Mayakovsky's love but his poetry too is vulgarized by "the uncrowned lord of the hearts."

The woman is in His power, and longing and sorrow call forth thoughts of suicide in the poet, whose "heart longs for the bullet / and throat yearns for a razor." During a stroll alongside the Neva his soul falls to the ice like a "frozen emerald." He finds a pharmacy, but when the pharmacist produces a bottle marked "Poison," he remembers he is eternal, the roof opens of its own accord, and he climbs up to heaven. Once there, he shrugs off his "baggage / of things / and an exhausted body" on a cloud. The contrast between the high-flown theme and the prosaic tone is huge! To begin with he is disappointed. Hinting that the "invincible enemy" is also within himself, he complains that there is not a single corner where he can sit and drink tea and read the paper in peace. But he gets used to it; life in heaven turns out to be a mirror image of life on earth, and here too one's existence is regulated from morning till night. Someone is repairing a cloud, another is shoveling coal into "the sun's oven." But what is he, the poet, to do? After all, he is "all about heart, / and where is the heart in those who lack a body?" When he wants to "stretch out the body on a cloud and watch you all," he is given to understand that this will not do at all. Heaven too has no place for a poet.

His existence drags itself out; one year is just like another; in the end his heart begins to pound in his body again, and Mayakovsky wants to return to earth. Perhaps everything there will be new, after "1, 2, 4, 8, 16, thousands, millions of years"? But when he tumbles down to the earth like "a painter off the roof," he soon realizes that everything has stayed the same; human beings are burdened by the same workaday tasks as before; it is "the same invisible baldhead / in charge / the chief choreographer of the earthly cancan"—now "in the form of an idea, / now like the Devil, / now like God behind a cloud." The Enemy comes in many guises!

When Mayakovsky reaches the Trinity Bridge he remembers how in his previous life he stood there staring down at the Neva and thinking about throwing himself into the water. In a dream vision he sees his beloved, he senses "almost the fragrance of her skin, / almost her breath, / almost her voice," his newly awakened heart misses a beat, and once again he is plagued by "earthly torments": "Long live / —once again!— / my madness!" he exclaims, with a nod to "A Cloud in Trousers." When he asks a passerby about Zhukovsky Street, he is told that for thousands of years it has been called after Mayakovsky, who "shot himself here at his beloved's door."

He creeps up the stairs and recognizes the apartment: the same bedroom, the same silk curtains. When he catches sight of a bald head shining in the moonlight, he takes his dagger and creeps closer, reverting back "into love and pity." But when he lights the lamp, it emerges that the apartment is occupied by other people, the engineer Nikolayev and his wife. He flees down the stairs and gets hold of the caretaker. The answer to his question, "where have they put her / from apartment forty-two," is that "according to the legend," she threw herself out of the window after him and "then they lay there / body to body."

Mayakovsky fled the earthly scene because of a love that was impossible and when he returns to earth his love is no longer there. Where can he go? To which heaven this time? To which star? Mayakovsky has no answer to give. Everything is doomed to perish, he says, because "he / who controls life / will burn out / [. . .] the last ray / of the last suns." He himself will die the love-death, "embraced by fire, / on the pyre of an impossible love / that never burns down"—a variation on the closing lines of the first section of "A Cloud in Trousers": "Moan / into the centuries, / if you can, a last scream: I'm on fire!"

"Man" is the culmination of the existential theme that characterizes Mayakovsky's writing from the very beginning: the solitary I who battles against the enemy of poetry and love and whose name is legion: "necessity," philistinism, the triviality of everyday life, what in Russian is called *byt*—"my invincible enemy," the "Ruler of All." The Russian philosopher Lev Shestov talks of the "tragic souls" who are doomed to fight a battle on two fronts: "both against 'necessity' and against their neighbors, who have no trouble at all fitting in and who, without knowing what they are doing, thereby take the side of mankind's worst enemy." Shestov was thinking of Dostoevsky and Nietzsche, but the description is equally valid for Mayakovsky, with his tragic worldview.

As the title suggests, "Man" is not about Mayakovsky in Russia, but man in the Universe. The problem is universal, existential, not private. Yet the poem is strongly autobiographical, as always with Mayakovsky. If the political events of the time are conspicuous by their absence in this poem, which was written during the most turbulent year in modern Russian history, Lili is present in the highest degree. References to her are numerous, from a mention of her exact address—even the apartment number!—to the whispering of the names of Mayakovsky's poems. In the rough drafts of the poem the allusions to Lili are even more obvious.

KINEMO

Mayakovsky's enthusiasm for the Poets' Café soon waned. As early as the beginning of January he was telling Lili and Osip that he was sick and tired of the place, which had turned into a "petty little bedbug hatchery." Lili was equally tired of Petrograd, but her mood improved after she and Osip decided to take a trip to Japan with the ballerina Alexandra Dorinskaya. On the way there they intended to call on Mayakovsky in Moscow; but the trip never came off, and neither did the visit to Moscow.

"I dreamed about you all night," Lili wrote two months later, "that you're living with some woman, that she's terribly jealous, and

In a letter to Lili from March 1918, Mayakovsky expresses, with a characteristic exaggeration, his disappointment with the fact that he has only received half a letter from her whereas Lyova has received a thousand and Mother and Elsa a hundred. Hence the happy expression on Lyova's face and the sad one on Volodya's.

you're afraid to tell her about me." Mayakovsky retorted: "I always sit three or four places away from women in case they breathe something noxious over me."

The woman that Mayakovsky sat several seats away from was an artist called Yevgenia Lang. They had known each other since 1911 and had now renewed their acquaintance in Moscow. Yevgenia would later talk about Mayakovsky's great love for her, but there is no evidence that he was any more intimately involved with her than with any of the numerous other women that he associated with. It was Lili he loved. The earliest surviving letter in which he addresses her alone—not Lili and Osip jointly—was written in mid-March 1918 and ends with the words "I'm not kissing anyone else or sending my regards to anyone in this [letter]—it's one of the 'to you, Lilya' cycle"—the same dedication that graced the title page of *Man*. From now on the tone is different from that of the earlier letters, which can best be described as rather noncommittal situation reports on life in Moscow. In a letter of March 1918 Lili, for the first time, calls Mayakovsky her "little puppy" and reveals that she is longing for him.

And yet it was Mayakovsky who played the active part. In March and April he wrote three letters to Lili without receiving an answer: "Why don't you write me a single word? [. . .] Is four hundred miles [the distance from Petrograd to Moscow] really so much? You shouldn't do this, my child. It doesn't suit you! Please write, I get up every day with the melancholy thought: 'What's up with Lilya?' Don't forget that besides you I don't need anything and nothing interests me."

A scene from *The Lady and the Hooligan*, where the leading female role is played by Alexandra Rebikova. Just as in many of Mayakovsky's poems, the hero perishes at the end of the film— when he tries to defend the schoolmistress's honor, he is stabbed to death.

Mayakovsky as Ivan Nov in *Not Born for Money*.

Lili replied that she was longing dreadfully for him and he was welcome to come to Petrograd and live with them. "I terribly love getting your letters, and I terribly love you." She always wore the ring he gave her with her initials L. Yu. B. in a circle, so that they read "lyublyulyublyulyublyu. . ." in eternity—that is, [in Russian] "I love." On the inside he had had his name engraved, *Volodya*. The ring that Lili gave Mayakovsky had engraved on it the Latin initials *WM*—Wladimir Mayakovsky, and on the inside, *Lili*.

Mayakovsky's only way of overcoming his longing for Lili, he wrote, was "kinemo." During March and April he wrote, in quick succession, two film scenarios on commission from the private film company Neptune, whose owner, the Antik family, used to visit the Poets' Café and had been impressed by Mayakovsky's theatrical talent.

The first film script, *Not Born for Money*, was based on Jack London's novel *Martin Eden*. The leading role was played by Mayakovsky himself, and part of the action took place in the Poets' Café, whose interiors were constructed in the Neptune film studio. Although the film ran for several years in Moscow and some provincial towns, it has not survived. What has survived is the second film—*The*

Lady and the Hooligan—after the Italian writer Edmondo De Amicis's short story "The Worker Schoolmistress." It was premiered at about the same time as *Not Born for Money*. In this film too the leading role was played by Mayakovsky.

Mayakovsky himself described his work for Neptune as "sentimental piecework." But that was much later, with the murky perspective of hindsight. In actual fact he had a long-standing interest in the expressive possibilities offered by film. As early as 1913 he wrote a scenario—*The Hunt for Fame*—and several articles about film, and according to some sources he had a small role in the film *Drama at Futurist Café No. 13*.

His casual mention of "piecework" was a reference to the end result, which Mayakovsky was dissatisfied with, as his original idea had been distorted by all the compromises he had been forced to agree to. In fact, *Not Born for Money* was a strongly autobiographical work which rang the changes on the themes of Mayakovsky's poetry. Right from the start Martin Eden's life story resembled Mayakovsky's, and as he made the hero a poet, the identification was even more obvious. Ivan Nov, who comes from a poor background, falls in love with a girl from a bourgeois family. When she rejects him he tries to win her love by beginning to study and to write poems. He begins to move in Futurist circles, becomes famous and soon also rich. Just like the real Mayakovsky, he exchanges his Bohemian attire for an overcoat and top hat.

But Ivan Nov is not happy; the girl he loves still doesn't want him. When she finally declares her love for him, he suspects that she is after his money, and no longer wants it. He considers taking his own life, but decides instead to fundamentally change it. He simulates suicide by setting fire to a skeleton, knocks a bust of Pushkin off its pedestal, burns his elegant clothes, puts on his old worker's blouse and wanders off, in a Chaplinesque closing scene, into the unknown distance.

Mayakovsky won praise for his acting and was said to have made "a very strong impression" and to "have what it takes to become a fine character actor." He wrote to Lili himself: "The film people say my acting skill is unprecedented. They tempt me with speeches, glory, and money."

LOVELAND

Mayakovsky succumbed to the temptation. The medium of film promised new creative challenges and moreover offered the opportunity to formulate what he could not express in his usual way because of the poetic drought that was afflicting him. In April he wrote to Lili: "I'm not writing any poetry [. . .]. By the summer I'd like to make a film with you. I'd write a screenplay for you." Lili replied that she would be delighted if he was to write a script for them both, if possible, one that could be filmed "in a week or two": "I terribly want to be in a film with you."

On 19 May the newspaper *Film World* reported that "the poet V. V. Mayakovsky has written the film script *Fettered by Film*," which had been bought by the Neptune company. "After I had acquainted myself with the technique of filmmaking I wrote a film script related to our [the Futurists'] innovative work in the field of literature," was how Mayakovsky defined his third film script, the first which was his from

The actress in *Fettered by Film*—played by Lili—leaves the cinema screen but longs to return. When Mayakovsky cannot find a screen for her, he instead hangs a white tablecloth on the wall (see p. 118).

beginning to end. He wrote it "in earnest, unbelievably inspired, like with his best poems," recalled Lili.

Fettered by Film is a truly original and innovative work, on the same level as the Futurists' foremost literary experiments. That it was of central importance for Mayakovsky is shown by the fact that in 1926 he wrote a variation on the theme: *The Heart of the Screen*, which, however, was never filmed.

The film's hero is an artist. He is troubled and wanders around

the city. He gets into a conversation with a woman who suddenly becomes transparent. But instead of a heart, what is visible is a hat, hat pins, and a necklace. When he gets home, his wife has also become transparent: she has saucepans instead of a heart. When he bumps into a friend, it emerges that the latter has a bottle of liqueur and playing cards where his heart should be.

On the boulevard he is accosted by a Gypsy woman who wants to tell his fortune. He takes her to his studio, but while he is painting her, she becomes translucent—instead of a heart her chest turns out to contain small change.

Everywhere in the city there are advertisements for a new film, *The Heart of the Screen*. The posters show a ballerina holding a heart in her hands. The film shows to full houses. The artist sees it too. When the film is over and the audience has left the auditorium, the artist goes up to the screen and continues to applaud. The ballerina appears on the screen, steps down from it, and goes up to the artist.* He takes her out onto the street, where it's noisy and raining. The ballerina shivers and disappears back in through the closed door. The artist pounds the door in despair, but it remains closed.

The artist falls ill, and his maid goes off to the chemist's to fetch medicine. On the way home she drops the packet, the paper tears, and she wraps the medicine up in a film poster which has fallen onto the pavement. When the artist opens the packet and leans the poster against the wall, the ballerina suddenly comes to life and approaches him. He is beside himself with joy and immediately recovers. At that moment she disappears, not only from all the posters but from the cinema screen itself. Panic breaks out in the film company, as the film is taking in a lot of money.

The artist suggests to the ballerina that she come with him to his dacha. He rolls her up like a poster and lays her carefully in his car. Once out in the countryside the ballerina begins to long for the film, and he pounces on everything that's white and reminiscent of a screen. Finally the artist pulls off the tablecloth, with china and all, and hangs it up on the wall. The ballerina promptly strikes a pose and asks the artist to find her a proper cinema screen. He says good-bye to her, journeys through the night to the empty cinema, and cuts out the screen with a knife.

Meanwhile the Gypsy, who is in love with the artist and intensely jealous, has made her way out to the dacha. When the ballerina goes

* The same trick was used much later by Woody Allen in the film *The Purple Rose of Cairo*, where the hero of the film suddenly begins to talk to a woman in the audience and climbs out of the screen. She has seen the film so many times that he has fallen in love with her. The couple walk out of the cinema, leaving the dumbfounded actors and producers behind.

for a walk in the garden, she cuts her down with a knife. The ballerina changes into a poster, nailed to the tree she had been leaning against. The terrified Gypsy rushes off to the film company to tell them where the ballerina is. But as soon as she has gone, the ballerina comes to life again.

The ballerina waits for the artist. Instead there enters "the man with the beard"—who once offered the film company *The Heart of the Screen*—surrounded by all the stars of the film together with the Gypsy, who has brought them there. The ballerina is pleased; she has been waiting for them. The man with the beard wraps her up in a strip of film, and she dissolves into it. Everyone leaves the dacha, except the Gypsy, who faints.

When the artist returns with the cinema screen, the ballerina has gone. He revives the Gypsy, who tells him what has happened. He throws himself at the film poster, and suddenly, down at the bottom, he sees the name of the film's country of origin, in very small print. The last scene shows the artist by the window of a train, in search of this country. According to Lili, it was called something like "Lyubly-andia," "Loveland" (on the model of *Laplandiya*, Lapland).

The film is about unrequited love, just like many of Mayakovsky's poems—and the film *Not Born for Money*. But the fact that the heroine is a ballerina underlines the autobiographical aspect and places it in the ranks of all his other "To You, Lilya" works.

LILI + VOLODYA = TRUE

Fettered by Film was finished by the beginning of June and marked the symbolic prelude to the new phase in the relationship between Mayakovsky and Lili which now commenced. On 17 June Mayakovsky left Moscow, and a week later he registered at the same address in Petrograd as Lili and Osip: 7 Zhukovsky Street, where he rented a one-room apartment on the same landing which was so small that the bath was placed in the hall.

The real Lyublyandia was called Levashovo, a village outside Petrograd where Lili, Osip, and Mayakovsky spent a holiday as a threesome. Mayakovsky's dream had been fulfilled: he had finally got the woman he had loved for three years but who did not love him, or, if she did, had until now not wished to confront her feelings. "She kept him at a distance for a long time," Roman Jakobson recalled. "But he was phenomenally persistent."

In Levashovo they rented three rooms with board. Mayakovsky painted landscapes, they picked mushrooms, and in the evenings they played cards, but not for money. Losing a certain number of points meant that the loser had to clean Mayakovsky's razors. Even more points lost meant having to chase the midges out of the room at night. The hardest punishment was going to the station to fetch the newspaper when it was raining. In between picking mushrooms, painting, and playing cards, Mayakovsky worked on a play, *Mystery-Bouffe*, a revolutionary fantasy staged on the first anniversary of the October Revolution.

What made Lili take the step of beginning to live openly with Mayakovsky as his wife, and why just at this point? Even if, as we saw, she had realized that he was a poet of genius, until now she had felt harassed by his assiduous courtship. "Not until 1918 was I sure enough to tell Osip about our love," she explained, adding that she would have left Volodya at once if Osip had thought it was wrong. Osip replied that she mustn't leave Volodya but she must promise him that they two would never live apart. Lili had never even considered this, she answered: "And so it turned out: we always lived together with Osya."

Such were the rules of play for the three of them. "Perhaps I wouldn't have loved Volodya so much if it hadn't been for Osya," Lili recalled. "I couldn't stop loving Volodya when Osya loved him so much. Osya used to say that for him, Volodya was not a human being but a happening. Volodya molded a lot of Osya's thinking [. . .] and I don't know two friends and comrades who were more faithful to each other than they were."

However sincere Lili's view of Mayakovsky was, it was refracted through the prism of Osya's pince-nez. She could not live without Osip; he was the framework of her life—but Osip could not satisfy her emotional needs. If he loved her, it was not with a burning, unselfish love like Mayakovsky's. Was it vanity that made Lili move Mayakovsky into the family? After all, he had written so many exceptional poems dedicated to her. But he would have continued doing that in any case, especially as pain and suffering were important fuels for his creativity. Was it Mayakovsky's fame she was after? But Mayakovsky was not particularly famous at this time, nor did he have much money. Perhaps it was love, in spite of everything, after two and a half years' hesitation, that made Lili give herself to a man whom, before the making of the film in May, she had not seen for six months. Even Elsa was obviously surprised when she visited her sister in Levashovo: "The subconscious conviction that other people's private life is something sacrosanct forbade me not only to ask what would happen later, and how life would turn out for my nearest and dearest friends, but even to pretend that I had noticed their new relationship."

LITTLE STRAWBERRY, MARRY ME!

Roman Jakobson (ca. 1920), who courted Elsa intensively but to no avail.

After her father's death in the summer of 1915 Elsa and her mother had moved to a little house in Zamoskvaretchie, a picturesque part of town on the other side of the Moscow River from the Kremlin. At the same time Elsa began to study architecture at Moscow's Construction Courses for Women. Her course certificate is dated 27 June 1918. One week later she left Russia to travel to Paris, where she was to marry a French officer. Elsa's visit to Levashovo was thus no courtesy visit, but a leave-taking; she went there to bid her sister farewell.

Elsa did not travel alone, but in company with her mother. The journey to Paris went via Stockholm, and on the way there they spent the night with Lili in Petrograd. "The apartment was empty," Elsa recalled: "Lili and Volodya's life together had just started, and they had gone off to Levashovo, outside Petrograd. To my mother, this change in Lili's life was a severe blow. She was not at all prepared for it. She did not want to meet Mayakovsky and was prepared to continue our journey without saying good-bye to Lili. I went off to Levashovo on my own."

The following day Lili came into the city to say good-bye. It was, Elsa recalled, "as if she had suddenly realized that I was really about to go, that I was about to marry an unknown Frenchman." Mayakovsky did not come with her, as Yelena Yulyevna had such negative feelings for him. It was unbelievably hot, cholera was raging, and fruit was rotting in the streets because no one dared eat it. "With a feeling of infinite sadness I watched from the deck as Lili stretched toward us and tried to hand us a parcel of invaluable meat. I saw her small feet in the thin shoes alongside a stinking, perhaps cholera-infected pool of water, her thin figure, her eyes."

Lili and her mother would have preferred to see Elsa married instead to Roman Jakobson, who for several years had courted her so assiduously that, as he wrote in a jocular verse, he had:

> Forgotten folklore, lost his way,
> Sitting beside you night and day.
> Sorrowful and sadly groanin',
> In lack of rum he downed some bromine.

But however flattered Elsa was by his attentions, she rejected Roman's courtship, which she later described in the chapter "Little Strawberry, Be My Wife" in the novel *Wild Strawberry* (Moscow, 1926), where Roman goes under the name of Nika:

> Nika and Little Strawberry were sitting opposite each other by the samovar drinking tea with jam and biscuits. They had just been bickering about modern literature and were now happy just to sip their tea and hold their peace.
>
> Nika put down the empty tea glass and finally opened her mouth:
>
> "Why don't you marry me?"
>
> Little Strawberry filled the teapot and put it on the samovar.
>
> "But, Nika, how could I marry you?"

"As people usually do, quite simply. You are to marry me, it's clear as daylight."

Little Strawberry was silent.

"You'll have a really nice time. I'll give you all the books you want, we can travel wherever you want . . .

"Listen, little strawberry, this is really stupid of you! Do you really not understand? Even when I was six years old, waiting for you in the glade at Vesnyaki, and you didn't come, I cried as if I had broken my favorite steam engine! Even then it was obvious. Don't be so stupid and stubborn; marry me."

MONSIEUR TRIOLET

Elsa's intended was instead a French soldier named André Triolet who had come to Russia in May 1917. He was a sergeant in the cavalry and was part of a military delegation sent by France, Russia's ally. It is unclear when he and Elsa met, but it may have happened at the home of Osip's cousins, the Rumer brothers, who lived on the same landing as Elsa's parents. André Triolet came from a prosperous family (porcelain manufacturers in Limoges), and his main interests were women, horses, and sailing. He was also an elegant dresser. That Elsa was dazzled by this dandy is easy to believe, but whether she loved him is more doubtful; nor were her family very enthusiastic. When Elsa called on Lili and Osip in Petrograd at the end of 1917 with Triolet in tow, Lili and Osip, who had been sitting in the next room playing cards, came out "to have a peep at him [. . .] without comment."

The circumstances surrounding Elsa's journey and her marriage leave many questions unanswered. Why does she refer to such a decisive life event only in passing in her memoirs? And why is there no other information available, for example, from Lili? Why did Elsa travel to Paris to get married instead of marrying in Moscow? The uncertainties in Elsa's depiction of the circumstances surrounding her marriage to Triolet are in direct proportion to the number of questions which a more thorough examination would generate.

Before Elsa and her mother left Moscow, they disposed of their furniture, including the grand piano, so that the "worker's family" that

The last known family picture before Elsa and her mother left Russia in the summer of 1918. Besides Lili, Elsa, and Yelena Yulyevna, we see Lev Grinkrug and Elsa's friend Tamara Beglyarova (standing).

because of the law on "densification" of dwelling places was already living in their building could have more room. At least according to Elsa's memoirs, where she also informs us that they planned to return after three or four months. To what? An unfurnished apartment lacking the grand piano with which the whole of Yelena Yulyevna's life was bound up? And with whom—her French soldier?

All of this is clearly a rationalization by Elsa, who when she wrote her memoirs was a celebrated member of the French Communist Party and did not want to give the impression of someone who had deserted Soviet Russia at a time when the country's red future hung in the balance.

In actual fact, Elsa and her mother *fled* Bolshevik Russia, something which Elsa later acknowledged privately. She "abhorred the Revolution," she admitted, and found it "very unpleasant." What she meant was not only the violence and brutality but also the poverty that descended overnight, the lack of food and general comfort, the everyday destitution. This was not for a spoiled girl from a sheltered bourgeois home. She therefore actively sought contact with the French officers in Moscow, in the hope of finding someone who could help her to leave the country.

But was it Elsa herself who took the initiative in leaving Russia? Or did that come from her mother, who was at least as terrified by the forward march of Bolshevism as her youngest daughter? During the spring and summer of 1918 the state of provisions in Russia deteriorated radically: "In a time when materialism was triumphant, matter had become an abstract concept," as Boris Pasternak formulated the paradox in his novel *Doctor Zhivago*. It also soon became clear that the country was heading for a political dictatorship. The bourgeois press had been forbidden to publish immediately after the Revolution, and the socialist newspapers were closed down in the summer of 1918. At the same time a civil war broke out between "Whites" and "Reds," as a consequence of which the young Soviet Republic's territory was soon reduced to an area no bigger than that of the principality of Muscovy in the fifteenth century.

In these circumstances there were many in the higher social classes who decided to leave the country. Among their number were Yelena Yulyevna's close friends the Jakobson family, who left Russia in the summer of 1918 with Roman's five-year-younger brother Sergei, at the same time as Roman was in hiding in the countryside because of his membership in the liberal cadet party. For Yelena Yulyevna and Elsa the last straw came when they had new and unwelcome neighbors imposed on them: not a "worker's family," as Elsa explained in her memoirs, but five Red Guards who terrorized both women to the point where they were forced to barricade their doors every night for fear of assault.

Alongside these practical considerations there was another factor which influenced the Kagans, mother and daughter, in their decision to emigrate: Vladimir Mayakovsky, whom both of them had given up hope of. Elsa had lost Mayakovsky to her great rival, her sister, Lili, and she was indifferent to other suitors, like Viktor Shklovsky. On the romantic front, then, there was nothing to keep her in Russia; quite the contrary.

As for Yelena Yulyevna, she disliked Mayakovsky not only because he was uncouth and impertinent, but also because in her eyes his relationship with Lili, who was married, was deeply immoral. The antagonism between the eldest daughter's open-mindedness and what she perceived as her mother's bigotry now came to a head. Yelena Yulyevna also had nothing to keep her in Russia. Her husband had been dead for three years, and during the six months since the Bolsheviks' seizure of power her whole world had collapsed, materially as well as ideologically. The decision to emigrate was made easier by the fact that her brother Leo Berman now lived in London, where he was branch manager for Lloyd's Bank in Whitechapel.

CATCH-22

The steamer *Ångermanland* on which Elsa and her mother left Russia departed from Petrograd on 10 July 1918. When the boat reached Stockholm, it was immediately placed in quarantine, as the cook and some of the passengers had gone down with cholera. "I shall never forget how disgusting I found the Swedish food, especially the pastries," was Elsa's verdict on Swedish cuisine. After a period in Stockholm Elsa and her mother traveled on to Bergen in Norway, from where they intended to proceed by boat to London, where Yelena Yulyevna's brother was waiting for them. However, it soon became clear that they had landed in a Catch-22 situation. In order to obtain an entry permit for France they had to spend some time in England, but in order to enter England they had to show documentation proving that they would be allowed into France: "PERMISSION PASS THROUGH ENGLAND NO SUFFICIENT STOP WE MUST HAVE PERMISSION TO ENTER ENGLAND AND STAY THERE TILL GET PERMISSION FROM FRANCE," Yelena Yulyevna telegraphed to her brother in London on 12 August.

During the summer Leo Berman contacted various official bodies in England on their behalf, to no avail. Finally, on 14 October,

Elsa photographed during her short stay in Stockholm in 1918, when she made her depressing acquaintance with Swedish pastries.

he wrote a letter to the deputy foreign minister in which he expressed the hope that the latter would realize the "exceptional circumstances of the case, involving as they do great hardship for a defenceless widow and her young daughter and affecting the well-being of a gallant French officer, Miss Kagan's fiancé." In the meantime, he explained, André Triolet had been conscripted into the French expeditionary force which in August had been disembarked in Archangel in order to attempt to liberate Russia from the Bolsheviks, which meant that the reason for requesting a French visa no longer applied. At the same time, his sister and niece could not return to Moscow, where their house had been requisitioned by the Bolsheviks and they had been deprived of their means of subsistence. As they could not stay in Bergen either, Berman asked the authorities to allow them to settle in England. Lloyd's Bank could attest they were "in possession of ample means," and he promised that he would personally take responsibility for them during their stay in England.

The letter had the desired effect, and Yelena Yulyevna and Elsa received their British visas. On 11 November 1918, a good four months after leaving Petrograd, they landed in England. At the beginning of 1919 André Triolet returned to Paris, but Elsa remained in London, and the wedding did not take place until August of that year. One reason for the delay was that Elsa seems to have had doubts. There is a good deal of evidence that the feelings which André gave expression to were not reciprocated by Elsa. Yelena Yulyevna, for her part, believed it was André who had doubts and that the reason was anti-

Elsa and André Triolet in their Tahiti home.

Semitism: "André does not love you enough to make him marry a Russian Jewess." But she was wrong on this score; the opposition came from André's father, who strongly opposed the marriage. When André, taking his father's opposition into account, proposed that instead of marrying they should live *en concubinage*, Elsa declined, on the grounds that she was "at heart, very bourgeois."

André and his mother eventually managed to overcome his father's opposition, and the wedding took place in Paris on 20 August, 1919. The financial settlement gave André 1,500 francs a month to live on. Further economic agreements had to do with their travel plans: 50,000 francs were put at their disposal in the Banque d'Indochine in Tahiti, and they received 10,000 francs for the journey. In October of the same year the bridal couple left for the French island colony where André intended to buy a plantation.

A GOOD RELATIONSHIP TO HORSES AND A BAD ONE TO GORKY

Lili's many suitors included Yakov ("Jacques") Izrailevich, who had mixed in the same circles as Osip and Lili even before the Revolution. "A real troublemaker, by no means without talent, in his way even cultivated, someone who squandered his money and his life"—is how he was characterized by Roman Jakobson, who describes how, at a party, Jacques teased him for flirting with his (Jacques's) aunt, who was a young woman. When Jakobson jokingly asked how he could believe that an honest woman would permit anything of that kind, Jacques replied: "Who has the cheek to call my aunt an honest woman?"

During the filming of *Fettered by Film* Jacques inundated Lili with love letters which were so long that she did not bother to read them, let alone reply to them. Nor did she tell Mayakovsky that Jacques was bombarding her with letters. But during the stay in Levashovo she received a letter in which Jacques demanded an immediate meeting. Mayakovsky was beside himself with jealousy and traveled in to Petrograd with Lili and Osip. "We were at home when Volodya came and told us that he had bumped into I[zrailevich] on the street (just think!), that I. had attacked him, and they had begun to fight," Lili recalled. "The militia came, they were both taken to the station, I. said they should call Gorky, whom he used to visit, and then they were released. Volodya was very grim; he told us about it and showed us his clenched fists, covered in bruises, he had hit I. so hard." "After this Gorky began to hate Mayakovsky," Jakobson recollected.

The incident bears witness to the intensity of Mayakovsky's jealousy but also to the emotions that Lili, at twenty-seven, was still capable of provoking in the opposite sex. The fact that her relationship with Mayakovsky was now a public fact added to the rumormongering—especially as Mayakovsky himself was not exactly known as a paragon of virtue. Rumors that they were living in a ménage à trois with Osip made for malicious gossip. If Gorky was a minor figure in the episode with Jacques Izrailevich, he played the main role in another drama which unfolded at about the same time.

Initially, the relationship between Mayakovsky and the commissar of enlightenment, Anatoly Lunacharsky, had been very good. But, as we have seen, Mayakovsky did not share the Bolsheviks' view of culture, and as a result relations gradually became "a little cooler, as we had different opinions about a lot of things," as Lunacharsky phrased it. However, it never came to an actual breach, and there was never any conflict with Osip. Mayakovsky was also united to Lunacharsky by less formal bands—they played billiards together as often as they could. So when Lili noticed that Lunacharsky hardly greeted them any more when they met, she was bewildered. When she told Shklovsky about this, his

Maxim Gorky drawn by Yury Annenkov.

reaction was one of surprise: Didn't she know that Gorky had told "everyone" that Mayakovsky had "infected a girl with syphilis and then tried to blackmail her parents"? The girl was said to be Sonya Shamardina, and the source of the rumor was her self-appointed guardian, Korney Chukovsky, who had jealously guarded her virtue during those winter months of 1914 when she had had an intimate relationship with Mayakovsky.

Lili immediately went to visit Gorky at his home, accompanied by Shklovsky. Gorky was clearly upset by the ensuing conversation and drummed on the table with his fingers. "I don't know, I don't know, I heard it from a very reliable comrade," he replied, but refused to name the "comrade"—that is, Chukovsky—who in his turn claimed he had got the information from a doctor in Moscow. However, Gorky promised to find out his address. When he had still not been in touch a couple of weeks later, Lili wrote to him: "Alexey Maximovich, I insist that you inform me of the address of that person in Moscow from whom you intended to find out the doctor's address. I am traveling to Moscow today to finally clear up this whole business. In my view it is not possible to postpone it."

Lili's letter was returned to her with Gorky's reply written on the back. Unfortunately he had not succeeded in finding out "either the doctor's name or his address, as the person who would have been able to tell me has gone off to the Ukraine on official duties." Lili told Lunacharsky the whole story and asked him to tell Gorky that the only reason he hadn't received a beating from Mayakovsky was that he was old and sick.

The rumor was false—Mayakovsky did not have syphilis and therefore could not have infected anyone. But quite apart from the degree of truth or otherwise in the rumor—why did Gorky spread it, and to none other than the people's commissar of enlightenment? After all, Mayakovsky and Gorky had been close to each other for several years on literary as well as political issues. Gorky had been quick to greet Mayakovsky as a promising poet, his publishing house Parus had brought out both the anthology *Simple as a Mooing* (1916) and the poem *War and the World* (1917), and, like Osip, Mayakovsky had collaborated with Gorky on his newspaper *New Life*. Gorky also used to drop in at the apartment on Zhukovsky Street. "He was round at our place I don't know how many times, but I can't remember what we talked about," Lili wrote. "All I remember is that I didn't like him. I disliked his diffident manner, which he played up and which struck me as phony; I disliked the way he drank his tea, leaning against the edge of the table, and the way he eyed me. I remember we played drafts with him, without much enthusiasm."

Lili's depiction of their relationship with Gorky smacks of rationalization, but her explanation of Gorky's changed opinion of Mayakovsky is as good as any: "Gorky couldn't forgive Mayakovsky for his desertion after he had taken him under his wing, and I[zrailevich] and Ch[ukovsky] took delight in setting them against each other."

On 9 July 1918 *New Life* had published Mayakovsky's poem "A Good Relationship to Horses," about an emaciated horse that falls down and dies—a common sight on the streets in that summer of famine. It was the last time that Mayakovsky and Gorky worked together. After Gorky helped to spread the rumor about Mayakovsky's syphilis, their relationship was destroyed for good. "I can't remember any individual that Mayakovsky spoke about in a more hostile way than Gorky," recalled Jakobson, who in the spring of 1919 witnessed an expression of this hatred. Mayakovsky, having won at cards, took Jakobson to a private, semilegal café in the center of Moscow. Sitting at the next table was Yakov Blyumkin, who in the summer of 1918 had murdered the German ambassador von Mirbach but been pardoned. Blyumkin was a Left Socialist Revolutionary, a Chekist, and a genuine revolutionary romantic who was often seen waving his revolver around—at Osip Mandelstam, among others, when Mandelstam criticized him for working for the Cheka. But at the same time he was an educated man, he had studied Old Persian, and on this occasion he was discussing the Avesta, the holy scriptures of the Iranian people, with Jakobson. But the conversation soon took another turn, Jakobson recalled, "and Mayakovsky suggested to Blyumkin that the two of them arrange an appearance directed against Gorky." According to Jakobson, Mayakovsky made "nasty jokes about Gorky" during the rest of the evening.

1. ТОВАРИЩИ! ПОЧЕМУ В ЕВРОПЕ
ДО СИХ ПОР НЕТ СОВЕТОВ,
А БУРЖУИ У ВЛАСТИ?

2. ПОТОМУ, ЧТО ТАМ ПРИМАЗАЛИ
К РАБОЧИМ МЕНЬШЕВИКИ-
РЕФОРМИСТЫ

3. ТРИ КОРОБА НАОБЕЩАЕТ ТАКОЙ РАБОЧЕМУ
А ГЛЯДИШЬ НА ДЕЛЕ - БУРЖУЮ
ДРУГ ИСТЫЙ

4. ЗАПОМНИТЕ ЭТО ТОВАРИЩИ
ЕДИНСТВЕННАЯ ВАША
РАБОЧАЯ ПАРТИЯ -
- КОММУНИСТЫ !

НАРКОМПРОС РОСТА № 5

5

COMMUNIST FUTURISM

1918–1920

The Bolsheviks' brutal propaganda awakens the darkest instincts of the masses.
Maxim Gorky, April 1918

Just as the anarchistic "Café Futurism" of Mayakovsky, Burlyuk, and Kamensky was flourishing as never before, a state institution was founded which would fundamentally change the rules of play for the Russian avant-garde: IZO (an abbreviation for Otdel Izobrazitelnykh Iskusstv [Section for the Visual Arts]). The initiative was a direct result of the cultural workers' negative attitude to the Bolsheviks' invitation of November 1917. Faced with this situation, Lunacharsky decided to create an organ that would be loyal to the new political power and whose main task would be to reform art education.

IZO was founded in Petrograd in January 1918, and initially it had seven members, among them artists like Natan Altman and David Sterenberg. The fact that there were only seven people at this point in time who

A typical ROSTA window. Here the workers of Europe are urged not to be seduced by "Menshevik reformists" when there exists a real workers' party made up of Communists.

wished, or dared, to collaborate with the Bolsheviks is significant in itself, but equally interesting is the fact that they were immediately attacked by conservatives as well as radicals for their "betrayal" of the cause of art. Despite this, the formation of IZO had two important consequences: the Union of Cultural Workers, the democratic association founded after the February revolution, lost its influence in one fell swoop, and the Academy of Art was shut down.

RED TERROR

"There is less and less revolutionary fervor," wrote the critic Yevgeny Lundberg in June 1918, "and so much hardship that people seem to age from one week to the next." It was a horribly exact observation. In the summer of 1918 there occurred several events that led to thoroughgoing changes in Russian internal politics. The civil war between the Red and White armies was stepped up, and foreign troops invaded the country. In June all right and center Socialist Revolutionaries and Mensheviks were excluded from the workers' councils, the soviets, which meant that there was only one legal party left alongside the Bolsheviks: the Left Socialist Revolutionaries. After their attempt to topple the Bolshevik government during the Fifth Soviet Congress at the beginning of July, they were excluded too. During the summer virtually all non-Bolshevik newspapers were banned, the tsar and his family were executed, the Bolshevik leaders Volodarsky and Uritsky were murdered, and on 30 August the Socialist Revolutionary Fanny Kaplan tried to murder Lenin. Finally, at the beginning of September, and as a consequence of these events, the "Red Terror" was proclaimed by way of a Cheka decree.

All of this meant that after the summer of 1918 the Bolsheviks had a monopoly on political power in Russia, which forced people to make a final choice: for or against. The mobility between parties which had been possible during the spring was no longer feasible. Now there were only two camps: the White and the Red. On the other hand, the Bolsheviks now needed all the support they could get and therefore had to make their policies more attractive to other socialists. Nor could they continue to challenge the intellectuals in the same way as before.

In the political arena this meant a more tolerant attitude to the other socialist parties. The Mensheviks responded by acknowledging that the October Revolution was "historically necessary" and promising their "direct support for the armed forces of the Soviet government against foreign intervention." In return the Bolshevik party allowed the Mensheviks to resume their political activity, and some political prisoners were released. The Socialist Revolutionaries soon followed the Mensheviks' example. Thus, for a time, a political armistice prevailed, even if there was no doubt about who determined the conditions.

In the autumn of 1918, in connection with the Bolsheviks' policy of consolidation, the "creative intelligentsia" was also exhorted to take sides, and many skeptics and critics now abandoned their earlier opposition. This did not necessarily mean that they had become Bolsheviks, but for many the Bolshevik party seemed a better alternative than the one presented by the White side.

Maxim Gorky's reaction is particularly interesting. Hitherto Gorky had been relentless in his criticism of the Bolsheviks, whose policies he attacked time and again in his column Untimely Thoughts in *New Life*. In April 1918 he had even refused to take part in a debate with Grigory Zinovyev, the Petrograd party boss, arguing that "demagogues like Zinovyev lead the workers astray," that "the Bolsheviks' brutal propaganda awakens the darkest instincts of the masses," and that "Soviet policies mean the betrayal of the working class."

But in September Gorky had changed his tune and declared that "the terrorist acts against the leaders of the Soviet republic had finally induced him to tread the path of close cooperation with them." One month later, at the beginning of October, he chaired a mass meeting at which representatives of the Bolshevik party exhorted the "workers' intelligentsia" to give the regime their support. One of the speakers was none other than Zinovyev, who described the political situation in the following manner: "For those who wish to work with us, we will open the way. In a time like this neutrality is impossible. Schools cannot be neutral; art cannot be neutral; literature cannot be neutral. Comrades, there is no choice. And I would advise you to side with the working class."

In the same way as the political leaders turned to the socialist parties, IZO turned to "the workers and artists" and welcomed those who now, one year after the Revolution, were prepared to "serve the socialist motherland"—but the invitation was only for those who supported "contemporary art" and who wanted to "create a new art." In other words, the aesthetic course was clear: Realists and other artists of a traditionalist outlook need not bother!

Many heeded the call, and during the autumn the teaching staffs in Petrograd and Moscow were complemented by some of the leading contemporary artists: Kazimir Malevich, Pavel Kuznetsov, Ilya Mashkov, Robert Falk, Alexey Morgunov, Olga Rozanova, Vasily Kandinsky, and others. IZO became a stronghold for the avant-garde artists—or Futurists, as they were generally called. At this time the term "Futurism" was used in a wider meaning than before the Revolution, and especially before the war, when the name designated Cubo-Futurists and other groups who called themselves Futurists. From the autumn of 1918 onward, "avant-garde," "left-wing art," and "Futurism" became more or less synonymous denominations.

ART OF THE COMMUNE

Mayakovsky and Osip were both socialists but were closer to Gorky and Menshevism than to Communism. In autumn 1918, however, they too went over to IZO. This indicated not only a new political orientation but also that they had abandoned the principle that art should be independent of the state, one of the main points in the manifesto published in the *Futurists' Newspaper* in March that same year.

One of the first issues discussed by the Petrograd IZO was the need for a mouthpiece in which they could propagate their ideas. December 1918 saw the publication of the first number of the weekly magazine *Art of the Commune* (use of the word "commune"—after the Paris commune—was widespread in the young Soviet state, and it was often used as a synonym for "Communism"). In January 1919 it was complemented by a similar publication in Moscow called *Art*. The editors of *Art of the Commune* were Brik, Natan Altman, and the art historian Nikolay Punin, and contributors included Malevich,

Chagall, and Viktor Shklovsky. Mayakovsky published his poems as leaders in the newspaper.

The most important point in the IZO members' program was the struggle against the influence of the cultural heritage on the art and culture of the new society. In articles and poems they launched scathing attacks on what they perceived as an obsolete aesthetics and its influence on contemporary culture. The "new" or "young" art which was to replace the old was, of course, "Futurism." Futurism was, in their opinion, the most advanced contemporary aesthetics and therefore the only art form worthy of the proletariat, historically the most advanced class. Futurism was thus equated with proletarian culture. These positively charged terms were not more narrowly defined but used mostly as slogans. Whatever was "new" and experimental was explained as Futurist, and therefore also proletarian. Just as the war, the Revolution created a reality which could not be described by traditional means, and the Futurists' claim to represent a suitable aesthetics linked directly into the argumentation in Mayakovsky's articles from the autumn of 1914 (see the chapter "A Cloud in Trousers").

There was yet another important ingredient in the Futurists' aesthetics. They emphasized professionalism, talent, and quality and criticized the tendency to approve of all expressions of "proletarian art" so long as the artist had the correct proletarian ideology and/or class background. For the Futurists, with their awareness of form, such an ideology was utter nonsense. Mayakovsky, for example, declared that "the approach of the poet to his material must be as conscientious as that of a welder to his steel," a notion which was directly opposed to the amateurish view of form-related questions prevalent among the proletarian writers.

During the course of a few months IZO grew into a significant force in cultural life. It took responsibility for art education throughout the Soviet republic and for the purchase of new art for museums, and propaganda for its ideas was published in newspapers published and financed by the Commissariat for Popular Education. Despite this, there was dissatisfaction with the pace of development. In actual fact, little had changed since the spring of 1918. Accordingly, in December, at the same time as the magazine *Art of the Commune*

Commissar of Enlightenment Anatoly Lunacharsky drawn by Yury Annenkov.

started to come out, Mayakovsky, Brik, and other members of IZO organized a series of talks and poetry readings in working-class areas of Petrograd. They felt strongly the need for a social base; they had to show the critics—and not least the workers!—that they were as close to the proletariat as they themselves maintained.

As a result of these worker contacts a Communist-Futurist collective (Komfut) was founded in January 1919, consisting of a couple of IZO members—including Brik—and several workers. Mayakovsky wholeheartedly supported their activities but could not officially take part, as he was not a member of the party, in contrast to Osip, who is thought to have joined the Bolshevik party at the same time as he began working for IZO. The *Komfuters* claimed that the cultural policies of the Bolsheviks were not in the least revolutionary, that the cultural revolution was lagging behind the political and economic upheavals, and that "a new Communist cultural ideology" was needed—which was simply a new expression of the demand for a spiritual revolution.

The Komfut was envisaged as a party collective within one of the Communist Party's local branches in Petrograd, but it was refused registration on the grounds that such a collective could "create an unwanted precedent for the future." This repudiation of Komfut was one example among many of the hardening attitude toward the Futurists within the party and government circles. The criticism had got under way in connection with the anniversary of the Revolution, when some avant-garde artists had decorated the streets in Petrograd with Cubist shapes. For their opponents, these decorations were typical examples of the "incomprehensibility" of Futurism. Moreover, the Futurists were criticized for having "occupied" IZO with the aim of having Futurism recognized as "state art."

At the beginning of 1919 the attacks became more frequent and intensive. So, for instance, it was decided that the Futurists were "on no account" to be entrusted with the decorations for the First of May celebrations in 1919. The last nail in the coffin was hammered in by Lenin himself, who attacked them for having "used the educational institutions of the peasants and the workers" for "their own private tricks" and for presenting "the most absurd doodles" as something new and proletarian. The result was that the Futurists were deprived of their magazines and lost almost all their influence within the Commissariat of Enlightenment. In December Lunacharsky stated with satisfaction that the intelligentsia's changed attitude had now made it possible to create a "balanced" staff within IZO. The avant-garde's time as state cultural ideology was over in Russia.

DOGS AND CATS

In the winter of 1918 the German army was dangerously close to capturing Petrograd, and in March the government moved to Moscow, which after a hundred and six years became Russia's capital again. When Mayakovsky and the Briks moved there the following winter, it was because Moscow was where the cultural struggle was now being fought out.

During their early days in Moscow they shared an apartment in Poluektov Lane in the city center with the artist David Sterenberg and his wife. Apart from Levashovo in the summer it was the first time that Mayakovsky and the Briks shared a dwelling. The apartment had lots of rooms, but in order to keep warm they squashed up together in the smallest one, where they had two beds and a folding bed. "We covered the walls and the floor with mats to prevent drafts," Lili recalled. "In one corner there was an oven and a stove. We seldom used the oven, but we lit the stove—morning, noon, and night—with old newspapers, broken boxes, whatever we could lay our hands on." It was a hungry time, and on one occasion things were so desperate that Lili was forced to trade a pearl necklace for a sack of potatoes.

Living with them in the little apartment was their setter Shenik ("Puppy"), which Mayakovsky had found in the village of Pushkino outside Moscow, where they spent the summer of 1919. In a letter written in the spring of 1918 Lili had called Mayakovsky her "puppy" ("Shenok"), but from now on he came to be identified with a particular dog. "They were very like each other," Lili recalled. "They both had big paws and big heads. They both went around with their tail in the air. Both of them whined when they wanted something and didn't stop till they had got their way. Sometimes they simply took it out on the first person to come along, just to score a point. We started to call Vladimir Vladimirovich 'Shen.'"

From now on Mayakovsky signed his letters and telegrams with this nickname and often added a drawing of himself as a puppy. "Animals were the constant topic of conversation in our life," Lili confided. "Every time I came home Volodya, would ask if I had seen any 'interesting dogs and cats.'" Shen was the first of several dogs in the "family," which enveloped itself in a thoroughgoing animal symbolism:

Mayakovsky was a puppy, Lili was a pussycat, Osip a tomcat. Like Mayakovsky, Lili and Osip signed their letters with drawings, and later on Lili even had a special "pussycat stamp" made.

They rented the dacha in Pushkino together with Roman Jakobson, who remembers how they spent the time discussing literary questions. At this time Jakobson was working on Mayakovsky's rhymes, and Mayakovsky in his turn was keenly interested in questions to do with the structure of verse. The conversations were so intense that Lev Grinkrug could not resist the ironic comment: "We all like Mayakovsky, but does that mean that we have to excerpt his rhymes?" Osip by this time

Lili, Lyova, and the setter Shenik outside the apartment in Poluektov Lane, 1920.

had become more and more interested in the sociological aspects of art and questions concerning production and consumption, supply and demand. When not talking about literature and art they played croquet and sunbathed. The mood was relaxed, and Lili liked to go around in minimal clothing. Once when she discovered a man standing by the fence glowering at her, she shouted: "Have you never seen a naked woman before, eh?"

The dog and cat symbolism hints at an intimacy in the relations between Mayakovsky and Lili that did not reflect the whole truth. Mayakovsky's jealousy meant that he often felt hurt and offended, and they had so many scenes that they even kept a record of "acts of war between Lily and Volodya." Hanging from a string fastened to a little notebook was a pencil which Lili used to write peace treaties and an eraser so that Mayakovsky could rub out injuries he felt he had suffered. In the summer of 1919 the conflicts became so acute that Lili no longer wished to stay under the same roof as Mayakovsky. Jakobson reported to Elsa in Paris: "Lily tired of Volodya long ago; he has turned into a real bourgeois philistine who is only interested in feeding and fattening up his woman. This of course is not Lili's style." The upshot was that in the autumn of 1919 Mayakovsky moved out of the apartment in Poluektov Lane, and a few months later, in the winter of 1920, they separated.

As we have seen, in a Moscow which was suffering from a lack of housing there had been a move to "densify" larger apartments "with the intention of improving the living conditions of the working class," as it was claimed. The owner of the apartment and his family were usually allowed to keep one of the rooms (if it was a large family, possibly two), while the others were occupied by homeless working-class people. The kitchen, toilet, and bathroom (if there was one) were shared. Mayakovsky was helped by Roman Jakobson, whose neighbor at 3 Lubyanka Passage, a kindly bourgeois called Yuly Balshin, feared that his apartment was going to be "densified" with complete strangers. When he asked Roman if he knew anyone of a placid disposition who might conceivably move in, Roman recommended Mayakovsky, prudently omitting to mention that he was a poet.

So the experiment of living with Lili very soon collapsed. What was the cause? Had Mayakovsky really turned into a bourgeois philistine, as Jakobson maintained? Perhaps there is something in that. Mayakovsky had pursued Lili for several years, and when he was finally accepted, it was like getting a family—for the first time. Perhaps it was his eagerness to safeguard his new-won happiness that made him careful in a way that Lili interpreted as "philistine." "He was incredibly frightened of Lili," Jakobson recalled: "It only took a rebuke from her to make him break down."

The most likely explanation, however, is that what made Lili tire of Mayakovsky was his jealousy, an emotion she deeply despised. Before they moved in together she had been able to satisfy all her romantic needs without his knowing all the details, but now that they were living together he was constantly confronted with her promiscuity. When Lili was asked in later life if Mayakovsky knew of her romances she answered: "Always!" To the follow-up question about how he reacted, the answer was: "He was silent." Mayakovsky's way of dealing with his feelings was to suppress them, and it was not a good way.

When he was not being silent, he could react with feigned cynicism—like in the summer of 1919, when Osip brought the conversation round to Antonina Gumilina, an artist Mayakovsky had been seeing before he met Lili. According to Jakobson, Gumilina was one of the models for Maria in "A Cloud in Trousers," and her paintings had only one theme: herself and Mayakovsky. One day Osip came home and talked about having seen a series of sketches of an erotic nature depicting Mayakovsky and Gumilina herself. The person who had shown them to him was Gumilina's husband, the artist Eduard Schiemann. None of the paintings have survived, but Jakobson, who went to one of her exhibitions, remembered one of them: a room in the morning, she is sitting on the bed arranging her hair while Mayakovsky stands by the window dressed in trousers and shirt, and with cloven hooves. . . . Elsa remembered another, *The Last Supper*, in which Mayakovsky sits in Christ's place at the table. Gumilina also wrote lyrical prose, including a piece called "Two Hearts in One," about herself and Mayakovsky, which, however, has not been found.

When Lili asked what had happened to Gumilina, Osip replied that she had committed suicide. "How could you not throw yourself out of the window with a husband like that?" Mayakovsky commented, with feigned indifference. For someone who was himself a perpetual candidate for suicide, the conversation was a bit too close to the bone, especially as there was reason to believe that it was love of him that had induced her to take her own life. "Her life belonged to Volodya," Elsa concluded, "whatever the motive [. . .] for her suicide was."

A MAN OF ACTION

However much Mayakovsky wanted to, he could not share Lili's attitude to love and unfaithfulness—let alone live with it. He had lots of fleeting relationships himself, but at heart he was a prude who prided himself on never having written anything indecent. Jakobson has described a visit to an exhibition of erotic engravings in 1919 in the company of Lili, Osip, and Mayakovsky. Mayakovsky was embarrassed and felt very ill at ease, while Lili and Osip commented on the pictures

Nikolay Punin, one of Lili's lovers, photographed in 1920.

with worldly nonchalance and bought an engraving showing "the young Pushkin" in different sexual positions, which they gave to Roman as a gift. The inscription "To Romik" on the underside of the etching was also signed by Mayakovsky, probably only after a hard struggle with his conscience.

Apart from the difficulties experienced by every married couple, in Lili's case there was a complication of a more deep-seated nature. It concerned the sexual incompatibility that existed between her and the two men she lived with. Osip did not desire her physically; Mayakovsky did, but obviously suffered from some form of sexual handicap. According to Lili he was simply "a torment in bed." Given all the women that Mayakovsky had relationships with over the years, it is hard to believe—although it has been suggested—that this was due to impotence. Although Elsa too complained that he was "not good in bed," explaining that by this she meant he "wasn't indecent enough"—the disorder seems to have shown itself mainly in his relationship with Lili. According to Viktor Shklovsky, Mayakovsky suffered from premature ejaculation, a conclusion which is backed up by Lili's (subsequently destroyed) diary, according to which Mayakovsky's sexual shortcomings "were perhaps because of his strong feelings for me."

Lili was promiscuous by nature, and the problems in her relations with Mayakovsky did not make things any easier. She sought out new contacts. According to Jakobson's memories of the year 1919, there was a period when Lili was "so unfavorably disposed toward Volodya that she couldn't hear talk of art or poetry or to talk about artists or poets herself without 'animal' irritation, and she fantasized instead about 'men of action'"—her "new style" was *affairs* which did not disturb the order of things.

One of these "discreet affairs" was with Nikolay Punin, the art historian, director of the Russian Museum in Petrograd, colleague of Osip and Mayakovsky in IZO, and one of the foremost exponents of the culture of the avant-garde. Punin was married, but the marriage was on the rocks. A note in his diary indicates that he and Lili had already had some sort of relationship in Petrograd, but it is only in the spring of 1920 that the relationship gets into focus. A short encounter on 20 May is followed by a long reflection in Punin's diary:

> Her pupils merge into her eyelashes and darken when she is roused. She has a triumphant glance. There is something insolent and charming in her face with its painted lips and dark eyelids[. . . .] This "most fascinating woman" knows a great deal about human love and physical love. [. . .] I can think of no other woman that it would give me greater satisfaction to possess. Physically, it is as if she was made for me, but she talked about art and I could not [. . .] If we had met ten years ago it would have been an intensive, long-term and solid relationship, but it seems I cannot fall in love so sweetly, so unreservedly, so humanly, so tenderly, as I love my wife.

When they met again, two weeks later, Lili told him of her feelings after the previous meeting. Punin noted: "When a woman [. . .] who is helpless and who clings on to life loves in this way, it is dismal and dreadful—but when Lilya B., who knows a great deal about love, who is strong and steadfast, spoiled, proud, and controlled, loves in this way—it is fine." As they were drawn to each other for different reasons, they could not agree on the conditions of the relationship. Lili wanted to talk about art, while Punin's interest in Lili was of a more primitive male kind: "I told her that she only interested me physically and if she was ready to accept me in that way, then we could see each other. Anything other than that I neither could nor would agree to. If she did not accept that, I asked her to ensure that we did not see each other. 'We will not see each other,' she said by way of farewell and put down the receiver."

It was Punin who put an end to the "relationship" and not the other way round. Lili was not used to this and she reacted with hysteria. Punin's notes show that it was not sex that was the most important ingredient in Lili's relations with men. What really interested her was the confirmation of her attractiveness to and power over men, and in this endeavor sex was only one of several weapons.

Lili was well read, quickwitted, provocative, and stimulating, but there were gaps in her education, and her knowledge was unsystematic. Her intellectual inferiority complex led her to be drawn to men who were her intellectual superiors, and Punin's frank declaration that Lili's body attracted him more than her ideas was a devastating blow to her self-esteem. Her statement that they would never see each other again did not reflect her true feelings, and she continued the battle to win his love. "L. B. talked about how her feelings were still unchanged and about how she 'howled' because of me," Punin noted in his diary in March 1923: "'Above all,' she said, 'I had no idea how to behave with you. If I act, you close up and go away, and when I'm passive you don't react either.' What she doesn't know is that I don't love [her] any more, and on the whole nothing could have come of it without love, whatever she, Lilya, was like. [. . .] Lilya B. still believes I am not indifferent, that I am not like a stone in my attitude to her. She caressed my hand and wanted me to kiss her, but I thought of An. and didn't do it."—"An." was an abbreviation for the poet Anna Akhmatova, whom Punin, despite being married, had started an affair with the previous autumn and whom he would live with until 1938.

A PRAGUE ROMANCE

Despite the territorial change that had taken place in the autumn of 1919, Mayakovsky had continued to call on Lili and Osip almost daily, just as he had done in Petrograd. But nothing was as it had been before, as emerges from Lili's desperate attempt to initiate a relationship with Punin. And at the beginning of 1920 something happened which made Lili think about leaving Soviet Russia for good. As the country was under blockade, she considered a marriage of convenience with Roman Jakobson, who left for Prague in May 1920.

Roman had graduated from the university in 1918 and had been handpicked for doctoral studies at Moscow University. This had the advantage, among other things, that he was excused from military service, which during the civil war meant serving at the front. But as he had been struck down in the winter of 1919 with typhus—which had reached epidemic proportions in Russia—he was unable to hand in the documentation in time and risked being seen as a deserter. However, after a period as an employee of the State Fuel Commission, he was saved by the university principal, who arranged the necessary papers.

Instead of a risky existence at the front, Roman was offered unexpected work in the press bureau of the Soviet Republic's first diplomatic mission in Reval (Tallinn), which was to be set up in the winter of 1920. When he asked why he had been offered the job, the Commissariat of Foreign Affairs official replied that no one else had been willing to travel for fear of being blown to bits by the White army once they crossed the border. "The journey took a long time," Jakobson recalled. "We had to travel a large part of the way [. . .] by sledge, as the roads had been destroyed during the civil war. Everybody from the mission was there, even the typists." Instead of bombers, the delegation was greeted in the border town of Narva by Estonia's minister for war and sandwiches with sausage and ham. "The bosses restrained themselves, but the girls threw themselves at the sandwiches as if they hadn't eaten for two years—however much they had been exhorted to be on their best behavior."

After spending some time in Reval Roman returned to Moscow, where a Polish researcher offered him the chance to travel to Prague with a Red Cross mission. Their task was to repatriate Russian prisoners of war who had been left behind after the war and to try to set up diplomatic ties with Czechoslovakia. As Jakobson's university course included studies in Czech, he struck a deal with the leader of the delegation, Doctor Gillerson, that he could study at the Charles University if work allowed. At the end of May he traveled back to Reval to wait there for the mission from the Red Cross, and on 10 July 1920 he arrived in Prague.

It was in connection with Roman's trip to Prague that Lili suggested they should contract a fake marriage so that she could leave Soviet Russia. "It was only by pure coincidence that it didn't come off," Roman reported to Elsa in Paris. Roman left Moscow in May

1920, but Lili's desire to emigrate is documented even earlier. In October 1919, that is, at the same time as she and Mayakovsky split up, Boris Pasternak wrote the following dedication to Lili on the manuscript of his poetry collection *My Sister Life*: "May the rhythm of this October bagatelle / serve as rhythm / for your flight from the land of bungles / to Whitman's land. / And in the same moment as the Red Army's helmets / begin to glitter here, / may your cheeks take on the red flush / of a Chicago dawn."

The idea of emigration was thus no sudden whim connected with Roman's departure; it had been in Lili's mind for at least seven or eight months, since the autumn of 1919. Pasternak's dedication reveals that Lili wished to move to Whitman's country, not to Western Europe, where her mother and sister lived. Why to the United States, where she had neither relatives nor other contacts? Moreover, her languages were French and German. The question has no answer.

And why in any case did she want to emigrate and abandon Osip and Mayakovsky? One important reason, of course, was her complicated relationship with Mayakovsky. She worshipped him as a poet, but as a man and a husband he fell far short of her ideal. Lili's immediate environment no longer provided her with the stimulation she needed to breathe. To these private disappointments can no doubt be added a general dislike of developments in Russia, not least in the arena of cultural politics. For twelve months, from the winter of 1918 to the winter of 1919, the Futurists—among them Lili—had found themselves in the center of cultural politics and had occupied important positions in the cultural bureaucracy. By the autumn of 1919 all this was over. At the same time the civil war was still raging with unabated intensity and the food situation was catastrophic. For a woman with Lili's material demands, the lack of comforts must surely have been an important factor behind her wish to leave the country.

But perhaps there was something else that led her to conclude it was best to leave? Lili had a big secret which she carried all her life, and which only one other person was privy to: Roman Jakobson, who once, "by pure chance," was witness to an event which, if it had become known, "would completely change Lili's life story." He never revealed what it was all about, but when asked how the secret would change her life story if it came out, he replied: "In the way that changes change things." Did the episode that Jakobson witnessed play a role in Lili's plans to emigrate?

Whatever deliberations lay behind Lili's desire to leave Russia, she was not alone in having such thoughts. Her sister, Elsa, had already left, her mother too, as well as Jakobson's parents and several others of her close acquaintances—and many more would follow during the coming years. It was a period marked by civil war, political uncertainty, and economic chaos, a time when no one knew what the future would look like. One alternative was to bide one's time abroad—not necessarily emigrate for good—then return home if things developed in a satisfactory direction. It was a survival strategy that many people adopted during these years.

DARK FORCES . . .

But Lili did not emigrate. Instead, only a week or so after Jakobson's departure, a change occurred in Brik's and Mayakovsky's life, the significance of which can hardly be overstated. On 8 June 1920 Osip was taken on as an investigator in the security police's department for "economic speculation."

Having for years been completely engrossed in his new literary and poetical-theory interests, Osip suddenly got a job with the feared Cheka! How did this come about? It was hardly the kind of service that was openly advertised. Nor was the Lubyanka a workplace that one visited in person to ask for a job. Such enthusiasts were automatically turned away. So someone must have recruited Osip. Whoever it was, and however the recruitment was done, it is clear that by the spring of 1920 Osip was regarded as sufficiently reliable to be entrusted with a post in the security service. After a while he was assigned to the "Secret Department's 7th Section," where it seems that, among other things, his remit was to keep an eye on former "bourgeois"—persons whom the Bolsheviks, with their social background, were not well acquainted with. Whatever the assignment was, Pasternak, who often visited the Briks during these years, said it was "creepy" to hear Lili say: "Wait a bit, we'll eat shortly, as soon as Osip gets home from the Cheka." And it wasn't long before someone—according to some accounts, the poet Sergey Yesenin—composed the following epigram, which was attached to their door one day: "You think that Brik lives here, the noted linguist? / Here lives an interrogator and a Chekist."

In a short time Osip's life—and thereby Lili's and Mayakovsky's lives too—changed fundamentally. From having considered life as an émigrée, Lili now had to do a complete rethink. Osip's work meant privileges but also falling into line. He was now not only a member of the increasingly omnipotent party but also a soldier in an army whose main task was to defend the state and the party against its enemies, real and—at least as often—fictitious. He had taken an irrevocable step: from now on the only option was a life in the world's first workers' state.

. . . AND LIGHT

It is unclear whether or not it was the requirements of their new life that led to a strengthening of relations between Mayakovsky and Lili, but that this actually happened is indisputable. Since the spring of 1919 Mayakovsky had been working on a long revolutionary epic, "150,000,000," which he finished in March 1920. After this, in April, he wrote a poetic tribute for Lenin's fiftieth birthday, but during the summer of 1920, which was also spent in Pushkino, his poetry took on a lyrical tone, suggesting a newfound harmony. He wrote a number of shorter poems on the themes of love and nature which were close stylistically to his prerevolutionary poetry; but above all he wrote the poem "An Extraordinary Adventure Which Befell Me, Vladimir Mayakovsky, in a Summer Cottage."

The poem is in the form of a conversation with the sun, whom Mayakovsky invites into his dacha in Pushkino for a chat. He is irritated by its eternal round, from sunrise to sunset, which he compares with his own daily stint. Since the autumn of 1919 he has been writing and designing hundreds of propaganda posters for the telegram bureau ROSTA (see page 159), and this work has squeezed all the juice out of him. They are soon on intimate terms and come to the conclusion that both of them are doing the same job, namely, to "sing in a gray tattered world":

When, in 1923, Mayakovsky published his poem "An Extraordinary Adventure . . ." as a separate book (with the title *The Sun*), the illustrations were provided by his old Futurist companion Mikhail Larionov. When, many years later, Larionov presented Roman Jakobson with one of the original drawings, he wrote on the back that it depicted Mayakovsky and was made in 1912.

Always to shine,
to shine everywhere,
to the very deeps of the last days,
to shine—
and to hell with everything else!—
That is my motto—
and the sun's!

(TRANS. GEORGE REAVEY)

The "conversation with the sun" was the first poem in a good two years which was not concerned with topical (especially cultural-political) issues. It breathed of belief in poetry and his own ability and marked a much-needed break from the poetic emergency service he had devoted himself to since the outbreak of the First World War.

In September 1920, after spending the summer in Pushkino, the Briks moved to Vodopyany Lane on the corner of Myasnitskaya Street, in the center of Moscow. The large apartment, which was occupied by the lawyer Nikolay Grinberg, his wife, and two children, was to be "densified," and Lili, Osip, and Mayakovsky were allotted three of the eight rooms. In this case too, the intermediary may have been Roman Jakobson, who was a university friend of the son of the family. Mr. Grinberg was a Socialist Revolutionary and, along with the rest of his family, spent some time in prison.

Off the long corridor to the right was the largest room—the former dining room—which was dominated by an enormous table with a samovar and ten chairs. This was Lili's room. The grand piano was also here, with a telephone on it. Behind a screen was Lili's bed, over which there hung a sign: "Do not sit on the bed." From the dining room a door led to the former boudoir, where Osip now took up residence. Here, there was a divan, a table and bookshelves. "[In the study] old-fashioned furniture," reported a visiting Italian journalist: "Masses of books. An enormous supply. Everything higgledy-piggledy, in heaps on the floor, arranged any old how on the bookshelves. [. . .] It was as if a devastating hailstorm had swept over the furniture, over the shelves, over the divans heaped with paper, over the dusty chairs, over the Cubist paintings that hung on the walls."

The third room, opposite the dining room on the other side of the corridor, officially belonged to Mayakovsky. There lived the housekeeper Annushka, who in the little maid's room behind the kitchen reared a piglet which in the autumn of 1921 tumbled out of the window and ended up on the dinner table.

The apartment was soon turned into a meeting place for disputatious, card-playing, tea-drinking breakfast-, lunch- and dinner-guests. Night and day, people on different errands passed through these rooms. "A brothel is a veritable church compared to this place," Mayakovsky complained mildly: "At least people don't go there in the middle of the day. But people visit us night and day, and, moreover, for free." When the card playing was at its most intensive—which it was most of the time—a sign saying "The Briks are not receiving visitors today" was hung on the door.

Mayakovsky kept his room in Lubyanka Passage but continued to call on Lili and Osip every day, and sometimes spent the night there. The fact that his relations with Lili had now been restored emerges from an entry in the diary of Korney Chukovsky, who in the autumn of 1920 invited Mayakovsky to Petrograd to perform at the House of

Art. Ever since Chukovsky's role in the "syphilis affair" the relationship between them had been frosty, and to begin with Mayakovsky was reluctant. But when he found out that there was a billiard table there, he gave up his resistance. On 5 November Chukovsky noted in his diary: "He arrived in the company of Brik's wife, Lilya Yuryevna, who is quite wonderful with him: friendly, cheerful, and unaffected. It's obvious that they are welded together in a close friendship—and for such a long time: since 1915. I would never have believed that someone like Mayakovsky would have been able to live in wedlock for so long with one woman. But now one is struck by what no one noticed before: the genuineness, constancy, and solidity in everything he does. He is faithful and reliable: all his contacts with his old friends, Punin, Shklovsky, and others, have remained good and sincere."

Chukovsky's diary entries make a strange impression. Was it he who was being naive, or was it Mayakovsky and Lili who were showing off? Was it this sort of facade that made Lili indignant about Mayakovsky's "philistinism" in the summer of 1919? That the truth was more complicated is clear from a note that Chukovsky wrote two days later. When Lili told him that Mayakovsky "now speaks well of everybody, praises everybody, and likes everybody," he replied that he had noticed this and took it to mean that Mayakovsky had become "sure of himself." "No," was Lili's response, "he doubts himself every minute of the day."

Lili was right: Mayakovsky was as insecure as ever, both about his creative talent and his relationship with her—or, more accurately, about her feelings for him. In other contexts he concealed his insecurity behind a facade of insolence and aggression; in relation to Lili, this was transformed into tenderness and an almost slave-like dependence. Viktor Shklovsky has described how Lili once left her handbag in a café and how Mayakovsky went back to fetch it. "Now you'll have to lug that handbag about with you for the rest of your life," the writer Larissa Reisner commented drily. "Larissa, I am ready to carry this handbag in my teeth," replied Mayakovsky. "Love knows no offences."

The outward harmony that Lili and Mayakovsky radiated in the autumn of 1920 hardly reflected the reality—Mayakovsky had no hopes of any constancy in their relationship, yet it presaged the beginning of the happiest and most conflict-free period of their entire life together.

КОММУНАЛЬНЫЙ ТЕАТР МУЗЫКАЛЬНОЙ ДРАМЫ

7, 8 НОЯБРЯ н/с.

МЫ ПОЭТЫ, ХУДОЖНИКИ, РЕЖИССЕРЫ и АКТЕРЫ ПРАЗДНУЕМ ДЕНЬ ГОДОВЩИНЫ

ОКТЯБРЬСКОЙ РЕВОЛЮЦИИ

Революционным спектаклем.
нами будет дана:

I КАРТ. БЕЛЫЕ И ЧЕРНЫЕ БЕГУТ ОТ КРАСНОГО ПОТОПА.

II КАРТ. КОВЧЕГ. ЧИСТЫЕ ПОДСОВЫВАЮТ НЕЧИСТЫМ ЦАРЯ и РЕСПУБЛИКУ. САМИ УВИДИТЕ ЧТО ИЗ ЭТОГО ПОЛУЧАЕТСЯ.

III КАРТ. АД В КОТОРОМ РАБОЧИЕ САМОГО ВЕЛЬЗЕВУЛА К ЧЕРТЯМ ПОСЛАЛИ

IV КАРТ. РАЙ. КРУНЫЙ РАЗГВОР БАТРАС МАФУСАИЛО

V КАРТИНА. КОММУНА! СОЛНЕНЫЙ ПРАЗНИК ВЕЩЕ и РАБОЧИ

РАСКРАШЕ МАЛЕВИЧЕ ПОСТАВЛЕ МЕЙЕРХОЛЬДО и МАЯКОВСКИ РАЗЫГРАНО ВОГНЫМИ АКТЕРАМ

,,!МИСТЕРИЯ БУФФ!"

ГЕРОИЧЕСКОЕ, ЭПИЧЕСКОЕ и САТИРИЧЕСКОЕ ИЗОБРАЖЕНИЕ НАШЕЙ ЭПОХИ, СДЕЛАННОЕ

В. МАЯКОВСКИМ.

Билеты на 7-е и 8-е ноября в распоряжении ЦЕНТРАЛЬНОГО БЮРО.

9-го ноября „МИСТЕРИЯ-БУФФ" открытый спектакль.
НАЧАЛО В 6½ ЧАС. ВЕЧЕРА.

6

NEP AND THE BEGINNINGS OF TERROR

1921

I am afraid that we will not get any real literature until we are cured of this new kind of Catholicism, which fears every heretical word as much as the old kind did. And if the sickness is incurable I am afraid that Russian literature has only one future: its past.
Yevgeny Zamyatin, "I Am Afraid," 1921

After a long spell of maintaining a wait-and-see policy toward the Bolshevik revolution Mayakovsky chose sides in the autumn of 1918, after a year's delay. On the first anniversary of the seizure of power his play *Mystery-Bouffe* was performed at the Theater of Musical Drama in Petrograd. The director was Vsevolod Meyerhold, and the decor and costumes were by Kazimir Malevich. The piece was a sort of medieval mystery play with elements of farce (buffonade). The action is simple. After the destruction of the world by a tidal wave, there are seven "pure" couples and seven "impure" ones left on the ark. The "pure" ones are dif-

On the poster for the play *Mystery-Bouffe*, which was staged on the first anniversary of the Revolution on 7 November 1918, "the old world" is crossed out.

ferent sorts of bourgeois, like for example the British prime minister Lloyd George and a Russian speculator. The "impure" are proletarians representing various trades. The pure ones deceive the impure ones, who throw them overboard. Eventually the proletarians end up in the promised land, with "trains, trams, and cars surrounded by rainbows, and in the midst of everything a garden of stars and moons crowned by the shining crown of the sun."

Mayakovsky himself played the part of the Commonest of All Men, who does not drown in the water or burn in fire but is "the unquenchable spirit of eternal rebellion." He preaches about "an earthly paradise" in which the workers' hands are not calloused by work and pineapples are harvested six times a year. As a part of Mayakovsky's oeuvre, *Mystery-Bouffe* has a certain interest, but it is not a significant work. With its biblical structure it is reminiscent of the proletarian poets' naive world of fantasy, where there was no better metaphor for the future Commune than the conventional biblical Paradise of old. The play was certainly not an example of the avant-garde aesthetics which Mayakovsky embraced.

During work on the production Mayakovsky encountered active opposition from both the actors and the theater bureaucrats, and there were only three performances. However traditional—and reasonably recognizable—the action was, the critics maintained that it was incomprehensible both to themselves and to the "masses."

Thus, Mayakovsky's attempt to cosy up to the Revolution by hailing its first anniversary failed, and the result was the struggle for Futurism's aesthetic ideals which he carried on in the newspaper *Art of the Commune*, which was described in the last chapter. As the position of the avant-garde was undermined in the course of 1919, Mayakovsky was forced to acknowledge that the struggle was hopeless; the enemies of the spiritual revolution had won. The Symbolist writer Andrey Bely, who hoped that the deposition of the monarchy would lead to a spiritual rebirth, believed that that very year of 1919 signified a "definite disillusionment regarding the possibility of a Spiritual Revolution." For Mayakovsky too, 1919 was a year of disillusionment—he realized that the spiritual revolution was not only far off, it was not even desired.

What should he do? In the autumn of 1919 Mayakovsky began

working for the Russian news agency ROSTA (the predecessor of TASS). He wrote and drew propaganda posters that were hung up in the windows of the agency's branches in central Moscow. Many of them were also duplicated. The posters were mostly contributions to the struggle against the White army in the civil war which was raging. It was an activity that was to dominate his life for a good two years. Lili also took an active part in producing the posters. Mayakovsky sketched the outlines and Lili filled in the colors.

Employment in this state institution provided both wages and food. The task had indisputable ideological aspects, but in a starving Moscow the material advantages were at least as powerful an incentive. An important reason why Mayakovsky began to work for ROSTA was also surely that he realized how pointless it was to formulate the problems of art in the heaven-storming way he had done in *Art of the Commune*. Instead he now devoted himself to practical work.

However, the drudgery on ROSTA did not mean that he abandoned his ideas. For Mayakovsky, Futurism was not a school of poetry but a way of conducting himself toward life and art. The Futurists had always opposed conservatism and rigidity. The struggle for the new and against the old was a constituent part of Mayakovsky's life and work. In one of the last issues of *Art of the Commune*, Nikolay Punin wrote that it was the Revolution that was dear to the Futurists' hearts, "the *revolution* itself," he italicized, "*and not present-day Soviet society*." The words could have been written by Mayakovsky.

HOOLIGAN COMMUNISM

After his vacillation during the first year of its existence, Mayakovsky chose to give his wholehearted support to the Bolshevik regime. But the enthusiasm was not mutual: he had to struggle constantly to get his books published, and the opposition from the cultural bureaucrats in the party and the state made him despair. Jakobson remembered how, during a break from working on ROSTA posters, Mayakovsky drew the following cartoon: while the Red Army is successfully penetrating a fortress defended by soldiers drawn up in three ranks, Mayakovsky is trying in vain to fight his way through to Lunacharsky, who is being defended by three ranks of secretaries.

In Soviet cultural history, 1921 is a turning point. It was in that year that the Bolshevik party showed for the first time that it wanted full control over cultural life and had no intention of tolerating deviations from the norm of realism. In Mayakovsky's case, 1921 was the year in which it became clear that the top party leadership's attitude toward him was not only negative but actually hostile. This insight would significantly affect his future actions in relation to the authorities.

At the same time as Mayakovsky was toiling on ROSTA, he was working on his verse epic "150,000,000." The poem, which was published without an author's name, began with the words "150,000,000 is the name of the author of this poem." In other words, it was Russia's population of one hundred and fifty million people which was declared to be the author of the epic; Mayakovsky's name was nowhere to be seen. It was of course a rhetorical trick—no one could doubt that Mayakovsky was the author of this glowing revolutionary poem, especially as he often recited it in public.

The first time Mayakovsky gave a reading of the poem was at Lili and Osip's home in Poluektov Lane. There were about twenty people present, among them Lunacharsky, who had been invited in the hope that he would help to get the poem printed. The people's commissar of enlightenment said he was glad that Mayakovsky was extolling the Revolution but at the same time declared that he was not sure if this was sincere or merely rhetoric. Mayakovsky stressed that the Revolution could not be described by naturalistic means but only as an epic, and Osip objected that it was not possible to make such a distinction in art. In Lunacharsky's recollection, Brik believed "that it is not interesting to ask if the column represented in the scenery is of real stone or if it is painted in oils, or if the poet is honest when he writes or if he is lying, pretending." The contrast between the formalistic view of a work of art as an artifact and the aesthetics of realism could hardly have been more clearly illustrated.

Lunacharsky's reaction was ambivalent, and this influenced the poem's fate. In April 1920 Mayakovsky delivered the manuscript to the literary department of the Commissariat of Enlightenment, LITO, the official censor of all literature published by the newly founded state publishing firm, Gosizdat. LITO forwarded the manuscript to the publishers with the recommendation that it be printed "as soon as possible" given the poem's "unique agitatorial importance"—but they waited until 31 August before doing this, that is, after four months' delay. On 20 October, nothing having happened in the meantime, Mayakovsky wrote to Gosizdat complaining that he was being obstructed by the bureaucrats and asking for his poem to be returned if they had no plans to publish it. But the manuscript was neither published nor returned, so that Mayakovsky was forced to write to the publishers again. On 22 November the poem was finally sent off to be set in type. But then there was silence again, and in April 1921, a year after Mayakovsky had handed over the manuscript, he wrote a long letter to the press agency in the Central Committee of the Russian Communist Party, describing yet again the opposition he was encountering from the board of the publishing house. When the book appeared at the end of that same month, it was in a print-run of only five thousand—although LITO had recommended that it be published in the biggest edition possible (which ought to have meant at least twenty-five thousand copies).

The case of *Mystery-Bouffe* was even more complicated. At the end of 1920 Mayakovsky finished off a new version of the play, which was staged by Meyerhold on 1 May 1921. Gosizdat did not want to print it, but Mayakovsky managed to place it in a double issue of the magazine *Theater Herald*. The magazine was published by Gosizdat, which nevertheless refused to pay the fee, whereupon Mayakovsky took the matter to court. In August the court found the defendants liable to pay out the money, but the firm refused and Mayakovsky got his fee only after the failure of an appeal against the verdict.

On the same day that the verdict was announced, an article was printed on the front page of *Pravda* with the headline "Enough of 'Mayakovskery'!" It was written by a leading party functionary, Lev Sosnovsky (a member of the party presidium and head of the party's propaganda bureau, Agitprop) and it ended with the words "Let us hope that it will soon be mayakovskery that ends up in the dock."

The slogan was a startling one, as it showed the party so clearly opposing a particular aesthetic trend. But it had firm ideological roots. As we saw, criticism of Futurism had gathered pace as the civil war neared its end and the political leadership had more time to devote to cultural politics. The clearest expression of this negative attitude was Lenin's reaction to the publication of "150,000,000." As soon as the poem came off the presses Mayakovsky sent it to the party leader with a "Communist-Futurist greeting." The dedication was signed not only by Mayakovsky but also by Lili and Osip together with several other Futurists. Lenin was incensed, and his wrath was directed against Lunacharsky:

> Are you not ashamed at having voted for the publication of Mayakovsky's 150,000,000 in 5,000 copies?
>
> Rubbish, stupid, stupid beyond belief and pretentious.
>
> In my opinion only 1 out of 10 of such things should be printed and *not more than 1,500 copies* for libraries and oddballs.
>
> And Lunacharsky should be horsewhipped for Futurism.

Lunacharsky's reply mirrors the ambiguity of his position: "I am not all that enamored of this book, but [. . .] when the author himself recited it, it was a big hit, even among the workers." This answer did not appease Lenin, who, in order to satisfy himself that the error would not be repeated, insisted to the head of Gosizdat that "this must be stopped": "Let us agree not to publish these Futurists more than twice a year and in *not more than 1,500 copies.* [. . .] Is it not possible to find some reliable *anti*-Futurists?"

Lenin's remark was not made public until 1957, but it was no secret to his contemporaries. During the *Mystery-Bouffe* trial, the prosecution alleged that it was in fact Lenin's verdict on 150,000,000 that lay behind Gosizdat's refusal to print the play, and Lenin's negative attitude along with the article about "mayakovskery" were referred to in a Berlin newspaper in the autumn of 1921. By that point Lenin's attitude had also become that of the party. "The Party as such, the Communist Party," Lunacharsky wrote in an article, "is cool or even hostile in its attitude not only to Mayakovsky's earlier works but also to those in which he appears as the herald of the revolution." This latter comment reflects Lenin's oral remark when he got his hands on a copy of 150,000,000: "This is very interesting literature. It's a special form of Communism. It's hooligan Communism."

Российская Социалистическая Федеративная Советская Республика.

Пролетарии всех стран, соединяйтесь!

Товарищу Владимиру Ильичу
с Комфутским приветом
Владимир Маяковский

150.000.000

Л. Брик
Ося Брик
Борис Кушнер.
Б. Пастернак
Д. Штеренберг
Нат. Альтман

ГОСУДАРСТВЕННОЕ ИЗДАТЕЛЬСТВО
1921

The poem "150,000,000" with "a communist-futurist greeting to comrade Vladimir Ilyich [Lenin]" from Mayakovsky and his friends, among them the Briks.

FAR EASTERN FUTURISM

Mayakovsky was both indignant and despairing. Here he was, putting his talent at the service of the Revolution, but instead of being welcomed with open arms he was meeting opposition from the highest political quarters. For ideological reasons he wanted to have his work printed by Gosizdat, but now he was forced to think again. If he could not get himself published in his homeland, he would have to try elsewhere. When in May 1920 Jakobson moved to Prague, he was given the manuscript of "150,000,000" in order to try to have the poem printed in Russian in Czechoslovakia. Mayakovsky also took organizational precautions. In response to a party decree of December 1920 which declared that Futurism was "absurd" and "perverse," in January 1921 Mayakovsky, Osip, and Lili along with a few others started up a second Komfut group. But this organizational initiative also came to nothing, apart from the fact that from now on, the Futurists came to be known as "Komfuters."

Mayakovsky found it impossible to tamely accept the growing opposition toward him in Moscow. He was, he wrote, sick and tired of his "three-year-long Golgotha walk"—that is, since 1918—and in March 1921 he contacted a Futurist group in Chita, in Russia's Far East, which called itself Tvorchestvo — "Creation." Chita was the capital of the so-called Far Eastern Republic, created in April 1920 by Alexander Krasnoshchokov, who in the spring of 1917 had returned after fifteen years as a political émigré in the United States and shortly afterward had been accepted by the government in Moscow. The Far Eastern Republic encompassed pretty well the whole of eastern Siberia, and its main purpose was to serve as a neutral buffer zone between the Red Army and the anti-Bolshevik Japanese forces that were occupying Vladivostok and other parts of the Russian Pacific coast. The republic had its own constitution and a "bourgeois" democratic government. It was led by a newly fledged Bolshevik— Krasnoshchokov—but the government included representatives of the farmers' party as well as Socialist Revolutionaries and Mensheviks. And Krasnoshchokov's closest colleague was the prominent anarcho-syndicalist Vladimir "Bill" Shatov, who had also spent ten years as a political émigré in America and filled prominent posts such

Alexander Krasnoshchokov speaking to the people from a freight car after the Red Army seized Chita on 1 November 1920.

as minister for war and for transport. In the Far Eastern Republic, there was also full freedom of expression and a free press.

Conditions here were thus reminiscent of those prevailing in Russia in the winter of 1917–18, and not only as regards the political situation. The literary situation too was guaranteed to make Mayakovsky feel nostalgic. The Tvorchestvo group consisted of several of his literary brothers-in-arms, who for various reasons had ended up in eastern Siberia during the world war and the civil war. Here was David Burlyuk, who had left Moscow the day after the Cheka's raid on the anarchists in April 1918 from fear of being arrested. Other members were the poets Nikolay Aseyev and Sergey Tretyakov, whom Mayakovsky had known for many years and who had not been able to return to Moscow because of the civil war. Tretyakov was vice-commissar for enlightenment in Krasnoshchokov's government.

The group was led by the Marxist critic—and old Bolshevik—Nikolay Chuzhak, editor of the periodical *Tvorchestvo* and the newspaper *Dalnevostochny Telegraf* (Far Eastern Telegraph). For him, Mayakovsky was the great literary model, and Burlyuk published his first recollections of Mayakovsky and Futurism in the group's periodical. Chuzyak was also the first—and last—to attack Sosnovsky for talking about "mayakovskery." The canvassing for Mayakovsky as the great

The Tvorchestvo group, the heralds of Futurism in the Far East, photographed in 1922. *Sitting, from left:* Nikolay Aseyev, Sergey Tretyakov, Vladimir Sillov, and his wife, Olga. The man with a moustache in the upper row is Nikolay Chuzhak.

poet of the Revolution also took place through lectures and poetry readings, and in December 1921 Tretyakov staged the tragedy *Vladimir Mayakovsky* with himself in the leading role. This very Nietzschean play had only been performed once before, in Petersburg in 1913, and the similarities between Mayakovsky and Nietzsche were commented on by the critic Vladimir Sillov—a mere twenty-year-old— who later, in the twenties, was to be involved with Futurist circles in Moscow but who is known to history for more sinister reasons—of which more in the chapter "At the Top of My Voice."

"The story of Mayakovsky's *Mystery-Bouffe* and, above all, of his latest poem," wrote Chuzhak, "*will in time be entered in the revolutionary annals of Russia as a page of shame.*" As "150,000,000" was finally published in Moscow, it never appeared in Chita. But Mayakovsky and his Futurist friends in Moscow maintained contact with the Tvorchestvo group and complained in their letters that "people with atrophied powers of receptiveness and psychological inflexibility have interposed themselves between the masses and the new art and are trying from on high [. . .] to impose on them their own obsolete view of art and to shield them from the new art by bureaucratic means." In Chuzhak's and Mayakovsky's vocabulary, the opponents of Futurism were nothing more than "Arakcheyevs"—a reference to the "iron count" Alexey Arakcheyev, the reactionary and tough-minded adviser to Alexander I.

Toward the end of the summer of 1921 Mayakovsky was so frustrated that he decided to travel to Chita to join his supporters there. The plan was that he would travel with Krasnoshchokov, who was in Moscow during the summer, but the latter's position was uncertain, he was unable to leave, and before long he was toppled (see the chapter "Free from Love and Posters"). Another reason why Mayakovsky was unable to set off was, ironically enough, the lawsuit against Gosizdat over *Mystery-Bouffe*. Instead, it was the "Siberians" who returned to Moscow, the following year, when the Far Eastern Republic was incorporated into the Russian Soviet Republic. The only one who did not return was Burlyuk, who instead moved to Japan and, a few years later, to New York. As he had been indulging in dubious economic actions in connection with the anarchists' occupation of houses in the winter of 1918, he feared unpleasant consequences if he returned to Moscow.

THE THIRD REVOLUTION AND THE FOURTH INTERNATIONAL

For Mayakovsky, the party bureaucracy's attitude to Futurism was yet another confirmation that the Revolution was on the wrong track. A fundamental change was as necessary as ever, and in the winter of 1920 Mayakovsky revisited the idea of a spiritual revolution in a long poem, which he worked on for three years and which was originally entitled "Fourth" and then "Fifth International." He was unsure what to call it, but whatever number he chose, the title is noteworthy: in opposition to Lenin's Third International, Mayakovsky sets up his own international, a spiritual one. The subtitle, "Open Letter from Mayakovsky to the Central Committee of the Russian Communist Party Explaining Some of His, Mayakovsky's, Actions," shows that the poem was intended as a direct poetic parallel to the above-named letter to the party's Central Committee. The echo of the manifesto in *The Futurists' Newspaper* is clear:

October has not burned out!
The Communists
are drawn in bunches
to fall asleep
to Onegin,
Silva,
Igor.
You are on your way to the gorillas!
To a spiritual vacuum!

The Bolshevik revolution has not yet had any influence on cultural life, the masses are still fed with the "old culture"—a new revolt is needed:

Communards!
Prepare a new revolt
in the coming
Communist beanfeast.

This revolt must be of a particular kind—a spiritual revolution:

Shaking the heads with explosions of thought,
roaring with the heart's artillery,
rears out of time
a new revolution—
the third revolution
of the spirit.

Significantly, when the poem was published in 1922, "the gorillas," the "spiritual vacuum," and the "Communist beanfeast" were erased by the censor.

The most irreverent section of the poem the censor never had to consider, as it was not included in the final version and only survives as a rough draft. It depicts Mayakovsky's conversation with a Lenin who has become petrified into an insensible statue, a monument on a marble plinth, behind the thick walls of the Kremlin. His cast-iron heavy words fall like thunderclaps over the deserted city. He is watched over by ranks of secretaries and guards. "Can't they see that I'm busy being a statue?" he asks. But Mayakovsky is not held back by any inhibitions: "I who am entirely spirit through and through, who should I be afraid of?" When Lenin spots Mayakovsky, he asks him to sit down, but secretly he is thinking: "Only talks rubbish. Needs a thrashing"—a direct reference to Lenin's rebuke to Lunacharsky, who "should be horsewhipped for Futurism." The draft ends with Mayakovsky, with his "bawling uproar of song," taking Lenin's place: "Don't try to shake me off. / Today it's me who's the chairman / of the Council of People's Commissars."

The sarcastic tone is strengthened by the choice of motif: Lenin as a monument protected by the walls of the Kremlin—in Mayak-ovsky's writings the statue is always a negatively charged metaphor for stagnation and petrification. "The Fourth International" was, at least in the initial stages, conceived as a direct response to Lenin's outburst against him and must be seen against the background of Mayakovsky's conflicts with the party leadership in 1921. The party leader's cast-iron heavy rebukes are answered by the leader of the poetic avant-garde with poems paying tribute to the spiritual kernel of the Revolution and emphasizing the poet's right to speak with the representatives of authority on equal terms.

THE THIRD REVOLUTION AND KRONSTADT

During the civil war a series of coercive economic measures were introduced which fundamentally changed the rules of play. The means of production were nationalized, private trade was forbid-den, money as a method of payment was abolished, and labor was all but militarized. These policies would later come to be called "war communism." The consequence was that the food situation in the big cities in the winter of 1920–21 was as critical as in the months before the February revolution of 1917. Compared to 1913, industrial pro-duction had decreased by 82 percent and production of grain by 40 percent. The inhabitants of the towns fled to the countryside in the hunt for the necessities of life. Petrograd's population went down by 70 percent, and Moscow's by 50 percent. If the problems up to now had affected the towns most of all, the countryside also now began

to feel the effects of the mismanagement. As long as the war contin-
ued, the authorities could blame circumstances and their opponents,
but that was no longer possible. The Bolsheviks had never enjoyed
wide support among the people, and now the opposition spilled over
into armed struggle. Nothing like it had been seen since the peasant
revolts in the eighteenth century. The strength of the opposition is
borne out by the numbers of Red Army soldiers killed in 1921–22
during the struggle against the rebels: almost a quarter of a million.

In January 1921, at the same time as Mayakovsky and his friends
were attempting to set up a Komfut organization, a workers' uprising
erupted which was to cost many people their lives but also force the
Bolshevik regime to grant significant concessions. The background
was the authorities' decision to reduce by a third the bread rations in
Moscow, Petrograd, and other towns. Just as in the winter of 1917, the
protests began with demands for bread but gradually came to include
demands for political changes: a free vote for the workers' councils,
freedom of speech, and an end to police terror. The revolt began in
Moscow but soon spread to Petrograd, where the industrial workers'
rations had been reduced to a thousand calories per day.

The center of opposition was the naval base of Kronstadt, whose
ten thousand sailors had always been influenced by syndicalist and
anarchistic ideas. The leaders of the revolt exhorted the workers to
struggle against the Communists, who had given them not freedom,
but "daily bread in the form of the Cheka's torture chambers, whose
horrors are many times worse than those of tsardom." The "glorious
emblem" of the workers' state, the hammer and sickle, had been re-
placed by the bayonet and the iron bar, "created to defend the peace-
ful and carefree existence of the new bureaucracy, the Communist
commissars and functionaries." The greatest crime of the Commu-
nists was that they had interfered in the inner lives of the workers and
forced them to think the way they wanted them to. What the sailors
of Kronstadt had done with their revolt was to lay "the first stone of
the third revolution, which will free the laboring masses of their last

The monument to Karl Marx and Friedrich Engels in Moscow, inaugurated by Lenin on the first
anniversary of the Revolution, was immediately dubbed "Marx and Engels in the bathtub" by the
people.

chains and open a new broad path for the building of socialism." This new revolution is "an example of the new socialist building, which is the direct opposite of state Communism."

The third revolution! There was no organizational connection between the Kronstadt sailors and Mayakovsky, but they had in common an ideological grounding in anarchism and the general contempt for the bourgeoisie which is so typical of Russian radicalism. When Mayakovsky sent 150,000,000 to Lenin, the Kronstadt revolt was in full swing, and it is quite likely that the exaggerated aggressiveness with which the party leader reacted was motivated by concern that the situation was about to slip out of his control. If he overreacted to Mayakovsky, he did, with the help of Trotsky, the commissar for war, even more so to the Kronstadt sailors. On the night of 16–17 March the revolt was crushed with the help of fifty thousand Red Army troops. The Soviet rulers were not interested in any third revolution.

The attack on Kronstadt was carried out in the middle of the Tenth Party Congress, which took place in Moscow. Even if the revolt cost the lives of hundreds of sailors, and hundreds more were put in concentration camps, it had the consequence that Lenin and the party leadership were forced to think again. In order to put an end to the disturbances taking place all over the country it was decided that the arbitrary confiscation of grain—which deprived the peasants of their production and the urban population of their food—should be replaced with a tax. This meant an ideological U-turn, but in the face of an economic catastrophe with undreamed-of political consequences, there was no choice. The "economic breathing space" (as Lenin put it) which the party now opted for had the desired effect: the peasant revolt came to an end, and the basis was laid for an improved food-supply situation.

Some further reforms were unplanned but followed out of economic necessity. When the peasants won back the right to sell their own products, a market emerged, and with it a need for market relations in other areas too. Small-scale private and cooperative businesses were allowed, and the ruble was reintroduced as a means of payment. But the larger businesses remained in state hands, as well as the banks, foreign trade, and transport systems. The right of inheritance, which had been abolished in 1918, was partially restored. This hybrid of socialism and capitalism came to be called the New Economic Policy, shortened to NEP.

The economy picked up again, but the reforms were directly counter to the prevailing ideology, and the party leadership feared—rightly—that the partial revival of capitalism might threaten the party's monopoly position in society at large. The economic liberalization therefore had to be reinforced by tighter political restraints. "Discipline must be even firmer now. It is also a hundred times more necessary, for when the whole army is in retreat it does not know, it does not see, where it ought to halt: all it sees is the retreat," Lenin declared. "The danger is immediate." The result was that the Cheka (which from 1922 was called the GPU) was given increased powers, and the number of concentration camps grew from 84 at the end of 1920 to 315 three years later. During 1921 and 1922 the few remnants of civil liberties remaining in the country were crushed. The attacks were directed mostly against political rivals but also against the Orthodox Church and the intelligentsia.

In corresponding manner, the Tenth Party Congress forced through a ban on factions within the party, which meant that although individual members could express dissident views, they were not allowed to organize. The same kind of dictatorship that prevailed in society at large was also thereby introduced into the party, which moreover carried out a purge of its cadres in the summer of 1921. During the civil war party numbers had increased drastically and in 1921 had risen to almost three quarters of a million. Now that membership in the party no longer entailed risks and sacrifices, there was an obvious danger that it would attract careerists to a greater degree than before. The revolt in Kronstadt also provided a motive for examining party cadres. The purge began on the first of August, and between then and the beginning of 1922, 136,000 people were expelled from the party: that is, one fifth of the total membership.

The main thrust was directed against those who had served under the old regime, former members of other political parties, and Communist Party members in the civil service. The commonest reasons for expulsion were passivity (34 percent) and careerism, drunkenness, a bourgeois lifestyle, and so on (25 percent). One of those who were purged was Osip. No documentation survives, but according to reliable sources it was his "bourgeois past" which was held against him. Ironically, it was precisely in his capacity as an "expert on former bourgeois" that he had been employed by the Cheka in the first place. The fact that his expulsion from the party did not mean his having to give up this work shows that the link between the party and the security service was not as obvious as it would become later.

THE FIRST VICTIMS: GUMILYOV AND BLOK

Show trials as a way of attacking political opponents are a political genre that reached its apogee in the 1930s, but the method began to be practiced as early as 1921 as a direct consequence of the Kronstadt revolt and the subsequent economic "liberalization." The first of these cases was against something called the "Petrograd Combat Organization," which was said to be led by a geography professor, Vladimir Tagantsev. In June 1921 Tagantsev was arrested, accused of having helped intellectuals to flee the country and of possessing large sums of money. But for the Cheka, Tagantsev and two colleagues (who had already been shot dead) were not enough to frighten the intelligentsia; what was needed was a proper "conspiracy," which was duly fabricated.

Tagantsev was silent for forty-five days, right up until a new chief interrogator came on the scene: Yakov Agranov, a Chekist since May 1919, lead investigator into the circumstances surrounding the Kronstadt revolt, with specific responsibility for issues relating to the treatment of intellectuals. Agranov promised in writing that if Tagantsev revealed the names of everyone who was mixed up in the "combat organization," no death sentences would be carried out. Tagantsev took Agranov at his word and began to talk, in other words, to sign the minutes which his interrogators had already drawn up.

The case against the Petrograd Combat Organization would not have been written about at such length if it had not involved one of Russia's leading writers, the poet Nikolay Gumilyov, former husband of Anna Akhmatova, Russia's most popular female poet. Gumilyov was an anti-Bolshevik and monarchist but at the same time worked

Nikolay Gumilyov, the first writer to be executed in the Soviet Union, photographed with his wife, Anna Akhmatova, and their son Lev. On 16 August, as Gumilyov was held in a pretrial prison in Petrograd, Akhmatova wrote a poem containing the following lines: "Never again will you rise / from the cold snow. / The deep wounds from bayonets / and the roar of guns. / It's bitter, the gift / that I sewed for my friend. / The Russian soil loves blood, / blood is what it loves."

as a lecturer for Proletkult. He was also chairman of the Petrograd Section of the All-Russian Union of Poets and a member of the editorial committee of the state publishing house World Literature, led by Maxim Gorky. Gumilyov was arrested on the night of 5 August and executed by a firing squad three weeks later. On 1 September the Petrograd edition of *Pravda* carried the news that all members of the mythical "combat organization" had been executed: sixty-one individuals. About Gumilyov it was said was that he had "actively collaborated in the writing of proclamations with counterrevolutionary content and had promised, in connection with the revolt, to bring together a group of intellectuals and officer cadres with the organization." So much for Agranov's written promise.

Despite Gumilyov's political views—which he made no effort to hide—there is little evidence that he would have taken part in any conspiracy. The minutes of the interrogation are muddled, and the pen has been wielded by an almost illiterate hand. Seventy years later, in 1991, his sentence was quashed by the Supreme Court of the Soviet Union.

That the case against the Petrograd Combat Organization did not involve concrete accusations but was first and foremost designed to serve as a warning to others is shown by the fact that an intellectual with completely opposing political views—Nikolay Punin—was arrested on the same night as Gumilyov. This, if anything, was an irony of fate, as Punin, in the first issue of *Art of the Commune* in December 1918, had expressed himself about Gumilyov in a manner which could be interpreted as pure denunciation: "I confess that personally I have felt cheerful and uplifted all year, in part because certain 'critics' are no longer being published and certain poets (for example, Gumilyov) are no longer being read. And then, suddenly, I stumble across him in 'Soviet circles.' [. . .] This resurrection, when it comes down to it, is not surprising. To me, this is one of countless expressions of the reaction that never sleeps, that pokes its ugly snout in, now here, now there."

In contrast to Gumilyov, Punin was released. His release was facilitated after Lunacharsky was made aware of the case by Punin's wife—and by Osip, whose work for the Cheka was therefore of some use in this case at least. Punin was released—only to move in two years later with Anna Akhmatova, the murdered Gumilyov's first wife.

The execution of Gumilyov was the first murder of a writer in Soviet Russia and naturally caused alarm not only among Gumilyov's sympathizers. By executing Gumilyov the authorities demonstrated not only their contempt for human life but also their attitude to intellectual freedom and artistic creation. The message to the intellectuals was clear: you are dispensable.

There is no evidence as to how Mayakovsky reacted to Gumilyov's death, but the very fact that a fellow writer had been executed must have shaken him. Despite their differing views on political issues Mayakovsky liked Gumilyov's poems, and in that very year of 1921 his name had acquired special significance for Mayakovsky, not so much because of Gumilyov himself as because of his former wife. A few months earlier Korney Chukovsky had published an article that caused quite a stir, entitled "Akhmatova and Mayakovsky," in which the two poets were singled out as polar opposites of each other. While Akhmatova is the "prudent heiress to all the riches of prerevolutionary Russian literature," with the "soulful refinement" which is a result of "centuries of cultural traditions," Mayakovsky is a child of the age of revolution with its dogmas, bluster, and ecstasy. Akhmatova is moderate like Pushkin; with Mayakovsky, every letter of the alphabet is a hyperbole, an exaggeration. Both poets were equally dear to Chukovsky's heart. For him the question "Akhmatova or Mayakovsky?" did not exist—their methods of confronting reality complemented each other.

Although they really were each other's polar opposites, Mayakovsky had always liked Akhmatova's poems, which he used to quote (especially when he was depressed), and with this essay their names had been brought together in an unexpected way. After Gumilyov's execution it was natural that his thoughts were with her—especially after rumors that she had committed suicide from grief. "Every day just now there have been dire rumors about you which get more persistent and definitive by the hour," Marina Tsvetayeva wrote to Akhmatova in September. "I want to tell you that your only—as far as I know—true friend (a friend means taking action!) among the poets is Mayakovsky, who is going around [. . .] with the expression of a clubbed ox. *Broken-hearted with grief*—that's really how he looked. It was he who, through acquaintances, sent the telegram enquiring about you." It is hard to believe that Mayakovsky's distress was not as much the result of Gumilyov's actual death as of Akhmatova's rumored demise.

The lawsuit against Gumilyov coincided in time with Mayakovsky's lawsuit against Gosizdat, and to assume that he did not see a deeper connection between these events is hardly credible. Especially as this month of August offered yet another killer blow to Russian literature. Two days after Gumilyov's arrest one of Russia's foremost poets died: Alexander Blok.

Unlike many others of his generation of Symbolist poets, Blok wanted to see something positive in the revolutionary storms that were sweeping over Russia in 1917. He had a very weak grasp of political issues and saw the Revolution first and foremost as a force of nature, a cleansing thunderstorm. History had changed direction, and to oppose the Revolution would be like opposing history. His support for the Bolsheviks was a consequence of this view of history. Even when the library on his estate was burned down by his own peasants, he saw in this a redeeming conformity with the laws of history. In the winter of 1918 he published his epic poem "The Twelve" in the Revolutionary Socialist paper *Banner of Labor*. It was a paean to the Revolution in which twelve ragamuffins/Red Army soldiers/apostles wander through the city led by none other than Jesus Christ. The choice of the leader figure shows that Blok's attitude to the Revolution was complicated, but the Soviet authorities did not have much to choose from when it came to support from intellectuals and made a point of exploiting Blok's authority to the utmost. He was voted onto masses of committees and organizations and found employment in the Theater Section of the Commissariat for Popular Enlightenment.

During the first years of the Revolution Blok imagined he was still hearing the music of history and took an intense interest in events as they unfolded, but reality eventually caught up with him, and in January 1921 he made the following analysis of the situation of the poet in Soviet Russia: "*Peace and Freedom*. They are indispensable for a poet if harmony is to be released. But peace and freedom are also taken from us. Not outward peace, but the peace to create. Not a child's freedom, the freedom to do what one wants, but the freedom to create—inner freedom. And a poet dies because he no longer has anything to draw breath from: life has lost its meaning." The words were about Pushkin but just as much about himself.

Several months later Blok fell seriously ill. The illness was both physical and psychological in nature. His body had been weakened by lack of food and other privations, and he was assailed by asthma, scurvy, and heart problems. And his nervous system was at such a low ebb that for a while he was close to losing his mind. His death can thus be said to have had "natural causes," but these causes were conditioned by a particular historical and social situation. Documents which were marked "secret" until 1995 show that Blok's death could probably have been prevented, or at least postponed, if the top echelons of the political leadership had not wished otherwise.

When Gorky heard that Blok had fallen ill, he contacted Lunacharsky and asked him to arrange through the Central Committee of the party for Blok to be allowed to travel immediately to a sanatorium in Finland. The same urgent request was made to Lenin by

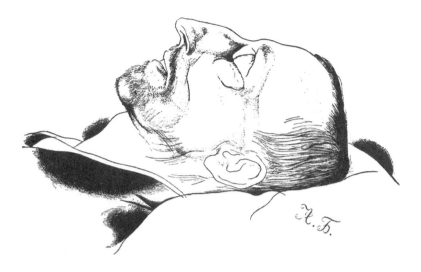

Alexander Blok on his deathbed, drawn by Yury Annenkov. To Blok, the Revolution was a purifying force of nature. However, it swept away not only the old world but also the poet himself.

the Petrograd Section of the Writers' Union. Lenin did not reply, and when the Central Committee reacted two weeks later, it was with an instruction that "A. A. Blok should be better provided for" rather than that he should be allowed to travel to Finland.

At the end of June the Cheka's foreign department let it be known that they saw no reason to let Blok travel abroad. Lunacharsky then went directly to Lenin and protested about Blok's treatment, "the without doubt most talented of Russia's well-known poets and the one who is most sympathetic toward us." That same day the deputy head of the Cheka, Vyacheslav Menzhinsky, reported to Lenin: "Blok is a poetic type. If he falls under the influence of some other version of events then obviously he will start to write poems directed against us. In my opinion we ought not to let him out, but to arrange good treatment in some sanatorium."

The Politburo followed Menzhinsky's recommendation. But Lunacharsky and Gorky did not give up, and Lenin, who earlier had opposed Blok's being permitted to leave the country, now changed sides and voted in favor. His wife, however, was not allowed to accompany him. The Politburo knew very well that Blok was too ill to travel on his own, but if he managed nevertheless to do so, it was good to have her still there as a hostage. This was a practice which the Soviet authorities over the years would polish to perfection. After repeated appeals from Gorky and Lunacharsky, Blok's wife was allowed to go with him. Permission was granted on 5 August. Two days later Blok died at the age of forty.

"A sort of endless song floated through him like a continuous stream," Chukovsky wrote of Blok in his diary: "Twenty years from 1898 till 1918. Then he stopped—and immediately began to die. His song was his life. When the song was finished, he was finished." Mayakovsky reacted to Blok's death with an obituary notice in which he praised Blok's poetic mastery and underlined his equivocal political views. At the very beginning of the Revolution he had met Blok on the street. Asked what he thought of the Revolution, he had answered, "Good," adding: "They've burned down my library out in the country." "The choice between celebrating that 'good' and complaining about the fire was one that Blok never made in his poetry." The obituary was printed in the propaganda bulletin *Agit-Rosta*, which hardly anyone read.

In Alexander Blok there died one of the foremost representatives of the great poetic tradition which had begun with Pushkin a hundred years earlier. But his death also marked the end of the time of hope and expectation which began with the revolutions of 1917 and the introduction of a new era in which citizens lived entirely by the grace of the party and the government. Tsardom had forbidden books; the Bolsheviks chose a more effective method: to do away with their authors. The Russian Soviet Republic was a new type of state, one in which the question of whether or not a dying citizen should be allowed to travel to a sanatorium in Finland was decided by the government, that is, the Communist Party.

GORKY AND LENIN

When Blok fell ill, Gorky acted to help him, but in Gumilyov's case he was passive. Not because he believed the charges against Gumilyov, but because the long-drawn-out and unsuccessful struggle on Blok's behalf made him realize that Lenin and his party comrades spat on those humanistic ideals which he represented, and he ran the risk of falling into disfavor himself at any time.

During the first year after the Bolshevik revolution Gorky had been strongly critical of the Bolshevik party's policies, but when in 1918 he did an about-face and chose to support the Bolsheviks in the struggle against the Whites, he did not have long to wait for his reward. He became head of the publishing firm World Literature, where he could find jobs for fellow authors suffering from hunger and other privations, among them Gumilyov and Blok. He was also entrusted with the chairmanship of the Commission for the Improvement of Scientists' Living Conditions, which was tasked with doling out food and clothing to those who needed them. During the next few years he functioned as a sort of middleman between the intelligentsia and the authorities, a sort of alternative minister of culture—a position he could assume thanks to his old relationship with Lenin.

In the summer of 1918 Gorky had been deprived of his newspaper *New Life* and thereby of the opportunity to attack the Bolsheviks openly, but his criticism of their policies, especially in relation to the intelligentsia, continued with undiminished strength, although now in the form of letters. Between 1919 and 1921 he penned countless missives to Lenin and other party functionaries begging for the release of imprisoned authors and scientists. His large apartment in Petrograd was a refuge for many who were persecuted by the regime, from writers and scientists to grand dukes. When ten leading scientists were arrested in September 1919 he protested to Lenin:

> What is this kind of self-defense apart from an expression of desperation, an admission of one's own weakness or—finally—a desire to be avenged for one's own lack of talent?
>
> I protest most vehemently against this tactic, which attacks the intellect of a people who are already spiritually impoverished.
>
> I know you will say the usual words: "the political struggle," "he who is not with us is against us," "neutral individuals are dangerous" and so forth. [. . .]
>
> I stand side by side with those people and prefer arrest and a prison sentence to participating—even tacitly—in the annihilation

of the best strengths of the Russian people. It has become obvious to me that "the Reds" are just as much enemies of the people as "the Whites."

Lenin's oral comment was that Gorky was "just as politically naive as he has always been." His written response was vintage Lenin. The arrests were correct and necessary, he maintained, continuing: "The intellectual powers of the workers and the peasants are growing and strengthening through the struggle to topple the bourgeoisie and their henchmen, the so-called intellectuals, the lackeys of capitalism, who see themselves as the nation's brain. They are not a brain, they are shit."

Despite Lenin's intransigence, the representations of Gorky and others were not without result. Many of the imprisoned scientists were released. The list of those whom Gorky saved from arrest, imprisonment, and death in those years is long. According to the opera singer Fyodor Chaliapin, Gorky's work to help persecuted fellow countrymen "was what gave most meaning to his life during the early years of Bolshevism." In the two-year-long struggle between Gorky and Lenin, both tested the limits of what was possible. How many could one arrest and execute? How many could one save?

As the political terror after the Kronstadt revolt intensified, Gorky's position finally became impossible. An internationally celebrated author—the nearest equivalent to his status would be that of Tolstoy decades earlier—who constantly criticizes the authorities is no politician's dream, least of all a dictator's. Moreover, Gorky's did not try to hide his opinions and actions; quite the reverse. As some intellectuals took a skeptical view of his contacts with the authorities, he was anxious to make his goodwill known. The above-mentioned letter, for example, was copied and disseminated and published in an emigrant newspaper in Prague. This kind of publicity was of course bad for Lenin's prestige, and it could not be tolerated in the long run.

If Gorky threatened to undermine Lenin's position with his constant protests, Lenin in his turn did everything to sabotage Gorky. An unparalleled example of this was the cynicism with which Lenin exploited Gorky's authority in connection with the nationwide famine that broke out in the summer of 1921.

The famine was the result of an unusually dry autumn in 1920, but it was exacerbated by the Bolsheviks' agricultural policy, which meant that the peasants' "surplus" was confiscated. As this was seldom the appropriation of overproduction but rather of essential reserves for food and sowing, catastrophe was inevitable. Worst affected were the black earth districts around the Volga, but the Donbass meadows and southern Ukraine were hit too. Before the Revolution production of grain in the affected areas had risen to 20 million tons per annum, but in 1921 it was down to 2.9 million tons. Faced with a problem that could not be solved by force, the political leadership was impotent. The press was forbidden to write about the failure of the crop, and the official reaction was to pretend that nothing had happened. Despite cases of cannibalism, and despite the fact that millions of starving peasants occupied railway stations in the hope of finding food elsewhere, the authorities refused to acknowledge the fact until the middle of July.

As such an acknowledgement meant admitting that the government's economic policies had failed, it was decided to take indirect action. On 13 July Gorky (with Lenin's approval) published an appeal in which he asked for aid to be given to the victims of the famine, and a week later the government approved the founding of the All-Russian Committee to Aid the Starving (in Russian, abbreviated to Pomgol): a voluntary, nongovernmental organization. The committee included Gorky and two other writers, Alexey Tolstoy and Boris Zaytsev, as well as several scientists, among them professor Sergey Oldenburg, one of those who had been arrested in September 1919 and whom Gorky had helped to free. The most sensational names were Sergey Prokopovich, a minister in the provisional government, and his wife Yekaterina Kuskova, along with one of the leaders of the cadet party, Nikolay Kishkin. These people helped to legitimize the work of the committee and make it easier to attract help from abroad. (In order to ensure that Soviet Russia's first volunteer organization was not indulging in any political freewheeling, it was supplemented by a "cell" consisting of twelve highly placed members of the Communist Party, including Lev Kamenev.)

Gorky and the committee turned to the whole world for help. Anatole France, H. G. Wells, John Galsworthy, Upton Sinclair, and other internationally renowned authors participated in the relief work at Gorky's request. The International Red Cross, led by Fridtjof Nansen, responded to Gorky's appeal, as did the American trade secretary, Herbert Hoover, who was the head of the ARA (American Relief Administration), an organization that had been founded to distribute food and medicine in Europe after the war. But Hoover insisted on two conditions: that they should be allowed to act independently, and that all American citizens in Soviet prisons be freed. Lenin wrote in a letter to the Politburo that Hoover ought to "*get a public slap on the face* so that *the whole world* sees it," but he had no choice but to accept these conditions. The agreement between the ARA and the Soviet government was signed in Riga on 21 August. The American Congress gave an initial capital sum of $18.6 million, and this was boosted by private contributions and by $11.3 million from Soviet gold reserves.

At the very moment the agreement was signed, the committee members were arrested and the newspapers were exhorted by Lenin to "make the utmost effort to mock and harass them at least once a week for two months." "They are arresting people in their hundreds here," Gorky wrote to his wife on 24 August. "Last night the whole city was reverberating with the noise of the Cheka's cars." Even Gorky himself was subjected to a house search and summoned for interrogation by the secret police.

Up until now Gorky, who was seriously ill with a lung complaint, had not wanted to accept Lenin's comradely recommendation that he ought to travel abroad for the sake of his health. "Don't pester me about traveling abroad," he wrote to Lenin in July, "instead, give me more freedom of action." But then came the deaths of Blok and Gumilyov, and the deception with Pomgol. When Gorky bumped into Kamenev in the Kremlin, he said to him, with tears in his eyes: "You have made me an agent provocateur." On 16 October 1921, Maxim Gorky left Russia. Lenin did not want him in the country any more, but neither did he want him as an enemy and potential leader of the large émigré community. Officially, therefore, Gorky went as the representative of Soviet Russia. He was to collect food, medicine, and money for his starving homeland. It was "a convenient pretext and at the same time a real and very appropriate task," as a Gorky specialist has put it. However one looks at it, it was yet another expression of the duplicity in Gorky's character—of what the poet Vladislav Khodasevich called his "ambiguous attitude to truth and lies."

Blok's death, the execution of Gumilyov, the dissolving of Pomgol . . . "This month of August marked a borderline," Nina Berberova recalled, "everything that happened afterward was simply a continuation of this August."

М. Ларионов.

20-11.1922

DRANG NACH WESTEN

7

1922

Solemnly raising index-lined verse
I swear—
I love
immutably, truly.
Vladimir Mayakovsky, "I Love"

The legal proceedings against Gosizdat over *Mystery-Bouffe* in August–September 1921 showed clearly that Mayakovsky's efforts to convince the authorities and party bureaucrats of his poetic greatness had been in vain. The conclusion he drew was that he had to make himself independent of the state cultural bureaucracy and seek other ways of publishing his work. As the New Economic Policy had not yet had an impact on the publishing industry, the alternative had to be sought abroad. That Mayakovsky, by this stage, was "in flight" is evidenced both by the fact that he sent his works to Prague (Jakobson) and Chita (Chuzhak) and by the fact that he had well-advanced plans to travel to the Far East and join up with his old Futurist comrades there.

During his stay in Paris, Mayakovsky met with his old friends Natalya Goncharova and her husband Mikhail Larionov, who had left Russia even before the Revolution. Larionov, who had already portrayed Mayakovsky once, now did it again, this time in a more realistic manner.

Mayakovsky did not make it to the Far East. Instead, at the beginning of October 1921 Lili traveled to Riga. Apart from a natural desire to travel abroad for the first time in eight years and to be able to live a normal "bourgeois" life for a while, she also had other motives for her journey. One of them was to call on her mother, who was living with her brother Leo at 90 Canfield Gardens in West Hampstead, an overwhelmingly Jewish neighborhood in London. But an application for a United Kingdom visa could not be made in Moscow, as the country had not accorded Soviet Russia diplomatic recognition. The reason that Lili chose Latvia as a springboard for her English ambitions was that she had relatives there. Her mother had been born in Riga, and her aunt Elsa Hirschberg lived there. But there was another, at least equally important reason for the trip: to try to find a publisher willing to publish Mayakovsky's poetry. For centuries there had been a large Russian colony in Latvia, and since the Bolshevik revolution it had substantially increased in size.

LILI IN RIGA

Even if the political situation had become normalized to some extent since the end of the civil war, a Soviet citizen could not leave the country just like that, that is, without permission from the Cheka. Blok's case affords tragic proof of this. Conventional tourist trips of the kind that subjects of the tsar had been able to indulge in were a luxury that belonged to a vanished age. But Soviet Russia's prohibitionist mentality was merely a part of the problem. The Soviet authorities' reluctance to let its citizens out was matched by other countries' reluctance to let them in. In order for Lili to travel to Riga, therefore, a special arrangement had to be made: she was appointed a member of the Soviet Russian diplomatic mission in the Latvian capital.

The arrangement shows what good contacts the Briks and Mayakovsky had in the Soviet Foreign Commissariat at this time, despite Mayakovsky's conflicts with the cultural bureaucracy. No one could be appointed to the Soviet Russian trade mission without approval from the highest quarters. Whatever function—if any—Lili fulfilled in the mission, her position brought with it obvious advantages, among them the opportunity to use the diplomatic pouch. This was important not only because of the poor postal service but also because the censors—both Latvian and Soviet—opened all letters to and from Soviet Russia. Since nearly all correspondence with Moscow went through diplomatic channels, Lili's three-and-a-half-month-long stay in Riga is unusually well documented. Although many letters never reached their addressee, as many as fifty-eight items have survived. She could also use this route to send food, clothes, and money to her "little beasts"—as she called Osip and Mayakovsky—in Moscow.

Through the diplomatic pouch she could also maintain contact with her mother, who was employed in a Soviet-owned trading company in London. During the civil war and the British-supported intervention, trade between Soviet Russia and Great Britain (like that with most other countries) had declined, but since the end of the fighting and with Soviet Russia's plans for international revolution put on ice, both countries were interested in resuming contact. The Soviet state was in dire need of consumer goods, and Britain, which was in the midst of an economic crisis, saw a chance here to create new job opportunities. October 1920 saw the setting-up of Arcos (the All-Russian Cooperative Society), and in March 1921 a trade agreement was signed between the two countries. The agreement implied a de facto recognition of Soviet Russia, and the head of the trade delegation, the skillful diplomat Leonid Krasin, who had brought it about, functioned to all intents and purposes as the Soviet ambassador to Great Britain.

Arcos, which was housed in the same property in Moorgate Street as the Soviet trade mission, was regarded by the British secret service as a cover organization for business which could not be carried on openly, including the purchase of matériel for the Red Army, and it was under constant surveillance. Yet by no means all those who worked there were Communists. Among those with no party allegiance was Lili's mother, who had worked for the firm right from the start and who, apart from her work as a clerk, regularly entertained her Arcos colleagues with her piano playing. She had probably obtained the post thanks to Osip's and Mayakovsky's good contacts in Moscow—among them the writer and journalist Mikhail Levidov, who had worked on Gorky's newspapers, had been head of the foreign desk at ROSTA, and by this time was working as the news agency's correspondent in London.

It was her mother's job with Arcos and her closeness to Krasin which made Lili hopeful that obtaining a visa for the UK would be a mere formality. For safety's sake, however, she also asked Elsa to help her with the entry visa to France. When it became clear that neither of them could do anything, Mayakovsky tried to organize a posting from Moscow. Rabis (an artists' union) asked the Foreign Trade Commissariat to arrange a business trip to London for "the artist Lili Brik" so that she could visit a craft exhibition and explore the possibility of cultural exchanges. The Foreign Trade Commissariat in turn asked Krasin in a telegram to approve "TRANSFER COLLEAGUE RIGA DEPARTMENT ARTIST LILI BRIK LONDON." However, nothing happened during Lili's almost four-month-long stay stay in Riga.

Why was Lili so keen to travel to London, where she had never been before? If the intention was to see her mother, they could just as easily have arranged a meeting in Berlin, for which it was much easier to obtain a visa. Elsa could also have come and visited them there. Considering Lili's strained relationship with Yelena Yulyevna, this eagerness to get to London is hard to understand. Was it simply the desire to travel and experience something new? In several letters she talks about traveling to Vienna, another city she had no obvious ties to.

Was it perhaps that Lili had not entirely given up all thought of emigrating? In that case, London would have been a tempting alternative given that she had a place to live organized. There is also reason to believe that Yelena Yulyevna had managed to bring some assets out with her when she left Russia in 1918. The money and clothes that she sent to Lili in Riga and Osip in Moscow indicate that she was not without means. That thoughts of emigration were not alien to Lili emerges from a letter of 6 November 1921, in which she assures Mayakovsky of the opposite: "Don't be sad, my puppy! I shan't forget you—I shall return without fail." But perhaps there were other motives altogether behind her desire to visit London. At the end of 1920 her uncle Leo had been sentenced to five years' imprisonment for forgery, which must also have been a hard blow for her mother.

In Riga Lili booked into the Hotel Bellevue, where she was given a small room on the sunny side. The period before her trip to Riga seems to have a nerve-wracking one for her, and in several letters she insists that she is feeling better now. She is seeing relatives and soon makes acquaintances and even admirers. While she herself is "faithful," she is clearly anxious that Mayakovsky will not be:

> My beloved Shenik! Don't cry because of me! I love you so terribly strongly, and forever! I'll come without fail! I'd come now if I wasn't ashamed to. Wait for me!
>
> Don't betray me!!!
>
> I'm terribly afraid of that. I am faithful to you *absolutely*. I now know lots of people here. I even have some admirers, but there's not one of them I like to even the slightest degree. By comparison to you all of them are fools and freaks! After all, you are my beloved Shen, so how could I like them? Every evening I kiss the bridge of your nose! I don't drink at all! I don't want to. In a word: you'd be satisfied with me.
>
> My nerves have had a good rest. When I arrive I'll be in a good mood.

Marital fidelity was not Lili's strong point. But during their separation in the autumn of 1921 it is clear that she is genuinely frightened of losing Mayakovsky. "Write honestly," she exhorts him. "Don't you sometimes live more easily without me? Are you never glad that I've gone away?—There's no one tormenting you! No one being capricious! No one wearing out your already worn out little nerves! I love you, little Shen! Are you mine? Do you need nobody else? I'm completely yours, my own child!" But at the same time she cannot resist occasionally showing her teeth, like when she hears by way of rumor that Osip and Mayakovsky have held a party and that Mayakovsky has been drinking himself "sick" and has been spotted in "tender poses" with a Miss Ginzburg: "In two weeks I shall be in Moscow, and I shall pretend with regard to you that I know nothing. But I *demand* that *everything* which I might not like be *absolutely* liquidated. There must not be a *single* telephone call, etc. If *all this* is not put into effect down to *the very tiniest detail*, I shall have to part from you, which I abso-

Lili photographed during her second visit to Riga, in the spring of 1922.

lutely don't want, because I love you. You're really fulfilling the conditions 'not to get drunk' and 'to wait' well. I have fulfilled both of them *to this very day*. As for the future—we'll have to see." Mayakovsky was distraught over the "fantastic nonsense" that Lili had heard and assured her that none of his relationships "goes beyond flirtation."

In any case, he added jokingly, since finding a new billiard hall he had not had time for any womenfolk. Generally speaking, the letters exude an air of love, harmony, and good humor. They also give a good picture of how the threesome functioned. In her letters Lili turns to either Mayakovsky or her "boys" and "beasts" together. "I am living a blameless life! Love me! Don't forget me! Don't deceive me! Write about everything! Till death us do part, your pussycat Lily [drawing of a cat]. I kiss all your little paws, your coats, the bridges of your noses, your little tails, your fur, your skulls! [drawing of a cat]. "My dears!" she writes in another letter: "My beloved ones! Lights of my life! My little suns! My little kittens! My little puppies! Love me! Don't betray me! If you do I'll tear off all your paws!" In one letter she addresses Osip directly: "You swine of a kitten!" she reproaches him: "Again you haven't written! How are you getting on without me? I get on very badly without you! Absolutely boo-hoo-hoo! There aren't any little kittens in the whole of Riga! There are lots of puppies but no kittens! What a shame!" She kisses his "little tail" and signs herself "your wife." Her reproaches were justified. With a few exceptions Osip played no part in the correspondence except as the object of Lili's and Mayakovsky's feelings.

Lili received money from her mother in London and from Misha Grinkrug, who had emigrated to Berlin—and even from Mayakovsky in Moscow, for perfume. She herself was constantly sending parcels to Moscow by diplomatic pouch, to Mayakovsky and Osip but also to Lyova Grinkrug. Foodstuffs such as herring, porridge oats, tea, coffee, cocoa, chocolate, sugar, flour, lard, and caramels, and Havana cigars. But also practical things like suspenders, suit material, razors, and rubber mugs. Mayakovsky also ordered a rubber bathtub—he refused to use hotel bathtubs and instead had a little rubber bathtub which he folded up in his room. However, such a commodity Lili could not find.

MAF

Lili devoted the early part of her stay in Riga to her efforts to get to London. But as soon as it became clear that there was no prospect of the journey's coming off, she spent all her time on the other purpose of the trip: promoting Mayakovsky's work. In October and November two articles about modern Russian literature, the first of them about Mayakovsky, were printed in the Russian-language newspaper *Novy Put* (New Path), which was published by the Soviet trade mission. The articles were signed L.B. Even if it is not certain that it was Lili concealed behind these initials, it was no coincidence that they were published during her stay in Riga. For Mayakovsky and his circle enjoyed ideological supporting fire in Riga in the shape of Grigory Vinokur, who was employed in the trade mission. Vinokur, a young linguistics researcher from Moscow who had ended up in Riga just as Roman Jakobson had in Prague, had two appreciative articles about Mayakovsky published in the newspaper in the course of that year, one of them a review of 150,000,000.

Lili also made contact with Riga's avant-garde circles and got to know a Jewish Futurist poet, B. Livshits (not to be confused with Benedikt Livshits, Mayakovsky's Futurist colleague), secretary of Arbeiterheim, a Jewish educational organization which was close to the Latvian Communist Party. Livshits was translating "Man" into Yiddish, and, according to Lili, was writing a big article about Mayakovsky. "They forced me to recite 'The Flute' to them and went mad with delight about it." Presumably it was her contacts with these circles that inspired Lili to have a new edition of *The Backbone-Flute* printed in Riga. "I want to print 'The Flute' here," Lili wrote to Mayakovsky at the end of October. *"Send me permission for the importation of five thousand copies."*

A couple of weeks later she told him, "I think we'll manage to print anything we like here, and without having to pay immediately!" and she asked her "boys" to send her not only Mayakovsky's books but also, among others, Pasternak's *My Sister Life*. She had made the acquaintance of a *"very important capitalist,"* the owner of a large printing business, who was prepared to publish the Futurists' books if he could finance the venture by printing Russian textbooks (for export to Soviet Russia). The capitalist in question was called Vasily Ziv and had moved to Riga from Petrograd in 1921. For the whole thing to work, Ziv wanted someone in Moscow to assume responsibility for this exclusively, in return for *guaranteed* payment in money and food. "I would like you to agree to be that person, Volosik," Lili exhorted Mayakovsky. "In the first place it's very interesting, and in the second place it would give you the possibility of giving up the posters completely."

Mayakovsky reacted with enthusiasm to the suggestion that he become the publisher's representative in Moscow and immediately contacted the Foreign Trade Commissariat, where the initiative was greeted positively. As there was a paper shortage in Russia, this type of cooperation over borders was becoming common—even Gosizdat was having books printed abroad which were then imported into Russia. Since the import authorization was being drawn up by Gosizdat, Mayakovsky was worried about possible obstacles, but the whole thing passed off painlessly thanks to Lunacharsky, whose support had immediately been canvassed.

Mayakovsky and Osip saw the potential in Lili's initiative right away and decided not only to request permission to import books but also to found a new publishing house, in order to supply a platform in Moscow for "Comfuturism." On 28 November 1921 the government issued a decree which, in line with the direction of NEP policy, allowed the setting-up of private and cooperative publishing firms. That same day, Mayakovsky and Osip applied to Lunacharsky for permission to found a publishing house, MAF, an abbreviation for "Moscow—in the future: International—Association of Futurists." In the memorandum they wrote: "The firm's aims are to publish a journal, collections of articles, monographs, collected works, textbooks, etc., designed to promote the basic values of the Communist art of the future and to show what has been achieved toward this. In view of the difficulties involved in printing our books in Russia, publication will take place abroad and the books will be imported and distributed in the Russian Soviet Republic. The firm will be founded with private capital." Among the names of the authors they intended to publish were Pasternak, Mayakovsky, and Khlebnikov.

Despite support from Lunacharsky, the Riga project came to nothing. Mayakovsky received an advance in foreign currency in Moscow, but the whole thing came to grief because Ziv turned out to be mainly interested in publishing physics and mathematics textbooks, where he could turn a large profit with long print-runs. The publication of the Futurists' works was simply a way of assuring himself of such orders. "For the publisher the main thing is profit!" Lili reported at the beginning of December. "Best of all is orders from the government for textbooks." But orders for textbooks had to go via Lenin's wife Nadezhda Krupskaya, and here Mayakovsky was powerless. Madame Krupskaya shared her husband's distaste for the Futurists, whom she had described in an article in *Pravda* in February 1921 as exponents of "the worst elements in the old art" and "utterly abnormal, perverted feelings."

LILI AND LENIN

While Lili was in Riga, life in Moscow went on as usual, without much of note happening. Mayakovsky took part in some public discussions about contemporary literature and gave a rare performance together with his old Futurist colleagues Kruchonykh, Kamensky, and Khlebnikov. The latter even stayed in Vodopyany Lane for several weeks during Lili's absence. Osip and Mayakovsky went out occasionally, but their sole topic of conversation, Mayakovsky assured her, was— Lili: "Theme: the only *person* in the world is kitty." Otherwise they stayed at home, Mayakovsky drawing and Osip reading Chekhov aloud. "I'm still your same Shen," Mayakovsky wrote to Lili, "I spend my whole life thinking about you, I'm waiting for you and I adore you. Every morning I come to Osya and I say 'it's boring brother cat without Liska' and Oska says 'it's boring brother pup without Kiska.'"

During the autumn and winter Mayakovsky continued to write and draw propaganda posters on current themes: "Decree concerning the foodstuffs tax on eggs," "Help the starving!," "The New Economic Policy shows that we are on the right path," and so on. But he soon got a commission of a different kind: "Write some poetry *for me*," Lili urged him at the end of October. He immediately accepted the challenge. "I'm terribly happy that you're writing, Volosik," Lili wrote only a week or so later: "You absolutely must write something for my return!" "The long poem is advancing extremely slowly," Mayakovsky replied, "a line a day!" And a few weeks later again, on 22 November: "I'm worried that I shan't be able to write a poem for you before you arrive. I'm trying terribly hard."

Despite these creative agonies, we can take it that the poem was finished by the time Lili returned to Moscow at the beginning of February 1922. For Mayakovsky, writing poems to Lili was the best way—perhaps the only way—to assure himself of her love, and he knew that he could not give her a better welcoming present. "I Love" came out at the end of March in a separate edition, as number 1 of MAF's publications. The poem was dedicated to L. Yu. B.

"I Love" is quite a bit shorter than "The Backbone-Flute" and "A Cloud in Trousers" and also less complex. It begins with the characteristic Mayakovskian observation that love is the prisoner of reality, of life. "Any man born is entitled to love, / but what with jobs, / incomes, / and other such things / the heart's core grows harder / from day to day." Love can be bought, but not for one who, like the poet, is incapable of governing his heart. Women cannot handle his exaggerated feelings and recoil in fear. But then "you"—that is,

Lili—appears and sees through everything, sees the boy behind the tortured, bellowing giant. She takes his heart and plays with it as if with a ball. "She must be a lion tamer / a girl from from the zoo!" other women are heard to exclaim. But Mayakovsky rejoices: "I didn't feel it— / the yoke! / Oblivious with joy, / I jumped / and leapt about, a bride-happy redskin, / I felt so elated / and light." When the poet returns to "her," it's like returning home: "Solemnly raising index-lined verse / I swear— / I love / immutably, truly."

"I Love" is perhaps Mayakovsky's sunniest poem, filled with love and self-confidence, free of gloom and suicidal thoughts. It reflects a happy and harmonious period in the relationship between himself and Lili, possibly the most conflict free in the whole of their life together. "Mayakovsky often said of this poem that it was a 'mature' work—presumably because it . . . deals with happy love," Lili wrote. That the feeling of happiness and harmony may have been the result of their living apart from each other during this time is another matter.

The publication of the poem coincided with the end of an important stage in Mayakovsky's career as an author and artist. In February 1922 he produced his last ROSTA poster. The period of agitation in Russian politics was over, and life was now characterized by the conditions which had been created under the NEP. Moreover, the situation on the publishing-house front had changed completely, giving authors new opportunities for making money. As a consequence of the decree of 28 November 1921, during the following year no fewer than two hundred private and cooperative publishing firms were registered, of which seventy came to function in practice. This meant that Mayakovsky was no longer dependent on Gosizdat but could turn to other publishers to get his work published. But even more important than the economic factors was a purely political intervention in his literary career, also this time by Lenin.

On 5 March the official government newspaper *Izvestiya* printed Mayakovsky's poem "In re Conferences," a witty and furious attack on the bureaucratization of Soviet society. "Comrade Ivan Ivanych" and his colleagues attend so many conferences that they have to divide themselves in the purely physical sense in order to cope: "Every day / they have to go to / a score of conferences. / So whether they want to or not / They're forced to split themselves in two. / From the waist here, / the rest / over there."

The poem ends with Mayakovsky's dream of a conference-free society: "Oh, at least / one more conference / to put an end to all conferences!"

The following day Lenin gave a speech to the Communist Section of the Metalworkers' Union. "Yesterday, by chance, I read Mayakovsky's poem on a political theme in *Izvestiya*," he said, continuing: "I am not one of those who admire his poetic talents, although I willingly confess my lack of expertise in this field. But it has been a long time since I last felt such enjoyment from a political and administrative standpoint. In his poem he ridicules all conferences and pokes fun at Communists who simply attend one conference after another. I can't comment on the poetry, but as far as the politics is concerned, I can guarantee that he is absolutely correct."

If Lenin's criticism of "150,000,000" had made Mayakovsky persona non grata within the cultural bureaucracy, his positive comments about "In re Conferences" had the opposite effect. For a poet who wanted nothing more than to put his pen at the service of the Revolution, Lenin's reaction was a pure gift. And Mayakovsky understood the political signals. As early as 2 April he had another poem on the same theme printed in *Izvestiya*: "Bureaucratiade." Before this, he had only occasionally managed to publish in the government newspaper, which now in short order published six of his newly written poems. "It was only after Lenin drew attention to me that *Izvestiya* started publishing me," Mayakovsky himself commented. The effect of Lenin's praise was actually—as Nikolay Aseyev put it in a letter to his Futurist colleagues in the Far East—so enormous that it "put [all] other literary events in the shade," among them the publication of *Stavrogin's Confession*, a newly discovered manuscript by Dostoevsky.

At the same time the whole thing was degrading, as Mayakovsky had been put—and had put himself—in the position of being dependent on the leader's favor. Did he realize this? And did he realize how devalued his poetic talent—and his status as a poet—would be as a result of writing such political verse? Others did. Among those who were concerned about Mayakovsky's growing inclination toward utilitarian art and political loyalism were Boris Pasternak and Osip Mandelstam, two of the country's leading poets, who refused to adapt their poetry to the requirements of the hour and of the party.

Pasternak was, as we saw, a great admirer of Mayakovsky, but after the "uncreative" "150,000,000" he felt he had "nothing more to say to him." In a verse dedication to Mayakovsky in *My Sister Life* in 1922 he wondered why the latter chose to squander his talent on the Central National Economic Council's problems with balancing the budget and suchlike: "I know your way is true, / but how did you let yourself be driven in / under the arches of such a poorhouse / on your sincere way?"

Osip Mandelstam, whose own attitude to the Revolution, to "the noise of time," was inquiring and more sympathetic than anything else, captured Mayakovsky's dilemma precisely when he wrote that same spring: "The extensive widening of the poetic road admittedly takes place at the expense of intensity, depth of content, poetic culture." To "address oneself to a public wholly unprepared for poetry," he goes on, "is as thankless a task as trying to perch on a pin." A poetry bereft of its poetic culture ceases to be poetry. According to Mandelstam, Mayakovsky is a poet whose lines are technically masterful and crammed with hyperbolic imagery. "It is therefore completely wrong for Mayakovsky to renounce all claims on the estate of poetry," he concludes, with a form of words that Mayakovsky himself would later echo with his declaration that he had set "my heel / on the throat / of my own song."

Mayakovsky was aware of the difficulty of being the poet of the masses without renouncing poetic quality, but he was honest in his ambition to put his pen at the service of the people with everything that this implied in terms of simplification of form and content. And although he subdued his lyrical impulses, he had enough breath left in his windpipe to produce glowing love poetry. In actual fact, the epic-historic alternated with the lyrical throughout Mayakovsky's career, as if for the sake of inner balance; he needed both of them. "A Cloud in Trousers" (1915) was followed by "War and the World," which was written in the years 1916–17, then "Man" (1917), followed by *Mystery-Bouffe* (1918) and "150,000,000" (1920–21), a poem which in its turn was followed by "I Love" (1922).

BACK IN RIGA

On 1 May 1922 a "formal reception" was held for Anatoly Lunacharsky in the little apartment in Vodopyany Lane. The discussion centered around Futurism and the relationship between "eternal" art and the present. "Everybody descended on Lunacharsky, who simply sat and waved them off," reported Nikolay Aseyev. Was it Lenin's praise of "In re Conferences" that gave them courage? Despite the harassment Lunacharsky acknowledged that all of the "most brightly shining and resounding of our generation" were represented in that little room. Among the poets present were, besides Mayakovsky and Aseyev, Pasternak and Khlebnikov.

Lili was not with them; she had gone back to Riga in the middle of April to try to reach an agreement with the publisher Ziv. She had barely arrived when she sent "the beasts" in Moscow sandals, German magazines, musical scores, and books. Osip got spectacles with spare lenses, Mayakovsky and Lyova Grinkrug received packs of cards. Chocolate, jars of preserves, and liqueur were to be shared with their housekeeper Annushka, Rita Rayt (their mutual friend who, the previous summer, had translated *Mystery-Bouffe* into German), and Aseyev and his wife. "I've been several times to the cinema, once to the circus, once to the theater. Deadly boring! I can't manage to get anything done!—They won't give me material on credit! And I can't get the money!! [. . .] All in all—I'm out of luck! My room is revolting!"

Ziv was no longer interested, and Lili was hoping to be able to return to Moscow as early as 6 May. Instead, on 2 May, the day after the reception for Lunacharsky, Mayakovsky traveled to Riga, where Lili had arranged performances for him. It was Mayakovsky's first trip abroad. Officially he was traveling as an employee of the Commissariat for Enlightenment, so it was thanks to Lunacharsky that Lili and Mayakovsky were able to spend nine days together in the Hotel Bellevue in Riga.

Mayakovsky was supposed to give a lecture, but he was forbidden to appear in public by the strongly anti-Soviet Latvian authorities. Similarly, almost the whole of the second edition of the poem "I Love," which had been printed by Arbeiterheim during his stay in Riga, was confiscated by the police. These setbacks inspired, on the one hand, an ironic but one-track poem about "democracy" and "freedom of speech" in the Latvian republic and, on the other hand, a tribute, in the form of an interview, to the Soviet authorities for their attitude to him: "The Soviet government, despite difficulties and lack of understanding of my writings, has done masses of favors to me and helped me. Nowhere else would I ever have received such support."

LONDON

The summer of 1922 was spent once again in Pushkino, for the fourth year in a row. They followed the usual routines, rising early to eat breakfast on the veranda: fresh bread and eggs, fried and served by Annushka. On the days when Mayakovsky did not travel into town he went out into the forest equipped with a little notebook. Just as he was accustomed to striding to and fro in a room in the house mumbling lines of verse to himself, so he now hammered out the rhythm on a path or in a glade. When he was not writing poetry, he picked mushrooms with the same compulsiveness with which he took money off his opponents in a game. If it rained, they passed the time by playing cards or chess. When Osip was involved in an absorbing game of chess with one of their guests, Mayakovsky (who did not play chess) would pounce on Rita, who was spending the summer with them. But Rita did not play cards and Mayakovsky would invite her to play anything at all, as long as they played something. When she lost, her punishment would be to clean Mayakovsky's razors for a whole week. Mayakovsky shaved every morning, even when he was in a hurry or traveling, and because of his hypochondria he refused to use a dirty razor.

The usual rhythm was broken in August when Lili went to Berlin. Germany and Russia had resumed diplomatic relations in April of that year, which made it significantly easier for Soviet citizens to travel there. In Berlin she went around with Lyova Grinkrug, who was in the German capital to see his brothers. She lived a flirtatious life, buying two new dresses and "a fantastic leather coat." As she was also thinking, as usual, of those back home—Osip and Mayakovsky received stylish shirts and ties and Rita got a blue velvet hat—her money soon ran out.

At the same time as Lili was living the high life in Berlin in company with Lyova and other Moscow friends, Osip and Mayakovsky were entertaining at home, just as they had done during her time in Riga. Usually they would receive visits on Sundays from their closest friends, seven or eight people. But now there were sometimes so many guests that not even Mayakovsky knew who all of them were, and Annushka tore her hair out in frustration.

The intention was that Osip and Mayakovsky would follow Lili to Germany. On 15 August she sent them entry permits and wrote that if they would only inform the German legation that they were ill and needed to travel to the spa Bad Kissingen, "you should get your visas very quickly." "Illness" was a pretext to ease the process of obtaining a visa. There was never any question of traveling to a sanatorium, as is evident from the wording of this letter from Lili: "On the way to Kissingen stop over in Berlin; you'll find you can stay there for as long as you need to."

The journey to Berlin was intended to take place at the beginning of September but for some reason was postponed. Not until a month later did Mayakovsky and Osip get away, via Estonia. There was obviously no problem obtaining a German visa, but to enable them to enter Estonia the Soviet authorities designated them "technical personnel" at the Soviet legation in Reval.

Meanwhile Lili had managed to visit her mother in England. Her entry into the country had been made possible by her formal appointment on 19 August to the Soviet trade delegation in London. It was Lili's first meeting with her mother since July 1918, that is, in four years. "Elsa's coming tomorrow—interesting," Lili wrote from London at the end of August with a remarkably offhand choice of words. Nothing is known about how the reunion turned out. But there is no reason to believe that her mother had reconciled herself to the thought of Lili's and Mayakovsky's unconventional living arrangements, which by this time were both a public and a poetic fact. Her youngest daughter's situation also left much to be desired. After a year in Tahiti Elsa and André had returned to Paris, where they separated at the end of 1921. After the separation Elsa moved to London, where she worked for a while in an architect's practice but was so poorly paid that, according to her own account, she could

When Lili came to London in 1922, it was the first encounter in four years with her sister and mother.

not even afford lipstick. Her change of address was not, however, motivated solely by her failed marriage to Triolet, but also by the fact that her mother needed company and support after uncle Leo had ended up in prison.

If Lili did not go into precise detail in her letters to the boys in Moscow, she was all the more candid in her reports to Rita: "I would like to stay in London for another two or three months," she wrote on 22 September. "During the day I walk and go to museums, and at night I go dancing!" Lili threw herself enthusiastically into the carefree, many-faceted life that London offered, which in Russia was only a memory. In London there were silk stockings and other luxury goods, and as usual she was the object of men's attention. On the plane from Moscow to Königsberg a man had fallen head over heels in love with her, and her dancing partner Lev Herzman, who worked at Arcos, managed to become her lover before she left London. At the same time she was worried about Mikhail Alter, an acquaintance from Riga, where he was attached to the press bureau of the trade delegation. He was now receiving treatment for his diseased lungs in St. Blasien, and she was keen to call on him before traveling to Berlin to meet up with Osip and Mayakovsky.

Lili was a long way from Moscow and the reality there, not least the literary feuds, and she was enjoying that: "There are no Futurists here and I am awfully glad about that," she reported to Rita. As soon as Rita received the letter she phoned Mayakovsky and Osip, who rushed over to read it dressed in pink shirts and trilbies that Lili had bought them in Riga. Rita insisted on reading the letter aloud, as it contained material that did not concern them. In this way she could exclude information about Lili's romantic adventures. But when she came to the bit about the Futurists, she began to hesitate, and Mayakovsky told her brusquely to read the whole thing. When Osip said that he shouldn't force her, he replied, downcast: "I'm sure she's glad to be free from us Futurists." Rita remembered that she was shocked by Mayakovsky's prescience and the almost exact repetition of the wording in Lili's letter.

Mayakovsky's downcast mood is understandable. On the one hand he suspected that behind Lili's attitude to Futurism there also lay a change in her attitude to him, and on the other hand it was precisely in his capacity as a Futurist and representative of the new revolutionary aesthetics that he was traveling to Berlin. "I am traveling to Europe as a victor, to view and take the pulse of art in the West," he had explained in an inteview before he left Moscow with Osip on 6 October.

After a few days in Reval, where Mayakovsky gave a lecture about "proletarian poetry" at the Soviet legation, they continued their journey by boat to Stettin and by train to Berlin, where they were met by

Lili and Elsa. All four of them stayed in the Kurfürstenhotel on the Kurfürstendamm, in the center of a Berlin which at this time contained several hundred thousand Russian émigrés. In the area around the Kurfürstendamm itself the Russian element was so strong that locals dubbed the street "Nepsky Prospect" (after the NEP). According to one popular anecdote a poor German was said to have hanged himself from grief at never hearing his mother tongue spoken in this neighborhood. There were Russian restaurants and cafés here, Russian bookshops, Russian schools, Russian football teams, and Russian tennis clubs. And here were also several Russian publishing firms and a series of Russian-language newspapers and magazines. If Paris was the political capital of the Russian emigration—and would remain so—Berlin, from 1921, was its cultural center.

After diplomatic relations were established between Soviet Russia and the Weimar Republic, the Russian part of Berlin was filled with writers and intellectuals making good use of their newly won—relative—freedom to travel. Many also felt the need for a breathing space after all the years of hardship. One who was attracted by the inspirational cultural milieu in Berlin was Boris Pasternak, who spent a good six months in the city in 1922–23. Another was Andrey Bely, who was in Berlin from 1921 to 1923. Just as Berlin was developing into the cultural capital of the Russian emigration, Smena vekh (New Milestones), a group which stood for closer links between the emigrants and the Soviet authorities, moved from Paris to Berlin, and with it came one of its supporters, the author Alexey Tolstoy, who in 1924 returned to the Soviet Union. The writer Ilya Ehrenburg arrived from Paris at the same time.

The rich and fruitful intercourse between writers from the Soviet Union and those who had emigrated was specific to Russian Berlin during the years 1921 to 1924. The Petrograd-based House of Art had a branch in Berlin, where meetings took place on Fridays in the Café Leon in Nollendorfplatz. Taking part in these lecture and discussion evenings were writers like Pasternak, Mayakovsky, Sergey Yesenin, Andrey Bely, and Igor Severyanin, and artists such as Alexander Arkhipenko, Natan Altman, Naum Gabo, and El Lissitzky. There were also lectures by some of Russia's leading philosophers and theologians. This unique political and cultural coexistence was made possible partly by the relative degree of freedom of speech and of travel which obtained for a short while in the Soviet Union, partly by the fact that many writers were deeply insecure about where their future lay: in emigration, or in a Bolshevik Russia.

VITYA AND ROMA

Many Russian writers had emigrated; others had ended up in the German capital by other, more complicated routes. One of these was Maxim Gorky, who settled in Saarow, a suburb of Berlin. Another was Viktor Shklovsky, who not only refused to acknowledge the October Revolution but fought against Bolshevism with weapon in hand. As chairman of the armored section of the Socialist Revolutionaries' military organization, he became deeply involved in the spring of 1918 in an attempted coup against the Bolshevik regime, and in several bombings. When the conspiracy was discovered, he went underground. Once he hid in the home of Roman Jakobson. On one occasion when Roman was about to go out, Shklovsky asked what he should do if the Chekists came. "Pretend you're a paper and rustle," was Jakobson's brisk but rather perilous recommendation. In October 1918 Shklovsky fled to Ukraine, but a few months later he returned to Moscow, where he decided to lay down his arms.

"There are no victors; it is time for reconciliation," Shklovsky wrote in February 1919, at the same time as the Socialist Revolutionaries were granted a political amnesty. But three years later the leader of the party's military organization, Grigory Semyonov, brought out a book in Berlin in which he revealed hitherto unknown facts about their terrorist activities in the years 1917–18. On the list of active terrorists was the name of Viktor Shklovsky.

As early as December 1921, on the initiative of Felix Dzerzhinsky, the head of the Cheka, the Soviet government had decided to pursue legal action against the Socialist Revolutionaries. The information in Semyonov's book was like manna from heaven, but as the book's author now worked for the Cheka, it came as no surprise. The lawsuit was one strand in the political tightening-up which followed in the footsteps of the New Economic Policy. A week before the book came out, Lenin wrote to the justice commissar that he wanted "to stage

The literary theoretician and socialist revolutionary Viktor Shklovsky portrayed by Yury Annenkov in 1919.

a series of *show trials*" in Moscow, Petrograd, Kharkov, and other important cities. The aim was to use the party to "apply pressure" to the revolutionary tribunals in order to "improve the work of the courts" and "intensify the oppression." The trials were to be "terrifying, loud, and *nurturing*." On 28 February it was made known that thirty-four leading right-wing Socialist Revolutionaries were to be tried, accused of counterrevolutionary activity, including terrorist actions directed against the Soviet government.

To be on the safe side, in the middle of March Shklovsky fled over the ice to Finland, where after two weeks' quarantine in the village of Kellomäki he moved to an uncle in another small village, Raivola. From there he wrote to Gorky in Berlin: "They wanted to arrest me, searched everywhere for me, I hid for two weeks before I was finally able to flee to Finland. [. . .] I don't know how I'll be able to live with-out my homeland. Come what may, up till now I have managed to avoid Gumilyov's fate." But the price of flight was a high one. On 22 March his wife was arrested in Petrograd to be held as a hostage. In Raivola, Shklovsky continued working on his autobiographical novel *A Sentimental Journey*, which was finished that same summer in Berlin, where he moved after his stay in Finland.

If Viktor Shklovsky's flight from Soviet Russia was dramatic, Roman Jakobson's early days in Prague were no less eventful. The Red Cross mission, which was the Soviet state's first representation in Czechoslovakia, soon became the meeting place for left-wing circles in Prague and was labeled a nest of Bolsheviks by the right-wing Czech press. This was not so strange given that the head of the mission, Dr. Gillerson, was a prominent Bolshevik with a history of membership in the Jewish Socialist organization Bund. Jakobson soon realized how politically loaded his post there was. As he wanted to study more than anything, he asked to be allowed to leave the mission, a request which was approved in September 1920. But he jumped from the frying pan into the fire: a newspaper interpreted his ambition to study as an attempt by the Bolshevik regime to infiltrate the Charles University. On 14 November Roman reported to Elsa in Paris: "I don't know if you know it or not, but in September I was strongly attacked here for my participation in the Red Cross mission. The newspapers were crying out about 'the boa constrictor grasping in its tenacious embrace the local professors' (this is me), and so on, the professors vacillated whether I was a bandit or a scholar or an unlawful mongrel, in the cabaret they were singing little songs about me—all of this was not very witty. The situation was complex, but it seems to me that be my fate is to tightrope walk in inconceivable situations." "I took the first available opportunity to wind up my job," he wrote at the same time to his academic colleague Grigory Vinokur in Riga: "Despite everything, I am a philologist and not a bureaucrat." In the end the professorial council accepted Jakobson's candidature and he was allowed to pursue his doctoral studies at the university.

Jakobson's difficulties during his early days in Prague were a consequence of the political chaos in Europe and Russia after the First World War, which made life insecure and unpredictable for so many people. The situation can hardly be better described than in Roman's first report to Elsa in a letter of September 1920: "Really, each one of us lived not one but ten lives in the last two years. In the last few years I, for example, was a counterrevolutionary, a scholar (and not the worst), the scholarly secretary of Brik, the head of IZO, a deserter, a gambler, an irreplaceable specialist at the Fuel Commission, a writer, a humorist, a reporter, a diplomat, in every sort of romantic *emploi*, and so on and so forth. I assure you, I was indeed a *roman d'aventures*. And so it was with practically all of us."

Jakobson belonged to a generation who were programmatically radical without necessarily being defined in party-political terms. The distinguishing feature of Russian radicalism was that it was deeply antibourgeois and at the same time strongly eschatological: the world was to be changed in one leap, not through slow and patient labor. This is why the messianic form of marxism—Communism—found its most fertile soil in Russia. Among the generation which came to maturity around the time of the First World War, there was also a strong conviction that it was young people who were "today's legislators," in Jakobson's words, and that nothing was impossible: "We didn't feel ourselves to be beginners. It seemed quite natural that we, the boys in the Moscow Linguistic Circle, should ask ourselves the question: 'How should one transform linguistics?' The same occurred in all other fields."

At the same time Jakobson had a characteristic which he described as "decisive in his life": lack of engagement. "I can appear in any role whatsoever, but they are only roles (involving no commitment)," he wrote. "Philology is also a role like any other, even if it is my favorite role." He is like an spectator at a game of chess who is interested in the game but not in the result: "One watches out of curiosity, feels sorry for the loser, enjoys the winner's clever chess, and works out moves for both white and black. One can even sit down for a bit and make a few moves for one of them. Such is my attitude to the politics of the day."

It was this relativism—defined by Brik as "diplomatic talent"—that led to Jakobson's being viewed with suspicion by many people. For even if he did not become engaged in the politics of the day, he was compromised by his closeness to Mayakovsky and the circle around him. He also made contact at an early date with avant-garde circles in Prague, and in February 1921 he was able to report to Mayakovsky: "Today you got a real going-over in the government newspaper. The mildest expression was 'bastard.' Your popularity is growing in left-wing circles. A translation of your *Mystery* is going to be performed in a major theater here on the first of May, and there's going to be an almighty row about the performance. Their best dramaturge, Dvořák (now a Communist), keeps repeating, irrespective of which play he's writing about in the Prague press, that compared with you it's bourgeois rot. [. . .] In the next few days a reading of your poems is being organized for the workers in a factory complex in Brno."

Jakobson did what he could to popularize the new Russian art and literature in Czechoslovakia. Among other things, he saw to it that fragments of "150,000,000" were translated into Czech (the poem was published in its entirety in 1925) and he learned the language so quickly that after only six months in Prague he was able to publish a poem by Khlebnikov in his own translation. Despite his close personal relationship to Mayakovsky, it was Khlebnikov who interested Jakobson most as a poet. In Khlebnikov's advanced formal experiments he found nourishment for his own ideas about poetry as an essentially linguistic activity. While still in Moscow he had worked on an edition of Khlebnikov's works and written a foreword which he now published in book form in Russian in Prague: *The Newest Russian Poetry: An Outline.*

Although Jakobson was allowed to begin studying at the Charles University, he was bored during his early days in Prague and longed to go home. Sending his book about Khlebnikov to Osip in Moscow in January 1921, he complained in the covering letter that Czechoslovakia was a "country of small shopkeepers": "I am sick of it and would like to see something on a bigger scale, but I'll probably return home." The notion of returning to Moscow recurs in several letters from this period. Jakobson longs for the intellectual intercourse with Osip and the other Formalists. Their work in linguistics and poetics was groundbreaking and anticipated developments in other countries by several years. Jakobson has a bad conscience about having forsaken the circle that fostered him: "Have I deceived Moscow, friends in Moscow, the Circle?" he asks rhetorically in a letter to Vinokur in the winter of 1921, and answers his own question: "No, I am coming back. But now, after my pleasant conversation with M. in Reval, my return has become *particularly* dangerous, and this has nothing to do with my having given up my work [at the mission]." Nevertheless he hopes to be able to travel home again at the latest by the spring of 1922, "with new research capital" in his luggage.

Irrespective of who "M." was and what the "pleasant" conversation was about, Roman's life soon took another turn. When Soviet Russia's first diplomatic envoy arrived in Prague in the summer of 1921, Jakobson was appointed to the legation, where among other things he worked as a translator. He badly needed money—there was one period when he was so short of funds that he could only eat every other day. The reason he remained in Prague after this, although his work at the legation took valuable time away from his research, was partly that he soon managed to take his place in Czech academic life, partly the growing political repression in Russia. Gumilyov's execution and Shklovsky's flight were clear signals that any return to that country was "particularly dangerous."

BERLIN

A few days after their arrival in Berlin, Mayakovsky and Brik participated in the opening of the first exhibition of Russian art in the west since the Revolution, arranged by the Commissariat for Enlighten-

(Over) In the collection *For the Voice*, El Lissitzky recreated Mayakovsky's poems with graphic and typographic means. The book is designed as a telephone book, but the letters are replaced by graphic symbols and the titles of the poems. The illustration shows the poem "But Could You?" from 1913: "I suddenly smeared the weekday map / splashing paint from a glass. / On a plate of aspic / I revealed the ocean's slanted cheeks. / On the scales of a tin fish / I read the summons of new lips. / But you / could you perform / a nocturne / on a drainpipe flute?"

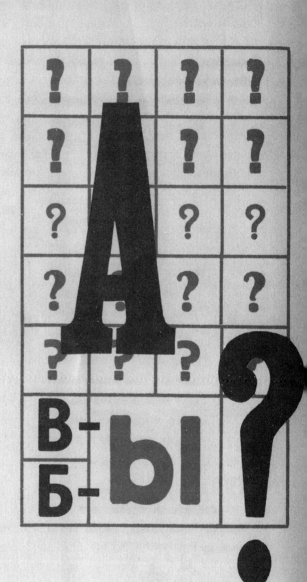

а ВЫ МОГЛИ БЫ ∎ ?

Я сразу смазал карту будня,
плеснувши краску из стакана.
Я показал на блюде студня
косые скулы океана.
На чешуе жестяной рыбы
прочел я зовы новых губ.
А вы
ноктюрн сыграть
могли бы
на флейте водосточных труб?

41

ment in a private gallery, Van Diemen. As well as paintings by more traditional artists, the exhibits included the first showings of works by the leading exponents of the Russian avant-garde: Malevich, Tatlin, Kandinsky, El Lissitzky, Chagall, Rodchenko, and Burlyuk. Mayakovsky was represented by ten of his ROSTA posters.

Apart from his short stay in provincial Riga, this was Mayakovsky's first proper trip abroad. Berlin made a gloomy impression on him. The city certainly seethed with life but was also marked by the poverty and social unrest which were a legacy of the war. He was "dejected like a vulnerable little child, captivated and gripped by the city's vivid ungraspability," Pasternak reported to a friend in Moscow. During the galloping inflation in those years, even Soviet citizens could lead a life of luxury in Germany. At regular intervals Mayakovsky had a florist deliver enormous flower arrangements to Lili, who in turn bought a fur for Rita Rayt for the equivalent of one dollar. And he always ordered masses of food although they only ate in the best and most expensive restaurants, like Horcher. "Ich fünf portion melone und fünf portion kompott," he would say, with the help of the German that Rita had tried to teach him during the summer. "Ich bin ein russischer dichter, bekannt im russischen land; I may not eat less." In the same way he often asked for two beers, "für mich und mein Genie"—according to Pasternak, an expression characteristic of Mayakovsky's "confounded conceit."

During their time in Berlin, Mayakovsky and Osip took part in several discussions and poetry readings at the Café Léon and other places, and Osip gave two lectures about the Bauhaus. Mayakovsky was also preoccupied with his various publishing projects. He signed a contract with the pro-Soviet publishing house Nakanune for a selection of his poetry and arranged the private printing of *Dlya golosa* (For the Voice), one of Russian Constructivism's most successful efforts in the field of graphic art. The book consisted of poems which were suited to being read aloud, and the lines of verse were phrased typographically by El Lissitzky so that the reader could follow the rhythm and intonation with his eye.

The day before Mayakovsky went to Paris, he gave Lili this portrait, with the dedication "Beloved red-haired Kitty, you are mine. / See you again in two weeks' time."

ия любимого кисика рыжего
ду две недели увижу его

17/XI

Mayakovsky and Osip also spent a lot of time with the representatives of the German political and artistic avant-garde, among them George Grosz. Mayakovsky received from Grosz a copy of the graphic portfolio *Ecce homo*, published by Malik Verlag, a Communist publishing house founded and led by Wieland Herzfelde, brother of the photographer and collage artist John Heartfield. (Two years later the latter designed the German edition of 150,000,000.) Grosz and Heartfield were among the left-wing artists whom Mayakovsky and Osip would propagandize for when they returned to Moscow.

Lili, who had been living a carefree, independent life in London for over a month, soon tired of Mayakovsky and his jealousy, just as she tired of having to interpret for him the whole time. Not so with Osip, who spoke fluent German and was well acquainted with German culture. "He was," Lili declared, "very unlike Mayakovsky," who, instead of getting to know the German capital, preferred to sit in his hotel room and play cards. Such behavior was typical of Mayakovsky, who was more or less indifferent to anything which did not absorb him privately or professionally. Although this was his first real trip abroad, he took no interest in the culture, architecture, history, and so on, of the country other than on a very superficial level, to the extent that it might be useful for his writing.

While Elsa and Lili were out from morning till night, at museums, on shopping expeditions and in dance halls, Mayakovsky spent nearly all his time at the card table. "I dreamed of being able to show him all the important things in Berlin," Lili recalled, "but he didn't want to see anything. A friend from Moscow was staying in our hotel, and Mayakovsky played cards with him all day long." Lili got tired of this, just like Elsa, who was if anything even more irritated by his eternal card playing:

Things went wrong for us from the very beginning. We avoided each other, didn't speak. In his room in the hotel, cards were played. Volodya was a compulsive gambler, he gambled constantly and about anything, cards, mah-jongg, billiards, made-up games. Before Berlin, I had only known him the way he was with me, and, moreover, as a poet, I knew him very intimately without really knowing him. [. . .] In Berlin, I lived side by side with him for the first time, day after day, and the eternal card playing irritated me to the point where [. . .] before long I rented a couple of furnished rooms and moved out of the hotel. There were lots of people at my housewarming. Volodya came with his pack of cards. I begged him not to start playing. Volodya was irritated and muttered something about lack of hospitality. [. . .] He went off, swearing that it was for ever and ruining the whole evening. What a gloomy and difficult man he was!

Mayakovsky's relationship with both Lili and Elsa was thus strained to breaking point. When the impresario of the Ballets Russes, Sergey Diaghilev, who lived in Paris but was visiting Berlin, invited Mayakovsky to Paris and promised to take care of his visa, he therefore immediately said yes. At the end of November he spent a week in Paris, where he saw again his old artist friends Mikhail Larionov and Natalya Goncharova and got to know some of the most prominent names in contemporary art: Igor Stravinsky, Picasso, Léger, Braque, Robert Delaunay, and Jean Cocteau. He also attended the funeral of Marcel Proust. That Paris attracted him in a different way from Berlin emerges from the fact that he wrote no fewer than four long—if superficial—articles for *Izvestiya* and even a little book, *A Seven-Day Inspection of French Painting* (which, however, only appeared posthumously). In contrast, he wrote only two short reports about Berlin, one of which was about the art exhibition in the Galerie Van Diemen. Clearly it was not only Lili who breathed a sigh of relief when deprived of Mayakovsky's demanding presence. Out of reach of her prying eye, he also felt freer and more independent.

200

Elsa was irritated by Mayakovsky's manic card playing, but that was not the only thing that set her nerves on edge. At this point in time she had separated from André and was uncertain about her future. Where? With whom? She still had feelings for Mayakovsky, and old memories were stirring again. By choosing Lili instead of her, he was indeed one of the reasons for her leaving Russia. The situation was complicated by the fact that she was being assiduously courted in Berlin by two other men, Roman Jakobson and Viktor Shklovsky.

Shklovsky had barely landed in Berlin from Finland before Jakobson was back in touch. "He sends me one telegram in the morning and one in the evening," Shklovsky informed Gorky in September 1922. "I love him like a lover." As youngsters, Jakobson and Shklovsky had initiated the research into poetic language and founded Formalism in the field of literary theory, but for several years they had been starved intellectually. They needed the stimulus of each other, and now that they once again had the opportunity to communicate, they didn't let a single day go to waste. As soon as he was able to, Shklovsky went to see Jakobson in Prague.

A month after Shklovsky's visit to Prague, Jakobson came to Berlin. It was only an eight-hour train journey from Prague, but he does not seem to have been in the German capital all that often, although his parents and brother lived there. "Roman is boozing something awful," Shklovsky reported, once again to Gorky. At this point Jakobson was twenty-six years old and had been living in Prague for two years. But he was not happy and was drinking, although this did not affect his intellect or capacity for work. "Roman was red faced, starry eyed, and squinting with one eye. He drank a lot but always kept a clear head. Only after the tenth glass did he button up his jacket the wrong way," recalled Ilya Ehrenburg, who was struck by the fact that Roman "knew everything"—"the structure of Khlebnikov's poems, old Czech literature, Rimbaud, and the intrigues of [Lord] Curzon or [Ramsay] MacDonald."

When Roman traveled to Berlin in October 1922, it was to meet Mayakovsky, Osip, and Lili, whom he had not seen since May 1920— and Elsa, whom he had not seen since the summer of 1918.

One reason for Jakobson's drinking was his love for Elsa, which had not faded with the years. Even before he left Moscow, Lili had impressed upon him that he should not forget Elsa was married. But instead of heeding her admonition Roman bombarded Elsa with declarations of love and begged her to move in with him in Prague. "I'm waiting for you, as I did four years minus one week ago," he wrote in December 1920, referring to his courtship of her in 1916. "What I then proposed remains in force in all its details." But Elsa

One in a series of photographic portraits that Elsa made after she returned from Tahiti to Paris in 1921.

seems to have had her doubts (her letters have not survived), and in 1922 Jakobson married a twenty-three-year-old Russian medical student he had met in Prague, Sonya Feldman. Marriage, however, did not prevent him from continuing to pay court to Elsa: "I'll never be able to convince either you, or myself, or Sonya that I love her as I love you," he wrote to her in January 1923. "When I spent days with you in Moscow, I forgot the address of the university. Thus, my philological school is Pyatnitskaya, Golikovsky Lane [where Elsa lived]. I am fashioned by you, Elsa." That Elsa was not unmoved by Roman's single-minded courtship emerges from a diary entry she made shortly after receiving the letter. "It seems to me as if Romik might have given me my life back after all."

It was with this emotional baggage that Roman saw Elsa again in October 1922, after four years' separation. To his disappointment he found that he was not the only one who was in love with her. Viktor Shklovsky, who had already been courting Elsa in Russia, fell hopelessly in love with her in Berlin. He was poor and only had the one shirt collar which he washed every evening and "ironed" by fastening it while still wet to the mirror in his hotel room—all in order to save money so that he could buy flowers for Elsa. Every morning when she opened the door of her room in the boardinghouse, there would be a fresh bouquet of flowers lying across the shoes that she had left out for polishing.

If Roman found it hard to get used to the idea that he had a rival, he found it even harder to accept that Shklovsky was creating literature out of his love for Elsa, which was as unrequited as his own. "I am sick of the fact that Vitya wants to put you and me on the stage then get hold of a press pass to the drama if he doesn't succeed in obtaining a minor role," Roman wrote to Elsa in March 1923. What he was getting at was the book Shklovsky was working on, which came out in Russian in Berlin in the summer of 1923: *Zoo; or, Letters Not about Love*—an epistolary novel about unrequited love. The book is strongly autobiographical. Shklovsky is Shklovsky, the woman he writes to, Alya, is Elsa, and the third member of the love triangle, whose name is not given, is Roman.

The book is a motley blend of personal portraits, reflections on literary theory, depictions of the city, and so forth. But all these are merely metaphors for his love for Alya, which he has forbidden himself to write about. And the metaphorization is total: even Alya is a metaphor, a realized metaphor. She stands for bourgeois Europe and its civilization, symbolized by good table manners and ironed trouser creases. The author himself presses his trousers by laying them under the mattress of his bed at night.

To that extent, *Zoo* is an artificial construct of a book, drawn up in accordance with the rule book of Formalism. According to the same rules, biographical data are of minor importance to the genesis of works of literature. Of this, however, *Zoo* was an eloquent disclaimer. Without his all-consuming passion for Elsa, the book would not have come about. The prohibition against writing about love was not only a literary device but also an unusually good example of repression. "I dedicate the book to Elsa Triolet and name it The Third Héloïse," read the dedication printed on the title-page. Héloïse was an anagram of the loved one's name, but in contrast to the first Héloïse, Abélard's, and the second, Rousseau's "new Héloïse," this addressee was not even in love with the sender of the letter.

When in February 1923 Shklovsky sent chapters of the book to Gorky for publication in his newspaper, he explained away a scandal he had caused during a public lecture by saying he was ill at the time: "I had a fever of 82.61 (a certain telephone number)." The telephone number was Elsa's. "To cut a long story short," Shklovsky continued, "I am in love, very unhappy in my love, and how I am to extricate myself from this I do not know."

Not even Alya's measured reactions are a literary construction: her letters are genuine; they were written by Elsa, who did not return Shklovsky's love but on the contrary was irritated by his intrusive courtship. Whatever she thought about her private letters' being publicized in this way, the publication would change her life. When Gorky found out that the letters were not imagined but written by Elsa, he wrote to her and advised her to begin writing—which she duly did. "I have brought her to life and I swear by my honor and my intuition, which has never deceived me, that she is very gifted," Shklovsky wrote to Gorky. But when Elsa's first book, *On Tahiti*, came out in Moscow in 1925, it was not Shklovsky but Jakobson that she invoked, by choosing a ditty he had written as a motto: "I'd rather hide it, sweetie / that I love you from my heart. / But when you go off to Tahiti / I'll weep buckets when we part."

Jakobson was upset that Shklovsky was making their mutual feelings for Elsa into public property: "I don't wish to write letters to you for publication, as certain acquaintances do," he commented ironically in a letter to Elsa. "For me you are not a literary motif or a poetic heroine." But Jakobson was hardly surprised by the device, as Shklovsky in January 1922 had published an "Open Letter to Roman Jakobson" in the Moscow journal *Book Corner*, a letter in which—against the background of the NEP reforms—he exhorted Jakobson to return to Russia:

> Come back.
> Without you, we are missing a handsome and high-spirited beast from our menagerie. [. . .]
> Come back.
> You'll see how much we have achieved together—I'm just talking about us philologists.
> I'll tell you everything when we're standing in the long queue for the house of Science. We'll have plenty of time to chat.
> We'll install a tiled stove for you.
> Come back.
> It's a new era here, and we must all cultivate our gardens as best we can.
> It's better to repair one's own broken roof than to live under a stranger's.

Jakobson did not return, and one of the reasons was surely that Shklovsky's flight from Russia a couple of months after the publication of the letter showed how much his optimism was worth. When Jakobson published his book *On Czech Verse, Especially in Comparison with Russian* in Berlin in 1923, the same year in which Shklovsky's *Zoo* appeared, he included a printed dedication: "To V. B. Shklovsky (in place of a reply to his letter in *Book Corner*)." The message was unambiguous: it was possible to work, and to work well, under a stranger's roof. By that stage Shklovsky had already decided to go back to Petrograd, where his wife was still being held as a hostage.

The last letter in *Zoo* is an application to VTsIK, the All-Union Central Executive Committee, to be allowed to return home.

"Vitya is a strange fellow," Brik commented ironically. "He hasn't studied grammar. He doesn't know that there are inanimate words and that VTsIK is an inanimate noun. Inanimate objects don't have a sense of humor, so one should not joke with them." But the Central Executive Committee proved to be a grammatical exception, and in October 1923 Shklovsky was reunited with his wife in Petrograd.

BOLSHEVIK HUMANISM

Although Mayakovsky's visit and the exhibition of contemporary Russian art naturally aroused the interest of Berlin's Russian circles, the big topic of conversation in the autumn of 1922 was another event: the expulsion from the Soviet Union of more than one hundred and sixty philosophers, writers, historians, economists, jurists, mathematicians, and other intellectuals. The idea of exiling them was Lenin's, and the task was handed to the Cheka, which in May set up a special commission with the remit of collecting information on "anti-Soviet elements." Dissatisfied with the tempo of the work, Lenin wrote to Stalin in July that "it would be good to send a few hundred of these gentlemen abroad without mercy. Let us cleanse Russia for a long time hence."

This move, unparalleled in history, was yet another step in Lenin's and the government's deliberate policy of crushing all political opposition before it even arose. Leon Trotsky was shameless enough to present it as an expression of "Bolshevik humanism." The "elements" whom the government chose to exile were, according to the commissar for war, politically insignificant but potential weapons in the enemy's hands in the event of a further outbreak of war: "And then we will be forced to shoot them according to the laws of war. This is why we prefer to send them out in good time, while things are peaceful."

At the end of September two contingents were sent to Riga and Berlin by train. Shortly afterward, thirty persons and their families were put on a boat to Stettin, among them the philosophers Nikolay Berdyayev, Semyon Frank, Sergey Trubetskoy (the philol-

Тов. Ленин ОЧИЩАЕТ
землю от нечисти.

On this poster from 1920, Lenin cleans the earth of all sorts of "impurity," in the shape of capitalists, priests, and others. Two years later, the time had ripened for new categories: scholars and writers.

ogist's namesake), and Ivan Ilyin. On the other boat, which left in November, were seventeen persons with their families, including two other outstanding philosophers, Lev Karsavin and Nikolay Lossky. As Russia's leading thinkers were being sent into exile *in corpore*, the ferries came to be known as "philosopher ships," although many other professional categories, such as writers, were also represented. The period of exile was officially limited to three years, but they were told unofficially that it was forever.

At a stroke Lenin had freed Russia of its intellectual elite and the country's most independently minded thinkers. As many unwanted "elements" had chosen to emigrate during those years, the sum total for the year 1922 was impressive. Five years after the Revolution Russia had been bereft not only of its leading philosophers and scientists but also of its best prose writers: Ivan Bunin, Maxim Gorky, Alexander Kuprin, Alexey Remizov, Dmitry Merezhkovsky, Boris Zaytsev—along with a future master, Vladimir Nabokov. Someone with Lenin's attitude to the intelligentsia—"shit"—had every reason to feel satisfied with the results of the cleansing program.

As poetry is concerned, the picture was not so uniform. Marina Tsvetayeva, Konstantin Balmont, Igor Severyanin, Zinaida Hippius, and Vladislav Khodasevich emigrated, and Pasternak and Bely treated themselves to brief breathing spaces in Berlin, but among those who remained, apart from Mayakovsky, were major poets such as Osip Mandelstam, Boris Pasternak, Anna Akhmatova, Nikolay Klyuyev, and Sergey Yesenin.

Out of these, however, it was only Mayakovsky who wholeheartedly supported the Revolution. How did he react to the influx of exiled Russian intellectuals into Berlin while he was in that city? We do not know—he does not mention this unparalleled measure in his newspaper reportage. Even if he did not have any ideological common ground with the deportees, there were nevertheless writers among them, his professional colleagues. But Mayakovsky was on the other side of the barricades and saw their exile, one may surmise, as something that was necessary for the survival of the Revolution. The fact that a writer like Mayakovsky—like other Soviet writers— failed to protest when the country's government took upon itself to exile the country's leading intellectuals *in corpore*, however, bears witness to the moral devaluation that had taken place in Bolshevik Russia. In tsarist times a similar move on the part of the authorities would have aroused vociferous protests.

This silence is evidence of the fear that the Bolshevik party had managed to implant in the intellectuals and the population at large—a result of the Cheka's successful work. For those who had chosen to side with the Revolution it was natural to support, or at least to accept, the activities of the Cheka. Mayakovsky was neither a member of the party nor an employee of the security service, but in a poem written in September 1922 he praises, for the first time, the Cheka—which at this point had been renamed the GPU—as society's weapon in the struggle against economic speculation. "At that time we regarded the Chekists as saints," Lili commented much later.

At this point Brik's work for the GPU was no secret either in Russia or in emigrant circles. In March 1922 the Russian Berlin newspaper *Voice of Russia* reported that "it is said of Brik that he ended up in the Cheka because he wished to avoid going to the Front. As a member of the Party he had to choose between the Front and the Cheka—he preferred the latter." However much credence one gives to these comments, it is a fact that by 1922 it was widely known—the article was reprinted in a Russian newspaper in Paris a few days later—that Osip was working for the Soviet secret police.

Whatever his work assignments looked like, Osip—whenever he found it possible and convenient—also used his influence to the benefit of people who had become the object of the GPU's attentions. As we saw, in the summer of 1921 he prevailed on Lunacharsky to set Punin free, and in that same year he helped Pasternak's parents and sisters to obtain passports so they could leave Russia. In a letter from Riga in the autumn of 1921 Lili asked Osip to "find out from the Cheka" about an acquaintance who had been arrested, the implication being that he should try to set him free. A woman whose friend had been arrested, and who knew that Mayakovsky knew someone who might be able to help get him released, describes a visit to Vodopyany Lane:

> "My dear," said Mayakovsky, turning to [Lili], "this is something that only Osya can help with . . ."

"I'll call for him . . ."

Her whole being radiated a single overwhelming desire to be of assistance, an unforced, joyful goodwill. [. . .]

I had to tell the whole sad story all over again and repeat my plea.

With great dignity, without in the least demeaning himself or butting in, Mayakovsky added:

"Please, Osya, do what you can."

And the lady turned to me so sweetly and said encouragingly:

"Don't worry. My husband will give the order and your friend will be released."

Without rising from his armchair B[rik] lifted the telephone receiver.

The story is creepy for two reasons: first, because it shows how chance, that is, contacts, decided who lived and who died, and second, because of the naturalness with which Mayakovsky and Lili reacted to the situation. That Osip was a Chekist was nothing for them to be ashamed of.

For those living outside the borders of the Soviet Union it was not so self-evident that the Cheka's activities should be viewed with benign approval. In the course of conversations in Berlin, Jakobson was shocked by Osip's talk about "several rather gory episodes" he had witnessed in the Cheka. "'Now there's an institution where a man loses his sentimentality,'" was Osip's summing-up. According to Jakobson, this was the first time that Brik made "an almost repulsive impression" on him: "Working in the Cheka had really ruined him." Considering Brik's well-attested unsentimental disposition, we can take it that the episodes which made him lose his sentimentality were indeed "rather gory."

GPU IDENTITY CARD 15073

A job with the Cheka opened a lot of doors. On Osip's application for a foreign passport for the trip to Berlin, under the heading "List of documents produced," we find a reference to his GPU identity card with the number 24541. What neither Jakobson nor anyone else knew—it was not revealed until the early 1990s—was that Lili's name also cropped up in this context. When she applied for a foreign passport to travel to England in July 1922, she made reference at the same point to her GPU identity card (number 15073). This did not necessarily mean that she was employed by the security service. Her ID card had been issued five days before her application was filed, which suggests that it was primarily intended to speed up the bureaucratic process. But who issued it? This was still a rather ascetic time, and it is unlikely that Osip would have allowed himself such a nepotistic liberty. Who was the high-ranking GPU official who dared to issue an ID card which was a mere formality and did not reflect the true situation? Or did it? Did Lili have tasks to perform for the GPU?

These questions may appear provocative, but if one bears in mind some circumstances surrounding Lili's first trip to Riga, they are not unmotivated. When she traveled there in October 1921, she was accompanied on the train by a young employee of the Foreign Commissariat whose services she was to find extremely useful. Lev Elbert in fact traveled back and forth between Riga and Moscow and functioned as a courier between Lili and the "beasts" back home. But his post with the Foreign Commissariat was only a cover; in actual fact, Elbert worked for the Foreign Department of the Cheka. Latvia, by virtue of its geographic position, was an important base for the Cheka's operations in Western Europe. Was it a coincidence that he and Lili traveled to Riga on the same train? Like so many other enthusiastic Bolsheviks, Elbert was very young, only twenty-three, he came from Odessa on the Black Sea, this was his first foreign assignment and of course he had no knowledge of Riga—in contrast with Lili, who had a large part of her family there. Given Osip's work for the security service it is entirely possible that he knew about Elbert's true function, but did Lili know too? Is it even possible that they worked together? Or did he simply use Lili in order to penetrate the circles she moved in (which also included Russian emigrants)?

The questions have no answers but must nevertheless be posed—not least because that man who because of his way of talking through his teeth bore the nickname "the Snob" would, later in the twenties, be part of the entourage of GPU men with whom Mayakovsky and the Briks surrounded themselves.

CROSSROADS BERLIN

The meeting in Berlin signified a crossroads for all concerned. Elsa remained in the city, heeding Gorky's advice; in time she would become both a prolific and to some extent even successful writer. Roman chose not to obey Shklovsky's exhortation to return to Moscow, influenced probably by Osip's "gory episodes" and by the deportation of intellectuals. He remained in Prague. Shklovsky himself could not settle in the West, among other reasons, because he knew no foreign languages, and the following autumn he returned to the Soviet Union, although he realized—as he wrote to Gorky—that he would "be forced to begin to lie" and did not anticipate "anything good." He would be proved right on both counts. For the Briks and Mayakovsky, their direction of travel was clear: back to Moscow and the struggle for Futurism, which by this point defined itself largely as Constructivism and Production Art.

No fewer than four books would be the direct or indirect result of the meetings in Berlin, all of them with biographical content. Shklovsky wrote *Zoo*, about himself, Elsa, and Jakobson, who in turn dedicated his study of Czech verse to Shklovsky. Elsa wrote the autobiographical book *The Wild Strawberry* with herself and Roman in the leading roles—and Mayakovsky wrote a poem which would be the culmination of his lyrical oeuvre and at the same time signal the beginning of the end of his relationship with Lili.

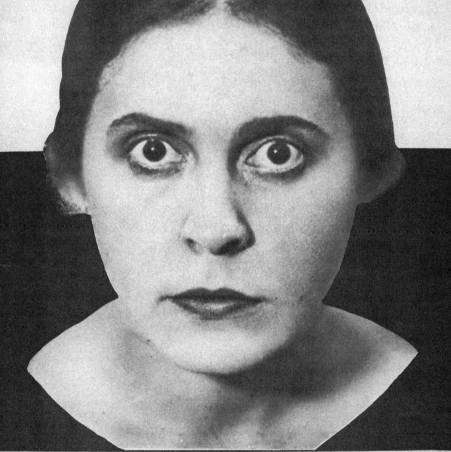

8

ABOUT THIS

1923

**Revolutions shake the bodies of kingdoms,
the human herd changes drovers,
but you,
uncrowned lord of the hearts,
not a single rebellion can disturb!**
Vladimir Mayakovsky, "Man"

After their return from Moscow in the middle of December 1922, Mayakovsky and Osip reported to the Institute for Artistic Culture (Inkhuk) on their impressions from Berlin and Paris and showed original works and reproductions of Pablo Picasso, Fernand Léger, George Grosz and other French and German artists.

The degree of interest in what Mayakovsky in particular had to relate about his first trips abroad was enormous. On 24 December *Izvestiya* printed his reportage "Paris (Notes of a Human Goose)" and three days later "Autumn Salon." And when he appeared in the Polytechnic Museum to deliver his lectures "What Is Berlin Doing?" and "What Is Paris Doing?," mounted police were called in to maintain order. There was com-

Alexander Rodchenko's cover of *About This*.

plete chaos in the packed auditorium, two people were sitting on each chair, the gangways were crammed, and enthusiastic listeners sat on the dais dangling their legs.

Lili also sat on the dais, behind the lectern, where chairs had been set out for friends and acquaintances. Expectations were screwed up to fever pitch, but when Mayakovsky—to thunderous applause—began to speak about Berlin, Lili became upset. She thought he was just repeating what he had heard from others instead of relating his own impressions; she also knew that he had spent most of his time at restaurant tables or in poker games in his hotel room. "To begin with I listened in consternation and dismay, but then I began to interrupt him with hurtful, but, as I thought, justified comments." Mayakovsky, alarmed, shot furtive glances at her while the Young Communists on the edge of the dais, not wishing to miss a single word he said, tried noisily but in vain to silence her.

The scandal was a fact. In the interval Mayakovsky said not a word to Lili, while the organizer, Fyodor Dolidze, did his level best to calm her down and persuade her not to make any more scenes. When she refused, he saw to it that she remained in the artists' dressing room during the second part.

"When I got home, I couldn't sleep, I was so disappointed," Lili recalled. She took so many tranquilizers that she slept through till noon the following day. When Mayakovsky appeared that evening, he asked if she was planning to come to his next lecture, about Paris. No, she replied. "Shall I cancel it then?"—"You do what you want," was Lili's reply.

Mayakovsky knew that he had more to relate about Paris than about Berlin and did not cancel the lecture. But he drew his own conclusions from Lili's criticism. While his reportage from Paris was published in a prominent position in *Izvestiya*, the article "Today's Berlin" was included in material which the news agency of the Central Committee's Department for Agitation and Propaganda sent out to the provincial press.

When Mayakovsky talked about Paris on 27 December, Lili stayed at home. Next morning they had a long and wearing discussion. Rita, who visited them that same morning, noticed that both Lili and Mayakovsky were red eyed. "We had a long conversation, very young and very difficult," Lili recalled. "We both cried." The result was that she showed Mayakovsky the door.

In a letter to Elsa in Berlin, Lili justified her decision by saying she found Mayakovsky's eternal card playing "repulsive." No doubt his gambling excesses during the Berlin trip had got on both their nerves, but this argument is remarkable given that both Lili and Osip were passionate card players. They played every evening, often right through the night. Why was she suddenly so upset by Mayakovsky's card playing? The other argument in the letter to Elsa was that Mayakovsky devoted himself far too much to *khaltura*. Exactly what she was getting at with this Russian word (which can be translated as "a botched job" or "a job on the side, "moonlighting") is unclear, but it may well have been his propaganda poems and political posters—which, by implication, hindered him from writing love lyrics, by implication, to her. It emerges from other sources that Lili also thought Mayakovsky drank too much.

When at a later date she tried to explain the origins of the conflict, she did it in more ideological terms. It was triggered, she wrote, by their mutual feeling that their life together had become stale and that they had to reconsider their positions. Everything had become routine: love, art, revolution. They had got used to each other, to being fed, clothed, and shod and to drinking tea with jam at prescribed times of day. In short, they had let themselves be "bourgeoisified." The paradox is that if anyone was to blame for Mayakovsky's "bourgeoisification," it was Lili. It was she who had transformed the shabby bohemian into a British-style dandy and who bought him shirts, ties, and suit material in Riga, Berlin, and London. It was he who had adopted her customs, not the other way round. But the NEP brought the issue to a head: what should be the attitude of a person of radical views, a Communist, to this hybrid form of capitalism and socialism? Once when Lili took Rita with her to a newly opened private restaurant known for its fine porcelain, she let slip a comment about how pretty it was, adding: "But of course I wouldn't start collecting it myself." No, to the circle around Mayakovsky it was unthinkable to collect porcelain from tsarist times; it was simple, modern design that counted.

In actual fact all these explanations—both at the time, in letters to

Elsa, and later, in memoirs—are fictionalizations of a conflict which had significantly deeper roots, namely, Mayakovsky's and Lili's irreconcilable views on love and jealousy. Mayakovsky thought that if Lili really loved him, then she needed to belong only to him, and that was an attitude she could not share. To her, jealousy was an outdated emotion which encroached on the erotic freedom she perceived as the natural right of an individual in the modern world. They had often quarreled about this issue over the years, and now the conflict reached its culmination.

Lili had shown Mayakovsky the door several times before, but never in the same dramatic way, or with the same dramatic consequences, as now. As soon as he reached the street below, he went into a café and drew up a long letter to her:

Lilyok
I see you've made a firm decision. I know that all my pestering you is painful to you. But Lilik what happened to me today is too terrible for me not to clutch at this last straw letter.

I have never felt so wretched—I really must have grown up too much. Earlier whenever you banished me I believed that we would meet again. Now I feel as if I've been completely torn away from life, as if there will never ever be anything else again. There is no life without you. I always said it, always knew it, now I feel it feel it with my whole essence, everything everything which I thought about with pleasure now has no value—it's revolting.

I'm not threatening, I'm not extorting forgiveness. I shall do nothing, nothing to myself—I'm too terrified for Mama and [my sister] Lyuda. . . . Also sentimental adulthood. I cannot promise you anything. I know that there is no promise you would believe in. I know that there is no way of seeing you, of being reconciled that would not be a torment to you.

And yet I am not capable of not writing, not begging you to forgive me for everything.

If you made your decision with difficulty, after a struggle, if you want to try one last time, you'll forgive me, you'll write.

But even if you don't reply *you* are my only thought, as I loved you seven years ago so I love you this very second, whatever you may wish, whatever you may order I shall do it this very moment, I shall do it with rapture. How terrible it is to part if you know that you are in love and that the parting is your own fault.

I'm sitting in a café and howling, the waitresses are laughing at me. It's terrifying to think that all the rest of my life will be like this.

I'm writing only about myself, not about you. It's terrible to think that you are calm and that every second you are further from me, and that it'll only take a few more for me to be forgotten completely.

If this letter causes you to feel anything other than pain and revulsion answer it for the sake of Christ, answer it immediately, I'm going to run home and wait. If you don't it will be a terrible terrible grief to me. (30–32)

I kiss you. Completely yours.

Me.

It's now ten o'clock. If you don't reply by eleven I'll know there's no point in waiting.

The letter was delivered by messenger to Lili, who either dialed Mayakovsky's telephone number, 30–32, or told him in some other way that there was some "point in waiting." From a second letter, written the same day, we learn that Lili—probably influenced by the implied threat of suicide—converted the breakup into a two months' divorce:

I shall be honest down to the smallest trifles for two months. I shall measure people by their attitude to me during these two months. My brain tells me that you shouldn't do a thing like this to a person. Despite all the conditions of my life, if this were to happen to Lichika, I'd put a stop to it that very day. If Lilik loves me, she'll (I feel this with my whole heart) put a stop to it, or alleviate it in some way. She must sense this, understand it. I shall be with Lilik at 2:30 p.m. on 28 February. If Lilik does not do anything even an hour before the end of my sentence, I shall know I am a loving idiot and for Lilik a rabbit being used in an experiment.

The arrangement was as follows: Mayakovsky promised that for two

The windows of the apartment in Vodopyany Lane where Mayakovsky hoped to catch a glimpse of Lili: "With the palm of the street corner against the windowledge / I shuffled and pulled windowpane after windowpane from the pack. / I staked my whole life on the window-cards," he wrote in "About This."

months he would "voluntarily" (his own choice of word) confine himself to his study in Lubyanka Passage, not playing cards or going off or visiting Lili—against a promise from her to reconsider her decision to break off their relationship if this two months' "incarceration" led to the desired result. Mayakovsky was to use the time to think how he would "change his character." Lili was "no saint" either, she liked "drinking tea," she admitted that—but she set no conditions for herself. She was just an ordinary human being, while Mayakovsky was a revolutionary poet and had to set an example.

Although Lili forbade Mayakovsky to write to her except when he "absolutely had to," a large number of letters and notes survive from this two-month-long divorce. Sometimes Lili replied with shorter messages. Mayakovsky delivered his letters via the housekeeper Annushka, but Osip and Nikolay Aseyev were also employed as messengers. Sometimes, "when he absolutely had to," he phoned. He sent her flowers and birds in a cage as a reminder of his own imprisonment, which he compared to that of Oscar Wilde in *Reading Gaol*. And he sent her both the books which appeared during their separation:

the anthology 13 *Years' Work* and *Lyrics*, which contained all the love poems associated with Lili together with the printed dedication "To Lilya." Mayakovsky's study was only five hundred meters from Lili and Osip's apartment, along the same street, but his suggestion that they should take a walk together was not taken up. Instead they met once by chance at Gosizdat. He went almost every day to Vodopyany Lane, where he stood for hours staring up at Lili's window in hopes of catching a glimpse of her. On at least one occasion he sneaked up the stairs and listened at the door, but then turned away.

The contrast with the life Lili was leading was enormous. "I'm in an excellent humor, having a good rest," she reported to Elsa, continuing: "My tics are completely gone. Enjoying my freedom! Have taken up ballet again—practicing every day. We dance in the evenings. Osya is an ideal partner. [. . .] We have even hired a pianist. [. . .] Materially, I am very well off—getting money from Lyova, he has lots just now."

During his strolls under Lili's window Mayakovsky was able to see for himself what kind of life she was living in his absence, with constant guests, music, and dancing—the one-step and two-step were the fashion. And soon the jealousy which he had promised to fight against broke out again with full force: "You won't reply because I'm already replaced, because I no longer exist for you, because you wish I'd never existed." Lili denied that she had anyone else—at the same time as her self-esteem led her to chide Mayakovsky for paying attentions to other women, with the same threatening tone she had used during the trip to Riga when she reproached him for enjoying himself in her absence: "I know of all your lyrical doings with all the details."

Mayakovsky's reaction was one of despair: "You ought to find out about my present life in order to have some idea about any 'doings.' What's terrible is not being suspected, what's terrible is that despite all my infinite love for you, I cannot know everything that may sadden you."

LOVE IS THE HEART OF EVERYTHING

The letters that Mayakovsky sent to Lili during their "divorce" are sincere enough, but his innermost thoughts he confided to a diary which he began writing on 1 February, after thirty-five days of "incarceration." It has been preserved but is not accessible in its entirety for research. Even in abbreviated form, however, it is a harrowing document, written by a man on the brink of complete collapse, perhaps even suicide. The complete text is a formidable denunciation of Lili, whom he accuses of being completely indifferent toward him and of having ruined his life. He was weeping aloud when he wrote it, the pages are stained with tears and the large, sprawling letters are printed by the hand of a desperate man.*

He assures her that he will take his punishment as something he has deserved but he does not wish to run the risk of incurring such a thing again: "The past for me before 28 December, for me with regard to you until 28 February, does not exist, either in words, or in letters, or in actions." If he sees a vestige of his "daily routines" recurring after this date, he promises to take himself off. "My decision to spoil your life in no way, not even by my breathing, is the main thing. The fact that you feel better off without me for even a month, even a day, is a good enough blow."

The central passages in the diary consist of Mayakovsky's analysis of his love for Lili and hers for him. Under the heading "Do I love you?" he writes:

I love you, I love you, despite everything and because of everything, I have loved you, I love you and I will love you, whether you're foul to me or affectionate, whether you belong to me or to someone else. All the same I love you. Amen. It is ridiculous writing about it, you know it yourself. [. . .] Is love the sum total of everything to me? Yes, only in another sense. Love is life, love is the main thing. My poetry, my actions, everything else stems from it. Love is the heart of everything. If it stops working, all the rest withers, becomes superfluous, unnecessary. But if the heart is working, its influence cannot but be apparent in all the rest. Without you (not without

* When I published the correspondence between Mayakovsky and Lili in 1982 in Russian (in English in 1986), I had access to the abbreviated version which Lili Brik prepared in 1956 for publication in a volume of memoirs which never appeared. A few years later I was given an opportunity to read the complete version but was not permitted to make notes.

you because you've "gone away," without you inwardly) I cease to exist. That was always the case, it is so now.

Lili's view of love is analyzed under the heading "Do you love me?":

> It's probably a strange question for you—of course you love me. But do you love *me*? Do you love me in such a way that I can sense it constantly?
>
> No. I've already said so to Osya. You don't feel love toward me, you feel love toward everything. I too occupy my place in it (perhaps even a large place), but if I come to an end I'll be removed, like a stone from a stream, and your love will go on washing over all the rest. Is this bad? No, for you it's good, I'd like to love in that way.

He wishes he "could love in that way too," Mayakovsky writes, explaining: "There are no ideal families. All families break up. All there can be is ideal love. But you can't establish love through any sorts of 'musts' or 'must nots'—only through free competition with the entire world." It was an attempt to accept Lili's view of love, but it was doomed to failure.

ONE MINUTE PAST THREE

During the whole period of his "divorce" from Lili, Mayakovsky oscillated between hope and despair. When he received a letter from Lili on 7 February suggesting they travel to Petrograd together on the twenty-eighth, his hope was rekindled. At the same time he realized that the possibility they might continue to live together just as before was the result of *her* initiative, of *her* wish. His reaction can be gleaned from the diary:

> We separated in order to think about life in the future, the one that didn't want to prolong our relationship was you, suddenly you decided yesterday that you can have a relationship with me, so why is it that we didn't go off yesterday and we're only going in three weeks' time? Because I'm not allowed to? This thought should not even occur to me, or my sitting here will become not something

voluntary, but an incarceration, something I will not agree to even for a single second.

I shall never be able to be the *creator* of relations, if you can just crook your little finger and I'll sit at home howling for two months, and then you'll crook another one and I'll break out without even knowing what you think, and rush off abandoning everything. [. . .]

I'm going to do only what results from my own desires.

I'm going to Petersburg.

I'm going because I've been busy working for two months, I'm tired, I want to have a rest and have some fun.

It was an unexpected joy for me that this coincides with a desire on the part of a woman whom I like terribly to do a little traveling.

Although Mayakovsky tried to make Lili's decision into his own, he did not want to believe that the trip would result in a resumption of the relationship with "this woman [who] tires of everything quickly." And he vacillates again between the hope that everything will be as it was before, even if subject to new conditions, and the suspicion that Lili has had second thoughts about the trip but is hesitating to tell him. In his darkest moments he even believes that she is actually planning to "condemn him to death" by telling him to "go to hell" when they see each other on the twenty-eighth. But she is not planning anything of the kind, she assures him. "Volosik, my child, my puppy, I *want* to go with you to Petersburg on the twenty-eighth. Don't expect anything bad! I believe that things will be good. I embrace and kiss you warmly. *Your* Lili."

As the time for their reunion drew near, Mayakovsky's nerves were at breaking-point. When he learned that the train would not be departing until five hours after the expiry of their enforced separation, at eight in the evening, he was in despair: "Just think, after traveling for two months, to spend two weeks driving up to the house and then to wait another half a day for the signal to change!"

At last the twenty-eighth arrived, Mayakovsky collected the tickets and sent them to Lili with the following message: "Dear Child, I'm sending the ticket. The train leaves at 8 precisely. Let's meet in the carriage." Later that day he sent a further message to Lili with a quotation from the revolutionary march "Warszawianka": "The

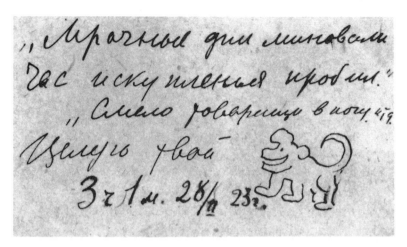

The scrap of paper from 28 February with the quotation from the famous revolutionary march "Warszawianka."

days of gloom are past, / The hour of atonement has tolled." "Boldly comrades in step and so on." The signature is a drawing of a happily barking puppy and the time is given to the minute: 3.01 28/11 23.

"If [Volodya] [. . .] realizes that the game is worth the candle, I'll take him back after two months," Lili wrote to Elsa on 6 February: "If not, so be it!" And she continues: "It's been over a month. He walks to and fro under my windows day and night, *never* goes away anywhere and has written a lyrical poem of 1,300 lines!! So it hasn't been a complete waste of time!"

Lili's conclusions are cynical, but not as cynical as they might appear. She was tired of Mayakovsky as a lovesick suitor but at the same time she knew that if anyone was capable of getting him to write anything other than propaganda verses it was herself. If she could not love Mayakovsky as a man, she loved him sincerely as a poet. Herein lay her great importance, not to say mission: to waken his lyrical talent—or, to use his own expression, "the heart's engine"—into life.

"We traveled by horse-drawn carriage," recalled Rita, who kept Lili company to the station. "It was cold and drafty but Lili suddenly took off her hat, I said: 'Look out, you'll catch a chill' and she rammed the hat down on her head again, it was obvious how nervous she was." Having reached the station they saw Mayakovsky on the platform.

Lili kissed Rita goodbye. "On my way out I turned round and saw Lili walking toward the carriage and Mayakovsky standing on the step, motionless, as if turned to stone . . ."

As soon as the train moved off Mayakovsky recited his poem to Lili, leaning against the door of the compartment. "When he had finished reading, he was so relieved that he burst into tears," she remembered. The poem was "Pro eto" (About This), perhaps Mayakovsky's greatest poetical achievement.

ABOUT THIS

The idea for a poem about love had been in Mayakovsky's mind since at least the summer of 1922, when he wrote in his brief autobiography "I Myself" (intended as a foreword to a four-volume edition of his works which never appeared): "Planned: about love. An enormous poem. Will be finished next year." We do not know the "plan" of this poem, but that it must have been different from the one which resulted from the separation from Lili is obvious as the thematic basis of "About This" is precisely that separation. Given the homogeneity of Mayakovsky's imagery and symbolism we cannot exclude the possibility that some of his ideas and images may have been present in earlier drafts; however, it was the separation from Lili that unleashed his creativity and made him set pen to paper.

"About This" is dedicated "To her and to me." "About what—about this?" is the interrogative heading of the prologue:

> In this theme,
> so private,
> so petty,
> sung over
> before and again,
> I've spun round,
> a poetical squirrel,
> and want to keep spinning some more.

When *About This* was published as a book in the summer of 1923, it included "photo montages" by Alexander Rodchenko. Here is the one illustrating the section about "the Man on the bridge."

What kind of theme is it that "is both Buddha's prayer / and a slave's knife itching for Master's neck"? That will "grab a cripple by the elbow / drag him to a piece of paper" and order him to take up his pen? That "came along, / rubbing out any others / and alone / became near and dear." In the last line of the prologue Mayakovsky indicated with dots what kind of theme it was that made him grasp his pen:

> This theme put a knife to my throat.
> Like a blacksmith's hammer
>   ringing from heart to skull.
> This theme darkened my day, and tells me:
>   Strike the dark with lines pulled from your brow.
>   The name
>   of this
>   theme is:
>   . . . . . . !

(TRANSLATION OF THE EXCERPTS FROM "ABOUT THIS" IN THE PRECEDING PART OF THIS SECTION BY VAL VINOKUR)

The heading of the poem's first section, "The Ballad of Reading Gaol," is borrowed from Oscar Wilde's ballad, which was rendered into Russian by the Symbolist poet Valery Bryusov and which affected Mayakovsky deeply:

> Yet each man kills the thing he loves,
>   By each let this be heard,
> Some do it with a bitter look,
>   Some with a flattering word,
> The coward does it with a kiss,
>   The brave man with a sword.

In Wilde's poem it is a soldier who has been condemned to death for killing his lover. Mayakovsky, on the other hand, is condemned to death because he has killed his love by loving too much, because of his gloom, and because of his jealousy. Even if the "Lilya" of the first draft is replaced by the pronoun "she" in the final version, the autobiographical component is unmistakeable:

She.
　　Lying in bed.
He.
　　Telephone on the table.
"He" and "she," that's my ballad.
　　Not terribly new.
　　What's terrible is
　　　"he" is me
　　and "she" has to do with me.

It's Christmas Eve. Mayakovsky's room in Lubyanka Passage has been transformed into a prison cell, and the telephone is his last straw. He rings the operator and asks to be connected to Lili's number, 67–10. The two blazing arrows—the trademark of L. M. Ericsson—set not only the telephone but the whole poem on fire. The ringing shakes Moscow like an earthquake. The sleepy female cook who replies that Lili doesn't want to talk to him is immediately transformed into d'Anthès, Pushkin's nemesis in the duel of 1837; the telephone receiver into a loaded revolver, and Mayakovsky himself into a weeping bear. (The bear metaphor was borrowed from Goethe, who depicts himself as a jealous bear in the poem "Lili's Park.") His tears become a flood and the pillow an ice floe gliding down the river Neva. He sees himself on the bridge over the Neva as he was seven years previously, prepared to throw himself into the water—the image is borrowed from "Man"—and he hears his own voice, which "prays and pleads":

　—Vladimir!
　　Stop!
　　Don't leave me!
　Why didn't you let me
　　throw myself over then?
　Let my heart be crushed against the pillars?
　I've stood here for seven years.[*]

---

[*] In the draft of the poem this reads "five years," which is the correct time lapse. "Man" was published exactly five years before "About This" was written. But by then

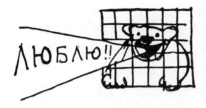

On 19 February, Mayakovsky sent Lili a letter with the sender's address "Moscow. Reading Gaol"—a direct reference to Oscar Wilde's poem. The letter was signed: "Your Shen, alias Oscar Wilde, alias the prisoner of Chillon"—an allusion to Lord Byron's poem "The Prisoner of Chillon," from 1816. The speech bubble reads: "I love!!"

I look down into the water,
Lashed to the railing by the hawsers of my verses.
For seven years, exposed to the water's merciless gaze.
When,
oh when will my chains be smashed?

The poet on the bridge wonders if his contemporary I has also surrendered to bourgeois family domesticity, and threatens him:

—Don't try to sneak away!
It was I
who called you.
I'll find you.
Torment you.
Persecute you.
Take your life!

Until love comes and saves the man on the bridge, the man from "seven years back," the author of "About This," will also "wander around / loveless": "Even beyond your grave you'll remember / the waves that surged in 'Man.'"

The second section, "Christmas Eve," depicts Mayakovsky's efforts to involve his family and friends in an attempt to save the man on the bridge, that is, himself. But in vain. Nobody understands him. First he sets his hopes on a young man he sees walking toward him: "He is Christ. / He looks like our Savior!" But he turns out to be a

---

Mayakovsky had already published his autobiography "I Myself," in which he dates "Man" to 1916—for obvious political reasons; he was careful to place this Jesus parallel on the right side of the October Revolution.

Young Communist who, before Mayakovsky's eyes, takes his own life because of a disappointment in love—yet another doppelgänger: "To that degree / he looked like me." The boy's farewell letter ("I beg you, don't blame anyone . . .") was one that Mayakovsky would have reason to remember seven years later.

After this Mayakovsky turns to his family, to his mother and sisters, and asks them to come with him to the bridge. But they do not understand him either and he wonders reproachfully:

> Have you replaced love with tea?
> Are you darning stockings instead of loving one another?

He takes his mother on a trip round the world—everywhere, people are drinking tea! "Even the Negro / caressing his Negress in the Sahara / is lapping his tea in a woolly headed gang," and under October's "punitive and judgmental" wing the bourgeoisie have set out their best porcelain. There is no help to be found anywhere. Finally he sees himself come running with Christmas presents under his arm and he realizes that he himself is one of "them." And when he comes home to Fyokla Davydovna and her husband ("the Joneses") he understands that nothing has changed, despite the Revolution. Icons hang on the wall beside the contemporary saviors: "Marx has been stretched between the red shafts of the frame, / even he a draft beast for philistines." And people are drinking tea: "In pools of tea with outstretched handles / the samovar took the whole world in a shining embrace."

The worst thing is that he recognizes himself:

> But most dreadful of all:
>   same height,
>   same skin,
> clothes, yes,
>   the same gait as mine!
>   So I recognized
>   in one of them
> —just like twins—
> myself—
>   it was
>   myself.

The doppelgänger motif again! Redemption, in other words, can only be found in himself. And the only place where Mayakovsky can go to search for it is with her. In the section "No Way Out" he steals away to Lili's house and up the stairs to her apartment to get her to save the potential suicide on the bridge:

> I go softly
>   in stocking soles
> up ice-cold stairs slippery with spittle.
> The pains in my heart don't die away
> but forge link after link.
>   Just so
>   came Raskolnikov
>   after murdering
>   to ring the bell again.

The reference to Raskolnikov is no coincidence—"About This" is packed with references to Dostoevsky, who was Mayakovsky's favorite author. This is true not least of the very title, "About This" (*Pro eto*), which is borrowed from *Crime and Punishment*. Raskolnikov consistently uses the words *about this* (in italics) to describe what he has done—the murder of the moncylender and her sister. Mayakovsky recognized himself in Raskolnikov: the overheated passion for an idea, the obsession with performing deeds that will change the world, the refusal to be dragged down into the misery and routine of daily life.

Lili has guests; they are dancing and yelling. The fragments of conversation the poet overhears through the door are trivial and banal, and he is gripped by the terrifying insight that she too belongs to "them"—just like the heroine in "A Cloud in Trousers" and the red-haired woman in "The Backbone-Flute" with "a lawful wedded husband and scores on the piano." Yet it is she who has saved him from suicide:

> My life has been filled with the clutter of apartments . . .
> It has shouted:
>   make up your mind

The photographs for the collages in *About This* were not taken by Rodchenko but by Avraam Sterenberg, brother of the painter David Sterenberg, with whose family Mayakovsky and the Briks shared the apartment in Poluektov Lane in 1919–20. This photo was used in the collage where Mayakovsky is waiting for the phone call from Lili.

from the window
straight down to the street!
I have fled the siren-call of windows gaping wide,
loving, I ran.

He has never betrayed their love in his poetry. And when he curses
the "daily sludge" he is so repelled by, he makes an exception for her:

—Look, my love, even when
I thunder in verse against the horrors of everyday,
I protect her whom I love
and skip over
your name
in my curses.

But Lili does not help him either, and soon his doppelgänger pops up
again and explains that it is naive of him to believe he could succeed
where no one else has succeeded:

Seven years I've stood here,
I'll stay for two hundred,
nailed fast
and constantly waiting.
Year after year on the bridge,
laughed at,
despised,
in the role of savior of earthly love
I shall stand.
I stand here for all.
I shall atone for all,
weep for all.

The man on the bridge is nailed fast, crucified, and suffering for all
mankind—just like the poet in "A Cloud in Trousers" and "Man."
The crucifixion metaphor continues in the following section.
During his trip through Russia and Europe Mayakovsky gets stuck
on the cupola of Ivan the Terrible's church tower in the Kremlin.

He tries to balance with his arms outstretched like a cross, but before long "friends and acquaintances / from every corner of the universe" catch sight of him, spit on their hands, and pound his cheek until it is transformed into a dishcloth. They challenge him to a duel, smacking his face not with a glove but with a whole shopful of gloves. His despairing explanation that he is "only poetry, only soul" is answered with a reference to the poet and hussar Mikhail Lermontov, who was killed in a duel in 1841: "No! / For hundreds of years you have been our enemy. / We've already come across one like you— / a hussar!"

Mayakovsky's punishment for daring to challenge the world order, personified in "Man" under the name "Ruler of All," is death, and his execution is dreadful in its prolonged horror:

> Harder than driving rain
> and the thunder's lightning-fireworks,
> simultaneously, eyebrow
> to eyebrow,
> from each weapon,
> from every battery,
> from each Mauser, each Browning,
> from a hundred paces,
> from ten,
> from two,
> shot after shot rings out
> right beside me.
> They pause to draw breath, but then
> begin to spray lead again.
> Fill his heart with lead!
> Take aim, fire!
> Fire till he finally stops twitching!
> When it comes down to it
> everything comes to an end.
> Even twitches come to an end.

When the slaughter is over, his opponents slowly draw back, "savoring every detail." Left behind on the church tower "shone the poet's tattered remains / fluttering in the wind like a bloodred flag"—a clear reference to "A Cloud in Trousers," in which the poet cuts the soul out of his breast and stamps it into a bloody banner.

His martyr's death prepares the way for the poet's continued journey, into the future. The last section of the poem is in the form of a petition to an unknown chemist in the thirtieth century. He looks down on Earth from the perspective of Charles's Wain—the Great Bear! His manifesto against "the tyranny of the everyday" is a rhetorical masterpiece. His ancestor was raised to the nobility and he himself has never stood on a workshop floor—

But with my breathing,
    my heartbeat,
        with my voice,
with every sawtooth set on edge,
with the holes of my nostrils,
        the nails of my eyes,
    my teeth, ground down and grinding still,
with goose pimples,
        my gathered eyebrows' concentrated rage,
with trillions of pores
        yes,
          with all my pores,
in the summer,
        autumn,
           winter,
              spring.
when I'm awake,
    when I'm sleeping,
    I shall never accept,
    always hate all
    of this.
All,
    that has been hammered into us
        of the slavery of the past,
all,
    that like swarms of weeds

has eaten its way in
     and taken root like everyday tyranny
even here
    in our red-flagged society.

Mayakovsky wants another life and weighs up different alternatives. If he believed in a life after this one, there would be no problem, but his opponents are not to have the pleasure of seeing "how, silenced by your shots, I fall." The attack on him was a failure, although only a few "tatters of poet" remained. He also rejects suicide: "a crooking of the finger / then the bullet shows / the way / to the life to come / in the form of / a shot." No, everything he "believed in / and believes in is / this world." So when, under the heading "Faith," he asks the chemist to revive him, it is a question of resurrection in flesh and blood. Influenced by the Russian philosopher Nikolay Fyodorov's ideas about "resurrecting the dead" and by Einstein's theory of relativity—which he discussed enthusiastically with Roman Jakobson in the spring of 1920—Mayakovsky believed in a future world where all the dead have been resurrected in the physical sense:

Air to air,
    like stone to stone,
untouched by decay and putrefaction,
in all its splendor
     through the centuries it arises—
the workshop for human resurrection.

He develops the concept under the heading "Hope," where he asks the chemist to implant a new heart in him, to give him blood transfusions and hammer ideas into his skull: "I never lived my life on earth to the full, / never managed / to have my fill / of love." If it proves difficult to find work for him, he can always take a job in a zoo, as he is so fond of animals.

With this, we are into the final section, "Love," which is a summary of the whole poem. In a vision of extraordinarily lyrical power Mayakovsky sees himself reunited with Lili in a new life, free from "everyday garbage," in a love which is no longer *eros* but *agape*, where

narrow family solidarity has been replaced by fellowship among all
mankind:

Perhaps,
    one day
        perhaps, along the walkways of the zoo,
she will come—
    for she loved animals too—
        wandering through the park,
like in the photo
    in my drawer,
        smiling.
They will certainly resurrect her—
    she is so pretty.
    . . .
Resurrect me
    at least
        because I
            as a poet,
waited for you,
freed myself from all the everyday muck.
Resurrect me
    at least for that!
Resurrect me—
    I want to live out the rest of my life!
So that love is not changed into a lackey
    to marriage,
        bread
            and lechery.
So that love with a curse
    climbs up out of its bed
to wander through the universe's infinity.
So that the day
    doesn't have to go begging for food,
grizzled and ragged in the highway's dust.
So that

with the first cry:
—Comrade!—
the earth turns round and is changed.
So that we avoid living
 fettered to the household hearth.
So that
from now on
  we are like brother and sister,
so that
 our father at least
  might be the world
and the earth our mother.

LEF

Mayakovsky and Lili spent a few days together in Petrograd, in a hotel, to avoid "every imaginable Chukovsky type" finding out that they were in the city. They wanted to avoid the sort of gossip that Korney Chukovsky had so generously disseminated five years earlier. When Rita called on Lili, on the same morning on which they returned to Moscow, she was greeted on the threshold with the words "Volodya has written a poem of genius!" That very evening some friends and colleagues gathered to hear Mayakovsky recite his latest poem, and at a reading the following evening the apartment was chock full. The news spread quickly: Mayakovsky had written a poem of genius.

Among those who were the first to hear "About This" were Anatoly Lunacharsky, Viktor Shklovsky, and Boris Pasternak. "The impression it made was stunning, enormous," recalled the wife of the people's commissar. "Anatoly Vasilyevich was quite captivated by both the poem and the performance." The recital of "About This" finally persuaded him what an "exceptional poet" Mayakovsky was.

The poem is best known in the edition published at the beginning of June 1923 with an ingenious photomontage by Alexander Rodchenko. But it had already been published on 29 March, in the periodical *Lef*.

The photo of Lili in the Berlin Zoo, about which Mayakovsky writes in "About This": "Perhaps, / one day / perhaps, along the walkways of the zoo, / she will come— / for she loved animals too— / wandering through the park, / like in the photo / in my drawer, / smiling.

Lef—standing for *Levyi Front Iskusstv*, "Left Front of the Arts"—was a new attempt to build a platform for Futurist aesthetics. During his separation from Lili, Mayakovsky had not only worked on "About This" but had also, to the best of his ability, shared in the planning of the first number of the periodical with Osip, who visited him just about every day. Lili took part in the work too, by translating texts by George Grosz and the dramatist Karl Wittfogel which were published in the first issues.

Shortly before the "divorce" from Lili, Mayakovsky had sought permission from the Party's Propaganda Section to publish a magazine, and in January 1923 Gosizdat promised to come up with the money. The ideological driving force behind Lef was Osip, but Mayakovsky's name was the selling point, and he was appointed editor in chief. The Lef group brought together large sections of the Russian avant-garde: the poets Nikolay Aseyev and Sergey Tretyakov, artists like Alexander Rodchenko and Anton Lavinsky, theoreticians like Osip, Boris Arvatov, Boris Kushner, and Nikolay Chuzhak, a man of the theater like Sergey Eisenstein (who had not yet started making films), and the filmmaker Dziga Vertov.

Lef campaigned for a new aesthetics which, rather than reflecting life, helped to "build" it—"life building" was a key term. While earlier literature was at best nontendentious and inclined to promote passive acceptance, and at worst antirevolutionary, the new literature would serve socialist requirements. But however utilitarian it was, in order to "influence" its readers it had to be formally high class—a guarantee of quality that only the Futurists could give.

In the realm of art, the equivalent to this aesthetics was Constructivism and Production Art. Instead of painting, artists were supposed to devote themselves to practical activity and work closely with the factories and workshops: designing work clothes, reading rooms, and textiles. "The impression is growing that painting is beginning to die out," Osip wrote in a programmatic article, "that it is irretrievably bound up with the forms of the capitalist system, its cultural ideology, and that calico material is becoming the focus of artists' attention—that calico and what can be done with it are the high points of artistic endeavor." The model that was held up was Alexander Rodchenko, who put the ideas of Lef into practice with

Lili with a copy of *About This*. Photograph by Alexander Rodchenko, 1924.

his innovative graphic designs (as well as working on *About This* he designed the covers for *Lef*).

In the realm of literature, OPOYAZ was exhorted to devote more attention to the sociological aspects of literature. In film, it was the formal and technical possibilities of the medium that were emphasized at the expense of storytelling: the "camera eye," with its "visual energy," ought not to reflect reality but, with the help of the technique of montage, create a new reality, an artifact.

It was around this artistic platform that the Futurists now gathered, in hopes of obtaining a frontline position in Soviet cultural life. It was of course an illusion, as the leading party ideologues were now—after the aesthetic free-for-all of the early years of the Revolution—heading in the opposite direction: toward ninteteenth-century realism. This was also Lunacharsky's position. The party's decision to bankroll *Lef* was thus not an expression of goodwill, being dictated instead by purely practical considerations. In the current competitive climate within the publishing industry the party was anxious to support those groups which had declared themselves loyal to the Revolution. Among the latter was Lef, but also their declared opponents among the proletarian writers, whose magazine *On Guard* also received a publication subsidy.

Even among the contributors to *Lef*, there were obvious aesthetic differences. Despite its praise for utilitarian art, *Lef* published experimental poems of a traditional Futurist nature, and one of its contributors was Boris Pasternak, whose poetry was regarded by many as individualistic and overly aesthetic. The conflicts within the editorial board emerged clearly as soon as the first number appeared, and the cause was—"About This."

One of Lef's declared aims was to combat *byt*, that is, daily life with its routine and its insipidity—Mayakovsky's "invincible foe" in "Man." One of the three manifestos which formed the introduction to the first issue of the magazine stated that Lef, which had opposed *byt* before the Revolution, "will fight against the remnants of this *byt* today." "Our weapon," they wrote, "is example, agitation, propaganda."

It was this pledge that Nikolay Chuzhak took as the starting point for his critique of "About This" in the second number of *Lef*:

A sentimental romance. . . . Grammar-school girls weep buckets over it. . . . But we, who know other things by Mayakovsky and a lot more in general, are not in the least bit moved by this in the year of 1923.

Everything in this "Mystery" is connected with *byt*. Everything is driven by *byt*. "My" home. "She," surrounded by friends and servants. [. . .] Dances the one-step. [. . .] And "he" stands eavesdropping at the door, rushes around with his genius from one bourgeois boor to another, talks about art to them, enthusiastically makes a fool of himself [. . .] and comes to the conclusion: "Nowhere to go!" [. . .]

At the end of the poem, we are told, there is "a way out." This way out is *the belief that "in the future everything will be different," there will be some kind of "terrific life."* [. . .] It looks to me as if this belief comes from *despair*, from the fact that "there is nowhere to go." [. . .] This is *not a way out but a hopeless situation.*

Byt had always been Mayakovsky's existential enemy, and when he discovered to his horror that nothing had changed with the Revolution, he renewed his attacks on its various manifestations. In the poem "About Trash" (1921), for example, the Revolution is threatened by the Soviet citizen with Marx on the wall, a canary in a cage, and a cat which lies purring on a copy of *Izvestiya*. The third revolution which Mayakovsky had evoked in "The Fourth International" was still conspicuous by its absence.

Chuzhak was an inflexible ideologue, deaf to more subtle intellectual reasoning, not to mention poetry. But in this case he hit the target. Mayakovsky really believed that the "red-flagged society" offered no better way out than the situation before the Revolution. The same force that ruled life and love before Communism still reigned supreme. The only hope, therefore, lay in a distant future in the thirtieth century, which "will chase away / masses of rubbish which has cut our hearts asunder."

For Chuzhak it was sacrilege not to believe in the Revolution's potential to overcome *byt*: "The time for drinking toasts with the Great Bear is over, as far as Futurism is concerned. What is needed is not some waving of the arms in 'eternity' (which in practice is the same as 'yesterday') but a tenacious bit of building work 'today.'" In the discussions which followed this criticism Mayakovsky toned down the private motifs in "About This" and maintained that the main theme was in fact *byt*—"that *byt* which has not changed in the least, that *byt* which is our worst enemy because it turns us into philistines." But however honest he was in his desire to overcome *byt,* he knew deep inside that this was demagoguery. That force which he personified in "Man" under the name of the "Ruler of All" is not socially determined but part of man himself, of human nature.

9

FREE FROM LOVE AND POSTERS

1923–1924

For all kinds of dead meat
                    I feel disgust!
I worship
            all that is life!
Vladimir Mayakovsky, "Jubilees"

Nikolay Chuzhak found it hard to see how Mayak-
ovsky could reconcile Lef's theories about utilitarian
art with the individualistic stamp of "About This." His
criticism was ideological and grounded in the demands
of orthodoxy. As if that wasn't enough, Mayakovsky
was also told that the poem was "incomprehensible."
Criticism for incomprehensibility had dogged Mayak-
ovsky all through his career and was a consequence of
his striving to renew the means of poetic expression.
Before the Revolution he had been able to dismiss such
reproaches as expressions of "reactionary" or "bour-
geois" taste, but now that they were coming from the
workers, he found them deeply hurtful. After all, it was
the working class that he saw as his employers.

Mayakovsky's standard reply was that "comprehen-

Osip Brik with a "Lef eye" — photo montage by Alexander Rodchenko 1924.

sibility" was a question of knowledge. When, at the beginning of May, he recited "About This" to an audience of workers in Moscow, he said: "The first thing I want to direct your attention to, comrades, is your remarkable slogan 'I don't understand.' You should try out that slogan in some other context! The only way I can answer that is by saying: 'Read on.'" According to Mayakovsky—and Lef—the workers and the Futurists were fighting the same battle. The goal of the working class was to build Communism, and the Futurists wanted to create a culture that would be in harmony with this new society. The problem was that the enthusiasm was not mutual. While the Futurists did all in their power to get the workers on their side, the workers saw Futurism as an expression of a basically bourgeois aesthetics.

Although Mayakovsky tried to justify "About This" with the argument that the poem was about the struggle against *byt*, there is no doubt that he was influenced by the criticism. After this, he devoted almost all his energy to writing "utilitarian" poetry. He became a kind of poetic journalist. This was entirely in line with Lef's theories, which saw journalism as a model genre in the battle to raise people's consciousness and level of education. During the remainder of the year he wrote about forty poems, all of them on topical themes. With reference to Easter he agitated against religious holidays and in favor of Communist ones ("The 25th of October / is the Commune's Sunday. / Our place is not in some grubby church"), he wrote no fewer than three May Day poems, he attacked Britain and France for their anti-Soviet policies and wrote satires against the political leaders of these countries, and he hailed the newly founded Soviet air force. When the first bulletins on Lenin's illness were issued in March 1923, he commented despairingly on them in the poem "We Don't Believe It!"

Mayakovsky may have been adapting himself thematically, but at the same time he was steadfast in respect of the linguistic laboratory work he had always been devoted to. New content demands a new form! One of the three May Day poems—appropriately enough, the one which was printed in *Lef*—is nothing more than a lengthy discussion about the form of poetic language. Whereas most May Day poems consist of tired clichés, he wishes to put together a celebration "without meter at least, / at least without rhyme." In terms of content too, the poem has a surprise in store. On this May Day, Mayakovsky wants to celebrate the month of *December*: "Long live the cold and Siberia! / The cold, which shaped the will into iron." It was not the spring month of May that once inspired the working class to rise up, but the deportations to frozen Siberia. The concept is original, but what is really new about this May Day poem is something else: Bolshevik implacability, which appears for the first time here in Mayakovsky's work:

> Down with weakness!
> Long live hate!
> The hate of the millions for the hundreds.
> the hate that forged solidarity.

Was the rancorous choice of words an attempt to adapt himself to a level that "the masses" could understand, to express himself "comprehensibly"? Whatever the motive, his tone bears witness to the fact that not even a poet like Mayakovsky was able to defend himself against the brutalization of politics and language that had taken place since the Bolsheviks had taken power.

The attempt to write unrhymed verse was natural for a poet who was constantly experimenting with form, but since masterfully orchestrated and structured rhyme was the very basis of his genius, unrhymed verse remained the exception in his work. Thematically, however, he continued his struggle to realize the ideas of Lef. The antilyrical tendency found its most powerful expression in the poem "To the Workers in Kursk, Who Mined the First Ore, a Provisional Memorial Raised by Vladimir Mayakovsky." The title refers to the exploitation of ore deposits at Kursk in the Urals, which got underway in 1923. The poem was written in the autumn and published in number 4 of *Lef*, which appeared at the beginning of January 1924. The title is redolent of the eighteenth century and is in fact an ode—a new kind of ode, to the miners and to the working class in general. Like "About This," it was dedicated to Lili: a recognition of the fact that she was the main source of inspiration for all his poems.

In the Kursk poem, belief in the future of the mining industry is contrasted with the current stagnation in the field of literature.

Lunacharsky had just exhorted authors to "learn from the classics"—but nobody would dream of telling the miners to abandon iron and go back to "ivory, / to the mammoth"! This prompts Mayakovsky to ironic comments about authorial anniversaries and all the statues of authors which adorn the boulevards of Moscow—a fate which, by implication, awaits him too.

What should a memorial to thirty thousand workers in Kursk look like? "No Merkurov / tries to convey / the smoke's beard, / the body of the factory's roar," wrote Mayakovsky, with a gibe at the most popular sculptor of the time. The miners have no need of any traditional tributes; their memorial is the fast train built from the ore they have mined, which rushes along so fast that the magpies have no time to bespatter it with their droppings. Nor do they need to endure any saccharine anniversary speeches; their tribute is "the tractor's rumble," the most persuasive anniversary speaker of all.

The poem is a development of a central motif in Mayakovsky's writings: the *statue* as a symbol of stagnation and reaction, of the society of old. "With its belief in the future, [the poem] was greeted by the young people with a storm of enthusiasm," recalled a young girl who was present when Mayakovsky read it at a student club—Natalya Bryukhanenko, whom we shall have the opportunity to return to later. The Kursk poem was the absolute antithesis of "About This" and represented a repudiation of the lyric and a belittling of literature as such, even of Lef's theories. When the miners' contributions to Communism are compared with those of the members of Lef, it is to the advantage of the former. The music from millions of cranes in Kursk, it is asserted, is "better than all Lef members / who have dealt / the Russian's sluggish taste / a mortal blow." This choice of words is in complete harmony with the antipoetic ideas of Lef and added yet another stone to the self-destructive building that Mayakovsky, through his struggle against the lyric poet within himself, had for some time been busy erecting. There would be many more.

WHEREVER YOU'RE FROM, BUY IN MOSSELPROM

The multiplicity of publishing houses created by the NEP meant that the literary groupings could engage in debate and argument

"From the old world / only the cigarette Ira is left." Advertisement for Mosselprom. Text by Mayakovsky and design by Rodchenko.

in a civilized fashion, that is, with words. With the exception of the deportation of the philosophers in the autumn of 1922, the Communist Party also maintained a healthy distance between itself and both literature and its practitioners, and insofar as it tried to regulate cultural life, it did not do so, as it would in the thirties, with the help of prison and a shot in the head. This pluralism was one positive side of the New Economic Policy. Another was that the economy soon got back on its feet again after the economic chaos of wartime communism. But there were also less positive aspects. The NEP generated its own bourgeoisie—the *NEP-men*—who often exceeded their tsarist counterparts in thoughtlessness and vulgarity. The vodka and champagne flowed in private restaurants and clubs, while large sections of the population lived, as before, in destitution. The contradictions stuck out like an eyesore, not least for those who had done their bit for the Revolution and who believed that it would lead to the end of capitalism and the introduction of new forms of production. "Many people with a revolutionary past felt they had been sidelined," was how Nikolay Aseyev summed up the mood of the time: "Many lives were crushed under the weight of the growing contradictions."

It is against this background that we have to see the next step in a utilitarian direction by Mayakovsky, in the summer of 1923, when he set about the task of writing advertising verses, which he sometimes illustrated with his own drawings. In this work he collaborated closely with other artists such as Alexander Rodchenko and his wife, Varvara Stepanova.

According to Mayakovsky, advertising was an important weapon in the struggle against private business and for state and cooperative products. During the next few years he produced hundreds of examples of advertising copy for everything from babies' pacifiers to cigarettes, from galoshes to caramels. His main patrons were the warehouse GUM and Mosselprom, Moscow's state-owned wholesalers. His slogan "Wherever you're from, / buy in Mosselprom!" became the firm's official motto and could be read on placards and on house walls.

Mayakovsky loved playing with words and produced ingenious rhymes with the speed and frequency of a conveyor belt. But many were critical, thinking he was wasting his talent on trivia. According to Mayakovsky, however, the advertising verses were a natural part of the work of the poetic laboratory, and the renowned Mosselprom verse was an example of "poetry of the very highest quality." A skeptical reply from Roman Jakobson was parried with the words "You will understand later." And indeed, several extracts from the advertising verses were later integrated into Mayakovsky's "real" poetry.

The advertising copy was in fact a logical continuation of his poster work during the First World War and wartime communism: it was applied poetry. Like these activities too, his advertising work meant a significant contribution to the household budget.

THE MAN FROM CHERNOBYL

In the letter that Lili wrote to Elsa during her separation from Mayakovsky she assured her sister: "I have no love affairs at all. Now that Volodya is no longer here I have more men running after me than ever before. But I am steadfast!"

This was a truth in want of significant modification. A year or so earlier, Lili had become acquainted with a man who met most of her requirements for intelligence, education, style, and—social class. He was Alexander Krasnoshchokov, former head of government in the Far Eastern Republic, a person with a life story which was exceptional even for this exceptional epoch.

Krasnoshchokov was Jewish, and his original name was Avraam Moiseivich Krasnoshchok. He had been born in 1880 in a Ukrainian

Alexander Krasnoshchokov, Lili's lover, 1922–24.

shetl called Chernobyl, which a century later would become known for quite different reasons. His father was a tailor. At the age of sixteen Avraam joined an underground social-democratic group. After being arrested and exiled several times, in 1902 he fled Russia and made his way via Berlin to New York, arriving there the following year. There, he changed his name to Tobinson, after his mother's given name Toiba—"Krasnoshchokov" was too difficult to write and pronounce in English.

To begin with, Tobinson worked as a tailor and painter, but he had higher aims in life and in 1912 he graduated in law and economics from the University of Chicago. During the next few years he worked as a lawyer specialising in trade-union and immigration issues, and he was one of the founders of the Chicago Working Men's Institute, where he lectured in economics and law. When the Left-Wing Section of the American Socialist Party was founded in 1904, he lost no time signing up for it. He was also a member of the American Federation of Labor and the anarcho-syndicalist trade union Industrial Workers of the World (IWW), he knew Joe Hill, the legendary labor agitator, and he wrote articles for the party and trade-union papers in Russian, Yiddish, and English.

After the February revolution, like so many other Russian émigrés he chose to return home. Landing in Vladivostok at the end of July 1917, he immediately joined the Bolshevik Section of the Social Democratic Party. It was not long before full-scale war broke out in the Far East between the Reds and the Whites, supported by foreign interventionary forces. On several occasions Krasnoshchokov avoided death by a hair's breadth, and he soon acquired the status of a hero. In April 1920 he proclaimed the Far Eastern Republic, becoming both leader of the government and foreign minister. In Vladivostok and later—after the city had been captured by Japanese troops—in Chita he came into contact with the "Far Eastern Futurists" Aseyev, Tretyakov, Chuzak, and others, and through them, indirectly, with Mayakovsky, whom he got to know in Moscow in 1921.

Krasnoshchokov was a dynamic and single-minded individual with a view of how the new society should be organized that was quite different from the prevailing opinion in Moscow. As we saw earlier, the Far Eastern Republic consisted not only of Bolsheviks but also of representatives of other parties and tendencies, including anarcho-syndicalists like "Bill" Shatov. In the United States Krasnoshchokov had kept company with another anarchist, Emma Goldman, who was also a Russian émigré. When he was in Moscow in the summer of 1920 to discuss the future of the Far Eastern Republic, he looked up Goldman, who had just been sent back to Soviet Russia by the American authorities. The legendary anarchist drew the following portrait of her colleague from the workers' university and the IWW:

> He had travelled from Siberia in his own railroad car, bringing plenty of provisions and his own cook, and he would give us our first real feast in Soviet Russia. Krasnoshchokov had remained the same free and generous fellow he had been in the States, but we could not alter our plans and we had only a few hours to spend with him. [. . .] Free speech and press prevailed in his part of Russia, he assured me, and there was every opportunity for our propaganda. [. . .] He needed our help and we could count on him. [. . .] "Free speech and free press—how does Moscow stand for that?" I asked. Conditions were different in that far country, Krasnoshchokov explained, and he had been given a free hand there. Anarchists, Left Socialist Revolutionists, and even Mensheviki were co-operating with him and he was proving that free expression and joint effort were giving the best results.

The Far Eastern Republic had been set up by Krasnoshchokov in politically chaotic circumstances in Siberia in the spring of 1920 and had been recognized by both Soviet Russia and Japan. But it lay in Russian territory and existed only by the grace of the Kremlin, and as the civil war calmed down the leadership in Moscow began to worry that the republic would declare independence, which would mean that Russia was deprived of an enormous land area. When Krasnoshchokov's enemies in the government of the Far Eastern Republic accused him of anarcho-syndicalist sympathies and separatist tendencies, it was a charge that the leadership in Moscow was not slow to exploit. Quite independently of the degree of truth in the charge, it is clear that Krasnoshchokov's view of socialism differed from that of the Bolshevik regime, and in the summer of 1921 he was recalled to the capital.

In September he was formally deposed as head of the government of the Far Eastern Republic, which in November of the following year was incorporated into the Russian Federation.

Lenin, who held Krasnoshchokov in high esteem, later regretted that he and the Politburo had removed this "clever, energetic, knowledgeable, and experienced" person who "knows every language" and who had been an "intelligent leader of the Far Eastern Republic, where he organized nearly everything himself." Lenin's high regard for Krasnoshchokov can be seen in the fact that as early as the end of 1921 he appointed him second people's vice-commissar for finances. But in this post, too, Krasnoshchokov encountered opposition, and he only lasted a few months. It was said that he had not wished to understand how the "Soviet system" functioned. Yet his knowledge of economics was so great that his services could not be dispensed with for long, and in November 1922 he became head of the newly founded Industry and Commerce Bank, whose purpose was to provide investment capital for Soviet businesses. A token of his ability and capacity for work is that in 1923 he published a book directly linked to his new work assignment, *Financing and Granting of Credit in Industry*.

Lili probably first met Krasnoshchokov in the summer of 1921, which is when Mayakovsky also got to know him. However, they did not become more closely acquainted until the following summer, when Krasnoshchokov rented a dacha in Pushkino, not far from Mayakovsky and the Briks. At this juncture Krasnoshchokov was forty-two years old, tall and broad shouldered, charming, well read, and cultivated, giving off an aura of adventure and heroism. Moreover, he had power. In August 1922, when Osip and Mayakovsky were about to apply for foreign passports to enable them to travel to Germany, it was Krasnoshchokov that Lili advised them to contact.

She would not have given such a recommendation if she had not been convinced that Krasnoshchokov had the power to help. She was; she knew that if she or someone close to her turned to him, he would do what he could. Mayakovsky knew this too, and he knew why—it must have been with mixed feelings that he asked for help from the person who was the object of Lili's latest passion. His autobiography "I Myself," in which he revealed that he was planning an "enormous poem" about love, was written in Pushkino that very summer.

Suddenly, the love affair between the charismatic politician and Lili, who was equally famed for her own merits, was on everyone's lips. When the confrontation between Mayakovsky and Lili took place in December 1922, it was in the dark shadow of her passion for "The Other Big One," as she called Krasnoshchokov in letters to Rita.

MOSCOW–KÖNIGSBERG

Lili and Krasnoshchokov were one of the most talked-of pairs of lovers in Moscow, and Lili made no secret of the relationship; that would have been against her nature and principles. But if she was not disturbed by the gossip that followed in the wake of the affair, she certainly was worried by the rumors of financial irregularities which were soon being spread about Krasnoshchokov. Given the large sums of money at his disposal in his capacity as head of the Industry Bank and general representative for the Russian-American Industrial Corporation, the charges seemed to many to be quite plausible. In any event, the wide currency given to the rumors bore witness to the fact that Krasnoshchokov had powerful enemies within the party and government apparatus.

Whether or not it was the rumors about Krasnoshchokov that made Mayakovsky, Lili, and Osip leave Moscow on 3 July 1923 is impossible to say. The trip seems to have been planned since at least the beginning of May. But the fact is that, barely six months after their previous visit to Germany, they went there again; this time, for a change, flying from Moscow to Königsberg. For the time, it was an exclusive means of travel, and Mayakovsky would later depict his first-ever flight in the poem "Moscow–Königsberg."

To begin with they spent some time in the southern German spa Bad Flinsberg. Roman Jakobson, who visited them there, remembered that Mayakovsky played cards the whole time and "won money at cards from some sort of rich émigré who had managed to bring a colossal amount of platinum out of Siberia." From there they traveled to the seaside resort of Norderney on one of the Frisian Islands off the North Sea coast of Germany. There they were joined by Viktor

Shklovsky and Elsa from Berlin, and Yelena Yulyevna, who came over from London. She had seen Lili in London the previous year, but it was the first time since her emigration in 1918 that she met both of Lili's men. One may assume that by this time she had accepted their unusual family model, if not exactly with joy, then at least as an unavoidable fact of life.

"He is young, like a sixteen-year-old, and full of high spirits," was Shklovsky's impression of Mayakovsky. During the daytime they swam, caught crabs, and sunbathed. "Mayakovsky played in the sea like a little boy." He had with him a pocket edition of Heine's *Die Nordsee*; he loved Heine and declaimed his poems in a thick Russian accent without really understanding what he was reading. He was himself so taken with the unique beauty of the Frisian sand dunes that after only a few days he wrote a poem, "Norderney," which was printed in *Izvestiya* on 12 August. In the evenings they dined in restaurants. Lili and Elsa, as usual, made good use of the dance floor until late into the night, but with partners other than Shklovsky and Mayakovsky, neither of whom liked dancing.

The photographs from the beaches of Norderney convey the impression of a cloud-free summer idyll, but of course this was not the case. The tensions between the vacationers were too great for that. Shklovsky's roman-à-clef *Zoo* had come off the presses only a few weeks earlier, and the fact that his love for Elsa was now public knowledge could hardly avoid affecting their mood. Moreover, he was still as hopelessly in love with her as she was averse to him. Relations between Mayakovsky and Lili were under a cloud because of her passion for Krasnoshchokov, and Mayakovsky's relationship to Elsa was still strained after the conflict in Berlin the previous autumn. Lili had tried to bring about a reconciliation between them, but according to Elsa it was "a poor sort of peace, for appearance's sake." Although she fell seriously ill immediately after arriving in Norderney, Mayakovsky was ostentatiously indifferent to her.

According to Lunacharsky's letter of recommendation to the Foreign Commissariat with respect to the visit to Germany, "the well-known Communist poet Mayakovsky" was making the trip as

In July 1923, the old friends Lili, Osip, Mayakovsky, and Roman Jakobson met in the German spa resort Bad Flinsberg.

Norderney, summer 1923. Mayakovsky and Lili with Yelena Yulyevna and Raisa Kushner, wife of the Lef member Boris Kushner.

a representative of the People's Commissariat of Enlightenment: "The aims of his trip to Germany have the full support of the commissariat. They are also motivated by the ambition to enhance our cultural status abroad." As Soviet citizens, especially those with a reputation like Mayakovsky's, often had "disagreeable experiences of various kinds" abroad, Lunacharsky asked the Soviet Foreign Office to supply Mayakovsky with an official passport. Lili and Osip were also presumably provided with similar documents.

Mayakovsky's position within Soviet literature was so unique at this time that he was regarded almost as a natural resource, at least by Lunacharsky. But what were the actual aims of his trip? He spent at least seven of his ten weeks in Germany relaxing in spas and seaside resorts. He gave only one poetry recital (in Berlin) and seems to have written only two poems—"Norderney" and "Moscow–

Königsberg"—which moreover had little propaganda value in the West, as they were in Russian.

Was it really in order to strike a blow for Soviet culture that Mayakovsky traveled to Berlin? Or was it the case that foreign trips had become a necessity for him, a sort of breathing space? There is a good deal of evidence for that. "I need to travel," he explained. "The company of living creatures is almost more important to me than reading books." On 15 September, the same day on which he left Berlin, he sent a letter to David Burlyuk in New York. He would very much like to come and see him "in two or three months," if only Burlyuk could arrange an American entry visa for him. "Today I'm going to Moscow for three months," he wrote—which points to the fact that his next foreign trip was already planned, whether to America or not.

A SHOW-TRIAL

Mayakovsky returned to Moscow on 17 or 18 September. The following day, Krasnoshchokov was arrested, accused of a number of different offenses. He was supposed to have lent money to his brother Yakov, head of the firm American-Russian Constructor, at too low a rate of interest, and to have arranged drink- and sex-fueled orgies at the Hotel Europe in Petrograd, paying the Gypsy girls who entertained the company with pure gold. He was also accused of having passed on his salary from the Russian-American Industrial Corporation ($200 a month) to his wife (who had returned to the United States), of having bought his mistress flowers and furs out of state funds, of renting a luxury villa, and of keeping no fewer than three horses. Lenin was now so ill that he had not been able to intervene on Krasnoshchokov's behalf even if he had wanted to.

His arrest was a sensation of the first order. It was the first time that such a highly placed Communist had been accused of corruption, and the event cast a shadow over the whole party apparatus. Immediately after Krasnoshchokov's arrest, and in order to prevent undesired interpretations of what had happened, Valerian Kuybyshev, the commissar for Workers' and Peasants' Inspection, let it be known that "incontrovertible facts have come to light which show Krasnoshchokov has in a criminal manner exploited the resources of the economics department [of the Industry Bank] for his own use, that he has arranged wild orgies with these funds, and that he has used bank funds to enrich his relatives, etc." He had, it was claimed, "in a criminal manner betrayed the trust placed in him and must be sentenced to a severe punishment."

Krasnoshchokov was, in other words, judged in advance. There was no question of any objective legal process; the intention was to set an example: "The Soviet power and the Communist Party will [. . .] root out with an iron hand all sick manifestations of the NEP and remind those who 'let themselves be tempted' by the joys of capitalism that they live in a workers' state run by a Communist party." Krasnoshchokov's arrest was deemed so important that Kuybyshev's statement was printed simultaneously in the party organ *Pravda* and the government organ *Izvestiya*. Kuybyshev was a close friend of the prosecutor Nikolay Krylenko, who had led the prosecution of the Socialist Revolutionaries the previous year, and who in time would turn show trials and false charges into an art form.

When Krasnoshchokov was arrested, Lili and Osip were still in Berlin. In the letter that Mayakovsky wrote to them a few days after the arrest, the sensational news is passed over in total silence. He gives them the name of the civil servant in the Berlin legation who can give them permission to import household effects (which they had obviously bought in Berlin) into Russia; he tells them that the squirrel which lives with them is still alive and that Lyova Grinkrug is in the Crimea. The only news item of greater significance is that he has been at Lunacharsky's to discuss *Lef* and is going to visit Trotsky on the same mission. But of the event which the whole of Moscow was talking about, and which affected Lili to the utmost degree—not a word.

Krasnoshchokov's trial took place at the beginning of March 1924. Sitting in the dock, apart from his brother Yakov, were three employees of the Industry Bank. Krasnoshchokov, who was a lawyer, delivered a brilliant speech in his own defense, explaining that, as head of the bank, he had the right to fix lending rates in individual cases and that one must be flexible in order to obtain the desired result. As for the charges of immoral behavior he maintained that his work necessitated a certain degree of official entertainment and that the "luxury villa" in the suburb of Kuntsevo was an abandoned dacha which in addition was his sole permanent dwelling. (It is one of the ironies of history that the house had been owned before the Revolution by the Shekhtel family and accordingly had often had Mayakovsky as a guest—see the chapter "Volodya"). Finally, he pointed out that his private life was not within the jurisdiction of the law.

This opinion was not shared by the court, which ruled that Krasnoshchokov had lived an immoral life during a time when a Communist ought to have set a good example and not surrender to the temptations offered by the New Economic Policy. Krasnoshchokov was also guilty of having used his position to "encourage his relatives' private business transactions" and having caused the bank to lose 10,000 gold rubles. He was sentenced to six years' imprisonment and in addition three years' deprivation of citizen's rights. Moreover, he was excluded from the Communist Party. His brother was given three years' imprisonment, while the other three coworkers received shorter sentences.

Krasnoshchokov had in fact been a very successful bank director. Between January 1923 and his arrest in September he had managed to increase the Industry Bank's capital tenfold, partly thanks to a flexible interest policy which led to large American investments in Russia. There is a good deal of evidence that the charges against him were initiated by persons within the Finance Commissariat and the Industry Bank's competitor, the Soviet National Bank. Shortly before his arrest Krasnoshchokov had suggested that the Industry Bank should take over all the National Bank's industrial-financial operations. Exactly the opposite happened: after Krasnoshchokov's verdict was announced, the Industry Bank was subordinated to the Soviet National Bank.

There is little to suggest that the accusations of orgies were true. Krasnoshchokov was not known to be a rake, and his "entertainment expenses" were hardly greater than those of other highly placed functionaries. But he had difficulties defending himself, as he maintained not one mistress but two—although he had a wife and children. The woman who figured in the trial was not, as one might have expected, Lili, but a certain Donna Gruz—Krasnoshchokov's secretary, who six years later would become his second wife. This

When Lili and Elsa showed Nadezhda Lamanova's dresses in Paris in the winter of 1924, it attracted the attention of both the French and the British press, where this photograph was published with the caption "SOVIET SACK FASHION.—Because of the lack of textiles in Soviet Russia, Mme. Lamanoff, a Moscow fashion designer, had this dress made out of sackcloth from freight bales."

fact undoubtedly undermined his credibility as far as his private life was concerned.

By the time the judgment was announced, Lili had been in Paris for three weeks. She was there for her own amusement and does not seem to have had any particular tasks to fulfill. But she had with her dresses by the Soviet couturier Nadezhda Lamanova which she and Elsa showed off at two soirees organized by a Paris newspaper. She would like to go to Nice, she confided in a letter home to Moscow on 23 February, but her plans were frustrated by the fact that Russian emigrants were holding a congress there. She was thinking of traveling to Spain instead, or somewhere else in France, to "bake in the sun for a week or so." But she remained in Paris, where she and Elsa went out dancing the whole time. Their "more or less regular cavaliers" were Fernand Léger (whom Mayakovsky had got to know in Paris in 1922) and an acquaintance from London who took them everywhere with him, "from the most chic of places to the worst of dives." "It has been nothing but partying here," she wrote. "Elsa has instituted a notebook in which she writes down all our rendezvous ten days in advance!" As clothes are expensive in Paris too, she asks Osip and Mayakovsky to send her a little money in the event of their managing to win "some mad sum of money" at cards.

When she was writing this letter, there were still two weeks to

Circular 795 from the British Home Office preventing Mayakovsky from entering British territory.

SECRET.   B. 795/H.O. (17a)

9th February, 1923.

DECARDED
Vladimir MAYAKOVSKY.
30 JUN 1960

Born in Bagdady on 7/6/1894.

In 1907 became a member of the Bolshevist faction of the Russian Social Democratic Party (now re-christened Communist Party). Under the *nom-de-guerre* "Comrade Constantine" took part in active revolutionary propaganda among the Moscow workers. Was elected member of Moscow Committee of Bolshevist party (in 1907) together with LOMOFF, SMIDOVICH, etc. Later was arrested and imprisoned by the Russian Imperial police. Was set free in a few months, re-arrested and served 11 months in Bytirki prison in Moscow. Began to write poetry, became Russia's first futurist poet. During war took active part in definite propaganda, together with MAXIM GORKI, etc.

When Bolshevists came to power in October, 1917, immediately offered his services to Proletcult for propaganda work.

In 1919 became one of the principal leaders of the "Communist" propaganda and agitation section of the "Rosta" (Russian Telegraph Agency) In 1921 began to write for Moscow Iszvestia, chiefly unsigned propaganda articles.

He should not be given a visa or be allowed to land in the United Kingdom : all British Overseas Countries also warned accordingly.

W. HALDANE PORTER,
H.M. Chief Inspector, Aliens Branch, Home Office.

Home Office Ports.
Scotland House.
Passport Control for all Controls and Consuls
Military Controls.
India Office.

MAYAKOVSKY, | 23 | M. | Ru | Commu- | Bol. | RD. | B. 795
VLADIMIR | | | | nist

go before Krasnoshchokov's trial. "How is A[lexander] M[ikhai-lovich]?" she asked, in the middle of reporting on the fun she was having. But she did not receive a reply, or if she did, it has not been preserved. On 26 March, after a month in Paris, she took the boat to England to visit her mother, who was in poor health, but that same evening she was forced to return to Calais after being stopped at passport control in Dover—despite having a British visa issued in Moscow in June 1923. What she did not know was that after her first visit to England in October 1922 she had been declared persona non grata, something which all British passport control points "for Europe and New York" had been informed of in a secret circular of 13 February 1923.

"You can't imagine how humiliating it was to be turned back at the British border," she wrote to Mayakovsky: "I have all sorts of theories about it, which I'll tell you about when we I see you. Strange as it may seem, I think they didn't let me in because of you." She guessed right: documents from the Home Office show that it was her relationship with Mayakovsky, who wrote "extremely libellous articles" in *Izvestiya*, which had proved her undoing. Strangely enough, despite being refused entry to Britain, she was able to travel to London three weeks later. The British passport authorities have no record of her entry to the country. Did she come in by an illegal route?

At the same time that Lili traveled to Paris, Mayakovsky set out on a recital tour in Ukraine. Recitals were an important source of income for him. During his stay in Odessa he mentioned in a newspaper interview that he was planning to set out soon on a trip round the world, as he had been invited to give lectures and read poems in the United States. Two weeks later he was back in Moscow, and in the middle of April he went to Berlin, where Lili joined him about a week later. According to one newspaper, Mayakovsky was in the German capital "on his way to America."

The round-the-world trip did not come off, as Mayakovsky failed to obtain the necessary visas. It was not possible to request an American visa in Moscow, as the two countries lacked diplomatic ties. Mayakovsky's plan was therefore to try to get into the United States via a third country. Britain's first Labour government, under Ramsay MacDonald, had scarcely recognized the Soviet Union (on

1 February 1924) before Mayakovsky requested a British visa, on 25 March. From England he planned to continue his journey to Canada and India. In a letter to Ramsay MacDonald, Britain's chargé d'affaires in Moscow asked for advice about the visa application. Mayakovsky was not known to the mission, he wrote, but was "a member of the Communist party and, I am told, is known as a Bolshevik propagandist." Mr. Hodgson would not have needed to do this if he had known that on 9 February, the Home Office had also issued a secret circular about Mayakovsky, "one of the principal leaders of the 'Communist' propaganda and agitation section of the 'ROSTA,'" who since 1921 had been writing propaganda articles for *Izvestiya* and "should not be given a visa or be allowed to land in the United Kingdom" or any of its colonies. In Mayakovsky's case the circular was sent to every British port, consulate, and passport and military checkpoint, as well as to Scotland House and the India Office. But in the very place where people really ought to have known about it, His Majesty's diplomatic mission in Moscow, they were completely unaware of it.

While he waited for an answer from the British, Mayakovsky made a couple of appearances in Berlin where he talked about Lef and recited his poems. On the 9 May he traveled back to Moscow in company with Lili and Scotty, the Scotch terrier she had picked up in England, tired of waiting for notification that never came. When he got to Moscow he found out that on 5 May London had instructed the British mission in Moscow to turn down his visa application.

VLADIMIR ILYICH

The preliminary investigation and subsequent trial of Krasnoshchokov caused a great stir, but it would certainly have got even more column inches if it had not been played out in the shadow of a significantly more important event. On 21 January 1924, Vladimir Lenin died after several years of illness.

Among the thousands of people jostling one another in the queues which snaked around in front of Trade Unions House, where the leader of the Revolution lay in state, were Mayakovsky, Lili, and Osip. Lenin's death affected Mayakovsky deeply. "It was a terrible

morning when he died," Lili recalled. "We wept in the queue in Red Square where we were standing in the freezing cold to see him. Mayakovsky had a press card, so we were able to bypass the queue. I think he viewed the body ten times. We were all deeply shaken."

The feelings awakened by Lenin's death were deep and genuine, and not only for his political supporters. Among those queuing were Boris Pasternak and Osip Mandelstam, who shared a far more lukewarm attitude to the Revolution and its leader. "Lenin dead in Moscow!" exclaimed Mandelstam in his coverage of the event. "How can one fail to be with Moscow in this hour! Who does not want to see that dear face, the face of Russia itself? The time? Two, three, four? How long will we stand here? No one knows. The time is past. We stand in a wonderful nocturnal forest of people. And thousands of children with us."

Shortly after Lenin's death Mayakovsky tackled his most ambitious project to date: a long poem about the Communist leader. He had written about him before, in connection with his fiftieth birthday in 1920 ("Vladimir Ilyich!"), and when Lenin suffered his first stroke in the winter of 1923 ("We Don't Believe It!"), but those were shorter poems. According to Mayakovsky himself, he began pondering a poem about Lenin as early as 1923, but that may well have been a rationalization after the event. What set his pen in motion was in any case Lenin's death in January 1924.

Mayakovsky had only a superficial knowledge of Lenin's life and work and was forced to read up on him before he could write about him. His mentor, as on so many other occasions, was Osip, who supplied him with books and gave him a crash course in *Leniniana*. Mayakovsky himself had neither the time nor the patience for such projects. The poem was written during the summer and was ready by the beginning of October 1924. It was given the title "Vladimir Ilyich Lenin" and was the longest poem Mayakovsky ever wrote; at three thousand lines, it was almost twice as long as "About This." In

Mayakovsky with Scotty, whom Lili bought in England. The picture was taken in the summer of 1924 at the dacha in Pushkino. Scotty loved ice cream, and, according to Rodchenko, Mayakovsky regarded "with great tenderness how Scotty ate and licked his mouth." "He took him in his arms and I photographed them in the garden," the photographer remembered. "I took two pictures. Volodya kept his tender smile, wholly directed at Scotty." The photograph with Scotty is in fact one of the few where Mayakovsky can be seen smiling.

The line to the Trade Unions' House in Moscow, where Lenin was lying in state.

the autumn of 1924 he gave several poetry readings and fragments of the poem were printed in various newspapers. It came out in book form in February 1925.

So the lyrical "About This" was followed by an epic poem, in accordance with the conscious or unconscious scheme that directed the rhythm of Mayakovsky's writing. If even a propaganda poem like "To the Workers in Kursk" was dedicated to Lili, such a dedication was impossible in this case. "Vladimir Ilyich Lenin" was dedicated to the Russian Communist Party, and Mayakovsky explains why, with a subtle but unambiguous reference to "About This":

> I can write
>> about this,
>>> about that,
> but now
>> is not the time
>>> for love-drivel.
> All my
>> resounding power
>>> as a poet

I
    give to you,
        attacking class.

In "Vladimir Ilyich Lenin" Lenin is portrayed as a Messiah-like fig-
ure, whose appearance on the historical scene is an inevitable con-
sequence of the emergence of the working class. Karl Marx revealed
the laws of history and, with his theories, "helped the working class
to its feet." But Marx was only a theoretician, who in the fullness
of time would be replaced by someone who could turn theory into
practice, that is, Lenin.

The poem is uneven, which is not surprising considering the for-
mat. From a linguistic point of view—the rhyme, the neologisms—it
is undoubtedly comparable to the best of Mayakovsky's other works,
and the depiction of the sorrow and loss after Lenin's death is no less
than a magnificent requiem. But the epic, historical sections are too
long and prolix. The same is true of the tributes to the Communist
Party, which often rattle with empty rhetoric (which in turn can pos-
sibly be explained by the fact that Mayakovsky was never a member
of the party):

I want
    once more to make the majestic word
        "PARTY"
            shine.
One individual!
    Who needs that?!
The voice of an individual
    is thinner than a cheep.
Who hears it—
    except perhaps his wife?
   . . .
The party
    is a hand with millions of fingers
clenched
    into a single destroying fist.
The individual is rubbish,

the individual is zero . . .
We say Lenin,
        but mean
                The Party.
We say
    The Party,
        but mean Lenin.

One of the few reviewers who paid any attention to the poem, the proletarian critic and anti-Futurist G. Lelevich, was quite right in pointing out that Mayakovsky's "ultraindividualistic" lines in "About This" stand out as "uniquely honest" in comparison with "Vladimir Ilyich Lenin," which "with few exceptions is *rationalistic* and *rhetorical.*" This was a "tragic fact" that Mayakovsky could only do something about by trying to "conquer himself." The Lenin poem, wrote Lelevich, was a "flawed but meaningful and fruitful attempt to tread this path."

Lelevich was right to claim that "About This" is a much more convincing poem than the ode to Lenin. But the "tragic" thing was not what Lelevich perceived as such, but something quite different, namely, Mayakovsky's denial of the individual and his importance. In order to "conquer" himself, that is, the lyrical impulse within himself, he would have to take yet more steps in that direction which he would in fact do, although it went against his innermost being.

If there is anything of lasting value in "Vladimir Ilyich Lenin," it is not the paeans of praise to Lenin and the Communist Party—poems of homage are seldom good—but the warnings that Lenin, after his death, will be turned into an icon. The Lenin to whom Mayakovsky pays tribute was born in the Russian provinces as "a normal, simple boy" and grew up to be the "most human of all human beings." If he had been "king-like and god-like" Mayakovsky would without a doubt have protested and taken a stance "opposed to all processions and tributes":

I ought
    to have found words
            for lightning-flashing curses,
    and while

                    I
          and my yell
                    were trampled underfoot
    I should have
          hurled blasphemies
                    against heaven
    and tossed
          like bombs at the Kremlin
                    my: NO!

The worst thing Mayakovsky can imagine is that Lenin, like Marx, will become a "cooling plaster dotard imprisoned in marble." This is a reference back to "The Fourth International," in which Lenin is depicted as a petrified monument.

    I am worried that
                    processions
                              and mausoleums,
          celebratory statues
                    set in stone,
    will drench
          Leninist simplicity
    in syrup-smooth balsam—

Mayakovsky warns, clearly blind to the fact that he himself is contributing to this development with his seventy-five-page long poem.

The fear that Lenin would be canonized after his death was deeply felt—and well grounded. It did not take long before Gosizdat (!) began advertising busts of the leader in plaster, bronze, granite, and marble, "life-size and double life-size." The busts were produced from an original by the sculptor Merkurov—whom Mayakovsky had apostrophized in his Kursk poem—and with the permission of the Committee for the Perpetuation of the Memory of V. I. Lenin. The target groups were civil-service departments, party organizations and trade unions, cooperatives, and the like.

The Lef members' tribute to the dead leader was of a different nature. The theory section in the first issue of *Lef* for 1924 was devoted

After his return from Berlin in May 1924, Mayakovsky met with the Japanese author Tamisi Naito, who was visiting Moscow. Seated at the table next to Mayakovsky and Lili is Sergey Tretyakov's wife, Olga. To left of Naito (standing in the center) are Sergey Eisenstein and Boris Pasternak.

to Lenin's language, with contributions by leading Formalists such as Viktor Shklovsky, Boris Eikhenbaum, Boris Tomashevsky, and Yury Tynyanov—groundbreaking attempts to analyze political language by means of structuralist methods. Lenin was said to have "decanonized" the language, "cut down the inflated style," and so on, all in the name of linguistic efficiency. This striving for powerful simplicity was in line with the theoretical ambitions of the Lef writers but stood in stark contrast to the canonization of Lenin which was set in train by his successors as soon as his corpse was cold.

This entire issue of *Lef* was in actual fact a polemic against this development—indirectly, in the essays about Lenin's language, and in a more undisguised way in the leader article. In a direct reference to the advertisements for Lenin busts, the editorial team at *Lef* in their manifesto "Don't Trade in Lenin!" sent the following exhortation to the authorities:

We insist:

Don't make matrices out of Lenin.

Don't print his portrait on posters, oilcloths, plates, drinking vessels, cigarette boxes.

Don't turn Lenin into bronze.

Don't take from him his living gait and human physiognomy, which he managed to preserve at the same time as he led history.

Lenin is still our present.

He is among the living.

We need him living, not dead.

Therefore:

Learn from Lenin, but don't canonize him.

Don't create a cult around a man who fought against all kinds of cults throughout his life.

Don't peddle artifacts of this cult.

Don't trade in Lenin.

In view of the extravagant cult of Lenin that would develop later in the Soviet Union, the text is insightful to the point of clairvoyance. But the readers of *Lef* were never to see it. According to the list of contents, the issue began on page 3 with the leader "Don't Trade in Lenin!" But in the copies that were distributed, this page is missing and the pagination begins instead on page 5. The leadership of Gosizdat, which distributed *Lef*, had been incensed by the criticism of the advertisements for Lenin busts and had removed the leader. As if by some miracle, it has been preserved in a few complimentary copies which made it to the libraries before the censor's axe fell.

STRETCHED OUT LIKE JEALOUSY'S SKIN
THE BEAR CLAWS THE PARQUET

That the theme of statues became of topical concern to Mayakovsky at just this point in time was not solely because of Lenin's death. The question also had a personal dimension. At the age of thirty he was indisputably the most successful Soviet poet. Among his contemporaries were Boris Pasternak and Sergey Yesenin, Osip Mandelstam and Anna Akhmatova, all of them distinguished poets. In this company he was perhaps not the leading light, but he was undoubtedly one of the best, and unlike the others he had actively placed himself on the side of the new social order. The leading representatives of the Soviet state had in their turn showered their blessings on him: not just Lenin and Lunacharsky, but also Leon Trotsky, the commissar for war, who had hailed Mayakovsky as a "colossal talent" who had "taken the Revolution on board in a more natural way than any other Russian poet." So the risk that Mayakovsky himself might be turned into a monument was not insignificant.

In the spring of 1924, at the same time as Mayakovsky was beginning to plan the Lenin poem, he was working on another poem on the theme of monuments and jubilees. The 125th anniversary of the birth of Alexander Pushkin was celebrated on 6 June 1924—an event which gave Mayakovsky an excuse to reflect on Russia's national poet.

If Mayakovsky himself was quite clear about his attitude to Pushkin, outsiders had good reason to be puzzled. In December 1918, in his poem "Too Early to Rejoice," he had turned against his fellow poet with the words "But why not attack Pushkin? / And other classic generals?" These lines incensed Lunacharsky, who believed that such contempt for the classics was not in the interests of the working class. Instead of automatically dismissing the great writers of the past, one ought to learn from them. Mayakovsky defended himself by saying that it was not Pushkin the poet he was opposed to, but rather Pushkin the *monument*, and that it was not the older literature in itself that he and the Futurists attacked but the fact that it was held up as a model for modern literature. Besides, he stressed, his words should not be interpreted literally.

In actual fact, Mayakovsky loved Pushkin. During his work on the poem "Yubileynoe," which was written for the 125th anniversary, Osip read *Eugene Onegin* aloud to him, and although Mayakovsky already knew the whole long verse novel by heart, he disconnected the telephone so as not to be disturbed. However, in the aesthetic atmosphere created by the Revolution and encouraged by the Lef group themselves, to openly declare one's love for Pushkin was not without its complications. In order to justify his positive attitude to the poet, Mayakovsky had to make him into a colleague and comrade-in-arms, a fellow member of Lef. Pushkin was therefore said to have waged the same battle to renew the language of poetry in the 1820s as Mayakovsky was doing a hundred years later, and if he had been living now, Mayakovsky would have made him a fellow editor of *Lef* and had him write both propaganda poems and advertising slogans.

This was an idea that the literary theoretician and "Young Formalist" Yury Tynyanov picked up on in an essay on contemporary literature, "A Transitional Period," written in the same year, 1924. He saw Mayakovsky's advertising slogans as a necessary linguistic laboratory exercise which had a direct counterpart in Pushkin's experiments in "low genres," like, for example, verses in a poetry album.

The title "Yubileynoe" is ironic—it can perhaps be translated as "Jubilees"—and reflects Mayakovsky's attitude to such celebrations. The poem is in the form of a conversation with Pushkin, whom Mayakovsky pulls down from his plinth in Tver Boulevard in Moscow so he can have a chat with him: "Like you / I too have / eternity before me. / What odds does it make, then / if we lose / an hour or two?" It then develops along two main threads. One of them deals with the danger of becoming a monument, a fate which has befallen Pushkin and which threatens to affect Mayakovsky himself:

Perhaps
   I am
      the only one
             who is really sorry
that you are not
      alive among us today.
I
   would like
      to know you
         here in life.
Soon
   I shall also die
      and become silent.

> After death
> > we shall
> > > almost stand side by side:
> you at P
> > and I
> > at M.

Mayakovsky loves Pushkin "living / and not mummified," as a poet who also like himself lived a stormy life before he "became hard-backed / and anthology-lacquered." When he finally sets Pushkin back on his plinth, it is with an invocation:

> According to precedence
> > I ought
> > > already, here in life, to have a statue—
> I would
> > stuff it full
> > > of dynamite and blow it up!
> For all kinds of dead meat
> > I feel disgust!
> I worship
> > all that is life!

The other main thread concerns the ever-topical opposition between the lyric poet and the poet of social criticism. "To dream is dangerous," Mayakovsky writes, "and equally pointless are imaginary visions," when there are "masses of workaday tasks / that need / to be done"—

> But it can't be helped
> > that rhyme's gills
> > > sometimes flap on those of us
> who keep house
> > on the sandy strands of poetry.

The Futurists have "time and again attacked the lyric with their bayonets" in the hunt for "a language / which is exact and naked"—

But poetry
> is a crafty piece of devilry:
it's simply there—
>> not much we can do about it.

Lyric poetry exists because love exists—even in the new society, despite all its ascetic ideals:

They say
that I am thematically I-n-d-i-v-i-d-u-a-l!
Entre nous . . .
> so that the censor doesn't delete it,
let me tell you:
> they even
>> say
that someone saw
> two lovesick members
>> of the Executive Committee.

The tone is ironic, but Mayakovsky's reflections on love and poetry had an impeccably concrete background. A year or so after the separation which generated "About This," in the spring of 1924, the relationship with Lili had undergone a new crisis, more grave than any previous one. Her affair with Krasnoshchokov was so serious that she made up her mind to break off with Mayakovsky. As she found it hard to tell him face to face—"it's too difficult to talk"—he was told in writing. "You promised me that when I told you, you wouldn't make a fuss. I don't love you any more. I get the feeling that you also love me a lot less and won't be tormented." As Mayakovsky later remarked that the terrier Scotty was the last thing that he and Lili "did together," the rift can be dated to their stay in Berlin at the beginning of May.

The relationship between Lili and Mayakovsky was established and well known, and her affair with Krasnoshchokov was one of the most discussed in Moscow. Therefore, one did not have to be overly perceptive to grasp the background to the following lines in "Jubilees," with its direct references to "About This":

I
am
now
free
from love
and posters.
Stretched out like jealousy's skin
the bear lies
and claws the parquet.
. . .
So much has happened:
the waiting under a window,
letters,
a quivering jelly of nerves.

Pushkin had died in a duel with his wife's lover, Baron d'Anthès. In the poem he is compared to Lili's latest suitor, whose name contemporary readers had no difficulty making out:

Nor
today
do we suffer from a lack of
seductive types
who chase
our wives.

The rift between Lili and Mayakovsky caused a sensation in wide circles and shook their closest friends. "NB! Lili has left Mayakovsky," reported Shklovsky—who at this point had been repatriated to his native land—to Roman Jakobson in Prague. "She is in love with (has snared) Krasnoshchokov. Don't say anything to Elsa, if you have any contact with her at all."

Why did Shklovsky not want Elsa to find out that Lili had broken up with Mayakovsky? Because she might be sorry or upset? Because Mayakovsky and Elsa still had feelings for each other and the news might inspire vain hopes of winning him back? Or because he thought that it might be possible to repair the relationship again, as had happened so often before, and that it would be foolish to trouble Elsa for nothing?

Shklovsky had good reason for his caution. Lili had broken up with Mayakovsky, but this did not mean the end of their life together— even if nothing would be the same again.

10

AMERICA

1925

**We kiss
your long-legged women
—illicitly!—
on Hudson's shore.**
Vladimir Mayakovsky, "A Challenge," 1925

Mayakovsky loved Lili just as much as ever and was devastated that she had rejected him. As early as the end of May, after only a few weeks in Moscow, he asked Lunacharsky for a letter of recommendation to the Soviet overseas legations, which seems to indicate that he was planning a trip abroad again in the near future in order to escape from his grief. However, the trip did not come off. The summer was spent as usual at Pushkino, but in contrast to previous years Mayakovsky only went out there on the weekends—he spent the weekdays in his room in Lubyanka Passage.

This was Krasnoshchokov's first summer in custody. The Lefortovo prison, which according to a Cheka report was notorious for its dirt, dampness, stench, and bad air, was the worst conceivable environment for someone with Krasnoshchokov's weak lungs. After his

A well-tailored Mayakovsky visiting New York.

request for a transfer to another prison was turned down, he managed instead to obtain permission to work in his cell. He translated Walt Whitman into Russian and wrote a book, *The Modern American Banking System*, which was finished in November 1924. When it appeared two years later Krasnoshchokov explained in the foreword that the delay was because of "circumstances beyond my control." The place where the book was written was indicated with the initials L. I, an abbreviation which most people had no problem deciphering as "Lefortovo. Izolyator—solitary confinement wing."

Lili visited him as often as she could, equipped with food parcels and books. Her concern for Krasnoshchokov also led her to take responsibility for his fourteen-year-old daughter, who moved into the dacha in Pushkino. Alexander Mikhaylovich was married with two children, Luella and Yevgeny, born in Chicago in 1910 and 1914, respectively. Luella was called after Llewelyn Park in New Jersey, where her parents liked to walk. During their first few years in Russia the family had lived together, but in December 1922 Krasnoshchokov's wife, Gertrud, a Polish Jew, returned to the United States with her son while Luella, at her own request, stayed behind with her father in Moscow. It does not take much imagination to realize what made Krasnoshchokov's wife leave the Soviet Union.

During one of their first days in Pushkino Lili said to Luella: "They'll tell you that I kiss men in every doorway. Don't believe them, get to know me instead." Lili gave Luella two lots of her own underclothes and sewed dresses for her herself—simple, sack-like lengths of material without sleeves and with a deep décolletage, in accordance with the utilitarian aesthetics of the time. During the daytime they sunbathed naked on the grass. "Lili became very sunburned and was as dark as a Negro," Luella recalled. "It was a kind of sport—we competed to see who could get brownest."

In the evenings they played chess or dominoes or sang, all except Mayakovsky, who was not only unmusical but also completely indifferent to music. When he came on a visit he would bring seven chocolate bars for Luella, one for each day of the week.

At the end of August Mayakovsky went off on a month-long reading tour in southern Russia and the Caucasus. Clearly he wanted to get away from Moscow and from a relationship that was not over, but

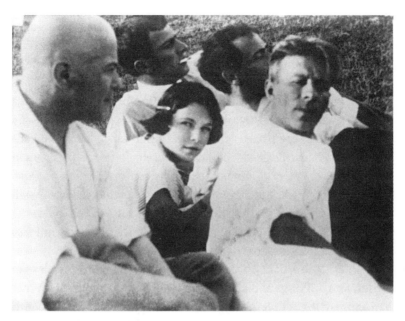

Luella Krasnoshchokova in Pushkino with Viktor Shklovsky, Mayakovsky, Nikolay Aseyev, and, partly hidden, Boris Kushner. Photograph by Alexander Rodchenko in 1924.

the parameters of which had fundamentally altered. He needed time to ponder the new situation. When he came back, Lili and Luella had moved from Pushkino to a dacha warm enough to stay there during the winter. The house was in the suburb of Sokolniki, far from the center of Moscow, but near Luella's school and the prison in which Krasnoshchokov was incarcerated.

If the choice of location was decided by this consideration, the actual move was motivated by other factors. Mayakovsky had his room in Lubyanka Passage and in addition was registered in the apartment in Vodopyany Lane. But there was a serious housing shortage in Moscow, and to be registered at two addresses simultaneously was regarded as an impermissible luxury. The authorities therefore wanted to deprive Mayakovsky of one of his rooms. (Boris Pasternak was also threatened at this time with being evicted from the apartment in which he lived with his family.) Although he took the matter to court, the result was that he was forced to give up the room in Vodopyany Lane. Since the apartment also served as the editorial office and committee room for Lef, it was impossible for Lili and Osip to go on living there under such conditions. However, by making the housekeeper Annushka Osip's secretary and enrolling her in the Writers' Union, they managed to hold on to one of the rooms in Vodopyany Lane.

In Sokolniki they rented the whole of the lower flat, which consisted of a large dining room, two small rooms for Lili and Osip, and a room so small that there was only room for a bed. When Mayakovsky came to visit, he spent the night in the dining room, which conveniently enough also boasted a billiard table. He preferred the room in Lubyanka Passage, not only because of its central location but also because there he was not constantly reminded of the reason why Lili had broken off their relationship.

But was it really a question of a *breakup*? Their letters from this time contain the same tokens of tenderness as before. "My own dear and sweet little whale, I miss you terribly terribly," Mayakovsky writes, and Lili hugs and kisses him in her answering letters. What had happened was that Lili no longer saw Mayakovsky as "husband" or "lover" but as a beloved friend—and a poet whom she sincerely admired. To break off with him completely would be to destroy a life which they had built up together with Osip over many years and whose main ingredient was not physical love but shared ideals and interests. If Mayakovsky wished to be part of this life, he now had to get used to the fact that the situation had regressed to something reminiscent of the period before 1918.

WORLD TOUR PLANS

Mayakovsky had only been back in Moscow for about a month before he went abroad again. On 24 October he headed for Paris, via Riga and Berlin. The day before his departure he received a message from Lili where she expressed the hope that they would see each other soon, perhaps in America. Their changed relationship obviously did not preclude them from traveling together. That was an important signal to Mayakovsky. On the same day Lunacharsky, Mayakovsky's eternal guardian angel, wrote a letter to the finance department of the Economic Council in which he asked that the poet be allowed to keep his room in Lubyanka Passage during his trip abroad. The threat of eviction hung over Mayakovsky the whole time.

When Mayakovsky reached Paris on 2 November, he was not met as usual by Elsa, as his telegram had not arrived in time. He was therefore obliged, with the help of his nonexistent French, to take a cab from the station to the little Hôtel Istria in Montparnasse where Elsa had been living since her return from Berlin earlier that year. "Inside, it reminds you of a tower," Elsa recalled. "A narrow stairwell with a narrow set of stairs, five landings without corridors, around each landing five separate doors, and behind each door a little room. All the rooms have striped carpets, in each room there is a double bed, a bedside table, a little occasional table, two chairs, a cupboard with mirror, a washstand with hot water, and on the floor, a small yellow and worn patterned rug."

The room was indeed very small. "Vladimir Mayakovsky is the greatest Russian poet of the present day," noted a young Russian émigré writer, Vladimir Pozner, who called on him at the hotel on behalf of the magazine *Le journal littéraire*. "He is so tall that even when he's seated you feel like asking him to sit down." It was so cramped that there was not room for the poet and his shoes in the room at the same time, the awestruck Pozner reported with a degree of exaggeration. "They stood outside the door, and in order to let me in Mayakovsky was forced to lie on the bed." When the interview was over, Pozner left Mayakovsky "enveloped in clouds like an Olympic god": "I had never seen him take or light a cigarette, they appeared by themselves in the corner of his mouth." Once outside the room, Pozner knelt down to examine Mayakovsky's shoes and managed to ascertain, with a mixture of horror and admiration, that they were size 46.

Mayakovsky himself described the room as follows in the poem "Verlaine and Cézanne":

> I bump into
> the table,
> against the edge of the cupboard—
> measure out four meters for myself each day.
> I'm short of space here
> in the hotel Istria—
> at the fag-end
> of rue Campagne Première.

Mayakovsky's room was on the same landing as Elsa's, and he became so fond of the Istria that he chose to live there during all his future visits to Paris. Several well-known artists put up there in those years, among them Francis Picabia, Marcel Duchamp and Man Ray, as well as the famous model Kiki. Montparnasse was full of artists' studios, and moreover it was near the cafés of the Boulevard Montparnasse— the Rotonde, the Select, the Dôme, and, from 1927, La Coupole— where artists and writers met.

But in the autumn of 1924 Paris was only a halfway house. The plan was that from here, Mayakovsky would make yet another attempt to start his world tour. He was not allowed to enter Canada, that he knew, and the United States had not yet established diplomatic relations with the Soviet Union. The French too were on their guard against someone they saw as a Bolshevik agitator, and they wanted Mayakovsky expelled from their country. Nevertheless, he managed to have his residence permit extended and spent a month and a half in Paris doing—very little. "I'm terribly tired and I'm consciously giving myself 2 or 3 weeks rest—and then I'll write for everywhere at once," he explained in a letter to Lili. He was indeed inspired to write several "Paris poems," but none of them were published until the following spring. He also met artistic colleagues like Picasso and Robert Delaunay, and he became particularly friendly with Fernand Léger. "These two giants did not need to talk to each other in order to agree," recalled Elsa, who was helped by Léger to show Mayakovsky around Paris. He also gave a couple of newspaper interviews in which among other things he claimed that Russia was enjoying a literary renaissance, that poetry was becoming more accessible, and that the people themselves now had the opportunity to judge it, as poems were being read in front of enormous crowds. As for French literature, he said there was nothing he could say, as he did not know the language. "I bow to the great literature of France, I admire it, and I hold my peace."

Mayakovsky seems to have spent most of his time in cafés and restaurants. On one occasion he persuaded Elsa to come with him to Maxim's, but he was in a filthy mood, bawled out the waiter, and in general behaved boorishly. Elsa danced all evening with a gigolo whom Maxim employed and whose services were added to the bill.

Presumably those evenings when Mayakovsky was not sitting in a restaurant were spent at the gaming tables. And even if he was not sitting at gaming tables, he would still be gambling, on everything that came his way. One night on the way down from Montmartre he caught sight of a shop selling funeral accessories with a sign in the form of a golden wreath. "Volodya, with perfect aim, threw his walking stick through the hole in the wreath, another person in the company picked it up and also tried to throw it through the wreath," Elsa recalled. Immediately a competition was initiated, rules were drawn up, and so on. "Volodya beat everybody. He had good eye-hand coordination and anyway the wreath was almost at the height of his shoulder."

During the daytime he walked—and shopped, always with Elsa. "We devoted my very first day here to your purchases," he wrote to Lili. "We ordered you a splendid little case and bought hats. [. . .] I sent the perfume (only not a liter, I couldn't manage that), a bottle, if it gets through in one piece I'll gradually send more of the same." For Osip he bought shirts and a chess set. Mayakovsky took delight in practical, well-made artifacts and also bought a few things for himself. On the recommendation of—and with money supplied by—André Triolet, whom Elsa was once again seeing, he had shirts made in an elegant atelier in the Place Vendôme; at J. M. Weston on the Boulevard Malesherbes he bought shoes fitted with heel- and toe irons ("They last for eternity!"), at Old England he bought ties, stockings, pajamas, and a collapsible rubber bathtub. At Innovation he bought dressing cases, drinking glasses, knives, forks, and spoons in leather cases, and more besides. Because of his fear of germs he made sure he was always well supplied with such accessories. "Volodya washed his hands like a doctor before an operation, he drowned himself in eau de cologne, and God forbid that you should cut yourself in his presence!" Elsa recalled. "Once he made me wash my hands with iodine because the color had run from the twine around a parcel."

Elsa was at his side the whole time, as guide and interpreter. In Paris he expressed himself, as he put it, "in triolet." He was irritated beyond measure by his lack of language skills. He, a poetic genius, a pyrotechnic display of witticisms, word games, and brilliant rhymes in his mother tongue, was sentenced to total dumbness abroad! He got worked up about not understanding and not being understood and often reacted with insults and abuse which Elsa or whoever was interpreting for him was too embarrassed to translate.

"I had a really tough time with him," Elsa remembered. "It was tough having to traipse round the city every evening and to have to put up with his heavy silences or the kind of conversations where it would have been better if he had held his tongue! And when we were with other people, it was even more awkward than when we were alone. Sometimes Mayakovsky would suddenly and ostentatiously clam up—clam up at the top of his voice, so to speak. Or he would suddenly dispatch some highly respected fully grown adult to get cigarettes for him."

All of this exemplified for Elsa Mayakovsky's ability to stretch his own and other people's nerves to the breaking point when he was in a bad mood. "Mayakovsky wouldn't make a scene because his soup was too salty [. . .] but he was hugely demanding of people close to him. He had to have power over their hearts and souls. He had, to an extreme degree, what the French call *le sens de l'absolu*, he demanded absolute, maximum emotions both in friendship and in love [. . .], without concessions, without compromises, without any allowances whatsoever." Depending on whether he felt himself loved or abandoned, he swung between manic exaltation and deepest depression, sometimes "zum Himmel hoch jauchzend," sometimes "zum Tode betrübt," as Elsa, with the wisdom of hindsight, put it—sometimes storming heaven, sometimes grieved unto death.

Relations between Mayakovsky and Elsa were still unresolved. Only three days after his arrival in Paris she confided to her diary: "I am very fond of him and grateful that he loves Lili—and me into the bargain. Obviously 'into the bargain,' despite all the speeches he makes to me. How he reacts to the least little thing, with what vehemence! How vehemently he reacts to nothing at all! With his enormous body! [. . .] He, who thinks of himself as tender and kind to a fault! There is something of that in him too, but not only that. . . . How will things go between him and me?"

The difficult sides to Mayakovsky's character were nothing new for Elsa, who had known him for ten years by now. They had flown at each other in Berlin in 1922, and living together in the summer of

1923 had not led to any improvement in relations. However, during their stay in Paris in the autumn of 1924 Mayakovsky, according to Elsa, had been "especially gloomy"—a judgment shared by the artist Valentina Khodasevich, who happened to be in Paris at the same time and who also occasionally acted as interpreter. He was, she recalled, "gloomy and bad tempered." The reason was his breakup with Lili, which Elsa was of course aware of.

After only a week in Paris it was clear to Mayakovsky that his travel plans would be difficult to implement. But he could not return home right away, as he was ashamed to face both Lili and the publisher he had promised material to. After all, it was not the first time he had informed the press that he was going to travel to the United States. And what was there for him to do in Moscow, he asked rhetorically in a letter to Lili, continuing: "I cannot write, and as for who you are and what you are I still have absolutely, absolutely no idea. Because there really is no way to console myself, you are dear to me and I love you, but all the same you are in Moscow and you're either someone else's or not mine. Forgive me—but I feel so wretched."

He also worried in a masochistic way about Lili's own feelings, about her "affairs of the heart and your circumstances," as he put it, referring to her affair with Krasnoshchokov. "What can be done about it?" replied Lili. "I cannot give up A.M. while he is in prison. It would be shameful! More shameful than anything in my entire life. Put yourself in my place. I can't. Dying would be easier." But although Mayakovsky longed fiercely for Lili, he did not accept her explanation:

> Your last letter is very painful and incomprehensible for me. I didn't know how to reply. You write about *shame.* Are you really trying to tell me that that is *all* that binds you to him and *the only thing* that prevents you from being with me? I don't believe you!—And if that is the case, it really is so unlike you—so indecisive and so immaterial. This is not a clarification of nonexistent relations—it's my sorrow and my thoughts—pay no attention to them. Do what you like, *nothing will ever change my love for you in any way.*

The letter ends with a despairing plea: "Love me a little, my child!"

No reply to this letter has survived. On the other hand, there is a letter from Lili which crossed with the one from Mayakovsky, and in this letter Krasnoshchokov is not mentioned at all. Instead she writes about everything else under the sun: about problems with *Lef*, which Gosizdat wanted to close down, about "umpteen problems" with the nap on a fur coat which had been sewn on wrongly, about the Dobermann pinscher which she had been given by Alter, her old acquaintance in Riga, and which had taken the place of Scotty (who had died), about the Lef people who sat up playing cards till seven in the morning. She also wondered what kind of haircut Mayakovsky was sporting—whether his hair was long or cropped.

A letter full of mundane concerns and utter banalities—like most of Lili's letters. But her silence about Alexander Mikhaylovich was not due to a general disinclination to broach the subject, nor was it down to delicacy. Lili had every reason to exercise caution, especially on paper. Her relationship with Krasnoshchokov was in a completely different dimension from her earlier flings. Alexander Mikhaylovich was a high-ranking Communist functionary who had been imprisoned for misappropriation of state funds. Moreover, her connection with the case was not of a purely private nature. Osip figured in the margins of the affair as the lawyer who had drawn up the regulations governing Yakov Krasnoshchokov's construction firm American-Russian Constructor. The relationship thus had a political dimension which was not to be taken lightly.

Perhaps this is what Mayakovsky was getting at when he said he was uneasy not only about her "affairs of the heart" but also about her "circumstances." There is no doubt that the Krasnoshchokov affair also cast a shadow over Mayakovsky and the Briks, who moreover no longer enjoyed the same protection as before. On 1 January 1924 Osip had been sacked from the GPU as a "deserter." The background to this curt formulation is said to be that he had been absent from far too many operations by declaring himself on sick leave. If this is correct, then it undoubtedly redounds to his credit. Perhaps there was also not the same need as previously for his expertise as a "specialist in the bourgeoisie."

L'EUROPE GALANTE

On 13 December 1924, a week before Mayakovsky left Paris, he sent a telegram to Lili: "TELEGRAPH IMMEDIATELY DO YOU WANT EVEN A LITTLE SEE ME? KISS YOU. VOLODYA." Lili answered the same day: "VERY MUCH WANT SEE YOU. MISS YOU. KISS YOU. LILI."

Whatever his reception was like, Mayakovsky must have been in a wretched mood when he stepped off the train in Moscow a few days before New Year's Eve. The trip had been a total fiasco. Paris was meant to have been an intermediate stop on his world tour but instead he had remained there for six weeks waiting for a visa that never arrived. He had fled Moscow, Lili, and Krasnoshchokov with the intention of being away for a long time, but instead he was forced to return home with his tail between his legs.

If Mayakovsky was moody and depressed, Lili was not a much better case. "Volodya's back," she reported to Rita, adding: "We will probably be going to Paris in six weeks' time. A. T[obinson] is very ill. He's in the hospital. I hardly see him at all. I have suicidal thoughts. I don't want to live."

Krasnoshchokov had been struck down with pneumonia in November and was near death. He was therefore transferred to the state hospital in the center of Moscow, and in January 1925 he was pardoned. Why he was released after only six months in jail is unclear. All that can be said with certainty is that it must have happened on orders from the highest political authority. Clearly Krasnoshchokov was no longer seen as a threat. The punishment meted out to him had also been much harsher than in other corruption cases. The fact that GPU chief Felix Dzerzhinsky was also given the task of finding accommodation for Krasnoshchokov possibly signaled a degree of repentance on the side of the government.

The pardon was encouraging, but the situation continued to be complicated for all concerned. Krasnoshchokov was in the hospital, Mayakovsky was jealous and depressed, and Lili was on the brink of suicide. As if this was not enough, Lili fell seriously ill at the beginning of February. "I'm actually spending my third week in bed," she told Rita on the twenty-third. "It appears I've had a large cyst and the lump has gone and got inflamed." Lili was in the care of Isaak Braude, one of the leading gynecologists in Moscow, and Mayakovsky waited on her "like a children's nurse."

Her convalescence took time and was hardly made any easier by the fact that the Krasnoshchokov case, shortly after his pardon, was raised to the status of literature. In February 1925 the young dramatist Boris Romashov premiered his play *A Soufflé* at the Theater of the Revolution in Moscow. The play was based on the trial of Krasnoshchokov. The main characters were the bank director Koromyslov and his lover, the actress and ballerina Rita Kern. Koromyslov was portrayed as a degenerate Communist, but most of all as the victim of a group of corrupt people, including his brother. "Maybe I was deluded about business affairs, maybe I misunderstood what was going on around me, but I have never betrayed the interests of the workers," he says. Even if the female lead was supposed to have been modeled on both Donna Gruz and Lili Brik, the public of course only made the connection to Lili, not only because the play's heroine was a ballet dancer like Lili but because out of the two of them Lili was the only one who was known to the public.

The play was commissioned by Olga Kameneva, political leader (*politruk*) of the theater and a hard-nosed ideologue. The fact that Kameneva—the sister of Leon Trotsky—had despised and opposed Futurism ever since the Revolution may also have played a part. By attacking Krasnoshchokov and Lili she was also, indirectly, attacking the group around Mayakovsky. The staging of the play, which was performed over a hundred times, was in any event a stab in the back for Krasnoshchokov from the side of the party leadership.

By this time Mayakovsky's status was such as to make his cohabitation with Lili and Osip a matter of interest and controversy, and not only in Russia. In January they received a visit from Paul Morand, a forty-year-old French diplomat who in recent years had also become known as a writer. Morand's interest in Russia was dictated not only by curiosity about Bolshevism but also by the fact that his father had been born and brought up in St. Petersburg, whence his grandfather Adolphe Morand had fled in the mid-nineteenth century. Although Paul Morand himself was born in France, part of his identity was undoubtedly Russian.

When Morand turned up at the apartment that the Briks and May-

Lili and Mayakovsky in the "salon" in Vodopyany Lane where Paul Morand visited them.

akovsky shared on one of the last days of January 1925, he had already been in Moscow for several weeks and knew very well whom he was calling on. Through his reading, and through listening to gossip, he was knowledgeable down to the last detail about this notorious "marriage cartel."

The epithet is Morand's and is taken from his fictional account of his visit to Moscow, "I Burn Up Moscow." The story's main characters are Vasilissa Abramovna, her husband, Ben Moïsevich, and "the red poet" Mardochée Goldwasser, who lives in a "love tryst" in the same apartment. That Mayakovsky was the model for Goldwasser was actually confirmed by Morand himself. That he too was allotted a Jewish name is in all likelihood because of the conspicuous number of Jews in the ranks of leading Bolsheviks, especially during what Morand called "the Trotskyist phase 1917–25." "I Burn Up Moscow" is a piece of glittering literary journalism, full of accurate observations and well-directed jibes and characterized by a distinctive style. "He made the French language jazz," was Louis-Ferdinand Céline's description of Morand's verbal artistry.

Morand's portraits are not pure depictions—Ben Moïsevich, for example, has borrowed some traits from Krasnoshchokov, whose daughter Luella moreover figures as the family's "adoptive child." And they have several characteristics borrowed from other people altogether. The depiction of Moscow too is characterized by several artistically motivated factual errors. However, what is important is not these aberrations but the insightful portrayal of the thoroughly politicized and paranoid Soviet society as well as the generally ac-curate descriptions of the main figures. Morand discovers that all of them, himself included, are hopelessly in love with the seductive and loose-living Vasilissa, who belongs to "the usual type that all men think they have owned"; he records Goldwasser's purchase of expensive perfumes for her in Paris, something that chimes with her "precious few political convictions" ("although she called herself a Communist"); he also notes Ben Moïsevich's good contacts in the security service. If the observation that there was a bust of Lenin in the room is true, this is a piquant reminder that theory and practice do not always go hand in hand.

Goldwasser is described as a "giant" with "an open, likeable appearance," a poet with "an original style" who writes everything from political plays and advertising slogans for state-owned industrial products to atheistic children's songs and poems glorifying the use of manure in agriculture. He is, writes Morand, "too artistic by nature" to be free from neuroses. In Goldwasser's case the neuroses take the form of hypochondria. "His fear of germs is well known. This Communist washes every object he comes into contact with, sterilizes his cutlery, wears rubber gloves, opens doors at a height where no one else can touch them." He is the richest of the three family members and supports the others: "This is the first country I have visited where a poet pays for other people." A large part of his income undoubtedly derived from writing books and giving lectures, but a lot of it also came from gambling. When the playing cards were produced late at night, noted Morand, Goldwasser was "a player of genius who places his stakes ruthlessly."

"I Burn Up Moscow" was published in the magazine *Demain* in April 1925 and in the book *L'Europe galante*, which came out later that year. As representatives of "the first workers' state," Lili, Osip, and Mayakovsky were naturally extremely upset at being depicted as representatives of postwar "racy Europe"—and at how they themselves were portrayed. Elsa found the story anti-Semitic, and Mayakovsky was of the opinion that Morand was "obviously a particularly vile piece of work." According to Elsa, Mayakovsky thought for a time about penning a response in which he would counter Morand page by page and describe "how it actually was," but nothing came of these plans.

LITERATURE AND REVOLUTION

The day after Mayakovsky returned to Moscow, on 28 December 1924, he took part in a meeting about the design of the Soviet pavilion at the International Exhibition of Modern Industrial and Decorative Arts which was due to open in Paris the following spring. The committee also included, among others, Alexander Rodchenko and the architect Konstantin Melnikov, who designed the pavilion. Mayakovsky was responsible for the layout of the advertising at the exhibition. In January 1925 it was decided that the USSR should be represented by seventeen original posters from different branches of industry, among them Mayakovsky's own.

On 12 January Mayakovsky collected a new foreign passport, which may indicate that he had been thinking of returning to Paris soon, perhaps even before the exhibition was officially opened at the end of April. By contrast with Rodchenko, who had already traveled there in March, Mayakovsky did not leave until the end of May. There were several reasons for this. For one thing, the Soviet pavilion was not ready until the beginning of June; for another, the cultural-political situation demanded his presence in Moscow.

In the winter of 1925 it was well known in cultural circles that the Communist Party was preparing a document in which it would set out its view of current developments in literature. Against this background, the Lef writers felt the need to clarify their position with regard to both organization and ideology. Mayakovsky and Brik had always recommended a loose association of avant-garde artists united by a common vision of how the new culture should look: Futurists, Constructivists, Formalists, and other pioneers of new forms (like Boris Pasternak). The original idea was that Lef should function as a platform not only for Russian avant-gardists but for the international avant-garde in general. Among those considered as potential collaborators on the journal were George Grosz, Tristan Tzara, Fernand Léger, and two old Futurist colleagues who now lived abroad—Burlyuk and Jakobson. One predecessor—and model—was

Leon Trotsky (1879–1940) was one of the central figures of the Russian Revolution, Bolshevik Russia's first war commissar and a brilliant writer, both on political and literary issues. After being exiled in 1929, he was banned in the Soviet Union and all traces of his influence were deleted, including his contacts with Mayakovsky. In Mayakovsky's Collected Works, there is a letter with the heading "Letter about Futurism." It is dated 1 September 1922 but has no addressee. In actual fact, it was addressed to Trotsky, who two days earlier had written to Mayakovsky to ask if there were any "survey article that explains the main poetical features in Futurism." "Could you not yourself in a few words if not characterize then at least list the main features of Futurism?" Trotsky finished. It is this letter that Mayakovsky's letter was an answer to. The reason why Mayakovsky, who was no letter writer, responded so quickly and at such length—the letter is several pages long—was that he knew Trotsky was working on a book that contained a chapter about Futurism and himself. The answer is an enumeration of the basic aesthetic ideas of Futurism, with the stress on literature as a "verbal art," where the most important component is the work with the word (neologisms, sound repetitions, rhythm, syntax, etc.). The drawing by Yury Annenkov was made when Trotsky was at the height of his power, in 1923, when his book Literature and Revolution was published.

ю. Анненков
1923

the journal *Vyeshch-Objet-Gegenstand*, three issues of which appeared in Berlin in 1922 with Ilya Ehrenburg and El Lissitzky as editors and Mayakovsky as one of the contributors. Although some issues of *Lef* contained contributions from abroad, the journal never developed into an international organ.

Despite ideas about a looser association, as early as the autumn of 1923 Lef was forced by the cultural-political situation into an alliance with its direct opponents in MAPP, the Moscow Section of RAPP, the Russian Union of Proletarian Writers. Given their diametrically opposed views on literature, the alliance implied fundamental concessions on both sides. For the proletarian writers content was significantly more important than form, while the Lef school, as before, stressed the decisive importance of form. What united MAPP and Lef was the struggle for what was seen as "Communist art" and criticism of so-called fellow travelers—the term had been coined by Trotsky and meant writers who were not Communists yet were not hostile to the Revolution: poets like Sergey Yesenin and prose writers like Boris Pilnyak, Yevgeny Zamyatin, Mikhail Zoshchenko, Vsevolod Ivanov, Isaak Babel, and others. The alliance was in other words no love affair but built on purely strategic considerations. By coming together they hoped to gain greater influence on the formulation of Soviet cultural politics.

However, this did not come off, partly because Lef was incapable of sorting out its internal contradictions. During the winter and spring of 1925 organizational questions were discussed at a number of meetings between the group around Mayakovsky and the one which supported Nikolay Chuzhak and his demand for a firm organizational structure and a more unified and binding aesthetic program. But no compromise could be reached.

The Communist Party was striving for reconciliation and consolidation on the writers' front and had little sympathy for radical left-wing ideas of the kind championed by Lef and MAPP. When the resolution "Regarding the Party's Policy in the Area of Literature" was published in July 1925, reactions from most quarters were positive—but not from Lef, which had hoped that the party would grant them a central role in the development of the new culture. Instead, Lef was not mentioned at all. The proletarian writers also had cause for dissatisfaction. Although their importance was acknowledged, they were criticized for their indifference to the cultural heritage, for "Communist arrogance," and for their attempts to create a "proletarian hothouse of literature." The actual winners from the resolution were the much-decried "fellow travelers," who, instead of being attacked, were said to play an important role during the transition period between bourgeois and Communist culture.

The most important aspect of the resolution was that the party espoused "free competition between different groupings and currents." "Even if the party supports proletarian and peasant-proletarian literature materially and morally and helps 'fellow travelers,' etc., it cannot grant a monopoly status to any one group, however proletarian its ideological content may be." "The party by and large cannot commit itself to supporting any particular direction in the area of *literary form*. Even if the party steers literature by and large, it is just as unable to support any *individual* literary faction [. . .] as it is to solve questions of family life by resolutions."

The resolution was largely drawn up by Nikolay Bukharin, the spokesman for a "soft" line in literary questions, and it was seen as "liberal" both by contemporaries and by later commentators. And so it was, in the sense that it refused to give preference to one grouping or the other. But there is an element of duplicity in the resolution. On the one hand the party expresses itself in favor of "free competition"; on the other hand it claims to "steer literature." This contradiction is an echo of the ideas in Trotsky's book *Literature and Revolution* (1923), in which he laid down that "art is not an area where the party is called on to give orders"—at the same time declaring that "nor, in the area of art, can the party for one single day restrict itself to liberal *laissez-faire* principles."

Along with Lunacharsky and Bukharin, Trotsky was one of the few genuinely educated persons in the party leadership—and his analysis of contemporary literature bears witness to a significant sharpness of mind, not least in his article about Futurism and Lef. At the same time as he was expressing his support for linguistic experimentation and theories about the connection between art and industrial production, he was criticizing the Lef writers for refusing to see man's inner life, his psyche, as a worthy subject for artistic creativity.

"An intelligent article," commented Mayakovsky, who had had some dealings with Trotsky, for example, during his work on the book. And yet Trotsky was one of those who laid the foundations for the Soviet tradition of valuing artistic works for their political and not for their aesthetic value: an approach which would have consequences that were devastating for Russian literature and fatal for its practitioners. But just as alarming as the party's ambitions to steer cultural life was the eagerness with which many writers jostled for position as the favorites of the state and the party—the same writers who, with the same frenzy and conviction, had fought against tsarist censorship and the Bolsheviks' attempts to take over cultural life directly after the Revolution of 1917. Had Mayakovsky repressed his proud slogan from 1917: "There is no room for politics in art"?

BACK TO PARIS

Several writers and critics commented on the resolution, among them Osip, who latched on to those points on which the party might be said to have supported Lef indirectly, especially on the question of literary form. Mayakovsky made no comment. The resolution was published in *Pravda* and *Izvestiya* on 1 July, by which time he was already treading the deck of an Atlantic steamer en route to Mexico.

On 25 May Mayakovsky had gone to Paris in order to try yet again to travel on from there to the United States. He should have left on the twentieth but gambled away the money for the trip and remained in Moscow for a few days longer to try to win the money back. In order not to commit the same faux pas as last time, when he was forced to return to Moscow with his errand unaccomplished, he had written off the idea of requesting an American visa. Instead he had decided to try to get into the United States by means of a detour, via Mexico, which had recognized the Soviet Union the previous year. As he learned after only a week in Paris that his papers were ready, we may assume that he had been in contact with the Mexican authorities already in Moscow.

Since the first ship to Mexico did not leave until two weeks after Mayakovsky's arrival in the French capital, he remained in Paris for the time being. As he had done on his earlier visit, he spent a lot of time

Mayakovsky portrayed by the photographer Pierre Choumoff in Paris in 1925, as serious and concentrated as in all other photographs—and in life. He rarely laughed. "He was mostly silent, then he would say something and everybody would burst out laughing," according to Rodchenko. "We laughed, he just smiled and observed . . ."

with Léger and other artists and had the opportunity to experience every side of Paris: from the cheapest dives in Montmartre, where the pimps fought each other to the death before his eyes, to the most distinguished *quartiers* and the most luxurious restaurants. One evening he met Filippo Tommaso Marinetti, the leader of the Italian Futurists, whom he had not seen since Marinetti's visit to Russia in 1914.

Unfortunately we know nothing about their conversation, which was conducted "in triolet." Elsa said she remembered only how Marinetti tried to prove to Mayakovsky that Fascism was the same to Italy as Communism to Russia, and Mayakovsky claimed that he had nothing to talk to Marinetti about and that they only "exchanged some polite phrases in French." But according to one newspaper report the conversation was intended for publication, which suggests that there was more substance to it than this. However difficult it is to imagine how a restaurant conversation could be resurrected in print, this piece of information is interesting. Elsa's partial memory loss and Mayakovsky's terseness perhaps suggest that the two poets had more in common than otherwise. Evidence of this is the "futuristic good wishes" to "my dear Mayakovsky and marvellous Russia with its energy and optimism," as Marinetti jotted down in Mayakovsky's notebook. If the meeting was as positive as the greetings indicate, Mayakovsky had no reason to advertise it.

"I am even more bored than usual here," he complained to Lili. "[. . .] I sleep twice a day, have two breakfasts, wash, and that's all." Not even the Soviet pavilion at the Paris exhibition, which was officially opened on 4 June, gave him any pleasure, although he won a silver medal for his advertising posters. But the exhibition was "a very tedious and pointless place," and he was "sick to death of it," "especially of the conversations going on around it." He saw a Chaplin film, gave a poetry reading, and as always bought presents for Lili and Osip (who this time got a suit). No doubt he exaggerated his wretchedness in the letters to Lili to gain her sympathy. At the same time as he was complaining about the famous "Paris spring" (which "is quite worthless, since nothing blooms and all they do is mend the streets everywhere"), he was courting some pretty young Russian émigrées, presumably not only because of their bilingualism.

Mayakovsky did not know himself how long he planned to be

away from Moscow; everything depended on how his America plans developed. But he had plenty of money with him in Paris—25,000 francs—which represented about a year's salary for a French teacher but almost three times the annual salary of a Soviet citizen. 25,000 francs corresponded to about 2,400 rubles, which shows what a special position Mayakovsky occupied. The largest sum a Soviet citizen was allowed to transfer to a single individual abroad was 200 rubles per month.*

The amount may seem large, but it had to last for several months, and boat tickets were dear. He was therefore trying, he told Lili, "not to spend any money." He told her he was making a living by having poems published in the *Paris News*, a newspaper which had been started up by the Soviet embassy as a counterweight to the many "White Russian" publications in Paris. Several of the Paris poems which Mayakovsky had begun during his previous visit to the French capital were published here. He was paid two francs a line. He was in dire need of it, as his whole capital apart from three francs had been stolen from him on 10 June.

"The thief took the room opposite mine in the Istria," he reported in a letter to Lili, "and when I popped out for twenty seconds on business connected with my stomach he extraordinarily skillfully swiped all my money and wallets (with your photo and all my papers!) and skedaddled from the room in an unknown direction. All my statements to the authorities had no effect, only they said that all the signs pointed to its being a thief who is notorious for this sort of thing. I'm young enough not to care about the money. But the thought that my journey would be curtailed and that once again I'd come back like a fool to be made a laughingstock by you put me into an absolute frenzy."

It may seem strange that Mayakovsky had the whole of his traveling funds, 25,000 francs, in his wallet. Was he really robbed? Or did

---

* The ruble's value was established by the Soviet State Bank and was thus arbitrary. After the First World War the franc had fallen in value, and one therefore received ten francs for one ruble. As the ruble was not convertible, anyone leaving the Soviet Union had to buy foreign currency first. The reason for the favorable "rate of exchange" was partly that the Soviet authorities did not want the small numbers of their citizens allowed to travel abroad to be seen as poor, but rather to serve as living examples of the progress of the Soviet economy.

Mayakovsky and Elsa on flying tour in Paris in June 1925. Between them are the artist Robert Delaunay, the writers Iwan and Clare Goll, and the artist Valentina Khodasevich, who was working in Paris at the time. The French-German poet Iwan Goll was a great admirer of Mayakovsky and had translated parts of "War and the World" into German.

he gamble the money away? There is no evidence to support such a hypothesis apart from the fact that he was a manic gambler. And if he had gambled the money away, he would never have had the courage to admit it to Lili but would have had to come up with another explanation, especially as he had already gambled his funds away a few weeks earlier in Moscow.

Whatever the reason for the disappearance of the money, in March Mayakovsky had managed to reach an agreement with Gosizdat about an edition of his collected works in four volumes. The agreement had come about despite stiff opposition from the publishing house, which was still unfavorably inclined toward him. It was signed and sealed only after Lunacharsky had affirmed that "people at the top of the party are very well disposed" toward Mayakovsky, and after major concessions from the author, who accepted the unusually low fee of twelve kopecks per line. Now, with Lili's help, he could sign for an advance of 2,000 rubles, the equivalent of about 21,000 francs, that is, almost the entire sum he had lost. The rest Mayakovsky had to borrow from "Elsa's André" and from Russians staying in Paris in connection with the world's fair. Even this round of borrowing was transformed by Mayakovsky into a wager. When he and Elsa came across a Russian in some café they would size him up: if the amount he later lent them was closer to Elsa's estimate of his means, she would receive the difference. If it was closer to Mayakovsky's guess, the money would be his.

Mayakovsky managed to put together the sum required to enable him to continue the journey, and on 21 June, at St. Nazaire, he boarded the twenty-thousand-ton *Espagne*, which was to take him to Mexico. A few days later Elsa traveled to Moscow, where she was met not only by Lili and Osip but also by Yelena Yulyevna, who was taking the opportunity of visiting her hometown during Mayakovsky's absence. It was the first time that Elsa and her mother had visited Soviet Russia since 1918.

WITH CLICKING HEELS ON BROADWAY

The voyage to Veracruz in Mexico took eighteen days. "I can't say I've had a very jolly time on the steamer," Mayakovsky wrote to Lili on 3 July as they were approaching Cuba. "Twelve days of water is fine for fish and professional discoverers, but for landlubbers it's too much. I haven't learned to speak French and Spanish, but on the other hand I have perfected the expressiveness of my face, since I communicate by miming."

The miming came in useful during his poker playing, to which, according to a Mexican newspaper, he devoted a large part of his time, as he could not make conversation with any of his fellow passengers, being the only Russian on the boat. But Mayakovsky was also working. However, none of the six poems he produced represents a high point of his authorship. On the contrary—with the exception of isolated verses, one might talk about a sort of intellectual devaluation, like when he makes fun of six nuns who are traveling on the boat: "Instead of the well-known / symmetrical places / where women have bulges / they have a hollow: / in the one / a silver cross, / in the other / medals / with [popes] Leo and Pius." It was cheap point scoring which went down well with an uneducated working-class public but was unworthy of the author of "Man" and "About This."

If Paris was a halfway house on the way to Mexico, Mexico was only a stage on the planned journey to the United States, perhaps even on a round-the-world trip. When asked by journalists if he had any assignments to carry out for his government and whether he was a party member, Mayakovsky stressed that he had "long ago abandoned all public assignments" and that his stay in Mexico was "of a purely literary nature, without any political significance." This cautious—and not entirely truthful—reply was intended not so much for Mexican newspaper readers as for the American immigration authorities. It was Mayakovsky's position as a Soviet poet and a mouthpiece for Communism that was the major hindrance to his getting a visa for the United States, and he was well aware of this.

David Burlyuk had lived too short a time in America to be able to invite Mayakovsky in. Instead he asked one of his artist friends to send an invitation. But this did not help, and a couple of weeks later Mayakovsky turned in despair to the French embassy in Mexico City with a request for a visa to France. "If the United States doesn't come off, I'll leave for Moscow about 15 August and arrive between 15 and 20 September," he wrote to Lili. But the very next day, 24 July, he visited the American consulate in Mexico City and filled in an application form for temporary residence in the United States. He described himself not as a writer but as an artist who wished to come to the United States to exhibit his work. This time things went better, and Mayakovsky was given an entry visa valid for six months. Half of the $500—half an annual salary in America!—demanded from him as a pledge he borrowed from an employee at the Soviet embassy in Mexico City. On 27 July 1925 Mayakovsky crossed the border into the United States of America at Laredo, and three days later he was in New York.

The first person Mayakovsky contacted in New York was of course David Burlyuk, whom he had not seen for seven years. "It was with

Mayakovsky and David Burlyuk at Rockaway Beach in August 1925.

a special emotion that I heard his sonorous, manly, deep bass voice on the telephone," his old Futurist friend recalled. "I rushed down into the subway and hurried off to Fifth Avenue, where Mayakovsky was staying. From a long way off I saw a large 'Russian' foot stepping over the threshold and a couple of heavy cases that had got stuck in the door."

If the American authorities had not realized it before, they were soon made aware that the foot belonged to a poet and not to an artist. Vladimir Mayakovsky, "Soviet Russia's best-known poet of the last decade," whose poems "are printed in editions of millions in the new Russia," was portrayed and interviewed in several newspaper articles, most of them published in the Communist press. But readers of the *New York Times* were also able to read the following: "The most popular poet in Russia, Mayakovsky, is also one of the richest—so far as riches are permitted in his land. [. . .] The last book brought him something like $10,000 in American money. Mayakovsky is one of the champion card players. He loses in cards much more than he makes by his pen, and lives on his winnings." The reporter also pointed out that the Russian proletarian poet "likes to dress like a dandy and orders his clothes from the best tailors in Paris," and that he "loves comfort and luxury and at the same time despises them."

Despite the obvious errors and exaggerations it is worth noting that Mayakovsky's reputation as a cardsharp had reached far beyond the confines of Russia. One must however not forget that his "riches" were in rubles, not in convertible currency, and therefore relatively worthless outside his homeland.

Mayakovsky had a series of well-received performances in New York, and during a tour in the eastern United States he visited Cleveland, Detroit, Chicago, Philadelphia, and Pittsburgh. He recited poems and talked about the Soviet state and his impressions of the United States. When he appeared in the Central Opera House in New York, two thousand people turned up. "He is as simple and enormous as Soviet Russia itself," the Jewish Communist newspaper *Freihait* reported: "Gigantic of build, with powerful shoulders, a simple jacket, large close-cropped head and broad Russian nostrils. [. . .] The enormous auditorium listened with rapt attention to Mayakovsky's poems, masterfully performed by the poet himself."

Even if "every poem evoked volleys of thunderous applause which seemed as if they would never cease" from "New York's revolutionary workers," not all were equally enthusiastic. One critic thought that the author of "A Cloud in Trousers" had wasted his talent during the last seven years, in other words since the Revolution—that "his muse has abandoned him."

In his interviews and appearances Mayakovsky criticized American technology and industrialization from both an ideological and an aesthetic viewpoint. Magnificent material results had been achieved, but people had not reached the same level and were still stuck in the past. "Intellectually, New Yorkers are still provincials," he said in his first interview. "Their minds have not accepted the full implications of the industrial age." The city is "unorganized," is not "the full grown, mature product of men who understood what they wanted and planned it out like artists." When the industrial age comes to Russia it will be different, it will be "planned—it will be conscious." As examples Mayakovsky cites the skyscrapers, which the Renaissance masters could only have dreamed of and which with their fifty stories defy the laws of gravity. But the American architects seem not to understand what a miracle they have brought about, decorating them with "obsolete and silly Gothic or Byzantine ornaments." "It's like tying pink ribbons on a steam dredge, or like putting Kewpie figures on a locomotive," he said, offering as an alternative the art of Futurism and the industrial age, whose ground rule is functionalism. "Nothing superfluous!" According to Mayakovsky, "art must have a function." Just as he had trimmed away the rhetoric from his poetry to make it what it now was, so Futurism was "for technique, for scientific organization, for the machine, for planfulness, for will power, for courage, for speed, precision and for the new man, who is armed with all these things."

Mayakovsky's America poems are also strongly ideological, but the imagery is fresh and the rhymes—often on English words—ingenious. And in two of the best poems—"Brooklyn Bridge" and "Broadway"—he cannot restrain his childlike enthusiasm for America's technological marvels and the seething life of its great city: "You look left: / good lord! / You look right: / oh my lord!! / There's something to see here for that lot in Moscow. [. . .] This is New York. / This is Broadway. / How do you do! / I'm bewitched / by the city of New York" ("Broadway").

A BOAT CAPSIZES

Mayakovsky wrote about his impressions of America not only in poetry but also in a long piece of travel reporting, *My Discovery of America*, which came out in book form in August 1926. The American trip made a deep impression on him, and after his return to the Soviet Union he gave many lectures in which he described his experiences and impressions. But there were two incidents he never referred to, either in print or during his public appearances—incidents that were as overwhelming as the very encounter with the United States.

The person who had helped Mayakovsky with his visa and who had arranged an apartment for him on Fifth Avenue (no. 3, right by Washington Square) was Isaiah Khurgin, who had an apartment of his own in the same block. Khurgin was a mathematician and an astronomer and had come to the United States in 1923 as head of the American branch of a German-Russian transport company. As the organizations responsible for Soviet trade with the United States were not very efficient, he suggested to Krasin, the commissar for foreign trade (who had previously been head of Arcos in London), that a new limited company be set up, and May 1924 saw the founding of the American Trading Corporation (Amtorg). The firm began with a start-up capital of $1 million, and after one year it had a turnover of 50 million. By the time of Mayakovsky's arrival Khurgin had earned a good reputation in New York financial circles and was described as a "happy-go-lucky, intelligent, clear-sighted, ironic personality." Since Amtorg was an offshoot of Arcos's USA branch, it is not too bold to suppose that the contact with Khurgin was established via Krasin (whom Mayakovsky had met in Paris) or someone else connected with the firm, perhaps even Yelena Yulyevna herself, who still worked in Arcos's London office.

Irrespective of the warmth of their relationship, Lili and Mayakovsky regularly exchanged letters and telegrams when they were traveling. But during his two-month stay in New York Mayakovsky did not write a single letter to Lili, only fourteen brief and uncommunicative telegrams. The first telegram was sent on 2 August: "DEAR KITTY. NO DETAILS YET. JUST ARRIVED. KISS YOU LOVE YOU." But he had not "just arrived"; he had come to New York four days earlier. This was not like Mayakovsky, who normally sent a telegram as soon as he arrived! Lili replied the following day with a letter in which she asked him to "please send me a visa and moneys" and continued: "Don't dare to forget me!!! I love you and kiss you and embrace you." In a telegram sent the same day she repeats that she "VERY MUCH WANT COME NEW YORK." Three days later Mayakovsky replied: "TRYING HARD GET VISA. IF CAN'T WILL SELF COME HOME." Then there is silence from Mayakovsky *for a whole month*. For once it is Lili who persecutes Mayakovsky with letters and telegrams, not the other way round. When he never answers, she finally telegraphs desperately: "WHERE HAVE YOU GOT TO?" The telegram is signed Lili, and not with the usual "Your Kitty."

When Mayakovsky replied two days later it was with the following telegram: "DEAR KITTEN TRAGEDY KHURGIN UPSET VISA BUSINESS PLANS . [. . .] ANSWER TENDERLY PLEASE. LOVE YOU KISS YOU."

What had happened was that Isaiah Khurgin had been drowned, along with Efraim Sklyansky, on 27 August during a boat trip on Long Lake outside New York. Sklyansky had come to the United States three days earlier in his capacity as head of a Soviet textile trust. According to the official report, the accident had been caused by a sudden storm, but after his flight from the Soviet Union in 1928 Stalin's secretary Boris Bazyanov maintained that it was an instance of a political murder ordered by Stalin, who in January 1925 had sacked Trotsky as commissar for war and initiated a campaign against the "Trotskyists" in the party. Sklyansky was one of Trotsky's closest associates and had been his deputy in the Revolutionary War Council. The technique of disguising a murder as an accident was also used when Mikhail Frunze, Sklyansky's successor in the war council and Trotsky's successor as war commissar, "died" two months later on the operating table.

Khurgin's death caused deep gloom in the Russian colony in New York. He had been popular, and no one seems to have believed that his death was an accident. Nobody grieved more than Mayakovsky, who according to witnesses stood on permanent vigil by the coffin.

He also made a speech at the funeral and followed the urn with Khurgin's ashes to the Soviet steamer which was to take it back to Russia. But he never wrote a line about Khurgin's death. He could not write the truth, and he did not want to lie. With Khurgin, evidently, there disappeared Lili's last chance of obtaining an American visa.

ELLY

Shortly after the deaths of Khurgin and Sklyansky, Mayakovsky was at a cocktail party at the house of the radical American lawyer Charles Recht, who was a consultant to Amtorg and the IWW (Industrial Workers of the World) and who had had a finger in the pie when Mayakovsky received his visa. It was at Recht's place that he had spent his first evening in New York. At the party he met a young Russian woman, "Elly," whom Khurgin had known but refused to introduce to Mayakovsky, with the excuse that he was certainly "an amusing person" but also a "devourer of women's hearts." But now they met. When she said she had never seen him perform, either in New York or in Moscow, but that she had read his poems, he replied: "That's what *all* the pretty girls say. When I pin them down to tell me what poems they have read, they say, 'Oh, a long one and a short one'!" Her reply—"I don't know any short ones—except your advertising slogans"—must surely have impressed Mayakovsky.

"Elly"'s real name was Yelizaveta. She had been born in the village of Dovlekanovo in the Urals in October 1904. When she became acquainted with Mayakovsky she was thus only twenty. Her parents, Peter Henry and Helena Siebert, were both descendants of German Mennonites—a pacifist Protestant sect—who had moved to Bashkiria at the end of the eighteenth century at the invitation of Catherine the Great to develop agriculture and set up workshops. Although the Mennonites preached simplicity and their lifestyle was sternly God fearing, Yelizaveta's father was a rich man who owned large tracts of land and had business interests both inside and beyond Russia. The family were bilingual—at home they spoke German, outside the home, Russian. Yelizaveta in addition received tuition in English and French.

When the Revolution and the civil war broke out, the Siebert fam-

Бурлюк 1925 г.
сем. В Ниагедаше
кепте с мол.
новыми

Елизавета Алексеевна
Mrs Эжонс

[из Доблеканова Сад.З.Ш.С.]

W. Маяковский
6/Х . New York

During one of their visits to the summer
camp Nit Gedaige, Mayakovsky and
Burlyuk both made portraits of Elly
Jones—just as they had portrayed
Mariya Denisova eleven years before
(see pp. 22–23). Mayakovsky's drawing
(*bottom*) was published in a Russian
émigré newspaper in New York in 1932.

ily lost all its assets. The young Yelizaveta worked for several years with homeless boys in Samara and as an interpreter for the American Relief Association, which was led by the Quaker Herbert Hoover (see the chapter "NEP and the Beginnings of Terror"). During her work with the ARA in Moscow she met the English accountant George E. Jones, whom she married in May 1923 when she was only eighteen. They moved to London and from there on to New York. But the marriage was not happy. It seems that Jones had married Yelizaveta—or "Elly," as she came to be called in the West—to help her leave Russia. After a while in New York they separated and Jones rented an apartment for her on Seventy-First Street. To earn money, Elly, who was slender and well built, worked as a model.

Her first meeting with Mayakovsky ended dramatically. He invited Elly to lunch, but on the way from Recht's apartment Elly felt unwell from drinking the "bathtub gin" that she had been given (it was the time of Prohibition). Mayakovsky and a girlfriend of Elly's took her to Mayakovsky's apartment, where she fell asleep. Early next morning, on Mayakovsky's initiative, they took a taxi to the structure that impressed him more than any other in New York, just as it did most other Russians. "He was just so *happy* to be walking over the Brooklyn Bridge," Elly recalled.

To begin with, Mayakovsky's interest in Elly was probably motivated mainly by practical considerations. He spoke no English, and in his jacket pocket he carried a piece of paper with the only sentence he could pronounce: an apology for not taking people by the hand when he greeted them. Elly, who was fluent in both Russian and English, was an ideal interpreter, not least when it came to buying clothes, makeup, and other feminine accessories. "I can see why he has a reputation as a 'lady-killer,'" Elly noted in her diary after he asked her during a cocktail party at Recht's if she would come with him to buy presents for his "wife." "Right away he establishes that he is married. Yet he insists on getting my phone number." The message was plain: we can amuse ourselves while we are in New York, but another woman is waiting in Moscow. After their first dinner in private, however, Elly's suspicion abated. "He was absolutely correct with me, and I had a wonderful time . . . interesting . . . without having anything to drink."

When they parted Mayakovsky declared that he wanted to meet Elly again the following day. The utilitarian attitude had gone; his emotions had gained the upper hand. "He called for me every morning and we spent the day together, reading and walking. Going places. Being invited here and there. Almost every day we went somewhere. He took me with him everywhere he could and never left me alone." Although the relationship very soon became intimate they were careful not to flaunt it. Elly was still married to George Jones and only had a temporary residence permit in the United States. If he had divorced her—as he threatened to do when they quarreled—she would have found it difficult to remain in the country. Mayakovsky had to be careful too. If his affair with a Russian émigrée got out it would not only have been harmful to his image as a proletarian poet, but also would directly have endangered his life. If he did not know it before, the "drowning accident" in Long Lake demonstrated that the GPU's arm extended far beyond the confines of the homeland. "We always used the formal 'you' when we were around other people," Elly recalled. "He and Burlyuk never called me anything but Yelizaveta Petrovna, as a matter of respect. He kissed my hand in public in front of other people. To Americans he only called me Mrs. Jones."

The official Soviet annals of Mayakovsky's stay in New York note only his performances and meetings with American Socialists and Communists. But what else was he doing? "Mayakovsky was always working. That is, he composed his work orally, mumbling," Elly recalled. "He particularly liked to walk on Fifth Avenue by day and Broadway by night." The clicking noise from the metal fittings on his shoes was something that stuck in her memory. For the most part they ate in cheap Armenian and Russian food outlets or in a restaurant for children on Fifth Avenue. "He moved around the East Side the whole time, i.e., in the Russian and Jewish quarters, where he treated himself and his friend Burlyuk to cheap lunches," a fellow countryman reported home to Moscow. Mayakovsky was short of money, and his travel funds soon gave out. "He was," Elly declared, "the poorest man" she had ever met.

They were often invited out to parties: one evening, to the Negro Club in Harlem. The men wore tuxedos, the women, evening gowns—except for Mayakovsky, Burlyuk, and Elly, who moreover were the only white people at the party. Neither Mayakovsky nor Elly danced: in his case, because he didn't enjoy it; in hers, because dancing was regarded as a sin in the environment she grew up in. On one occasion they were at the home of the journalist Mike Gold, editor of the newspaper *New Masses*. Another time they ended up in an elegant luxury apartment in Gramercy Park in south Manhattan, where a woman asked Mayakovsky to say what he thought about his fellow poet Yesenin, who had just been in the United States with his wife, the dancer Isadora Duncan. "The language barrier precludes me from doing justice to the subject," Mayakovsky explained. The party was boring, and after a while he got up and explained in Russian that Yelizaveta Petrovna was a little tired and that he had to take her home. He preferred being with Elly rather than with people he could not talk to and who often saw him as an exotic attraction: a poet, and a Russian to boot! In the short story "How I Made Her Laugh," Mayakovsky gave a humorous depiction of how he felt:

> It is possible that foreigners respect me, but it is also possible that they take me for an idiot. I'll say nothing about Russians for the present. Try to put yourself in the following situation in America. They have invited a poet—a genius, so it's said. Genius, that's even more than being famous. I arrive and say:
>   "Giv mi pliz sam ti!"
> OK. I get my tea. Wait a bit, then say again:
>   "Giv mi pliz . . ."
> I get more tea.
> I just carry on, with different voices and forms of words:
>   "Giv me da sam ti, sam ti da giv mi," I say. And so the evening passes.
> Spry, respectful old men listen reverently and think: "A real Russian, not an unnecessary word. A thinker. Tolstoy. The North."
> The American thinks for his work. It would never occur to an American to think after six o'clock.
> Nor does it occur to him that I don't know a word of English, that my tongue is leaping and writhing like a corkscrew from my desire

to say something. [...] It would never occur to an American that I am bringing forth wild, hyper-English phrases in spasms:

"Jes wyte pliz faiv dabl arm strong..."

And it seems to me as if the girls with their meter-long legs held their breath, enchanted by my pronunciation, enraptured by my sharp-wittedness, subdued by the depth of my thought, and as if the men shrank in everyone's sight and were transformed into pessimists because of the total impossibility of competing with me.

But the ladies bestir themselves after hearing for the hundredth time that request for tea, pronounced in an agreeable bass voice, and the gentlemen withdraw to the corner and jest respectfully at my speechless cost.

"Translate for them," I yell at Burlyuk, "that if they knew Russian, then without dirtying my shirtfront I would transfix them with my tongue to the cross on their suspenders, I would make this whole collection of insects rotate on the spit of my tongue..."

And the conscientious Burlyuk translates:

"My eminent friend Vladimir Vladimirovich would like another cup of tea."

Mayakovsky spent a lot of time in radical Jewish circles and had a few poems published in Yiddish translation in the newspaper *Freihait*. On the weekends he occasionally traveled to an open-air camp which belonged to *Freihait*—Camp Nit Gedaige—sixty kilometers north of New York on the Hudson on one occasion in company with Elly and Burlyuk. Here he and Elly were allotted the same sleeping tent, which embarrassed both of them. She did not wish to be seen as Mayakovsky's "sex partner." They quarreled and on Elly's initiative took the last train back to New York, where she refused to let him go home with her or follow him to his apartment. Despite her youth Elly was a woman of great integrity and firm character.

This in all probability was not the first time they had fallen out. The upshot of the story was typical for Mayakovsky, who demanded of his friends that they stand by him in all kinds of situations, and of his lovers that they should belong only to him. When it came to conflict he reacted with emotional blackmail, and in the case of Elsa and Lili he had even threatened suicide. He did not go so far with Elly, who promised him that they "would be together the whole time, only them." But the pattern was the same.

Three days had passed without any contact between them when, early one morning, Mayakovsky's landlord phoned Elly to say that Mayakovsky was very ill and was not going out. When she reached the apartment on Fifth Avenue she found Mayakovsky lying on the bed with his face to the wall, "absolutely sick." "I had seen him like that. Just so depressed." Elly warmed a little chicken soup she had bought and brought with her. "Don't go to work," Mayakovsky entreated her. "Don't go. Don't leave me. I don't want to be alone—please. I'm sorry if you were hurt. I was insensitive."

But Elly had to go; she had a job to do. But she promised to come back when she was finished. When she came back in the evening, to her surprise Mayakovsky was standing waiting for her. "He took my hatbox in one hand and held the other. Everything was fine after that." Once again Mayakovsky had received proof that he was loved, or at least that someone was thinking of him.

After this crisis Elly moved down to Greenwich Village to be nearer Mayakovsky. But even if he and Elly met just about every day during his stay in New York and were often seen together, there were few people apart from Burlyuk who knew how close they were to each other. Nor does Elly figure in Mayakovsky's poetry, other than indirectly, in the poem "A Challenge": "We kiss / your long-legged women /—illicitly!— / on Hudson's shore." (In the rough draft the plural pronoun is replaced by the first person singular: "I.")

What was it that Mayakovsky saw in Elly, apart from her external assets, her big eyes, her buxom body, her youth? Like so many of her generation, Elly had seen and experienced more in her few years than a person normally experiences during a whole lifetime. When the Bolshevik revolution broke out she was only thirteen. The Revolution propelled her and her closest family into a life of chaos, uncertainty, and insecurity—life could be all over at any time. In order to survive, she was forced to rely on herself. The privations and hardships she lived through during the six years she remained in Russia sharpened her senses and made her strong. If one adds to that an inborn intelligence and a strong character, it is easy to un-

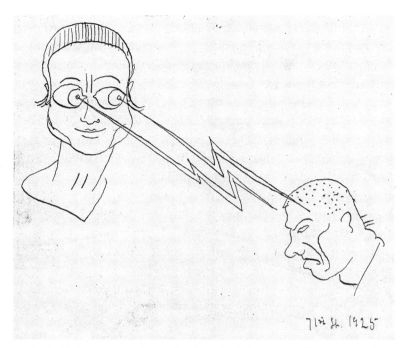

Judging by this drawing by Mayakovsky, the relationship between him and Elly was extremely charged.

derstand that Mayakovsky saw in Elly a sort of Lili: intelligent, well read, independent, demanding. These were qualities which Mayakovsky found irresistibly fascinating. It was such women he was drawn to.

When, on 28 October, Mayakovsky boarded the steamer *Rochambeau*, which was to take him to Le Havre, it was not only because duty called but because he could not have stayed any longer in New York even if he had wanted to. He simply could not afford to. The reason why he gave so many readings was that he constantly needed to replenish his funds. But toward the end of October his money began to run out, and not only because living in New York was expensive. On 22 September Lili told Mayakovsky that she had obtained a visa for Italy. She was going to travel to the health resort of Salsamaggiore near Parma. During the month of October Mayakovsky telegraphed her a total of $950, which almost corresponds to his original travel funds of 25,000 francs. Where did the money come from? He was not well paid for his appearances. Some of the money he borrowed, as emerges from surviving receipts. He also undoubtedly won some it by gambling. But the fact remains that when Mayakovsky left New York he was as good as broke.

Despite this he bought warm clothes for Elly before his departure—it had suddenly become cold in New York, colder than in living memory. In Bloomingdale's they shopped for a brown wool dress and "the cheapest tweed coat we could find," according to Elly. "Then he paid my rent for a month—fifty dollars, or whatever it was." He stinted on himself instead. Contrary to his usual custom he bought himself a simple and cheap jacket, and if he had left Paris in first class, he spent the eight days of the return journey in a cheap berth in the very bottom of the ship, under the dance floor—"in the worst cabin / of all cabins."

There were many who came to the quay to say their farewells. Elly did not want to come, but Mayakovsky persuaded her. He kissed her hand and went on board. When the ship had put out, Charles Recht drove her home. "I wanted to throw myself on the bed and cry [. . .] but could not," Elly recalled. "My bed was covered with flowers—forget-me-nots. He had so little money. But he was that way." That's what he was like: not a few flowers or a bouquet but a bed "covered with flowers." It was typical of Mayakovsky's tendency to overdo things: when he was courting a woman he gave her not one basket of flowers but several; not one box of chocolates but ten; he bought not one lottery ticket but the whole lottery . . .

The relationship with Elly was the longest and most intense that Mayakovsky had had since his meeting with Lili in 1915. For a year or more he had no longer felt any obligation to be faithful to Lili. "We broke up completely," he confided to Elly and told her that Lili had attempted suicide by taking a medicine which for a short while made her blind. Yet Mayakovsky was still jealous of her. While waiting for a Mexican visa in Paris he learned from acquaintances that Lili had holidayed on the Volga. "It's funny that I learned about that by chance from acquaintances," he reproached her. "Because I'm interested in knowing it, if only from the point of view of learning you must have recovered!" He knew, or suspected, that Lili had not spent the holiday on her own.

Lili's reply was telling: "Write in detail *how* you're living. (*With whom* you can omit.)" They both had countless erotic adventures. The difference was that Mayakovsky suffered dreadfully from knowing about Lili's affairs with other men while Lili seems rather to have been grateful for his affairs with women—as long as these did not threaten their life together with Osip. They gave her both the moral right and the practical freedom to devote herself to her own affairs. In any case, a fling on the other side of the globe was hardly anything to worry about! However, the relationship with Elly Jones was to have more far-reaching consequences than any of the parties involved could have guessed.

11

NEW RULES

1926–1927

We must live *together*; we must travel *together*. Or, we must part—a last time and forever.
Lili to Mayakovsky

With what feelings did Mayakovsky leave the North American Continent? During his four months in Mexico and the United States both the agitator and the lyric poet in him had been able to satisfy their needs—the former in poems and public appearances, the latter in the private sphere. In addition to the love affair with Elly Jones the trip had offered large doses of nostalgia in the form of David Burlyuk, whom Mayakovsky saw more or less daily. Burlyuk helped to organize several of his readings and provided the illustrations for two of his poems which were published as separate books during his stay in New York.

But however politically "progressive" Burlyuk was, the old friends did not of course talk only, or even mainly, about politics. Nor were the poems that Burlyuk illustrated propaganda pieces, but "An Extraordinary Adventure…" (Mayakovsky's conversation with

Mayakovsky, Shklovsky, and Rodchenko photographed in 1926 by Varvara Stepanova in the garden before the house in Gendrikov Lane.

the sun; see page 152) and another nonpolitical poem, "Christopher Columbus." Burlyuk was not only "the father of Russian Futurism"; he was also in a certain sense Mayakovsky' father, for he it was who had discovered the latter's talent for poetry and made him into a writer. They had fought together for the aesthetic ideals of Futurism and, after the Revolution, for the liberation of art from the state. Burlyuk was one of Mayakovsky's closest friends. If there was anyone he could open his heart to, it was him. When he confided to Burlyuk during his stay in New York that he "had been bored for the last seven years," these words cannot simply be dismissed as an expression of tiredness, depression, or temporary mental aberration. Moreover, the comment tallies well with a form of words in the "diary" which Mayakovsky wrote during his separation from Lili in the winter of 1923, where he talks of "a horror that stretches from 1917 up to today and which is now indivisible."

Mayakovsky's split personality, the contradictions in his attitude to his work and his homeland, emerge with full force in the poem "Back Home!," which he began work on during the voyage from New York. The poem is a paean to the Communist task of reconstruction, and Mayakovsky underlines that the poet's contribution to the Revolution is at least as important as that of the worker, although they have approached Communism from different directions:

> Proletarians
>   arrive at Communism
>   from below—
> by the low way of mines,
>   sickles
>   and pitchforks,
> but I,
>   from poetry's skies,
>   plunge into Communism,
> because
>   without it
>   I feel no love.
>
> (TRANS. GEORGE REAVEY)

Just as in "About This" Mayakovsky sees the new Communist society as a precondition for true love. At the same time he develops another theme from earlier poems: that poetry must be subordinated to politics and the poet must carry out what contemporaries called "social commissions" (cf. page 399). He feels like "a Soviet factory / manufacturing happiness," he wants the State Planning Commission to set him annual tasks, the "commissar of the times" to "command his thoughts," the factory committee to "lock my lips" when work is over, his "pen to be on a par / with the bayonet," and Stalin, on the orders of the Politburo, to give a speech about "verse in the making." (That he envisaged Stalin and not someone else as the speech maker was not because of any particular sympathy for Lenin's successor as party leader but because Mayakovsky needed a good rhyme for *stali*, "steel." Stalin was not known for his pronouncements on literary questions.)

Mayakovsky had never gone as far as this before in self-effacing denial of poetry. And the frightening thing is that he did it without external pressure; there was no demand from official quarters for such orthodoxy. The impulse came from within. Mayakovsky knew with what suspicion he was regarded in many circles, and his declaration was a way of showing that he was no fellow traveler but more Communist than the party itself.

And yet Mayakovsky seems, in his innermost self, to have doubted the effect of his oath of loyalty, its political correctness notwithstanding. With his strong need to be understood and respected he feared that the reaction would be the opposite one, as emerges from the final verse of the poem:

> I want to be understood by my country,
> but if I am not understood—
>   so what?
> I must pass by my homeland
>   off to the side,
>   just like the slanting rain.

Just as interesting as Mayakovsky's doubts about whether his poetry had any place in the new society is the fact that he later deleted these lines—on the advice of Osip, who thought that a poet "for whom the

goal of his whole work, his life, is at any price to be heard and under-
stood by his country" could not write in this way. Although Mayak-
ovsky was very attached to these lines, he agreed to delete them. By
doing this he also annulled the contrast between ambivalent feelings
which is so characteristic of his best poems. (The same ambivalence
is reflected, by the way, in the rough draft of the poem, which shows
that in the fourth line of the verse the poet hesitated between two
diametrically opposed epithets—"homeland" and "foreign land.")

THE UNFINISHED NOVEL

What Mayakovsky gave expression to in a deeper sense in "Back
Home!" was the alienation that all poets feel, irrespective of which
country they live in, and which Marina Tsvetayeva summed up in the
words "Every poet is at heart an emigrant, even in [his own home-
land]." But when Mayakovsky wrote the poem, there were also per-
fectly concrete reasons, alongside this existential alienation, why he
did not feel appreciated in his homeland.

"After a short stay in Paris V. V. Mayakovsky is hastening to Mos-
cow, where he must see to the publication of his *Collected Works*," the
New York–based Russian newspaper *Russky Golos* (Russia's Voice)
announced on the day that Mayakovsky left New York. Although
he had delivered the manuscript of the first volume before leaving
Moscow five months earlier, it had never gone for typesetting. And
although the contract had been signed after major concessions on
Mayakovsky's part, the publisher's marketing department wanted to
tear it up, arguing that there was "insufficient demand" for Mayak-
ovsky's books, of which there were "large amounts of surplus stock."
Mayakovsky could show that this was because of poor marketing, but
after his homecoming he was nevertheless forced to renegotiate the
contract and agree to more distant publication dates, which meant
that the first volume came out only three years later, in December
1928.

Despite his setbacks with Gosizdat, directly after his return May-
akovsky signed a contract for four new books, among them a report
on his trip to America. The books also included a novel of about four
hundred pages, which he promised to have finished by April 1926.

"Are you writing the novel?" Lili asked in a letter to Mexico. This he obviously was. In an article in a Russian newspaper in New York, Burlyuk revealed that Mayakovsky was in the throes of writing a novel but did not wish to say what it was about. According to Burlyuk, who "had been lucky enough to listen to it," it depicted life in Russia but also contained something about America. The idea of a novel was not a new one for Mayakovsky but can be traced back to at least 1923. After his return from the United States notices appeared in the press announcing that the novel was set in Moscow and St. Petersburg during the years from 1914 "till our day" and that it depicted "literary life and daily life [*byt*], the struggle between different schools, etc." But the book was never written.

"I finished it in my head," Mayakovsky explained later, "but didn't transfer it to paper because during the process I was seized with hatred of the fictive element and began to long for concrete names, facts, etc." Instead he considered writing about the same things in the form of a "literary biography." But that did not come off either. Why? The likeliest explanation is that his temperament and lifestyle did not allow a project requiring so much time. Mayakovsky wrote his poems in his head before committing them to paper, but a novel demanded other working methods. Mayakovsky was used to working quickly and seeing quick results. How was someone so impatient that he hardly ever finished reading a book (according to Lili) or only ate fish completely filleted of bones, as it took too long otherwise (according to his sister Lyudmila), going to find peace to write a novel?

DARLING, I WON'T TORMENT YOU ANY MORE

"Let's meet somewhere *not in Moscow, abroad*," Lili wrote on 26 July to Mayakovsky, who was then still in Mexico. She had been quite prepared to call on Mayakovsky in the United States but, as we saw, those plans came to naught. "IF YOU DON'T SEND VISA WILL GO ITALY SEPTEMBER," she telegraphed on 13 August. She had recovered from her gynecological operation and claimed to be "healthy in every way," but as "the Italians" had promised her a visa she felt obliged to go to the mud baths at Salsomaggiore. On 22 September she told Mayakovsky that her papers were in order. The plan was that Mayakovsky would join her in Italy. "STAYING ONLY FOR VISA," he telegraphed Lili a month later from New York, not entirely truthfully.

In the event Mayakovsky had to leave New York without any Italian visa in his pocket. Shortly after landing in Paris on 6 November he received a letter from Lili in which she informed him that she was going to travel to Rome to try to get a visa for him there. "Telegraph whether you have any money. I'm completely in rags—I've worn everything into holes. We should buy everything in Italy—it's much cheaper. It would be good if I could get you a visa, so you could come and fetch me here! [. . .] I miss you incredibly! We could spend about ten days traveling round the Venices—and then go home! I've got a splendid present waiting for you in Moscow." But obtaining the visa, it transpired, would take several weeks, and Lili and Mayakovsky met instead in Berlin on 14 November. They had not seen each other for almost six months.

Mayakovsky was the first to arrive in the German capital. When Lili stepped off the train, he was so agitated that he lost his cane. He had got her room in the Kurfürstenhôtel ready for her, and when she opened the door in she was met by baskets and vases of flowers and a whole tree with flowering camellias. Presents from Mexico were lying everywhere: wooden toys, a bird made from real feathers, a colorful rug, a box with different-colored cigarettes from Havana. There was also a newfangled American gadget in the form of a folding travel iron. Lili in her turn gave Mayakovsky a Persian elephant with bronze inlay.

They were overjoyed at meeting again, at the presents, at the solicitude that the presents bore witness to. Lili put on a violet dress and lit up a violet cigarette. They talked nonstop. Everything was just like before. Or was it? As usual they had separate rooms in the hotel. After dinner Mayakovsky came over to Lili's. According to the account she gave later, he did not come into the room but leaned against the doorpost and said softly: "Good night, darling, I won't torment you any more." He had realized that Lili would leave him for good if he continued to force himself on her against her will. After ten years Mayakovsky knew Lili well enough to be aware that their relation-

When Mayakovsky returned from America, his friends came together to welcome him home. *Standing, from left:* Mayakovsky with his present from Lili, the bulldog Bulka, Osip, Boris Pasternak, Sergey Tretyakov, Viktor Shklovsky, Lev Grinkrug, Osip Beskin, and Pyotr Neznamov. *Sitting from left:* Elsa, Lili, Raisa Kushner, Yelena Pasternak, and Olga Tretyakova.

ship was entirely dictated by Lili's feelings and wishes, not by his. His remark meant the irrevocable end of their physical relationship.

He also knew her well enough to know she would not react with indignation to the episode with Elly. The code guiding their relationship dictated that they keep each other apprised of their respective "affairs." That Mayakovsky told Lili about Elly therefore seems beyond doubt. When he took an anonymous Wasserman test at the Institute for Medical Diagnostics in Berlin to find out if he had syphilis, we can rest assured that this took place with Lili's knowledge, if not on her initiative. Mayakovsky's nonexistent German in any case excludes the possibility that he could have consulted the doctor by himself. The result was negative.

After four days in Berlin Lili and Mayakovsky traveled home to

Zhenya photographed by Rodchenko in the studio of his wife, Varvara Stepanova, in 1924, the year before she joined fortunes with Osip. She is dressed in a sport costume designed by Stepanova for the students of the Academy for Social Training. On the wall to the left are some of Rodchenko's advertisement posters.

Moscow, via Lithuania. They were met at the station by Osip and Elsa, who remembered that Lili stepped down from the railway carriage wearing a jacket of squirrel skin. After a month abroad she was no longer "threadbare.". . . After her came Mayakovsky, who was greeted on reaching Sokolniki by the barking of Lili's "fantastic present"—the bulldog Bulka.

Their homecoming had not only pleasant surprises in store, however. If Mayakovsky had not realized it earlier, he was now left in no doubt that the rules of play for their "marriage cartel" had definitely changed. What made him realize this was not so much Lili's fleeting passion for the publisher Osip Beskin—whom she lived with for a while at the beginning of 1926—as the more revolutionary change that had taken place in Osip's life. In January 1925 he had become acquainted with a young woman, the twenty-five-year-old Yevgeniya ("Zhenya") Sokolova, who was married to the film director Vitaly Zhemchuzhny. In the libertine culture that dominated the cultural circles in Moscow in the twenties Osip was an exception. Although Osip and Lili had not been intimate for over ten years, the fact that a young librarian had managed to awaken his slumbering sexuality was a severe affront to Lili—especially as Zhenya was a woman of a quite different kind from those the Briks were used to socializing with in their salon: quiet and reserved. "I can't understand what he finds to talk to her about," was her testy comment about Zhenya, whose lack of "elegance" also upset her.

Lili, who had always successfully managed to tame her "beasts" into submission—and who had never objected Mayakovsky's affairs with women—was now forced to accept that Osip, whom she had loved since childhood, had found a woman who released his emotions. For Osip the encounter with Zhenya was nothing short of a "miracle," as he wrote in a poetic greeting to her twenty days after their first meeting—had he believed in God, he would have gone down on his knees to him for allowing their paths to cross.

WE MUST LIVE TOGETHER!

However difficult Lili found it at first to accept Osip's newly awakened emotions, the whole thing was made easier by the fact that Zhenya never moved in with "the family." Their life as a threesome could thus continue as before. And that was the most important thing.

The relationship of Lili, Osip, and Mayakovsky had never been a "ménage à trois" in the physical sense and now it was no longer even a "ménage à deux." There is no doubt that Lili's theories about free love caused Mayakovsky endless suffering, but the foundation of their life together was a partnership of a much deeper kind. However distraught Mayakovsky was because of all Lili's affairs, he knew that no one appreciated his poetry more than she did. And however tired Lili became of Mayakovsky's childish petulance, jealousy, and impossible demands, she knew what a central role she played in his creativity. As for Osip, she had loved him all her life—in the same way as she admired Mayakovsky for his poetry, she looked up to Osip for his erudition and intellectual brilliance.

The third factor in the equation, Mayakovsky's relationship to Osip, was characterized by tenderheartedness and deep friendship. It was Mayakovsky who had awakened Osip's interest in poetry and thereby steered his life in a new direction. Osip's intellect, which hitherto had been directed toward law and corals, came henceforth to be focused on literary and literary-theoretical questions, and during the twenties he developed into one of the country's leading cultural idcologists. The source of inspiration for his theorizing was primarily Mayakovsky and his poetry.

At the same time as Mayakovsky, in Lili's words, "changed Osip's thinking," so Osip had a colossal importance for Mayakovsky's development. Mayakovsky read little and unsystematically while Osip was a great reader who went the round of secondhand booksellers every day and in time put together a significant library. Mayakovsky had complete trust in Osip's taste and competence in aesthetic questions. It was a rare sort of relationship, based on friendship, affection, humor, common interests, and the political conviction that they were on their way to creating a better world.

If Mayakovsky was the poet and Osip the cultural theorist, Lili was the chief ideologue with regard to questions of how they should live their lives. Here, she was just as influenced by ideas stemming from the revolution in equality between the sexes and women's liberation as by her innate need for freedom. In order for their partnership to function, she decided that they should be able to do as they wished during the daytime but that they should try to spend the evenings, and—if possible—the nights under the same roof. Some time after their separation in 1923 Lili formulated her ideas in a letter to Mayakovsky:

> You and I cannot go on living the way we've lived up till now. I absolutely refuse to! We must live *together*; we must travel *together*. Or, we must part—a last time and forever. Which I do not want. We must stay in Moscow now; get the flat sorted out. Do you really not want to live a human life with me?! And then, starting from our shared life, everything else will follow. [. . .]
>
> We should start doing all this straightaway, if, of course, you want to. I want to very much. It seems both fun and interesting. I could like you now, I could love you, if you were *with me* and *for me*. If, regardless of where we had been and what we had been doing during the day, we could lie side by side *together* in the evening or at night in a clean, comfortable bed; in a room with fresh air; after a warm bath!
>
> Isn't that right? You think I'm complicating matters again, or being capricious.
>
> Think about it seriously, like an adult. I've thought about it for a long time, and *for myself I've decided*. I would like you to be glad about my desire and my decision, and not simply to go along with them! I kiss you, your Lili.

The letter is remarkable, coming as it does from a woman who reproached *Mayakovsky* for surrendering to the temptations of bourgeois life. But it is interesting as a declaration of intent. The relationship of Lili, Osip and Mayakovsky was an example of a modern family setup, a way of living which corresponded to Chernyshevsky's revolutionary ideal. This family structure had by now taken on almost emblematic status and might not be upset, however great the stresses it was exposed to in the form of Lili's need for erotic and intellectual stimulation and Mayakovsky's uncontrollable jealousy. By conducting all their "affairs" outside the home, the "family" could be kept intact. It was a stratagem on Lili's terms, a way of guaranteeing that the freedom she had always taken pains to assure herself was not threatened. Mayakovsky knew this, and he also knew that if he did not accept it, the relationship between Lili and himself was over for good.

CHANGEZ VOS DAMES!

The "marriage cartel" of Lili, Osip, and Mayakovsky may have been one of the period's most talked-about examples of modern family structure, but free-love relationships were nothing unusual in the first workers' state, especially in literary and artistic circles. Osip Mandelstam lived together with his wife and the poet Mariya Petrovykh in a relationship which was applauded by his wife, who could only see this trinity as something positive. Maxim Gorky was married but lived openly with the actress Mariya Andreyeva and later with Baroness Mariya Budberg. During those years when Nikolay Punin lived with Anna Akhmatova they had dinner every evening with Punin's former wife. The list can be extended and completed with the great nineteenth-century figures Chernyshevsky, Turgenev, and Nekrasov. "The moral and sexual aspects of such unions did not bother me in the least," commented Emma Gerstein, a close friend of the Mandelstams. "We lived in the epoch of the sexual revolution, we were freethinking, young, with a natural and healthy sensuality. [. . .] The only criterion for how one should behave in private life was for us individual taste—one was allowed to do what one wanted."

This behavior had its origins in the general loosening of the bonds of convention which took place after the middle of the nineteenth century (see the chapter "Lili") and which was given official sanction after the Revolution by new marriage laws. According to the first, adopted in 1918, only civil marriage was allowed, not church marriage, it became easy to divorce, and "legitimate" and "illegitimate" children were given equal status in law. In the next marriage act, from 1926, the legislation was liberalized to the extent that it was legally insignificant whether a marriage was registered or not: the main thing was that a man and a woman who lived together regarded themselves as married. The procedure for obtaining a divorce was made even simpler; it was enough that one of the parties declared

A modern woman posing in 1924 for a modern photographer, Alexander Rodchenko.

that he or she wished to separate—the other did not even need to be present, let alone give consent. This marriage act also legalized free abortion.

The new legislation was built on ideas with their roots in the founding fathers of Marxism, and particularly Friedrich Engels. Connubial and sexual freedom were part of the general freedom which would be achieved in the new society and the spokespersons for free love were quick to draw parallels between private ownership in the old society and monogamy (i.e., ownership of women) and the public ownership and the free love of free individuals in the Communist society. During the first decade after the Revolution the Communist Party was also careful not to interfere in citizens' private lives. Commissar of Enlightenment Lunacharsky declared in 1923 that state regulation of the individual's life "endangers Communism" and that "the morality of Communist society will be found in the fact that there will be no precepts; it will be the morality of the absolutely free individual." There should, he enjoined, be "no pressure of public opinion either; there must be no *comme il faut!*"

One of the leading propagandists for free love—or, more accurately, for free sexual expression—was the veteran Communist Alexandra Kollontay, according to whose "water-glass theory" people in a society liberated from bourgeois moral principles ought to be able to satisfy their sexual needs as easily as drinking a glass of water. Sexual promiscuity was as much a right for women as for men.

It is hard to say how much currency Kollontay's water-glass theory enjoyed, but it was taken up largely by intellectuals and by the young. One Young Communist, for example, revealed that he no longer visited prostitutes because he could now sleep with any young woman whatsoever! And in 1927, when the students at ten schools of higher learning in Odessa were asked the question "Does love exist?" only 60.9 percent of the women and 51.8 percent of the men answered in the affirmative.

The sexual theories of Kollontay and other radicals followed logically from Marxism's ideas about the free—or liberated—individual in the Communist society: admittedly extreme but difficult to refute with Marxist arguments. As Communism and sexual freedom were seen as going hand in hand (like the old sexual morality and bourgeois society), all opposition to "the new morality" was regarded as prejudiced and reactionary.

Ten years after the revolution Anatoly Lunacharsky, who to begin with had praised sexual freedom in the name of "the natural human being," had taken a decidedly more sober stance, and when in a lecture in 1927 he summed up the "Marxist" view of the relations between man and woman, he did so with an ironic paraphrase:

> Husband, wife, children—husband and wife who bear and rear children, this is a bourgeois business. A Communist who respects himself, a Soviet person, a leading member of the intelligentsia, a genuine proletarian ought to be on his guard against such a bourgeois business. "Socialism," say such 'Marxists,' "brings with it new forms of relationship between man and woman—namely free love. A man and a woman come together, live together while they like each other—and after they no longer like each other—they part. They are together for a relatively short period, not setting up a permanent household. Both the man and woman are free in this relationship." [...] "A genuine Communist, a Soviet person," they say, "must avoid a pairing marriage and seek to satisfy his needs by *changez vos dames*, as they said in the old cadrille, with a definite changing, a freedom of the mutual relations of the husbands, the wives, fathers, children, so that you can't tell who is related to whom and how closely. That is social construction."

However ironic Lunacharsky' description, it tallied very well with the ideals which Lili embraced and which had support from the Soviet legal code—thus far: the marriage act of 1936 represented revenge for the traditional view of marriage and family.

IN THIS LIFE TO DIE IS NOT SO HARD

On the morning of 28 December 1925, Russia awoke to dreadful news: the poet Sergey Yesenin had been found dead in the Hôtel d'Angleterre in Leningrad, thirty years old. He had hanged himself from the water pipe in his room.

Sergey Yesenin was in many ways Mayakovsky's opposite. If May-

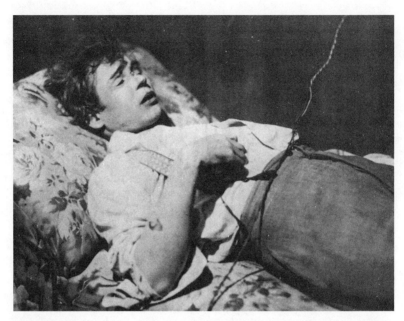

Sergey Yesenin took his life by hanging himself on the water pipe in the Hôtel d'Angleterre with the help of an electric cord.

akovsky was the poet of the big city and the Revolution, Yesenin was the poet of the dying Russian countryside. Their contacts over the years were confined mostly to polemics, especially at the beginning of the twenties, when Yesenin for a time allied himself to the Futurists' opponents, the Imaginists. When asked during his American trip what he thought about Yesenin, Mayakovsky replied that he was "talented but conservative" and that he "mourned the demise of the wealthy peasants of the old countryside at the same time as Soviet Russia's struggling proletariat was forced to fight against this countryside because the wealthy peasants hid bread instead of delivering it to the starving cities."

On one occasion he indulged himself in a joke about Yesenin's drinking habits which was unworthy but not unwarranted. Yesenin lived a dissipated life, not least during his short marriage to the expansive and eccentric dancer Isadora Duncan. Their European roundtrip in Duncan's five-seater Buick was framed by scenes, smashed-up restaurant interiors, and Yesenin's drunken binges.

In the autumn of 1925 Yesenin was at such a low ebb that he

was assailed by delirium tremens and hallucinations, and on 26 November he was admitted to a psychiatric clinic in Moscow. His condition was exacerbated by epilepsy (which, like his alcoholism, seems to have been hereditary) and a melancholia so deep that it brought on suicidal thoughts. The door to his room in the hospital was therefore kept permanently open. On 21 December Yesenin broke off his treatment on his own initiative and left the clinic—perhaps because he had heard that he had only six months left to live. A couple of days later he traveled to Leningrad, where he took his own life.

For Mayakovsky, who constantly entertained suicide as an option at the back of his mind, Yesenin's death released a series of defense mechanisms. In the preceding few years several great poets had died: Gumilyov, Blok, Khlebnikov—but none of these losses evoked the same tortured reaction from Mayakovsky as Yesenin's suicide. Although, according to Lili, "on principle he never expressed himself positively" about Yesenin, he regarded him as "devilishly gifted" and moreover as something of a soul mate, equally vulnerable, equally vehement and uneven in temper as himself, equally restless and desperate in his searching. Yesenin's first wife, the actress Zinaida Reikh, who later married Vsevolod Meyerhold, said that she "did not perceive any difference" between the mental state of Yesenin and Mayakovsky: "A violent inner unrest, a feeling of dissatisfaction and fear in face of the fading fame of their youth."

When Yesenin took his own life, the identification became even stronger, especially as Mayakovsky was hardly unaware that it was not his first suicide attempt. This was clear, if nowhere else, from Yesenin's poems, where the suicide motif is just as common as in Mayakovsky's own. Just like Mayakovsky, Yesenin was, in the poet Anatoly Mariengof's definition, "manic" in his suicidal thoughts.

Before he hanged himself, Yesenin made a shallow cut on his arm and wrote a farewell poem in his own blood which ended with the lines "To die in this life is nothing new, / but neither is it new to live." The day after his death the poem was printed in all the newspapers. "After these lines," commented Mayakovsky, "Yesenin's death became a 'literary fact.'" It was only by transmuting Yesenin's death into literature, by objectifying it, that Mayakovsky could cope with his feelings. At the end of January he left on a three-month-long reading tour in southern Russia. Yesenin's suicide was a constant presence, both for himself and for the public, and when he was asked a question about Yesenin during an appearance in Kharkov, he gave the irritable answer: "After death I don't give a damn about monuments and laurel wreaths. . . . Take care of your poets!"

In order to be able to deal with Yesenin's suicide, he tried to write about it, but the work went slowly. Although he thought about the subject every day during the long tour, he "couldn't come up with anything sensible." The only thing that occurred to him was "a lot of devilish nonsense in the form of blue faces and water pipes." The reason he was unable to write, he confided, was "the all-too-great similarity between the subject matter and my own predicament. The same hotel room, the same pipes, and the same enforced solitude." Even if Mayakovsky is referring here to the superficial similarities— the traveling poet in a lonely hotel room—it is clear that Yesenin's suicide inspired thoughts in him that he would have preferred to avoid. It happened at a time when the conditions of his own life had fundamentally altered and the future was uncertain. He was to live beside Lili in the same apartment but no longer as her husband. What form would his life take, and who would fill the emotional vacuum left by Lili?

After trying to write something for three weeks, at the end of March Mayakovsky delivered the poem "To Sergey Yesenin" to the printer's. It enjoyed enormous success and circulated in transcript even before it was published. "It was immediately clear how many wavering individuals [Yesenin's] powerful verse—precisely, *verse*— would tempt to the noose or the revolver," Mayakovsky wrote in his essay "How to Make Verse," which in large part is concerned with his work on the Yesenin poem. "And this verse cannot be annulled by any newspaper analyses or articles. This verse must and can be fought with verse and *only with verse*."

The aim of Mayakovsky's poem was "in a well-reasoned way to paralyze Yesenin's last lines, to make Yesenin's ending uninteresting," in his own words, "since [. . .] laboring humanity [. . .] demands that we celebrate the joy of life, joy in the difficult march toward Communism."

Mayakovsky's way of making "Yesenin's ending uninteresting" was to paraphrase the last lines of Yesenin's poem:

> In this life,
>> to die is not so hard.
> To build new life
>> is significantly harder.

The lines are an answer not only to Yesenin's poem but also to the deeply felt hurt to which Mayakovsky gives expression in the introduction to the poem:

> You have disappeared,
>> they say,
>>> to another world.
> Emptiness . . .
>> You fly,
>>> push your way in among the stars.
> Where there are neither advances
>> nor pubs.
> Sobriety.
>> No, Yesenin,
>>> this
>>>> is not mockery.
> The lump in my throat
>> is sorrow—
>>> not laughter.
> I see in front of me
>> how with your mangled arm
> you set
>> the sack
>>> with your legs swaying.

The one who expressed the idea that Yesenin's suicide could tempt vulnerable people "to the noose or the revolver" knew very well that he himself belonged to this company. If there was one thing that the poem "To Sergey Yesenin" was designed to "annul" it was

Mayakovsky's own suicidal thoughts. A year later, during a visit to Leningrad, he asked his driver to make a detour to avoid the Hôtel d'Angleterre—he could not face the thought of seeing the building where Yesenin had taken his own life.

GENDRIKOV

In order to realize Lili's vision of how they ought to live, they needed another, bigger apartment. As long as they were living in such cramped conditions, only parts of the program could be carried out. They spent the evenings together, at the card table, or out, but Mayakovsky mostly spent the nights in his room in Lubyanka Passage.

Immediately after his return from the United States, in December 1925, Mayakovsky was allotted an apartment in Gendrikov Alley in the Taganka district, some way from the center of Moscow. It was not large—three bedrooms of ten square meters each, a living room that measured fourteen, a little kitchen—but they did not have to share it with other people. It was their own apartment, their new joint dwelling, where Lili's theories could be put to practice. But before this the apartment had to be renovated and put in order, which took almost six months.

It was in order to finance the renovation that Mayakovsky set

out in January on his reading tour. Before leaving he asked Lunacharsky—for the umpteenth time!—to intervene to prevent him from losing his apartment, this time in Gendrikov Alley. He was successful in this, and thanks to a decision of the Moscow soviet he also managed to deflect the threat of "densification." Instead he "densified" the apartment in the way he himself wanted, by ensuring that Lili and Osip were registered there too.

In Mayakovsky's absence it was Lili who looked after the practical task of putting the apartment in order. "Dear sunray," he wrote from Baku on 20 February, "I'm very sorry for

The house (*opposite*) in Gendrikov Lane. Mayakovsky's and the Briks' apartment was on the second floor. The rooms were small, and every inch had to be utilized. Mayakovsky had a special wardrobe made, with a mirror and a folding dressing table (*above*). The photograph at top shows the sitting-room and Mayakovsky's room.

Elsa and Lili at the dacha in Pushkino in 1925, when Elsa visited Russia for the first time since 1918.

you having to deal with all the bother about the flat on your own. And I'm very envious of you because that kind of bother is interesting." He sent her money as soon as he earned it. The money was needed—the apartment was in a lamentable state, with lice crawling behind the wallpaper—and everything had to be replaced and redone. And as the rooms were so small, the furniture had to be specially ordered.

Lili took care of everything; she went around workshops, ordered bookshelves and cupboards, discussed shapes and sizes with the carpenters. For the external door she ordered a plate with the names "BRIK. MAYAKOVSKY." The Steinway had to be sold, as there was no room for it, and books which could not be accommodated in Osip's room were placed in two specially made padlocked bookcases on the cold landing outside the door. "The design principle was the same as when 'Cloud' was published, 'nothing superfluous,'" Lili recalled. "Nothing decorative—mahogany, paintings, ornaments. Everything was new, even knives and forks, and we only had what was really essential. The walls were bare. Except that over V.V.'s and O.M.'s couches there were textiles from Mexico and over mine an old pearl-embroidered rug with a hunting motif which Volodya brought back from Moscow for me when we lived in Petrograd. On the floor, colorful Ukrainian rugs for the sake of warmth, and in Vladimir Vladimirovich's room there hung two photographs of me which I gave him as a birthday present the same year we met."

At the end of April, at the same time as the poem "To Sergey Yesenin" came out as a separate book with a cover by Alexander Rodchenko, Mayakovsky, Lili, and Osip were able to move into the newly renovated apartment. Elsa, who had been in Moscow since the previous summer and who had stayed alternately in the house in Sokolniki and in Mayakovsky's room in Lubyanka Passage, had by then returned to Paris after eight months in her homeland. In the meantime she had made her debut as a writer with the fictionalized travel account *On Tahiti*, which appeared in Leningrad in 1925 with Roman Jakobson's jocular lines as their epigraph (see the chapter "*Drang nach Westen*"). The private and the literary could not be kept apart: in the autobiographical *Wild Strawberry*, which came out in 1926, she transmuted Roman's passion for her into literature (see the chapter "The First Revolution and the Third") in the same way as Shklovsky had done with his feelings for Elsa in *Zoo*.

DOCHKA

The move had been a major financial outlay for Mayakovsky, who in addition got a nasty surprise from the tax authorities that same spring. They wanted to tax him in the same way as private small businessmen and artisans, and as Mayakovsky did not keep a cashbook, he had to give detailed justification for his allowances—travel, office materials, help with typing, and so on—in several petitions to the tax office. He also did it in verse, with the poem "Conversation with the Tax Collector about Poetry," in which he shows that the poet, unlike other people, "is always / indebted to the universe / paying / interest / and fines / for his grief." In the end he managed to obtain a reduction of 50 percent for "production costs" (and for maintenance of his mother), so that his gross income of 9,935 rubles for six months was reduced to a taxable income of 4,968 rubles.

While Mayakovsky's expenses, for himself and others, were always considerable, he had a very irresponsible attitude to money. He was both generous and extravagant and could without a second thought wager large sums on the turn of a card, or a game of billiards. The *New York Times* revealed that he was "one of the richest" poets in Russia. But how much money did he actually earn? Mayakovsky's returns to the tax office make it possible to arrive at a rough approximation of his income. According to the man himself, his income of 9,935 rubles for the fourth quarter of 1925 and the first quarter of 1926 was 3,000 rubles higher than normal, as during this period he had sold his *Collected Works* to Gosizdat. His normal income over a six-month period was therefore around 6,000 rubles, that is, 12,000 a year. This should be compared to the annual wage of an industrial worker, which was around 900 rubles. So Mayakovsky earned a good thirteen times more than the worker. As another comparison, the voyage from New York to Le Havre cost 400 rubles.

If the renovation of the apartment had emptied Mayakovsky's wallet, it had exhausted Lili's strength, and shortly after the move she went to the Black Sea for a few weeks' holiday. When she returned home it was Mayakovsky's turn to travel south, this time for readings in the Crimea. He left Moscow on 19 June. In Yalta he received a letter from Lili reporting on how she and Osip were spending their days. "On Mondays the cream of literary, artistic, political, and financial Moscow gather at our place," "on Sundays we drive to the races," "on the other days Osya visits his women friends" (!) and Lili herself drives around calling on various "bigwigs," among them Alter, in the dacha quarter Serebryany bor. "Now try to avoid envy, Volosit," she exhorts Mayakovsky.

According to the rules that Lili had drawn up, all three members of the family were free to devote themselves to their own relationships, as long as this did not disturb their life together. Osip spent more and more time with Zhenya, and Lili had possibly continuing contact with Krasnoshchokov, who had returned from his Crimean sanatorium in the autumn of 1925 and begun working as an economist

Lili and Luella photographed by Alexander Rodchenko.

on the cotton committee of the Commissariat for Agriculture. That same year his wife and son came on a visit from the United States, but hopes of a reconciliation came to nought—after only one and a half months in Moscow they traveled back to New York, where Gertrud was employed by Amtorg. In connection with his new job, Krasnoshchokov was allotted an apartment in Moscow, to which he moved with his daughter Luella.

Mayakovsky was of course jealous, however much Lili urged him not to be. But by the time he received her letter, in the middle of July, his life had been enriched—and complicated—by an event which to some degree put such concerns in the shade. On 15 June Elly Jones in New York had borne him a daughter, who was christened Helen Patricia and called Elly like her mother. The news came as no surprise to Mayakovsky, who knew or suspected that Elly was pregnant. It was probably this that the wording of his New Year telegram hinted at: "WRITE EVERYTHING. EVERYTHING. HAPPY NEW YEAR." But Elly did not write, from fear that the information would be snapped up by the Soviet censorship. When on 6 May she finally told Mayakovsky about her imminent confinement and asked him for financial assistance she did it in general terms, without mentioning what the money would be used for: "I have to pay the hospital $600 in three weeks. If you can, send it to the following address: [. . .] I think you understand my silence. If I die—*all right*, if not, we'll meet." Mayakovsky replied with a telegram in which he told her that "objective circumstances" prevented him from sending money, however much he wanted to.

Although he had to be very careful, Mayakovsky contacted Elly as soon as he found out he was going to be a father. "I was so happy with your letter, my friend! Why, why didn't you write earlier?" she wondered reproachfully on 20 July. "I am still very weak. Can hardly walk. Can't manage to write very much. I don't want to think about my nightmarish spring for then I am just sad. I'm alive at least. I'll soon be well. Forgive me for making you sad with my stupid letter." She had been waiting for a long time for letters from him, she continues, but perhaps they remained in the desk drawer? "Oh, Vladimir, do you really not remember the dear paw? You are strange, you are. One day maybe we both ought to go and call on Freud."

Mayakovsky's reaction to the event is only casually registered in one of his notebooks from 1926, in which he wrote the word *dochka*, "a little daughter," on an otherwise empty page. But from Elly's letters to him it emerges that he had plans to visit New York. "I am quite sure that we can arrange a visa for you. Telegraph if you have finally decided to come." The person who was to help with the formalities was, just like before, the lawyer Charles Recht.

But Mayakovsky never made it. The "objective circumstances" which had prevented the transfer of money to the United States were even more "objective" when it came to his own possibilities of obtaining transport. How could he have justified such a trip, and at such short notice? He could not declare the real motive to either the Soviet or the American authorities, or even to his friends. It would be a good two years before Mayakovsky managed to see his daughter (who officially had George Jones as her father).

For the time being he found release for his paternal feelings in writing for children, something which by his own account he devoted himself to "with special enthusiasm." Shortly after his daughter's birth he wrote a film script, *Children*, about the starving family of an American miner. The mother's name is Elly, and the daughter is called Irma—which suggests that he had not yet been told her real name. The story is full of clichés about the inhumanity of capital-ism, but when Mayakovsky has Irma invited to the Soviet Union to meet Russian Pioneers it is not the ideologue talking but the father dreaming of meeting his daughter one day.

One measure of the depth of Mayakovsky's anguish at not hav-ing contact with his child is an event which took place the following year in Prague. When the one-year-old son of the folklorist Pyotr Bogatyryov came rushing into the room, Mayakovsky shouted irri-tably: "Take him out!" Roman Jakobson, who described the episode, interpreted this aggressive reaction as an expression of Mayakovsky's dislike of children, whom, according to Jakobson, he regarded as a "continuation of daily *byt*." It is possible that Jakobson was right. But he did not know that Mayakovsky had a daughter in the United States and that the shout might just as well well have been a shout of despair.

Lili knew that Mayakovsky had had an affair with Elly, but when did she find out that he had become a father? At the end of July she came to the Crimea to work as assistant director during the filming

Lili and Mayakovsky at the seaside resort Chair in August 1926.

of *Jews Work the Land*, a film about the attempt to set up Jewish farm-
ing settlements in the Crimea, with a script by Shklovsky. After the
filming was finished, Lili spent fourteen days with Mayakovsky at
the pension Chair in the Crimea. Perhaps it was then she found out
that Elly had borne Mayakovsky a daughter.

I'M TRAVELING AROUND LIKE A MADMAN

Although they had just moved into a new apartment, both Lili and
Mayakovsky were absent from Moscow a great deal during this
year, in Mayakovsky's case for a whole five months. After returning
from the Crimea at the end of August he made several trips out into
the country during the autumn. A letter to Lili from Krasnodar in
Ukraine gives a picture of the hectic life he was leading:

I'm traveling around like a madman. I've already read in Voronezh, Rostov, Taganrog, Rostov again, Novocherkassk, and twice more in Rostov; now I'm sitting in Krasnodar; this evening I shall not so much read as wheeze—I'm begging the organizers not to take me to Novorossiysk, but they're begging me to go to Stavropol as well.

It's rather difficult reading. I read every day: for example, on Saturday I read in Novocherkassk from 8:30 in the evening until 12:45 at night, and they asked me to appear again at 8:00 in the morning in the university and at 10:00 at the cavalry regiment, but I had to refuse because at 10:00 I left for Rostov and read at RAPP from 1:30 till 4:30, and then at 5:30 in the Lenin workshops, which I absolutely couldn't refuse: it was for the workers and free!

These trips continued during the winter and the whole of 1927, when Mayakovsky was absent from Moscow for all of 181 days, visited forty towns, and delivered over one hundred readings. "I am continuing the interrupted tradition of the troubadours and the meistersingers," he declared. His appearances involved an enormous strain; they lasted on average for three hours and were followed by questions and heckling by the public. That same year, moreover, Mayakovsky wrote seventy poems, twenty articles and essays, three film scripts, and a long poem, "Good!," for the tenth anniversary of the October Revolution. It was impressive, but it took its toll of his strength.

What made him shoulder this almost inhuman workload was a combination of several factors. In the first place, he wanted to meet his public and disseminate his poems and his aesthetic message. He was a born platform poet, and this was the breath of life to him. In the second place he needed to earn money. And third, work was a way of repressing thoughts of the life Lili was leading in Moscow—while his own life "from the spiritual and romantic point of view" was "pretty awful."

But neither did Lili confine herself to Moscow the whole time. Europe was tempting, as always, and on 16 January 1927, the same day on which Mayakovsky set off on one of his reading tours—this time in the towns on the Volga—Lili took the train to Vienna. Nothing is known of her stay there or of her reasons for traveling to Austria, except that she met Elsa, who had gone to the health spa of Franzensbad in Czechoslovakia to seek a cure for the rheumatism she had developed in Tahiti, and to work on her new book *Camouflage Color*. The only witnesses to her three-week-long stay in Vienna are some telegrams in which she begs Mayakovsky and Osip to send money. In order to do this, the permission of the authorities had to be obtained, and on 3 February Mayakovsky was able to tell her that he had sent $205 to the Arbeiterbank in Vienna and would send the rest "any day."

LETTER TO MAXIM GORKY

Since the beginning of 1925 the group around Mayakovsky had lacked a mouthpiece for their aesthetic ideas. *Lef* had died a natural death: the seventh and last number came out in January 1925. A planned eighth number was never published. Encouraged by the party resolution on literature, which completely ignored Futurism and Lef, Gosizdat had found it possible to cease publication. The fact that the cancellation of *Lef* coincided with the publisher's decision to postpone Mayakovsky's *Collected Works* was probably no coincidence.

If the word "Futurism" had had dubious publicity value even at an earlier stage of the Soviet cultural debate, it was now genuinely counterproductive. During an appearance in New York in October 1925, when it was already clear that Gosizdat wanted to break its contract for the collected works, Mayakovsky explained:

> Futurism had its place and has made itself immortal in literary history, but in Soviet Russia it has had its day.
> The Soviet Union's striving and labor is mirrored not in Futurism but in Lef, which celebrates not naked chaotic technology but rational organization. Futurism and the work of building the Soviet Union [. . .] cannot go hand in hand. From now on [. . .] I am against Futurism. From now on I shall fight it.

This was verbal hairsplitting. The important thing was not what the "Futurists" called themselves, the important thing was the stress on literary innovation, and this remained unaltered. In the winter of 1926 Osip and three poets (Aseyev, Pasternak and the Constructivist Ilya Selvinski, who was close to the Futurists) visited Leon Trotsky to complain about the difficulties experimental writers were experiencing in getting published. Even if Trotsky belonged to the opposition within the party, his position in issues pertaining to culture was sufficiently strong to justify a visit, particularly as Brik at this point was declaring that he had "had enough of it" and was himself supporting the opposition.

Mayakovsky, who had been in contact with Trotsky several times before, was not present, probably because the meeting took place while he was out of town. Perhaps it was pressure from Trotsky (who immediately called a meeting with leading cultural bureaucrats) which in September 1926 led to the Lef group's being able to conclude an agreement with Gosizdat about the publication of a new monthly journal, *New Lef*, with a print run of fifteen hundred. It extended to only three printed sheets, forty-eight pages, significantly less than "old *Lef*," which sometimes contained several hundred pages.

In the editorial in the first number, which came out in January 1927, the justification given for the initiative was that the situation in the cultural sector in recent years had changed into "a swamp that threatens to approach the level of the prewar years" and that *Lef* was "a stone thrown into this swamp of life and art." It ended with a rallying cry to other cultural workers to come to the defense of revolutionary aesthetics: "Our constant struggle for quality, industrialism, constructivism (i.e., purposefulness and economy of the artistic expression) provides a parallel in today's situation to the fundamental political and economic watchwords in the country and ought to entice all practitioners of the new culture over to us."

The editorial was followed by a poem of Mayakovsky's in which he criticized Maxim Gorky for remaining abroad instead of returning to his homeland and joining in the work of "building tomorrow's world." The fact that "Letter from the Author Vladimir Vladimirovich MAYAKOVSKY to the Author Alexey Maximovich GORKY" was published in such a prominent place was a deliberate challenge, as the poem had previously been turned down by *Izvestiya*, which in turn led Mayakovsky to cease publishing his works in the government organ.

As a leading symbol of non-Bolshevik socialism, Gorky had left a large vacuum behind him when he had moved abroad in 1921. "I don't know what would have been left of the Revolution for me, or wherein its *truth* would have resided, if you had not existed in the history of Russia," Pasternak wrote to him. "The whole of Soviet Russia thinks constantly of you," Yesenin told Gorky shortly before he took his own life, and the prose writer Mikhail Prishvin flattered him jokingly with the comment that he was now so important that he quite simply could not come home, as he would be "torn to pieces."

If Yesenin or Pasternak could possibly have talked Gorky into coming home, Mayakovsky's chances of doing so were minimal. Relations between himself and Gorky had been dreadful since the row over Mayakovsky's alleged syphilis. Mayakovsky was one of the few authors whom Gorky, that dedicated letter writer, never exchanged a letter with. And although Gorky followed and commented on literary developments in the Soviet Union with close attention, he never uttered a word about Mayakovsky's writings (which, in view of Mayakovsky's position, was an impressive achievement).

Nor was Mayakovsky's "Letter" so much an exhortation as a reproach. For Mayakovsky, Gorky's absence from his homeland was just as much an act of treachery as Yesenin's suicide. After several years in Germany, Gorky had lived since 1924 in Sorrento, not far from the island of Capri, where he had spent seven years in exile, from 1906 to 1913. "It's a pity, comrade Gorky / that you / are not to be seen / where we are building nowadays. / Do you think / the view is better / from Capri's cliffs?" But his criticism was not only motivated by political differences. The old wounds had not healed, as can be seen in the opening lines of the poem:

> Alexey Maximovich,
>> as I remember
>>> something in the style of a punch-up
> or a quarrel
> flared up
>> between us.
> I went away
>> in my threadbare trousers
> and you were carried off
>> in international railway carriages.

Mayakovsky could never forgive Gorky either for interfering in his private life or for what he saw as political treachery. When he read "Letter" at Roman Jakobson's house in Prague in April 1927 and the ambassador of the Soviet Union, Antonov-Ovseyenko, sprang to Gorky's defense, Mayakovsky objected irritably: "Then what's he dawdling around there for?" Whereupon, according to Gorky, he vented his feelings about Gorky, describing him as a "fundamentally immoral being."

That the animosity was mutual emerges from the fact that Nikolay Aseyev, during a visit to Gorky in Sorrento in the autumn of that same year, did not even dare mention Mayakovsky by name. In his desire to try to reconcile the two authors, he read poems by Mayakovsky without mentioning who had written them but was interrupted the whole time by Gorky under various pretexts; Mayakovsky's style was unmistakable. "Instead of reconciling Gorky to Mayakovsky I succeeded in turning Gorky against myself," Aseyev noted, resigned. If he had known about Gorky's reaction to Mayakovsky's "Letter"— "Mayakovsky has always been a hooligan and as far as I can judge will remain one until he dies"—he would probably never have ventured on his attempt at reconciliation.

HOW ARE YOU?

During the autumn and winter of 1926–27 the apartment in Gendrikov Alley was transformed into the Lef group's headquarters. Lef-Tuesdays were arranged every week and were attended by everyone close to the group—Aseyev, Tretyakov, Pasternak, the young poet Semyon Kirsanov, Shklovsky, the theater director Meyerhold, Vitaly Zhemchuzhny, and Lev Kuleshov. Had it not been for the size of the living room and the word's aura of a vanished epoch, the event could have been called a "salon."

According to Lef's new theories, the modern writer was expected to employ genres which were grounded not in an imaginary reality but in facts: reportage, newspaper sketches, memoirs, and biographies. In accordance with this aesthetics, photographs and films were held up as model art forms. One person who was particularly interested in film was Osip, who at this time was collaborating on several film magazines, advocating the type of "ethnographic documentary film" of which *Jews Work the Land* was an example.

Mayakovsky, who had been captivated from an early date by "ki-nemo" (see the chapter "The First Revolution and the Third"), also latched on to this new interest in film, perhaps inspired by Lili's participation in *Jews Work the Land*. Within the course of a year or so he wrote no fewer than nine scenarios, of which however only two were filmed. *Children* reached the cinema screens in the spring of 1928.

Among those film scripts which were never realized was a new version of *Fettered by Film* with the title *The Heart of the Film* and a completely new script, *How Are You?*, both of which date to the autumn of 1926. The rhythm of Mayakovsky's writing dictated that "Vladimir Ilyich Lenin" should be followed by a lyrical work. And so it was, but this time it was not in a poem but in a film script that Mayakovsky's innermost feelings found expression. *How Are You?*, which depicts "24 hours in a person's life" in "five film episodes," is closely related to his lyric poems "Man" and "About This," both thematically and in terms of imagery. Just as in those works, the central character, "a man," bears the author's own name. The autobiographical background is further underlined by the names on the doorplate: BRIK. MAYAKOVSKY. Even if Mayakovsky in his propaganda poems too often turned to the world in the first person, when he cast off the role of agitator he was more nakedly personal and self-revealing than ever.

How Are You? is a variation on two of the leitmotifs in his work: the feeling of not being appreciated and loved, and suicide as an alternative way out. Mayakovsky is a poet—a "factory without chimneys and smoke"—who writes poetry no one wants. "I have no need of your poems," explains a tea-drinking paterfamilias with porcine features who suddenly changes into an orangutan. The image seems to be borrowed from "About This." The only ones who are interested in poetry are the workers, represented in this scenario by some Young Communists. When Mayakovsky goes up to the newspaper office to sell a poem, the following scenes take place:

38. Mayakovsky enters the editor's room. On the way in he grows and finally fills the whole door frame.
39. The editor and the man shake hands. The man shrinks to the

same size as the editor. The editor is a newspaper bureaucrat. Asks him to read.

40, 41, 42. The editor, who is his own height, becomes smaller and smaller and finally becomes quite tiny. Mayakovsky attacks him with his manuscript, grows to an enormous size, becomes four times bigger than the editor. By now a little chessman is sitting on the editor's chair.

43. The poet reads with an audience in the background.

44. When the editor has finished listening, he stretches, looks through the manuscript, pulls a cross face, and starts attacking the poet. Mayakovsky becomes small. The editor becomes huge, four times as big as the poet. The poet stands like a little chessman on a little chair.

45. The editor gives his criticism with a family of orangutans in the background.

The whole thing ends with the editor giving Mayakovsky an advance of ten rubles, but the cashier's office is shut, and he can't get any money.

The scene is a condensed description of the humiliation which Mayakovsky constantly felt himself subjected to by the editorial staff of newspapers and publishers. Even if his vulnerable psyche often blew up conflicts to unreasonable proportions, the opposition he encountered from the cultural bureaucracy was only too real. "I remember once when he came back from Gosizdat, where he had waited for someone, queued at the cashier's office, and tried to prove something which didn't need to be proved," Lili recounted. "When he came home, he threw himself his whole length on the couch and literally began to howl at the top of his voice: 'I can't stand it . . . any more . . .' Then I burst into tears out of sympathy and concern for him and he forgot about himself and jumped up to comfort me."

Lili feared for Mayakovsky's life. But in *How Are You?* it is not Mayakovsky who commits suicide but his former girlfriend. He reads about the suicide in the newspaper:

122. The newspaper is unfolded, becomes a corner, like an enormous screen.

123. Out of the newspaper's dark corner there emerges a girl, in her despair she lifts her hand with a revolver in it, the revolver is aimed at her temple, she presses the trigger.

124. Mayakovsky throws himself through the newspaper, like a dog tearing apart the paper in a hoop in the circus, and rushes into the room formed by the newspaper.

125. He tries to grab the hand with the revolver and move it aside, but it is too late—the girl falls to the floor.

126. The man steps backward. His face expresses terror.

The idea of suicide was almost obsessive with Mayakovsky, and one of the poems he most liked to read during his performances at this time was "To Sergey Yesenin." But in the film script it was the shade of another suicide that plagued him: Antonina Gumilina, who took her life for his sake in 1918, an event which he never managed to repress (see the chapter "Communist Futurism").

A LION IN THE MENAGERIE

How Are You? was a commissioned work. Lev Kuleshov was to have directed the film, and his wife Alexandra Khokhlova was to have played the part of the girl who takes her own life. The scenario was never adapted for the screen but was in a way brought to life anyhow: Kuleshov and Lili fell madly in love and their romance had nearly fatal consequences.

Lev Kuleshov was twenty-eight years old and thus eight years younger than Lili. Despite his youth he had been working in films for many years and was one of the directors who contributed to the revolutionary development of the art of film which took place in the Soviet Union in the nineteen twenties. His pupils included directors like Dziga Vertov (*Cine Eye*), Sergey Eisenstein (*The Strike, The Battleship Potemkin*), and Vsevolod Pudovkin (*The Mother*). Kuleshov himself made his mark in 1924 with *Mister West's Remarkable Adventures in the Land of the Bolsheviks*, with a script by Aseyev and with his wife in one of the roles.

Kuleshov was crazy about Lili, wrote madrigals for her, made a fine photographic portrait of her, and gave her a brooch of his own

Lev Kuleshov on his motorcycle. The photo was taken by Alexander Rodchenko in 1927.

design, in the shape of a lion (in Russian, *Lev*). Lili was equally blinded by Kuleshov, who was stylish in the manner of a Hollywood star. He hunted, loved sports, and drove round Moscow on his motorcycle, often with Lili in the sidecar.

If motorcycles were unusual in the Soviet Union in the twenties, private cars were a more or less unknown—and ideologically dubious—luxury. But Kuleshov—and Lili—were desperate to have a car and when on 15 April 1927 Mayakovsky traveled abroad, along with the usual orders for clothes and perfume he was given yet another task, to buy "a little car": "We've thought about the make a good deal. And we've decided that best of all would be a little Ford. (1) It would be best of all for our roads, (2) it's the easiest to get spare parts for, (3) it's not smart, it's a working car, (4) it's the easiest to drive, and I absolutely want to drive it myself. *Only you absolutely must buy* a Ford of *the latest model, with the stronger reinforced tyres*, with a complete set of all the instruments and as many spare parts as possible."

"We" who had "thought a good deal" were of course Lili and Kuleshov, for whose motorcycle she also asked Mayakovsky to "buy everything" she had written down on the list he was given to take with him: "We do a great deal of driving on it." Not even Kuleshov's actress wife was forgotten: Mayakovsky was asked to buy her whitening agent for her teeth.

On this occasion Mayakovsky's foreign trip took him to Warsaw, Prague, Berlin, and Paris. During the month or so that he was away, he seldom sent a telegram to Moscow and wrote only one letter—an answer to Lili's instructions about the Ford, which reached him when he arrived in Paris on 29 April. "The moment I tumbled into the Istria they brought me your letter," he told her. "I hadn't even had time to take my hat off. I went wild with joy and from then on I led my life according to your instructions—I looked after Elsa, thought about the car, and so on and so forth." He went on to complain about his life, which was "utterly repulsive and unbelievably boring" and declared that he would do anything to shorten his stay "in these rotten abroads."

The letter was never finished or sent, but the Ford (a sports model) was bought and delivered to Moscow. Mayakovsky was extremely generous and always came back from his foreign trips with casefuls of presents. "How thoughtful he was, how he always fulfilled everyone's wishes!" recalled Alexander Rodchenko, to whom Mayakovsky brought back camera parts from Germany which he had also taken the trouble to obtain an import licence for—something he also had to do for Kuleshov's Ford. However, the purchase of the car reflected not only his all-around generosity but also his desire to constantly please Lili. It is not hard to imagine what this effort cost him in this particular case, not only in terms of willpower but presumably also in ready money.

For Lili it was natural to live out her relationship with Kuleshov quite openly. It was also a way of showing Mayakovsky that their love affair was definitely over. Mayakovsky was forced to play along—his hateful jealousy must not triumph! So the summer was spent as usual in Pushkino, although with breaks for trips away: at the beginning of July, Lili and Kuleshov left for a two weeks' holiday in the Caucasus, and a few weeks later Mayakovsky himself went off on a six-week-long reading tour. But when they were in Pushkino together they socialized as if it was the most natural thing in the world: picking mushrooms, playing mah-jongg, a game that Lili's mother had brought back from London, and table tennis, a novelty introduced by Kuleshov which Mayakovsky had insisted that the latter teach him to play. They played for a whole day and night, for money; at the beginning Mayakovsky lost "astronomical sums," but the upshot was that he won it all back and a bit more besides.

That their "pussycat family" had been augmented with a male lion was a development whose charm Mayakovsky found it hard to appreciate, especially as it was known that Kuleshov's sexual preferences were at least as "indecent" as those that Harry Blumenfeld had once exposed Lili to in Munich. On 14 November Alexander Rodchenko's wife, the artist Varvara Stepanova, noted in her diary that Mayakovsky was "in very a bad shape" and "his nerves at breaking point": "He has begun to have problems with his sight, the doctor has prescribed spectacles. The reason is his nerves." Even if Mayakovsky had an incredibly demanding program in connection with the anniversary of the Revolution, it is difficult not to see his mental collapse as also being a result of factors other than physical exhaustion.

He was not the only one to be suffering, however. The open promiscuity embraced by Lili and Osip was also hard to swallow for Ku-

The young Lef member Vasily Katanyan and his wife, Galina, had different opinions of the morals embraced at the dacha in Pushkino. Ten years later, they separated and Katanyan moved in with Lili.

leshov's wife, who came from a "good family." On her father's side she was descended from the well-known medical family of Botkin, and on her mother's side from the family which had founded the Tretyakov Gallery in Moscow. Her husband and Lili unashamedly indulged themselves in their mutual passion before her eyes. When at the end of July Vasily ("Vasya") Katanyan, a young member of the Lef group from Tbilisi, and his wife Galina paid their first-ever visit to the dacha in Pushkino, they were struck by the "well-dressed, elegant women and men" sitting on the terrace. Galina recalled:

> Kuleshov and Khokhlova came on a visit. Lili and Kuleshov immediately went upstairs and stayed up there for a long time. The same thing happened when Zhemchuzhny and Zhenya called round. Osya immediately disappeared upstairs with Zhenya, who blushed with embarrassment and joy. Khokhlova, quite indifferent, chatted to the ladies on the terrace, while Zhemchuzhny, who was obviously not so used to this, strode up and down in the garden, alone and gloomy. I was a little disturbed by what I had seen, and on the

Lili and Osip with Alexander Rodchenko and his wife, Varvara Stepanova, at the dining table in Gendrikov Lane (in 1926 or 1927). During the second half of the 1920s, the garçon haircut was popular with the Lef wives, and Lili had her hair cut for the first time. Osip was against it since he—"a known reactionary when it comes to women," according to Stepanova—was of the opinion that "women with short-cropped hair immediately look like hookers."

way home I asked Vasya what it was all about. Vasya thought for a moment then explained to me that modern people must be above jealousy, that it is petit bourgeois to be jealous.

Khokhlova's "indifference" was hard won, for she also had no desire to appear "petit bourgeois." In actual fact she was suffering unspeakably and on one occasion tried to take her own life. She "was stopped on the threshold of suicide," Lili recounted, "literally when she was in the process of laying hands on herself." Thus Alexandra Khokhlova managed to play in real life the part that she was not able to play in the film—with the same man in the director's chair. Lili found it hard to understand Khokhlova's reaction, which to her was an expression of "stone-age morality." Osip's contribution to the family dramaturgy was *Cleopatra*, a film script with Kuleshov as director and Khokhlova in the leading role, which like *How Are You?* never reached the cinema screen.

The Lef group practiced an aesthetic and morality of their own and were so tightly welded together that one can almost talk of a sect. "Apart from [the Lef people] I knew hardly anyone," Lili commented. "I met other people on the tram, at the theater. But the Lef people grew up in each other's sight. Lef began, without using that name, as early as 1915, with 'A Cloud in Trousers,' with Volodya's readings, and developed by way of Kom-Fut and *Art of the Commune*. [. . .] It was an association of like-minded, gifted Soviet people." United by common ideas and common enemies, they went around together night and day. When not discussing art, literature, or film, they played board games. "Mah-jongg is one of the Lef group's favorite occupations," Varvara Stepanova noted in her diary: "They all play it. There are two groups: the fanatics—Volodya, Kolya [Aseyev], Lilya—and the classics—Vitaly, Osya, Lyova. Rodchenko has a special playing style—individual. They play till 6–7 in the morning, sometimes 17 hours on end." The same information is given in Lili's diaries—the Lef people sit up and play for nights together. Just as there was a Lef aesthetic and a Lef morality, so, with the passing of years, there developed a definite Lef lifestyle.

NATASHA

Scenes like the one described by Galina Katanyan drove Mayakovsky mad with jealousy, but on the day that the Katanyans visited Pushkino Mayakovsky was not there but away on his reading tour in Ukraine, the Crimea, and the Caucasus. On 25 July he and Lili met at the station in Kharkov; Lili was on her way home to Moscow from her holiday with Kuleshov. When Mayakovsky asked her to stay for one day in Kharkov so that he could recite a new poem to her, she promptly threw her traveling bag out of the carriage window before the train could continue on its way. Mayakovsky was beside himself with joy—whatever Lili had going with Kuleshov or other men, he was wholly dependent on her ear, her admiration. "Of the hotel, I remember the traditional water jug and the glass on the table we sat at—and immediately, that same night, he read out the newly finished chapters 13 and 14 of the poem 'Good!'"

"Good!" was Mayakovsky's tribute to the tenth anniversary of the October Revolution, a poem as voluminous as "Vladimir Ilyich Lenin."

The chapters he read to Lili in the hotel in Kharkov dealt with their life together in Poluyektov Alley in the hungry winter of 1919/20:

> Twelve square arshins
>   of living space.*
> Four
>   in the room—
>   Lilya,
>   Osya,
>   me
> and the dog
>   Shenik.

It was a happy time, despite all the hardships, despite the fact that "hunger's abscess" had changed Lili's shining eyes into "peering slits":

> If
>   I
>   have had something to write,
> if
>   I
>   have had something to say
> it is those
>   eyes-skies that are to blame,
> my
>   darling's
>   eyes.
> Almond-brown,
>   round,
> burning
>   like fire.

He remembers how he managed to find two carrots, which he gave Lili in order to get some vitamins into her and get her swollen eyes to open again. He has, he writes, been "a lot in warm countries"—

---

* An arshin corresponds to 0.71 meters.

But that winter
　　　for the first time
I understood
　　　the meaning
of warmth
　　in love,
　　　　friendship,
　　　　　family.

This unreserved declaration of love for Lili—and Osip—was written
during one of the worst crises to date in Mayakovsky's life, when Lili
was openly living with another man. Was it an expression of will-
power or did it reflect his true feelings? The answer is: both.

If Kuleshov was also on that train, we must suppose that he con-
tinued on to Moscow without Lili. After Lili too had moved on, and
after he had given several readings, Mayakovsky traveled to Yalta in
the Crimea. On the same day he sent an express telegram to Mos-
cow: "MOSCOW. GOSIZDAT. BRYUKHANENKO. LONGING. TRAVEL
THIRTEENTH MEET SEVASTOPOL. BUY TICKET TODAY. TELE-
GRAPH DETAILS YALTA HOTEL ROSSIYA. COLOSSAL GREETINGS.
MAYAKOVSKY."

The recipient of the telegram was Natalya Bryukhanenko, a twenty-
one-year-old student who worked in the Gosizdat library. That May-
akovsky sent her an express telegram asking her to come eleven days
later was due partly to the fact that train tickets had to be purchased
ten days in advance, and partly to the express telegram's being the
natural form of communication for the impulsive and impatient poet.
After Natalya failed to buy a ticket the same day, she received a new
express telegram two days later: "EXPECTING TELEGRAM ARRIVAL
TIME DAY. COME SOONEST. HOPE TO BE TOGETHER WHOLE YOUR
HOLIDAY. LONGING TERRIBLY. MAYAKOVSKY."

Mayakovsky had got to know the tall, stylish Natalya—Natasha,
as she was called—at Gosizdat in the spring of 1926 and had imme-
diately taken her with him to a café where he was to meet Osip. With
childlike directness he pointed at Natasha and said: "A big, good-
looking woman like this is just what I need." When Osip had left he

Natasha Bryukhanenko in 1927, when she and Mayakovsky were forming plans for the future that made Lili act accordingly.

asked her to come with him to Lubyanka Passage, where he offered her champagne and chocolates and read her his poems—in a low, almost whispering voice. "Then he came up to me, all of a sudden loosened my long plaits and started asking me if I could become fond of him." When Natasha told him she wanted to leave, Mayakovsky did not protest. On their way down Mayakovsky warned Natasha against touching the banisters since a venereologist lived in the apartment below and she wasn't wearing gloves.

Natasha was disappointed that such an "unusual poet" had shown himself to be such a "normal man," and when they emerged on to the street she told him so. "What did you expect? That I would have a golden belly like Buddha?" Mayakovsky replied, gesturing as if he was painting his belly.

This episode shows us Mayakovsky captured in a flash: his hypochondria, his impatience and impulsiveness, his need for instant gratification, the sudden, often brusque shifts from one emotional state to another. Everything or nothing—and now, not later! Mayakovsky's inability to control his feelings scared people off, especially women, which meant that for all his reserves of tenderness he found it difficult to get his own need for tenderness and love satisfied. It was in this way that, eleven years earlier, he had "attacked" Lili, who responded by keeping him at a distance for several years.

Natasha became frightened and they did not see each other for another year, until June 1927, when Mayakovsky called at the publisher's to collect the fifth volume of his *Collected Works* (the first one to appear). When he caught sight of Natasha, he reproached her for having fled from him "without even waving your paw." "That same day he invited me to dinner," she recalled: "I thanked him and promised never to flee from him again."

The second meeting with Natasha took place when Lili's romance with Kuleshov was in its most intensive phase and Mayakovsky needed a "big, good-looking woman" even more than he had the year before. "From that day we met a great deal, more or less every day," Natasha recalled. Mayakovsky loathed being on his own; loneliness made him depressed. One might think that his manic need for company would have made it hard for him to work, but not so. Unlike most writers he did not work in his room and at fixed times. He worked constantly, during walks, alone or in company, beating out the rhythm of the words with his stout walking stick. Sometimes he took out a notebook and wrote down some rhyme. The Czech artist Adolf Hofmeister was struck by the fact that Mayakovsky "could not be unoccupied for a second" but drank and smoked and drew the whole time, and Natasha recalled that, while waiting for a meal in a restaurant, he would fill the paper napkins on the table with one drawing after another. It was only when he was reading proofs or indulging in some other less creative activity that he sat at his desk—but even then he preferred somebody by his side.

Natasha had agreed to Mayakovsky's conditions, so now he summoned her to Yalta. When she arrived at the station in Sevastopol at seven o'clock in the morning Mayakovsky was waiting on the platform, sunburned and dressed in a gray shirt with a red tie and gray flannel trousers.

They spent a month together: the whole of Natasha's vacation and a bit more besides. She was present at his readings in various towns in the Crimea—and later in the Caucasus—and they were in each other's company the whole time. Once when they were traveling by bus to Yalta Mayakovsky booked three seats so that they would not be too cramped. He demonstrated the same generosity—or hyperbolism—on Natasha's name day. As soon as she awoke, she was presented with a bouquet of roses so large that it could only be accommodated in a pail. And when they were walking along the promenade by the quay, Mayakovsky went into every shop and bought bottle after bottle of the most expensive eau de cologne. When they could not carry any more, and Natasha begged him to stop, Mayakovsky went instead into a kiosk and began buying flowers. When she reminded him that there was already a whole pailful of flowers in their hotel room, he replied: "*One bouquet* is nothing. I want you to remember that you got not one bouquet but a whole *kiosk-full of roses* and *all* the eau de cologne in the whole of Yalta!"

There was nothing furtive about Mayakovsky's relationship with

Natasha. She visited him not only in his study but also in Gendrikov Alley and in Pushkino. And as we have seen, during her vacation in the Crimea and the Caucasus she hardly moved from his side. But if Osip had met Natasha on at least one occasion, Lili had never seen her, since she was traveling with Kuleshov when the romance with Natasha began. But Lili kept herself well informed about most of what went on and of course knew that Mayakovsky was in love. Only a few days after Natasha's arrival in the Crimea she sent him a long letter which ended—after a series of more or less trivial bits of news (about Bulka and her pups, repairs to the apartment, and various messages from the publisher)—with an appeal which despite the jocular tone exudes an air of deep seriousness:

> I love you terribly strongly. Please don't get seriously married, because everyone is assuring me that you're terribly in love and will definitely get married! All three of us are married to each other and to get married any more is a sin.

Mayakovsky replied with a telegram which began with instructions for the printing of his "October poem"—which here received its final title, "Good!"—and ended with the following greeting: "KISS MY ONLY KITTY OSYA FAMILY." When Mayakovsky and Natasha returned to Moscow on 15 September they were met at the railway station by Lili—and Rita. "It was the first time I saw Lili," Natasha recalled, but "only for a second, as I immediately withdrew and went home." The fact that Lili took Rita with her suggests that she did not find the situation easy to deal with.

Mayakovsky and Natasha continued to meet, going for walks and to the cinema, where they saw Eisenstein's *October: Ten Days That Shook the World*. On her birthday, 28 November, she received greetings by telegram from Mayakovsky, who was off on his travels again, and a money order for 500 rubles. Early the next morning Natasha phoned Lili to ask for Mayakovsky's address so she could thank him. Lili was sleeping but asked no questions and said only: Rostov, hotel such-and-such. She reacted, in other words, as she had expected Kuleshov's wife to react, with understanding and not with jealousy.

No doubt it was already clear to her that the young librarian posed no threat to the Mayakovsky-Brik trinity. By regarding Lili as a confidante and not as a rival, Natasha was also behaving in accordance with Lili's rulebook. Perhaps she already suspected what she would later be forced to acknowledge, namely, that there was only one woman Mayakovsky truly loved.

12

TATYANA

1928–1929

To love
　　　is to spring up
　　　　　　from bedsheets
torn by insomnia,
　　　jealous of Copernicus,
　　　　　　regarding him, not the neighbor's husband,
as
　　　your true
　　　　　　rival.

Vladimir Mayakovsky, "Letter from Paris
to Comrade Kostrov . . ."

The autumn and winter of 1927 were largely dominated for Mayakovsky by his revolutionary poem. His own view of "Good!" was that it was "a manifesto, a sort of 'A Cloud in Trousers' of its time," but reactions were mixed. For Lunacharsky it was "the October Revolution cast in bronze," "a magnificent fanfare for our anniversary, without a single false note." Mayakovsky's opponents, on the other hand, especially within RAPP, seized every opportunity to attack him. Mayakovsky, it was said, was in actual fact "far from understanding

Tatyana Yakovleva in 1932.

the October Revolution, its content and nature." What he wrote was nothing more than "cheap anniversary trumpery."

At the same time there were more discerning commentators, like the critic of the Kharkov newspaper *Proletarian* who declared that the epic was quite simply not Mayakovsky's strongest genre: "He goes astray here the whole time and is not capable of rising above journalism of a decidedly low standard. The poet can get worked up about his lyrical 'constitution,' he can try to fight it, but to overcome it is clearly not given to him."

When Mayakovsky delivered the poem to members of the Communist Party's Moscow Section in October, he asked the audience before the reading to tell him if it was comprehensible or not. In the course of the subsequent discussion he was criticized—as usual—for his individualism, for "depicting individual heroes but not showing the masses," but the majority thought that the poem was fine both as regards form and content. And to his great joy, no one claimed that it was "incomprehensible." After the meeting a resolution was adopted to the effect that "Good!" was "a step forward and deserves to be utilized in practical applications as a means of artistic agitation."

However satisfied Mayakovsky was with the reaction of the party collective, he knew that it was not representative. During his readings he could not help noticing, time after time, how eagerly his opponents tried to get at him and what malicious pleasure they felt when they thought they had succeeded. There were literary rivals among the hecklers but also those who had come merely to provoke a scandal. Mayakovsky was a brilliant performance poet, and his readings often developed into pure show, not least because of his preeminent ability to parry interjections from the audience. His powerful bass voice contributed to the effect, drowning out everything and everyone. Questions were put either orally or on pieces of paper which were handed up to the platform. "Ha, nobody reads you, nobody asks for you. Take that, take that!" a librarian exulted in Leningrad, and in Baku Mayakovsky received a scrap of paper with the following comment: "When a person's soul is empty, there are two alternatives: to be silent, or to shout. Why have you chosen the second alternative?" The reply was vintage Mayakovsky: "The questioner has forgotten

One of Mayakovsky's favorite venues was the Polytechnic Museum in Moscow. Here he is seen reading the poem "Good!" on 20 October 1927, two weeks before the tenth anniversary of the Revolution.

that there is a third alternative: to ask such empty-headed questions." The audience split its sides.

With his lightning-swift and crushing put-downs, Mayakovsky could mostly turn the discussion to his advantage, but often the questions were so vile that he felt as if his whole life was being called in question. Was this the reward for his unconditional commitment to the Revolution and the working class? The readings often lasted for hours, and afterward he was worn out, "milked dry," as he said to Natasha Bryukhanenko. During his hundreds of appearances over the years he collected so many scraps of paper—around twenty thousand—that he thought about drawing up a "universal answer" to his questioners. If it had ever been written it would probably have contained the following views, formulated in the first issue of *New Lef* in 1928 under the heading (framed by quotation marks) "The Workers and Peasants Do Not Understand You": "I have never yet seen anyone boast as follows: 'Look how clever I am—I don't understand arithmetic, I don't understand French, I don't understand grammar!' But the cheerful slogan: 'I don't understand the Futurists' has been heard for fifteen years. Sometimes it quietens down, but before long it resounds again, just as excited and cheerful as before. People have made a career out of this slogan, gathered the masses around them, become leaders of whole movements."

The whole of Mayakovsky's life and poetry was about politics, the building of Communism, and the poet's place therein. But if he readily commented on topical issues, the big political processes are conspicuous by their absence both from his poetry and his correspondence—despite the fact that the years 1927–28 were characterized by events which changed Soviet society fundamentally. At the same time as the celebrations of the anniversary of the Revolution which Mayakovsky paid homage to in "Good!," Stalin was implementing a brutal purge of his opponents. On 14 November the leaders of the so-called left-wing opposition were thrown out of the Communist Party, and two months later their leader Leon Trotsky was banished to Alma-Ata in Kazakhstan along with about thirty other members of the opposition. Once the left-wing opposition had been crushed, Stalin took on the right-wing opposition, led by Nikolay Bukharin, who was gradually neutralized in the course of 1928.

Developments on the economic front were at least as thoroughgoing. Although the New Economic Policy was constantly said to form the basis for the building of socialism, in practice an economic policy was implemented which was directly contrary to the basic ideas behind the NEP: in 1927–28 the first steps were taken toward a forced industrialization and compulsory collectivization of agriculture.

SHAKHTY

The radical economic changes led to mistrust and unrest in the workplaces, where people were uncertain which rules of play applied. The dissatisfaction found expression in heated discussions and letters to the authorities, and even strikes. In order to divert attention from the real problems, the party leadership initiated a campaign with the aim of showing that the difficulties were the result of a political conspiracy. In March 1928 the security service (which since 1924 had been called the OGPU) claimed to have uncovered a plot by so-called bourgeois specialists employed in the mines in the town of Shakhty in the Donets Basin in Ukraine. ("Bourgeois specialists" was the name given to engineers and other educated workers whom the Communist regime chose to cooperate with after the Revolution, in the absence of experts of their own. As late as 1927, only 1 percent of party members had a higher education.) The engineers and technicians were said to be controlled by a counterrevolutionary center in Paris and were accused of having blown up and destroyed mine shafts in a bid to sabotage the Soviet economy.

The trial took place between 18 May and 6 July 1928 in an atmosphere of political paranoia. The activities of the Communists in France had led to diplomatic complications with Paris. Relations with Poland had been damaged since the murder of the Soviet ambassador Pyotr Voykov in June 1927 in the middle of negotiations about a nonaggression pact. And when that same year the Soviet Union tried to export the Revolution to China, it suffered a monumental rebuff. The worst reverse, however, was the raid carried out by the British authorities on 12–15 May 1927 on Arcos, which was suspected of having acquired a secret document from the British Air Ministry.

The action, which led Great Britain to break off diplomatic relations with the USSR, also involved one of the main characters in this book—Lili's mother, who ended up on the blacklist of "bad Communists" who were to be expelled from England. During an interrogation by MI5, Yelena Yulyevna gave assurances that she was not a member of Arcos's Communist cell and that she "takes no interest whatever in politics," that she "is of a bourgeois family and that her husband was a supporter of the Czarist regime," and that she "lost all the property left by her husband as a result of the Russian Revolution." Whether it was these arguments or the fact that she was "a good pianist and has played at gatherings of the Arcos club [. . .] and has also trained the Arcos choir" that most impressed her interrogators is unclear, but the result was that Yelena Yulyevna was struck off the list and allowed to remain in England.

Because of all these international developments, by the time of the Shakhty trial the Soviet citizens had been for a long time exposed to propaganda warning of imminent war. The danger was not real, but the propaganda contributed to the xenophobic atmosphere surrounding the trial. In the dock sat fifty-three Russian and three German mining experts. The nature of the charge was given as "sabotage," a concept which was employed here for the first time. The prosecutor was Nikolay Krylenko, an old hand at show trials; the judge—a novice, Andrey Vyshinsky, who during this case laid the foundation for a brilliant career as a judicial executioner during the show trials of the thirties. The only evidence presented to the court was the confessions that had been extracted by threats and torture. Eleven individuals were sentenced to death, but for those who in the course of the trial had betrayed their colleagues, the sentence was commuted to hard labor. The case was given wide publicity and was used to whip up hatred against the "saboteurs"—imaginary and real—who were said to be threatening the building of socialism.

EMPERORS AND SABOTEURS

One of those who condemned the mine saboteurs was Mayakovsky, whose poem "The Saboteur" was printed in *Komsomolskaya Pravda* the very day after the verdict. The engineers were accused of having repaid the generosity of the Soviet government—liberal food rations and fine apartments—by sabotaging work in the mines, seduced by foreign capital. The poem is primitive and politically naive, possibly written on commission—the daily newspaper *Komsomolskaya Pravda* was Mayakovsky's main source of work at this time. But that is no excuse. Nor is it an excuse that he was only one voice in the chorus of the self-righteous: there were poets who realized that the threat to the country was not a few mining engineers in Ukraine but fabricated legal proceedings of the sort that the Shakhty trial exemplified.

One of these was Boris Pasternak, who summed up the situation concisely in a letter to his cousin Olga Freidenberg the week before the Shakhty trial: "As you know, the terror is back again, without the moralistic reasons and justifications for it that they found for it the last time, when trade, careerism, and an insignificant 'sinfulness' were rampant. It is no longer a question of the same puritanical saints who then acted like avenging angels. On the whole, a dreadful confusion holds sway, waves roll by which have no relation to the times, no one understands anything." Another poet who opposed the move toward a police state was Osip Mandelstam, who involved himself in the case of six high-ranking bank officials who had been sentenced to death. His—very Mandelstamian!—course of action was to send his book of poetry to Nikolay Bukharin, the editor in chief of *Pravda* and a member of the Politburo, on the same day as the Shakhty trial. The book contained a dedication, the essence of which was that "everything in this book is a protest against what you are trying to do." Remarkably enough, the protest was effective. A while later, Bukharin informed Mandelstam that the death penalty had been commuted to hard labor.

Mayakovsky was neither opportunistic nor cynical, but he was politically naive, in his desire to build a new and better society, blind to events which in reality militated against such a development. Nor was he a philosophically analytical person, like Pasternak. But bloodthirsty he was not. And deep inside he understood what Pasternak had realized: that violence was no alternative.

The complicated psychological processes that Mayakovsky was suffering are reflected in two poems he wrote during a four-day visit to Sverdlovsk in Siberia in January 1928. "The Story of the Smelter Ivan Kozyryov about How He Moved into a New Apartment" tells of a worker who, having been allotted a bright new apartment with hot and cold running water by the workers' cooperative, feels as if he has "paid a visit to socialism." The poem is a tribute to the Soviet authorities, just like the hundreds of other edifying verses Mayakovsky wrote during these years. But at the same time he wrote a poem of a quite different kind, "The Emperor," which was published a few times during his lifetime but which remained unknown to all but specialists well into the 1950s.

Sverdlovsk was formerly called Yekaterinburg and was the place where the Russian tsar and his family were executed in the summer of 1918. The poem begins with a reminiscence. It is Easter or

Christmas, Moscow's streets are full of police constables, and a lan-
dau passes Mayakovsky containing "a young officer with a neatly
trimmed beard." In front of him sit his four "little daughters," his
dochurki—Mayakovsky uses the affectionate diminutive form of the
word for "daughter." In the next clip we find ourselves in Sverdlovsk.
Mayakovsky and the chairman of the city soviet go off to look for the
mine shaft where the bodies of the royal family were dumped. "The
universe is wrapped in snow"; all one can see is "the traces of the
bellies of wolves / on the spoor of wild goats." But at last they find the
spot they have been looking for: "by the root, / under the cedar, / is a
path, / and here the emperor / was buried." The only thing marking
the place is "flags" of "dark clouds," filled with "birds' lies, / of the
croaking of one-headed crows"—instead, by implication, of the im-
perial standard adorned with the double-headed eagle.

It is a threatening and suggestive image. Of what? Of the fall of
tsardom? Naturally. But perhaps it also hinted at something else.
Several lines in the rough draft of the poem suggest this: "I vote
against. / [...] Living they can be sent to a zoo / among the hyenas
and wolves. / And however little one gets out of the living / one gets
even less out of the dead. / We have turned the course of history. /
Say farewell for ever to the old. / A communist and human being /
must not feel bloodlust." What Mayakovsky is expressing here is a
forbidden idea, namely, that the murder of the tsar and his family
was unethical—and not unethical in the most general terms but in
terms of Communist morality

What kind of lies did the one-headed crows croak? The lies of mur-
der? The lie that it was right to execute the emperor and his "little
daughters"? Is it Mayakovsky the father speaking, seeing four little
girls being mown down before his eyes in a hail of bullets in the cel-
lar of Ipatyev's house in Sverdlovsk in the summer of 1918? During
his visit to Warsaw in the spring of 1927 Mayakovsky met the Soviet
Union's ambassador to Poland, Pyotr Voykov, who was assassinated
in Warsaw in June of that same year. Voykov was one of those who
organized the murder of the royal family, and the man who obtained
the acid which was used to destroy the bodies. Did he describe to
Mayakovsky how the execution took place? Did he reveal where the
remains had been flung?

We do not know, but one thing is clear: the starry Siberian nights put Mayakovsky into a contemplative frame of mind which along with the ambiguous "Emperor" also generated the following elegiac lines—directed to Lili, presumably:

It's already one o'clock and you have gone to bed
The silver waves of the Milky Way traverse the night
I'm in no hurry, there's no need
To wake you and trouble you with express telegrams

PASTERNAK THE CATALYST

The years 1927–28 saw great upheavals not only in the political sphere but also in the realm of literature. Right from the beginning of the twenties literary life had been characterized by strife between different coteries. Between the politically orthodox proletarian authors of RAPP and the aesthetic dogmatists in Lef there was a spectrum of lesser groupings and associations—along with authors who belonged to no group at all. The latter included the "fellow travelers" who had long been championed by the critic Alexander Voronsky and his magazine *Red Virgin Soil*. When Voronsky was dismissed from his post in 1927 after going over to the Trotskyist opposition, the fellow travelers found a new mouthpiece: the newly launched magazine *Novy Mir* (New World), whose editor in chief, Vyacheslav Polonsky, detested the extremism of RAPP and Lef and stood for a liberal middle way, with respect for the classics.

The basis of Lef's aesthetics was what in the language of the time was called "social commissioning": the artist's task was to fulfil the "commissions" issued by time through the proletarian state. Mayakovsky's ROSTA posters were held up as a classic example of such an artistic attitude. Out of this basic idea came the theory of "literature of fact," according to which, in Aseyev's words, "imagination can deceive, while reality, underpinned by facts, necessarily leaves traces in art." Instead of novels and short stories—journalism, instead of painting—photography and documentary films. This "antiromanticism" was itself in essence a form of romanticism: a veneration of the new socialist reality, which was not to be distorted by the imagination

Boris Pasternak, who had a better understanding than most people of the processes going on in the Soviet Union.

of individual authors—a dream of being able, with pure facts alone, to represent "reality itself."

The Lef writers barely managed to launch their program in the first number of *New Lef* before Polonsky unleashed a frontal assault on it. Polonsky was an opponent of all forms of literary coteries—what in Russian is called *gruppovshchina*—and he saw theorizing and sectarianism as damaging to literature. Mayakovsky, Aseyev, and Pasternak scored triumphs when they acted as individuals, but when they performed as members of a group and spokesmen for a theory their individuality was suppressed, with the ensuing results. According to Polonsky, the idea of "social commissioning" meant that the artist had to adapt himself to the demands and taste of the patron (i.e., the era, and in this case, the state). "Art, after all, has never been advanced by those who have obediently executed 'commissions' but by rebels, those who have set their face against outmoded concepts of taste, and who have toppled accepted idols and distanced themselves from established forms."

"Social commissioning" was an expression of servility, according to Polonsky, who believed that the true artist's transition to socialism *must* be difficult: "The proletariat has no need of people who are prepared to write what the proletariat wants and in the way it wants—at the same time as they remain distanced from the proletariat socially, psychologically, and ideologically." One example of a poet who, in Polonsky's opinion, had a difficult inner struggle to understand the political processes in the Soviet Union was Boris Pasternak, who came to serve as a sort of catalyst for the aesthetic conflict between himself and the Lef people. Pasternak had been present when *New Lef* was planned, and when the first number came out in January 1927 he contributed an extract from his poem "Lieutenant Schmidt." But according to Polonsky, Pasternak had never been a Futurist and was not one "now that Futurism's rotting corpse is beginning to stink."

As a consequence of his reasoning, Polonsky maintained that a grouping like Lef was unnecessary under socialism. The Lef writers (through Aseyev) countered this by pointing out that Polonsky, in *Novy Mir*, had published fellow traveler Boris Pilnyak's "The Story of the Unquenched Moon," which covertly describes the murder of the war commmissar Mikhail Frunze, as ordered by Stalin (see pages 329,

455). That was a comment which, in the prevailing political climate, bordered on informing. In this conflict, Pasternak chose Polonsky's side, and in June 1927 he walked out of Lef, which "repelled" him "with its exaggerated Sovietness, i.e., groveling servility, i.e., partiality for revolt with an official mandate for revolt in their pocket." According to Pasternak, Mayakovsky's own poetry was proof of how "simplistic" Lef's theories were. "I had always thought that Mayakovsky's innate talent would explode one day, that it would be forced to blow up these storehouses of chemically pure nonsense, dreamlike in its meaninglessness, which he has voluntarily decked himself out in over the last decade, until he became unrecognizable," he wrote to a woman friend in May 1927, adding: "In my feelings for him I have simply lived with this hope."

Pasternak would see his hope fulfilled, but only a year or so later. He had wanted Mayakovsky to be the first after himself to break with Lef, but two others got there first: Sergey Eisenstein was hurt and incensed that Mayakovsky had criticized his film *October: Ten Days That Shook the World* for "aestheticism" and jumped ship in the spring of 1928. In Shklovsky's case the immediate cause was a conflict with Lili, who had come to play an ever-more-active role in Lef. When Osip and Zhemchuzhny criticized one of his film scenarios in an editorial meeting, he lost his temper, and matters were not improved when Lili, to pour oil on troubled waters, suggested they discuss "any other bad film script whatsoever."

Shklovsky sprang to his feet, yelled at Lili that "the hostess"—or "housewife"—versions differ—ought to know her place and not stick her nose in when "working men are talking," whereupon he left the room. The following day he wrote to her and begged forgiveness but Lili was implacable. "I felt dreadfully distressed and let down by the ones closest to me," she commented later. "I didn't want to live. For the first time I felt that no one needed me. Osya didn't understand me this time either."

Mayakovsky was not present, but when he heard what had happened, he was distraught and, as always, took Lili's part. On 26 September, only about a week after the scene between Lili and Shklovsky, he explained in the course of a performance entitled "To the Left of Lef" that he was leaving the group. The news came as a shock. He had not discussed this in advance with anyone, apart from Osip. Several members of Lef suspected that private motives lay behind the drastic step. For Aseyev, it was obvious that the breach was Mayakovsky's way of avenging Lili, and Shklovsky himself explained that "Lef fell apart or was destroyed because it was impossible for Lili to sit in the same room as me." Lili was in no doubt that she was the reason for Mayakovsky's leaving the group: "No woman can resist when she hears: 'I will avenge you even it means that I will die doing so.'"

Hard-hitting discussions were a part of the Lef culture, and it may therefore seem strange that Lili reacted so vehemently to Shklovsky's words. The reason was that they were uttered at a time when she was sorely disappointed that her contributions to Lef, far from being properly appreciated, were being severely called in question. When, during one of their many rows, Kuleshov shouted at Lili, "Nobody likes you, your Lef friends can't stand you!" she had not wanted to believe him, but Shklovsky's attack confirmed that he was right. "Hadn't I corrected all Volodya's proofs?" Lili asked rhetorically—

> Hadn't I worked night and day on ROSTA? Hadn't I taken care of his affairs when he was away on all his trips? I worked for Gosizdat, in the children's books department, I reedited adult books for children, and I made a good job of it, but I was forced to write "Edited by O. Brik and N. Aseyev," although they neither wanted to nor could do it, and the people at the publisher's were very pleased with my work. But I had no name.
>
> When Zhemchuzhny and I had written the film scenario *The Glass Eye* and we were asked to make a film out of it, they tried every day to force me off the project. Midway through the rehearsals an order came that the whole project was to be entrusted to Zhemchuzhny immediately because I had got the job through contacts and I lacked the necessary qualifications. It was unbelievably difficult finishing the thing off. [. . .] During the editing Zhemchuzhny started working on a new film and I finished the editing of *The Glass Eye* all by myself—but I didn't get any more commissions.

However provocative Shklovsky's outburst was, or seemed to be, it

Alexander Rodchenko's cover of *New Lef*, number 9 (1928), which no longer had Mayakovsky as an editor. The last issue edited by him was number 7 (1928).

was hardly the reason for Mayakovsky's breach with Lef but rather the trigger—a good excuse.

The official reason Mayakovsky gave for his departure was that all "literary coteries have outlived themselves" and that one must distance oneself from "literary sectarianism." The wording here reminds one of Pasternak's views, but Mayakovsky's aim in cutting his links with Lef was diametrically opposed to his. It was not increased space for the individual he was seeking, but an even closer relationship with the "social commissioner." "Literature as an end in itself must give way to the work of social commissioning," he explained, "and not only commissions from newspapers and magazines but from all economic and industrial institutions in need of a well-turned phrase." Accordingly, he exhorted the Lef writers to carry on with their innovative work—only not in "laboratories" but out in the field—in newspapers, films, and radio. At the same time as Mayakovsky was condemning Lef as a coterie, he was thus continuing to defend its aesthetics, an aesthetics which was fundamentally Futurist. "We really are different," Mayakovsky commented to Pasternak in the context of the Lef conflict. "You love the electricity in the sky; I love it in the electric iron."

Along with his defection, Mayakovsky also made the surprising declaration that he was giving "an amnesty to Rembrandt" and that "we need the song, the poem, and not only the newspaper," a statement which was as shocking to his circle as the defection itself. But the amnesty was not because he had changed his opinion; it was based on the insight that if he wanted to continue to play a role in cultural politics he must—at least in his rhetoric—cosy up to the ideological middle ground. However tactical this move was, for someone who had once regarded "Rembrandt" and "Raphael" as hateful symbols of an obsolete aesthetic it was nevertheless a capitulation.

If the Rembrandt amnesty was scarcely meant in all honesty, there is every reason to take his comment about "the need for the song, the poem," seriously. Even if Mayakovsky did not want to admit it openly, he was tormented by the thought that the constant production of topical verses was hindering him from writing "proper" poetry. In private he would sometimes give vent to his fear that he was finished as a poet. In the spring of 1927, when Ilya Ehrenburg looked in on him

early one morning at the Hotel Istria in Paris, his bed was untouched. Mayakovsky had not slept, was very gloomy, and immediately asked, without even greeting him: "Do you also think that I wrote better before?"

Mayakovsky had not written any lyric poetry since "About This," and the image of him as "herald of the Revolution" was the dominant one in the second half of the decade. It was otherwise with Pasternak, who, despite having dealt with the theme of the Revolution in poems such as "1905" and "Lieutenant Schmidt," was still primarily seen as a *poet*. "Since 1922 Mayakovsky has been discussed seriously in terms of 'wherever you're from, buy in Mosselprom,' while Pasternak's poems

ДРУЖЕСКИЕ ШАРЖИ
Бор. Ефимова

In connection with its tenth anniversary in the fall of 1927, the government newspaper *Izvestiya* published this cartoon featuring its contributors. Mayakovsky depicted here is the biggest and the loudest, but he is not first in line. The drum is instead beaten by Demyan Bedny, the Party's favorite writer, a diligent producer of politically correct verses who had an apartment in the Kremlin and close contacts with Stalin. Although Bedny was an inferior poet, Mayakovsky envied him his position.

are circulated in transcript before they are even published," the poet Benedikt Livshits reported to David Burlyuk in the winter of 1926.

For Mayakovsky, the intensive production of journeyman verses was an economic necessity. At this time he was a full-time member of the staff of *Komsomolskaya Pravda* (which was published by the party's youth organization, Komsomol), but he was paid only seventy kopecks per line. He was sometimes therefore forced to write up to three poems a day—an amount which might cause the richest lyrical source to dry up. But was it only his finances that decided the direction of his poetic creativity? Or was the topical verse a means of escape from the realization that he did not know what he should write about, that he lacked a *theme*? By choosing to comment on issues of the day he obtained a new theme every day for free. It was convenient, and probably also necessary in a situation where Lili was no longer around to act as a catalyst to his need for lyrical expression.

"Volodya is working without a goal. The newspaper work is his salvation," Osip commented. Mayakovsky had experienced a similar creative crisis before: in the years 1919–21, when, apart from the poster texts, he wrote only about twenty poems. After this poetic drought, however, he succeeded once again in composing himself for great poetry, in poems like "150,000,000" and "I Love." "Perhaps yet again he will find a way out of the situation," Viktor Shklovsky hoped in the autumn of 1928. Shklovsky maintained that Mayakovsky had got himself into a poetic "dead end" and that this was one of the explanations for the crisis within Lef (along with his own row with Lili). He would turn out to be right, and more quickly than he could have expected. As would become evident, Mayakovsky had already found a "way out of the situation."

A LITTLE RENAULT

The foreign trips continued during 1928. In mid-April Lili traveled to Berlin, where she met her mother. That relations with Yelena Yulyevna were still cool emerges from Lili's exclamation in her first letter home to the "beasts" in Moscow: "It's good that Mama is leaving!!" Yet it was not primarily in order to see her mother that Lili was in Berlin. For some time now she had been working on the film *The Glass Eye* (see above), which she wrote and directed together with Lef member Vitaly Zhemchuzhny, husband of Osip's Zhenya. The film was a parody of the commercial movies which filled the cinemas and at the same time "propaganda for the newsreel film." It was precisely in order to buy foreign newsreel films—which were to be incorporated into *The Glass Eye*—that Lili was in Berlin. The producer was the Film Company for International Workers' Aid, which Lili hoped would meet the expenses. "Osip, think of my cinema business!!!" she wrote. "It'll be a shame if I can't manage to buy anything! After all, it isn't that much money! Persuade the board." It would appear

The signature in Mayakovsky's letter to Lili of 28 April 1928 was a sick Shen.

that the film company came up with the money, for the film was shot in August, edited during the autumn, and premiered in January 1929. Osip's film script *Cleopatra* fared less well when Lili tried in vain to interest German directors in it.

Back home in Moscow, Mayakovsky was in bed with a bad dose of flu, but the intention was that he would follow Lili to Berlin as soon as he was well again. He was then to bring with him, Lili wrote, "(1) some *soft* caviar; (2) 2–3 boxes (square metal ones) of fruit drops; (3) 2 pounds of sunflower seeds and (4) a hundred (4 boxes of 25) Mosselprom cigarettes." Lili herself sent a scarf to Osip and a pair of driving gloves to Kuleshov. But Mayakovsky's recovery took its time, and the trip never came off.

Lili therefore continued on to Paris by herself and stayed there for ten days. At this time Elsa was living in very straitened circumstances and earning her living by making necklaces of artificial pearls and sometimes even of macaroni. The correspondence between Paris and Moscow was largely concerned, as always, with financial matters, this time with Elsa as the focus. Mayakovsky sent her money from Moscow, and Lili gave her ten pounds to last for two months. Their mother received financial assistance too. But neither did Lili forget herself: "I've bought a dozen stockings, six changes of underwear (three black, three pink), 2 pairs of plaited shoes, night slippers, handkerchiefs, a bag." Where did the money come from? When Lili was in Paris she borrowed money for her purchases, which she then transferred from Berlin on the way home to Moscow. Did they have money in Berlin? Was that why Yelena Yulyevna met Lili there and not in Paris, which after all was much nearer London?

The summer of 1928 was again spent in Pushkino, but Maya-kovsky also managed a three-week reading tour of the Crimea. On the same day on which he returned to Moscow, 11 August, Lili reported to Osip, who was on holiday with Zhenya, that "Volo-dya has come home determined to build a house and import a car from abroad." The same day she reported his travel plans in more detail in a letter to Rita: "In six weeks he is traveling via Japan to America. Perhaps not to Amer-ica, actually, but to Europe—but definitely to Japan."

This time the preconditions for a round-the-world trip were bet-ter than ever. In June the editors of *Komsomolskaya Pravda* and the central committee of the youth wing of the Communist Party turned to various authorities with the following request:

Although he was sick, Mayakovsky visited the May First celebrations in Red Square, where he was caught by Rodchenko's camera with the eternal cigarette in the corner of his mouth.

Comrade Mayakovsky is being sent by the central committee of the *Komsomol* and the edi-tors of *Komsomolskaya Pravda* to Siberia-Japan-Argentina-USA-Germany-France, and Turkey to write despatches to our newspaper from all over the world delin-eating the lives and living conditions of young people. We regard this trip as being of unique significance, and we beg you to help Comrade Mayakovsky in every way possible to arrange the trip.

Despite this powerful support the round-the-world trip did not come off this time either. When Mayakovsky traveled to Paris via Berlin on 8 October, the only one of his summer plans that remained was the decision to buy a car. Each time he went abroad, he was given a detailed wish list by Lili, and this time it ran as follows:

In Berlin:
- Knitted dark-blue suit (not for pulling over the head). To go with it, a wool scarf and jumper, to wear with a tie.
- Stockings—very fine, not too light (I'll send some with this).
- Drrr . . . —two short and one long.
- Dark blue and red glossy taffeta.

In Paris:
- 2 woollen dresses of very soft material for special occasions.
- One very elegant, eccentric, of crêpe georgette with petticoat. If possible, bright and colorful. Preferably with long sleeves, although without will be all right. For New Year's Eve.
- Stockings. Pearl necklace (if they're still in fashion, and if so, blue). Gloves.
- Small fashionable objects. Handkerchiefs.
- Handbag (a cheap one from Berlin will also be fine, in which case, from [the department store] KDW).
- Perfume: Rue de la Paix, Mon Boudoir and what Elsa recommends. As much as possible and different ones. 2 Arax powder compacts. Brun eyebrow pencils, Houbigant eyebrow pencils.

The car:
- Preferably with a roof—conduite intérieure—with all spare parts, two spare tyres, boot at the back.
- If not Renault, then [drawing].
- Toy for the rear window.
- Clock that needs winding just once a week.
- Car gloves.

Lili's order for "drrr"—the onomatopoeic description of zippers—had already been taken care of in Berlin, and they were immediately sent to Moscow with an acquaintance. But most important of all, of

"It's an attractive car, you probably know what it's like yourself," Mayakovsky wrote to Lili on 12 November. "Of course the drawing is clumsy but I gave away the photograph from the catalog with the order and I haven't got hold of another one yet. I asked them to make it a gray one, they said if they can manage it, if not it'll be dark blue."

course, was the car, for which Mayakovsky had obtained an import licence before his departure. After arranging a Ford for Kuleshov Lili now wanted a car of her own. The purchase was to be financed in large part by Mayakovsky's sale of the German rights to all his hitherto unpublished works to the Berlin publishing house Malik, which had published 150,000,000 in German four years earlier. The publishers were interested but wanted to bide their time until the play Mayakovsky was working on was finished. So there was no money to be had in Berlin.

Mayakovsky had hardly reached Paris when he received a letter from Lili in which all the details of her shopping list were repeated, with certain additions: front and rear bumpers, extra headlights at the side, electric windshield wipers, a light at the back with a "stop" sign, electric indicators showing which way the car was turning, a warm cover to stop the water from freezing. "The color and shape (closed . . . open . . .) I leave to your and Elsa's taste. Only it mustn't look like a taxi. Best of all would be a Buick or a Renault. Only *not* an *Amilcar*! Tomorrow morning I'm starting driving lessons." "All my hopes are pinned on Malik," Mayakovsky replied. "They want to sign a contract with me—depending on the quality of the play." He was making strenuous efforts to finish it and in the meantime had to content himself with going around "licking my lips at cars," in one instance, at a car show.

Lili was disappointed: "Puppy! BOO-HOO-HOOOO-HOOOOOO! . . . ! . . . ! . . . Volodya! Boohoohoohoohoohoohoo-hoo-hoo!!!" she replied on 28 October. "Are we really not going to have a little car?! But I've learned to drive so brilliantly! Please!" Mayakovsky did what he could to indulge Lili's desires, and in order to finance the purchase of the car he tried to interest the film director René Clair in a film script he was working on. "What happened with René Clair?" Lili wondered uneasily. "If there isn't enough money, then at least send (through Amtorg) 450 dollars for a little Ford with no spare parts."

Although the film project came to nothing, Mayakovsky was able to send Lili a telegram on 10 November: "BUYING RENAULT. HANDSOME GRAY BRUTE 6 HORSEPOWER 4 CYLINDERS CONDUITE INTÉRIEURE." The money—he announced several days later—he would "scrape together and earn with the help of some good souls." He enclosed a drawing of the car and explained that he was staying a bit longer in Paris "to collect the car from the factory myself and get it crated up and sent off or else it'll drag on for months." Meanwhile he was slaving away on the play and the film script: "That'll be the first petrol Renoshka tries to wolf down."

The model Mayakovsky bought was the cheapest one and cost 20,000 francs, which corresponds to about 10,000 euros in today's values. The car was delivered to Moscow in January 1929.

THE IDEAL AND THE BEDCOVER

The manuscript that Mayakovsky tried to interest René Clair in was called "The Ideal and the Bedcover" and it survives as a short draft in French:

> Mayakovsky loves women. Women love Mayakovsky. As a person of refined feelings he seeks the ideal woman. He has even begun to read Tolstoy. He fashions ideal beings for himself, he vows that he will only commit himself to a woman who corresponds to his ideal, but he is always coming across other women.
>
> One such "other woman" got out of a Rolls one day and would have fallen if the idealist had not caught her in his arms. His relationship with her, vulgar, sensual, and stormy, is exactly the sort of relationship that Mayakovsky wanted to avoid. This relationship weighed on him all the more because, when he rang a telephone number in a letter he by chance had got in his hand, he had been enchanted by a deep, masculine, and bewitching woman's voice. It never developed beyond conversations, letters, and the sight of a fleeting figure that held out a letter to him. With even greater rage

he returned to his unavoidable lover, in the constant hope of being able to leave her, attracted by the unknown woman he loved.

Years of inquiries, which his lover did all she could to obstruct, finally persuaded the unknown woman to give in. She said she was his, and he cleansed himself by breaking with his earthly love. Shrouded in mystery, he is taken to the place where he is to have the fantastic meeting with the unknown woman. Full of happy anticipation Mayakovsky goes to encounter the beginning and end of his life.

The first turn of the head—and the unknown woman turns out to be the same woman he had spent all those years with and whom he has just left.

The poet is torn between physical love ("the bedcover") and pure love ("the ideal")—the text reflects the same longing for the ultimate love that we meet in all the love poems of Mayakovsky, "eternally / wounded by love." Even if the main character bears the same name as the author, it would be a mistake to infer too exact parallels with his real life. Mayakovsky lived "all those years" with Lili, and Lili wanted a car—if not yet a Rolls Royce—but their relationship was not "vulgar" but the direct opposite. No, the lover in this scenario is not a flesh-and-blood woman but a metaphor for physical love, *eros*, which is set against the *agape* of ideal love—as so often in Mayakovsky. But in one respect "The Ideal and the Bedcover" was autobiographical: it reflected Mayakovsky's longing for a new love just at this time, in the autumn of 1928.

THE TWO ELLYS

If Mayakovsky kept Lili informed about his doings in connection with buying the car, he was more reticent about other things. "*Go and rest somewhere!*" Lili urged him in her first letter to Paris. "Kiss Elsa, tell her *to send you off for a rest*." "Unfortunately I'm in Paris, which has bored me to the point of insensibility, nausea, and revulsion," replied Mayakovsky, adding, "Today I'm off to Nice for a couple of days (lady acquaintances have turned up), and I'll decide where to have a holiday. I'll either base myself in Nice for four weeks, or I'll go back to Germany. I can't do any work at all unless I get a break!"

Mayakovsky's "lady acquaintances" were two French-speaking young ladies whom Mayakovsky took with him to conceal the real reason for the trip, namely, to meet Elly Jones and the daughter they had had together, who were spending the autumn in Nice. The trip had not been planned in advance—it was a mutual acquaintance from New York, whom Mayakovsky bumped into in Paris, who told him that the two Ellys were in France.

The visit to Nice was to be a short one. Mayakovsky left Paris on 20 October and was back already on the twenty-fifth. What we know about the meeting of Mayakovsky, Elly, and their daughter we know from the account Elly gave to her daughter, Patricia, half a century later. According to Elly, they stood for a long time embracing before taking themselves off to Mayakovsky's hotel room, where Elly spent the night on account of the pouring rain. They talked the whole night long in floods of tears and fell asleep in each other's arms only as dawn broke. But they did not have intercourse. Elly found it hard to resist Mayakovsky's advances but was afraid of becoming pregnant again. It was clear to both of them that they could never raise a family either in the United States or the USSR. Their relationship had no future.

The day after his return to Paris Mayakovsky wrote a letter to his "two sweet Ellys," the only one which has survived:

I'm already dying to see you both again. Dreaming of being able to come and see you for at least another week. Will you receive me? And embrace me?

Please answer. Paris 29 rue Campagne Première Hotel Istria.

(Just hoping this doesn't just remain a dream. If I can I'll travel to Nice Wednesday-Thursday.)

I'm sorry that the sudden and unexpected trip didn't give me the opportunity to puff out my cheeks with well-being. What would you have thought about that?

Hope I can stretch out in Nice and show myself off to you in all my smiling beauty.

Please write immediately.

I kiss all eight of your paws.

When Mayakovsky visited the two Ellys in Nice in October 1928, it was the first and only time he saw his daughter.

Almost simultaneously, on 27 October, Elly wrote Mayakovsky a letter of which only the envelope survives. When she received Mayakovsky's letter two days later she composed a new one in which she wrote: "Of course we'll be delighted, you monster! [. . .] Send a telegram as soon as you have decided. We'll meet you! [. . .] The four paws are sleeping! They kissed the right cheek for Volodya, the left one for mama. Then, lest there should be any misunderstanding, they spent a long time explaining that Volodya's kiss was on the right cheek. [. . .] If you can't come, you should know that there will be two very disappointed Ellys in Nice, and in that case write often to us. Send a snowball from Moscow, I think I would be crazy with joy if I came there. I dream about you the whole time!"

Mayakovsky did not return to Nice, nor does he seem to have answered the letter from Elly, whose next letter (the first page of which is missing) is a mixture of expressions of tenderness and reproaches. It is dated 8 November and postmarked the eleventh:

You said: "We should be able to live so much yet." Now I say: "If everything you said here was *out of politeness*, carry on being polite if it isn't awfully difficult for you." You can't imagine how frayed my nerves have been this week! I don't know what you are thinking of—it's hard enough for me as it is—I don't love you *a lot*, I simply just love you. Why make it even more painful for me? In that case you needn't have come. Or written the first letter either. I asked you to send a telegram! Didn't have time? Have you already forgotten your two Ellys? Or perhaps you didn't like my letter? Or is it not interesting to call on two women who have a cold? Who moreover issue bourgeois orders of conduct.

Dear one! Please (the child says: bitte, bitte, bitte) never leave me in ignorance. I'm going quite crazy! And if you don't want to write, say so: this is my last letter—don't feel like writing. Or something like that. But to listen and worry about every step in the corridor, every knock on the door, is terrible. [. . .]

[The child] kept running out to the balcony the whole time, thinking that you would come by car. Then I cried and she comforted me and threatened that I wouldn't get any goodies. I tried to explain the whole thing, saying that "Volodya ist dumm und ungezogen," not only has he not come, he hasn't written either. She obviously agreed that that was uncouth, but she said forcefully that "Volodya ist nicht dumm." [. . .]

I had already started longing less for you, but then you came and now I miss you terribly and long for Russia. [. . .]

Seriously, Vladimir, don't make your girlfriend sad, you who are prepared to give your liver to a dog*—and we ask so little. We are also animals, with legs, with eyes! Unusual animals, I assure you— if not in a cage. And it is awfully necessary for our peace of mind that we know people are thinking of us—think of us at least once a month (the child's birthday is the fifteenth)! Write, and if you don't have time cut out something you've written in magazines or news-papers. Books, you've promised them. [. . .]

Take care of yourself, promise! Pray "the person you love" to for-bid you to burn the candle at both ends! What's the point? Don't do it.

Come here! Only without an interpreter! Every minute you are here will be, if not filled, at least occupied!

It is clear from the next-to-last sentence that Mayakovsky did not hide from Elly the fact that the only woman he really loved was Lili. However masochistic his love for her was, especially at this time, it was a fact that women he courted had to reconcile themselves to. When the affair with Natasha Bryukhanenko ended in the spring of 1928 it was after the following conversation between herself and Mayakovsky:

"You think I'm nice and pretty and you say you need me. You even say I have good legs. So why don't you say you love me?"

"I love Lili. I can like all the other ones or like them A LOT, but only love them in second place. Do you want me to love you in sec-ond place?"

"No! In that case it would be better if you didn't love me at all, I said. Like me A LOT instead."

* A reference to the following lines in "About This": "I love animals. / When I see a cur— / there is one outside the bakery / without a hair / I'm ready / to cut out my own liver. / What's mine is yours / my dear!"

Natasha went on seeing Mayakovsky and also became a friend of Lili and Osip. This was exactly how Lili wanted it, and as it happened so often: Mayakovsky's girlfriends became hers too. It was an arrangement which in Elly's case, for obvious reasons, was unthinkable.

A BEAUTY STEPS INTO THE ROOM . . .

Elly's letters to Mayakovsky were not addressed to Paris but to Lubyanka Passage in Moscow, which shows that he had no intention of staying in the French capital but was thinking of returning to Moscow. Why? Couldn't he cope with the situation, emotionally or practically? Was it a way of escaping from an impossible equation?

But Mayakovsky did not travel back to Moscow, as he had told Elly he would. On the same day on which he returned to Paris, 25 October, Elsa had an appointment with Dr. Serge Simon, and she asked Mayakovsky to go with her. While they were sitting talking, a young woman came in. "When I entered the salon," the woman related later, "I saw the doctor, Elsa Triolet, and a tall man, very elegantly dressed in a well-cut suit, fine shoes, sitting in an armchair looking rather bored. As soon as I came in he fixed me with an alert and sober gaze. I immediately recognized the short crew cut and the handsome, strong facial features—it was Mayakovsky." When Mayakovsky heard her name—Tatyana—he knew at once who she was: the girl that several of his Russian acquaintances in Paris had told him about and to whom he had sent his anonymous greetings.

The young girl had a dreadful cough, but despite his hypochondria Mayakovsky offered to see her home. It was cold in the taxi, and he took off his coat and laid it over her legs. "From that moment I was aware of a tenderness and consideration which it was impossible not to respond to," Tatyana recalled.

The meeting at Dr. Simon's had been arranged. Elsa was friendly with the doctor's Russian wife, Nadezhda, and had told her that Mayakovsky was bored in Paris and needed someone to go out with. Tatyana, whom she had got to know shortly before, was exactly his type of woman: Russian speaking, pretty, and moreover interested in poetry. So when Tatyana phoned to complain of a bad dose of bronchi-

Tatyana Yakovleva around 1928.

tis and Dr. Simon asked her to come and see him immediately, his wife contacted Elsa and invited her and Mayakovsky the same evening. . . . It was not the first time that Elsa had gone in for such matchmaking, but it was the first time that the chosen person had fulfilled all the specified criteria.

Elsa's explanation of why she wanted to introduce Tatyana to Mayakovsky is probably correct. But why was she in such a hurry, why did it have to happen on the same day that he came back from Nice? Tatyana was very active in Russian circles in Paris and the meeting could have been arranged at any time in one of the cafés in Montparnasse. Were there other motives for Elsa's action? Had Elsa—and by the same token Lili—learned of the meeting in Nice? Was it in order to distract him and make him stop thinking about the Ellys that Tatyana was required? Was Lili afraid that Mayakovsky would be tempted to accompany his daughter and her mother to the United States? Was it Lili who—in a letter or telephone conversation that is lost to posterity—asked Elsa to find a woman for him? In that case her appeal would coincide with Elsa's interest in keeping Mayakovsky in Paris, where she was living in poverty and Mayakovsky's wallet made her existence significantly more bearable. In that case Elsa must have been panic stricken when Mayakovsky stepped off the train from Nice and declared that he was thinking of returning to Moscow.

At the time of her meeting with Mayakovsky, Tatyana Yakovleva was twenty-two years old and according to Elsa "full of youthful daring." She had "endless joie de vivre, spoke breathlessly, swam, played tennis, had countless admirers." She was born in 1906 in St. Petersburg, but from 1913 she lived in Penza, 350 miles southeast of Moscow, where her architect father, Alexey Yakovlev, had been commissioned to design the new town theater. The family also had another daughter, Lyudmila, known as "Lila," who was two years younger than Tatyana. Two years later the parents divorced and the father moved to the United States. Shortly afterward the mother married a rich entrepreneur who lost his fortune in the Revolution. In 1921 when southern Russia was hit by famine, he died as a consequence of malnourishment and tuberculosis, whereupon the mother married again for the third time.

In 1922 Tatyana also fell ill with tuberculosis, probably infected by her stepfather, and her paternal uncle Alexander Yakovlev, who lived in Paris, ensured with the help of his friend André Citroën, the industrialist, that she could come to France. When she arrived in Paris in the summer of 1925 she had just turned nineteen. Her paternal grandmother, "Babushka," and her aunt Sandra, an opera singer who used to perform with Chaliapin, had already been living in Paris for some years.

Tatyana spent the first few years trying to regain her health and was not allowed to go out in the evenings, but when she finally surfaced in Paris's inner circles, she was an immediate success. She was tall, about five feet ten, with lovely long legs and a degree of sex appeal which had men queueing for her favors, among them the Russian oil magnate Mantashev. Thanks to her looks she soon found work as a film extra and as a model with Chanel, and in addition she advertised stockings on posters which could be seen all over Paris. She also made a living as a milliner, which was later to become her profession. Her uncle Alexander was a well-known explorer and a successful artist who knew *tout Paris*, and through him she came into contact with cultural celebrities like the writer Jean Cocteau and the composer Sergey Prokofiev (with whom she played Brahms four-handed the evening before she met Mayakovsky).

Whatever motive Elsa had for pairing off Mayakovsky and Tatyana, her hopes of a lighthearted flirtation came to nought: Mayakovsky and Tatyana fell madly in love with each other and started meeting daily. After his meeting with Tatyana Mayakovsky had no contact with Moscow for about two weeks. When he finally sent Lili a telegram it was to tell her he was in the process of buying the Renault. What he did not tell her was that the person helping him to choose the color of the car was his new love. But if Lili was unaware of Tatyana, Tatyana knew all about her. Just as he had done with Elly, he talked constantly to Tatyana about Lili, whom, in Tatyana's words, he "adored as a friend," although they had not lived together for several years.

"They were a brilliant couple," recalled an acquaintance who often saw them together: "Mayakovsky very stylish, a big man. Tanya was also good looking—tall, slim, and a good match for him. Mayakovsky gave the impression of being quiet, in love. She was captivated and full of admiration for him, proud of his talent." However, neither Mayakovsky nor Tatyana had any interest in showing off their relationship: she, because her strongly anti-Soviet family had been at great pains to get her out of the Soviet Union, and Mayakovsky, because a Soviet proletarian poet ought not to be seeing a Russian émigrée girl. Yet politics does not seem to have played a major role in their relationship. They mostly talked instead about poetry. Mayakovsky was impressed not only by Tatyana's external charms but also by her phenomenal memory for poems, which she could recite from memory for hours. She also wrote poetry herself but did not dare tell him.

Sometimes they met in company with other people in the better-known cafés, but they mostly went to cheaper places where they could be anonymous. Mayakovsky used to phone Tatyana in the mornings, when Babushka did not answer the phone, in order to arrange when and where they would meet in the evening. Sometimes he waited in a taxi outside the front door and they drove to the theater or went to see Elsa or other friends who knew about their relationship. "Babushka and Auntie are 'traditionalists,'" Tatyana wrote to her mother in Penza, "and of course do not understand this type of person, and his poems are incomprehensible to them." However, when Mayakovsky went to her home to pick her up, he was "unbelievably amiable."

"He is the first individual who has succeeded in leaving an impression on my soul," Tatyana reported to her mother. "He is the most gifted person I have ever met and moreover in an area that interests me." Even if Tatyana, for safety's sake, did not use the word "love," there can be no doubt that her feelings for Mayakovsky went deep. But when, after a few weeks' acquaintanceship, he asked her to become his wife and come back to Moscow with him, she went on the defensive. Her reaction released his dormant lyrical powers and during the night he wrote a poem which he read out to her the following day when they met in a restaurant and which ends with his answer to her evasive reply:

> You don't want to?
>> Spend the winter in this city then—
> that insult can be added
>> to our joint account.
> Sometime,
>> however,
> I will come nevertheless
>> and take you
> alone
>> or Paris with you.

Shklovsky had been proved right: Mayakovsky had found a "way out of the situation." "Letter to Tatyana Yakovleva" was one of two lyric poems which Mayakovsky wrote during the autumn he spent in Paris. The other was "Letter to Comrade Kostrov from Paris about the Nature of Love," which was finished later, shortly before his journey home.

In "About This" Mayakovsky had asked Lili the rhetorical question: "Where, / my love, where / have I once / betrayed / our love / in my song?" He had never done this hitherto—all his poems were dedicated to her, and the first volume of his *Collected Works*, which came out while he was in Paris, began with the printed dedication "To L. Yu. B." So all his writings were dedicated to Lili. But with the poem to Tatyana, Mayakovsky "betrayed" Lili for the first time in his "song." It was the first love poem since 1915 which did not have Lili as the object of his lyricism, and it was one of his finest ever:

Only you
        match me for height,
come, stand beside me,
                brow against brow,
I want to talk for a bit
        about this
                crucial evening
like one human being
                to another.

Women like Tatyana, "of our long-legged sort," are needed in poor, suffering Russia:

You who went
        through the snowstorm
                and typhus
On those legs
        so many times
must not
        let them be caressed
by oil barons
        in salons by night.
Forget all that.
        Your eyes are on fire
and the arcs of your eyebrows uncurve into lines.
Come here instead,
        here where my big
clumsy hands
        stretch out to you.

Despite his reluctance to advertise his relationship with Tatyana, Mayakovsky read the poem not only to Elsa but also in Russian circles in Paris. Tatyana, not unnaturally, was both embarrassed and flattered that his love for her had been given the status of poetry, and it seems like he came close to persuading her after all to go back to Moscow with him: "He made me long so much for Russia and for all of you," Tatyana wrote to her mother: "I was on the verge of going back."

She did not do so; instead, they agreed to try to see each other again as soon as possible. Before leaving Paris, Mayakovsky instructed a florist to deliver a bouquet of roses to Tatyana every Sunday morning until he returned. Every bouquet was accompanied by a calling card with verses and drawings on the back.

Mayakovsky left Paris on 3 December, and as soon as he arrived in Berlin next morning he sent a telegram to Tatyana and phoned her. In a letter to her mother Tatyana described the conversation as "one long cry of anguish." On 8 December he was back in Moscow, from where, two days later, he sent her the first volume of his *Collected Works* with the dedication: "I send / my works / to my dear friend, / May they take my place / until we meet / again in May. / Or why not in March? Because of the almanac and the map?" On his very first day in Moscow he looked up Tatyana's sister Lyudmila, who wanted to move to Paris. Tatyana had asked Mayakovsky to help her obtain an exit visa.

As long as Mayakovsky was in Paris, Lili remained in blissful ignorance about Tatyana. In his one and only letter to Lili, on 12 November, he reported: "My life is rather strange, with no events but many details which are not material for a letter and can only be told when I sort through my cases which I am going do not later than the the eighth or tenth [of December]." If this statement did not make Lili particularly uneasy, Mayakovsky's plea that she should "transfer by telegraph thirty rubles to Lyudmila Alexeyevna Yakovleva, flat 3, 52 Krasnaya Street, in Penza" must have made her suspect that something was up. This was the first she had heard about any "Yakovleva"!

Elsa normally kept Lili informed about most of what was going on, but not this time. What had been envisaged as a distraction had developed into a serious relationship, and the blame was hers. If Elsa did not dare inform her sister about the love drama in Paris, Mayakovsky no sooner got home than he told Lili all about Tatyana—in the same way that he always told her everything. "He came home [. . .] elated and in love," Lili recalled. "The girl was a beauty, gifted, pure, one of us, Soviet. Preferred him to all the oil barons. He was the first one she had given herself to. Loves him, is waiting for him. Isn't dependent on anyone. Works." But this time he was disappointed by her reaction. Lili soon came to realize that Tatyana was not just a passing fancy, but that Mayakovsky loved her and really meant to try to get her to move to Moscow. On 17 December Lili sounded the alarm in a letter to Elsa: "Dear Elsa! Please write and tell me what kind of a woman this is that Volodya is eating out his heart for, that he is thinking of bringing here to Moscow, that he is writing poems to (!!), and who, after so many years in Paris, faints when she hears the word *merde*! I find it difficult to believe in the innocence of a Russian milliner in Paris! DON'T TELL ANYONE that I'm asking you about this and write giving me all the details. Nobody reads the letters I get."

Lili's distrust of Tatyana's "innocence" shows that she saw her as a gold digger, but it was not true. Mayakovsky satisfied a need in her that none of her other suitors could supply. "I still really long for him," Tatyana wrote to her mother on Christmas Eve 1928. "The people I go around with are mainly 'society people' who have no need to use their brain or any other cobwebbed thoughts or feelings." On the same day Mayakovsky wrote to Tatyana that he bore her name like a "banner over the city hall" and did not intend to lower it by a millimeter. And a week or so later:

> The lines from you are more than half of my life in general and all of my private life.
>
> I don't like explaining myself on paper [. . .] but if I was to write down all the conversations I've had with myself about you, all the unwritten letters and unspoken endearments, then my collected works would swell threefold, and that only in the form of lyrics!
>
> My dear!
>
> I really don't like being without you. Think again and collect your thoughts (and then your things) and open your heart to my hope that I can take you in my arms and lead you here, to me, in Moscow. [. . .] Let us turn our separation into a test.
>
> If we love each other—why do we squander our love and our time by meeting via telegraph poles?

On New Year's Eve the mood in the apartment in Gendrikov Alley was subdued. Mayakovsky was thinking the whole time about

Tatyana, and when, toward the stroke of midnight, he became "awash with longing," Lili could no longer restrain her jealousy, shouting at him: "If you're so miserable why don't you just go to her now?" Osip was in somber mood too, with their whole way of life now in the balance.

Mayakovsky would gladly have gone back to Paris and Tatyana immediately, but it was impossible. The play he had been working on during his stay in Paris was finished and was due to be performed in Meyerhold's theater. He would leave as soon as the rehearsals of *The Bedbug* were over. Meanwhile, he assured Tatyana, his work and his thoughts about her were his "*only* joy."

LETTER TO COMRADE KOSTROV ABOUT THE NATURE OF LOVE

"Letter to Tatyana Yakovleva" was not printed during Mayakovsky's lifetime. This was presumably at the request of Tatyana, who had not approved of his reciting the poem in Russian circles in Paris. But the other Paris poem, "Letter to Comrade Kostrov from Paris about the Nature of Love," was published in the January issue of the magazine *Molodaya Gvardiya* (Young Guard). Taras Kostrov was the editor of the magazine and had commissioned the Paris poems from Mayakovsky. "Letter to Comrade Kostrov" went off like a bomb and brought impassioned protests from the proletarian writers in RAPP, for whom the very theme was impermissible for a writer who claimed to be a communist.

Lili could not protest publicly but was extremely upset by what she regarded as Mayakovsky's betrayal of her—especially the lines "the heart's / stalled engine / has been / started up again," which were a blow to her status as his muse. The fact that he had written the poem at all was bad enough. Now that it was in print, what before had been merely the stuff of rumor was proved beyond doubt: namely, that the fuel for the engine of the poet's heart had been supplied by someone other than Lili.

After a reference to their first meeting at Dr. Simon's—"Just think: / a beauty / walks into the room / in furs / and pearls clad"—"Letter to Comrade Kostrov" continues with a definition of love which belongs among the most powerful in the history of Russian lyric poetry:

To love
  means
    to rush out
every night
    into the pitch-black darkness
and with a flashing axe
        chop wood
your muscles
    rippling.
To love
  is to spring up
        from bedsheets
torn by insomnia,
    jealous of Copernicus,
            regarding him, not the neighbor's husband,
as
  your true
      rival.

By publishing this tribute to the power of love Mayakovsky risked further undermining his reputation as a proletarian poet, something he was of course aware of. He was incredibly touchy about any hints that he was not living in the way his critics thought he ought to, and his love affair with a "White" émigrée made him an easy target for attacks. His purchase of a car was also a sensitive issue in a country where the number of private cars could be counted on the fingers of one hand. That Mayakovsky realized the Renault would be counted against him is clear from the poem "Answer to Future Gossip," in which he defends himself by claiming that "the steering wheel, / the springs, / the spokes" had been paid for by "two thousand six hundred sleepless lines of poetry": "I will not escape / all the malicious gossip. / So what? / Please forgive me / that I / brought back a Renault / from Paris / and not perfume / or ties."

The poem was written before the car was delivered to Moscow, and it was printed in the January issue of the newspaper *Behind the Wheel*. But it is hard to believe that it would have lessened people's mistrust of Mayakovsky, especially as everyone knew that the purchase of the car did not exclude imports of either perfume or ties.

PHILISTINUS VULGARIS

At the same time as the lyric poet in him was triumphing in his love poems to Tatyana, Mayakovsky was working on his most antilyrical work to date. The play *The Bedbug* was finished by the end of December 1928 and was greeted with enthusiasm by Vsevolod Meyerhold, who ten years earlier had directed *Mystery-Bouffe*. The work of staging the play—the decor, costumes, rehearsals—was carried out in record time, little over a month. The music was written by the young composer Dmitry Shostakovich.

In the updated version of his autobiography, written in April 1928, Mayakovsky stated that his tribute to the Revolution, "Good!," was to have been followed by a poem with the title "Bad." It was never written—instead, Mayakovsky wrote *The Bedbug*, in which the main character, the vodka-drinking, guitar-strumming, and mawkish Communist Party member Prisypkin is a vulgarized variant of the Soviet citizen whom Mayakovsky parodied in "About This." Prisypkin abandons his old love, the working-class girl Zoya Beryozkina, who in desperation tries to kill herself, in order to marry the cashier and manicurist Elsevira Renaissance. During the wedding, which is held in a hairdressing salon, a fire breaks out and everyone dies.

Fifty years later Prisypkin is found deep-frozen in the cellar of the house, drowned by water from the fire hoses, and the Institute for the Resurrection of People is given the task of thawing him out. But along with Prisypkin, they revive a louse, "an extinct and, at the beginning of the century, very popular insect," which spreads plague in the form of phenomena which by 1979 have long been obsolete and are found only in dictionaries: love, romance, suicide, dancing, tobacco, vodka . . . When a young girl begins to dance the Charleston and to mumble poems, the professors declare that she has been hit by something called "love"—"an ancient sickness, when the human sex drive, rationally spread out over one's whole life, is suddenly condensed into one week in a single inflammatory process which leads to irrational and incomprehensible acts." And when the professor's assistant—who is none other than an aged Zoya Beryozkina—admits that fifty years earlier she attempted suicide because of love, he replies: "Nonsense . . . Love should be used to build bridges and bear children." The responses echo with private references: to Tonya Gumilina, who committed suicide for Mayakovsky's sake—and to Elly/Patricia, the fruit of his own love.

When the louse is finally caught, it is packed off along with Prisypkin to a zoo: "Different sizes, but basically the same: the famous *Lusus normalis* and *Philistinus vulgaris*." Locked in a cage with his guitar, his vodka bottles and his cigarettes, Prisypkin—"the creature," as the director of the zoo calls him—is exhibited to a curious public. Special filters ensure that his vulgar speech reaches the onlookers in a censored form. Sometimes he "smokes," sometimes "he stimulates himself" with the help of a vodka bottle. When the director encourages him to say something, Prisypkin turns to the watching public and shouts: "Fellow citizens! Brothers! My friends! My dear ones! Where do you come from? How many of you are there?! When were you all thawed out? Why am I alone in this cage? Come here and keep me company! Why must I suffer?"

If the louse is a metaphor for Prisypkin, Prisypkin is a caricature of Mayakovsky, the poet who, with his dreams of "an absurd love," suffers for all mankind. To underline the parallel, Mayakovsky insisted that the actor playing the leading role should learn to imitate his mannerisms. In *The Bedbug* the poet settles the accounts with his youthful dreams of a bright future and an all-redeeming love. In the play, the Communist future is a soulless, mechanized society in which love has been reduced to pure physiology, to the sexual drive. The dream of resurrection in "About This," where Mayakovsky meets his beloved in the future "along the walkways of the zoo" is grimly parodied in *The Bedbug*, where the poet's reawakened alter ego is kept locked in a cage along with a poisonous insect. In "Man" Mayakovsky declares that he is "only heart," but in the society of the future no one knows what heart is. And if he believed, in 150,000,000, that "in the new world / roses and dreams soiled by poets / will burst forth / to the delight / of us / grown-up children," the reality of the year 1979 is now rather different: "Roses are found only in gardening books, and dreams only in medicine, in the chapter on hallucinations."

The Bedbug sucked all the energy out of Mayakovsky, who worked on it day and night and got hardly any sleep. But the work was tax-

Mayakovsky with the theater director Vsevolod Meyerhold and the composer Dmitry Shostakovich during the rehearsals for *The Bedbug*. *To the right:* Alexander Rodchenko, who designed the costumes for the second part of the play, which takes place in 1979.

ing not only physically but also because the play was a variation on the basic theme of his writing just as this theme had come to the fore again for the first time in ages. Tatyana was in his thoughts all the time, and it was with the Waterman pen she had given him as a present that he finished writing the play. "HOPE COME RESTORE HEALTH REST BEGINNING FEBRUARY. ABSOLUTE RIVIERA. HELP ARRANGE WITH ELSA. TELEGRAPH WRITE LOVING LONGING KISS YOUR VOL," ran the telegram he sent her on 13 January. To Natasha Bryukhanenko, who visited Mayakovsky in January, he declared in "friendly confidence" that he would shoot himself if he did not soon manage to see the woman he was in love with. But

Natasha immediately betrayed his confidence: frightened that he might take his own life, she immediately phoned Lili and told her everything.

Mayakovsky could not leave before the premiere of *The Bedbug*, which took place on 13 February and which with a few exceptions was a critical success. The very next day he left Moscow—three months earlier than planned. He sent Tatyana a telegram from the Russian border: "LEAVE TODAY WITH STAY FEW DAYS PRAGUE BERLIN." Mayakovsky's reason for making a detour via Prague and Berlin, despite his longing for Tatyana, was financial. On 1 February he had signed a "general contract" with Gosizdat which gave the publisher the rights to "all works, published and unpublished, together with those works which the author may come to write during the duration of the contract," that is, for four years. In return the publisher would pay Mayakovsky a monthly salary of around 1,000 rubles, which would give him "the opportunity to work without stress and without having to waste time on hackwork." However, in view of his future plans the contract with Gosizdat was unsatisfactory, and he was in great need of other sources of income.

This was why Mayakovsky went to Prague, where there was some interest in putting on a production of *The Bedbug*. When he got there, Roman Jakobson had arranged for him to read the play to the people responsible for drawing up the repertoire at the Vinohrad Theater. But although they were impressed both by the innovative dramaturgy and Mayakovsky's masterly performance, no contract was signed, and Mayakovsky left Prague after only one day. He "was in a hurry to head west," according to Jakobson, who also recollected that he spoke openly of his love for Tatyana: "I am in love, and that puts everything else in the shade."

On this visit to Prague Mayakovsky was given a much cooler reception at the Soviet legation than two years earlier. Jakobson did not know "whether it was because of him or because of me," although he heard visitors from Moscow saying that "it is already seen as advantageous and popular to pound" Mayakovsky and that "everybody who felt like it jumped on him."

If Prague was a disappointment, Mayakovsky had all the more success in Berlin, where he signed the contract with Malik Verlag which he had been hoping to sign the previous autumn—a German variant of the general contract with Gosizdat. As soon as it was concluded he was free to travel on to Paris: "ARRIVE TOMORROW TWENTY-SECOND TWO O'CLOCK BLUE EXPRESS," he wired Tatyana on 21 February.

IN THE EVENT OF MY DEATH PLEASE INFORM . . .

"He was more in love when he came back than when he left," recalled Tatyana, who was given the manuscript of *The Bedbug* as a present. During the two months that Mayakovsky spent in France they saw each other every day. "V.V. takes up all my spare time," Tatyana revealed to her mother as an explanation for why she wrote so seldom. Their favorite places were La Coupole and the little restaurant La Grande Chaumière in Montparnasse. As the latest American and French films were not shown in the Soviet Union, they often went to the cinema, and the first talking picture that Mayakovsky saw was with Tatyana in the News cinema.

Just as before, they also saw something of Elsa, but not as often or intimately as in the autumn. Elsa was no longer living in the Hotel Istria. On 6 November 1928, shortly after Mayakovsky had got to know Tatyana, she had met the French surrealist poet Louis Aragon. It was love at first sight. The acquaintanceship with Aragon came at a time when Elsa was standing at a crossroads. Her marriage to Triolet was long dead, her private life was unhappy, she was short of money, and she only existed as a writer in the USSR. In the autumn of 1928 she had become so desperate that she asked Mayakovsky to help her return to her native country. Then, after a couple of ill-fated love affairs, she met Aragon, whom she moved in with after only a few months. Apart from the fact that Elsa's life changed in a trice, her new love also meant a restoration of the balance in the eternal rivalry with her elder sister: she too was now living with a great poet.

Mayakovsky and Tatyana spent their holidays at Le Touquet or Deauville on the French Atlantic coast, where they could go about undisturbed and where the casinos offered enticing opportunities to bolster their finances. Mayakovsky was a generous, not to say extravagant, suitor, and his wallet became thinner with every passing day. He had been hoping for money from Gosizdat, but on 20 March Lili informed him that his request to transfer money to Paris had been turned down. This was a major setback which Mayakovsky attempted to compensate for at the gaming table. But the turn of the dice was not in his favor. On one occasion he lost all his money at roulette and they were forced to hitchhike back to Paris. "He was really brilliant at all kinds of games," Tatyana recalled, "but there were some there who played even better."

Two days after receiving the news about the canceled money transfer, Mayakovsky traveled to Nice, "as long it [the money] lasts," he told Lili in the only (surviving) letter from this stay in Paris, "and it looks as if it will only last for a little while." The excursion to Nice had two aims: he wanted to try his luck in the casino in Monte Carlo, and he hoped to be able to see his American girlfriends.

The trip turned out badly on both counts. Mayakovsky gambled away his last few pennies in Monte Carlo and was forced, hungry, to borrow money from the artist Yury Annenkov, who had been living in France for several years and whom he bumped into in Nice. Asked by Mayakovsky when he intended to return to Moscow, Annenkov replied that he had no intention of doing any such thing as he wished to continue being an artist. "Mayakovsky clapped mc on the shoulder," Annenkov recalled, "became suddenly somber and said in a hoarse voice: 'But I'm going back. . . because I have already stopped being a poet.' There followed a truly dramatic scene: Mayakovsky burst into tears and whispered, barely audibly: 'Nowadays I am. . . a functionary.'"

As for his two Ellys, for the last month they had been living with a female friend in Milan. When they returned to Nice in mid-April so that the girl could get a little sun before they traveled back to the United States, Mayakovsky was no longer there. "She hasn't forgotten you yet, although I never talk about you," Elly wrote in reply to a letter from Mayakovsky which has not survived. "When we were out walking in Milan the other day she suddenly said: 'Der große Mann heißt Volodja.' You told me long ago that no woman has been able to withstand your charm. You are obviously right!"

If Elly had formerly entertained hopes of a life together with Mayakovsky, she had now given up such thoughts. Instead she gave him her new address in New York and ended with an ill-omened suggestion: "Listen, write this address down in your notebook, under the heading 'In the event of my death please inform'—us too. Take care."

Mayakovsky did as Elly asked and wrote the words in his notebook. But what reason did she have to suspect that he might soon die? After all, he was only 35. A letter of Elly's in which she writes of a female friend that "she is *also* a candidate for suicide" (my italics) suggests that Mayakovsky's suicidal disposition was no secret to her. Presumably he had talked to her about his attempts at and constant thoughts about suicide. But there is also another possible explanation for her anxiety, namely, that Mayakovsky was afraid he might be killed. The twenties were a time of widespread lawlessness and banditry, they had had several attempted burglaries in both Sokolniki and Gendrikov, and Mayakovsky always carried a knuckle-duster and a loaded pistol on him. With his poetry and his challenging and provocative style, he stirred up strong feelings, and on one occasion a madman had tried to shoot him.

Lately, the political situation in the USSR was aggravated by an intense political power struggle. In January Trotsky had been expelled from Kazakhstan to Turkey, and in April Bukharin was sacked from the editorship of *Pravda*. The consolidation within the party and government apparatus corresponded to a similar centralization of economic power. The NEP was definitely finished, agriculture was being collectivized, and industry nationalized. The mood in the country became more and more claustrophobic, the authorities saw enemies everywhere, informing was rampant, and the newspapers were filled with articles about children who had distanced themselves from their—by implication, counterrevolutionary—fathers. Mayakovsky's relationship with Tatyana was of course carefully monitored by OGPU agents in Paris, and it is hard to believe that he would not have known or at least suspected that his movements were being followed by the Soviet security service. His efforts to help Tatyana's sister to leave the Soviet Union also of course attracted attention: the Soviet Union's leading poet colluding with a prominent Russian émigré family!

Elly's letter enticed his suicidal thoughts to the surface, and the conversation with Annenkov brought to the fore both his split personality and the complexity of the poetic and political tasks he had set himself. It is clear from his scanty and meager correspondence with Lili from around this time that their relationship had cooled significantly. Against this background, the relationship with Tatyana simply *had* to succeed! She *must* become his wife and come back with him to the Soviet Union! But Tatyana hesitated, and her mother in Penza was extremely apprehensive: "I have certainly not decided to set off or, as you put it, 'rush' after M.," Tatyana wrote soothingly to her shortly before Mayakovsky arrived in Paris in February, "and he is not *coming to fetch me* but coming *to me*, and just for a short visit." She did not want to get married just now, she explained, but if she were to do so it would be with Mayakovsky. "He is so intelligent" that her other suitors are worthless in comparison. Marriage to Mayakovsky would also have the advantage that she would get the chance to see her mother again.

Mayakovsky inundated Tatyana with tokens of love and proposals of marriage, but was it Tatyana he loved—or love itself? "Volodya has written a lovely poem to Tatyana. Poor, poor Tata!" Elsa noted in her diary on 3 December 1928, the same day on which Mayakovsky left Paris. "One could write a novel about it. In reality, it can't be expressed better than Volodya does it in his poems. But how awful it is to know someone like I do—when, what, how—all that, I know him without having to exchange two words with him, it's enough that I see the position he finds himself in. His cunning and his aggressiveness, like a wild animal, either it's about billiards or love. And now Tata, young, beautiful, dearly loved by one and all."

For Elsa, Mayakovsky's relationship to Tatyana was a variation on a theme that she and Lili were only too familiar with: a storm of emotions demanding an immediate and wholehearted response. Did Tatyana understand this? And did she understand that she was the object not so much of Mayakovsky's love as of his *need for love*? Hardly. Overwhelmed by the intensity of his courtship and flattered by the attentions of one of the leading poets in the Russian language, she was not to know that *all* the women whom Mayakovsky courted were exposed to the same emotional assault.

And how intimate was the relationship? According to what Mayakovsky told Lili, he was the first man Tatyana had "given herself to," something Lili found hard to believe. Such a beautiful woman with so many suitors, and moreover with the reputation of a femme fatale!? If so, this was an expression of chastity or coyness that Lili found hard to understand. According to Tatyana, however, they did not go to bed with each other during Mayakovsky's first stay in Paris: "He was [. . .] a born hunter, he liked conquering, he had a need of it," she explained in an interview many years later. "If I had gone to bed with him the first time perhaps he wouldn't have come back."

Whatever the degree of intimacy in their relationship may have been, Tatyana wavered under the strain of conflicting feelings in the spring of 1929 when Mayakovsky stepped up the pressure and "tried desperately to persuade [her] to return to Russia." At the same time he explained to her, just as he had done to Annenkov, that he was "disappointed" about many things in his homeland. On this occasion too, Tatyana was unable to make up her mind. Was it Mayakovsky's growing skepticism about developments in the Soviet Union that made her hesitate? The alternative, that he would stay in France, was out of the question. That would have meant the end for him as a poet; without the Soviet atmosphere he could not breathe, and without Lili and Osip he could not function as a poet. No one understood his personality and no one appreciated his poetic greatness like they did, and however difficult his relationship to Lili was, no one was closer to him than she was. Perhaps it was that insight that held Tatyana back.

Mayakovsky left Paris on one of the last days of April. His farewell party was held in his favorite restaurant, La Grande Chaumière. Present at the dinner—apart from Tatyana—were Elsa and Aragon and a few other people, among them the Soviet Russian author Lev Nikulin and an acquaintance who was an "automobilist" and who, after the dinner, gave the company a lift to the Gare du Nord and the Berlin train. "Mayakovsky and his girlfriend wandered up and down the platform hand in hand until it was time to board the train," Nikulin recalled. Mayakovsky was supposed to come back to Paris in October, when they would get married.

Before leaving Paris, Mayakovsky sent a telegram to Lili asking her to transfer 100 rubles to Negoreloye, the railway station on the border with Poland. He was broke and needed money to pay for the last lap home.

13

THE YEAR OF THE GREAT CHANGE

1929

We are better off than ever and better than anywhere else. Human history has never known such a boost before.
Mayakovsky to Tatyana in the summer of 1929

"I was sad when Volodya read 'Letter from Paris about the Nature of Love' to me," was Lili's later summing-up of her reaction. This was a euphemism. She was not sad but disappointed and upset. The poem was an acknowledgement of Mayakovsky's feelings for Tatyana and a dreadful blow to Lili's ego. It was the first time that her place in Mayakovsky's poetry and life had been called in question, and she was shaken. The fragile mental state in which she obviously found herself in the winter of 1928–29 was exacerbated by the fact that her relationship with Kuleshov had ended and no satisfactory substitute had as yet appeared. At the age of thirty-seven, had she lost her power of attraction? During Mayakovsky's stay in Paris Lili fell hopelessly in love with another film director, Vsevolod Pudovkin,

Mayakovsky's last passion, the young actress Veronika Polonskaya.

who had made his name in 1926 with a film version of Gorky's novel *The Mother*, following this two years later with the film *Storm over Asia*, an international success based on a scenario written by Osip.

Pudovkin was also someone to Lili's taste: a man of the world who spoke excellent French and was a dedicated tennis player. He was married but did not live with his actress wife. Everything therefore seemed ideally set up for a love affair, according to Lili's plan, without jealous scenes. There was only one jarring note: unlike most other men, Pudovkin was not receptive to Lili's charms, which led her to attempt suicide. She took an overdose of the sleeping pill Veronal; attempts to revive her succeeded, but her recuperation took several months. When Mayakovsky returned from Paris, Lili told him everything. The interesting thing is not her honesty—they had after all agreed not to hide anything from each other—but Mayakovsky's reaction: "He gave a start," Lili recalled, "and left the room without hearing the end of the story." Any talk of suicide awoke dark thoughts in him.

Family relations were in other words strained to the limit by 2 May, when Mayakovsky came home from Paris, fully resolved to return there in October to marry Tatyana. Conversations over the dinner table in Gendrikov Alley were long and despairing. From Lili's notes we can conclude that she tried to persuade Mayakovsky that Tatyana was not the person he thought she was, that she had other lovers, and if they were married she would never go back to Moscow with him. But his relationship with Tatyana was stronger than the one with Natasha, and Mayakovsky did not give in to Lili's arguments. On 8 May—one day late—he congratulated Tatyana on her twenty-third birthday, and on 15 May he sent her both a letter and a telegram. They were answers to a letter from Tatyana which has not survived but in which she seems to have reproached Mayakovsky for not writing: "Only now has my head cleared a bit so that I can think and write a bit. Please don't complain and scold me—I've been through so much unpleasantness, from gnat sized to elephant sized, that really no one has the right to be angry with me." And he continued with the following situation report:

1) I love Tanik very much and wholeheartedly.
2) Have just begun working, will write out your *The Bathhouse*.

3) Lilichka [Tatyana's sister] exploded and became angry because I didn't immediately take her to the Eiffel Tower, but now she has calmed down and will content herself for the foreseeable future with traveling to Sochi, for which she is leaving in a couple of days. Hoping to be able to talk your mother into going too, will refer to your order that she is to rest. We'll see each other there anyway.

4) Yesterday I got a letter from your mother, she asks about you— will reply to her today.

5) I'll send the books today, volume 4 and two issues of *Young Guard* with *The Bedbug*.

6) Leaving Moscow around 15–25 June for Caucasus and Crimea—readings.

7) Write to me *always* and *compulsorily* and send telegrams, without your letters I quite simply cannot live.

8) I long for you something awful.

9,10,11,12, etc. I love you always and all of you a lot and wholly and completely.

Tatyana's letters have not survived, but her feelings emerge from a letter which she wrote to her sister at the same time: "Write and tell me what kind of mood he is in and how he looks. It is terribly dreary without him. There are few people of his caliber here." She sent her sister three pairs of fine stockings, a pair of beige-gray shoes and a pistachio-colored dress which Mayakovsky promised to help her get through customs. His concern for Tatyana's mother and sister were truly touching.

Lyudmila seems to have made it to the Crimea, but not her mother. "I was very sorry that you didn't want to go to the Crimea, I had dreamed so much about it," Tatyana wrote to her. "V.V. also sent me a sad letter. He was so keen to arrange it. After all, the only agreeable thing he can do for me during such a long absence is to look after yourself and Lilyushka. That is exactly what I admire about him. An infinite goodness and thoughtfulness." (Lyudmila's ungrateful reaction when Mayakovsky proved unable to arrange immediate transport to Paris makes it hard to free oneself from the thought that she saw his "goodness" first and foremost as an opportunity to further her own ends.)

They had agreed to write to each other often—every three days—but it didn't happen. After Mayakovsky's letter on 15 May there was a break of three weeks in the correspondence. They did not write, or the postal service failed to function, or the letters were stopped by the censor, or they have not survived.* But there is also another explanation for the silence, and it has a name: Veronika Polonskaya, a young actress at the Moscow Art Theater.

NORA

Veronika—or "Nora" as her friends called her—had one of the leading roles in Lili and Zhemchuzhny's film *The Glass Eye*, which had its premiere in January. Despite her age—she was born in 1908—the lovely Nora had been married for four years to an actor colleague at the Art Theater, Mikhail Yanshin, but the marriage was not happy, and they lived largely their own lives. To Lili, who got to know her during the making of the film, Nora represented a potential object of Mayakovsky's insatiable need for stimulants in the form of female beauty and attention. Mayakovsky found it easy to fall in love, and Lili hoped that Nora would divert his thoughts from Tatyana. All that was needed was a suitable opportunity to introduce them to each other.

Such an opportunity presented itself on 13 May, when Lili and Osip saw to it that they met at the Moscow hippodrome. "Look how disproportionate Volodya's body is," Osip pointed out to Nora. "So big—and such short legs." Mayakovsky was six feet three, but because of his large upper body he was seen by many as a giant. By Nora too, whose first impression was that he was "big and uncouth, in a white coat, with his hat pressed down over his forehead and a cane that he waved around vigorously the whole time." She was also startled by his "loudness," by his "quite unique way of making conversation."

Nora's husband and the writers Yury Olesha, Boris Pilnyak, and Valentin Katayev were also at the racetrack, and they agreed to meet up at Katayev's later that evening. Mayakovsky promised to call

---

* After Mayakovsky's death Lili destroyed Tatyana's letters. Tatyana kept Mayakovsky's letters and telegrams to her, but a number of them were lost in the course of her flight to the United States in the Second World War.

Veronika Polonskaya in Lili's film *The Glass Eye*.

round for Nora with his car after her performance but got caught up in a game of billiards, so Nora drove to Katayev's with her husband. When she got there she was told that Mayakovsky had phoned several times, asking for her. After yet another telephone conversation he finally turned up in person. When Nora asked why he had not come to fetch her, he replied: "There are things in a man's life that he can't fight against. So don't be angry with me."

As always when Mayakovsky fell for a woman, he had to have his own powers of attraction acknowledged at once, and he asked her to meet him the next day. They met in the afternoon and went for a walk. "This time Mayakovsky made a completely different impression on me from the day before," Nora recollected. "He was not in the least like the Mayakovsky of the day before—vehement, noisy, highly strung in the company of other writers." Instead he was "unbelievably gentle and delicate, and he spoke about the simplest and most mundane things." After several days of chatting and walks, Mayakovsky invited Nora up to the room in Lubyanka Passage, where, with his "strong, deep voice of which he had such mastery," he recited his poems to her—"with incredible expressiveness, with the most unexpected emphases."

The rest is Mayakovsky in a nutshell. When Nora answered the question "Do you like my poems, Veronika Vitoldovna?" in the affirmative, he began "suddenly and insistently" to embrace her, and when she protested he became "incredibly surprised and hurt like a child." He "became sullen and dejected" and said: "Oh well, give me your paw, it won't happen again. If you're so sensitive!" But Nora had already realized that if Mayakovsky so wished, he could—as she put it—"become a part of my life," and a few days later they shared a bed for the first time. Afterward, when he saw her home, he suddenly started dancing the mazurka by himself in the middle of Lubyanka Square—"big and uncouth, but very light footed and comical at the same time."

It took a lot to make Mayakovsky take a single dance step, but here he was breaking into a mazurka in the center of town! It says something about his emotional state at the time, but also bears witness to his well-known "shamelessness." Infantile egocentric that he was, he always behaved as if the people around him did not exist. He was completely free from embarrassment; he would take his shoe off in the middle of the road when he got gravel in it, and he talked loudly on the telephone about the most intimate matters, ignoring the fact that strangers could hear what he was saying. We see here an important trait of Mayakovsky's character: his inability to play the hypocrite, to be cunning or false, to indulge in intrigues. He was unable to pretend.

Just like everyone else, Nora too was struck by the abrupt changes of Mayakovsky's moods. "I never saw Mayakovsky calm or balanced. Either he was in high spirits, loud, happy, unbelievably charming, and either reciting individual lines of verse the whole time or singing the same verses to melodies he had made up himself—or he was in a black mood, and at such times he could be silent for hours at a stretch."

Mayakovsky with the actress Anel Sudakevich in Khosta in August 1929.

Despite the difficulties resulting from Mayakovsky's character, their relationship became more intense during the summer. In July Mayakovsky went off on his annual reading tour of the Crimea, where Nora was holidaying with some girlfriends from the Art Theater. They had several days together in Sochi and Khosta, but about a week later, when they were to meet in Yalta, Nora fell ill and could not come. Mayakovsky was beside himself with anxiety and bombarded her with express telegrams, one of them so long that the telegraphist was dumbfounded. He begged her to come—if she did not, he would come to her in Sochi—but Nora sent a telegram in reply saying it would be best if they saw each other at home in Moscow. There was already a lot of talk about their relationship, and she was worried that the gossip would reach her husband, who seems to have been one of the few people who knew nothing.

On 22 August Mayakovsky was home again. Six days later, when Nora came back to Moscow, he met her at the railway station, "exalted" and "more loving than ever." In his hand he held two roses—instead of the huge bouquet he had wanted to give her. The reason was—he confided to Nora's mother—that he did not want to look like "a lovesick schoolboy."

Nora had never had cause to doubt Mayakovsky's feelings, and by this time she was ready to share her life with him. But although he would have "made me happy" if he had "asked me then to be his," to her great sorrow he never talked about their "future relations." What was holding Mayakovsky back was, of course, Tatyana, whose existence Nora must have been aware of, as one of his poems to her— "Letter to Comrade Kostrov"—was in print and well known. This made it impossible for him to lie about her. For Nora to have agreed to be with Mayakovsky, then, he must have persuaded her that the relationship with Tatyana belonged to the past. However, Tatyana did not belong to the past, but in the highest degree to the future. "Don't be sad, my child, it is simply not possible that we will not be together for all time," Mayakovsky wrote to her on 8 June, just as his courtship of Nora was reaching its height. "You ask me about the details of my life. There are no details." With Mayakovsky, the word "details" often signaled that he had something he neither wished nor was able to tell. In this case, the details that did not exist were—Nora. Mayakovsky's letters were never very substantial, and Tatyana's curiosity can easily be explained by a general interest in knowing something about his life. But the most plausible explanation is that she had heard rumors about Mayakovsky's affair with Nora—from Elsa, who in turn was kept informed by Lili, whose interest in ensuring that Tatyana's feelings for Mayakovsky cooled should not be underestimated.

During the summer Mayakovsky worked intensely on his new play, *The Bathhouse*, a sequel to *The Bedbug*. But he wrote hardly any poetry, or at least none that he himself could feel proud of. "Haven't written a line of poetry," Mayakovsky complained to Tatyana. "After your poems all others seem insipid. Burying myself in work with the consolation that it won't be long till October. [. . .] My dear, beloved Tanik, please don't forget me. I *love* you as much as ever and am dying to see you." A month later, on 12 July, he reproached her for hardly ever writing, and went on: "I can't imagine [life] without you longer than till October (as we agreed). In September I'm going to begin attaching wings to myself for my aerial attack on you." The declarations of love continued in a letter written four days later: "When I think of those people who are nicest and dearest to me, I think of you. My child, please love me. I have an absolute need of that." He longed, according to his letter, "regularly" for her, and "during these last days not only regularly but even more often." And he listed his arguments for why she ought to marry him and return to the USSR:

> We are better off than ever and better than anywhere else. Human history has never known such a boost before.
>
> I rejoice to be part of this field of force as if it was an enormous present. Tanik! You are a girl with many talents. Become an engineer. You can do it. Don't put all your energy into hats.
>
> Please excuse this lecturing (so unusual for me).
>
> But I would like it so much!
>
> Tanka—an engineer somewhere in the Altai Mountains! Couldn't you be that!

Whatever Tatyana thought of the suggestion, and whatever rumors she had heard about Nora, she was looking forward to their reunion in Paris: "I'm waiting with great joy for his arrival in the autumn,"

she wrote to her mother. "There is no one of his caliber here. In his
attitude to women in general (and to me in particular) he is a gentle-
man through and through."

Mayakovsky's claim in the June letter that he had "not written a
line of verse" was no longer true a month later. During his stay in the
Crimea he wrote "Poem about the Soviet Passport," which begins
with a furious attack on bureaucracy: "Like a wolf / I could gnaw /
bureaucracy / to bits. / I lack respect / for authority. / To hell / with
all kinds / of papers!" There is one exception, however: the Soviet
passport. With dizzying hyperbole Mayakovsky describes how the
passport official on the train, with yawning indifference, checks the
documents of Britons, Americans, Poles, "Danes and all other con-
ceivable kinds of Swedes" while he takes Mayakovsky's "red giant
passport" "like a bomb, / like a hedgehog, / like a double-edged razor,
/ like a two-meter-long / rattlesnake / with 20 stings." "To hell / with
all bloody papers!'—

> But this . . .
>   I pluck out
> of my wide trousers
>   the double
> of the priceless load.
> Read,
>   envy—
>   I
>   am a citizen
> of the Soviet Union.

The summer of 1929 was one long wait for the opportunity to frighten
the French border police once again, but on 28 August, according
to Lili's diary, Lili and Osip had "a conversation with Volodya about
how he had been replaced in Paris." The information presumably
came from Elsa, who supplied Lili with news from Paris in the same
way that Lili reported to her from Moscow. Information about Tat-
yana's life doubtless also came from Soviet agents in Paris and was
forwarded to Lili via her and Mayakovsky's friends in the security
service. And there was this and that to tell. Just as Mayakovsky, with

Lili got her driver's license in June 1929 as one of the first women to do so in the Soviet Union. During a ride in Moscow, she ran over a young girl, who was injured but survived. The matter was taken to a "people's tribunal," and Lili was acquitted. "One of the members of the court telephoned me in a lyrical tone of voice! It was so unexpected that I lost my head," Lili noted in her diary, adding: "Volodya was jealous." On one occasion, Lili asked Rodchenko to take photographs of her with the car during a trip to Leningrad (pp. 449–51). "We took pictures in Moscow in one dress, then I changed clothes, we went to fill up at Zemlyanoy val, he took pictures from the backseat, and so on. . . . We agreed that we should travel a distance, he would take photographs and then go back while I continued. But I didn't get any further, the road turned out to be terribly bad, the car started to sneeze, and moreover it seemed boring and lonely to travel so far on my own."

apparent unconcern, was courting two women at the same time, so Tatyana was operating with a reserve list of at least three admirers. One of them was the grandson of Ilya Mechnikov, the Russian Nobel laureate in medicine, and with the same given name. "I have a mass of stories just now," she confided to her mother in February 1929, even before Mayakovsky's second visit to Paris. "Even if I wanted to be together with M., how would things go then with Ilya, and besides there are another two as well. A vicious circle!" One of the two other

suitors was Bertrand du Plessix, a French *vicomte* working as an attaché at the French embassy in Warsaw.

This is what Lili and Osip's "conversation with Volodya about how he had been replaced in Paris" was aimed at: to convince him that Tatyana had given him up and that there was no point in his going there. They no doubt tried to persuade him instead to confine himself to Nora, who after all loved him so sincerely. But the conversation seems not to have had the desired effect, for the following day Mayakovsky sent a telegram to Tatyana: "LONGING UNSPEAKABLY WRITE MORE OFTEN KISS LOVE FOR EVER YOUR VOL."

The emotional double-entry bookkeeping that Mayakovsky was practicing in the summer of 1929 points to deep confusion, almost desperation—all the more so as in addition to Tatyana and Nora the accountancy contained a third column, for Lili. What form would

his life, his future, assume? Should he establish a family along tra-
ditional lines? There is much to suggest that he longed for that. Or
should he continue to live in the "marriage cartel" he had lived in
since 1918? Despite everything he loved Lili more than anything else
and Osip was his closest friend and adviser. These questions were
not easy to answer even for someone with a more stable psyche than
Mayakovsky.

THE PRIMACY OF THE GOAL

The same conflicts that complicated Mayakovsky's private life also
marked his literary and public activities. When he walked out of
Lef the previous autumn, his motivation was that all "literary co-
teries have outlived themselves." Accordingly, the winter of 1929

was the first time since 1912 that Mayakovsky had not had a group around him, which was hard for such a fire-eater. Despite the assertion that "literary coteries" belonged to the past, as soon as he came back from Paris he founded a new group, Ref: the Left Front of the Arts, Lef, had become the Revolutionary Front of the Arts, Ref. The difference between the old group and the new one was not just the change of a consonant—its whole direction was new. The old questions "what?" and "how?" were replaced by the new slogan *"for what?"* "We maintain," Mayakovsky explained, *"the primacy of the goal over content as much as form."* Art was a tool in the class war, and "only those literary methods which lead to the goal are good." From now on they repudiated "the naked fact" and declared that art should be "tendentious and goal oriented." Ref's goal was "[the] struggle against apoliticism and a conscious orientation of art toward agitation and propaganda for the work of building socialism." Despite the fact that the members of Ref (who were more or less identical with the members of Lef, minus Shklovsky, Tretyakov, and a few others) were not party members, they claimed henceforth to "unconditionally follow the party."

In contrast to Lef, Ref played no role in literary politics, especially as the planned Ref almanac never appeared. Perhaps it was as one of the founders maintained: that the group came together largely by chance, because Mayakovsky longed to get back to the literary battlefield, to polemic and debate.

Whatever the explanation looked like, Ref's theories reflected the continued Sovietization of society. When Mayakovsky wrote to Tatyana that "human history has never known such a boost" as in the USSR, he was perfectly justified in doing so. As Stalin put it, 1929 was "the year of the great change": in some ways more revolutionary than the year of 1917. In order to industrialize the country, five-year plans were drawn up and agriculture was forcibly collectivized. In the wake of these changes a five-day continuous working week was introduced, followed by a free day which thus could fall on any day of the week whatsoever and not necessarily on a Sunday. "The Reform" was intended not only to raise productivity; it was also an effective tool in the struggle against religion, which was now intensified. Churches were torn down in quick succession, and the Easter of 1929 was the last one on which the bells of Moscow's churches were allowed to ring. A new calendar was also introduced which began in 1917 and not with the birth of Christ.

During 1929 one enthusiastic report about economic projects and advances followed another. The propaganda apparatus was working at full capacity, and the dominant mood in the land was of pioneering spirit and optimism. That the collectivization was brutal and bloody and the industrialization badly planned, few in society understood or wished to acknowledge. For those who believed in the socialist revolution, the changes really did represent a "boost." This was true not least of Mayakovsky, who, happy to be "a part of this field of force," made poetic contributions both to the five-day week and to the struggle against religion.

As a conscious part of the process of Sovietization, a massive "review and cleansing of the Soviet apparatus" was carried out in 1929 and 1930: that is, a purge of "foreign elements" within the commissariats and public institutions. Just as in the Shakhty trial, the main thrust was directed against "specialists" with a dubious social background and/or suspect political views. The most important thing was no longer professional competence but one's degree of loyalty to state (i.e., the party's) policies.

Similar purges were carried out in the cultural and scientific fields. In the spring of 1929 a campaign was launched against the Academy of Sciences, which was regarded as advocating "apoliticism." Several prominent scientists were accused of sabotage, and the Academy was reorganized. The same measures were taken in the Institute for Art History, one of the last bastions of the Formalists. The management of the Moscow Art Theater was replaced, and in Leningrad the director of the Pushkin House (the city's leading literary archive) was removed and sent into exile abroad.

Another element in the policy of repression was the Commissariat of the Interior's ban (a secret at the time) on the founding of new literary, artistic, or scientific organizations. The most striking expression of the new social climate was the removal of Anatoli Lunacharsky from the post of people's commissar of enlightenment. Officially, Lunacharsky resigned on 13 September, but the Politburo's decision was taken on 15 July, and only two weeks later his

Yury Annenkov's drawing of Yevgeny Zamyatin, who as early as in 1921 feared that "Russian literature has only one future: its past."

successor was appointed: Andrey Bubnov, a political hack and true supporter of Stalin.

At the end of August, when the ideological offensive on the cultural sector which had been initiated in the spring of 1929 culminated in a vehement campaign against Boris Pilnyak and Yevgeny Zamyatin, the "liberal" Lunacharsky was gone and no longer able to exert his influence. The authors were accused and found guilty of allowing their works to be published abroad: in the case of Pilnyak's story *Ma-*

hogany, by a—pro-Soviet!— publishing firm in Berlin, while parts of Zamyatin's anti-utopian novel *We* were printed in a Russian émigré magazine in Prague. The campaign was coordinated and carried on simultaneously in several newspapers. It was led by RAPP but was initiated at the highest political level (unlike other literary groupings, RAPP was under the direct control of the Central Committee of the party).

The attack on Pilnyak and Zamyatin cast a shadow over the "fellow traveler writers" as a group, and soon Mikhail Bulgakov, Andrey Platonov, Ilya Ehrenburg, and Vsevolod Ivanov were also drawn into the debate. That Zamyatin and Pilnyak in particular were chosen as the main "fellow travelers" was however no coincidence, as both carried ideological baggage which made them particularly vulnerable. As early as 1921, Zamyatin had expressed his doubts about the future of Russian literature under the new Soviet orthodoxy in the article "I Am Afraid" (cf. the quotation on page 157), and the following year he was arrested to be exiled along with other intellectuals on the "philosophy ship"—a fate, however, which he escaped after the intervention of fellow writers. In 1924, when the novel *We*, which depicts life under communism in the twenty-sixth century, was banned by Soviet censorship, Zamyatin gave up hope of being published in his homeland and it was published instead in Prague in 1927, both in Czech and Russian, with the assistance of Roman Jakobson.

It was this translation which, after a delay of two and a half years, was now laid to Zamyatin's charge. In Pilnyak's case too there is reason to believe that it was not the publication of *Mahogany* (with its depiction of the drabness of life in a provincial Russian town) which primarily got him into trouble but his "Story about the Unextinguished Moon," which had been printed in *Novy Mir* in 1926 and which had more or less openly fingered Stalin as responsible for the murder of the war commissar Mikhail Frunze. The story was dedicated to the critic Alexander Voronsky, who had supplied Pilnyak with his factual basis. When Voronsky was arrested the following year, accused of "Trotskyism," Pilnyak thereby became automatically associated with the Trotskyist opposition.

Then, in 1926, after several humiliating apologies, Pilnyak was allowed to return to the literary field. The time had not yet come for

Yury Annenkov's drawing of Boris Pilnyak, one of the best representatives of the young Soviet prose.

a campaign of the type that got under way in the summer of 1929. The novelty here was partly that it was incited by the highest echelons of the party, partly the character of the charge itself: Never before had a writer been condemned for having his work published abroad. Another novelty was that the writers' organizations expressed solidarity not with the victims, but with the persecutors. Zamyatin was chairman of the Leningrad Section of the All-Russia Writers' Union, Pilnyak of the Moscow Section, but both were forced out of their posts: the former on the insistence of the board, the latter of his own accord and under protest. "For the first time since the birth of Russian literature, *Russian writers have not only acknowledged that censorship is useful but have also condemned the attempt to avoid it by publishing abroad,*" a critic declared in the Russian émigré newspaper *Latest News* (Paris), continuing: "What representatives of the imperial power failed to achieve over hundreds of years, what the most rabid 'spiritual obscurantists' never even dreamt of during the era of reaction, the Bolsheviks have achieved in a very short time and in a very simple way: by declaring that writers are collectively responsible for each other. The significance of the Bolsheviks' innovation in censorship is not a slight one: rights over a book have been replaced by rights over its author."

As a part of the campaign, RAPP exhorted "all writers' organizations and individual writers to make clear their attitude to the actions of Yevg. Zamyatin and B. Pilnyak." One of the many writers who obeyed was Mayakovsky, who answered on Ref's behalf with a manifesto whose heading—"Our Attitude"—was a direct reference to the exhortation from RAPP. After nonchalantly declaring that he had not read either Pilnyak's *Mahogany* or "other stories by him or many others," he spelled out his point of view with the following argument: "I see a completed work of literature as a weapon. Even if the work is classless (such a thing does not exist, but maybe Pilnyak thinks it does), the handing-over of this weapon to the White press means a strengthening of the enemy's arsenal. At a time when the clouds are piling up, this is equivalent to surrendering one's first line of defense." When Mayakovsky discussed the question with Lili and Osip that same evening, he granted himself the very right which he denied to Pilnyak. "For him," Lili noted in her diary, "it wouldn't be so terrible to be published by a White publisher, as it wouldn't be the publisher compromising him but the other way around."

What was forbidden for a "fellow traveler" was thus permitted for a "revolutionary" writer like Mayakovsky. His attitude shows that he had entered dangerously far into a territory which no writer ought to tread. After once before having defended writers against the state, he now sided with the latter. The fact that he thought he could do this without even having read Pilnyak's story testifies to a desperate need to distance himself from "fellow traveling," with its ever stronger ring of political opposition, but also to the moral devaluation which not only Soviet society but also Mayakovsky went through at this time.

THE CANCELED TRIP

Mayakovsky's stance in the Pilnyak debate cannot be excused, even if it was adopted at a time when many Soviet citizens, under the duress of external pressure and their own insecurity, began to lose their political and moral compass. His attitude was perhaps also influenced by the fragile psychological state in which he found himself in the late summer of 1929, brought on by the uncertainties governing his private life. Throughout the whole of September he received no letters from Tatyana, something he complained about in telegram after telegram. His last telegram was returned with the information that the addressee was unknown, but after a month or so she finally resumed contact.

"Is it really only because I am 'stingy' with words that you don't write?!" Mayakovsky asked in his answering letter on 5 October. For himself, he suspected that Tatyana—just as Lili had said—had given up on him. "Or is it perhaps rather that French poets (or even people with more common trades) are closer to your heart now. But *even if this is so* nobody, nothing can ever convince me that you are therefore less close to me and that it's all right to not write or to torture me with other methods." She ought to remember that she is his "dearest" for "at least 55 years" and he refuses to believe that she "doesn't give a damn" about him.

The letter contains no mention of any trip to Paris. On 8 September Lili noted in her diary: "Volodya moved me. Doesn't want to travel abroad this year. Wants to travel round the USSR for 3 months. This is the result of our heart-to-heart chat [on 28 August]." But eleven days later, on the nineteenth, according to the same diary Mayakovsky was no longer talking "about 3 months in the USSR but is thinking of a spring trip to Brazil (i.e., Paris)."

What had happened? After all, in his letter of 12 July Mayakovsky had declared that he could not imagine a life without Tatyana longer than till October and that he would begin to don his "wings"—that is, make the travel arrangements—in September.

Perhaps it was simply that he started rethinking as Tatyana was answering his letters and telegrams more and more sporadically. And that he was influenced by the news about Tatyana's life in Paris—generously conveyed by Elsa—that Lili supplied him with. Indeed, there were good reasons for such "information": "I have so many new friends that I can't count them," Tatyana wrote to her mother on 13 July. She was more popular than ever and amused herself as best she could. She went to the Atlantic coast every weekend, just as she had done with Mayakovsky, but now by car—and her plans for the summer were ambitious: "I'm going to cross the whole of France by car and perhaps the Mediterranean too by yacht."

It goes without saying that she was not planning to make these excursions on her own. If Mayakovsky had access to this or similar information, there was no reason for him to cling to the hope that Tatyana would become his wife—especially as he certainly knew in his innermost heart that he would never manage to persuade her to return to the Soviet Union with him. The fact that his relationship with Nora—which of course by this time was known in Paris—hardly helped to convince the already vacillating Tatyana of the advantages of sharing her life with him was something else he could not shut his eyes to.

It sounds reasonable enough: Although Mayakovsky still claimed that he loved Tatyana, the problems were too numerous and too great, and the whole thing quite simply petered out. "I thought he didn't want the responsibility of being saddled with a girl, even if he loved her," Tatyana recalled much later. "If I had agreed to go [back with him], he would have been forced to marry me, he wouldn't have had any choice. I thought he had simply taken fright."

This interpretation is contradicted by what Lili says about Mayakovsky's intention to go "to Brazil (i.e., Paris)" the following spring. If he had given up hope of Tatyana, there was no reason to plan a trip to Paris. But why did he not go there in the autumn of 1929? Why does he say nothing about "wings" in the October letter, which instead contains the following enigmatic sentence: "It is not possible to relate and describe all the sorrows which make my life even more taciturn"? His "taciturnity" was also noted by Nora, according to whom he became very bad tempered immediately after his return from the Caucasus: "He was very concerned about something and was often silent. He brushed aside my inquiries about the reason for his moods with jokes."

What sort of "sorrows" was it that made him "even more taciturn," that is, that could not be mentioned? Of all the unresolved mysteries in Mayakovsky's biography it is the question marks surrounding his postponed Paris trip that are hardest to straighten out.

One thing is beyond dispute: Lili did not want Mayakovsky to marry Tatyana, and she did what she could to prevent such a development. But what exactly did she do? Was her opposition confined to "heart-to-heart chats" and the dissemination of "news" that Tatyana had thrown him over for someone else? Or did she take more drastic measures to stop him?

For a long time there was a widespread belief that Mayakovsky did not make it to Paris because he was denied an exit visa. But a refusal presupposes an application, and no application papers are preserved in any Soviet archive. Lili declared she would "stake her head on it" that he never received a refusal—for the simple reason that he never filed an application. For her, it was unthinkable that Mayakovsky should be denied exit papers: "He could travel wherever he wanted, whenever he wanted, to any part of the world whatsoever." (What Lili meant was that Mayakovsky could always be sure to get a *Soviet foreign passport*—however, he could not travel "wherever he wanted," as he was not allowed into every country, e.g., Great Britain.)

There is a lot to be said for the theory that Mayakovsky never applied for a passport because he had shelved his plans to travel to Paris.

But why would he have done that? And was it of his own free will? Of course not. The most reasonable interpretation is that Mayakovsky really was denied an exit visa but that it was done *orally*, with the security service making it clear to him that there was no point in submitting an application. "The refusal [. . .] was conveyed in a humiliating manner," Galina Katanyan recalled. "He was made to come back several times. And he was refused in the same way as every other Soviet citizen—without any reason given."

What Galina Katanyan calls a "refusal" was thus an oral one. The person who told her about the "refusal" was an acquaintance who bumped into Mayakovsky coming out of the OGPU's headquarters at the Lubyanka "looking ghastly." Although they knew each other, Mayakovsky failed to greet him. Moisey Gorb—as he was called— had worked several years for the OGPU. Perhaps it was during his time as a Soviet agent in Berlin, from 1926 to 1928, that he became acquainted with Mayakovsky and the Briks. In the autumn of 1929 he was employed as deputy chief of the OGPU's Foreign Department with responsibility for the activities of Soviet agents in France. If anyone knew about the circumstances relating to Mayakovsky's canceled Paris trip it was he. In any event, if we want the answers to the questions surrounding this affair, it is within the walls of the Lubyanka that we ought to look.

"THE SNOB," "YANYA," AND "ZORYA"

The main reason why Mayakovsky could "travel wherever he wanted, whenever he wanted" was the protection he enjoyed within the OGPU. For the Lef writers and their sympathizers there was nothing shameful about associating with the representatives of the security organs. On the contrary, the Chekists were seen as heroes in the common struggle for Communism. To judge Soviet citizens' view of the OGPU from the perspective of our present knowledge of the 1930s' purges is deeply unhistorical.

Osip had not worked in the security service since the end of December 1923, but of course he still had his contacts there. However, apart from Lev Elbert, "the Snob," who in 1921 accompanied Lili on the train to Riga (see the chapter *"Drang nach Westen"*), no named

Mayakovsky with the Chekist Valery Gorozhanin in the summer of 1927.

Chekists crop up in Mayakovsky's life story until 1926. Then, during a visit to Kharkov, he met Valery Gorozhanin, one of the heads of the Ukrainian OGPU. They soon became friends, and during Mayakovsky's stay in Yalta the following summer they wrote a film script together. Called *Engineer D'Arcy*, it was based on an idea by Gorozhanin about how the British took control of Persian oil at the turn of the century. If Gorozhanin has a place in Mayakovsky's biography, however, it is not first and foremost because of this scenario (which was never filmed) but because he gave Mayakovsky a Mauser pistol—a present for which the latter thanked him by dedicating to him the poem "Dzerzhinsky's Soldiers," written for the security service's tenth anniversary in the autumn of 1927.

Even if the poem should be seen against the background of the strong international pressure on the USSR in 1927 (see the previous chapter), it is incontrovertible that with this tribute to the security service and its counterespionage, Mayakovsky was treading new poetic territory. That it happened just now was no coincidence. The publication of "Dzerzhinsky's Soldiers" in fact coincided with the increasing intimacy at this time between leading representatives of the OGPU and Mayakovsky and the Briks. Although it is natural to see this intimacy as an attempt at infiltration on the part of the security organs, the interest was far from being one sided. In the summer of 1928 the Chekists crop up in the poem "An Event in the Country" as guests in the dacha at Pushkino, where along with Mayakovsky they amuse themselves by filling with lead the tree stump which is the target for their Browning and Mauser pistols.

The key person in this infiltration project was Yakov ("Yanya") Agranov, who ever since the Revolution had been working closely with both Lenin and Stalin and had occupied leading positions in the security service. His special area was the surveillance of intellectuals. We remember him from the interrogations of the leaders of the Petrograd Combat Organization in 1921, the same year in which he led the investigation into the circumstances surrounding the Kronstadt rebellion (see the chapter "NEP and the Beginnings of Terror"). It was also Agranov who prepared the lawsuit against the right-wing Socialist Revolutionaries of 1922 and who put together lists of the writers, philosophers, and scientists who were shipped out of the Soviet Union that same autumn (see the chapter "*Drang nach Westen*").

Details of Agranov as a person are scanty, as they are of most others in his line of work. He was small and insignificant, had "thin and attractive lips" which formed themselves into "a smile which was now cunning, now questioning," but at the same time he was described as "an intelligent person." Whatever qualities qualified Agranov for the tasks he was given, he was eminently successful at worming his

The only known picture where Yakov Agranov is seen with Mayakovsky was taken on the terrace of the dacha in Pushkino. Among the guests are (*from left in the lower row*) Alexander Rodchenko, Luella, Agranov (*in suit and tie*), Semyon Kirsanov, Mayakovsky (*with Bulka in his arms*), Vasily Katanyan, Osip and his Zhenya, Mayakovsky's sister Olga (*with her arms on the railing*), and Zhenya's husband, Vitaly Zhemchuzhny.

way into Moscow's literary circles. His acquaintances there included not only Mayakovsky and the Lef group but also Leopold Averbakh, the leader of RAPP and Mayakovsky's deadly enemy—as well as a "fellow traveler" like Boris Pilnyak. Agranov was also a member of the artistic council at Meyerhold's theater and, along with others, an honored guest at Meyerhold's "Friday salon."

Although it was thus not only the Briks' apartment that was infiltrated, it is these contacts that have aroused the most interest. This is partly because of the circumstances surrounding Mayakovsky's canceled Paris trip but also because of the persistent rumors suggesting that Lili provided Agranov with information about the sentiments among intellectuals and moreover that for a while she was in an intimate relationship with him. Even if the substance of the rumors is debatable, they cannot be dismissed as wholly unfounded. There is a good deal of evidence that Lili did in fact forward information to the security services which she thought would interest them. Pasternak would later speak of the Briks' apartment as a "branch of the Moscow police," and Rita Rayt described how Lili once tried to "recruit" her to infiltrate Russian émigré circles in Berlin. Rita did not decline, but during her preliminary interview she exhibited such nervousness that she was regarded as unsuitable for the job. Whether this commitment on Lili's side meant that she was employed by the security organs or helped out from pure idealism—like Mayakovsky, she saw the Chekists as frontline soldiers of the Revolution—is yet another question in search of an answer.

It is unclear when Agranov first turned up in the Brik-Mayakovsky family. One hypothesis is that it was Gorozhanin who introduced him. In any case, the first time he is named in connection with Mayakovsky is in 1928, at one of Lef's weekly meetings, when Mayakovsky announced that Agranov, a "comrade" who "worked on literature issues in the security service," would be present. "Nobody was surprised. At that time Soviet people and particularly the Lef group regarded the security organs with total trust and respect," recalled the Lef artist Yelena Semyonova.

From that day Agranov was present at each Lef meeting, always together with his young wife Valentina, sometimes dressed in a military shirt, sometimes in civilian dress. Although he conducted himself discreetly and according to Semyonova "never butted into discussions," he soon came to play an important role behind the scenes. According to a diary entry by Varvara Stepanova he is supposed to have advised Mayakovsky to issue an open letter before his break with Lef in September 1928. Mayakovsky paid no heed, but the fact that a high-ranking representative of the OGPU allowed himself—and was allowed—to express opinions on the subject testifies to the fact that a new era was dawning. Yet Agranov's presence in Gendrikov Alley and Pushkino was advantageous not only to himself. At the same time as he was enabled to carry out his surveillance mission in an effective manner, the Lef people could look to him for a certain degree of political protection.

If it was "Yanya" who took the pulse of literary life in Moscow in general and in Lef circles in particular, the corresponding task in Paris was carried out by "Zorya." Zakhar Volovich was appointed secretary to the Soviet general consulate in Paris in February 1928 but was transferred a month later to the legation. In actual fact Volovich was the head of the OGPU's Paris department, which was housed in the same building. In France, however, "Zorya" was not known by his real name, but was called Vladimir Yanovich. His main assignment was to monitor political developments in France. In this he was helped by his wife Faina ("Fanya") who was a specialist in codes and head of the photographic section. Their immediate boss in Moscow was none other than Moisey Gorb.

Mayakovsky socialized with the Voloviches in Paris in the autumn of 1928 and spring of 1929, and when "Zorya" and "Fanya" visited Moscow in September 1929, they met again. They were also visible guests in Gendrikov Alley, and thanks to them Lili was able to keep in touch with Elsa by diplomatic post.

In other words, Mayakovsky's relationship with Tatyana was no secret to the OGPU. In Paris their movements were followed by Soviet agents, and in Moscow "Yanya" was kept informed down to the smallest detail. The fact that several of Mayakovsky's and Tatyana's letters never arrived was surely due to their being held up by the censor. Thus the "competent organs" (as they are called in Russian) had no need to ask Lili if they wanted to know about Mayakovsky's intentions with regard to the Paris trip in October 1929. The Soviet authorities had good reasons for preventing the trip. The most important was their fear that he would remain abroad if Tatyana did not wish to return to the Soviet Union, and that was a risk they could not take. Mayakovsky was a matter of national concern.

This mistrust on the part of the authorities was perceived as a pure insult by a poet who saw himself as the servant of the Revolution and who, that same summer, had proudly depicted the horror of the foreign border police on seeing the "hammer-and-sickle-adorned Soviet passport." Although Mayakovsky sent his "Poem about the Soviet Passport" to the magazine *Ogonyok* in July 1929, it was put aside until after his death, which makes it reasonable to see a connection between their rejection of it and his canceled Paris trip. To allow the publication of a poem in which Mayakovsky sang the praises of the Soviet passport at the same time as he was being denied one might well have been seen as cynical even by a government which was growing more and more ruthless with every passing day.

MADAME DU PLESSIX

If Mayakovsky was devastated to hear that he was not to be allowed to travel to Paris, what would Tatyana think? It was not just that Mayakovsky did not turn up—she was not told why not! He could not admit to the real reason, partly because he was ashamed of having been denied an exit visa, partly because he did not want the refusal to be exploited by émigré circles in Paris. Moreover, he must have suspected that his letters to Tatyana were being read not only by the addressee.

According to Tatyana herself, she did in fact find out the real reason why Mayakovsky failed to come to Paris—from Elsa, who was also undoubtedly no slouch when it came to imparting details of the attractive young woman who used to be seen in Mayakovsky's company in Moscow. When her old suitor Bertrand du Plessix offered her his hand in marriage, she therefore felt "quite free" and accepted. "He called on us quite openly, there was no reason to be underhand with him, he was a Frenchman, and unattached, not like Mayakovsky."

The proposal was made at the beginning of October, after Tatyana had learned that Mayakovsky would not be coming. She had known du Plessix for a year—he was, we may remember, one of the suitors on her reserve list—but as he was stationed in Warsaw, they cannot have seen each other very often. Yet it is hard to believe that she would have accepted a proposal from a man she knew so little. One must assume therefore that they had met in between times—it was probably du Plessix who took the wheel during that summer's motoring holiday. Elsa is not a reliable witness in questions relating to Tatyana, but when she writes that the latter "continued to meet her future husband during the affair with Mayakovsky" there is every reason to take her at her word. That Tatyana was going out with du

Tatyana and her husband, Bertrand du Plessix.

Plessix at the same time as she was making plans for a future with Mayakovsky is however something that she would never admit.

The wedding took place in Paris on 23 December, after which the newlyweds went off on their honeymoon trip to Italy: Florence, Naples, Capri. "I didn't love him," she said later about du Plessix. "In a manner of speaking it was a flight from Mayakovsky."[*]

Just as it was Elsa who told Tatyana that Mayakovsky would not be able to come to Paris, so it was Elsa again who told Lili about Tatyana's future husband. "Letter from Elya about Tatyana: she is of course about to marry a French viscount," Lili noted in her diary on 11 October, continuing: "Nadya [Sterenberg] said I went pale, something I never normally do. Can imagine Volodya's anger and shame. Today he went to Peter [St. Petersburg/Leningrad] to perform." Later, she would describe the scene as follows:

> There were several of us sitting quietly and peacefully in the dining room in Gendrikov Alley. Volodya was waiting in the car. He was about to go to Leningrad to give some performances. His packed and locked cases were on the floor. Then someone came with a let-

---

[*] In the course of my conversations with Tatyana in New York in the winter of 1982 it emerged clearly that Mayakovsky was the great love of her life, and likewise that she was ignorant of the fact that Mayakovsky had a daughter in the United States, which I informed her about.

ter from Elsa. I slit the envelope open and as always started reading the letter aloud. After various bits of news Elsa wrote that Tatyana Yakovleva [. . .] was going to marry a viscount, I think it was, that she would be married in a church, in a white dress with fleur d'or-anges, that she was beside herself with anxiety lest Volodya should find out and create a scandal which could hurt her and even make the marriage crack. At the end of the letter, therefore, Elsa asked us not to say anything to Volodya. But the letter had already been read out. Volodya had a face like thunder. He rose and said: "Well then, it's time for me to go."—"Where are you going? The car hasn't come yet." But he took the cases, kissed me, and went out. When the chauffeur came back, he said he had met Vladimir Vladimirovich on Vorontsov Street, he had slung the cases into the car with a thud and given the chauffeur a proper bawling-out, which had never happened before. Then he was silent the whole way. But when they got to the station he said: "I'm sorry, Comrade Gamazin, don't be angry with me. My heart is sore."

According to Lili, she phoned Mayakovsky the following morning at the Hotel Europe in Leningrad and explained that she was worried about him. He is supposed to have answered with a phrase from an old Jewish anecdote ("So what, this horse is done for, I'll have to switch to a new one") and assured her that she had no need to worry. When she asked if he would like her to come to Leningrad, he was delighted, and she set off that very evening. Mayakovsky had lots of readings to give, sometimes two or three a day, and almost every time he inserted something about viscounts or barons into his commentaries: "We work and toil, we aren't French viscounts," and so on.

This is the "official" version, from Lili's memoirs. But to judge from her diary, the telephone conversation only took place six days later, on 17 October: "Worried about Volodya. Rang him this morning in Leningrad. Happy that I'm coming. Asked if he hadn't thought of putting a bullet in his forehead because of Tatyana—in Paris they're worried. Says: 'Tell those idiots that this horse is finished and I've switched to a new one.' In the evening I went to Peter." And according to the same diary it was only in a letter from Elsa received on 1

December that Elsa says Tatyana "is getting married in a white moiré dress with fleur d'oranges."

The discrepancies and obscurities may seem marginal, but they are not. Among the "several of us" who, in Lili's version, were present when she read out the letter on 11 October were, according to one source, Nora and her husband. So when Mayakovsky learned about Tatyana's marriage it was in the presence of the woman he had been courting for six months. It is not hard to imagine what a blow to his self-esteem such an affront represented! And what did Nora think?

In the sixteen-hundred-page edition of the correspondence between Lili and Elsa there is not a single letter from between 19 June 1929 and 15 April 1930—not even those letters which Lili refers to in her diary—which suggests that they contained such sensitive information (especially regarding Mayakovsky's canceled trip) that there were good reasons to destroy them. The fact that Lili subsequently mixed up two letters, one with information that Tatyana was about to marry and the other with details of her dress, is neither strange nor significant and can be a pure memory lapse. Her claim that she immediately rushed after Mayakovsky to Leningrad, however, hardly stems from a defective memory—after all, she had access to her diary when she wrote her memoirs—but rather to the fact that reality looked different. That Lili only phoned Mayakovsky six days later suggests that his reaction was much more violent than she admitted. Was there something in the letter suggesting that Lili had something to do with the canceled Paris trip and therefore indirectly with Tatyana's decision to marry du Plessix? If Lili's diary had survived intact we might perhaps have had the answer, but it is only available in edited form. In connection with the Moscow trials at the end of the thirties, she got rid of any information that could hurt herself or others.

Despite its gaps, however, the diary casts a certain light over events in the autumn of 1929. At about the same time as Mayakovsky found out that it would be best to put his travel plans out of his mind, Lili and Osip were planning a trip to see Yelena Yulyevna in London. This shows that they saw Mayakovsky's passport problems as a special case and not as an expression of a general hardening of attitudes which could cause difficulties for them too. On 19 September they collected the forms for a Soviet exit visa, and on the twenty-seventh they applied for a British entry visa, but as Great Britain resumed diplomatic relations with the Soviet Union only a week later, the application was made via the Norwegian legation. Their applications were refused, on the grounds that circular B.795 was still in force and moreover "it is noted that Mrs Brik is the daughter of Mrs. Helen Kagan, who figured in the MI5 'Black List' at the time of the Arcos raid." As we can see, the counts against Lili were not only the Home Office circular from 1923 but also the fact that her mother had been classed as a "bad Communist" in connection with the Arcos affair. Of course, Lili knew nothing of this when she wrote in her diary on 10 October: "We were turned down for Engl. visa." Even less could she had guessed that the difficulties Mayakovsky had encountered would also come to affect them, of which more in the next chapter.

THE LAST NIGHT WITH THE GANG

On 23 October, two days after Mayakovsky and Lili returned from Leningrad, the Ref group took the decision to organize a retrospective exhibition of his work. The exhibition was Mayakovsky's answer to the mistrust from the side of the authorities which the refusal to sanction his Paris trip implied. By assembling the whole of the work he had produced he wanted to show what he had done and what he had meant for the Revolution and Soviet society over two decades. *20 Years' Work* was the name of the exhibition, whose opening was scheduled for the end of 1929. But the work went more slowly than anticipated, one reason being that the material was comprehensive and difficult to collect, and the opening was postponed for a month.

However, the planned anniversary party went ahead on 30 December 1929, the day before New Year's Eve—a jocular but conscious break with tradition. "Bought 2 mattresses for sitting on at Volodya's anniversary," Lili noted in her diary on 28 December, and on the following day: "Bought ice cream and fruit for tomorrow. Where will I find room for 42 people?!" Everyone was asked to bring champagne with them, and not one bottle per couple but one per person. "Kruchonykh really doesn't want to buy Abrau [champagne], says he's frightened he'll get drunk and say something stupid," Lili noted. His nightmares came true: the bathtub was filled with forty bottles of snow-chilled champagne, people partied the night away, despite the ascetic culture of Lef many got drunk, some fell asleep, others crept home on all fours in the ice-cold night.

As the dining room in Gendrikov Alley was only fourteen square meters in size, the table was moved out and cushions and mattresses placed on the floor and along the walls. Posters by and photographs of Mayakovsky were attached to the walls and a long placard with the object of the party's name in capital letters: M-A-Y-A-K-O-V-S-K-Y, to the ceiling. Meyerhold had brought with him costumes, waistcoats, wigs, hats, shawls, false beards, masks, and more besides from his theater, and he officiated as dresser himself.

Most of the guests were friends and colleagues from the Lef group, but there were also representatives of the "competent organs" like Gorb, "the Snob," Gorozhanin, and "Yanya," with their wives—as well as people with whom Mayakovsky was linked by complicated and emotional bonds: Natasha Bryukhanenko, Nora Polonskaya (with husband), together with Lev Kuleshov and his wife Alexandra Khokhlova. Also present was Krasnoshchokov's daughter Luella. The more unusual guests included the young Turkish poet Nazim Hikmet and Yusup Abdrakhmanov, a high party functionary.

The makeup of the party was intended as a surprise for Mayakovsky, who was not present during the preparations, spending the day instead in Lubyanka Passage. When he arrived in the evening, dressed up, newly shaven, and with a smile on his lips, the guests broke into a congratulatory cantata, written by Semyon Kirsanov, with accordion accompaniment by Vasily Kamensky. The chorus was sung by all, and went:

Vladimir Mayakovsky.
We honor you today.
From all your friends:
Hurrah! Hurrah! Hurrah!

The verses, including the following, were rendered by Galina Katan-yan, who was a professional singer:

Tuneful the cantata's screech,
Tuneful the cantata's screech.
With choir led by Osya Brik,
With choir led by Osya Brik!

And Lili Yuryevna sets the pace,
Lili Yuryevna sets the pace,
For she can sing both alto and bass,
Yes, she can sing both alto and bass!

And Meyerhold's not on his own,
No, Meyerhold's not on his own.
Of costumes he's given us a loan,
Of costumes he's given us a loan.

After the cantata Mayakovsky was offered a chair, on which he sat down back to front, donning a large goat's head of papier-mâché. The cantata was sung again, followed by fresh tributes in the form of ingenious addresses. Aseyev, for example, portrayed a hostile critic who delivers himself of a mass of platitudes but finally realizes he has mistaken the identity of the object of the celebrations. Each time he was addressed, Mayakovsky brayed in response from inside his goat's mask. Everybody was having a great time, people were dancing in every room and even on the landing, Kamensky was playing the accordion, and people were playing charades in which Mayakovsky had to try to work out which of his poems was being alluded to, including the following: one of the guests sat down at a table, another gave him paper and a pen, then left. Mayakovsky guessed right: the scene was from "Conversation with the Tax Collector . . .": "Here's my pen, comrades, try writing yourselves!"

But although the party had been devised in his honor, and although he tried to play along, the accounts of eyewitnesses are unanimous that he was in very low spirits. "His expression was grim even when he was dancing with the enchanting Polonskaya in her red dress, with Natasha Bryukhanenko, or with me," noted Galina Katanyan, who also recalled that Lili commented on his moroseness with the French expression "il a le vin triste," meaning literally that wine had made him gloomy. Nora sat alongside Mayakovsky the whole time, talking to him and explaining that she loved him in such a loud voice that the other guests could hear her. "I don't understand why Volodya was so gloomy," Lev Grinkrug commented to Nora. "Even if he has problems he ought to be happy that a woman he loves is so openly declaring her love for him."

By the small hours of the morning many of the company were drunk, Mayakovsky was sitting alone at the table with the presents, sipping his wine, and Galina Katanyan "had a momentary sensation that he was very lonely, cut off from the rest of us, that we were all strangers to him." When asked to recite some poems he was at first unwilling, but let himself be persuaded. The poem he chose, "A Good Relationship to Horses," depicts a horse who falls on a street in Petrograd during the famine of 1918. Cackling passersby gather round the horse, and the only person not laughing is Mayakovsky, who recognizes himself in the horse:

> I went up to the horse and saw
> how tear after tear
> trickled down its nose
> and disappeared in the hairs . . .
>
> And some kind of sorrow
> common to all animals,
> splashed out of me,
> floated out with a swish.
>
> Stop now, horse,
> horse, listen to me—
> do you think you're worse than them?
> My child,
> we all have a bit of horse in us,
> each in his own way is a horse.

"He sounded gloomier than usual," recalled Pavel Lavut, Mayak-ovsky's "manager," and according to the writer Lev Kassil, after May-akovsky had given a lackluster reading of another poem, he went into another room, where he stood for a long time leaning against a chest of drawers with a glass of tea in his hand. "There was," Kassil noted, "something helpless, lonely, depressing" about him.

Mayakovsky was lonelier than ever. Tatyana had left him (with the generous help of the Soviet authorities), Nora did not want to leave her husband for him, and in the United States a little girl was growing up whose mother had written to him as recently as October—the letter has not survived, but whatever it contained it was a reminder that he had a daughter whom he knew he would never see again. "I never thought one could have such strong feelings for a child," he told Sonya Shamardina, one of the few people to whom he confided his secret. "I think about her the whole time." And he suffered from not being able to help her: "I can't afford it, I don't have enough money, you see. I have two families—mama and my sisters and then my own family. So I can't help my daughter. But even if I had been able to, it would have been impossible."

As far as Lili was concerned—the woman whom Mayakovsky re-ally loved—she spent the whole evening unself-consciously flirt-ing with the high-ranking party functionary who was her latest conquest. Of all Lili's suitors, the Kirghiz Yusup Abdrakhmanov (1901–38) was the most anonymous and the most mysterious. Since 1927 he had been chairman of the Council of People's Commissars in the newly founded autonomous Kirghiz Soviet Republic and a member of the Central Executive Committee of the Soviet Union. During one of his visits to Moscow he got to know Mayakovsky and Lili, but when exactly he fell under her spell is unknown. From a letter written by Osip to Zhenya it emerges that Yusup spent a few days with Lili in Leningrad at the end of June 1929. Otherwise he is named only in connection with this party, and only as one of those present.

The silence surrounding his name does not mean his presence was not noted. On the contrary, with his stylish but exotic appear-ance and his little *tiubeteyka* (the traditional Kirghiz hat) on the crown of his head, he was an exotic bird in this tightly knit circle of writers and artists. The concealment is due more to the fact that his presence was perceived as embarrassing, both for Lili, whose flirts were usually of a different sort, and for Mayakovsky, who at his own party was forced to look on while Lili, never far from Yusup's side, at regular intervals took the pipe from his mouth, wiped it with her handkerchief and took a few puffs herself. Mayakovsky's reaction when Yusup presented him with a little wooden sheep with a paper round its neck, on which he was asked to write something about sheep (an important industry in Kirghizstan) says it all. Instead of putting it with the other presents he laid it aside without even looking at it.

"We played cards till the first trams started running, but I waited politely till everyone had gone"—with those words Lili ended her note about the party in her diary. What she does not mention is an incident which occurred right at the end of the party, in the small hours, when many people had already left. Boris Pasternak suddenly turned up, with Shklovsky in tow. Neither of them had been invited—on the contrary, the organizers had originally thought of poking fun at Pasternak by having one of the speakers parody his very individual way of speaking. But this was omitted, and now Pasternak had come to congratulate Mayakovsky and be reconciled to him. "I have been longing to see you, Volodya," he said. "I'm not here to have a fight, I only want to embrace you and congratulate you. You know yourself how much you mean to me." But Mayakovsky turned away and said, without looking at Pasternak: "He hasn't understood anything. He'd better leave. He thinks it's like a button that you rip off today and sew back on tomorrow . . . They rip people away from me so that my flesh comes away too! . . . He'd better leave." Pasternak rushed out of the apartment without even picking up his cap. "There was an extraordinary silence in the room; everybody was silent," recalled Galina Katanyan, who had been woken by the noise. "Mayakovsky was standing leaning forward aggressively with his hands in his pockets and a chewed cigarette end in his mouth."

The anniversary party of 30 December was in many ways a counterpart to the New Year's party of 1915, which also took the form of a fancy-dress party in a cramped apartment with many of the same guests (see the chapter "A Cloud in Trousers). But while the New Year's Eve of 1915 was characterized by youthful happiness and Futurist expectations, what was planned as a triumphal summing-up of Mayakovsky's work during the preceding years turned into a joyless performance in which most of the participants had too much of *le vin triste*. Instead of helping to patch together the company which in later years had been exposed to such great strains, the "New Year Party" of 1929 was to be the last night with the gang.

14

AT THE TOP OF MY VOICE

1929–1930

My verse will reach you
      over the mountain ranges of centuries
and over the heads
      of governments and poets.

Vladimir Mayakovsky, "At the Top of My Voice"

Mayakovsky's friends, not least Lili, had arranged his anniversary party to please him, to make him forget about Tatyana and the setbacks and injustices of that autumn. But the party ended in anticlimax and was followed by a psychological hangover. On 3 January Lili noted in her diary: "Volodya is hardly ever at home." And four days later: "Had a long conversation with Volodya." What the conversation was about is not clear, but it is safe to assume that it was about Tatyana, who had got married on 23 December but whose marriage Mayakovsky, according to Vassili Kamensky, "for a long time did not want to believe in."

That the issue was still of immediate concern not just to Mayakovsky and Lili but also to the "competent organs" is shown by a letter about Tatyana that "the Snob" showed to Lili on 9 January and which she quotes

Mayakovsky photographed by A. Teryomin in 1929.

from in her diary. "T. has married a viscount with a villa by some lake. [. . .] Visited me and bragged about her husband being a trade attaché at the Fr. embassy in Warsaw. I said it's the lowest-ranking post—an insignificant police spy, basically. She went away and forgot with righteous indignation to pay me the 200 francs she owes me. Well, well, I suppose I can comfort myself with the thought that I have a viscount among my debtors." She does not mention who wrote the letter, but it must have been a contact in Paris, possibly Volovich.

TRIP AT THE STATE'S EXPENSE?

On the same day that Elbert showed Lili the letter about Tatyana, Mayakovsky went to Leningrad for a few days. He thus missed an item which was published on 10 January in his house organ, *Komsomolskaya Pravda*, and which was a grim reminder of his canceled Paris trip. "O. Brik and his wife L. Brik are planning a trip abroad. They are being sent by one and the same organization. The aim of the assignment is also the same. One must ask oneself, why not send just one of the Briks on the trip? And if an additional colleague is absolutely necessary, why should that function be fulfilled by L. Brik in particular and not by one of the other specialists in those questions which constitute the reason for the trip."

The same difficulties Mayakovsky had encountered had thus affected his closest friends. The background to the attack was that since Lili and Osip had been refused entry visas to Britain, they had applied for foreign passports in order to travel to Germany, a country they had previously visited without any problems. The organization which had given them the "assignment" was Ref. Their application went via the Commissariat of Enlightenment (Narkompros) and was submitted sometime after 23 December, when, according to Lili's diary, Mayakovsky "finally received the forms for the trip from Narkompros." But now their trip was being officially queried. Why?

The news item about Osip and Lili, "Married Couple Travel at the Expense of the State," was part of a larger article with the heading "Save Currency! Stop Foreign Trips for Outsiders," which in turn was subordinated to an overall heading: "Purge of Narkompros." The campaign of purges within the Soviet apparatus which was initiated in the spring of 1929 had now reached Narkompros, and Lili's and Osip's trip was cited as a typical example of how (badly) Narkompros's commission for foreign travel was functioning. The notice ended with the following conclusion: "We must see to it that more high-school students, young specialists from working-class backgrounds, are sent abroad, the kind of young people who genuinely need to gain knowledge in order to improve and expedite the work of building socialism in the USSR. The purge of Narkompros will put a stop to the shoddy work of the commission for foreign travel."

The attack on Osip and Lili was a consequence of the "internal audit" within Narkompros but must also be seen in the light of an event which occurred at the end of September and beginning of October 1929, when Grigory Besedovsky, a Soviet diplomat, defected in Paris and asked for political asylum in France. His defection, which caused a huge sensation in the West, reduced at a stroke the opportunities for Soviet citizens to travel abroad and led to the passing of what was in the West called the "Lex Besedovsky" (promulgated on 21 November 1929), according to which those who had "gone over to the enemy camp" and "refused to return to the Soviet Union" were declared to be outside the law (and thus could be sentenced to death).*

On 12 January *Komsomolskaya Pravda* was forced to acknowledge that Osip and Lili were not traveling at the expense of the state but at their own cost and two days later, on 14 January, the newspaper printed a letter to the editor written by Mayakovsky, who had rushed back to Moscow from Leningrad. Mayakovsky emphasized that "comrades Osip and Lili Brik have not requested and are not now requesting any 'state funding' or 'currency'" for their trip, as "their literary contacts with Communist and left-leaning publishing firms make it possible for them to live abroad for two months and to carry out the work they have planned without any cost in foreign currency to the state."

He went on to list Osip's contributions to "the art of the revolutionary left"—as well as Lili's: "codirector of the film *The Glass Eye*,

---

* This topic is touched on by Mayakovsky in a draft of a film script about love in a foreign country which can be dated to exactly this period: "He is required to return, otherwise he is a deserter."

poster painter (ROSTA), first translator of Grosz's and Wittfogel's theoretical works, regular participant in all manifestations of revolutionary art in connection with Ref." Only someone who is "totally ignorant"—Mayakovsky concludes—could call these comrades "outsiders." The letter was supplemented by a few lines from the secretaries of the Soviet Writers' Federation (Vladimir Sutyrin) and RAPP (Mikhail Luzgin), who announced their full support for "the comrades from Ref."

However, Mayakovsky's intervention had no effect, and he was forced to ask for an audience with Lazar Kaganovich in order to set out his case. Kaganovich was the secretary of the party's Central Committee and a member of the Politburo and thus belonged to the party's top echelon. It was not the first time that Mayakovsky had turned to a high-ranking party member—on several occasions he had waited on Lunacharsky and Trotsky. But then it had been about literary questions; now, it was an errand of a quite different kind, with quite different political implications. Before the meeting he jotted down in his notebook some talking points which give us a clue to how his argument ran:

> Ref's decision about L. Yu. and O. M. Briks' foreign trip in connection with a planned anthology of international revolutionary classics (contract with Gosizdat). Translations of Freiligrath, Herwegh, Prutz, Pottier, Eliot, Christo Botev, et. al.
>
> The reason we have chosen to support the Briks is because they speak German, French, English, can live 2 mo. without foreign currency, on the income from their contributions to our newspapers.
>
> Moreover, comrade L. Yu. Brik's mother works for Arcos (can offer certain assistance with travel, subsistence, etc.). [. . .]
>
> Obviously there are no objections from the side of the GPU.
>
> Result: articles in *Komsomolskaya Pravda*.
>
> No one has objections and no one is giving permission.

Given that Kaganovich, a former shoemaker, had never set foot in a school, there are good reasons for supposing that the information about comrades Osip and Lili Briks' education would activate his inferiority complex—but along with his oral argumentation Mayakovsky could show seven letters in favor of Osip's and Lili's trip, from, among others, RAPP, the Soviet Writers' Federation, the Steering Committee for Art and Literature (Glaviskusstvo), Narkompros, and the Central Committee Section for Agitation and Propaganda. On the same day, 27 January, Lili noted in her diary: "Today Volodya saw Kaganovich about our trip. It will probably be sorted out by tomorrow."

According to Lili's diary their passports should have been on their way on several occasions (3 February: "Volodya said that as far as our passports are concerned it's not a question of days but hours"; and on 6 February: "We've got our passports"), but this was wishful thinking. Although Osip and Lili's trip was backed by several official bodies which were subordinate to Narkompros—Glaviskusstvo's and the Commissariat's own commission for foreign trips—the route via the Commissariat of Enlightenment was closed, and they were forced to apply again from scratch, this time through VOKS (the National Association for Cultural Links with Foreign Countries). On 8 February VOKS approached the Foreign Commissariat, which the very next day applied to the German legation for Osip—"who is traveling to Germany for scholarly purposes"—and his wife to be granted a German visa. On 15 February Osip and Lili received their passports, and on the same day they ordered train tickets to Berlin.

The story of the Brik's visa illustrates that the social climate was quite different from what it had been only a year earlier. The campaign against Zamyatin and Pilnyak (and the latter's apology), the purges within the different academies, and the burgeoning cult of Stalin's personality (accentuated in connection with his fiftieth birthday on 21 December 1929) were clear indications of the growing political pressure—pressure which was making itself felt more and more on the nucleus of the avant-garde. On the same day that Mayakovsky called on Kaganovich, Viktor Shklovsky, who in 1928–29 had toyed with the idea of reviving OPOYAZ, published his article "Monument to a Scholarly Mistake," in which he distanced himself from Formalism and stressed the importance of "the Marxist method" for the study of literature.

It is therefore easy to interpret Osip's and Lili's passport problems as a consequence of the general tightening-up that took place in Soviet society at this time, not least the purge within Narkompros. But the fact that they were attacked publicly gives rise to questions that are not so easy to answer: how did it come about that Lili and Osip, with their contacts in the security organs, only received their visa after being criticized in *Komsomolskaya Pravda*? And how did Mayakovsky, who had been denied a visa himself only a few months earlier, suddenly become so influential that he could help Osip and Lili?

The answer to the first question is uncertain, even if conspiracy theorists might maintain that the obstacles placed in the way of their foreign trip were only a diversion aimed at freeing them from suspicion of collaborating with the OGPU. As for the second question, there may possibly be a less speculative answer. On 21 January the sixth anniversary of Lenin's death was commemorated at the Bolshoi Theater with a concert and poetry readings. It was a solemn occasion: in the box for honorary guests sat Stalin with his wife and other members of the Politburo of the Communist Party. Among the guests were the mediocre proletarian writer Alexander Bezymensky—and Mayakovsky, who despite his "Sovietness" had never before appeared in such a context. Mayakovsky read the third part of his poem "Vladimir Ilyich Lenin." His performance was broadcast on the radio, and all his friends sat at home and listened. "He performed well, as always," Galina Katanyan recalled, "the applause was prolonged but restrained, as befits a mourning ceremony, a solemn occasion." According to what people told Lili, who was not there, Mayakovsky had "made a huge impression on the government box." "Regina [Glaz, Lili's cousin] says that Nadezhda Sergeyevna [Alliluyeva, Stalin's wife] and Stalin liked Volodya a lot," she noted in her diary. "That he conducted himself very well and did not look or bow toward their box at all (acc. to N. Serg.)."

The information about Stalin's positive reaction came from the most reliable source imaginable. Regina Glaz was Lili's cousin and had been involved in the upbringing of Stalin's children. Accordingly, she was used to associating on a daily basis with Stalin's wife, Nadezhda Alliluyeva, who was strict with the children as she was worried that life in the Kremlin would make them spoiled. But Regina, who was an admirer of the German educationalist Friedrich Froebel (best known as the founder of the kindergarten), believed more in the carrot than the stick, and on one occasion when Stalin's son Vasily had behaved particularly well, he was rewarded by being taken for a drive with Lili in her Renault.

Mayakovsky himself did not make a fuss about his triumph; on the contrary. "Mayakovsky never usually talked about his successes, and he never mentioned his failures," Aseyev recalled. "He didn't like complaining." Instead, when he came home, he talked animatedly about some bigwigs who had waved their identity cards at the taxi stand in order to jump to the head of the line, and how, incensed by this, he had dragged them out of the vehicle. "He was far prouder of this feat than of his performance and his success at the government concert," recalled Galina Katanyan. "We never did get anything sensible out of him about what had happened at the Bolshoi Theater."

And yet we may take it that Mayakovsky was overjoyed, both about the invitation itself and the fact that his performance was so well received. His reticence was rather an expression of his general disinclination to share his experiences with others. The story of his success soon spread, and the reactions were not slow to come in. For one thing, *Pravda* got in touch and requested poems for its planned literature page. But when Mayakovsky learned that they were not interested in a more organized form of cooperation, but that he would be published on the same conditions as other poets, he turned down the offer. He thought highly of his deserts as a poet and did not intend to be treated like any old rhymester. However, turning down an invitation from the party organ was a challenging gesture which reinforced his reputation as a principled and generally troublesome person.

SPARSE BEARDS

Even by the standards of a workaholic like Mayakovsky the beginning of 1930 was an unusually strenuous time. In January, in addition to all the trouble he took helping Osip and Lili with their exit visa, he was working on three large projects: his retrospective exhibition, a new long poem, "At the Top of My Voice," and a new play, *The Bathhouse*, which he had been working on since his return from Paris in May.

The Bathhouse was a sequel to *The Bedbug*, but it contained a more direct criticism of the bureaucratization of Soviet society and the emergence of a new privileged class of high-ranking bureaucrats with party membership. The inventor Chudakov ("Eccentrikov") has invented a time machine which he needs help to finance, but Comrade Pobedonosikov ("Triumphalnikov"), the executive head of "coordination management," is not available for consultation. The only things he is interested in are documents, meetings, resolutions, payment of subsistence allowances, and holiday arrangements—as well as being immortalized in oils so that posterity can appreciate his greatness. Shielded "behind secretaries and documents," Triumphalnikov typifies the soulless, uneducated, vulgar, autocratic bureaucrat who, after the Revolution, "climbed the ladder of jobs and apartments."

When the time machine is finally set in motion, despite Triumphalnikov's opposition, there appears a "phosphorescent woman" from the future whose task is to select those who are worthy to accompany "the first ever time train" toward Communism. "The Future accepts everyone who has at least one trait in common with the local collective—the will to work, the spirit of self-sacrifice, eagerness for innovation. [. . .] Fugitive time cuts loose and dumps the ballast of rubbish, the ballast of the faint hearted." Triumphalnikov and his secretary Optimistichenko are keen to join in the march to Communism, but they are left behind. "Well then, let them find out what it feels like to sail without a captain and without a sail," Triumphalnikov shouts defiantly—but his defiance soon turns to despair and he turns to the audience with a rhetorical question which is also the play's closing line: "Would you maintain that I am not needed under Communism?"

Neither structurally nor thematically was *The Bathhouse* anything new for Mayakovsky, whose plays and poems without exception end with a vision of the future—positive or negative. But the political message was clearer than ever. The play's title refers to the expression "to give someone a flogging [with birch twigs, as in a sauna]," and there is no question as to who was the object of this treatment: Soviet bureaucracy. Only once before had Mayakovsky expressed himself so clearly—in the draft of "The Fourth International," when the person shielded behind rows of secretaries is none other than Lenin (see the chapter "NEP and the Beginnings of Terror").

When Mayakovsky read the play at Meyerhold's theater on 23 September, the director compared him to Molière: "This is a very big event in the history of Russian theater, a unique event, [. . .] a major emancipation from tradition, at the same time as [Mayakovsky] employs dramaturgical concepts which instinctively make one think of a master like Molière. [. . .] Mayakovsky launches a new epoch and [. . .] I think with horror of the fact that I as a director must have to do with this play. We always commit outrages on those writers whose plays we put on. Sometimes we correct something, sometimes we redo it. In this play nothing can be redone, so organically is it written."

If Meyerhold and other theater people—like for example Nora's husband, Yanshin—burned with enthusiasm for *The Bathhouse*, the public was unmoved. Before the play had its premiere at Meyerhold's theater in Moscow, it opened in Leningrad. "The public greeted Mayakovsky's play with icy reserve," the author Mikhail Zoshchenko recalled. "I don't remember a single burst of laughter. After the first two acts there wasn't a single clap. I have never witnessed a bigger fiasco." The press were as merciless as the public. "*The Bathhouse* attacks—or more accurately, tries to attack—bureaucracy," wrote *The Red Paper*. "But [. . .] the theme is treated in a static fashion, extremely superficially and one-sidedly. [. . .] The performance is so uninteresting that it is hard to write about it. The onlooker remains emotionally uninvolved and follows the action, which is often difficult to follow, with cold indifference." The same theme was repeated with slight variations by other newspapers: audiences were bored and the criticism of bureaucracy was "primitive."

Even if simple malice lay behind much of the criticism of *The Bathhouse*, there is no escaping the fact that, in many respects, it was justified. The play lacks any real action, the cast of characters is clichéd, and the repartee and jokes are sometimes strained. But even if formally it was rather lacking, there is no doubt that its message came through, at least to those for whom the birch twigs were intended. The censors sat on the play for two and a half months, and permission to perform it was only given after Mayakovsky had agreed to tone down some of the more critical passages.

That so much nevertheless remained bears witness to the position that Mayakovsky still retained. But it was rapidly eroding. The

An exhausted Mayakovsky at the exhibition *20 Years' Work*.

fiasco in Leningrad took place on 30 January, two days before the opening of the postponed exhibition *20 Years' Work* on the Moscow premises of the Soviet Writers' Federation. The exhibition was intended to embrace everything that Mayakovsky had created during his twenty years as an author and artist: books, drawings, posters, newspaper articles, and so on. (He had made his debut in 1912, but since he had brought this forward by four years in his anthology *Everything Written by Vladimir Mayakovsky 1909–1919*—see the chapter "The First Revolution and the Third"—the time frame given was 1909–29.)

Like *The Bathhouse*, *20 Years' Work* can be seen as an attack both on Mayakovsky's critics and on the bureaucracy whose grip he felt tightening both on himself and on society at large. "The reason I arranged it was that, because of my cantankerous disposition, people have thrown so much shit at me and bawled me out for so many sins, real and imaginary, that I sometimes feel all I want to do is to clear out for a couple of years just to avoid having to hear all the abuse," Mayakovsky explained with a choice of words which did not exclude his real motive: to show the authorities that they were wrong to question his patriotism and loyalty to the Soviet system. Perhaps he also entertained the hope that one day the travel ban would be rescinded.

However, this was a motive that could not be named out loud. When Osip tried in retrospect to explain Mayakovsky's eagerness to put on an exhibition of his "collected works," he pointed to another incentive, namely, that Mayakovsky "wanted recognition": "He wanted us, the members of Ref, to take on ourselves the organization of the exhibition—and he wanted representatives of the party and the government to come and say that he, Mayakovsky, was a fine poet. Volodya had tired of the struggle, the infighting, the polemics. He wanted a little peace and quiet and a modicum of security for his creativity." It is an explanation which, despite Mayakovsky's rebellious temperament, is not without foundation.

However, the Ref group did not take on any of the work of organization. Kirsanov and Aseyev did not approve the idea of showing off Ref by means of an individual exhibition, and they declined to help out, which led to an open falling-out with Mayakovsky. The exhibition committee (which consisted of Aseyev, Zhemchuzhny, and Rodchenko) did not meet once, nor did Mayakovsky receive any help from officialdom (the Soviet Writers' Federation). He was working against strong headwinds and had to gather in most of the material himself, sorting and arranging it later in his little room in Lubyanka Passage. Nora helped him when she had time, and so did Lili. Moreover, he had help from Natasha Bryukhanenko and Artyomy Bromberg, a young employee of the State Literature Museum who joined in on his own initiative. But they encountered opposition the whole time—for example, the printers refused to print the exhibition catalog, which instead was handed out in simple stenciled form. Right to the end Mayakovsky himself was occupied in pinning up posters, drawings, and the like on the walls and screens of the exhibition space.

On the day before the opening Lili noted in her diary: "It ought to have been a model exhibition, but it was interesting only because of the material. Since the business with Shklovsky I know just what these people are worth, but Volodya realized it for the first time today—how long for, I wonder."

That Osip was correct to assume that Mayakovsky was longing for official recognition is borne out by the guest list. It contains authors like Yury Olesha, Ilya Selvinsky, Alexander Fadeyev, Leonid Leonov, Fyodor Gladkov, Alexander Bezymensky, Mikhail Svetlov, Vsevolod Ivanov, Nikolay Erdman, and more, but also high-ranking OGPU operatives—apart from Yakov Agranov, the organization's deputy and assistant vice-chairmen, Genrikh Yagoda and Stanislav Messing; the head of the secret political department, Yefim Yevdokimov; and one of his closest subordinates, Lev Elbert ("the Snob")—as well as high functionaries within the state apparatus and several from the highest echelon of the party (Molotov, Voroshilov, Kaganovich). Stalin, strangely enough, did not receive a personal invitation, but two tickets were sent to his office.

None of the high-ranking state and party functionaries turned up to the opening. And of the authors who were invited, only Bezymensky and Shklovsky seem to have come. Instead, many young people came to the exhibition. "Full of people," Lili noted in her diary, but "only young ones." Among those of Mayakovsky's friends who put in an appearance—apart from Lili and Osip, who of course were there—were Kirsanov and Rodchenko and his wife, whom Mayakovsky nevertheless refused to talk to. "If it was only Ref that united us, then I would have quarreled with you too, but between us there are other ties," he explained to Osip. "Volodya was quite worn out and spoke in a dreadfully tired voice," recalled Lili, who also noted that he "was not only tired but also in a bad mood; he was irritated with everybody and didn't want to talk to anyone."

The boycott of the exhibition by other authors was so striking that Mayakovsky could not help touching on it in his opening address. "I am very pleased by the absence of all snobs and bloody aesthetes who don't mind where they go and whom they celebrate, as long as it's an anniversary. No authors? That's just fine!" And his disappointment that not a single high party functionary had responded to his invitation he dealt with by converting it to defiance: "So, the 'beards' have stayed away. Then we'll just have to get by without them."

TODAY'S PETRIFIED SHIT

Perhaps it was just as well that the "beards" missed hearing the poem that Mayakovsky performed in public for the first time that evening: according to Lili, "with great strain." "At the Top of My Voice" was intended as the introduction to a longer poem and was written specially for the exhibition. It was only finished a week before the opening, when he recited it to Lili and Osip, who liked it a lot. "The latest thing I've written is about the exhibition, as it makes clear what I'm up to and the point of my work," Mayakovsky explained. "Those people who get agitated about my literary and journalistic work have been claiming lately that I have quite simply forgotten how to write poetry and that I will get it in the neck from posterity as a result."

As we have seen, it was not only Mayakovsky's detractors who suspected he had "forgotten how to write poetry" but also several of his friends. In recent years he had put his poetry almost exclusively at the service of social and political reform projects and those looking for proof that he had done great damage to his poetic talent did not need to search too hard. One example was a poem about his joy at having managed to stop smoking, entitled "I Am Happy!" It may be that Mayakovsky did actually stop smoking (at least for a short time) and was pleased about it—but how could he give the poem a title which stood in such strident contrast to his real psychological state? It was typed up on 16 October 1929, less than a week after he had found out that Tatyana was going to get married, and it was clear that he was not going to get an exit visa. If the poem bore witness to anything, it was not to happiness, but to schizophrenia.

With "At the Top of My Voice" Mayakovsky made a comeback as a poet, and with a vengeance. This time, however, it was not a question of love lyrics but a summing-up of his work and a vision of how it would be judged by posterity. "At the Top of My Voice" was an *exegi monumentum* poem in which Mayakovsky, in imitation of

Horace—and, in the Russian tradition, Pushkin—erected a monument to himself for posterity. It was a sequel to his earlier poems on the same theme, but this time the monument was made of different material.

When, one day, posterity begins to root among "today's petrified shit," they will also ask about Mayakovsky, who knows how to talk about time and about himself, "mobilized and called up by the Revolution" as he was. For him too, "agitprop sticks in my throat" and he would love to cobble together romances, which would be both more profitable and more pleasant—

> But I
> > curbed myself
> > setting my heel
> on the throat
> > of my own song.
> . . .
> I'll clamber over poetry albums
> and talk like a living man
> > to another being full of life.
> I'll come to you
> > in a far-off Communist time,
> not like a verse knight,
> > in Yesenin's style.
> My verse will reach you
> > over the mountain ranges of centuries
> and over the heads
> > of governments and poets.
> My poem will reach you
> > but not in the form
> > of pretty verses,
> not like an arrow
> > from the strings
> > of Eros's lyre,
> and not like a worn old coin
> > to a coin collector,
> or like the light from a burned-out star.

My poem
    will thrust itself forward
        through the centuries
and stand there heavy,
    rough
          and clear as glass,
like an aqueduct
    that has survived into our time
placed there ages ago
    by Roman slaves.

His words are "not used to / caressing." He lines up his pages on parade, where they stand "heavy as lead / ready both for death / and for deathless honor." They are his "favorite weapons, / ready / with a battle cry / to go on the attack / with rhymes raised / like whetted lances"—and all "these troops / armed to the teeth / who for twenty years / have rushed on to victory" he gives "to the last page" to "the planet's proletarians." His verse is a solder who will die "like a nameless soldier / died attacking," and the monument Mayakovsky wishes to erect is not a stone or bronze statue to himself or his works but socialism itself, which he and the working class have built together:

I don't give a damn
    about all heavyweight bronze,
I don't give a damn
    about sickly marble worship!
Let's share the honors—
    we're the same sort, after all—
and let our
    mutual monument be
socialism
      built
      in battle.

The poem concludes with the wish that in future his works may be judged by the control commission of the Communist Party (CCC):

> When I appear
>> before the CCC
>> of a more enlightened future
> I will
>> lift up
>> over the heap of poetic robbers
> like a Bolshevik membership card
>> all hundred volumes
>> of
>> my party books.

A more definitive declaration of loyalty is hard to imagine, especially as Mayakovsky was not a member of the Communist Party—a circumstance which his enemies were not slow to point out in their eagerness to portray him as a "fellow traveler," a term with perilous implications. Mayakovsky himself defended his decision to remain outside the party with various arguments, for example, that "the Communists are inclined to compromise in questions of art and education," that he would be "sent away to catch fish in Astrakhan," and that "the discipline would force me to do 'office work,'" which "would be the same as converting an armored cruiser into a bicycle."

These are quotations from Mayakovsky's autobiography, and the responses changed when the question came up during an appearance in connection with the exhibition. The fact that he was "nonparty," he said, was "no coincidence" as "manners I adopted before the revolution are deep rooted" and "cannot be reconciled with organized work." But at the same time as he was afraid that the party would order him to "travel here and there," he explained: "I do not shut myself off from the party, on the contrary, I regard myself as duty bound to carry out all the decrees of the party even if I do not have a membership card."

According to Lili's diary, he thought about joining the party at this time. That he chose not to was perhaps partly because of his bourgeois "manners," but most of all because his whole being rebelled against any form of subordination and compulsion. If he had really wanted to join the party, he could have done so as a spokesman for the pure, idealistic Communism he believed in. But this the party in its turn was not interested in. It would have been welcome ten years earlier, but not any longer. What the party wanted now was exactly such careerists as Mayakovsky loathed and whom he excoriated in his plays and poems.

Mayakovsky did everything he could to convince the authorities that he was needed, and he gradually accommodated himself more and more to the demands of the party and the times. But it made no difference. At the same time as he was setting his heel on the throat of his song, the volume of the *Soviet Encyclopaedia* that came out in January 1930 declared that "Mayakovsky's rebelliousness, anarchistic and individualistic, is essentially petit bourgeois" and that "even after the October Revolution" Mayakovsky had "been opposed to the worldview of the proletariat." And the list of the sixteen major works about Lenin which the newspaper *Ogonyok* published on 25 January, four days after Mayakovsky's acclaimed performance at the Bolshoi Theater, found no place for "Vladimir Ilyich Lenin."

What Mayakovsky gave expression to in "At the Top of My Voice" was a feeling of being at the mercy of uncomprehending contemporaries, a feeling of loneliness and isolation. As if he wanted to say: "OK, nobody wants to understand me, but the time will come when I will be appreciated as I deserve. Just now, I don't give a damn about you." This feeling of desperation was born of concrete circumstances and events but was also an expression of the existential victimhood that pervades all of Mayakovsky's works. "At the Top of My Voice" was a political declaration of intent, but it resonates with the same pain and desperation that we encounter in his earliest poems—like "A Cloud in Trousers," in which the poet, mocked by his contemporaries like "a prolonged, dirty joke," moans "into the centuries" about another, better future. "It felt today as if he was desperately lonely," Lunacharsky remarked to his wife after visiting the exhibition. He was right: Mayakovsky was lonely, as "lonely as the last eye / of one who is going blind," like in the poem "A Few Words about My Mother," written sixteen years earlier.

It was too late for Mayakovsky to join the party; it was too late for a lot of things. What does a person do after writing a poem like "At the Top of My Voice," which was basically a leave-taking? Mayakovsky's public did not know the answer to the question—but he himself did.

CONSOLIDATION OF ALL THE FORCES OF PROLETARIAN LITERATURE

If Mayakovsky had not realized the full extent of the fiasco in Leningrad before, he became aware of it the day after the opening of *20 Years' Work*, when the rumor reached him that his play *The Bathhouse* might be closed after only a few performances. He wanted to go there but could not leave the exhibition, so Lili went instead. The rumor proved to be unfounded; although "audiences are staying away and the press is hostile," there were no plans to close the play. However, there had been several instances of censorship, Lili noted in her diary on 3 February. For one thing, the line "I get in on my party card" had been changed to "I get in on my tram ticket."

If the situation in Leningrad was thus more or less under control, on the same day that Lili arrived there Mayakovsky detonated a bomb in Moscow which sent both his friends and his enemies into a state of shock. On 3 February he applied for membership in RAPP. As we saw in the chapter "America," Lef had allied itself with MAPP (the society's Moscow Section) as early as 1923, mainly for tactical reasons: although they had different views on aesthetic questions, they shared the same political ideals, and for the Lef writers the alliance was also a part of their attempt to shake off the "fellow traveler" label.

And now Mayakovsky took the step of joining RAPP, an organization which over the years had devoted a large part of its more or less intellectual resources to aggressive attacks on Mayakovsky the "fellow traveler" and the aesthetics he stood for: "Lef cannot be reformed—Lef must be destroyed"; "the October Revolution has often attracted Mayakovsky's attention [. . .] but in all these works Mayakovsky is far from understanding the October Revolution, its content and nature"; "tasteless, ravaged, and hard to endure is how the world is presented by Mayakovsky's pen." And so on.

Why did he do it? One explanation was undoubtedly the feeling of isolation that he felt after being abandoned by his own people, the Ref group. But that was only the catalyst, the last straw. His painful decision had been a long time in the making and was not totally illogical, coming from someone who in the autumn of 1929 had asserted "the primacy of the goal over content as well as form" and declared that he "identified fully with RAPP on most issues" and that the or-

One of the few photographs with Lili, Osip, and Mayakovsky together was taken in 1928 or 1929, when the "pussycat family" was actually breaking up.

ganization's proletarian membership cadres "constituted the basis for the future of Soviet literature."

And yet his decision was not primarily motivated by inner conviction but more the result of strong external pressure. On 4 December *Pravda* had published a leading article with the heading "For a Consolidation of All the Forces of Proletarian Literature," which laid down that RAPP was the party's instrument in the field of literature. The article, which had the character of a directive, was reprinted in several literary magazines and was followed on 31 January 1930 by yet another leader on the same theme, phrased threateningly as follows: "The tense situation enforces a choice: either once and for all to enter the camp of the honest allies of the proletariat or to be shunted aside into the ranks of the bourgeois scribblers." That it was *Pravda*'s line of argument that made Mayakovsky take the step of joining RAPP is clear from the first sentence of his application, which was a direct reference to the first leading article: "With a view to implementing the slogan about the consolidation of all the forces of proletarian literature, I hereby apply for membership in RAPP."

The trick of referring to "the tense situation" and "external threats" in order to force the citizens to take sides one way or the other was good old Bolshevik tactics, and the campaign of consolidation of 1929–30 was a direct echo of the party's exhortation to the intelligentsia in the autumn of 1918: "In a time like this, neutrality is impossible. Schools cannot be neutral; art cannot be neutral; literature cannot be neutral. Comrades, there is no choice. And I would advise you to side with the working class" (see the chapter "Communist Futurism"). But there was a difference: while the situation in 1918 was characterized by real antagonism between the supporters and the opponents of the Bolshevik revolution, the "tense situation" which now existed was the result of inflammatory propaganda in the Soviet press, warning of an imminent attack on the Soviet Union by "the international bourgeoisie," something which in turn was said to lead to an intensification of the "class struggle" within the country.

In his application Mayakovsky explained that he was in complete agreement with the party line on literary-political questions, as it was represented by RAPP. As for "artistic differences of opinion," they could be solved "to the benefit of proletarian literature" within the parameters of the organization. He also believed that "all active members of Ref" ought to draw the same conclusion and join RAPP. Three days later Mayakovsky's application was unanimously approved, and on 8 February he declared at the Moscow Section's conference that he had joined RAPP because it gave him "the opportunity to harness my energies into working in an organization for the masses" and that "working for the masses leads to a change in all poetical methods."

A few days after Mayakovsky's application a couple of other writers, the Constructivists Eduard Bagritsky and Vladimir Lugovskoy, applied to become members of RAPP and were accepted. But the Ref writers did not obey Mayakovsky's exhortation. Osip had originally thought of keeping Mayakovsky company but remained outside for the time being, and other members of the group found themselves, according to Lili, "in a state of panic" after Mayakovsky's decision. Apart from the point at issue Mayakovsky had once again, just as in 1928, surprised his friends and brothers-in-arms with a drastic move without seeking their advice first. "We regarded it as undemocratic and pigheaded," Aseyev recalled. "Quite honestly, we felt abandoned in a thicket of contradictions. Where should we go? What would happen next? [. . .] Should we also join RAPP? But anyone who didn't come from a proletarian background was greeted there with ill will and suspicion." Most unforgiving of all was Semyon Kirsanov, who responded to Mayakovsky's refusal to greet him with a poem, "The Price of a Handshake," in which he declared that he felt like "soaking my hand in petrol, / scrubbing it with pumice / to scrape off all his handshakes from my palm."

The poem was printed in *Komsomolskaya Pravda* on the same day that one of the leading members of RAPP, the young prose writer Alexander Fadeyev, maintained in a newspaper interview that the fact that Mayakovsky "with his political views showed his closeness to the proletariat" did not mean that he was accepted with "all his theoretical baggage": "We shall accept him to the extent that he gets rid of that baggage," he explained, adding patronizingly: "We will help him with that." And if Mayakovsky had believed that as a member of RAPP he would automatically come to be regarded as a "proletarian writer," he was wrong, as an editorial in RAPP's journal *On Literary Watch* made quite clear.

The magisterial tone was dictated by the feeling of triumph which the RAPP people felt at the sudden and unexpected flip-flop by their sternest opponent. If Mayakovsky's decision had come as a surprise for the Ref writers, the upset and confusion were at least as great in RAPP. How should they deal with the situation that had arisen? What were they to do with a giant like Mayakovsky in their ranks? Instead of voting him onto their board, which would have been the natural thing to do, they chose to treat him like a schoolboy—despite the fact that the leaders of RAPP were considerably younger than himself (the chairman Leopold Averbakh, for instance, was only twenty-six). Aseyev recalled how Mayakovsky, "leaning against the platform lights, stared darkly at the person explaining the criteria for acceptance by RAPP while shifting his cigarette from one corner of his mouth to the other."

But however gloomy Mayakovsky was, he realized that membership in RAPP really did require a reappraisal of his entire "system of thinking about poetry," something he promised to engage with. He was also serious about his promise to "harness my energies into working in an organization for the masses." "Volodya is planning to take on a huge circle [of workers] from three factories to teach them to write poems," we read in Lili's diary on 8 February, and two weeks later he aired this ambition in public. But this was theory, declarations of intent—none of his projects came off. In practice Mayakovsky seems to have put as little effort into implementing his ideas as RAPP did into trying to reeducate him. "He was cheerful and went out of his way to demonstrate that he had done the right thing and that he was glad to have joined RAPP," Nora recalled. "But you could see that he was ashamed of it, that he wasn't convinced he had done the right thing for himself. And—although he didn't admit it even to himself—that they hadn't welcomed him into RAPP as they ought to have welcomed Mayakovsky."

TALKIES IN BERLIN

On the same day that Mayakovsky was accepted into RAPP, Lili and Osip received their exit visas, and on 18 February they boarded the train to Berlin. "We've been here for 3 days but it feels like 3 months," Lili noted in her diary on 22 February. "Been nowhere and seen nothing. Osya has got a coat and a hat—he looked too awful in his fur. There's nothing else I want, and we've no money anyway. Never again will I apply for permission to travel abroad."

These lines give a good picture of Lili's fickle state of mind, but they reflect only the first few days of their stay in Berlin. Even if her boredom sometimes shows through at a later stage too, her continuing diary entries bear witness to a life filled with activities. Along with their visits to restaurants and cabarets, Osip made his usual rounds of the secondhand bookshops buying Russian classics, and one day he visited the Reichstag—"the cheapest theater in Berlin, but without very much in its repertory," according to the Communist member who showed him around. Lili in her turn paid several visits to the zoo, where she had herself photographed with a lion cub which was sold a few days later to the zoo in Munich. "The keeper told me, with real grief in his voice: *Alle die kleinen verkauft*. I began to cry, and since then it has hurt me to look at the animals." The fickleness of her moods is illustrated by the fact that from time to time she spices up her diary with an anecdote, such as the following. The principal of a kindergarten asks a woman with lovely red hair: "Does your child have such fantastic hair?"—"No, he's dark haired."—"Does the father have dark hair?"—"I don't know, he had a hat."

Their acquaintances included German and Soviet film people (among them Eisenstein), and they often went to the cinema. They saw films with Chaplin and Greta Garbo and *Die weiße Hölle vom Piz Palü* with Leni Riefenstahl ("If sinners are tortured in Hell with films like that then it really is unbearable"), but most of all they were interested in the great novelty in the art of film, the talkie: *Liebeswalzer* ("about counts and princes—a parody, but still!"), *So ist das Leben*, *Zwei Herzen in Dreivierteltakt* (whose theme became a popular hit), and many others, including *Dreyfus*, where they glimpsed Albert Einstein in the audience.

Given the involvement of Lili and Osip in the Soviet film industry, one might say that their many cinema visits were in keeping with the "scholarly purposes" they had invoked as the reason for their trip. The serious part of their program also included Lili's negotiations on Mayakovsky's behalf with the Malik publishing firm and a meeting (it is unclear with whom) in which they decided to set up a company to produce sound films in the Soviet Union. Osip for his part put in an appearance at the Soviet legation's club in Berlin and gave a public lecture, in German, on "the newest literature produced during the building of socialism in the Soviet Union." According to Lili, the lecture was "brilliant" and the audience as good as it had been in the Polytechnic Museum in Moscow. But if Osip's performance was a success in Berlin, it caused disquiet among the members of RAPP in Moscow, who were concerned about Osip's orthodoxy. Had he really expressed himself as he ought to?

However profitable and productive Lili's and Osip's stay in Berlin was, the German capital served only as a intermediate stop on a

The photo of Lili with a lion cub at the Berlin Zoo that she sent to Mayakovsky. "How much I'd like a little lion cub like this one," she wrote. "You can't imagine what soft little claws they have!"

journey whose intended destination was London. The reason given for the trip to England was to visit Lili's mother, but there was also another motive behind their desire to get to London: they wanted to see Elsa and to get to know her husband Louis Aragon. Although their application for a visa was turned down in October, Lili and Osip did not give up hope, and on 5 March they made a further attempt, this time at the British legation in Berlin. This time things went better, and on 17 March Lili's mother sent them a telegram to inform them that a visa had been issued for both of them. The change in attitude by the British authorities can be seen in a decision from the Home Office according to which the instruction in circular B795 "should now be regarded as canceled and her [Lili's] name removed from the suspect index." However ignorant Lili may have been about the machinations surrounding the British visas for herself and Mayakovsky, she must have wondered why the British authorities suddenly changed their minds. Was the explanation simply that they wanted to improve relations with the Soviet Union after two years of diplomatic chill? Whatever the reason, she and Osip left Berlin on 30 March after walking out halfway through *For the Love of Anna* (the silent film version of *Anna Karenina* from 1927), with Greta Garbo and John Gilbert, which they found "comical." The sleeping car which took them to the Hook of Holland to catch the boat for England was German: "bracket lamps, hooks, and electric mains for all systems."

When they left Germany they had already spent a week in the company of Elsa and Aragon, who in view of the uncertainty surrounding Osip and Lili's trip to England had come to Berlin. The short time that they spent together in the Kurfürstenhôtel was enough for Lili to be impressed by her new brother-in-law. "Aragon is great," she noted. "A real pity that I can't manage to commit to memory everything he says." In another diary entry we read: "[Aragon] refuses to meet Eisenstein because he has shaken hands with Marinetti and been photographed with him." A member of the French Communist Party could not accept that a prominent representative of Soviet culture should be seen in the company of a pro-Fascist Italian Futurist. In truth, the times were politically explosive.

THE BATHHOUSE IN MOSCOW

On 17 March, the same day on which Lili and Osip in Berlin received the good news from Lili's mother, Mayakovsky awoke in Moscow in quite a different mood. The previous evening *The Bathhouse* had had its premiere in Meyerhold's theater and had been just as big a fiasco as in Leningrad. Two days later he wrote to Lili: "The day before yesterday was the premiere of *The Bathhouse*; I liked it with the exception of one or two details. In my opinion it's my first proper production. [Maxim] Shtraukh [who played Triumphalnikov] is excellent. It was funny how much the audience was divided—some said, 'We've never been so bored'; others said, 'We've never had such fun.' What else they're going to say and write I don't know."

Mayakovsky's comment about the audience at the premiere splitting into two equal camps was putting rather a gloss on things. At best, the reaction was "cool," in the words of Vasily Katanyan, something that cannot have escaped Mayakovsky either during the per-

formance itself or afterward, when he stood in the vestibule looking everyone who was leaving the theater in the eye. This impression was borne out by the reviews, which began to stream in a few days after the letter to Lili and which were utterly scathing. Mayakovsky's view of Soviet reality was said to be "mocking," the characters were "lifeless," and the play "superficial" and "bad," "lacking concrete class content," and it was dismissed as "a fiasco" which had nothing to do with "practical social reality."

If Mayakovsky had thought that his membership in RAPP would assure him of support from that quarter, he was gravely mistaken. A week *before* the premiere the RAPP critic Vladimir Yermilov had an article published in *Pravda* with the title "Concerning Petit Bourgeois 'Left-Wing' Sentiments in Literature," in which he castigated Mayakovsky for a "falsely 'leftish' tone, so familiar to us from areas other than literature," thereby indirectly coupling him with the "Trotskyist opposition." Meyerhold defended Mayakovsky in a newspaper article, and Mayakovsky himself responded by adding to the antibureaucratic posters hung up in the theater auditorium on the evening of the premiere one directed against "critics in the style of Yermilov / who help the bureaucrats with their pen."

This infuriated the RAPP leadership, and he was told to take the poster down, which was duly done. That the pugnacious Mayakovsky laid down his arms in this humiliating fashion shows that he had not only set his heel "on the throat of [his] own song" but also his whole personality. This was precisely what the leadership of RAPP was after—to take Mayakovsky down a peg. A further step in that direction was taken just a week or so after the premiere of *The Bathhouse*, when an expanded plenary session of RAPP declared that the magazine *Oktober*'s publication of excerpts from the play, which was said to be aimed at "the proletarian state" rather than the bureaucracy, had been a "mistake."

ON THE THRESHOLD OF MASS TERROR

In the prevailing situation Yermilov's article was nothing less than a *donos*, a political denunciation, something that both he and Mayakovsky were well aware of. The party's struggle against "the opposition" within science and culture had until now mainly involved exile, purges, and bans on publication, but more recently it had changed character, as was demonstrated by the arrest and execution of Yakov Blyumkin in the autumn of 1929. We remember Blyumkin from the first years after the Revolution as a theatrical, revolver-waving Chekist and terrorist, a habitué of the literary cafés and the friend of several writers, among them Sergey Yesenin, Osip Mandelstam—and Mayakovsky, who gave him some of his books with a written dedication. After the murder of the German ambassador von Mirbach in the summer of 1918, he fled Moscow, but the following year he was pardoned by Dzerzhinsky, the head of the Cheka, and during the twenties he enjoyed an outstanding career in the Cheka. Because of his knowledge of languages (apart from Hebrew he was fluent in several Oriental languages) he was given many tasks abroad, for instance in Palestine, Afghanistan, Mongolia, China, and India (where his job was to try to get the population to turn on the British occupying power).

Alongside its traditional activities the OGPU was also interested in suggestion and the possibility of exerting mass influence, and for a while Blyumkin was entrusted with infiltrating occult circles in Petrograd. Related to this rather odd genre of espionage were two expeditions to Tibet, organized by the OGPU in 1926 and 1928, to try to find the mythical city of Shambhala, whose inhabitants were said to possess telepathic powers. The official leader of the expedition was the well-known Russian artist and theosophist Nikolay Roerich, but the chief agent—well versed in the mysticism of the East—was Blyumkin, who appeared disguised either as a Mongolian officer or a lama, depending on his assignment.

Throughout the whole of his adventurous career Blyumkin was close to Leon Trotsky, and for several years he worked as his secretary. During Stalin's attacks on the opposition at the end of 1927 Blyumkin openly demonstrated his sympathy with it. Nevertheless, thanks to his good contacts in the OGPU he was given responsibility for the activities of Soviet agents in the whole of the Middle East. In order to finance this spy network he opened a bookshop in Constantinople specializing in old Jewish books (which the OGPU had stolen from the Lenin Library or confiscated from synagogues and other Jewish venues). Under the Azerbaijani-Jewish cover name of Jakub Sultanov he then traveled around Europe selling the books at the highest possible prices, something that tallied very well with the interests of his employers.

Significantly less admired in those circles was Blyumkin's meeting in April 1929 with Trotsky, who at this time was living in Constantinople and who persuaded him to join the struggle against Stalin. Once back in Moscow the ever-talkative Blyumkin could not keep quiet about his contacts with Trotsky and was betrayed and arrested—according to one account, at the home of the newly deposed People's Commissar of Enlightenment Anatoly Lunacharsky, with whom he stayed for a while. On 3 November 1929 he was executed on the direct orders of Stalin.

Blyumkin's execution shook his colleagues in the party and the security service. If a person with such good contacts in high OGPU circles could be put to death, anyone could meet the same fate. In the same way that the legal process against Krasnoshchokov was the first corruption case against a leading Communist, the execution of Blyumkin was the first death sentence against a sympathizer with the Trotskyist opposition—not counting secret assassinations. Trotsky exhorted his supporters in the West to protest against the murder of the "burning revolutionary," but without much success.

There are no references to Blyumkin's execution by Mayakovsky or his friends, which in view of its political explosiveness is not surprising. But it is hard to believe that it would not have stirred up strong feelings in him—and memories: of the anarchistic and libertarian socialism of the first revolutionary years, of a time when everything still seemed to be possible. The execution of Blyumkin was not only the death of an individual human being but also the brutal end of a revolutionary epoch and the dream of a freer form of socialism. A new era in the history of the Russian Revolution was in the offing: one of terror and mass executions.

If Blyumkin's death was a reminder of a vanished time and of an adventurer and revolutionary romantic whom Mayakovsky had not met all that often in recent years, another execution, which took place two months later, struck a direct blow at the innermost circle of the Futurists. Vladimir Sillov, born in 1901, was a member of both the Siberian Futurist group Tvorchestvo and of Lef, he wrote articles about Mayakovsky and Burlyuk and drew up bibliographies of the works of both Khlebnikov and Mayakovsky (the latter bibliography was printed in the first volume of Mayakovsky's *Collected Works*, which came out in November 1928). He was arrested on 8 January 1930; on the thirteenth he was sentenced to shooting by firing squad for "espionage and counterrevolutionary propaganda," and three days later the sentence was carried out.

What the non-party-member Sillov's "crime" consisted of is unclear. According to one source (the Trotskyist Victor Serge) he had done a favor for an OGPU man who supported the opposition. According to another (Trotsky's son) Sillov was executed "after a botched attempt to link [him] to some sort of 'conspiracy' or 'espionage.'" The "proof" may perhaps have been found in Sillov's diary, which was "the diary, not of a bourgeois, but of a dedicated revolutionary." "He thought too much," Pasternak reported to his father, "and that sometimes leads to this form of meningitis."

The news of Sillov's arrest and execution naturally became known immediately to his friends and colleagues, but we know as little about their reaction as in the Blyumkin case. According to one source Pasternak was struck by Kirsanov's indifference when the affair came up in conversation, "as if he was talking about a wedding or a new apartment." But the memoir that this relies on refers to an unnamed "old friend, a former Socialist Revolutionary" and may just as well refer to Blyumkin, someone who was not close to Kirsanov. Whatever the truth of the matter, what Pasternak perceived as indifference was more likely camouflaged terror.

If the reactions of the Ref set are unknown, Pasternak reacted with seismic sensitivity to Sillov's sentence—just as he had done in the Shakhty trial two years earlier. Faced with this, he wrote to Korney Chukovsky's son Nikolay, everything that happened earlier "pales in comparison and is eclipsed," continuing: "Of all the members of Lef in its present form he was the only honest, living, gently reproachful exemplar of the new [i.e., Communist] morality which I never aspired to as it is wholly incomprehensible and alien to my temperament, but whose (failed and exclusively verbal) embodiment the whole of Lef served, at the cost of suppressing either one's conscience or talent.

There was only one person who for a moment lent plausibility to this impossible and enforced myth and that was V[ladimir] S[illov]. To express it more exactly: In Moscow there was only one place I visited which made me doubt the rightness of my convictions. That was Sillov's room in the Proletkult block on Vozdvizhenka."

Although Pasternak was aware of the limits of what could be said, he gave proof, as usual, of an uncommon degree of civic courage: "I will break off my account of him here as I have said enough. But if even that is forbidden, i.e., that on losing people who are close to us we must pretend that they are still living and must not remember them and say that they are gone: if my letter leads to any unpleasantness for you, I beg you not to spare me but to point me out as the guilty party. It is for this reason that I am signing with my full name (I usually do it with an indecipherable signature or only with initials)."

After Sillov's death his wife attempted suicide by throwing herself out of a window—despite the fact that they had a little boy, which says something about her state of mind. How did Mayakovsky react to Sillov's death? To his wife's suicide attempt? Blyumkin's death was "understandable" in the sense that it involved a politically active opponent of Stalin. Sillov was a writer and friend, a "wonderful, cultivated, talented, to the highest degree and in the best sense of the word *progressive* human being," in Pasternak's definition. Could his execution inject anything other than fear into his closest circles? Hardly. If an individual like Sillov could be put to death, who was safe? The silence surrounding his death testifies to the atmosphere of fear which was already beginning to spread through Soviet society, in the winter of 1930, six years before the Great Terror which swept away millions of innocent people, among them hundreds of writers.*

* With his death Sillov became a nonperson not only for his contemporaries but also for posterity. In his memoir *Safe Conduct* (1931) Pasternak alludes to him under his wife's initials, O.S., but otherwise his name is not mentioned anywhere in the many memoirs which were written about Tvorchestvo and Lef. Not even his own wife names him in her reminiscences about her time in Siberia (at least not in the printed and presumably censored version which was published in 1980). The first time the initials O.S. were deciphered—thereby throwing light on Vladimir Sillov's fate—was in a scholarly article by Michel Aucouturier published in 1975.

15

THE FIRST BOLSHEVIK SPRING

1930

**I and my heart have never lived till May,
in that life we have lived
there are only a hundred Aprils.**
Vladimir Mayakovsky, "A Cloud in Trousers"

Tatyana's marriage meant that Paris was a closed chapter as far as Mayakovsky was concerned. If there was anything positive in this, it was that the emotional double-entry bookkeeping enforced by the parallel affairs with Tatyana and Nora were no longer necessary. At the beginning of 1930 the relationship with Nora intensified, and after the departure of Lili and Osip for Berlin it entered a decisive phase.

At this point Nora's marriage was purely formal and relations with her husband "good, friendly, but no more than that": "Yanshin regarded me as a little girl and was interested in neither my life nor my work, nor did I immerse myself in his life and thoughts." But although Yanshin himself was no exemplar of marital faithfulness, Nora was tortured by the thought that she was betraying him with Mayakovsky, especially as

Downtown Moscow on 17 April 1930.

they often went around as a threesome: to the theater, horse racing, restaurants, and gambling. However, Yanshin was so flattered at being seen in the great poet's company that he did not want to make an issue of Mayakovsky's evident interest in his wife.

If Yanshin chose to swallow his annoyance, Mayakovsky's "family," who after all had initiated the relationship with Nora, reacted positively to it as long as it followed Lili's rule that "extramarital" relations should not be cultivated within the walls of their home. So when Nora spent the night with Mayakovsky, it was in his study in Lubyanka Passage. Once, when Lili and Osip were in Leningrad and Yanshin was also out of Moscow, Mayakovsky suggested that she should sleep over in Gendrikov. When Nora wondered what Lili would say if she came home the following morning and found Nora there, he replied: "She'll say: 'Ah, you're living with Nora? . . . I'm all for that.'" Nora took this to mean that he "in a way was sorry that Lili Yuryevna was so indifferent to that fact." It was, she recalled, "as if he still loved her, which in turn was hurting my ego."

Lili had her lovers, Osip had Zhenya, Mayakovsky had Nora—everything was fine and dandy as long as the fundamentals of "family life" were not disturbed. When Lili wanted to put an end to Mayakovsky's relationship with Natasha Bryukhanenko she did it with the words "We are all three of us married to each other and to marry any more is a sin for us," and that basic rule still held good. "It seemed to me that Lili Yuryevna did not take his romances seriously and even encouraged them, as in my case—to begin with," Nora commented. "But if anyone started to interest him at a deeper level she became anxious. She wanted to be the only one, for ever, unique in Mayakovsky's life."

Five years had passed since Lili had broken off physical relations with Mayakovsky, and on at least two occasions he had been ready to leave his "pussycat family" to start one of his own. That in both Natasha's and Tatyana's cases it was Lili who with different methods had prevented such a development was no secret to Mayakovsky, who knew that he would never be able to leave their collective setup in Gendrikov Alley as long as Lili was keeping an eye on him. So when she and Osip went abroad he made haste to propose to Nora. If she accepted, he could present Lili with a fait accompli when they returned two months later. Mayakovsky had made Nora pregnant and she had had a difficult abortion, which had perhaps precipitated the proposal. (Interestingly enough Osip's Zhenya had had an abortion a few months earlier on the grounds of an ectopic pregnancy—one wonders how Lili would have reacted if both of her "beasts" had become fathers at the same time.) But Nora postponed the issue. She found it hard to take the step of leaving Yanshin; she promised Mayakovsky that she would be his wife, "but not now."

Nora's irresoluteness was partly due to her youth and her shyness, but also to Mayakovsky's mood swings and despotic attempts to monopolize her. If she failed to keep assuring him that she loved him, jealousy dug its claws into him. He waited for her every day in a café beside the theater, and whenever she was late, the same sight greeted her. Mayakovsky would be sitting at a café table wearing his broad-brimmed hat with his hands on his walking stick, chin sunk in his hands and his gaze directed at the door, waiting for her to come. If it was embarrassing for Nora, who had Yanshin and her reputation to think of, it was just as painful for Mayakovsky, who became a figure of fun to the waitresses in the café: a morose man of thirty-six who waited for hours for an actress barely half his age. When Nora asked him not to arrange for them to meet in the café, as she could not promise to come in time, he replied: "Never mind the waitresses, let them laugh. I'll wait patiently, just as long as you come!"

An illuminating example of Mayakovsky's egocentricity and egotism was his refusal to accept that Nora would not have sex with him after the abortion. She tried to explain to him that it was because of a temporary depression and that if he left her alone for a while and did not react "so impatiently and neurotically" to her "lack of interest in the physical side" then their relationship would soon get back to how it was before. "But my lack of interest made Vladimir Vladimirovich beside himself. He was often obstinate and even nasty," Nora recalled. Sex "played a very big role" in their relationship: "That's why Vladimir Vladimirovich was so pathologically neurotic toward me, and that was why I hesitated about leaving Yanshin and moving in with Mayakovsky, and put off taking a decision."

While they were waiting for the right moment to present itself they began looking for somewhere where they could live together. According to Nora they wanted two separate apartments on the same landing. "Of course it was absurd to go and wait for an apartment so as to let that decide whether or not we could live together," Nora recalled. "But it was necessary for me, as I was frightened of telling Yanshin the whole story and kept putting it off, and it had a calming effect on Vladimir Vladimirovich." As the Soviet Writers' Federation was in the process of building an apartment block opposite the Art Theater, Mayakovsky contacted the Federation's secretary—the same Vladimir Sutyrin who in the name of the federation had signed Mayakovsky's article in *Komsomolskaya Pravda* in connection with the attacks on Lili and Osip. He explained that he could no longer live in Gendrikov and therefore needed an apartment, preferably before Lili and Osip came back from abroad. When he heard it could not be arranged before the autumn, he replied: "Well then, then I'll rent something and in the autumn we can agree that you'll give me a place of my own."

A LAST STRAW

During the month of March Mayakovsky was busy with a new theater project, *Moscow Is Burning*, a "heroic piece set to music" about the revolution of 1905 written for the Moscow Circus. As the management of the circus was less interested in Mayakovsky's artistic intentions than in good ticket sales, they interfered with the rehearsals and tried to "normalize" the production, which made him upset and disappointed. These artistic setbacks were matched in the private sphere by the loneliness he experienced after Lili and Osip departed and his closest friends abandoned him—or he them, depending on one's perspective. One loyal friend who visited him almost every day was Lev Grinkrug, with whom he could satisfy his passion for gambling.

"I believe that I myself and our relationship were a sort of straw that he clung to," Nora declared in a form of words which is rather too self-effacing given Mayakovsky's feelings for her. They met as often as work—both his and hers—allowed, often, for respectability's sake, in company with Nora's husband. "We met daily, sometimes several times a day," Yanshin recalled. "By day, in the evenings, at night." One day when all three of them were out together Mayakovsky asked the other two to come home with him to Gendrikov Alley. After talking for a while and drinking a little wine they went for a walk with Bulka, and Mayakovsky gave Yanshin's hand a hard squeeze, saying: "Mikhail Mikhaylovich, if you only knew how grateful I am that you looked in on me. If you only knew what you have saved me from."

When Mayakovsky became reconciled with Kirsanov in mid-March, it was without much enthusiasm, as we see from a letter to Lili in which his old friend (and his wife) are described as "new faces" whom he has almost forgotten. Apart from the bulldog, Mayakovsky's only company in Gendrikov was a housekeeper—and the OGPU agent Lev Elbert, "the Snob," who camped out there for a short time after Lili's and Osip's departure. Why? To keep Mayakovsky company? Or was his presence connected to his professional duties? "You must tell Snob that I left my address, but nobody has come here and it's very bad," Lili wrote to Mayakovsky from Berlin. Did Lili have some "task" to perform in the German capital? It is tempting to give a conspiratorial twist to her enigmatic comment, but perhaps it was only about a present that was to be handed over? (The same question mark surrounds the "various errands and requests" that "Yanya" Agranov intended to convey to Lili and Osip before their departure for Berlin but which he failed to do because of his late arrival at the railway station. Would a professional agent assign secret tasks on a railway platform—and moreover arrive too late for the train? Hardly. It is more plausible that the "errands and requests" in question were of the same kind that Lili used to give Mayakovsky.)

The feeling of loneliness and isolation that Mayakovsky experienced during the winter of 1930 was exacerbated by a severe dose of influenza which afflicted him at the end of February and was slow to recede. For a hypochondriac like Mayakovsky the least little chill led to inadequate reactions, and he became frightened and depressed. He was particularly anxious about his voice, which was his work tool and part of his identity as a poet: "Losing my voice is the equivalent for me to Chaliapin losing his voice." Because of his smoking habit and the many tours and readings he was often afflicted with throat infections, and however hard the doctors tried to reassure him, he was always afraid that he had throat cancer or some other fatal illness. In March he was forced on several occasions to break off readings because of throat problems caused by influenza in combination with stress and overwork. On 17 March, during an appearance at the Polytechnic Museum, he performed "At the Top of My Voice" to show that he had not "become a newspaper poet," but he could not finish the reading. "An agitated, earnest, overwrought Mayakovsky gazed in a strange, absentminded way over the auditorium and recited each successive verse in an ever-weaker voice. Then he suddenly stopped, looked out over the hall with a dismal, drained expression and declared: 'No, comrades, I will not be reading any more verses. I cannot.' He turned round suddenly and went out into the corridors." Mayakovsky continued to be dogged by problems with his voice and a week later, during a performance in the Young Communists' House in the Krasnaya Presnya district, when he was asked to read his poems rather than comment on them, he replied: "I have come here although I am seriously ill, I don't know what is happening to my throat, perhaps I shall be forced to give up reading my poems for a very long time." After nevertheless reading several poems he was forced to bring his performance to an end, saying: "Comrades, perhaps we'll finish here, my voice has given up."

WHEN WERE YOU THINKING OF SHOOTING YOURSELF?

Throughout his career Mayakovsky had confronted his readers not only through his books but also from the stage. This live confrontation with his public was the breath of life to him: he loved to provoke and to bandy words. But there was a big difference between the bourgeois audiences of the first decade of the century, who enjoyed being heckled by the Futurist Mayakovsky and whose attacks he found it easy to parry, and his unimpressionable and often boorish Soviet listeners. Both the poet and his public were different, something that Mayakovsky emphasized at the Young Communists' House on the 25 March: "The old reciter of poetry, the old listener, who sat in salons (it was mostly young ladies and gentlemen in the audience), that reciter is dead once and for all, and it is only the working-class audience, only the working and peasant masses, those who are in the

Mayakovsky during the meeting between Russian and Ukrainian writers in the winter of 1929, when he was subjected to unprovoked attacks.

process of building socialism and who intend to spread it over the whole world, it is only they who should be our real poetry reciters, and these people's poet is going to be me."

But the "working and peasant masses" were no more willing than the critics to be convinced that it was Mayakovsky who was the leading Soviet poet, and by the end of the twenties sniping at Mayakovsky in an article or during one of his performances had became something of a sport. The Ukrainian poet Pavlo Tychina gives the example of a meeting between Russian and Ukrainian writers in the winter of 1929 where Mayakovsky, though not the main focus of attention, nevertheless and quite without provocation on his part became the target of attacks from several of the writers present.

The fact that the situation was even worse a year later was partly due to the polarization within the cultural sector but also to Mayakovsky himself, who by arranging a retrospective exhibition forced those around him to make up their minds one way or the other: for or against. A neutral stance was scarcely feasible any longer. Mayakovsky's hegemonic pretensions to be the leading Soviet poet made him an easy target for mirth and derision. On one occasion a young man came up to him and said: "Mayakovsky, we know from history that good poets tend to come to a bad end. Either they're murdered, or. . . When were you thinking of shooting yourself?" Mayakovsky gave a start and answered slowly: "If any more idiots are going to ask that, I might just as well shoot myself."

On 8 April Mayakovsky saw Alexander Dovzhenko's new film *Earth*, and after the screening he asked the director to call on him the following day: "Let's have a talk about it, maybe we can organize at least some little group of artists in the defense of art," he said, adding: "What's going on around us is insufferable, impossible." But there was to be no conversation with Dovzhenko; instead, on 9 April Mayakovsky took part in another "conversation" which merely confirmed the correctness of his analysis. The participants in the discussion were students at the Moscow Institute of Economics, where Mayakovsky was to perform on the same day on which he was supposed to meet Dovzhenko.

Mayakovsky normally looked forward to such meetings, but this time he was feverish from influenza and his eyes were shining when he arrived at the institute. There was not a trace of his usual fighting mood. He had scarcely entered the building before he rushed to the door on the other side of the auditorium to hide from the public gaze. He tugged at the door but it did not open. He rapped on it with his cane. In vain. He sank down on a bench. "It was as if he wanted to sleep or he was suffering from fever, from influenza," recalled Viktor Slavinsky, a young admirer of Mayakovsky who has preserved the memory of the performance for posterity. "He sat with his head bowed and his eyes closed, without taking his hat off."

The public was slow to arrive. There was no question of the kind of crush and excitement that usually accompanied Mayakovsky's performances. One possible explanation is that the students had other things to think of. They were to be sent out into the countryside to help the peasants on the collective farms, and they were busy with their exams. It was the first spring of the first five-year plan, the so-called First Bolshevik Spring. The Easter festival had had to give way to the spring sowing, and the ringing of church bells to the din of sowing machines and tractors.

Whatever the reason, Mayakovsky was forced to begin before the auditorium was full, and he started out by declaring that he had only been persuaded with great difficulty to turn up. "I had no desire to do it, I am tired of performing." His defiant claim "When I am dead, you will be moved to tears by my poems" caused some of the audience to burst out laughing. "But now," he continued. "while I am still alive, a lot of nonsense is being talked about me and I am getting a lot of abuse. There is a lot of tittle-tattle about poets. But out of all the talking and scribbling about living poets, most rubbish is circulated about me. For instance, I have been criticized because I—Mayakovsky—am supposed to have run around Moscow naked with the slogan 'Down with shame?'"

Many members of the audience were well inclined toward Mayakovsky, but some were only there to heckle. When he read out "At the Top of My Voice" and came to the lines "in squares / where they cough up tuberculosis / among whores, pimps / and syphilis" he was interrupted by protests about the "ugly words" and was forced to stop. Instead he read some other poems and then invited questions from the audience. One student declared that he didn't understand "A Cloud in Trousers." Mayakovsky did not respond. Another submitted a written query up to the stage: "Is it true that Khlebnikov is a poet of genius and that you, Mayakovsky, are pure rubbish compared to him?" Mayakovsky answered that he did not want to compete with other poets but that there was a shortage of good poets in the Soviet Union.

He was tired, and descending from the high rostrum, he sat down on a step and remained there, his eyes shut, scarcely visible to sections of the audience. A student called Zaytsev had the floor: "Comrades! The workers do not understand Mayakovsky because of the way he breaks up his lines." Mayakovsky replied: "In fifteen to twenty years the cultural level of the workers will be higher and everyone will understand my works." Another student, Mikheyev, turned the screw: "Let Mayakovsky prove that people will be reading him in twenty years' time." The audience laughed. Mikheyev went on: "If Comrade Mayakovsky cannot prove that, then he shouldn't go on writing."

The atmosphere became more and more heated. Another student, Makarov, declared: "Mayakovsky is a poet. I like poetry. I like reciting poetry. I like all poets, and can recite any poet you like. I have not been able to recite Mayakovsky for any audience." In response to a question about what he had written on Lenin, Mayakovsky read from "Vladimir Ilyich Lenin." He read with enormous power, and the audience responded with thunderous applause, which did not stop one student from climbing up to the podium and announcing: "Mayakovsky says he has been writing for twenty years. But he talks a lot about himself, praising himself the whole time. He must stop doing that. Mayakovsky must begin to devote himself to proper work." Mayakovsky pushed the student aside and replied, very upset: "The last speaker talked a lot of nonsense. In forty minutes I have not said a word about myself." A voice from the audience: "Prove it."

Mayakovsky asked those who did not understand his poems to put their hands up, which a quarter of the audience did. A drunk student called Krikun (which means 'loudmouth') was given the floor and declared that Mayakovsky certainly had the correct political outlook but that he "goes to extremes in his work, just like the members of the party in their political work." To illustrate this he cited a poem by Mayakovsky in which the word "ticktock" is repeated over one and a half pages. Mayakovsky jumped up to the rostrum and protested: "Comrades! He's lying. I have no such poem. No!!" The loudmouth refused to leave the rostrum and continued: "Mayakovsky's readability is limited because there are excesses in his work." Mayakovsky was livid: "I want to learn from you, but you must shield me from lies . . . Not abuse me for everything under the sun, for poems which I haven't written. I have no poems such as have been quoted here! Do you understand? There are none!!"

The atmosphere was red hot, with Mayakovsky and his hecklers spurring each other on. Instead of asking for the floor the students were shouting out from where they sat. One female student waved her arms wildly. Mayakovsky: "Stop waving your arms, it doesn't make the pears fall off the trees, and there's a human being standing here at the rostrum." Quoting from the students' own comments, he demonstrated what a poor understanding they had of poetry: "I am disturbed by how illiterate my listeners are. I had not expected such a low level of culture among the students at such a highly respected educational institution."

A student wearing spectacles shouted: "Demagogy!"—"Demagogy! Comrades! Is this demagogy?" Mayakovsky asked, turning to the audience. The student shouted back: "Yes, it is." Mayakovsky leaned forward from the rostrum and, in a thunderous voice, commanded: "Sit down!" The student refused to sit and went on shouting. The whole audience rose to its feet. "Sit down! I shall make you be quiet!" The din grew less, and everyone sat down. As on so many previous occasions Mayakovsky had emerged victorious from a duel with his public. But the price was high. He stumbled down from the stage and threw himself down on the step, quite worn out. When he left the building he left his cane behind, something which had never happened before.

Although Mayakovsky managed to get the better of his audience in the end, there had been occasions during the course of the evening when he had shown clear signs of weakness and had been forced onto the defensive, which was most unusual. This weakness was due not only to the influenza but also to other factors. A few days before his performance Mayakovsky had found out that the magazine *Press and Revolution* had decided to pay tribute to him with a portrait and a congratulatory caption: "*Press and Revolution* offers its warmest congratulations to V. V. Mayakovsky—the great revolutionary poet, the outstanding poetic revolutionary, the tireless poetic comrade-in-arms of the working class—on the occasion of the twentieth anniversary of his artistic and societal work." As his exhibition had suffered from an almost total press boycott, the initiative came as a welcome surprise—especially as Mayakovsky had never contributed to the magazine and the tribute was therefore not a result of back-scratching. It was to be printed on a special page before the editorial, giving it extra weight. When a member of the editorial staff phoned Mayakovsky and said he was about to send him a few copies, Mayakovsky replied that he would like to fetch them himself so he could thank the editors personally.

This he never needed to do, because when the magazine was distributed, the page with the tribute to him had been torn out. This action had been authorized by Artyomy Khalatov, the head of Gosizdat (the magazine's publishers), who in a letter had furiously attacked the senior editorial staff for daring to call a "fellow traveler" like Mayakovsky a great revolutionary poet and demanded to know the name of the author of this "outrageous tribute." The editors were also ordered to see to it that the page was torn out of all the five thousand—already bound—copies of the magazine, which was duly done.

For Mayakovsky, who immediately learned what had happened, Khalatov's action was yet another bitter confirmation that the brutal dispatch of *The Bathhouse* and the exhibition boycott were no coincidence but a deliberate expression of the authorities' attitude toward him. However powerful the head of Gosizdat, he would never have taken such a drastic step without sanction from higher echelons—with whom he had regular contact due to his position: at this very time he was, for instance, exchanging letters with Stalin about the necessity of purging from Gorky's memoirs of Lenin all references to Trotsky.

If the silence surrounding *20 Years' Work* and the criticism of *The Bathhouse* had failed to convince Mayakovsky that he was regarded with deep suspicion by the party's ideologists, a few words from Ivan Gronsky, editor in chief of *Izvestiya*, dropped during a nocturnal promenade in February, ought to have done so: "Vladimir Vladimirovich, your differences of opinion with the party over artistic questions, or, more accurately, ethical-philosophical questions, are deeper than you think."

When Viktor Slavinsky saw the state Mayakovsky was in when he arrived at the Institute of Economics he tried to cheer him up by telling him that he had seen the edition of the magazine containing the tribute to him at the printer's where he worked. But the reaction he got was the opposite of what he expected. Mayakovsky knew already that the page had been torn out, and the reminder only increased his irritation and contributed to his aggressive behavior during the discussions. Khalatov's letter was an unambiguous sign that he had fallen out of favor. Were the students' insults also an expression of this? Had they been ordered there to provoke him? Mayakovsky's instinct for self-preservation undoubtedly made him turn a blind eye to that possibility—a possibility which did not however escape the notice of Nikolay Aseyev, who on the subject of this very discussion evening suggested that "an audience can be formed on more than one criterion."

The audience at the Institute of Economics was young. It was

Mayakovsky's audience—it was the young people he put his faith in; it was they who were the future. If the older generation did not understand his poems, the next generation would! The reception therefore left him extremely distressed, and his closing words testify to his bitterness and resignation: "Comrades! Today we have met for the first time. In a few months' time we shall meet again. We have had a bit of a quarrel and a shouting match with each other. But the bad language was unjustified. You have no reason to be angry with me."

There was to be no further meeting. Five days later Mayakovsky was dead.

THE HUNDREDTH APRIL

On the same day that Mayakovsky was tussling with the students in the Institute of Economics, Lili and Osip had lunch in the House of Commons at the invitation of a couple of Labour politicians they knew. "We saw the Speaker's procession," Lili noted in her diary. "Listened for a bit. They lounge around and guffaw. The upper house is almost identical but a bit smaller and like a Pullman car." In the evening they went to the cinema and saw a Hollywood musical with "phenomenal numbers."

They were staying with Yelena Yulyevna, who had moved into a smaller flat in Golders Green with open fires and a garden. They passed the time in the same way as they had done in Berlin. Osip went hunting for books, and Lili did the rounds of the shops, especially Selfridge's, which according to Lili made the Berlin department stores pale in comparison. They bought gramophone records from the HMV label which they played on Yelena Yulyevna's portable gramophone. Just as they had done in Berlin, they went to cabarets and cinemas practically every day and saw among other things *The Love Parade* with Maurice Chevalier (who had "a delightful English accent"), and Eisenstein's latest film, *The General Line*. In the audience at the Soviet Embassy was George Bernard Shaw, who seems to have misunderstood the film's message (it was about the collectivization of agriculture) and according to Lili "just about died laughing." They ate in Chinatown and in Italian restaurants in Soho—the Savoy Hotel insisted on evening dress and they were not allowed in.

В. В. МАЯКОВСКОГО —
велиного революционного поэта,
замечательного революционера поэтического искусства,
неутомимого поэтического соратника рабочего класса —

горячо приветствует „Печать и революция" по случаю
20-летия его творческой и общественной работы.

The address in *Press and Revolution* that was torn out after political pressure.

They visited Windsor Castle and Eton, where "boys in tall hats" made Lili think of Dickens. They listened a lot to the radio, following the Oxford-Cambridge boat race and listening to Lloyd George's daughter talking.

They knew nothing about Mayakovsky's life in Moscow, because he did not write to them. Since landing in London on 31 March they had received only one telegram from Mayakovsky and Bulka—"kiss you love you miss you waiting"—dated 3 April and signed "Puppies." The "letter diet" was very strict this time: since leaving Moscow on 18 February they had received only two letters and four—equally uninformative—telegrams. "Volodya, I am quite amazed by your silence," Lili rebuked Mayakovsky, urging him to write. But Volodya had neither the desire nor the time; he was wholly taken up with fighting for his life as a writer and a human being—and with courting Nora, the "straw he clung to" in a situation which appeared more and more hopeless.

10 APRIL

The day after his encounter with the students, on 10 April, Mayakovsky received a postcard from Lili and Osip showing the House of Commons. Dmitry Bogomolov, a counselor at the embassy, added a "friendly greeting," and the Labour politicians R. C. Wallhead and W. P. Coates wondered when Mayakovsky intended to come to London.

But London was far from Mayakovsky's thoughts. That same day he received a visit from Natasha Bryukhanenko, who had helped him with the transcription of *Moscow Is Burning* and wanted him to correct and approve it. "Do it yourself," he replied. She protested but began to delete and substitute words in the text. When she asked what he thought about her suggested changes his reply each time was: "Fine" or "It makes no difference." "I don't remember the words exactly but I remember clearly his state of mind, his gloominess and indifference," Natasha noted in her memoirs. When she was about to leave, Mayakovsky asked: "Can you stay here instead of going home?" She declined. "I would even go so far as to ask you to spend the night here," said Mayakovsky. But Natasha had too much to do and could not stay on. It was the last time she saw him.

In the evening Mayakovsky was at Meyerhold's theater, where he saw *The Bathhouse*. "He stood looking very gloomy with his elbow leaning against the door frame, smoking," recalled an acquaintance who, to lighten the mood, congratulated Mayakovsky on the fact that the party organ *Pravda* had printed a positive review of the play, which was a sure sign that the campaign against him was over. "It's already too late," was Mayakovsky's answer.

11 APRIL

The day after the greeting from the House of Commons Mayakovsky received another postcard from Lili and Osip in which, with reference to his usual telegram message ("waiting love you kiss you") they urged him to find a new one: "We're fed up with this one." If Lili's opinion still meant anything to Mayakovsky, such a snub was hardly calculated to improve his mood—and he was in dire need of positive signals after breaking with his friends Kirsanov and Aseyev. If his relationship with the former was patched up to a certain degree already in March, his relationship with Aseyev was more complicated, if only because Mayakovsky and Aseyev had known each other longer and were closer to each other. The person who, in the absence of Lili and Osip, took on the role of mediator was Lev Grinkrug, who recalled:

For a long time neither of them would take the first step, although they both wanted a reconciliation. At the beginning of April I decided to try to reestablish the friendship between Mayakovsky and Aseyev, cost what it might. On 11 April I worked the telephone from morning till night phoning first one then the other. [. . .] Mayakovsky said: "If Kolya rings I shall immediately make it up with him and ask him over." When I told Aseyev this, he replied that "Volodya could ring"—if Volodya rang he would come at once.

And this went on the whole day. Finally, about seven in the evening, I said to Mayakovsky that I was tired of making phone calls: "Show a little generosity, ring Kolya and ask him over." Aseyev came, and in the evening we played poker, the five of us—Polonskaya, Yanshin, Mayakovsky, Aseyev, and myself. Mayakovsky played in a casual fashion. He was nervy, silent, not like himself.

I remember that before we started playing he broke up a wad of 300-ruble notes, but to say that he gambled the money away would be wrong—he quite simply gave it away, apathetically. This was so unusual for Mayakovsky, who usually had far too much of the gambler's temperament.

Aseyev (according to whom the telephone conversation took place the day before) was also struck by Mayakovsky's lack of commitment during the poker session. Normally he was vociferous, joking and threatening and making suggestions like "You might as well give yourself up alive." But this time he was "unusually quiet and lacking in initiative. He played listlessly, snuffled discontentedly and lost without the least attempt to try to change his luck."

That same evening Zhenya sent a letter to Osip in London. "It was the card game that brought about the reconciliation between Kolya and Volodya," she wrote, summing up: "What long years of friendship and working together failed to clear up was achieved by poker. It's disgusting."

After the card session Mayakovsky was supposed to perform at Moscow University, but he never turned up—something that seldom happened: he was very much a man of his word and given to punctuality. Lots of people had come to listen, and after an hour, when Mayakovsky had not yet arrived, his manager Pavel Lavut sent a car for him, first to Lubyanka Passage, then to Gendrikov. There were few private cars in Moscow at this time, so when the person who had been sent out to fetch him saw a Renault in front of him, he took it for granted that it was Mayakovsky's and asked his driver to intercept him. When Mayakovsky realized what was afoot he denied all knowledge of the performance at the university and after a heated exchange banged the car door shut and ordered his chauffeur to drive on.

Mayakovsky knew very well that he had a performance to give that evening, but in his depressed state of mind he had repressed the knowledge. When he was stopped on the road, Nora was sitting in the car and they were in the middle of a "stormy scene" which according to Nora had its origins in "absolute trifles": "He had been unjust toward me and really hurt me," she recalled. "We were both very upset and could not control ourselves. I felt our relationship had gone as far as it could. I asked him to leave me and we parted in total disagreement."

The "trifles" consisted of a lie that Nora had told Mayakovsky a few days earlier. Tired of his repeated demands that she should leave Yanshin, she had said that she was going to rehearse but instead had gone to the cinema with her husband. When Mayakovsky found out he took himself off to Nora's apartment late that evening and paced to and fro under her window. But when she invited him in he simply sat there dejectedly without saying a word. The following day he took Nora with him to the room in Lubyanka Passage, where he explained that "he couldn't stand lies," that he would never forgive her for this, and that everything was over between them. He gave her back the ring and the handkerchief she had given him and said that one of the two glasses they usually drank out of had been broken that same morning. "It was meant to be," he said, and smashed the other glass against the wall. He was also foul mouthed. "I burst into tears," Nora recalled, "Vladimir Vladimirovich came over to me and we made it up." But the reconciliation was short lived: "The very next day it was back to quarreling, torment, injustices."

After Nora's lie Mayakovsky would not trust her "for a minute." "He constantly rang the theater to check what I was doing, waited for me outside, and could not hide his feelings even from outsiders. He often rang me at home and we could talk for a whole hour. The telephone was in the room we all shared so I could only answer yes or no. He talked a lot, and incoherently, made accusations, and was jealous." Yanshin's relatives, with whom they shared the apartment, wondered what was up, and Nora's hitherto-so-tolerant husband began to express his displeasure at her meetings with Mayakovsky. Nora lived "in an atmosphere of constant scenes and reproaches from every direction," and 11 April saw the explosion in the form of the "stormy scene" which ended in "total disagreement."

12 APRIL

When Pavel Lavut called on Mayakovsky in Gendrikov the following morning at half past ten to discuss the canceled performance, he found him still in bed. On a chair beside the bed was a piece of paper which he was writing on. When Lavut made to approach him Mayakovsky turned the paper over and stopped him. "Don't come any closer, you'll catch something," he said darkly, adding: "I'm not going to perform. I'm not feeling well," he said: "Phone tomorrow." Lavut, who had been working with Mayakovsky for many years, was taken aback by his reception, which verged on the unfriendly, and concluded that it was caused either by problems with *Moscow Is Burning* or by the fact that Mayakovsky was still tormented by the affair of the tribute that had been torn out of *Press and Revolution*.

That same morning Mayakovsky rang Aseyev and was most insistent that Aseyev should organize a poker session at his house with the same crowd who had come the previous evening. According to Aseyev, the request was presented more like an order. But Aseyev could not get hold of Yanshin, who was involved in rehearsals, and the project came to nothing. As Aseyev recollected, Mayakovsky—who "normally bellowed into the telephone in distress when he didn't get his way"—reacted on this occasion without any show of emotion.

In the forenoon, despite his state of mind, Mayakovsky managed to take part in a discussion about authors' rights at the Soviet Writers' Federation, where both Shklovsky and Lev Nikulin were struck by his low spirits. The latter tried to lighten the mood by asking Mayakovsky if he was pleased with his Renault. "I thought that [. . .] it would distract him, as he liked to talk about technical things," Nikulin recalled. But Mayakovsky looked at him in mild surprise without replying, got up and walked out. "I saw him from the window, walking out of the front door with heavy steps."

In the middle of the day Mayakovsky rang Nora, during the interval in her matinee performance. He was upset and explained that he was feeling really unwell, and not just now but in general. Only Nora could save him. Without her the objects by which he was surrounded—the inkwell, lamp, pens, and books on his desk—were meaningless. Only Nora could bring them to life. Nora calmed him, assured him that she could not live without him either and promised to call on him after the performance. "Listen, Nora," Mayakovsky said suddenly, "I've named you in my letter to the government, since I regard you as my family. You won't protest about that, will you?"

Nora answered that she had no idea what he was talking about and that he could name her wherever he wanted.

When they met after the performance Mayakovsky had prepared himself meticulously and had even drawn up a plan for their conversation:

1) If one is in love every conversation is a pleasure
2) If not, the quicker the better
3) For the first time I do not regret the past if it happens again I shall act in the same way
4) I am not ridiculous if one knows about our relationship
5) What my unhappiness basically consists of
6) *Not jealousy*
7) Truthfulness humanity
   must never appear ridiculous
8) One conversation and I will be calm
   Just one thing, we didn't meet at 10 o'clock either
9) Went to the tram anxiety telephone you were and would not be there must have gone [to] cinema even if [you] weren't there Mikh[ail] Mikh[ailovich] walked [?] with me didn't phone
10) Why conversation beneath your window
11) I shall not commit suicide not give the Art Theater such satisfaction
12) There will be gossip
13) Card playing a way of meeting if I am not in the right
14) The car journey
15) What must be done No more talking
16) Split up at once or know what is going to happen

The conversation plan contains direct references to actual events and injustices—the waitresses who laughed at him in the café, the lie about the visit to the cinema, the pacing under Nora's window—but also two important points which indicate the way forward: they must stop talking and decide how they want things to be between them.

After the conversation it was as if the knots had unraveled. "Vladimir Vladimirovich became very loving. I begged him not to worry about me and said that I would be his wife. [. . .] But we must think about the best, most tactful way of tackling Yanshin." As Mayakovsky was in "an unpredictable, morbid state," Nora also asked him to promise to see the doctor and to go away for at least a couple of days to have a good rest. "I remember marking both these days in his notebook. They were 13 and 14 April."

In the car on the way home Nora thought she saw Lev Grinkrug on the pavement, but Mayakovsky was unsure if it was really him. "If it is Lyova, you'll rest on the thirteenth and fourteenth and we won't see each other," said Nora. Mayakovsky accepted the challenge, and they jumped out of the car and raced each other in the direction of the person whom Nora had taken to be Lyova, and who turned out to be the man himself. Grinkrug noticed that Mayakovsky was particularly agitated and said: "You look as if you had nothing to live for." Mayakovsky gave a wry smile and replied: "And perhaps I don't." But Nora had won the bet, and he promised her that he would go to the doctor and that he would rest for two days. He also promised to stay away from her. When he rang in the evening they had a long and agreeable conversation. Mayakovsky told her that "he was writing again, and he was in a good mood; that he now realized that he had been wrong about a lot of things and that it would be best if they took a break from each other for a few days."

13 APRIL

Although Nora would have preferred Mayakovsky not to ring her, he was in touch the very next day to ask if she would come to the races with him. Nora replied that she had already promised to go there with Yanshin and a few other actors from the Art Theater, and she reminded him of his promise not to see her for two days. Asked what she was doing in the evening, Nora answered that she had been invited to Valentin Katayev's but that she did not intend to go.

In the afternoon Mayakovsky looked in at the circus, where work on *Moscow Is Burning* was underway. The theater designer was his friend Valentina Khodasevich, whom he had seen a lot of in Paris in the autumn of 1924. The premiere was approaching, but work was going badly, and Mayakovsky was dissatisfied and stressed. It was four o'clock on the afternoon of 13 April and the rehearsals were over.

Suddenly Khodasevich heard a dreadful clattering noise which was getting louder and louder. It was Mayakovsky walking toward her and rattling his cane over the backs of the seats. He was wearing a black overcoat and a black hat; "his face was pale and angry," she recalled. "He greeted me without a suggestion of a smile."

Mayakovsky had come to find out when the dress rehearsal was to take place, but no one from the management was around to tell him. Instead he suggested to Valentina that they go for a ride in his car. When she replied that she could not get away because of her work on the scenery, Mayakovsky was beside himself and thundered: "No? You can't get away!? You don't want to?" His face, she recollected, was "completely white, contorted, his eyes seemed as if they were inflamed, burning, the whites brownish, like the martyrs on icons." He kept on tapping his cane rhythmically against the seat they were standing beside and repeated his question: "No?" She replied: "No," which was followed by something resembling "a whimper or a sob": "No? I get 'no' from everybody! Only 'no'! Everywhere 'no.'"

As he was speaking Mayakovsky was already on his way to the exit. His cane clattered off the backs of the seats. "There was something almost crazy about all this," recalled Khodasevich, who chased after Mayakovsky and raced him to his car. She promised to come with him but asked him to wait a few minutes while she had a word with the stagehands. When she came back, Mayakovsky seemed to have changed beyond recognition, "quiet, pale, but not angry, more like a martyr." Valentina had previous experience of his mood swings and was not surprised. They drove for a while in utter silence. Then Mayakovsky turned round, gave her a friendly look and said, with a guilty smile, that he would spend the night at Lubyanka Passage. He asked her to give him a wake-up call in the morning so that he would not miss the rehearsal. Then he told his driver to pull up and jumped out of the car almost before it stopped. On reaching the pavement he swung his cane so wildly in the air that pedestrians jumped out of the way in alarm. With the words "The driver will take you wherever you want to go! I'm going for a walk!" he headed off with large, heavy strides, while Valentina screamed "You boor!" after him. "This was all hateful, completely impossible to understand and therefore ghastly," she recalled. On the way back to the circus they passed Mayakovsky, who with head held high was still swinging his cane in the air like a horsewhip.[*]

Nora's going to the hippodrome with Yanshin and her theatrical friends was for Mayakovsky yet further proof of his outsider status, a feeling which was amplified later when he rang Aseyev and learned from his sister-in-law that he too was at the racecourse—the fact that he was there on his own account and not in company with Nora was of less importance here. Aseyev's sister-in-law was struck by the way in which Mayakovsky, usually so polite, spoke "so strangely" and asked after "Kolya" without any preliminary salutations. When he learned that Aseyev was not at home he was quiet for a bit then said, with a sigh: "Right then, so there's nothing to be done." The fact that Mayakovsky had tried so urgently over the last few days to get in touch with Aseyev, whom he had not seen for months, was a token of his desperation.

His reason for trying to find Aseyev was that he wanted to invite him over for dinner that evening to relieve his loneliness. For the same reason he tried during the day to contact Luella—also without success—and other friends. Obviously some had promised to come, for when Luella's husband (she had married in December 1929), unaware that Mayakovsky had been looking for her, called at Gendrikov around eight o'clock in the evening, Mayakovsky was sitting at a table ready laid, drinking wine, all on his own. "I had never seen Vladimir Vladimirovich in such low spirits," he remembered.

When none of his guests turned up, Mayakovsky went round to Katayev's, in hopes that Nora would show up there after all. When he arrived, the host was not yet at home, but the artist Vladimir Roskin had got there. He and Mayakovsky were old friends and colleagues and had collaborated on ROSTA and on the decor for *Mystery-Bouffe*. While they were waiting for Katayev they sat down to a game of mah-jongg. Roskin noticed right away that Mayakovsky was not his usual self. When he lit a cigarette, Roskin pointed out

---

[*] Vasily Kamensky describes a similar incident which is supposed to have taken place on 13 April. Mayakovsky asks his driver to stop outside the Writers' Club, reaches for the revolver in his hip pocket and makes to jump out of the car, but is stopped. But this may very well be a variant of the episode with Valentina Khodasevich.

that this was surprising, given that in his poem "I Am Happy!" he had proudly proclaimed that he had given up smoking. Mayakovsky replied that this did not apply to him, that *he* was allowed to smoke. "I realized then that I had just escaped a verbal assault, that on another occasion he would have annihilated me for my sarcasm with a devastating witticism."

When Mayakovsky then lost ten rubles, he immediately paid up and announced that he did not want to play any more. Roskin was pleased and said that instead of spending the money he would save it as a memento of all the losses and humiliations he had suffered at Mayakovsky's hands over the years. Mayakovsky went up to him, stroked his cheek and said: "We are both unshaven," then went into another room. Roskin was struck by his passivity, in the same way that Aseyev had been two days earlier. "I was absolutely astounded," he recalled. "It was not like him at all. He never as a rule gave his fellow player any peace if he had a chance of winning his money back, and he would always go on playing until the other player decided to give in, and when the money ran out he would fetch more, and dash off a poem to be able to take his revenge. I realized that he was in a very bad mood."

Katayev came home around half past nine, in company with Yury Olesha. Both writers belonged to the so-called Odessa school. Olesha had made his debut in 1927 with the novel *Envy* and Katayev the following year with his play *Squaring the Circle*. They belonged to a different circle altogether from Mayakovsky, and he saw very little of them, mainly because Lili did not want him to. The reason is unclear, but in a letter written in July 1929 to Mayakovsky (who at the time was in Yalta) Lili urged him to keep away from Katayev: "Volodik, please, please don't meet Katayev. I have serious reasons for this request. I met him at the Society of Dramatists and Composers, he's off to the Crimea, and he asked for your address. I ask you again: *don't meet Katayev.*"

Whatever reasons lay behind this urgent entreaty, Lili was right to be wary of Katayev, who, when he noticed that Mayakovsky was depressed, began to make fun of him. But Mayakovsky, that past master at bandying words, was—Roskin recalled—"taciturn, out of humor, and not in the mood for jokes."

Around ten o'clock, after the horse racing, Nora arrived in company with Yanshin and the actor Boris Livanov. When she came in, she was greeted by Mayakovsky with the words "I knew you would come here!" He was very somber, and also drunk, recalled Nora, who had never seen him in that state before. Mayakovsky certainly drank every day, but only wine and champagne, not vodka, and according to Nora he was hardly ever under the influence. But this evening he had already been drinking in Gendrikov while he waited for the guests who never came.

Both Nora and Mayakovsky felt offended and hurt. Nora, because Mayakovsky would not leave her in peace as he had promised; Mayakovsky, because she had deceived him when she said she was not going to Katayev's. They talked so loudly that the other guests could not help overhearing, not least Yanshin, who "saw everything and braced himself for a scandal." In the midst of their angry exchanges Mayakovsky suddenly let slip a "Dear God!" When Nora, taken aback, wondered how such a phrase could escape Mayakovsky's lips and asked if he was a believer, he replied: "Oh, these days I don't know myself what I believe in." After a while, to avoid attracting attention, Mayakovsky took out a finely bound notebook, wrote something in it, tore out the page, and handed it to Roskin to give to Nora, who was sitting three seats away. "It struck me as odd," said Roskin later, "that someone who was so fond of quality, in hard-wearing shoes, with an expensive fountain pen which he was ready to fall on his knees to get back, would without thinking rip out pages from such a book." Nora replied, and the altercation turned into an exchange of crumpled scraps of paper with Roskin as the intermediary. "A lot of what was written was hurtful, we insulted each other royally, in a stupid, sad, unnecessary way," Nora recollected.

The mood of irritation was heightened by the constant taunts from Olesha and Katayev. On one occasion when Mayakovsky left the table and went into the adjoining room, Katayev's wife became uneasy over his prolonged absence. "Don't worry," Katayev commented, "Mayakovsky won't shoot himself. These modern lovers don't shoot themselves." Nora went after Mayakovsky, who had heard everything. He was sitting in an armchair drinking champagne. When she sat down on the arm of the chair and stroked his head he replied with an irritated "Take your bloody legs away" and threatened to tell Yanshin about their relationship in front of all the guests:

> He was very brusque and insulted me in every possible way. But I no longer felt humiliated and hurt by his boorish ways and his insults because I understood that what I had before me was an unhappy, seriously ill person who at any moment could come out with the most ridiculous remarks, that Mayakovsky could precipitate an unnecessary scandal, behave in a manner that was unworthy of him and make a fool of himself in front of this chance company of people. [. . .] I was seized by such feelings of tenderness and love for him. I tried to talk some sense into him, begged him to calm down, was loving and tender toward him. But my tenderness irritated him and made him angry, furious.
>
> He pulled out a revolver and declared that he was going to shoot himself. Threatened to kill me too. Aimed the muzzle of the revolver at me. I realized that my presence was only making his nerves even worse and I decided not to stay there any longer [. . .].

The guests began leaving toward half past two in the morning. In the hallway Mayakovsky suddenly gave Nora a friendly glance and said: "Norkochka, please stroke my head. You are so good, really, so good . . ." The company left the party together: Mayakovsky, Nora and Yanshin, Roskin, and the journalist Vasily Reginin, who had arrived late, about half past midnight. Mayakovsky and Nora walked together, sometimes in front of the others, sometimes behind them. He was once again as brooding as a thundercloud, and again he threatened to blurt out everything to Yanshin; several times he called out to him, but when Yanshin asked what he wanted, he replied: "Another time."

Nora was crying and on the point of collapse. She went down on her knees to Mayakovsky and begged him not to say anything— which he agreed to on condition that she promise to meet him the following morning (i.e., later the same morning). She had a rehearsal with the director of the theater, Vladimir Nemirovich-Danchenko, at half past ten, and they agreed that he would come for her at eight o'clock. Before they parted at Nora's front door, he nevertheless said to Yanshin that he had to talk to him the following day.

At the same time as the nocturnal company was strolling home through the empty Moscow streets, Lili and Osip were sleeping on the boat from England to Holland, on the way to Berlin via Amsterdam. Luxury class, with a private bathroom, cost four guineas extra, Lili noted in her diary. They themselves were traveling in the cheapest class, but they had their own cabin and "it doesn't roll at all."

14 APRIL

Monday, 14 April, was an unusually sunny and pleasant spring day. It was also the first day of Easter week. At 9:15 Mayakovsky rang Nora and told her he would come and fetch her—by taxi, as his chauffeur had the day off. Nora met him at the front door and noticed that he looked worn out, which was not too surprising, as he had only slept for a few hours and moreover had alcohol in his body. "Look how sunny it is," she said, and asked if he was still brooding over "yesterday's nonsense." He couldn't care less about the sunshine, he replied, but "there'll be no more nonsense": "I have realized that I can't do it because of my mother, and she is the only person I care about. We can talk about all that when we get home."

At ten o'clock or a few minutes before, they reached Lubyanka Passage. Nora explained yet again that she had an important rehearsal at half past ten which she couldn't miss. Mayakovsky asked the taxi driver to wait and they went up to his room. "Not this theater again!" he exploded. "I hate it, to hell with it! I can't stand it any longer, I'm not going to let you go to your rehearsal or even to leave this room!" He locked the door from the inside and stuck the key in his pocket, so agitated and overwrought that he failed to notice he had still not taken off his coat and hat. Nora sat down on the divan, and Mayakovsky threw himself down on the floor beside her and began to cry. She removed his coat and hat, stroked his head and tried to calm him.

After a while there was a knock at the door. It was a courier from Gosizdat with a volume of the *Soviet Encyclopaedia*. Mayakovsky asked him to leave it with the woman who lived in the room next door, with whom he had left money in case he was away when the courier came. He was "very rude" to him, the neighbor recalled, but a few minutes later when he knocked on her door to ask for some matches he was "very calm." His nerves were strained to the utmost, and his state of mind veered from one extreme to the other. "Vladimir Vladimirovich strode quickly up and down the room, almost running," Nora recalled:

> He demanded that I stay in that room with him there and then, without explaining to Yanshin. Waiting for an apartment was stupid, he said. I ought to give up the theater immediately and not go to that day's rehearsal. He would go to the theater himself and say that I was not coming back. The theater would get by without me. And he would talk to Yanshin himself; he would never let me go to him again. He would lock me in the room, take himself off to the theater, and then buy everything I needed to live here. I would have everything I had at home. I mustn't be afraid to leave the theater. His attitude to me would soon make me forget the theater. He would devote his whole time to my life in its entirety, from its most serious aspects to the wrinkles in my stockings. I shouldn't be put off by the difference in our ages: he could be youthful and happy, after all. What had happened yesterday was repulsive, he realized that. But it would never be repeated. Yesterday we had both behaved stupidly, in a vulgar fashion, shamefully. He had been unforgivably brusque, and today he despised himself for it. But we shouldn't think about that any longer. That's right, just as if nothing had happened. He had already destroyed the pages of his notebook that contained yesterday's exchanges.

Nora replied that she loved him but that she could not simply stay there without talking to Yanshin, nor could she leave the theater. Did he not understand that this would create a vacuum in her life that would be impossible to fill? And that he would be the first to feel the effects? No, she had to go to the rehearsal, then she would go home and tell Yanshin everything, and in the evening she would move in with Mayakovsky for good. But Mayakovsky would not agree to this, insisting that everything should be done at once or not at all. When she repeated that she could not do what he wanted, the following dialogue unfolded:

"So you intend to go to the rehearsal?" he asked.
"Yes, I do."
"And you intend to meet Yanshin?"
"Yes."
"Very well! In that case you can go right now, at once!"
I said it was too early for the rehearsal and I would go in twenty minutes.
"No, no, go right now."
"But will I see you again today?" I asked.
"I don't know."
"But you can at least ring me about five o'clock?"
"Yes, yes, yes."

After this Mayakovsky strode quickly over to the writing desk. Nora heard the rustle of paper but could not see what he was doing, as his body was in the way of the desk. Then he opened the desk drawer, banged it shut again and went back to walking round the room.

"Will you not even see me out?" I asked.
He came toward me, kissed me and said quite calmly and with great tenderness:
"No, my girl, go yourself. . . . Don't worry about me . . ."
He smiled and asked:
"I'll phone. Have you got money for a taxi?"
"No."
He gave me twenty rubles.
"So you'll phone?"
"Yes, yes."

With that promise Nora left the room. When she was on the other side of the door she heard a shot. She screamed and rushed back inside. Mayakovsky was lying on his back on the floor with his head toward the door, a Mauser pistol beside him. "What have you done? What have you done?" she screamed, but received no answer. Mayakovsky looked at her and tried to lift his head, he seemed to want to say something, but, Nora recalled, "his eyes were already dead." Then his head dropped.

Nora rushed out of the room and called for help—"Mayakovsky has shot himself!" Those neighbors who were at home, who had heard the shot but not understood what had happened, rushed out of their rooms and into Mayakovsky's room together with Nora. One of them, the electrician Krivtsov, immediately rang for an ambulance: "Mayakovsky was lying on the floor with a gunshot wound in his chest," while "Polonskaya was standing on the threshold in floods of tears, screaming for help," he declared when interviewed by the police. The other neighbors urged Nora to go down to the courtyard and meet the ambulance, which only took five minutes to get there— events had thus unfolded with amazing speed, it was only about a quarter of an hour since Mayakovsky and Nora had reached Luby- anka Passage. Once inside the room, the doctors were able to confirm that Mayakovsky was dead. According to one of the neighbors, the son of the Yuly Balshin, who had rented the room to Mayakovsky in 1919, he survived for about five minutes after shooting himself.

According to what Nora told the police later, when she realized that Mayakovsky was dead, she became "unwell," left the apartment, and went off to the theater—in the same taxi that she and Mayak- ovsky had arrived in. Of course, there was no question of any re- hearsal. Instead, she wandered around the courtyard behind the theater while she waited for Yanshin, who was due at eleven o'clock. When he arrived, she told him what had happened and phoned her mother, asking her to come and take her home with her. She was soon tracked down and called back to Lubyanka Passage for questioning.

During her interrogation by the head of the investigative team, Ivan Syrtsov, Nora maintained that she "had not had a sexual rela- tionship with [Mayakovsky], although he was insistent, but I was not willing." She also declared that she had explained to him that "I do not love him, do not intend to live with him, and have no intention of leaving my husband." Asked what she thought was the motive for his suicide, she stated that this was "unknown" to her, but she assumed that "the main reason" was her "refusal to reciprocate his feelings, together with the fiasco of *The Bathhouse* and his delicate mental state."

As we can see, these statements differ fundamentally from the version she presented in her memoirs and from which the above quotations are taken. The simplest—and most plausible—explanation is that during the police interrogation Nora lied out of consideration for Yanshin, something that is substantiated by a contemporary source, according to which she is supposed to have told the chief investigator that she had lived with Mayakovsky but that she then asked him to omit this from the transcript of the interrogation. When her memoirs were written eight years later, she was long divorced from Yanshin and had no need for such precautions, especially as the memoirs were not written for publication.

THE NATIONALIZATION OF A POET

Pavel Lavut arrived shortly after the ambulance. The day before, he had agreed with Mayakovsky that they would meet in Gendrikov Alley at eleven o'clock. On arrival he was told by the shocked housekeeper, Pasha, that Mayakovsky had shot himself in the room in Lubyanka Passage, and he immediately took a taxi there. When he came into the room he saw Mayakovsky lying outstretched on the floor with his eyes half-open. When he felt his forehead, it was still warm. He grabbed the telephone on Mayakovsky's desk and phoned the Central Committee of the Communist Party, the Soviet Writers' Federation, and Mayakovsky's sister Lyudmila. While he was talking on the phone he saw through the doorway Nora, on tottering legs, being led into the apartment by the assistant to the director of the Art Theater on their way to the chief investigator, who was waiting in the adjoining room.

Soon "all Moscow" heard the news, which many at first believed to be an April Fool's joke, as 14 April was 1 April according to the old calendar (which the church still followed). A stream of Mayakovsky's friends arrived: Aseyev, Tretyakov, Katanyan, and Pasternak—whose initial reaction was to summon the widow of the recently executed Vladimir Sillov, "as something told me that this shocking event could help her find release for her own sorrow." The stairs were crowded with curious onlookers and newspaper reporters eager to cross-examine the neighbors about what had happened. Before long representatives of the security organs were also on the scene. The headquarters of

OGPU were just across the street, but their swiftness in arriving was not only because of their geographic proximity but because Mayakovsky's death was regarded as an affair of national interest. This is borne out not only by the number of their agents who hurried to the scene, but also by their rank. Alongside Yakov Agranov, who since October 1929 had been the head of the OGPU's "secret department," was a high-ranking official from counterespionage, Semyon Gendin, together with two heads of operations, Aliyevsky and Rybkin.

These two went through Mayakovsky's letters, which were then put in a drawer which was sealed. The Mauser pistol was confiscated by Gendin, and the chief investigator took responsibility for a sum of cash amounting to 2,500 rubles. When the medical examiners had done their bit, Mayakovsky's body was moved over to the couch to be photographed. After consulting over the telephone with Stanislav Messing, OGPU's deputy vice-chairman with responsibility for foreign espionage, Agranov ordered that the body be taken to the apartment in Gendrikov Alley. Mayakovsky's biography was now in the hands of the Soviet state in the shape of the OGPU, as the inquisitive journalists soon became aware. Later the same day a ukase went out to all newspaper offices to the effect that all information about the suicide had to go through the ROSTA news agency. Only one evening paper in Leningrad managed to print an announcement before the information clampdown came into force.

1,700 GRAMS OF GENIUS

Only a few hours after the fateful shot, Mayakovsky lay on the couch in his room in Gendrikov Alley dressed in a light-blue, open-necked shirt and with his body partially covered by a traveling rug. The little apartment gradually filled up with people in a deep state of shock. Aseyev threw himself on the normally so reserved Lev Grinkrug, who was weeping loudly, saying: "I shall never forget that it was you who reconciled us." Shklovsky was in tears; Pasternak was falling into everyone's arms and crying uncontrollably. When Kirsanov arrived, he went straight into Mayakovsky's room and rushed out again weeping. Mayakovsky's mother was grieving in silence. One of his sisters, Lyudmila, kissed her brother, and her tears ran down his dead face,

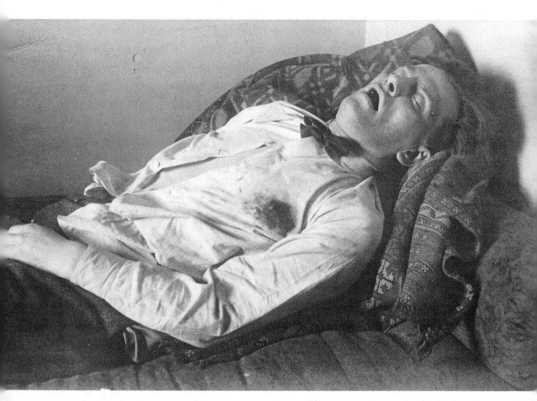

This photograph, taken after Mayakovsky was lifted from the floor and put on the couch in his room, was unknown for many years. It was found after the fall of the Soviet regime in the dossier about Mayakovsky's suicide kept in Nikolay Yezhov's archive.

while Olga was quite beside herself. She had arrived on her own, after her mother and Lyudmila. She was "noisy and demanding," Pasternak recalled, and "her voice floated into the room ahead of her":

> As she came up the stairs alone, she was talking loudly to someone, obviously addressing her brother. Then she actually appeared, walking past everyone, as if they were so much rubbish, and as she reached her brother's door she threw up her hands and stopped.
>
> "Volodya!" she screamed, and her voice rang through the entire house. A moment passed. "He won't speak!" she shouted even louder. "He's won't say anything. He won't answer. Volodya! Volodya!! How horrible!"

> She began to collapse. They caught her and quickly tried to bring her around. But she had hardly come to herself when she greedily moved towards the body and hastily renewed her unquenched dialogue, sitting at his feet.
>
> (*THE VOICE OF PROSE*, TRANS. CHRISTOPHER BARNES [1986])

Also present in Gendrikov, of course, was Yakov Agranov, who was taking care of the practical arrangements in consultation with the highest political and police authorities. From the following day onward Mayakovsky was to lie in state at the Writers' Club, and the funeral was arranged for 17 April. The date had been chosen to give Lili and Osip time to get back to Moscow. At this very moment they were in Amsterdam, where that very day they sent Mayakovsky a postcard depicting the *hollandse bloemenvelden*, blissfully unaware that it would never reach the addressee: "Volosik! It's absolutely great the way the flowers grow here! Real carpets—tulips, hyacinths, and narcissi. Whatever you turn to, everything Dutch is terribly indecent! We kiss your [i.e., Mayakovsky's and Bulka's] little muzzles. Lili, Osya."

Lili and Osip spent the day in Amsterdam sightseeing. The diamond workshop they wanted to visit was shut; instead, they met Hassidic Jews returning from the synagogue in black hats and with their prayer books under their arms. They were struck by the Corbusier-inspired architecture in the newly built districts and by the countless cigar and pipe shops. "We bought Volodya a cane and a box of cigars," Lili noted in her diary. "Now we're off to Berlin."

"On 15 April we arrived at the Kurfürstenhotel in Kurfürstenstrasse as usual," Osip recalled. "We were given a hearty welcome by the proprietress and the dog, Schneidt. The porter handed us a few letters and a telegram from Moscow. 'From Volodya,' I thought, stuffing it in my pocket without opening it. We took the lift up to our room, unpacked, and only afterward did we slit open the telegram." It was signed Lyova and Yanya, and read: "This morning Volodya took his own life."

"At our embassy they already knew everything," Osip further recollected. "They immediately arranged the necessary visas for us, and we traveled to Moscow that same evening."

The central role played by Agranov was a clear indication of the

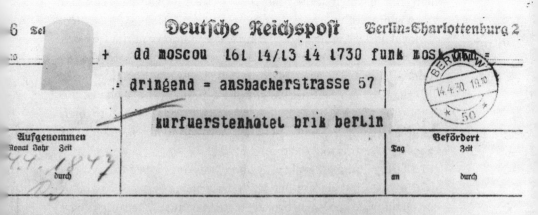

Deutsche Reichspost Berlin-Charlottenburg 2

6 Sel
+ dd moscou 161 14/13 14 1730 funk mos
dringend = ansbacherstrasse 57
kurfuerstenhotel brik berlin

Aufgenommen
Monat Jahr Zeit
durch

Befördert
Tag Zeit
an durch

= segodnia utrom volodia pokontschil soboi lewa fiania +

The telegram informing Lili and Osip about Mayakovsky's suicide, signed Lyova (Grinkrug) and Yanya (Agranov): "This morning Volodya killed himself."

state's takeover of Mayakovsky's biography, which started as soon as he was dead. Other signs of this process were the decision to take his death mask, a task carried out by the sculptor Konstantin Lutsky at 6:30 p.m., and the even greater infringement of Mayakovsky's privacy which took place an hour and a half later, when the head of the Brain Institute and his colleagues arrived to remove his brain.

The institute had been set up in 1928 to study the brains of geniuses with a view to discovering the materialistic foundations of their genius. The jewel in the institute's collection, which had by the way been the raison d'être for its foundation, was the brain which, six years earlier, had been removed from Lenin's cranium. Now it was Mayakovsky's turn. "The skull came apart and in it lay the brain," recalled the artist Nikolay Denisovsky, who was present during the operation as they were short of staff. "Then they took it out and said that this was really a large brain." The procedure made a gruesome impression on those who were present in the apartment, not least when the brain was borne out in a vessel covered with a white cloth.

Mayakovsky's brain turned out to weigh 1,700 grams. This was 360 grams more than Lenin's, which meant a bit of a headache for the ideologues of the Brain Institute, who had already had to wrestle with the problem that the weight of the brain of the leader of the Revolution was less than the norm—an embarrassing fact which was corrected by a downward adjustment of the normal weight of 1,395–1,400 grams to 1,300 grams.

Toward midnight Mayakovsky's body was transferred to the Writers' Club. But first yet another death mask had to be taken, as a bit of skin on the right cheek had been torn off, presumably because Lutsky had not used enough petroleum jelly. The person called in to take a new death mask was none other than Sergey Merkurov—the same Merkurov whom Mayakovsky had been ridiculing for years with his "antimonument poems": the very symbol of the "heavyweight bronze" and "sickly marble worship" he had so despised.

If anything deserves to be called "the irony of fate," it is this.

BLAME NO ONE FOR MY DEATH

However the authorities regarded Mayakovsky, they were now faced with an extremely embarrassing fait accompli, namely, that the poet of the Revolution had committed suicide and had done so during the first five-year plan, right in the middle of the country's definitive transformation into a socialist state. It was the second important suicide inflicted on the Soviet Union; the first being Sergey Yesenin's, five years earlier. But Mayakovsky's death was from an ideological perspective significantly more troublesome for the authorities, who were deeply worried about how the suicide would be perceived. Through its agents in the field, the OGPU tried to gauge the mood of the people. One common explanation was that the motives for the suicide were private and that "Mayakovsky shot himself because of a woman." It was an analysis which suited those in power and which also became the official one when news of Mayakovsky's suicide was made public in *Pravda* on 15 April:

Yesterday, on 14 April, at 10:15 a.m., the poet Vladimir Mayakovsky committed suicide in his study (3 Lubyanka Passage). According to what the head of the investigation, Comrade Syrtsov, has told our colleague, the early stages of the investigation show that the suicide was motivated by purely personal considerations, quite unconnected to the poet's public and literary activities. The suicide was preceded by a long-term illness from which the poet never properly recovered.

The phrase "long-term illness," which referred to influenza, breathed new life into the rumors about syphilis which had pursued Mayakovsky ever since Gorky and Chukovsky had first started spreading them in 1918 (see page 131). Even though the authorities were pleased to see the suicide ascribed to private motives, it was less agreeable that the great poet of the Revolution should be associated with a shameful illness. To prevent the further spread of the rumors, therefore, it was decided to carry out a postmortem on Mayakovsky, and this was done on the night of 16–17 April. The postmortem showed that there was no ground for the rumors, and this was immediately conveyed to those closest to Mayakovsky. However, this did not prevent Gorky from stating in a newspaper article that it was Mayakovsky's realization that he was "incurably ill" and that the illness "compromised his human dignity" which made him take his own life. "I knew the man and never believed him," he added for safety's sake in a private letter to Nikolay Bukharin.

The denial of the suicide's "connection with the poet's public and literary activities" may have been deeply un-Marxist, but it is supported by the farewell letter that Mayakovsky left behind and which Agranov laid hands on as soon as he saw it. On 14 April he read it out to several of Mayakovsky's friends and the following day it was printed in *Pravda* and a few other newspapers:

To everyone
  Blame no one for my death, and please don't gossip. The deceased really hated gossip.
  Mama, my sisters and comrades, forgive me—this is not a good method (I don't recommend any others) but I have no other way out.

Lili—love me.

Comrade government, my family is Lili Brik, mama, my sisters and Veronika Vitoldovna Polonskaya.

If you grant them a bearable life—thank you.

Give the unfinished poems to the Briks, they understand them.

As they say—
    "the game is over"
love's boat
has smashed against the reef of the everyday.
I'm quits with life
And there is no reason
To keep a record of pains
    cares and quarrels.
Be happy,
Vladimir Mayakovsky
    12/IV–30

Comrades in VAPP, don't call me a faintheart *
Seriously—there was nothing else to do
Greetings
Tell Yermilov I'm sorry I took the placard down, ought to have had
our quarrel out

                    VM

There are 2,000 rubles in the table drawer pay the tax with them.
Take the rest from Gosizdat

                    VM

As we can see, the letter is dated 12 April—it was this that Mayakovsky hid from Lavut when the latter called on him in the forenoon; it was this that he called his "letter to the government" when he spoke to Nora later the same day. The bullet which pierced his heart on the morning of 14 April had therefore been designed to carry out its task

---

* VAPP was the all–Soviet Union equivalent of RAPP, which was confined to the Soviet Russian republic.

two days earlier. The formula "Blame no one" was a standard phrase in such letters, but in Mayakovsky's case it was also an echo of the suicide's entreaty in "About This," written seven years earlier—see page 247.

A CRAFTY COMEDY

Mayakovsky's private motives were also underlined in the obituary "In Memory of a Friend" which was printed in the same issue of *Pravda* that carried the official death notice and was signed not only by Mayakovsky's writer friends but also by three Chekists: Agranov, Gorb, and Elbert. "For us, who knew and loved him, Mayakovsky and suicide are two irreconcilable things, and if suicide in general can never be justified in our circles, what words of anger and bitter reproach shall we not heap on Mayakovsky!"

No, suicide was something unacceptable in a socialist state, which explains the eagerness of the authorities to stress that Mayakovsky's death had its origins in his private life. Their eagerness was in direct proportion to the information of an opposite nature which they were privy to, thanks to their agents. Of the many intelligence reports that landed on Agranov's desk in the days after Mayakovsky's death, it was clear that in "writers' and artists' circles" people totally rejected "romantic motives" as the explanation for his suicide. "They are saying that the motive is much deeper and more important," wrote agent Petrov in a report. "Mayakovsky went through a crisis already long ago, and he no longer believed himself in what he wrote and hated it." What the papers had been writing was seen in these circles as "a crafty comedy for idiots": "For foreign countries, for public opinion abroad, Mayakovsky's death has to be presented as if it was a revolutionary poet who had died because of a personal drama."

On the day that Mayakovsky shot himself, the literary scholar Ilya Gruzdyev wrote to Gorky in Sorrento that "the suicide cannot be explained away by personal reasons," and according to agent Petrov several writers saw it as a purely political protest. The reactions were said to be identical in Moscow and in Leningrad. "One of the fundamental ideas behind these reactions is the claim that Mayakovsky's death is a challenge to the Soviet authorities and a condemnation of their policies in the field of literature," the same agent wrote in another report. "Another thesis is: 'If not even Mayakovsky could stand it any longer, that means that the situation in the literary world is really dreadful.'" According to the writer Anatoly Mariengof, Mayakovsky, during one of his last appearances, had let slip a comment about "how difficult it was to live and create in our 'hopeless time.'" Another writer, Lev Gumilyovsky, said that he shared the widespread belief that "the main reasons for the poet's death are sociopolitical" and that writers felt pressured to write "about prescribed, topical subjects." "A very large number of people are convinced that this death has a political background, that it is not about some 'love story' but about disillusionment with Soviet society." The times, Gumilyovsky continued, are "very difficult for an honest writer" and "very favorable to charlatans who regard themselves as writers only because RAPP has asked them to become members." Alexey Tolstoy, who had returned six years earlier from his self-imposed exile in Berlin, says that he is "ashamed of what he is writing," another writer states that he "forces himself to write stuff he doesn't want to write."

What must really have worried the authorities was reports about suicidal tendencies among writers. The novelist Panteleymon Romanov declared that "not so long ago I was in the same state of mind [as Mayakovsky] and came close to taking my own life," and some proletarian poets were even said to have planned to "commit collective suicide to show the outside world that writers in the Soviet Union are in a bad way and are persecuted by the censors." Most alarming were reports about the well-known prose writer and playwright Mikhail Bulgakov, about whom it was "definitely claimed" that he was "next in line to kill himself." He "is not allowed to travel abroad, and they are stifling him by not allowing his latest plays to be staged, although they are hypocritical enough to claim that we need Bulgakov and that we shall put on Bulgakov. But at the same time the theaters themselves are afraid of Bulgakov's very shadow and are avoiding him so as not to come under suspicion."*

---

* On 28 March Bulgakov had written to the Soviet government complaining that he was being denied the opportunity to work. On 18 April, the same day on which the report containing the information that Bulgakov was "next in line to commit suicide" was written, he received a phone call from Stalin, who promised that every-

17 APRIL

At six o'clock in the evening of 16 April the train from Berlin with Lili and Osip on board rolled into Negoreloye, the border station between White Russia and Poland which Mayakovsky had passed through so many times during his trips abroad. There they were met by Vasily Katanyan, who had received special permission to travel into the border zone "to meet the late Comrade Mayakovsky's family."

Apart from the telegram from Lyova and Agranov and a few notices in German newspapers, they did not know what had happened. Neither were they aware that Mayakovsky had left a farewell letter. Katanyan told them everything he knew and quoted the letter from memory, and at the railway station in Minsk they managed to get hold of the previous day's *Pravda*, where it was printed in full.

When they reached Moscow the following morning they were met by friends at the railway station. According to Luella, Lili had changed so much during those last few days that she scarcely recognized her. They went straight to the Writers' Club, which was housed in what had once been the palace of the Counts Sollogub, the model for the Rostov family home in Tolstoy's *War and Peace*. In the same room where a few months earlier the living Mayakovsky had recited "At the Top of My Voice," his coffin now stood on a red cube, lit by spotlights, lined with red material, and decorated with flowers and wreaths. Death had already managed to leave its imprint: his lips were blue; his hair contained traces from the making of the death masks.

"Lili's arrival precipitated a fresh outburst of despair from Olga Vladimirovna," recalled Vasily Katanyan. "She fell to her knees in the middle of the room and cried out: 'It is time to sit at someone else's feet! / I sing today / a painted woman / with fire-red hair . . .'" (from "The Backbone-Flute"). Mayakovsky's mother was calmer, simply saying to Lili: "If you had been here this wouldn't have happened." Osip, Lili, and Luella remained there for most of the day. From time

---

thing would come out all right—which in a manner of speaking it did. The next day he was made an assistant director at the Moscow Art Theater, although this post was a pure insult for a writer of Bulgakov's caliber.

Mayakovsky lying in state in the Writers' House in Moscow. *To the right of Lili and Osip,* Mayakovsky's mother; *standing to the left behind Osip,* Semyon Kirsanov; *in the shade,* Rita Rayt. The pair of eyes seen behind the lady in a beret to the right behind Osip belongs to Yakov Agranov.

to time Lili went and kissed Mayakovsky on the forehead, urging Luella to do the same: "Go up and kiss Volodya, my dear."

During the three days when Mayakovsky lay in state thousands of people filed past the coffin, which was guarded by an honor guard comprising both civilians and soldiers. Lili and Osip took their turn, as well as Luella, Pasternak, Aseyev, Kirsanov, Tretyakov, Kamensky, Rodchenko, Katanyan, and Lunacharsky, together with Mayakovsky's colleagues in RAPP: Yermilov, Libedinsky, Fadeyev, and Averbakh. Another member of the honor guard was Artyomy Khalatov, who only a week before had given orders that the tribute to Mayakovsky in *Press and Revolution* be removed. As chairman of the burial committee, Khalatov bore the greatest responsibility for the first three days of Mayakovsky's posthumous existence. How ironic can fate be allowed to get?

So ironic that Khalatov was one of the speakers at the memorial service, which started at three o'clock and which was opened by Sergey Tretyakov. The other speakers included the head of RAPP,

The memorial service in the yard of the Writers' House in Moscow. The speaker on the balcony is the former commissar of enlightenment, Anatoly Lunacharsky.

Leopold Averbakh, but also friends and sympathizers of Mayakovsky. Kirsanov read "At the Top of My Voice," and a deeply moved Lunacharsky made a speech in which he declared that Mayakovsky "was first and foremost a piece of intense, burning life" who became all the more so when he made himself into "the spokesman for a great social movement." "Listen to the resounding quality of his songs," urged the former people's commissar. "Nowhere will you find the least falseness, the least doubt, the least hesitation."

When the tributes were over, the coffin, draped in red and black, was carried out by "ten comrades," among them Osip, Aseyev, and

The coffin is carried to the truck. Among the bearers are, on the left side of the coffin, Artyom Khalatov in his Persian cap, on the right side, Nikolay Aseyev, and, behind him, Vasily Katanyan. Lili's Kirghiz friend Yusup Abdrakhmanov is seen right behind the coffin.

Tretyakov and the RAPP members Averbakh, Fadeyev, and Libedinsky. One of the other pallbearers was—Khalatov, who distinguished himself by failing to take off his Persian cap, a detail which was omitted from *Literaturnaya Gazeta*'s account of how the coffin, "swaying slowly," sailed forth "over the sea of bared heads." Out in the street mounted police tried to hold back the surging masses. People were hanging out of windows and trees and off lampposts, and the roofs of the houses were black with curious onlookers. The coffin was placed on a truck. "Alongside the coffin on the steel-gray platform," the newspaper account continued, "lies a wreath composed of sledge-hammers, flywheels, and screws. The caption reads: 'An iron wreath for an iron poet.' The truck begins to move off in the direction of Arbat Square, and after it follows the many-headed, boundless human crowd. As far as the eye can see the way is filled with tightly packed ranks of people, some of whom make their way along parallel streets and side alleys."

The truck which took Mayakovsky to his final rest had had a makeover by his artist friends Vladimir Tatlin, David Sterenberg, and "John" Levin and had been transformed into a steel-gray tank. Behind it there followed Mayakovsky's Renault and other cars containing, among others, Mayakovsky's mother and sisters. Lili and Osip made the whole of the long journey to the crematorium at the Don Monastery cemetery on foot, together with Luella. About sixty thousand people followed the truck, according to Olesha, who in a letter to Meyerhold (who was at a guest appearance in Berlin) described how the police shot in the air so that the coffin could be carried in through the door of the crematorium. There was an enormous crush of people. "We threw ourselves down on a bench, and Lilichka said she couldn't go any further and that we should stay sitting there till it was over," Luella recalled: "Alexandra Alexeyevna and Mayakovsky's sisters arrived in a car and continued straight in to the crematorium. Suddenly a mounted policeman called out: 'Brik, where's Brik, they're looking for Brik.' Alexandra Alexeyevna did not wish to take her leave of her son and allow the cremation to take place without Lili Yuryevna."

Inside the crematorium Mayakovsky's friends paid him a last farewell. Several of the funeral guests noticed the toe irons of his shoes, which were sticking up out of the open coffin and which Mayakovsky had said would "last for eternity." Then they played the "Internationale," which at this time was the national anthem of the Soviet Union; the coffin shook and sank slowly down toward the crematorium oven. Some of the guests went down a staircase to observe through a spyhole how the coffin and its contents were transformed into ashes—everything, except the metal fittings on his shoes, which indeed proved to be more durable than the poet's heart.

16

A GAME WITH LIFE AS THE STAKE

We are partly to blame. Because we did not write about his poetry, did not supply that wind that bears up the thin spider's web of poetic flight. But, alas, we are not held responsible. . . . He was tired of being a twenty-year-old when he was 36, he was a person who never grew older.

Viktor Shklovsky to Yury Tynyanov 1930/31

"Through his letter Mayakovsky united us for ever," Nora wrote in her memoirs. But the letter not only ensured her place in Mayakovsky's life story, it also resulted in her being singled out as the direct cause of his death—the "female" for whose sake he shot himself. Perhaps it was in order to defend her from such accusations that Mayakovsky included her in the list of his family, albeit only at the end, after Lili, his mother and his sisters—a canonization of their relationship which in its turn caused her marriage to Yanshin to be dissolved.

However, among the thousands of people who fol-

Toward the end of his life, Yefim Royak, a student of Kazimir Malevich's, made this gouache of Mayakovsky, blind to what was going on around him.

lowed Mayakovsky's coffin to the crematorium at the Don monastery Nora was not present. The decision to stay away was not her own but taken after pressure from Lili, who summoned her the same day. "We had a very honest conversation," Nora recalled. "I told her everything about my relationship with Vladimir Vladimirovich, and about 14 April. While I was talking she said several times: 'Yes, that's typical Volodya.' She told me about their relationship, about their breakup, about how he wanted to shoot himself because of her." Before they separated Lili impressed on Nora that she should "absolutely not" be present at the funeral as "the philistines' curiosity and interest" in her person could provoke "unnecessary incidents." "Don't poison the family's final farewell to Volodya by your presence," Lili urged her.

In the absence of a will Mayakovsky's farewell letter was the sole document with instructions about the disposal of his estate, and since Nora was named as a member of the family, she was in principle also entitled to a share. When she was summoned to the Kremlin a few months later to discuss the matter, she first consulted Lili, who advised her to waive her right of inheritance, that is, her entitlement to royalties from Mayakovsky's works—partly because his mother and sisters regarded Nora as the sole cause of his death and could not bear to hear her name mentioned, and partly because Lili had been asked by government sources to advise Nora to renounce her rights. Nora obeyed this time too, although she "felt as if by doing this I was drawing a line through everything that was then [. . .] so dear to me." Eight years later, when she committed her memoirs to paper, she could not free herself from the suspicion that Lili was guided by other considerations: namely, that if Nora were to achieve official status as Mayakovsky's "girlfriend," this would by the same token reduce Lili's role in his life story. It is hard not to agree with Nora's belated insight.

From the conversation in the Kremlin, Nora was given to understand that the authorities had no intention of respecting Mayakovsky's last will and testament. Instead, the government functionaries who met her hinted that she would be entitled to a holiday trip at the state's cost as compensation, an offer the cynicism of which she found devastating. Even after a further conversation with the same official the question remained unresolved. As far as Nora was concerned, that is to say. Through a decision taken by the All-Union Executive Committee and the Council of People's Commissars, Lili was granted half of Mayakovsky's royalties while his mother and sisters were to share the remainder. By this means Nora was deleted from Mayakovsky's life, and she was not to resurface until a good half century later, during the perestroika, when her memoirs were published. They came out in uncensored form only in the autumn of 2005.

Tatyana, who was living in Warsaw, found out about Mayakovsky's suicide four days later. "I am utterly devastated by today's papers," she wrote to her mother on 18 April. "For God's sake send me all the clippings from the fourteenth, etc. This is a dreadful shock for me. You understand. . ." Her sister Lyudmila, who, thanks to Mayakovsky's efforts, was now living in Paris, had sent a telegram to the Viscount du Plessix telling him not to show her any Russian newspapers, but it was no use, Tatyana reported to her mother, for "as well as the Russian papers, unfortunately, there are also foreign ones, so all their efforts were in vain."

The attempts by Tatyana's sister and husband to conceal the tragedy from her were prompted not only by concern for her mental health but also out of consideration for her physical state. She was in fact in the fourth month of pregnancy. "I was of course touched by their consideration," she wrote, " [but] I have been feeling fine physically the whole time." In her next letter, of 2 May, she returned to Mayakovsky's suicide, but only some way into the letter, among "other questions," in response to her mother's anxiety that it was she who had been the cause of it. "Dear little mummy, I have not believed for one second that it was I who was the cause. Indirectly, yes, since all of this naturally upset his nerves, but not directly, and in general it was not a question of a single cause but of several, plus his illness." That Tatyana's mother was seriously worried that her daughter was ultimately to blame emerges from the fact that she wrote to Vasily Kamensky and asked him to explain the reasons behind Mayakovsky's suicide, something that Kamensky said he was unable to do as he "still cannot view the matter calmly." "One thing is clear, however," he replied to her on 13 May, "and that is that Tatyana was one of the factors in the final equation": "I know this much from Volodya: he refused for a long time to believe in her marriage. Polonskaya was not of major importance. This last winter, Volodya (we met often) was more lonely than ever and could not find peace. He was extremely nervy and restless, and he was drinking."

WHAT DID THE OGPU KNOW AND WANT?

Although Mayakovsky wrote in his notebook that Elly should be informed "in the event of my death," she heard the news from her husband George Jones, who came home one day and told her curtly: "Your friend is dead." Many years later, with the help of the information in Mayakovsky's notebook, Lili tried to find out about Elly through the Soviet ambassador in the United States, but to no avail.

The reason why the attempts to find out about Elly came to nothing was that at that time she had remarried and had another surname, Peters. At least Lili knew that Mayakovsky had had a relationship with a Russian woman in New York which had resulted in a child. That was more than the OGPU knew. In their report on Mayakovsky's suicide, there is no mention of Elly Jones's name. Tatyana, on the other hand, immediately attracted the attention of the security organs. On 15 April—the same day on which a transcript of Nora's interrogation was delivered to Agranov—a secret agent with the code name Valentinov drew up a report containing information about Tatyana, her sister, and their mother. The date of the report suggests that it was commissioned immediately after Mayakovsky's suicide. According to the agent's information, after Mayakovsky met Tatyana in Paris he allegedly told his friends how "for the first time" he "had met a woman who was his match," and of "his love for her." But when he asked her to be his wife, she turned him down, as "she did not want to return to the USSR and do without the luxuries she had become used to in Paris." As for the "sudden [!] departure" of Tatyana's sister to Paris, it was said to have been made possible by Mayakovsky, or, possibly, by a well-known expert on antiques in Moscow.

The OGPU's interest in Tatyana can be explained by the fact that Mayakovsky's relationship with her was well known among a wide circle of people. Apart from any letters they may have found during their investigation, they also had access to photographs of her and her sister, as well as an invitation to Tatyana's wedding, which must have ended up with the OGPU via agents in Paris, possibly Zakhar Volovich.

The photo of Tatyana and the invitation to her wedding were handed over on 4 May to Semyon Gendin, whose role in the investigation of Mayakovsky's death is as central as it is mysterious. The fact that Agranov immediately rushed to the site of the suicide is not so strange; after all, he belonged to Mayakovsky's intimate circle of friends. But what function did Gendin have? It was he, we recall, who took charge of Mayakovsky's pistol after he killed himself. And it was after consulting with Gendin that the head of the investigation sent the transcript of Polonskaya's interrogation to Agranov. Who was Gendin? He was only twenty-eight years old but had been active in the Cheka for the whole of his adult life, since he was nineteen. And in February 1930 he had been appointed head of the Ninth and Tenth Sections of the Counterespionage Division with responsibility for the monitoring of Soviet citizens' contacts with foreigners and with "counterrevolutionary White émigrés."

It was in this capacity that Gendin joined in the search of Mayakovsky's room. What was it that he and the heads of operations, Rybkin and Alieyevsky, were looking for? Material compromising the Soviet government? Letters from foreign contacts—from Tatyana and her family, from Russian writers in exile? Or something even worse? Something which could cast a shadow over his and Brik's friends in the security service, whose hands—as Mayakovsky knew—were soaked in blood? Was the wording of his farewell letter, saying that he had no other way out, an expression of something more than that he had ended up on an existential one-way street? Did he feel snared in the security service's net? Did he know too much, and if he did, could there perhaps be evidence that had to be removed?*

Whatever the security organs were searching for, it is clear that they suspected there were more factors behind Mayakovsky's suicide than the purely private ones—a perception that was shared by Leon Trotsky, who refused to accept the official explanation that the suicide was "wholly unconnected to the poet's public and literary activities": "That's like saying that Mayakovsky's death had nothing to do with his revolutionary poetic works," the former war commissar commented from his exile in Constantinople. "That is both untrue and unnecessary. . . and stupid! '[Love's] boat has smashed against the reef of the everyday,' is what Mayakovsky wrote about his private life. That means precisely that his 'public and literary activities' *were no longer capable of elevating him sufficiently over everyday life [byt]* to save him from his painful inner urges."

VOLODYA OLD? NEVER!

In reality Mayakovsky's suicide was of course the result of a number of different factors: private, work related, literary-political—and purely political. During the last few years Mayakovsky had gradually come to realize that his services were no longer in demand, that he had no obvious place in the society which was taking shape and in which literature and literary politics were dominated to an ever-greater degree by individuals whose qualifications were not primarily literary. And the last six months had been one long succession of setbacks and defeats: the enforced breakup of the romance with Tatyana, the boycott of *20 Years' Work*, the fiasco with *The Bathhouse*, the

* The hypothesis occasionally put forward, that Mayakovsky did not kill himself but was murdered by the OGPU, is too speculative to be taken seriously, especially as it oozes anti-Semitism (at this time the OGPU had a strong Jewish component.) Even if Mayakovsky had influential enemies, it is difficult to see who would be interested in *murdering* him or motivated to do so. The threat posed by a possible marriage to Tatyana had after all been removed. And why choose an occasion when Mayakovsky was with Nora? These conspiracy theories find no support in the security service documentation about Mayakovsky's death, which was published in its entirety in the autumn of 2005.

humiliating capitulation to RAPP, the break with his closest friends, his persistent illness and his mental exhaustion, Nora's refusal to leave her husband when Mayakovsky demanded it.

Lili's initial reaction was one of dismay and shock. "Right now I understand nothing," she wrote to Elsa from Berlin on the very day that she received the news. "It is quite dreadful." When she wrote to her sister again two weeks later, she explained away Mayakovsky's suicide with "Volodya was terribly overstrained and couldn't cope with the situation by himself." If she and Osip had been in Moscow, "it would never have happened," she believed—a statement she repeated a further two weeks later, also this time in a letter to Elsa, adding: "I know exactly what happened, but in order to understand it one had to have known Volodya as I knew him. [. . .] Volodya behaved like a gambler, he used a brand-new revolver [actually, a Mauser pistol] which had never been fired before. Took out the magazine and left only one bullet in the bore, which means there's a fifty percent chance that it will just click. It did that thirteen years ago in Petrograd. Now he challenged fate for the second time.* He shot himself in Nora's presence, but she bears as much blame as an orange peel when one slips on it, falls over and dies."

Lili's conviction that Mayakovsky would not have shot himself if she and Osip had been at home was shared by many people, not only by Mayakovsky's mother, but also by Korney Chukovsky, who on 15 April wrote to Galina Katanyan: "I'm howling like an idiot these days. Convinced that it wouldn't have happened if Lili Yuryevna and Osip Maximovich had been here, in Moscow. . ."

The conclusion that Nora was no more to blame for Mayakovsky's suicide than an orange peel one trips over was, for all its flippancy, quite correct. Nora was the catalyst, no more. What Lili was getting at was that it was not first and foremost external factors that provoked his suicide but other, more deep-seated reasons. One of these, according to Lili, was Mayakovsky's fear of aging. He was terrified of becoming old and often returned to this theme in con-

* As we can see from the quotation below, and from the footnote on page 86, it seems that there were in fact at least two previous occasions.

versations with her. "Volodya old? Never!" was Lili's round-eyed re-action to Roman Jakobson's assertion that he could not imagine an old Mayakovsky: "He has already tried to shoot himself twice, both times leaving just the one bullet in the magazine. In the end, one of them will hit the target."

"It's not death that's terrible; the terrible thing is old age. An old person might as well just die," Mayakovsky declared, when he was thirty-three, to Natalya Ryabova, a girl he used to see during his visits to Kiev. When she asked him when old age begins, he answered that a man was old at thirty-five, a woman even earlier. "How many times did I not hear the word 'suicide' from Maya-kovsky," Lili wrote. "That he would take his own life. You're old at thirty-five! I shall live till I'm thirty, no more." His terror of be-coming old was closely connected to his fear of losing his attrac-tion for women. "Before the age of twenty-five a man is loved by all women," he stated shortly before his suicide to a twenty-five-year-old fellow writer. "After twenty-five he is also loved by all—except by the one he is in love with."

If anyone was conscious of the fact that Mayakovsky, in the words of Korney Chukovsky, was "a born suicide," it was Lili. But one did not have to know him so intimately to realize that the explanation for his killing himself lay in the internal conflicts that had always tortured him. For Marina Tsvetayeva, who since 1921 had been living in exile but who saw in Mayakovsky a poetic soul mate, his suicide was a tragic but logical result of the de-structive battle between the lyricist and the agitator within him. "For twelve years in a row Mayakovsky the human being tried to kill Mayakovsky the poet within himself; in the thirteenth year the poet stood up and killed the human being." This conclusion was shared by Pasternak, who thought that Mayakovsky shot himself "out of pride, because he condemned something within himself or around himself that his self-esteem could not become reconciled to."

If Mayakovsky's suicide was not entirely unexpected within his closest circle, it came as a complete surprise to those who only knew the public, extrovert side of him—the Futurist and Communist agi-tator, the strident performance poet, the brilliant polemicist. "Such

Mayakovsky as a eighteen-year-old art-school student. According to Viktor Shklovsky, he never grew much older.

a death is impossible to reconcile with Mayakovsky as we know him," commented Artyomy Khalatov, thereby showing that he did not know him at all. "To associate the thought of suicide with this figure is almost impossible," wrote Lunacharsky, and a leader in *Pravda* maintained that Mayakovsky's death was "so irreconcilable with the whole of his life, so impossible to discern in his writings." According to the journalist Mikhail Koltsov, it was not the real Mayakovsky who held the pistol but "someone else, by chance, who for that moment took over the weakened psyche of this social activist and revolutionary." "Incomprehensible," was the comment of the proletarian poet Demyan Bedny, who posed the rhetorical question: "What was it he was lacking?"—as if it was a question of insufficient material comforts.

THE GENERATION THAT SQUANDERED ITS POETS

Most insightful of all was Roman Jakobson, who was so shaken by Mayakovsky's suicide that he locked himself in his room in Prague in order to gather his thoughts about his dead friend. The result was a long essay, "On a Generation That Squandered Its Poets," written in May and June 1930. The generation in question was his and Mayakovsky's own, the generation which now, in 1930, was between thirty and forty-five years old, and which at the Revolution "was already formed, no longer formless clay, but not petrified either, still capable of absorbing influences and changing, still capable of understanding the world around them not statically but in its dynamics." It was a generation which, like that of the nineteenth-century romantics, burned itself out—or was burned out—in advance:

> The execution of Gumilyov (1886–1921), the long-drawn-out spiritual death-throes and unbearable physical agonies suffered by Blok (1880–1921), the painful privations and death after inhuman suffering of Khlebnikov (1885–1922), the planned suicides of Yesenin (1895–1925) and Mayakovsky (1893–1930). Thus vanished, during the twenties, between the ages of thirty and forty, poets who had

inspired a generation, and each and every one of them had a long-standing, clear-cut and insupportable sensation of being doomed. And it was not only those who were murdered or who committed suicide who went under but also those who were confined to a sickbed like Blok and Khlebnikov.*

Jakobson's article was the first serious attempt to analyze Mayakovsky's poetic world, and no one has done it better since. According to Jakobson, Mayakovsky's death was so intimately bound up with his poetry that it can only be understood in that light, and he rounded angrily on those who lacked sufficient insight to understand that. Of course it was Mayakovsky who fired the gun, no one else; everything can be found in his writings, which are "one and indivisible": "A dialectical development of one and the same theme. A symbolism of exceptional homogeneity."

While the connection between Mayakovsky's poetry and the Revolution are regarded as self-evident, critics—Jakobson believes—have overlooked another indissoluble connection in his writing, that is, "the revolution and the death of the poet." In Mayakovsky, the poet is a propitiatory sacrifice on the altar of a future resurrection: when "with rebellion / his advent announcing, / you step to meet the savior— / then I / shall root up my soul; / I'll trample it hard / till it spreads / in blood—and offer you this as a banner," he writes in "A Cloud in Trousers," and the image is developed in "About This," "where shone the poet's tattered remains / fluttering in the wind like a bloodred flag." Mayakovsky entertains the unshakeable belief that beyond "the mountains of sorrow" there is "a real earthly heaven"—but he himself will never come to experience this consummation; his lot is the redeemer's death.

---

* The feeling of being doomed was shared by many in this generation. When Meyerhold's wife, the actress Zinaida Reikh, expressed her condolences to Lili after Mayakovsky's suicide, it was with almost exactly the same words as in Jakobson's article: "I think it's the fate of some of us—born between 1890 and 1900—to age prematurely, to suck everything out of life at an early age." A few years later she herself was brutally murdered in mysterious circumstances. Someone else who talked repeatedly about the special nature of this generation to the author of this book was Nina Berberova—born in 1901.

The urge to commit suicide is the dark sounding board in May-akovsky's life, and the theme of suicide the leitmotif of his writings, from the first line to the last. The tragedy *Vladimir Mayakovsky*, the poem "Clearance Sale" ("Years and years from now / in short, when I am no longer alive— / dead from hunger, / or a pistol shot— / professors [. . .] will study / me / how, / when, / where I came from"), "The Backbone-Flute" ("More often I think: / it might be far better / to punctuate my end with a bullet" [trans. George Reavey]), "Man" ("The heart longs for the bullet / and the throat hallucinates about a razor"), the film *Not Born for Money*, "About This," the film script *How Are You?*, the unfinished play *Comedy with Suicide*, *The Bedbug*. The list of works and quotations is almost endless.

"The idea of suicide," Lili declared, "was a chronic disease with Mayakovsky, and like all chronic diseases it grew worse in unfavorable circumstances." Underlying the urge to suicide was not only the fear of aging but also the feeling of not being understood, of not being needed, of loving as few are capable of loving without feeling that he was loved in return.

Mayakovsky was a maximalist: he gave all that was in his power and demanded as much in return. "Countless numbers of people loved him and were fond of him," Lili wrote, "but that was just a drop in the ocean for someone with an 'insatiable thief' in his soul, who wanted everyone who didn't read him to read him, all those to come who didn't come, and that the one he thought didn't love him should love him." Love, art, revolution—to Mayakovsky, everything was a game with life as the stake. He played as befitted a compulsive gambler: intensely, without mercy. And he knew that if he lost, the result was hopelessness and despair.

Two weeks after his suicide, in the letter to Elsa, Lili said she was convinced that Mayakovsky would not have shot himself if she and Osip had been in Moscow. A quarter of a century later, in her memoirs, she toned down that statement with the qualification "perhaps": "If I had been at home then perhaps his death could have been postponed for a while longer; who knows?" She was right to do that. At heart she knew that sooner or later Mayakovsky would take his own life. The question was not *if* but *when* and *how*. This conviction was shared by Roman Jakobson, who toward the end of his own life summed up Mayakovsky's fate in the following words: "What he wrote in his farewell letter—'I have no other way out'—was the truth. He would have perished in any case, whatever happened, wherever he had lived, in Russia, Sweden, or America. He was a person who was singularly ill equipped for this life."

17

MAYAKOVSKY'S SECOND DEATH

Mayakovsky was and remains the best, most gifted poet of our Soviet epoch. Indifference to his memory and his work is a crime.

Joseph Stalin

In the years after Mayakovsky's suicide, the attitude toward him and his work was markedly cool. The political and literary establishment had in fact heaved a sigh of relief when this refractory giant departed the stage, and few had any interest in keeping his memory alive. His poems were seldom printed, and several of the measures that the government had decided on after his death were ignored. As the private and cooperative publishing firms had disappeared in connection with the first five-year plan, all decisions regarding publication were taken by the state-controlled publishing houses, where those who had despised and schemed against Mayakovsky while he was alive were still on the job.

Faced with this situation, Lili decided to write a let-

The Mayakovsky monument in Moscow was unveiled on 29 July 1958.
Photograph by Alexander Rodchenko's son-in-law, Nikolay Lavrentyev.

ter to Stalin. Few letters have played such a decisive role in deciding a poet's posthumous fate as this one, written five years after Mayakovsky's death:

> Dear Comrade Stalin!
> Since the poet Mayakovsky's death, all materials having a bearing on the publication of his poems and the preservation of his memory have been collected under my roof.
>
> I have his entire archive, rough drafts, notebooks, manuscripts, all his things. I am the editor of his works. People apply to me for materials, information, photographs.
>
> I have done everything in my power to ensure that his poems are printed, his possessions stored, and that the growing interest in Mayakovsky is satisfied.
>
> And interest in Mayakovsky is growing year by year.
>
> His poems have not aged, but are of great relevance today and a powerful revolutionary weapon.
>
> Almost six years have passed since Mayakovsky died, and he has no successor, but was and remains the greatest poet of our Revolution.
>
> However, far from everyone has realized this.
>
> It will soon be six years since he died, but only half of his *Collected Works* have been published and only in 10,000 copies.
>
> Negotiations for a one-volume edition have been in progress for over a year. The texts were delivered long ago, but the book has not even been sent for typesetting.
>
> His children's books are not published at all.
>
> Mayakovsky's books are not in the shops. It is impossible to get hold of them.
>
> After Mayakovsky's death and the government's decree it was decided to set up a Mayakovsky room in the Communist Academy, where all the material could be assembled. Such a room still does not exist . . .
>
> Three years ago the Workers' Council in the Proletarian District [of Moscow] commissioned me to restore Mayakovsky's last apartment to its original state and to set up a local branch library there named after Mayakovsky.

After a while I discovered that the Moscow Workers' Council had refused to contribute the small sum of money required.

It is a small wooden building consisting of four rooms (15 Gendrikov Alley). One of the rooms is Mayakovsky's. The library was to be set up in the other rooms. [. . .]

The room is very characteristic of Mayakovsky—simple, unpretentious, clean.

The little building may be pulled down any day now. Instead of regretting this in fifty years' time and then trying to collect objects with connection to the great revolutionary poet's life and work—is it not better to put everything back in its original condition while we are still alive?

After all, we are grateful today for the inkwell, table, and chair on display in the house at Pyatigorsk where Lermontov lived.

It has been suggested several times that Victory Square in Moscow and Nadezhdin Street in Leningrad should be called after Mayakovsky, but it has not happened yet.

This is the most important thing. In addition there are a series of trifles, like for example the fact that according to a decree by the People's Commissariat of Enlightenment the poems "Lenin" and "Good!" may not be named in the literature textbooks for 1935.

All of this taken together shows that our institutions do not understand Mayakovsky's enormous importance—his role as agitator, his topicality as a revolutionary.

There has been a lack of appreciation of the unique degree of interest shown in him by the Young Communists and Soviet youth in general.

This is why so little is published of him, and so slowly, instead of printing his selected poems in hundreds of thousands of copies.

This is why nobody is bothering to collect all the material relating to Mayakovsky before it is too late.

No one is thinking about preserving his memory for future generations.

I am not able by myself to overcome the lack of interest and the opposition on the part of officialdom, and so after six years I am turning to you, as I see no other possible way of ensuring that Mayakovsky's enormous revolutionary legacy is taken care of.

L. Brik

The letter is dated 24 November 1935. A few days later Lili was summoned to the Kremlin, where she was asked to present herself to Nikolay Yezhov, secretary of the Central Committee of the Communist Party and chairman of the party's Control Commission. Two years later Yezhov would be appointed commissar for internal affairs and lead the purges within the party, but for now he was just a simple—if high-ranking—party functionary: a very short, unconspicuous man with large gray eyes, dressed in a dark military shirt: "He looked like a model worker from a bad Soviet film," Lili recalled, "or perhaps even from a good one."

The conversation lasted for an hour and a half. Yezhov questioned Lili extensively, made notes, and asked if he might keep the memorandum she had drawn up with details of dates, editions, and so on. Then he read out Stalin's decision, printed in red pencil diagonally across her letter:

Comrade Yezhov, I want to draw your attention to Brik's letter. Mayakovsky was and remains the best, most gifted poet of our Soviet epoch. Indifference to his memory and his work is a crime. Brik's complaint is, in my opinion, justified. Contact her or summon her to Moscow. [. . .] See to it that everything we have left undone is done. If my help is required, I am ready.

Greetings!

J. Stalin

Stalin's words had an immediate effect. On 5 November, the second and third sentences of the decree were printed in *Pravda*, but instead of "the most gifted," there appeared "the gifted." A misprint? Or a continuation of the bureaucratic opposition that Lili complained of and that Stalin had now declared to be "a crime"? In any event, the correct wording—borrowed almost word for word from Lili's letter—

Stalin's resolution on Lili's letter.

24.11.35

Дорогой товарищ Сталин,

после смерти поэта Маяковского, все дела, связанные с изданием его
стихов и увековечением его памяти, сосредоточились у меня.

У меня весь его архив, черновики, записные книжки, рукописи, все
его вещи. Я редактирую его издания. Ко мне обращаются за матерьялами,
сведениями, фотографиями.

Я делаю всё, что от меня зависит, для того, чтобы стихи его пе-
чатались, чтобы вещи сохранились и чтобы все растущий интерес к Ма-
яковскому был хоть сколько-нибудь удовлетворен.

А интерес к Маяковскому растет с каждым годом.

Его стихи не только не устарели, но они сегодня абсолютно ак-
туальны и являются сильнейшим революционным оружием.

Прошло почти шесть лет со дня смерти Маяковского и он еще ни-
кем не заменен и, как был, так и остался, крупнейшим поэтом нашей ре-
волюции.

Но далеко не все это понимают.

Скоро шесть лет со дня его смерти, а "Полное собрание сочинений"
вышло только наполовину, и то — в количестве 10.000 экземпляров!

Уже больше года ведутся разговоры об однотомнике. Матерьял дав-
но сдан, а книга даже еще не набрана.

Детские книги не переиздаются совсем.

Книг Маяковского в магазинах нет. Купить их невозможно.

После смерти Маяковского, в постановлении правительства, было
предложено организовать кабинет Маяковского, при Комакадемии, где
должны были быть сосредоточены все матерьялы и рукописи. До сих пор
этого кабинета нет.

Матерьялы разбросаны. Часть находится в московском Литератур-
ном музее, который ими абсолютно не интересуется. Это видно хотя бы

13/29.XI.35.

was carried by *Pravda* on 17 December, the same day that Victory Square in Moscow was renamed Mayakovsky Square.

With this Mayakovsky began, in Boris Pasternak's words, to be "forcibly introduced like the potato under Catherine the Great." It was, he added, "his second death, and for this one he bore no blame." Pasternak's comment about Mayakovsky's "second death" referred to the fact that his position as the Soviet Union's number one poet demanded that his biography be remodeled according to the norms of Socialist Realism. He was now no longer a living poet but a monument having towns, streets, and squares named after it. His canonization happened at a time when the Bolshevik leaders were, in an almost manic way, crowning heroes and designating models. In every sphere of activity *one* example was paraded as the goal to aim at. Worker number one was called Stakhanov; the tractor driver with the same number—Angelina; the cotton picker—Mamlakat; the clown—Karandash; the radio announcer—Levitan; the theater director—Stanislavsky; the aviator—Tchkalov; the border police dog—Indus; and so on. In the same way, Soviet literature restricted itself to two model workers: poet number one was Mayakovsky, and prose writer number one—Maxim Gorky.

Mayakovsky's canonization meant that his works were published in mass editions, but apart from the academic editions the choice was very tendentious: the emphasis was laid on the politically correct works, while the youthful Futurist poems were in principle ignored. His political profile was also smoothed out. *The Bathhouse*, for example, could only be put on again after Stalin's death. Similarly, his relationship to Lili and Osip was toned down, until by the beginning of the seventies it was completely hushed up. A Soviet poet ought not to have such a complicated family life, especially not with Jews. A logical consequence of this policy was that the Mayakovsky museum in Gendrikov Alley, which had been set up as a result of Lili's letter, was closed in 1972. In order to totally expunge Lili from Mayakovsky's biography, great trouble was taken at the same time to find a replacement in the role of his great love. The choice fell on Tatyana Yakovleva. Given her life story, she was not the ideal alternative, but her background as a Russian émigrée was of little weight compared to the fact that there was not a drop of Jewish blood in her veins.

At the time of the fall of the Soviet Union the situation was quite absurd. Everyone who had played any part in Mayakovsky's biography knew that he had lived with Lili for the greater part of his life and dedicated not only individual poems but his collected works to her. And yet officially she did not exist. The picture of Mayakovsky was equally distorted. When the Soviet Union fell, Mayakovsky fell with it—heavily, as monuments do in revolutions—despised by generations of Soviet readers who had been force fed his poems. Although he was in many ways himself a victim, he was seen by most Russians as a representative of a hated social system. That he had written not only tributes to Lenin and the Revolution but also some of the finest love poems in the Russian language was something that few people realized. When the literary hierarchy was remodeled after the fall of the Soviet Union, Mayakovsky disappeared from the school curriculum as well as from the bookshop shelves. It was his third death, and he was not to blame for that one either.[*]

POSTSCRIPT

Despite all the absurd aspects of Mayakovsky's canonization there was a positive side too, in that most of his closest friends and colleagues survived the political purges of the thirties. They were simply regarded as indispensable witnesses to the life of the great poet.

The person who handed over Lili's letter to Stalin was possibly Vitaly Primakov, a top military officer whom Lili got to know in the autumn of 1930 and whom she thereafter joined her life with. Primakov was seven years younger than Lili, a hero of the civil war and a high-ranking officer but also a gifted author of short stories and poems. With his adventurous biography—military adviser in Sun Yat-

---

[*] In recent years, however, there has been a revival of interest in Mayakovsky in Russia. A sign of this is the publication of an academic edition of Mayakovsky's *Collected Works* in twenty volumes. The first two volumes came out in 2014. However, the print run is only 600 copies, whereas the last *Collected Works* (1955–61, in thirteen volumes) was printed in 200,000 copies.

Vitaly Primakov photographed a few years before he became acquainted with Lili.

sen's army in 1925–26, military attaché (and war leader) in Afghanistan in 1927, and military attaché in Japan in 1929–30—he was rather reminiscent of Alexander Krasnoshchokov. At the beginning of the thirties his work took him to different places within and beyond the Soviet Union, and Lili always accompanied him. For instance, they spent the spring of 1933 in Berlin, where Primakov was studying techniques of modern warfare at the German Military Academy. But their joint happiness was short lived. In August 1936 Primakov was arrested, unjustly accused of having participated in a military conspiracy against Stalin, and a year later he was executed.

After Primakov's death, which was a devastating blow for Lili, Vasily Katanyan from the Lef group moved into the apartment, which, just like before, had an additional occupant—Osip—whom Lili never left and never separated from.

During the thirties Osip was incredibly busy, writing articles about Mayakovsky and a host of opera libretti, film scripts, and adaptations of well-known novels for the theater. He also taught courses of literary theory and versification. During the war he wrote texts for so-called TASS windows, the equivalent of the ROSTA posters of the civil war. He died of a heart attack in February 1945, shortly before the end of the war. His Zhenya died almost forty years later, in 1982.

Lili survived Osip by over thirty years. She committed suicide in 1978, thereby fulfilling a prophetic dream she had on 4 June 1930; "I had a dream—I am angry with Volodya because he has shot himself, but he places a little pistol tenderly in my hand and says: 'But you'll end up doing the same thing.'" She did, but with the help of an overdose of sleeping pills rather than a bullet.

Vasily Katanyan, with whom Lili lived until her death, devoted

In connection with the eightieth anniversary of Mayakovsky's birth in 1973, the exhibition *20 Years' Work* was recreated in the same place as in 1930, the Soviet Writers' Union. This time, too, preparations were obstructed by influential circles within the Communist Party. Until the very last moment, for example, it was unclear whether Rodchenko's cover of *About This* would be included—after all, it showed the face of Lili Brik, who was at this time a persona non grata. Just like Mayakovsky forty-three years earlier, the writer Konstantin Simonov, who had forced the exhibition project through, had to do much of the practical work in order to get everything in place.

his whole life to Mayakovsky's writings and became best known for his *Chronicle* of Mayakovsky's life, which was published in several editions. He died two years after Lili, in 1980. His wife Galina, whom he left for Lili in 1937 and who could never forgive him for this betrayal, wrote some of the most insightful memoirs of Mayakovsky and the Lef circle. They could not be published until the advent of perestroika. She died in 1991.

Yelena Yulyevna returned to Moscow two years after Mayakovsky's death. Her last years were spent with her sister Ida Danzig in

Armavir, where Lili had had an abortion in 1906. She died of heart trouble in the winter of 1942.

Mayakovsky's youngest sister, Olga, died in 1949, and their mother in 1954, at the age of eighty-seven. The elder sister, Lyudmila, who lived on till 1972, lent herself at the end of her life to the campaign of persecution against Lili and Osip, and her letters to the general secretary of the Communist Party were a key factor in the closure of the museum in Gendrikov Alley. "The Briks are an antisocial phenomenon," she wrote to Leonid Brezhnev in 1971, "who serve only as demoralizing examples and strengthen anti-Soviet propaganda in the widest sense abroad. [. . .] I categorically and in principle oppose the preservation of any trace whatsoever of my brother in the Briks' former apartment."

Veronika Polonskaya's fate was to be played out entirely in Mayakovsky's shadow: the woman who was named in his farewell letter but whom nobody knew much about. Her marriage to Yanshin was dissolved, and she never had any significant career as an actress. Only after the publication of her memoirs, written in 1938 but not published until the eighties (in their entirety, in 2005), did she assume her rightful place in Mayakovsky's life story. She died in 1994.

If Nora's survival was guaranteed to some extent by her closeness to Mayakovsky, the same closeness by contrast posed a significant risk for Tatyana and Elly. As émigrées they were a disturbing ingredient in the great proletarian writer's biography and had every reason to exercise caution and not flaunt their romances with Mayakovsky.

In the autumn of 1930 Tatyana gave birth to a daughter, Francine, but a few years later she divorced du Plessix and married the artist and fashion illustrator Alex Liberman, of Russian-Jewish descent. In 1941 the family fled to New York, where Tatyana and Alex soon made a name for themselves as a milliner at Saks on Fifth Avenue and art editor for *Vogue*, respectively. After Stalin's death Tatyana gave the poem "Letter to Tatyana Yakovleva" and Mayakovsky's letters to Roman Jakobson, who published them in 1956 in a Russian émigré literary journal. In the sixties and seventies Tatyana kept a salon at her house in East Seventy-Third Street in New York which was reminiscent of Lili's in Moscow. Russian visitors included Mikhail Baryshnikov and Joseph Brodsky, whose poetry she adored. She died in 1991.

After Mayakovsky's death, Elly did a degree in Slavonic languages and worked for the rest of her life as a teacher of Russian, German, and French. She died in Pennsylvania in 1985. Four years later, during the perestroika, Elly junior chose to reveal her identity as Mayakovsky's daughter. The fact that it took her so long was because, after the canonization of Mayakovsky and, in particular, after Trotsky's murder in 1940, her mother was afraid of any kind of publicity. Mayakovsky was a Soviet hero who was not supposed to have kicked over the traces, least of all in America, and if Stalin found it possible to send killers to Mexico he would perhaps not hesitate to try to eliminate this stain on Mayakovsky's reputation. Elly, or Patricia J. Thompson—as she is officially known—is professor of feminist studies at Lehman College in the Bronx. In 1993 she brought out a little book about Mayakovsky, *Mayakovsky in Manhattan*, based on her mother's tape recordings.

Mayakovsky's daughter Patricia J. Thompson, photographed in 1999 with a bust of her father and her book *Mayakovsky in Manhattan*.

For another émigrée, Elsa, fate took a different turn. In the thirties she and Louis Aragon played leading roles in the French Communist Party, and over the years the couple achieved almost the same mythical status in France as Lili and Mayakovsky in the USSR. Aragon celebrated Elsa in his poetry and Elsa herself was eventually to become a successful author in French, awarded the Prix Goncourt in 1944. In 1939 she brought out a short memoir of Mayakovsky, *Maïakovski: Poète russe*. After the Soviet invasion of Czechoslovakia in 1968 their attitude to Soviet communism became more critical, and in her last book, *La mise en mots* (1969), Elsa wrote with surprising candor that she was a "Soviet idiot" and that it was her fault that Aragon had become a Communist.

Elsa, who had a weak heart, died in 1970, Aragon twelve years later—in the same year as Roman Jakobson, who in the thirties had become professor of Slavonic studies at the University of Brno, but who was forced to flee Czechoslovakia when the Germans invaded in 1939. In 1941, after two years in Denmark, Norway, and Sweden, he arrived in the United States, where after a while he was appointed to a post at Harvard. When he left Sweden, parts of his library were left behind, including Elsa's book about Mayakovsky, with the inscription "To dear Romik, about Volodya," which is now in the holdings of the Stockholm University library. When Jakobson died in Cambridge, Massachusetts, in 1982, he was generally known as one of the century's greatest and most innovative linguists.

Two years later Viktor Shklovsky died in Moscow. After the 1930 article "Monument to a Scholarly Mistake," in which he abandoned his Formalist convictions, he devoted himself more and more to biographical research and wrote among other things biographies of Leo Tolstoy and Sergey Eisenstein. He also wrote a good deal about film in general. However one judges Shklovsky's apostasy, it is impossible to deny the genuine originality of most of his works. This also applies to his memoirs, about Mayakovsky and others, despite the author's rather creative attitude to the truth. Shklovsky's nightmares that after returning to the Soviet Union he would be "forced to begin lying" were borne out in spades.

Roman Jakobson saved his life and his career by remaining abroad. Maxim Gorky, by contrast, having visited the Soviet Union in 1928 and 1929 (without once meeting Mayakovsky) and again in 1931, returned home for good two years later. If Mayakovsky was the number one Soviet poet, Gorky occupied the same position within Soviet prose. However, in contrast to Mayakovsky, whose profile could be trimmed as required, Gorky was still alive. Even if his room for maneuver was infinitely more restricted than it had been ten years earlier, his moral authority was a source of constant irritation to Stalin, and in 1936 he drew his last breath.

In the midthirties Socialist Realism was adopted as the only viable literary form, and Mayakovsky and Gorky were, as we have seen, designated its leading exponents. However implausible it seems today, the ideologically vacillating Boris Pasternak was once seen as the

The ninety-one-year-old Lev Grinkrug photographed in 1980 in his Moscow apartment with the Swedish edition of *About This*.

Soviet Union's model poet, a fate he avoided as a result of the canonization of Mayakovsky—something he personally thanked Stalin for. To be sure, he survived the purges, but in the thirties and forties he devoted himself primarily to translations—in particular, though not exclusively, to Shakespeare. At the same time he was quietly working on a novel, *Doctor Zhivago*, which played an important part in the Swedish Academy's decision to award him the 1958 Nobel Prize for literature, a distinction which the Soviet authorities forbade him to accept. He died two years later.

Most of the other key actors in this story about Mayakovsky and his circle fell victim to the Great Terror. Boris Pilnyak ("Japanese spy") was executed in 1938; Sergey Tretyakov ("German and Japanese spy") in 1939. In February of the following year Vsevolod Meyerhold was shot, and two weeks later his wife Zinaida Reikh was found knifed to death, with her eyes put out. Nor did the Chekists themselves escape the wave of terror which swept over the Soviet Union during these years. Zakhar Volovich and Moisey Gorb were executed by firing squad in the spring of 1937, as were Yakov Agranov (who had updated his CV in 1934 by signing Osip Mandelstam's arrest warrant and by participating in the "interrogation" of Lili's new husband Primakov two years later) and his wife Valentina in August 1938, and Nikolay Yezhov in February 1940.

Other victims of the terror included Alexander Krasnoshchokov, who in 1930 had married his former secretary Donna Gruz. Four years later the twins Lena and Natasha were born, thereby becoming Luella's half sisters. In July 1937 Krasnoshchokov was arrested for collaborating with Trotskyists, and in November it was Donna Gruz's turn. On 26 November he was executed and Donna was exiled for eight years as the wife of an enemy of the people.

Krasnoshchokov's daughter Luella married in 1929 and studied to be a zoologist. She died in St. Petersburg in 2002 at the age of ninety-two. Throughout her life she worshipped Lili—just like Lev Grinkrug, faithful friend and admirer for sixty-five years, from 1913 until Lili's death in 1978. Nine years later this gentle Russian nobleman died himself, at the age of ninety-eight, in a small apartment by the Concrete Factory bus stop in a suburb of Moscow.

Despite Mayakovsky's dominant position on the Soviet Parnassus for more than half a century, and despite the enormous amount of articles and books that have been written about him, the situation for scholars is far from ideal. Stalin's canonization of him in 1935 led to many of his works' being constantly published in new editions, but the poems that were regarded as less appropriate for a model Soviet poet were seldom or never printed. In the same way, information about Mayakovsky was censored, not least in memoirs of him. Everything that made the image of Mayakovsky as the great proletarian poet more complex was suppressed.

The situation improved after the Twentieth Party Congress in 1956 and the dismantling of the Stalin cult. Two years later the volume *New Materials about Mayakovsky* [Novoe o Maiakovskom] was published in the prestigious series The Literary Heritage (63; the numbers in parentheses refer to the bibliography below). It contained hitherto unknown texts by Mayakovsky and scholarly articles about his work, but also—and principally—125 of his letters to Lili Brik. The publication made the Communist Party's Commission for Ideology, Culture and International Relations adopt a resolution stating that the published letters "distort the image of the prominent Soviet poet" and that the volume as a whole is "an echo of the slanderous campaigns led by foreign revisionists." Volume 2, which was supposed to contain the memoirs of Lili and her sister, Elsa Triolet, never saw the light of day.

A fragment of Lili's memoirs was published instead in a book of over seven hundred pages that came out in 1963: *V. Mayakovsky Remembered by His Contemporaries* (V. Maiakovskii v vospominaniiakh sovremennikov) (107). Also published here were the memoirs of Viktor Shklovsky, Lev Grinkrug, Korney Chukovsky, Rita Rayt, Alexander Rodchenko, Sergey Eisenstein, Vsevolod Meyerhold, Sergey Tretyakov, Nikolay Ase-

yev, Vasily Katanyan, and other friends and colleagues of Maya-
kovsky. However, the volume was heavily censored, both by the
Soviet authorities and by the authors themselves. References to the
"complications" in Mayakovsky's biography were cut out, and sev-
eral of the individuals whom the reader has met on the pages of this
book were conspicuous by their absence: Elly Jones, Tatyana Ya-
kovleva, Veronika Polonskaya, not to mention politicians like Leon
Trotsky and Nikolay Bukharin.

Five years later, this volume was countered by the "anti-Brik
faction" with the volume *Mayakovsky Remembered by His Relatives
and Friends* (Maiakovskii v vospominaniiakh rodnykh i druzei [66]),
containing, among other things, a fierce attack on the Briks, who
were described as Mayakovsky's evil geniuses (58). The publication
of this book signified an escalation of the ideological battle being
waged around Mayakovsky (see the chapter "Mayakovsky's Second
Death"). An attempt to redress the balance was the volume *Vladimir
Majakovskij: Memoirs and Essays* (34), published (with contributions
in Russian and English) by myself and professor Nils Åke Nilsson in
Stockholm in 1975 (in the series Stockholm Studies in Russian Liter-
ature). Alongside memoirs of Lili and her husband Vasily Katanyan it
included articles by Russian and Swedish scholars. It also contained
Elsa Triolet's memoirs, written for the second volume of *New Mate-
rials about Mayakovsky*, which was never published.

Osip Brik's contributions to Russian culture was highlighted for
the first time in 1978, with Vahan D. Barooshian's *Brik and Mayak-
ovsky* (4).

During the 1970s the situation in the Soviet Union deteriorated to
the degree that Lili and Osip Brik were on the verge of being totally
eradicated from Mayakovsky's biography. As part of the battle to
counteract this development I published the full correspondence
between Lili and Mayakovsky, in all, 416 letters and telegrams, with
a lengthy introduction and extensive commentaries (36). It was a
measure I had encouraged Lili Brik to take, and the correspondence
was given to me by her husband after her death. When the book
came out in Russian in Stockholm in 1982, it was met with complete
silence in the Soviet Union—to mention it would have meant to rec-
ognize that Lili Brik had actually existed! In the next few years the

correspondence was published in several languages, such as Italian (Mondadori) and English (Grove Press, New York, and Polygon Press, Edinburgh). Six years later I published the correspondence between Mayakovsky and Elsa Triolet (37), and in 1992 a volume containing my interviews with Roman Jakobson about Russian Futurism as well as his letters to Elsa Triolet and his early articles on the Russian avant-garde (in English in 1997: *My Futurist Years* [38]).

With perestroika and the fall of the Soviet Union the situation changed radically. In 1991 my edition of the correspondence between Mayakovsky and Lili was published in the Soviet Union and Lili thus became "official." In connection with the hundredth anniversary of the poet's birth in 1993 hitherto-unpublished memoirs were printed, among them contributions by Ida Khvas (55) and Vera Schechtel (85), as well as a volume of memoirs by women who had been close to Mayakovsky: Lili, Elsa, Sonya Shamardina, Natasha Bryukhanenko, and others (48). In New York Mayakovsky's daughter put together the book *Mayakovsky in Manhattan*, based on tape recordings of her mother's recollections of Mayakovsky (100), and in far-off Kazakhstan Anatoly Valyuzhenich published a book with material by and about Osip Brik (110). The year 1999 saw the appearance of Vasily and Galina Katanyan's memoirs (47), and 2003 a volume containing memoirs of Lili along with extracts from her diaries and letters (11). In 2005 the single most important contribution to Mayakovsky research was published in Moscow: a volume containing material about Mayakovsky's suicide previously kept (or rather lost) in the archive of the interior commissar, Nikolay Yezhov (112): 600 pages with interrogation protocols, informers' reports, memoirs, and other documents related to the suicide.

The correspondence between Lili and Elsa in the years 1921–70, which appeared in Russian and French in 2000 (60, 61), is an important source which however only touches marginally on Mayakovsky, as only a handful of letters refer to the period before 1930. In recent years, several works have been published about Lili Brik, among them a book by Arkady Vaksberg (109) that is a valuable contribution to our knowledge of the role of the security organs in the 1920s in general and in the Mayakovsky-Brik "family" in particular.

As we can see, it is Lili who has attracted most attention in recent years, not Mayakovsky. This is due to two factors: the lack of interest in Mayakovsky after the fall of the Soviet Union and the newly won freedom to write about subjects that were once taboo. Here, Lili's colorful biography exerts an irresistible temptation—just like other women in Mayakovsky's life. The latest contributions to this genre—"Mayakovsky's women"—are the Mayakovsky Museum's slim volume *Tatá*, about Tatyana Yakovleva (98) and Yury Tyurin's little book on the same theme (101), together with Sofia Kovalenko's book about "women in Mayakovsky's life" (56). In 2005, in New York, Tatyana Yakovleva's daughter Francine du Plessix Gray brought out her book *Them*, about her mother and her stepfather Alex Liberman (22).

However, no real biography of Mayakovsky himself has ever been written. Viktor Pertsov's three-volume *Mayakovsky: Life and Work* (Moscow 1969–73) was published during the worst "stagnation years" and is hopelessly disfigured by the official view of Mayakovsky, whose greatness is measured only by his degree of loyalty to the Soviet regime (73). The same goes, although in a lesser degree, for Alexander Mikhaylov's biography *Mayakovsky* from 1988, written on the threshold of the new era but psychologically and ideologically totally rooted in the old, Soviet one (69). Yury Karabchiyevsky's *Mayakovsky's Resurrection* (published in Russian in Munich, 1985), on the other hand, is a furious attack on the official Soviet image of Mayakovsky, full of pain over Mayakovsky's fate and of poignant observations—but just as often unfair and unbalanced (43). And it is not a biography.

Vasily Katanyan's *Chronicle* (46) is a sort of biographical summary which came out in several editions—the latest in 1985—and which details Mayakovsky's life day by day. It contains quotations but no analysis. Although it is far from comprehensive, it has been a great help in the course of my work on this book.

If biography writing in the Soviet Union was hampered by the restrictions and taboos surrounding Mayakovsky's name, the absence of biographies in the West can best be explained by a lack of interest in him. The focus of Russian scholars in our part of the world has rightly been directed toward poets who were forbidden or persecuted in the Soviet Union—Anna Akhmatova, Boris Pasternak, Osip Mandelstam, Marina Tsvetayeva, and others—and who therefore could not be dealt with by Soviet scholars.

In 1970, Wiktor Woroszylski's *The Life of Mayakovsky* was published: an English translation of the original Polish edition of 1965 (115). This volume is a compilation of memoirs, letters, and other documents that illustrate Mayakovsky's life and work in a multifaceted and vivid way. However, it is a text anthology, not a biography. The same goes for Edward J. Brown's *Mayakovsky: A Poet in the Revolution* (1973)—a literary (formalistic) analysis of Mayakovsky's work with a pronounced antibiographical approach (12). Victor Terras, *Vladimir Mayakovsky* (1983), published in Twayne's World Author Series, is a short (150 pp.) but good introduction to Mayakovsky's work without biographical ambitions (99). In 1979, Ann and Samuel Charters published *I Love: The Story of Vladimir Mayakovsky and Lili Brik* (17). It is largely based on interviews with Lili Brik, most of them made with the help of Rita Rayt, some with mine. The book's stated aim is to describe "the love story between Lili Brik and Vladimir Mayakovsky," and Mayakovsky's literary, social, and political biography is touched upon only superficially. Unfortunately the book contains a number of factual mistakes, a result of the authors' lack of knowledge of the Russian language, a fact that also strongly reduced their access to sources (which in 1979 were in any case scarce).

The book that now weighs heavily in the reader's hand is not the first book about Mayakovsky, but it is, strangely enough, the first non-Soviet *biography* of him. The reason it has not been written before is that only in recent years has such a venture been made possible: in Soviet times too many sources were either unknown or inaccessible. Although the situation has improved radically since the fall of the Soviet Union, however, much source material has been lost forever. After the canonization of Mayakovsky in 1935 Lili burned the letters to Mayakovsky from Tatyana Yakovleva and Mariya Denisova (but, strangely enough, not those from Elly Jones). If this auto-da-fé was inspired by her wish to secure her role as the only muse in Mayakovsky's life (which, in principle, she was), the measures taken by her after the arrest of Vitaly Primakov in 1936 were dictated by fear and survival instinct. The memoirs that she began to write in 1929 and which are said to have comprised about 450 pages were destroyed—with the exception of the chapters dealing with the pre-revolutionary period, which are quoted in the chapter "Lili." And the diary she kept was reedited, and all facts and names that could compromise herself and others were deleted. The text that I have had access to is thus an edited version from 1936 or 1937.

This is what we know, from Lili herself and others. What we do not know is how many other sources were destroyed during the fifty years that the official Mayakovsky cult lasted. Mayakovsky was no prolific letter writer, but he undoubtedly wrote and received more letters than the ones that have been preserved.

Lili Brik's and Vasily Katanyan's papers are kept at the State Russian Literary Archive and were only recently made public to scholars. However, photocopies of parts of their archives have been in my possession since the 1970s. These and other unpublished materials are listed below under the chapter headings.

Printed sources are shown under the heading "Recurrent References and Other Sources of Interest." Some of these are mentioned again under individual chapter headings, though not sources which are utilized throughout the work (e.g. Lili's and Elsa's published recollections, Katanyan's *Chronicle*, and my edition of Roman Jakobson's memoirs). Mayakovsky's texts are cited from his *Collected Works* in thirteen volumes (Moscow, 1955–61) (65), and Lili's and Mayakovsky's letters from the correspondence (36).

RECURRENT REFERENCES AND OTHER SOURCES OF INTEREST

Translations of Mayakovsky's works by James H. McGavran III are taken from Vladimir Mayakovsky, Selected Poems, translated from the Russian by James H. McGavran III (Evanston, IL: Northwestern University Press, 2013).

Translations of Mayakovsky's works by George Reavey are taken from Vladimir Mayakovsky, *"The Bedbug" and Selected Poetry*, translated by George Reavey (1960; reprint, Bloomington: Indiana University Press, 1975).

Translations of Mayakovsky's works by Val Vinokur are taken from *Night Wraps the Sky: Writings by and about Mayakovsky*, edited by Michael Almereyda (New York: Farrar Straus Giroux, 2008).

1. Annenkov, Yury. *Dnevnik moikh vstrech*. Vols. 1–2. New York, 1966.
2. Aseyev, Nikolay. "Vospominaniia o Maiakovskom." (107)
3. Barnes, Christopher. *Boris Pasternak: A Literary Biography*. Vols. 1–2. Cambridge, 1989–98.
4. Barooshian, Vahan D. *Brik and Mayakovsky*. The Hague, 1978.
5. *Bol'shaia tsenzura: Pisateli i zhur-*

nalisty v strane sovetov 1917–1956. Moscow, 2005.

6. Brik, Lili. "Iz vospominanii." In *S Maiakovskim.* Moscow, 1934.

7. Brik, Lili. *Shchen (iz vospominanii o Maiakovskom).* Molotov, 1942.

8. Brik, Lili. "Chuzhie stikhi." (107)

9. Brik, Lili. "Predlozhenie issledovateliam." *Voprosy literatury* 9 (1966).

10. Brik, Lilya. "Iz vospominanii." (49)

11. Brik, Lilya. *Pristrastnye rasskazy.* Edited by Ya. I. Groysman and Inna Gens. Nizhniy Novgorod, 2003.

12. Brown, Edward J. *Mayakovsky: A Poet in the Revolution.* Princeton, N.J., 1973.

13. Bouchardeau, Huguette. *Elsa Triolet: Écrivain.* Paris, 2000.

14. Bryukhanenko, Natal'ya. "Perezhitoe." (49)

15. Burlyuk, David. *Fragmenty iz vospominanii futurista.* St. Petersburg, 1994.

16. Burlyuk, David, and Marusya Burlyuk. "Maiakovskii i ego sovremenniki." *Literaturnoe obozrenie* 6 (1993).

17 Charters, Ann, and Samuel Charters. *I Love: The Story of Vladimir Mayakovsky and Lili Brik.* New York, 1979.

18. Chukovsky, Korney. *Dnevnik 1901–1929.* Moscow, 1991. *Dnevnik 1930–1969.* Moscow, 1994.

19. Desanti, Dominique. *Les clés d'Elsa.* Paris, 1983.

20. Dinerstein, Yefim. *Maiakovskii i kniga.* Moscow, 1987.

21. *Dokumente zur sowjetischen Literaturpolitik 1917–1932.* Edited by Karl Eimermacher. Stuttgart, 1972.

22. Du Plessix Gray, Francine. *Them: A Memoir of Parents.* New York, 2005.

23. Erlikh, Viktor. *Russian Formalism: History, Doctrine.* The Hague, 1969.

24. Fleishman, Lazar. *Boris Pasternak v dvadtsatye gody.* Munich, [1981].

25. Fleishman, Lazar. *Boris Pasternak: The Poet and His Politics.* Cambridge, Mass., 1990.

26. Fleishman, Lazar. *Boris Pasternak i literaturnoe dvizhenie 1930-kh godov.* St. Petersburg, 2005.

27. Geiger, Kent. *The Family in Soviet Russia.* Cambridge, Mass., 1968.

28. Gladkov, Alexander. *Vstrechi s Pasternakom.* Paris, 1973.

29. Harding, Gunnar, and Bengt Jangfeldt. *Den vrålande parnassen: Den ryska futurismen i poesi, bild och dokument.* Stockholm, 1976.

30. Jakobson, Roman. *Jakobson-budetlianin.* (See 38)

31. Jakobson, Roman. "O pokolenii, rastrativshem svoikh poetov." In *Smert' Vladimira Maiakovskogo.* Berlin, 1931. In English: "On a Generation That Squandered Its Poets." (38)

32. Jakobson, Roman. "Novye stroki Maiakovskogo." In *Russkii literaturnyi arkhiv* (1956).

33. Jangfeldt, Bengt, ed. *Lili Brik: Mayakovskij; Ur Minnen.* Stockholm, 1974.

34. Jangfeldt, Bengt, and Nils Åke Nilsson, eds. *Vladimir Mayakovskij: Memoirs and Essays.* Stockholm, 1975.

35. Jangfeldt, Bengt. *Mayakovsky and Futurism, 1917–1921.* Stockholm, 1976.

36. Jangfeldt, Bengt, ed. *Love Is the Heart of Everything: Correspondence between Vladimir Mayakovsky and Lili Brik, 1915–1930.* New York, 1987.

37. Jangfeldt, Bengt, ed. *"Dorogoi diadia Volodia . . .": Vladimir Maiakovskii-El'za Triole; Pis'ma 1915–1917.* Stockholm, 1990.

38. Jangfeldt, Bengt, ed. *Iakobson-budetlianin: Sbornik materialov.* Stockholm, 1992; Moscow, 2012. English edition: *My Futurist Years.* New York, 1997.

39. Jangfeldt, Bengt. "Tri zametki o V. V. Maiakovskom i L. Iu. Brik." In *A Century's Perspective: Essays on Russian Literature in Honor of Olga Raevsky Hughes and Robert P. Hughes.* Stanford, Calif., 2006.

40. Jangfeldt, Bengt. "'Ostanovis', prokhozhii!': Fragmenty iz belletrizirovannykh vospominanii L. Iu. Brik o Maiakovskom." *Vademecum: K 65-letiiu Lazaria Fleishmana.* Moscow, 2010.

41. Katsis, Leonid. *Vladimir Maia-kovskii: Poet v intellektual'nom kontekste epokhi.* Moscow, 2004.

42. Kamensky, Vasily. *Zhizn' s Maia-kovskim.* Moscow, 1940.

43. Karabchiyevsky, Yury. *Voskresenie Maiakovskogo.* Munich, 1985.

44. Kassil, Lev. *Maiakovskii—sam.* Moscow, 1963.

45. Katanyan, Galina. "Azorskie ostro-va." In *Dom Ostroukhova v trubin-kakh.* Moscow, 1995. In a slightly different version, in no. 47.

46. Katanyan, V. A. *Maiakovskii: Khroni-ka zhizni i deiatel'nosti.* Moscow 1985. Italian edition (heavily shortened): *Vita di Mayakovskij.* Rome, 1978.

47. Katanyan, V. A. *Raspechatannaia butylka.* Nizhniy Novgorod, 1999.

48. Katanyan, V. V., ed. *Imia etoi teme: Liubov'!; Sovremennitsy o Maiakovs-kom.* Moscow, 1993.

49. Katanyan, V. V., ed. *Lilya Brik, Vlad-imir Maiakovskii i drugie muzhchiny.* Moscow, 1998.

50. Katanyan, V. V. *Lilya Brik: Zhizn'.* Moscow, 2002.

51. Kemrad, S., *Maiakovskii v Amerike.* Moscow, 1970.

52. Khardzhiev, Nikolay. "'Veselyi god' Maiakovskogo." (34)

53. Khodasevich, Valentina. *Portrety slovami.* Moscow, 1987.

54. Khodasevich, Vladislav. "O Maia-kovskom." In *Izbrannaia proza.* New York, 1982.

55. Khvas, Ida. "Vospominaniia o Maia-kovskom." *Literaturnoe obozrenie* 9–10 (1993).

56. Kovalenko, Svetlana. "Zvezdnaia dan'": Zhenshchiny v sud'be Maia-kovskogo.* Moscow, 2006.

57. Krusanov, Andrey. *Russkii avangard: Futuristicheskaia revoliutsiia 1917–1921.* Vol. 2, bk. 1–2. Moscow, 2003.

58. Lavinskaya, E. A., "Vospominaniia o vstrechakh s Maiakovskim." (66)

59. Lavut, Pavel. *Maiakovskii edet po Soiuzu.* Moscow, 1969.

60. *Lili Brik–Elsa Triolet: Correspon-dance 1921–1970.* Preface and notes by Léon Robel. Paris, 2000.

61. *Lilia Brik–El'za Triole: Neizdannaia perepiska 1921–1970.* Edited by V. V. Katanyan. Moscow, 2000.

62. *Literaturnaia zhizn' Rossii 1920-kh godov.* Vol. 1, parts 1–2. Edited by A. Galushkin. Moscow, 2005.

63. *Novoe o Mayakovskom.* Literaturnoe nasledstvo, vol. 65. Moscow, 1958.

64. Mackinnon, Lachlan. *The Lives of Elsa Triolet.* London, 1992.

65. Mayakovsky, Vladimir. *Polnoe sobranie sochinenii v 13-i tomakh.* Moscow, 1955–61.

66. *Maiakovskii v vospominaniiakh rodnykh i druzei.* Moscow, 1968.

67. *Mayakowski in Deutschland: Texte zur Rezeption 1919–1930.* Edited by Roswitha Loew and Bella Tschis-towa. Berlin, 1986.

68. Mazaev, A. I. *Iskusstvo i bol'shevizm 1920–1930.* Moscow, 2004.

69. Mikhaylov, Alexander. *Maiakovskii.* Moscow, 1988.

70. Mukhachov, B. I. *Aleksandr Kras-noshchekov.* Vladivostok, 1999.

71. Pasternak, Boris. *Collected Short Prose.* New York, 1987.

72. Pasternak, Boris. *The Correspondence of Boris Pasternak and Olga Freiden-berg, 1910–1954.* New York, 1982.

73. Pertsov, Viktor. *Maiakovskii: Zhizn' i tvorchestvo.* Vols. 1–3. Moscow, 1969–73.

74. Pipes, Richard. *The Russian Revolu-tion, 1899–1919.* London, 1990.

75. Pipes, Richard. *Russia under the Bolshevik Regime, 1919–1924.* London, 1994.

76. Polonskaya, Veronika. [Memoirs.] (112)

77. Punin, Nikolay. *Mir svetel liubov'iu: Dnevniki, pis'ma.* Moscow, 2000.

78. Rayt, Rita. "Tol'ko vospominaniia." (107)

79. Rayt, Rita. "Vse luchshie vospomi-naniia…" *Oxford Slavonic Papers* 13 (1967).

80. Rappoport, Alexander. "Ne tol'ko o Maiakovskom: Zapis' besedy s Iuriem (Iuliem—nast.) Borisovi-chem Rumerom 14 aprelia 1978 g." www.alrapp.narod.ru.

81. Rodchenko, Alexander. *Stat'i: Vospominaniia . . .* Moscow, 1982.
82. Rodchenko, Alexander. *Opyty dlia budushchego.* Moscow, 1996.
83. Schapiro, Leonard. *The Communist Party of the Soviet Union.* New York, 1971.
84. Shamardina, Sofya. "Futuristicheskaia iunost'." (48)
85. Shekhtel, Vera. "Byl u nas Maiakovskii . . ." *Literaturnoe obozrenie* 6 (1993).
86. Shklovsky, Viktor. *Tret'ia fabrika.* Moscow, 1926.
87. Shklovsky, Viktor. "O Maiakovskom." In *Sobranie sochinenii,* vol. 3. Moscow, 1974.
88. Shklovsky, Viktor. *Gamburgskii shchet.* Edited by A. Galushkin. Moscow, 1990.
89. Skoryatin, Valentin. *Taina gibeli Maiakovskogo.* Moscow, 1998.
90. Sokolova, Yevgeniya. "Dvadtsat' let riadom." (110)
91. Spassky, Sergey. *Maiakovskii i ego sputniki.* Moscow, 1940.
92. Spivak, Monika. *Posmertnaia diagnostika genial'nosti.* Moscow, 2001.
93. Stahlberger, Lawrence L. *The Symbolic System of Mayakovskij.* The Hague, 1964.
94. Stepanova, Varvara. *Chelovek ne mozhet bez chuda.* Moscow, 1994.
95. Stephan, Halina. *"Lef" and the Left Front of the Arts.* Munich, 1981.
96. Stites, Richard. *The Women's Liberation Movement in Russia: Feminism, Nihilism, and Bolshevism, 1860–1930.* Princeton, N.J., 1978
97. Struve, Gleb. *Russkaia literatura v izgnanii.* Paris, 1984.
98. *Tatá (Tat'iana Iakovleva).* Moscow, 2003.
99. Terras, Victor. *Vladimir Mayakovsky.* Boston, 1983.
100. Thompson, Patricia J. *Mayakovsky in Manhattan: A Love Story.* New York, 1993.
101. Tyurin, Yury. *Tat'iana: Russkaia muza Parizha.* Moscow, 2006.
102. Toman, Jindrich. *The Magic of a Common Language: Jakobson, Mathesius, Trubetzkoy, and the Prague Linguistic Circle.* Cambridge, Mass., 1995.
103. Triolet, Elsa. *Fraise-des-bois.* Paris, 1974.
104. Triolet, Elsa. "Voinstvuiushchii poet." (34)
105. Triolet, Elsa. *Écrits intimes 1912–1939.* Edited by Marie-Thérèse Eychart. Paris, 1998.
106. Trotsky, Leon. *Literature and Revolution.* Chicago, 2005 (1925).
107. *V. Maiakovskii v vospominaniiakh sovremennikov.* Moscow, 1963.
108. Vaksberg, Arkady. *Gibel' burevestnika.* Moscow, 1999. French edition: *Le Mystère Gorki.* Paris, 1997.
109. Vaksberg, Arkady. *Zagadka i magiia Lili Brik.* Moscow, 2003. French edition: *Lili Brik: Portrait d'un séductrice.* Paris, 1999.
110. Valyuzhenich, Anatoly, ed. *O. M. Brik: Materialy k biografii.* Akmola, 1993.
111. Valyuzenich, Anatoly. *Lilya Brik—zhena komandira.* Astana, 2006.
112. *"V tom, chto umiraiu, ne vinite nikogo? . . .": Sledstvennoe delo V. V. Maiakovskogo.* Moscow, 2005.
113. Volkov-Lannit, L. *Alexander Rodchenko risuet, fotografiruet, sporit.* Moscow, 1968.
114. Volkov-Lannit, L. *Vizhu Maiakovskogo.* Moscow, 1981.
115. Woroszylski, Wiktor. *The Life of Mayakovsky.* New York, 1970.

1. VOLODYA, 1893–1915

PRINTED SOURCES

Burlyuk, David. *Fragmenty iz vospominanii futurista.* (15)
Burlyuk, David, and Marusya Burlyuk. "Maiakovskii i ego sovremenniki." (16)
Kamensky, Vasily. *Zhizn' s Maiakovskim.* (42)

Khvas, Ida. "Vospominaniia o Maia-
    kovskom." (55)
Livshits, Benedikt. *Polutoraglazyi
    strelets*. Leningrad, 1933.
Mayakovskaya, Alexandra. "Detstvo i
    iunost' Vladimira Maiakovskogo."
    (107)
Mayakovskaya, Ljudmila. *Perezhitoe.*
    Tbilisi, 1957.

Pasternak, Boris. *The Voice of Prose*. Edited
    by Christopher Barnes. New York,
    1986.
Shekhtel, Vera. "Byl u nas Maia-
    kovsky. . ." (85)
Shamardina, Sofya. "Futuristicheskaia
    iunost'." (84)

2. LILI, 1891–1915

UNPUBLISHED SOURCES
The information about Lili's childhood
and youth comes from her unpub-
lished memoirs as well as from
transcripts of taped interviews.
Copies in author's archive.

PRINTED SOURCES
Azarkh-Granovskaya, A. V. *Vospomi-
    naniia*. Jerusalem, 2001.
Stites, Richard. *The Women's Liberation
    Movement in Russia: Feminism, Nihil-
    ism, and Bolshevism 1860–1930*. (96)

Triolet, Elsa. *Le premier accroc coûte deux
    cents francs*. Paris, 1945.
Triolet, Elsa. *Écrits intimes 1912–1939*. (105)
Valyuzhenich, Anatoly, ed. *O. M. Brik:
    Materialy k biografii*. (110)
Yablonskaya, M. N., and I. A. Yestafyeva.
    "Genrikh (Andrei) Bliumenfel'd
    (1893–1920)." *Panorama iskusstv* 13
    (1990).
Yangirov, Rashit. "Oleg Frelikh i Osip
    Brik . . ." In *6-e Tynianovskie Chteni-
    ia*. Riga, 1992.

3. A CLOUD IN TROUSERS, 1915–1916

UNPUBLISHED SOURCES
Brik, Lili. "Kak bylo delo." Copy in
    author's archive.

PRINTED SOURCES
Azarkh-Granovskaya, A. V. *Vospomi-
    naniia*. Jerusalem, 2001.
Khvas, Ida. "Vospominaniia o Maia-
    kovskom." (55)

Shklovsky, Viktor. *Tret'ia fabrika*. (86)
Toddes, E., ed. "Ustnye vospominaniia R.
    O. Iakobsona o Maiakovskom." In *7-e
    Tynianovskie Chteniia*. Riga, 1995–96.
Raskovskaya, M. A., ed. *Boris Pasternak
    i Sergei Bobrov: Pis'ma chetyrekh
    desiatiletii*. Stanford Slavic Studies,
    vol. 10. Stanford, Calif., 1996.

4. THE FIRST REVOLUTION AND THE THIRD, 1917–1918

UNPUBLISHED SOURCES
Brik, Lili. "Kak bylo delo." Copy in
    author's archive.

PRINTED SOURCES
Baranova-Shestova, I. *Zhizn' L'va Shesto-
    va*. Vol. 1. Paris, 1983.
Bouchardeau, Huguette. *Elsa Triolet:
    Écrivain*. (13)
Desanti, Dominique. *Les clés d'Elsa*. (19)

Grinkrug, Lev. "Ne dlia deneg rodivshi-
    isia." (107)
Jakobson, Roman. "Novyc stroki Maia-
    kovskogo." (32)
Jangfeldt, Bengt. "Notes on 'Manifest
    Letučej Federacii Futuristov' and
    the Revolution of the Spirit." (34)
Jangfeldt, Bengt. *Mayakovsky and Futur-
    ism, 1917–1921*. (35)

Jangfeldt, Bengt. "Russian Futurism, 1917–1919." In *Art, Society, Revolution: Russia, 1917–1921*. Stockholm, 1979.

Shamardina, Sofya. "Futuristicheskaia iunost'." (48)

5. COMMUNIST FUTURISM, 1918–1920

UNPUBLISHED SOURCES

Talova, M. A. "Vodop'iany pereulok i ego obitateli." Copy in author's archive.

P. 146. The etching, showing "The young Pushkin," has been preserved in a private archive.

P. 146. Lili's assertion that Mayakovsky was "a torment in bed" was conveyed to me by her stepniece Inna Gens.

P. 146. The information about Mayakovsky's sexual problems was confided to me in 1982 by Nina Berberova, who in turn heard it from Shklovsky in Berlin in 1922.

P. 150. The story about Lili's "secret" was told to me by Roman Jakobson in 1977.

PRINTED SOURCES

Azarkh-Granovskaya, A. V. *Vospominaniia*. Jerusalem, 2001.

Barnes, Christopher. *Boris Pasternak: A Literary Biography*. (3)

Chukovsky, Korney. *Dnevnik 1901–1929*. (18)

Ivanov, V. V. "Buria nad N'iufaundlendom." In *Roman Iakobson: Teksty, Dokumenty, Issledovaniia*. Moscow, 1999.

Jakobson, Roman. "Postscript." In *O. M. Brik: Two Essays on Poetic Language*. Ann Arbor, Mich., 1964.

Jangfeldt, Bengt, ed. *Iakobson-budetlianin: Sbornik materialov*. (38)

Krusanov, Andrey. *Russkii avangard: Futuristicheskaia revoliutsiia 1917–1921*. (57)

Punin, Nikolay. *Mir svetel liubov'iu: Dnevniki, pis'ma*. (77)

Teryokhina, V. N. "'Dvoe v odnom serdtse': Vladimir Maiakovskii i Antonina Gumilina." *Chelovek* 2 (1999).

Yangirov, Rashit. "Roman Grinberg i Roman Iakobson." In *Roman Iakobson: Teksty, Dokumenty, Issledovaniia*. Moscow, 1999.

Zolotonosov, M. *M/Z ili Katamoran*. St. Petersburg, 1996.

6. NEP AND THE BEGINNINGS OF TERROR, 1921

PRINTED SOURCES

Berberova, Nina. *The Italics Are Mine*. New York, 1992.

Jangfeldt, Bengt. "Mayakovsky and the Publication of '150 000 000': New Materials." *Scando-Slavica* 21 (1975).

Jangfeldt, Bengt. "Russian Futurism, 1917–1919." In *Art, Society, Revolution: Russia, 1917–1921*. Stockholm, 1979.

Jangfeldt, Bengt. "Eshche raz o Maiakovskom i Lenine (Novye materialy)." *Scando-Slavica* 33 (1987).

Mukhachov, B. I. *Aleksandr Krasnoshchekov*. (70)

Neizvestnyi Gor'kii. Moscow, 1994.

Pipes, Richard. *The Russian Revolution, 1899–1919*. (75)

7. *DRANG NACH WESTEN*, 1922

UNPUBLISHED SOURCES

Public Record Office. London. Records of the Security Service (KV2/484). (The British security service's file about Lili's and Elsa's mother Yelena Kagan, also containing documents concerning Elsa, Lili, Osip, and Mayakovsky. Declassified in 2002.)

PRINTED SOURCES

Chamberlain, Lesley. *The Philosophy Steamer: Lenin and the Exile of the Intelligentsia*. London, 2006.

Ehrenburg, Ilya. *Liudi, Gody, Zhizn'*. Vol. 1, bk. 3. Moscow, 1990.

Fleishman, Lazar. "Vysylka intelligentsii v russkii Berlin v 1922 g." In *Russkii Berlin: 1920–1945*. Moscow, 2006.

Galushkin, Alexander, "V. B. Shklovskii: Pis'ma k M. Gor'komu." *De Visu* 1(2) (1993).

Gindin, S., and E. Ivanova. "Perepiska R. O. Jakobsona i G. O. Vinokura." *Novoe literaturnoe obozrenie* 21 (1996).

Pipes, Richard. *Russia under the Bolshevik Regime, 1919–1924*. (75)

Pogorelova [Runt], Bronislava. "Valerii Briusov i ego okruzhenie." In *Vospominaniia o serebrianom veke*. Moscow, 1993.

Rayt, Rita. "Vse luchshie vospominania . . ." (79)

Raskovskaya, M. A., ed. *Boris Pasternak i Sergei Bobrov: Pis'ma chetyrekh desiatiletii*. Stanford Slavic Studies, vol. 10. Stanford, Calif., 1996.

Shklovsky, Viktor. *Gamburgskii shchet*. (88)

Skoryatin, Valentin. *Taina gibeli Maiakovskogo*. (89)

Triolet, Elsa. *Écrits intimes 1912–1939*. (105)

Vospominaniia ob Aseeve. Moscow, 1980.

8. ABOUT THIS, 1923

PRINTED SOURCES

Brik, Lili. "Predlozhenie issledovateliam." (9)

Jangfeldt, Bengt. "Maiakovskii i Goethe v parke Lili." In *Wlodzimierz Mayakowski i jego czasy*. Warsaw, 1995.

Rayt, Rita. "Vse luchshie vospominania . . ." (79)

Stephan, Halina. *"Lef" and the Left Front of the Arts*. (95)

9. FREE FROM LOVE AND POSTERS, 1923–1924

UNPUBLISHED SOURCES

Krasnoshchokova, Luella. Memoirs of Mayakovsky. Copy in author's archive.

Public Record Office. London. Records of the Security Service (KV2/484). [The British security service's file about Lili's and Elsa's mother Yelena Kagan, also containing documents concerning Elsa, Lili, Osip, and Mayakovsky. Declassified in 2002.]

PRINTED SOURCES

Argenbright, Robert. "Marking NEP's Slippery Path: The Krasnoshchekov Show Trial." *Russian Review* 61 (2002).

Aseyev, Nikolay. "Vospominaniia o Maiakovskom." (107)

Galushkin, Alexander. "Viktor Shklovskii i Roman Iakobson: Perepiska (1922–1956)." In *Roman Iakobson: Teksty, Dokumenty, Issledovaniia*. Moscow, 1999.

Goldman, Emma. *Living My Life*. New York, 1931.

Kleberg, Lars. "Notes on the Poem 'Vladimir Il'ič Lenin.'" (34)

Krasnoshchokova, Luella. "Iz vospominanii ob ottse i sem'e." *Dal'nii vostok* 4 (1990).

Mukhachov, B. I. *Aleksandr Krasnoshchekov*. (70)

Stephan, Halina. *"Lef" and the Left Front of the Arts*. (95)

10. AMERICA, 1925

UNPUBLISHED SOURCES

Krasnoshchokova, Luella. Memoirs of Mayakovsky. Copy in author's archive.

PRINTED SOURCES

Fleishman, Lazar. *Boris Pasternak v dvadtsatye gody.* (24)

Galushkin, Alexander. "Nad strokoi partiinogo resheniia: Neizvestnoe vystuplenie V. V. Maiakovskogo v TsK RKP (b)." *Novoe literaturnoe obozrenie* 41 (2000).

Jangfeldt, Bengt. "Aseev, Marinetti i Maiakovskii." *Russia* 5 (1987).

Jangfeldt, Bengt. "Mayakovsky and 'the Two Ellies.'" *Scando-Slavica* 37 (1991).

Kemrad, S. *Maiakovskii v Amerike.* (51)

Khodasevich, Valentina. *Portrety slovami.* (53)

Morand, Paul, *L'Europe galante.* Paris, 1925.

Pozner, Vladimir. "La littérature française jugée par les grands écrivains étrangers." *Le journal littéraire,* 29 September 1925.

Thompson, Patricia J. *Mayakovsky in Manhattan: A Love Story.* (100)

Trotsky, Leon. *Literature and Revolution.* (106)

Yangirov, Rashit. "Krymskii proekt i evrei-'zemlebory' v diskurse sovetskoi kinematografii." *Paralleli,* no. 1 (2002).

Yevdayev, Nobert. *David Burliuk v Amerike: Materialy k biografii.* Moscow, 2002.

11. NEW RULES, 1926–1927

UNPUBLISHED SOURCES

Katanyan, Galina. Memoirs. Copy in author's archive.

Brik, Lili. Unpublished memoir from the 1930s. Copy in author's archive.

P. 342. The assertion that Mayakovsky claimed to have "been bored" for seven years comes from Nikolay Khardzhiyev (who confided it to the author on 20 August 1976). According to Khardzhiyev, Burlyuk reported this in a letter (now lost) to Vasily Kamensky. See also a letter from Burlyuk's wife to a friend in the Soviet Union: "I once saw him [Mayakovsky] covering his face with his left hand, went up to him and said very, very quietly: 'Vladimir Vladimirovitch, don't be sad.' Mayakovsky came to and said, also in a quiet voice: 'Mariya Nikolayevna, for the last five years I have not known what to do with myself" (D. D. Burlyuk, Pis'ma iz kollekcii S. Denisova, Tambov 2011, p. 680).

PRINTED SOURCES

Bryukhanenko, Natalya. "Perezhitoe." (14)

Fleishman, Lazar. *Boris Pasternak v dvadtsatye gody.* (24)

Geiger, Kent. *The Family in Soviet Russia.* Cambridge, Mass., 1968.

Jangfeldt, Bengt. "Aseev, Marinetti i Maiakovskii." *Russia* 5 (1987).

Kuleshov, Lev, and Alexandra Khokhlova. *50 let v kino.* Moscow, 1975.

Lavut, Pavel. *Maiakovskii edet po Soiuzu.* (59)

Rodchenko, Alexander. *Stat'i: Vospominaniia . . .* (81)

Rodchenko, Alexander. *Opyty dlia budushchego.* (82)

Stepanova, Varvara. *Chelovek ne mozhet bez chuda.* (94)

Stephan, Halina. *"Lef" and the Left Front of the Arts.* (95)

Yefimov, Boris. "Poet, kakim ia ego znal lichno." http://1001.vdv.ru/books/efimov.

12. TATYANA, 1928–1929

UNPUBLISHED SOURCES

Shmakov, Gennady. Transcript of taped interviews with Tatyana Yakovleva. Copy in author's archive.

Public Record Office. London. Records of the Security Service (KV2/484). [The British security service's file about Lili's and Elsa's mother Yelena Kagan, also containing documents concerning Elsa, Lili, Osip, and Mayakovsky. Declassified in 2002.]

PRINTED SOURCES

Annenkov, Yury. *Dnevnik moikh vstrech.* Vol. 1. (1)

Barnes, Christopher. *Boris Pasternak: A Literary Biography.* Vol. 1. (3)

Bryukhanenko, Natalya. "Perezhitoe." (14)

Du Plessix Gray, Francine, *Them: A Memoir of Parents.* (22)

Fleishman, Lazar. *Boris Pasternak v dvadtsatye gody.* (24)

Fleishman, Lazar. *Boris Pasternak: The Poet and His Politics.* (25)

Galushkin, Alexander. "'I tak, stavshi na kostiakh, budem trubit' sbor . . .': K istorii nesostoiavshegosia voz-rozhdeniia Opoiaza v 1928–1930 gg." *Novoe literaturnoe obozrenie* 44 (2000).

Jakobson, Roman. "Novye stroki Maia-kovskogo." (32)

Jangfeldt, Bengt. "Mayakovsky and 'the Two Ellies.'" *Scando-Slavica* 37 (1991).

Serov, A. I., ed. "Pis'ma Benedikta Livshitsa k Davidu Burliuku." *Novoe literaturnoe obozrenie* 31 (1998).

Pasternak, Boris. *The Correspondence of Boris Pasternak and Olga Freidenberg.* (72)

Shukhayev, V. I., and V. F. Shukhayeva. "Tri vremeni." (66)

Tatá (Tat'iana Iakovleva). (98)

Thompson, Patricia J. *Mayakovsky in Manhattan: A Love Story.* (100)

Triolet, Elsa. *Écrits intimes 1912–1939.* (105)

13. THE YEAR OF THE GREAT CHANGE, 1929

UNPUBLISHED SOURCES

Brik, Lili. Unpublished memoir from the 1930s. Copy in author's archive.

Brik, Lili. Diaries. Copy in author's archive.

Public Record Office. London. Records of the Security Service (KV2/484). [The British security service's file about Lili's and Elsa's mother Yelena Kagan, also containing documents concerning Elsa, Lili, Osip, and Mayakovsky. Declassified in 2002.]

PRINTED SOURCES

Du Plessix Gray, Francine, *Them: A Memoir of Parents.* (22)

Duvakin, Viktor. [Taped interview with Lili Brik, 1973.] *Literaturnaia gazeta,* dossier, 5, 1993.

Fleishman, Lazar. *Boris Pasternak v dvadtsatye gody.* (24)

Gershteyn, Emma. "O Pasternake i ob Akhmatovoi." *Literaturnoe obozrenie* 2 (1990).

Kassil, Lev. *Maiakovskii—sam.* (44)

Katanyan, Galina. "Azorskie ostrova." (45)

Lavut, Pavel. *Maiakovskii edet po Soiuzu.* (59)

Neznamov, Pyotr. "Maiakovskii v dvad-tsatykh godakh." (107)

Polonskaya, Veronika. [Memoirs.] (112)

Skoryatin, Valentin. *Taina gibeli Maia-kovskogo.* (89)

Stepanova, Varvara, *Chelovek ne mozhet bez chuda.* (94)

Tatá (Tat'iana Iakovleva). (98)

Valyuzhenich, Anatoly. "Lilia Brik i 'kazakh Iusup.'" *Niva* 5 (2002).

14. AT THE TOP OF MY VOICE, 1929–1930

UNPUBLISHED SOURCES

Brik, Lili. Diaries. Copy in author's archive.

Mayakovsky, Vladimir. Memo before the meeting with Lazar Kaganovich. Russian State Literary Archive (RGALI), 2577-1-1158.

PRINTED SOURCES

Aseyev, Nikolay. "Vospominaniia o Maiakovskom." (107)

Aucouturier, Michel. "Ob odnom kliuche k 'Okhrannoi gramote.'" In *Boris Pasternak 1890–1960*. Paris, 1979.

Bromberg, A. G. "Vystavka 'Dvadtsat' let raboty.'" (107)

Maiakovskii delaet vystavku. Moscow, 1973.

Pasternak, Boris. *Collected Short Prose*. (71)

Lunacharskaya-Rozenel', Natalya, "Lunacharskii i Maiakovskii." (107)

Sheshukov, S. *Neistovye revniteli*. Moscow, 1970.

Tatá (Tat'iana Iakovleva). (98)

Yakimenko, Yu. N., "Iz istorii 'chistok apparata': Akademiia khudozhestvennykh nauk v 1929–1932." *Novyi istoricheskii vestnik* 1, no. 12 (2005).

15. THE FIRST BOLSHEVIK SPRING, 1930

UNPUBLISHED SOURCES

Brik, Lili. Diaries. Copy in author's archive.

Grinkrug, Lev. Memoirs. Copy in author's archive.

PRINTED SOURCES

Aseyev, Nikolay. "Vospominaniia o Maiakovskom." (107)

Fevralsky, Alexander. *Vstrechi s Maiakovskim*. Moscow, 1971.

Gronsky, Ivan, and Viktor Duvakin. "Nakanune tragedii." (112)

Khodasevich, Valentina. *Portrety slovami*. (53)

Pasternak, Boris. *Collected Short Prose*. (71)

Polonskaya, Veronika. [Memoirs.] (112)

Roskin, Vladimir. [Memoirs.] (112)

Skoryatin, Valentin. *Taina gibeli Maiakovskogo*. (89)

Spivak, Monika. *Posmertnaia diagnostika genial'nosti*. (92)

Sutyrin, Vladimir. [Memoirs.] (112)

Valyuzhenich, Anatoly. *Lilia Brik— zhena komandira*. (111)

16. A GAME WITH LIFE AS THE STAKE

PRINTED SOURCES

Jakobson, Roman. "On a Generation That Squandered Its Poets." (31)

Jakobson, Roman. "Novye stroki Maiakovskogo." (32)

Ryabova, Natalya. "Kievskie vstrechi." (48)

Tatá (Tat'iana Iakovleva). (98)

Chertok, Semyon. *Posledniaia liubov' Maiakovskogo*. Ann Arbor, Mich., 1983.

Chukovsky, Korney. *Dnevnik 1930–1969*. (18)

17. MAYAKOVSKY'S SECOND DEATH

PRINTED SOURCES

Du Plessix Gray, Francine. *Them: A Memoir of Parents*. (22)

Jangfeldt, Bengt. "Fången i Särna." In *Den trettonde aposteln*. Stockholm, 1995.

Mukhachov, B. I. *Aleksandr Krasnoshche-kov.* (70)

"V tom, chto umiraiu, ne vinite nikogo?" (112)

Valyuzenich, Anatoly. *Lilia Brik—zhena komandira.* (111)

Vaksberg, Arkady. *Zagadka i magiia Lili Brik.* (109)

ILLUSTRATIONS

The numbers indicate the pages on which the illustrations are found.

AUTHOR'S ARCHIVE

xii, 3, 7, 10, 11, 13, 16, 17, 20, 21, 22 (upper illustration), 27, 33, 43, 45, 46, 47, 54, 58, 70, 71, 78, 83, 87, 89, 94, 104, 107, 112, 113, 114, 122, 125, 128, 129, 134, 143, 146, 153, 156, 165, 166, 170, 175, 186, 192, 203, 212–13, 215, 219, 230, 236, 241, 243, 246, 256, 258, 262, 267, 269, 274, 276, 284, 286, 298, 301, 311, 319, 325, 331 (lower illustration), 340, 347, 356, 360, 361 (both illustrations), 365, 368, 380 (both illustrations), 381, 390, 400, 404, 406–7, 409, 412, 443, 445, 464, 478, 497, 502, 504, 517, 545, 552, 556, 565, 579 (photo by Bengt Jangfeldt), 583 (photo by Bengt Jangfeldt)

ANATOLY VALYUZHENICH'S ARCHIVE (ASTANA)

29, 30, 38, 49, 163

BRIK/KATANYAN ARCHIVE (MOSCOW)

24, 31, 88, 116, 117, 118, 280, 290, 362, 385, 416, 438, 449, 450, 451, 488, 510, 553, 554, 578

POLITICAL POSTER COLLECTION, "TOV. LENIN OCHISHCHAET" (UNCATALOGED), HOOVER INSTITUTION ARCHIVES

224

PATRICIA J. THOMPSON (NEW YORK)

337, 581 (© Lehman College)

PUBLIC RECORD OFFICE (LONDON)

281

RODCHENKO/STEPANOVA ARCHIVE (MOSCOW)

249, 348, 353, 377, 410, 431, 570

STATE LITERATURE MUSEUM (MOSCOW)

22 (lower illustration), 23, 331 (upper illustration)

STATE MAYAKOVSKY MUSEUM (MOSCOW)

322, 393, 420, 462, 468, 524, 543, 575

YURY ANNENKOV'S SKETCHES AND DRAWINGS FROM *DNEVNIK MOIKH VSTRECH* (NO. 1 IN "RECURRENT REFERENCES AND OTHER SOURCES OF INTEREST" ABOVE)

131, 140, 179, 207, 315, 454, 456

ACKNOWLEDGMENTS

To all the friends and colleagues who have contributed information and material during the writing of this book: Lazar Fleishman, professor of Russian literature at Stanford University and the world's leading specialist on the works of Boris Pasternak; Arkady Waxberg, journalist and author, unbeatable connoisseur of the dark sides of Soviet society; Rashit Yangirov, film and cultural historian with a unique breadth of scientific interests; the literary historian Alexander Galushkin, unsurpassed connoisseur of Viktor Shklovsky's life and works; Svetlana Strizhnyova, director of the Mayakovsky Museum in Moscow, and her colleagues; as well as Vera Teryokhina, Mayakovsky researcher and one of the editors (together with the author of this book) of the forthcoming academic edition of Mayakovsky's works in twenty volumes.

An extraspecial thank-you goes to Anatoly Valyuzhenich, electrical engineer in Astana, the capital of Kazakhstan, far from the center of Russian cultural life, who has devoted a large part of his own life to the life and works of Osip Brik. He has provided me with documents and information without which this book would have been thinner in every respect.

Another special thank-you is due to Alexander Rodchenko's daughter Varvara and grandson Alexander Lavrentiev. When I told them about my work on the book they immediately declared, with exceptional generosity, that my publishers might "of course" reproduce Rodchenko's photographs of Mayakovsky and his circle free of charge. The same is true of Inna Gens, widow of Vasily Katanyan junior—Lili Brik's stepson—who made his photographic archive available to the publishers and myself on the same generous conditions.

A finished book is always the result of teamwork. I particularly want to thank one person with whom I have collaborated many times before: Harry D. Watson, my translator, with his keen feeling for the nuances of my style.

Bengt Jangfeldt, 2006–13

601

Note: page numbers in italics refer to illustrations.